WEBSTER'S
FAMILY
ENCYCLOPEDIA

WEBSTER'S FAMILY ENCYCLOPEDIA

VOLUME 6

1995 Edition

Exclusively distributed by
Archer Worldwide, Inc.
Great Neck, New York, USA

Abbreviations Used in Webster's Family Encyclopedia

AD	After Christ	ht	height	N.M.	New Mexico
Adm.	Admiral	i.e.	that is	NNE	north-northeast
Ala.	Alabama	in	inches	NNW	north-northwest
Apr	April	Ind.	Indiana	Nov	November
AR	Autonomous	Ill.	Illinois	NW	northwest
	Republic	Jan	January	N.Y.	New York
at no	atomic number	K	Kelvin	OAS	Organization of
at wt	atomic weight	Kans.	Kansas		American States
Aug	August	kg	kilograms	Oct	October
b.	born	km	kilometers	Okla.	Oklahoma
BC	Before Christ	kph	kilometers per	OPEC	Organization of
bp	boiling point		hour		Petroleum Ex-
C	Celsius, Centi-	kW	kilowatts		porting Countries
	grade	lb	pounds	Pa.	Pennsylvania
c.	circa	Lt.	Lieutenant	PLO	Palestine Libera-
Calif.	California	Lt. Gen.	Lieutenant		tion Organization
Capt.	Captain		General	Pres.	President
CIS	Commonwealth	m	meters	R.I.	Rhode Island
	of Independent	M. Sgt.	Master Sergeant	S	south, southern
	States	Mar	March	S.C.	South Carolina
cm	centimeters	Mass.	Massachusetts	SE	southeast
Co.	Company	Md.	Maryland	Sen.	Senator
Col.	Colonel	mi	miles	Sept	September
Conn.	Connecticut	Mich.	Michigan	Sgt.	Sergeant
d.	died	Minn.	Minnesota	sq mi	square miles
Dec	December	Miss.	Mississippi	SSE	south-southeast
Del.	Delaware	mm	millimeters	SSW	south-southwest
E	east, eastern	Mo.	Missouri	SW	southwest
EC	European Com-	MP	Member of	Tenn.	Tennessee
	munity		Parliament	Tex.	Texas
e.g.	for example	mp	melting point	UN	United Nations
est	estimated	mph	miles per hour	US	United States
F	Fahrenheit	N	north, northern	USSR	Union of Soviet
Feb	February	NATO	North Atlantic		Socialist
Fl. Lt.	Flight Lieutenant		Treaty		Republics
Fla.	Florida		Organization	Va.	Virginia
ft	feet	NE	northeast	Vt.	Vermont
Ga.	Georgia	Neb.	Nebraska	W	west, western
Gen.	General	N.H.	New Hampshire	wt	weight
Gov.	Governor	N.J.	New Jersey		

Kiéber, Jean Baptiste (1753–1800) French general in the Revolutionary Wars distinguished for his suppression of the uprising in the Vendée (1793). He was recalled from retirement in 1798 and given command in Napoleon's Egyptian campaign. He became governor of Alexandria (1799) but was assassinated after recapturing Cairo.

Klebs, Edwin (1834–1913) Prussian bacteriologist, who, with Friedrich *Loeffler in 1884, isolated the bacillus responsible for diphtheria (the **Klebs-Loeffler bacillus**). He also demonstrated the presence of bacteria in infected wounds and showed that tuberculosis could be transmitted via infected milk, thus establishing the bacterial cause of certain diseases.

Klee, Paul (1879–1940) Swiss painter and etcher, born in Berne. After training in the Munich Academy, he worked initially as an etcher, influenced by *Beardsley and *Goya in the grotesque and symbolic character of his works. Returning to Germany (1906), he became associated with Der *Blaue Reiter and taught at the *Bauhaus school of design (1920–33), but remained an original and independent talent. Inspired by a visit to Tunisia (1914), he turned to painting. Initially he produced small watercolors in brilliant colors; after 1919 he used oils, incorporating signs and hieroglyphs to create a fantasy world influenced by children's art.

Klein bottle In *topology, a surface that has no edges and only one side. It is made by putting the small end of a tapering tube through the side of the tube, stretching it, and joining it to the large end. It was discovered by the German mathematician Christian Felix Klein (1849–1925).

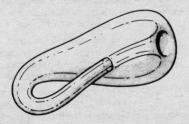

KLEIN BOTTLE *A solid with no edges and only one side.*

Klemperer, Otto (1885–1973) German conductor. He studied in Berlin and became conductor of the German Opera in Prague on the recommendation of Mahler in 1907. He was expelled by the Nazis in 1933 and became first a US and subsequently an Israeli citizen. He was principal conductor of the London Philharmonia Orchestra from 1959 until his death and is particularly remembered for his performances of Beethoven's symphonies.

Klimt, Gustav (1862–1918) Viennese Art Nouveau artist, who founded the Vienna Sezession (1897), an avant-garde exhibiting society. He achieved notoriety with the pessimistic and erotic symbolism of his murals for Vienna University (1900–03). Subsequent paintings and mosaics, allegories or female portraits, are characterized by large patterned areas often predominantly in gold, as in *The Kiss* (Vienna).

Klinger, Friedrich Maximilian von (1752–1831) German dramatist. After touring with a troupe of actors, he made a career in the Russian army. From his tempestuous play *Der Wirrwarr, oder Sturm und Drang* (1776), the *Sturm und Drang* movement took its name.

Klint, Kaare (1888–1954) Danish furniture designer, the originator of the contemporary Scandinavian style of design. Trained as an architect, he founded the Danish Academy of Arts in 1924 and became its first professor of furniture. His pioneering designs in natural unvarnished wood combined craftsmanship with modern functional needs and were influenced by *Chippendale as well as 20th-century styles.

klipspringer A small antelope, *Oreotragus oreotragus,* of rocky regions of S and E Africa; 24 in (60 cm) high at the shoulder, klipspringers have a matted bristly yellowish-brown speckled coat with white underparts. Males have short horns, ringed at the base. They are agile and aptly named "cliff-springers."

Klondike The valley of the Klondike River in NW Canada, in the central *Yukon, where gold was discovered in 1896. The subsequent gold rush opened up the Yukon, although the population dwindled when the gold started to run out (1900). The Klondike has passed into Canadian literature and song.

Klopstock, Friedrich Gottlieb (1724–1803) German poet. Inspired by what he felt to be his divine mission as a poet, he achieved success with his early epic *Der Messias* (1745–73) and later with his odes (*Oden*, 1771). In reacting against rationalism by emphasizing emotion and in his enthusiasm for nature, religion, and German history, he anticipated Romanticism. He also wrote plays.

klystron An electronic device used to generate or amplify *microwaves. It consists of a sealed evacuated tube in which a steady beam of electrons from an electron gun is alternately accelerated and retarded by high-frequency radio waves (velocity *modulation) as it passes through a cavity. The resultant radio-frequency pulses are picked up at a second cavity, either as a voltage oscillation or, if connected to a *waveguide, as electromagnetic waves. The second cavity can be tuned to the input frequency or a harmonic of it. *See also* magnetron.

knapweed One of several plants of the genus *Centaurea,* of Eurasia and N Africa, having knoblike purplish flower heads. The lesser knapweed (*C. nigra*), also called hardheads, is a plant of grasslands and open places and has been introduced to New Zealand and North America. Family: *Compositae.*

Kneller, Sir Godfrey (1646–1723) Portrait painter of German birth. Beginning a successful career in England (1674), he worked successively for Charles II, William III, Queen Anne, and George I. He founded the first English academy of painting (1711). His best portraits, those of the Whig Kit Cat Club (c. 1702–17) established a standard British portrait type, known as the kit cat (less than half-length but including a hand).

Knight, Dame Laura (1877–1970) British painter, famous for her scenes of circus, gypsy, and ballet life. She exhibited frequently at the Royal Academy, becoming a member in 1936. She was married to the portraitist **Harold Knight** (1874–1961).

knighthood, orders of Societies, found in many countries, to which persons are admitted as a mark of honor. In medieval Europe, companies of knights (e.g. the *Hospitallers) bound by monastic vows fought to defend Christendom (*see* Crusades). Subsequently, secular orders were instituted, usually by rulers who sought the sworn loyalty of their nobles. The most distinguished British orders are those of the Garter, the Thistle, and the Bath.

Knights of Labor US labor union, founded in 1869 in secrecy and designed to protect all who worked for a living. Its requirement of secrecy limited its growth, and it was not until Terence V. Powderly became its head (1879) the secrecy was dropped. The union then grew rapidly; by 1886 membership peaked at 700,000. Public opinion, especially after the *Haymarket Massacre (1886), subsequently turned against the union, which never recovered.

Knights of the White Camellia US secret society that advocated white supremacy. Established in 1867 in Louisiana, it sought to maintain the supremacy of whites in the South following the Civil War. Short-lived, it was dissolved by the early 1870s.

knitting The chain looping of yarn to form a network fabric that is more elastic than woven fabric; it is very suitable for clinging garments, such as sweaters and stockings. Hand knitting, using two or three needles, is an old craft. In addition to shaped flatwork in various relief patterns, tubular shapes can be knitted. Since the 19th century knitting machines have been developed.

knocking A metallic knock heard in gasoline engines as a result of combustion of the explosive charge ahead of the flame front. This is caused by local areas of high pressure in the combustion chamber. It greatly reduces the efficiency of the engine and is controlled by additives, such as *tetraethyl lead, to the fuel. Antiknock compounds that do not contain lead are being sought, owing to pollution of the atmosphere by lead.

Knossos The principal city of Minoan Crete, near present-day Heraklion. It was occupied between about 2500 and 1200 BC. Excavated and reconstructed (1899–1935) by Sir Arthur *Evans, the so-called Palace of Minos was luxurious and sophisticated. It is the probable original of the labyrinth in which, according to legend, *Theseus fought the *Minotaur. Frescoes showing processions, bull sports, and seascapes decorated its walls, there was an elaborate water system, and goods were imported from Egypt. About 1450 BC the palace was burned down and subsequent occupation levels show *Mycenaean influence. *See also* Minoan civilization.

knot (bird) A short-legged bird, *Calidris canutus*, that breeds in Arctic tundra and winters on southern coasts; 10 in (25 cm) long, it has a short black bill and its plumage is mottled gray in winter and reddish in summer. In winter, knots feed in flocks, probing mud and sand for snails, worms, and crabs. Family: *Scolopacidae* (sandpipers, snipe, etc.).

knot (unit) A unit of speed, used for ships and aircraft, equal to one nautical mile per hour (i.e. 1.15 mph).

knots Fastenings formed by looping and tying pieces of rope, cord, etc. The mathematical theory of knots, a branch of *topology, was developed mainly in the 20th century, and draws on *matrix theory, algebra, and geometry. A simple closed curve in space may be knotted in various ways, each with specific topological properties. These are classified by knot theory and can be expressed in matrix form.

Know Nothing Party US nativist political party, developed during the 1850s, that opposed the immigrants entering the US, especially Irish Roman Catholics. Also known as the American Party and Native American Party, it was founded in 1845 and acquired its name because members, pledged to secrecy, were to "know nothing" when asked about party policies. The party itself split after the 1856 elections and declined.

Knox, Henry (1750–1806) US soldier; first secretary of war (1785–94). As a colonel during the *American Revolution he brought back from Fort Ticonderoga captured British artillery that enabled the Americans to take Boston in 1776. A general from 1777, he went on to fight in almost every major battle during the Revolution. Named the first secretary of war under the Articles of Confederation, he stayed in that position when George Washington became president in 1789.

Knox, John (c. 1514–72) Scottish Protestant reformer. He was a Catholic priest before adopting the reformed faith in the 1540s. In 1547 he joined the

KNOTS

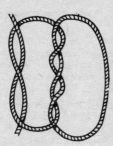

overhand knot *This is used either to make a knob in a rope or as the basis for another knot.*

reef knot *A nonslip knot for joining ropes of similar thickness.*

quick release knot *A tug on a will quickly unfasten this knot.*

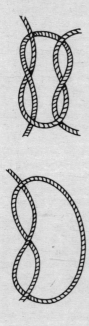

surgeon's knot *The extra twist in the first part of the knot prevents it from slipping loose while the second part is tied.*

bowline *A knot to form a nonslip loop.*

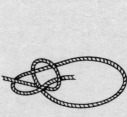

running bowline *A knot for making a running noose.*

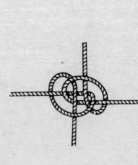

sheepshank *A means of temporarily shortening a rope.*

Hunter's bend *A strong, easily tied knot invented in 1978 by Dr Edward Hunter.*

KNOTS

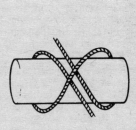

carrick bend *A knot well suited to tying heavy ropes together.*

rolling hitch *A quickly made and quickly unfastened knot for attaching a rope to a rail or another, standing rope.*

fisherman's knot *Used especially for joining lengths of fishing gut.*

anchor bend *A secure means of attaching a cable to an anchor.*

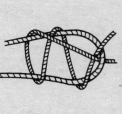

double sheet bend *This follows the same principles as the sheet bend.*

round turn and two half hitches *Used for similar purposes as the clove hitch, this knot does not easily work loose.*

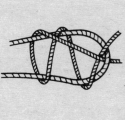

sheet bend *A knot for securely joining two ropes of different thickness.*

clove hitch *A simple knot for attaching a rope to a ring, rail, etc.*

Protestants after Wishart's execution in St Andrew's Castle. The castle was stormed by the French, who imprisoned Knox as a galley slave. After his release (1549) he became a chaplain to Edward VI in England and contributed to the revision of the Second Book of Common Prayer. On Queen Mary's accession he escaped to the Continent, where he met *Calvin in Geneva. Returning to Scotland in 1559, he became its leading reformer. In 1560 the Scottish Parliament adopted the *Confession of Faith* that Knox had compiled. His *First Book of Discipline* (1561) outlined a structure for the reformed Church of Scotland, embracing all aspects of life, including education and poor relief.

Knoxville 36 00N 83 57W A city in Tennessee, on the Tennessee River. It is the site of the University of Tennessee (1794) and the headquarters of the Tennessee Valley Authority. An inland port and agricultural trading center, its industries include meat packing and marble processing. Population (1990): 165,121.

koala An arboreal *marsupial, *Phascolarctus cinereus,* of E Australia. About 24 in (60 cm) high, koalas have thick grayish fur, tufted ears, a small tail, and long claws. Groups of koalas move slowly through eucalyptus forests, each adult eating more than 2.2 lb (1 kg) of the leaves every day. The pouch opens toward the female's tail and the young are weaned on half-digested eucalyptus soup from their mother's anus. Family: *Phalangeridae.*

kob An antelope, *Kobus kob*, of African savanna regions, also called Buffon's kob. Males stand about 35 in (90 cm) high at the shoulder; females are smaller. The coat ranges from orange-red to nearly black, with white markings on the face, legs, and belly and a black stripe down the foreleg.

Kobayashi Masaki (1916–) Japanese film director. He established his international reputation with *The Human Condition* (1959–61), a trilogy of films concerned with the dignity of the individual in modern society. His other films include *Kwaidan* (1964), an anthology of ghost stories, *Rebellion* (1967), and *Kaseki* (1974). *Harakiri* (1962), his finest film, examined Japanese warrior ethics.

Kobe 34 40N 135 12E A major port in Japan, in S Honshu on Osaka Bay. It forms the W end of the Osaka-Kobe industrial area and has two of the biggest shipbuilding yards in the country. Other industries include engineering, sugar, chemicals, and rubber. Its university was established in 1949. Population (1990): 1,477,410.

København. *See* Copenhagen.

Koblenz (Coblenz) 50 21N 7 36E A city in W Germany, in Rhineland-Palatinate at the confluence of the Rhine and Moselle Rivers. The seat of Frankish kings during the 6th century AD, it was annexed by France in 1798, passing to Prussia in 1815. Notable buildings, many rebuilt after World War II, include the Ehrenbreitstein fortress (c. 1000) and the birthplace of Metternich. It is a wine-trading center and manufactures furniture, pianos, and clothing. Population (1991 est): 109,000.

Koch, Robert (1843–1910) German bacteriologist, who was responsible for major discoveries in the study of disease-causing bacteria. As a young doctor, Koch successfully cultured the bacillus causing anthrax in cattle and determined its life cycle. Devising new and better culture methods, Koch succeeded in 1882 in identifying and isolating the bacillus responsible for tuberculosis. Koch investigated many other diseases including cholera, bubonic plague, and malaria. He was awarded a Nobel Prize (1905).

Köchel, Ludwig von (1800–77) Austrian naturalist and musical bibliographer. He compiled a thematic catalogue of Mozart's works, which was published in 1862; a particular work is referred to by a **Köchel number**, consisting of the letter K followed by the appropriate catalogue number.

Kodály, Zoltan (1882–1967) Hungarian composer. He was educated at Budapest University and conservatoire, where he developed an interest in Magyar folk music. In collaboration with *Bartók he collected and edited Hungarian peasant songs, which influenced his style of composition. He achieved international recognition with his *Psalmus Hungaricus* (1923); other works include the opera *Háry János* (1926), *Dances of Galanta* (1933), masses, chamber music, and orchestral music.

Kodiak 57 20N 153 40W A US island, off the S coast of Alaska in the Gulf of Alaska. First settled by Russians in 1784, it became a base for seal hunting and whaling. In 1964 it suffered an earthquake that lowered it by about 6 ft (1.8 m). Area: 3465 sq mi (8974 sq km). Population (1990): 6365.

Kodiak bear. *See* brown bear.

Koestler, Arthur (1905–83) British writer, born in Hungary. As a journalist in Berlin, he joined the Communist Party (1931) but left it in 1938. He settled in Britain in 1940, writing in English thereafter. His novel *Darkness at Noon* (1940), depicting the Moscow purge trials, calls on his own experience as a prisoner in the Spanish Civil War. His other novels include *Thieves in the Night* (1946) and *The Call Girls* (1972). His nonfiction was concerned with politics (*The Yogi and the Commissar,* 1945), scientific creativity (*The Sleepwalkers,* 1959; *The Act of Creation,* 1964; *The Ghost in the Machine,* 1967), and parapsychology (*The Roots of Coincidence,* 1972). His autobiographical volumes include *Arrow in the Blue* (1952) and *The Invisible Writing* (1954). His later books include *The Thirteenth Tribe: The Khazer Empire and Its Heritage* (1976) and *Janus: A Summing Up* (1979).

Koffka, Kurt (1886–1941) US psychologist, born in Germany, who was one of the founders of *Gestalt psychology. Among his works was *Growth of the Mind* (1921). He made an influential distinction between the behavioral and the geographical environments—the perceived world of common sense and the world studied by scientists.

Kohl, Helmut (1930–   ) German political leader, chancellor of West Germany (1982–90); chancellor of united Germany (1990–   ). He served in various state (Rhineland-Palatinate) and national political posts. He was head of Rhineland-Palatinate (1966–69) and a member of the federal legislature. Always active in the Christian Democratic Union (CDU), he became its chairman (1973). He lost the election for chancellor to Helmut Schmidt in 1976, but was elected to that position in 1982. He worked to unite East and West Germany in the late 1980s and was elected chancellor of the reunited Germany in 1990.

Köhler, Wolfgang (1887–1967) US psychologist and a founder of *Gestalt psychology. Kohler's experiments on problem solving in apes (*The Mentality of Apes,* 1917) led to his exploration of the physiological basis of perception and the process of learning.

kohlrabi A variety of *cabbage, sometimes called turnip-rooted cabbage. The green or purple stem base, which swells like a turnip, is used as a vegetable and as livestock food.

Kokand 40 33N 70 55E A city in NE Uzbekistan, in the Fergana Valley. Fertilizers and chemicals are produced. Population (1991 est): 175,000.

Koko Nor. *See* Qinghai, Lake.

Kokoschka, Oskar (1886–1980) Austrian expressionist painter and writer (*see* expressionism). In Vienna and Berlin, he specialized in probing portraits and allegorical poems, plays, and paintings, expressing the struggle of life. After World War I he taught at the Dresden Academy and traveled widely, painting landscapes and city views, particularly of London, where he lived (1938–53). From 1953 he lived and worked in Switzerland.

Kokura. *See* Kitakyushu.

kola (*or* cola) Either of two trees, *Cola nitida* or *C. acuminata*, native to West Africa and widely grown in the tropics, that produce **kola nuts**. These are rich in caffeine and chewed in Africa and the West Indies for their stimulating effects. Family: *Sterculiaceae*.

Kola Peninsula A promontory in the NW Russian Federation, between the Barents Sea to the N and the White Sea to the S. The area is largely granite but is mined for apatite (for its phosphorus) and nephelinite (for its aluminum). Tundra is extensive with some swampy pine and other forests in the S. The chief town is Murmansk. Area: about 50,182 sq mi (130,000 sq km).

Kolar 13 10N 78 10E A city in India, in Karnataka. To the NW lie the Kolar Gold Fields, which produce almost all India's gold output. Population (1981 est): 144,400.

Kolbe, (Adolf Wilhelm) Hermann (1818–84) German chemist, who became professor at Marburg University in 1851. He was one of the first chemists to synthesize organic compounds, his most important discovery being the Kolbe reaction, for synthesizing salicylic acid. This led to the large-scale manufacture of aspirin.

Kolchak, Alexander Vasilievich (1874–1920) Russian admiral. After the Russian Revolution (1917) he became leader of anti-Bolshevik elements at Omsk, clearing Siberia and linking with *Denikin in the south. However, Bolshevik counterattacks, discontent in his territories, and divisions among his followers destroyed Kolchak's forces. He was betrayed by the Allied powers to the Bolsheviks and shot.

Koldewey, Robert (1855–1925) German archeologist. After digging at several classical sites (e.g. *Baalbek), Koldewey excavated *Babylon (1899–1917). Here his training as an architect greatly facilitated recovery of the ancient street plan and reconstruction of the mud-brick buildings.

Kolhapur 16 40N 74 15E A city in India, in Maharashtra. An early center of Buddhism, its industries include sugar processing and textiles and it has a university (1962). Population (1991): 405,118.

Kolmogorov, Andrei Nikolaevich (1903–87) Soviet mathematician, who has made notable contributions to many fields of mathematics, particularly topology, probability theory, functional analysis, and geometry. His work in the branch of probability theory known as stochastic processes has found applications in the science of *cybernetics. He is the foremost Soviet mathematician of the 20th century and his influence on younger generations of mathematicians in the Soviet Union has been considerable.

Koloszvár. *See* Cluj.

Kolyma River A river in Russia. Rising in the Kolyma Range of NE Siberia, it flows mainly NE to the East Siberian Sea. Length: 1615 mi (2600 km).

Komeito A Japanese political party, known in English as the Clean Government Party, formed in 1964 by the Soka-gakkai, a branch of the extreme Nichiren Buddhists. It advocates the establishment of a nonaligned Japan free from extremes of wealth and poverty. Komeito rapidly increased its parliamentary representation to become Japan's third strongest political party. Accused of wishing to impose Nichiru Shoshu as the state religion and of reviving fascism, Komeito severed its links with the Soka-gakkai in 1970.

Komi Autonomous Republic An administrative division in Russia. It comprises chiefly tundra (in the NE) and coniferous forests. The administrative region was established in 1921 for the Komi people, who speak a Finno-Ugric language, and became an ASSR in 1936. Timbering and mining (notably of coal and oil) are the most important economic activities; livestock raising is the main branch of agriculture. Area: 160,540 sq mi (415,900 sq km). Population (1991 est): 1,265,000. Capital: Syktyvkar.

Komodo dragon A rare *monitor lizard, *Varanus komodoensis*, which, at 10 ft (3 m) long and weighing 298 lb (135 kg), is the largest living lizard. It has a stout neck and body, a long powerful tail, and short strong legs and is powerful enough to attack and kill a man. Komodo dragons feed mainly on carrion but also eat smaller monitors. They occur only on Komodo Island and some of the Lesser Sundea Islands of Indonesia. □reptile.

KOMSOMOL (All-Union Leninist Communist League of Youth) A Soviet organization for youths aged 14 to 28. Organized in 1918, its members fought in the civil war (1918–21). In 1992 it became a social organization to promote communist ideology through social activities.

Komsomolsk-na-Amur 50 32N 136 59E A city in W Russia, on the Amur River. It is named for the *KOMSOMOL, members of which built much of the city (founded 1932). Its industries, including engineering and machine building, are based on the Amurstal steelworks, located here; oil from Sakhalin is refined. Population (1991 est): 319,000.

Konakry. *See* Conakry.

Koniecpolski, Stanisław (1591–1646) Polish soldier and statesman. Koniecpolski fought many victorious battles against the Turks, Tatars, and Swedes. In 1632 he became commander in chief and subsequently influenced the government of Władysław IV (1595–1648; reigned 1632–48). Koniecpolski was extremely wealthy and acquired huge estates in Ukraine.

Koniev, Ivan Stepanovich (1897–1973) Soviet marshal. A commander in World War II in Ukraine and the southern front, he ended the war encircling Berlin from the south. He commanded all Warsaw Pact forces in Europe (1955–60).

Königsberg. *See* Kaliningrad.

Konoe Fumimaro, Prince (1891–1945) Japanese noble, who was prime minister three times. His first cabinet (1937–39) escalated the conflict between Japan and China; his second (1940–41) took Japan into alliance in World War II with Germany and Italy; and his third (1941) made the decision to attack the US. After Japan's surrender he avoided trial as a war criminal by committing suicide.

Kon-Tiki The name given by Thor *Heyerdahl to the raft built of nine balsawood logs on which, between Apr 28 and Aug 7, 1947, he and five companions traveled the 5000 miles (8000 km) between Peru and the Tuamotu islands near Tahiti. The purpose of the voyage was to demonstrate the possibility that ancient peoples of South America could have reached Polynesia. Kon-Tiki was an older name for the Inca creator god, Viracocha, allegedly known in Polynesia as Tiki.

Konya (ancient name: Iconium) 37 51N 32 30E A city in SW central Turkey. It is the center of the Whirling Dervish sect, and the monastery around the tomb of its founder is a religious museum. The town was visited by St Paul and was the capital of the Seljug kingdom of Rum. Population (1991): 513,346.

kookaburra A large gray-brown Australian *kingfisher, *Dacelo novaeguineae*, also called laughing jackass because of its chuckling call; 17 in (43 cm) long, it is arboreal and pounces on snakes, lizards, insects, and small rodents from a perch.

Köprülü A family, of Albanian origin, of viziers (public servants) of the Ottoman Empire. **Köprülü Mohammed** (c. 1583–1661), grand vizier (1656–61), reformed the Ottoman navy and economy. His son **Köprülü Ahmed** (1635–76), grand vizier (1661–76), conquered Crete. Ahmed's brother **Köprülü Mustafa** (1637–91), grand vizier (1689–91), instituted many financial and military reforms. Their cousin **Köprülü Hussein** (d. 1702), grand vizier (1697–1702), negotiated the Treaty of Karlowitz (1699), in which the Ottoman Empire lost much territory to Austria.

Koran (*or* Quran) The sacred scripture of Islam. According to tradition, the divine revelations given to *Mohammed (d. 632 AD) were preserved by his followers and collected as the Koran under the third caliph, Uthman (d. 656). Written in classical Arabic, they were arranged in 114 suras or chapters according to length, the longer ones first. Admonitions to worship God alone and legal prescriptions predominate. The Koran is one of the main sources of the comprehensive system of *Islamic law. Although the revelations were given to Mohammed piecemeal, Muslims believe that they exist complete in a heavenly book, which contains all that has happened and will happen in the universe.

Korbut, Olga (1955–   ) Soviet gymnast, who won international acclaim in the 1972 Olympic Games, when she was awarded gold medals for the beam and floor exercises and for the team event. In the 1976 Olympics she did less well, winning a silver on the beam.

Korcë 40 38N 20 44E A city in SE Albania. It is the commercial center of a large wheat-growing area. Population (1978 est): 50,900.

Korchnoi, Victor (1931–   ) Soviet chess player. An International Grandmaster, he became Soviet champion in 1960, 1962, and 1964. He left the Soviet Union (1976) and later lost a publicized match with *Karpov (1978).

Korda, Sir Alexander (Sandor Kellner; 1893–1956) British film producer and director, born in Hungary. After settling in London in 1930, he greatly boosted the British film industry during the 1930s and 1940s with a series of extravagant productions, including *The Private Life of Henry VIII* (1932), *The Scarlet Pimpernel* (1934), and *Anna Karenina* (1948).

kore (Greek: maiden) In archaic Greek sculpture, a draped standing female figure, derived originally (c. 650 BC) from Egyptian models. During the next two centuries the drapery, pose, and expression became increasingly naturalistic. *Compare* kouros.

Korea A country in NE Asia, occupying a peninsula between the Sea of Japan and the Yellow Sea, now divided (*see* below) into the Democratic Republic of Korea (North Korea) and the Republic of Korea (South Korea). Plains in the W rise to mountains in the N and E. Both North and South Koreans are ethnically related to the Mongoloid race. From the 1st century AD three kingdoms flourished in the peninsula: the Koguryo in the N, the Paechke in the SW, and the Silla in the SE. In 668 they were united under Silla and Buddhism became the state religion. The country long had ties with China but in 1905 became a Japanese protectorate, coming formally under Japanese rule in 1910. In 1945, following Japan's defeat in World War II, the Allies divided Korea at the *38th parallel. The communist Democratic People's Republic of Korea under *Kim Il Sung was established in the Soviet-occupied N and the Republic of Korea under Syngman Rhee, in the US-occupied S (1948). Soviet and US troops had withdrawn by 1949 and in 1950 the *Korean War broke out between North and South Korea, ending in 1953 with the country still divided.

OLGA KORBUT *Her performances did much to make gymnastics a popular spectator sport.*

Korea, People's Democratic Republic of (Korean name: Chosŏn) The division of Korea left the North with almost all the country's mineral wealth (coal, iron ore, lead, zinc, molybdenum, gold, graphite, and tungsten) and a large proportion of the industries, which had been developed by the Japanese. Although many of the industries were destroyed during the Korean War, reconstruction proceeded rapidly and factory output has expanded considerably in recent times. Textiles, chemicals, machinery, and metals are among the principal manufactures and all industry is nationalized. The rather sparse agricultural land was collectivized in the 1950s and is now almost all farmed in large cooperatives; mechanization has greatly increased production. Exports, mainly to communist countries, include metals and metal products. In 1991, North Korea signed an accord with South Korea that opened the way for future reconciliation discussions. North Korea was admitted to the UN in 1991, and it agreed in 1992 to allow the International Atomic Energy Agency to inspect North Korea's nuclear facilities but dragged its feet on compliance. President: Kim Il Sung. Official languge: Korean. Official currency: won of 100 jun. Area: 47,225 sq mi (122,370 sq km). Population (1990 est): 23,059,000. Capital: Pyongyang.

Korea, Republic of (Korean name: Han Hook) The repressive government led by the first president of South Korea, Syngman *Rhee, was ended by a military coup in 1961, followed by the rise to power of Gen. *Park Chung Hee, who was assassinated in 1979. The ruling party held the presidency in the bitter, violence-plagued 1987 election. The more densely populated South was primarily agricultural when separated from the North but the injection of US aid and other international assistance has led to the predominance of the industrial sector in recent times (especially textiles, chemicals, and food processing). Mineral resources are not large, although it has one of the world's largest deposits of tungsten. The main exports include clothes, plywood, textiles, and electrical goods. The 1988 Summer Olympic games were held in Seoul. In 1991, South Korea signed an accord with North Korea that paved the way for future reconciliation discussions. South Korea was admitted to the UN in 1991. President: Kim Young Sam. Official language: Korean. Official currency: won of 100 chon. Area: 38,002 sq mi (98,447 sq km). Population (1990): 43,919,000. Capital: Seoul. Main port: Pusan.

Korean The language of the Mongoloid people of Korea. It is probably distantly related to *Japanese and has a somewhat similar grammatical structure. The standard and official form is based on the dialect of Seoul. It is written in a phonetic script call onmun, devised in the mid-15th century to replace the Chinese characters in use before then. Korean literature also dates from about this time, with a royal college of literature being founded in 1420.

Korean War (1950–53) A military conflict between communist and noncommunist forces in Korea. In 1948, after a period of military occupation following World War II, two Korean states were established on either side of the *thirty-eighth parallel. In the north was the communist Democratic People's Republic allied with the Soviet Union and in the south was the Republic of Korea allied with the US. Growing tensions between the two Korean states led to the 1950 invasion of South Korea by northern forces joined by Chinese communist troops. The UN condemned the invasion, and the US and 15 other member nations sent military forces to defend South Korea, under the supreme command of Gen. Douglas *MacArthur of the US. The UN forces staged an amphibious landing at Inchon and eventually captured the North Korean capital of Pyongyang. With massive reinforcements from China, the North Koreans staged a counterattack, pushing back the UN forces and retaking the southern capital of Seoul. A stalemate developed between the contending armies after the fighting progressed slowly northward to the 38th parallel. Because MacArthur was intent on a direct confrontation with China, he was relieved of his command by Pres. Harry *Truman in 1951 and replaced by Gen. Matthew Ridgway. Peace talks were initiated, and an armistice between North and South Korea was signed in 1953.

Korematsu v. United States (1944) US Supreme Court decision that upheld the constitutionality of Pres. Franklin D. Roosevelt's relocation program of Japanese-Americans living on the West coast during World War II. Korematsu, a US citizen of Japanese descent, claimed that his rights under the 5th amendment were violated. The court, declaring the program "an emergency war measure," which would lessen the chances of domestic sabotage, voted in favor of the government's position.

Kórinthos. *See* Corinth.

Kornberg, Arthur (1918–) US biochemist, who discovered how DNA is replicated in bacterial cells. Kornberg and associates were able to reproduce the conditions necessary for DNA replication in a test tube. They found that the "building blocks" (nucleotides) of the new DNA strand were joined together by an enzyme—DNA polymerase I—using existing DNA as a template.

Kornilov, Lavrentia Georgievich (1870–1918) Russian general. After the Russian Revolution (1917) he led the anti-Bolshevik White armies in S Russia. After his death in action, the command was assumed by *Denikin.

Koroliov, Sergei Pavlovich (1906–66) Soviet aeronautical engineer, who designed missiles, rockets, and spacecraft. During the 1930s he headed development of the Soviet Union's first liquid-fuel rocket. After World War II he worked on ballistic missiles and later supervised the Vostok and Soyuz manned spaceflight programs.

Kortrijk. *See* Courtrai.

Koryŏ An ancient Korean kingdom founded and ruled by the Wang dynasty (935–1392). Both Buddhism and Confucianism were influential and Koryŏ was divided by rivalry between pacifist Confucianists and militarist nationalists. The weakened state succumbed to Mongol invasions in the 13th century and virtually became a Mongol dependency in 1231. The last Wang ruler was deposed by the *Yi in 1392.

Kos. *See* Cos.

Kosciusko, Mount 36 28S 148 17E The highest mountain in Australia, in SE New South Wales in the Snowy Mountains. It lies within the Kosciusko National Park, a popular area for winter sports. Height: 7316 ft (2230 m).

Kosciuszko, Tadeusz Andrezei Bonawentura (1746–1817) Polish general and statesman, who served in the American Revolution with George Washington (1776–83). Returning to Poland (1784), he distinguished himself in the war against the Russian invasion, which ended in the partition of Poland. Kosciuszko withdrew to Saxony but returned in 1794 to lead the revolt against the occupation. He was defeated and captured at Maciejourice and imprisoned until 1796.

Košice (German name: Kaschau; Hungarian name: Kassa) 48 44N 21 15E A city in E Slovakia. It has a 13th-century cathedral and a university (1959). One of the largest integrated iron and steel complexes in E Europe is situated here. Population (1991): 234,840.

Kosinski, Jerzy (Nikodem) (1933–91) US writer, born in Poland. Educated in Poland and the USSR, he became a US citizen in 1965. His works include *The Future is Ours* (1960) and *No Third Path* (1962), both written under the pseudonym of Joseph Novak; *The Painted Bird* (1965); *Steps* (1968); *Being There* (1971); *Cockpit* (1975); *Blind Date* (1978); *Passion Play* (1979); and *Pinball* (1982).

Kossuth, Lajos (1802–94) Hungarian statesman, who was one of the leaders of the Hungarian *Revolution of 1848. In March 1848, when Hungary was granted a separate government by Austria, Kossuth was appointed finance minister. He became governor of an independent Hungarian republic in April 1849. When Russia destroyed the republic in August, he left Hungary and lived in exile in Turkey, England, and Italy. After his death, his body was returned to Hungary.

Kosygin, Aleksei Nikolaevich (1904–80) Soviet statesman; prime minister (1964–80). Kosygin rose in the Communist party hierarchy in the 1940s as an expert in economic affairs. He served in the politburo (1948–1952), when he was demoted. In 1960 he was again elected to what was now the presidium and after Khrushchev's fall he became prime minister. He initially shared power with *Brezhnev but in the late 1960s Kosygin's influence declined.

koto A Japanese stringed instrument of the *zither family. The narrow sound board, 7 ft (2 m), has 13 strings, which the player, sitting on his heels, plucks with plectra attached to two fingers and the thumb of the right hand. □musical instruments.

Kottbus. *See* Cottbus.

Kotzebue, August von (1761–1819) German dramatist and novelist. He was a prolific writer of popular sentimental plays, most notably the comedy *Die deutschen Kleinstädter* (1803). He was assassinated as a suspected spy while working for the Russian tsar.

kouros (Greek: youth) In archaic Greek sculpture, a nude standing male figure, often more than life-size, derived (c. 650 BC) from Egyptian models. The modeling of the face and body became increasingly naturalistic. *Compare* kore.

Koussevitsky, Sergei (1874–1951) Russian composer. Originally a virtuoso double-bass player, he conducted the State Symphony Orchestra in Petrograd (now Leningrad) but left Russia in 1920. He worked in Paris and subsequently in the US, where he directed the Boston Symphony Orchestra from 1924 to 1949. He was an advocate of contemporary music and founded the Koussevitsky Music Foundation, which continues to commission new musical works.

Kovno. *See* Kaunas.

Kowloon. *See* Jiulong.

Koxinga. *See* Zheng Cheng Gong.

Kozhikode (former name: Calicut) 11 15N 75 45E A seaport on the W coast of India, in Kerala. Formerly famous as a cotton-manufacturing center (Calicut gave its name to calico), it was visited by the Portuguese explorer Vasco da Gama (1498) and in 1664 the British East India Company established a trading post here. Tea, coffee, coconut products, and spices are exported. Population (1981): 394,447.

Kra, Isthmus of The neck of the Malay Peninsula connecting it to the Asian mainland. It is occuped by Burma and Thailand and is 40 mi (64 km) across at its narrowest point.

Krafft-Ebing, Richard von (1840–1902) German psychiatrist, who studied many aspects of mental and nervous disorders. He established the link between syphilis and general paralysis of the insane and made pioneering studies of sexual aberrations in *Psychopathia sexualis* (1886).

kraft process An industrial process for producing cellulose for paper manufacture from pine-wood chips by digestion with alkali. Rosin and fatty-acid soaps are by-products. The pulp produced is especially strong, hence the name (German *kraft*, strong).

Kragujevac 44 01N 20 55E A city in E Yugoslavia, in Serbia. A former center of the Serbian struggle against the Turks, it was the capital of Serbia (1818–39). Its industries include a large car factory. Population (1981): 165,000.

krait A highly venomous snake belonging to the genus *Bungarus* (12 species) occurring in S Asia. Kraits have shiny scales and are usually patterned with blue-and-white or black-and-yellow bands; they prey chiefly on other snakes. The common blue krait (*B. caeruleus*) of India and China is 5 ft (1.5 m) long and its venom can be fatal to humans. Family: *Elapidae* (cobras, mambas, coral snakes).

Krakatoa (Indonesian name: Krakatau) 6 11S 105 26E A small volcanic Indonesian island in the Sunda Strait. During its eruption in 1883, one of the greatest ever recorded, 36,000 people were killed, many by the tidal waves that swept the coasts of Java and Sumatra. Today the island remains uninhabited.

KOUROS *The* Rampin Head *(Louvre, Paris), part of an equestrian statue from the Acropolis, Athens. Its "archaic smile" is typical of Greek sculpture of the second quarter of the 6th century* BC.

Kraków (*or* Cracow) 50 03N 19 55E The third largest city in Poland, on the Vistula River. It was the capital of Poland (1305–1609) and remains famous as a cultural center. The Jagiellonian University, one of the oldest in Europe, was founded here in 1364. Other notable buildings include the cathedral (14th century) and many architecturally distinguished churches. Its industry is based at Nowa Huta 6 mi (10 km) to the E. Population (1992 est): 751,000.

Kramatorsk 48 43N 37 33E A city in Ukraine, in the Donets Basin. An iron and steel center, it manufactures machinery and machine tools. Population (1991 est): 201,000.

Krasnodar (name until 1920: Ekaterinodar) 45 02N 39 00E A city in SW Russia on the Kuban River. It is the center of an agricultural region and food processing is the most important industry. Population (1991 est): 631,000.

Krasnoyarsk 56 05N 92 46E A city in Russia on the Yenisei River. It was founded in 1628, developing greatly after the discovery of gold in the region in the 19th century. It produces aluminum, having one of the largest outputs in the country, and has a notable hydroelectric station. Population (1991 est): 924,000.

Krebs, Sir Hans Adolf (1900–81) British biochemist, born in Germany. Working in Germany until 1933, Krebs discovered the cycle of reactions by which waste nitrogenous products are converted to *urea by the body. After his move to Britain came his major achievement—the *Krebs cycle. Krebs was awarded a Nobel Prize (1953) with Fritz Lipmann (1899–   ).

Krebs cycle (citric acid cycle *or* tricarboxylic acid cycle) The sequence of chemical reactions, taking place in the mitochondria of cells, that is central to the metabolism of virtually all living organisms. Named for its principal discoverer, Sir Hans *Krebs, the cycle involves the conversion of acetyl coenzyme A, derived from the carbohydrates, proteins, and fats of food, into hydrogen atoms or electrons, from which usable energy in the form of *ATP is produced by the *cytochrome electron transport chain. Intermediate products of the Krebs cycle are used for the manufacture of carbohydrates, lipids, and proteins by cells.

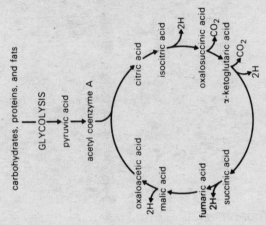

KREBS CYCLE *For every two atoms of hydrogen transferred, three ATP molecules are generated.*

Krefeld 51 20N 6 32E A city in NW Germany, in North Rhine-Westphalia on the Rhine River. It is known especially for its silk and velvet industries. It was the site of a Prussian victory (1758) during the Seven Years' War. Population (1991 est): 244,000.

Kreisky, Bruno (1911–90) Austrian statesman, Socialist chancellor (1970–83). After Austria fell to Nazi Germany, he escaped to Sweden (1938), where he lived until 1945. He was foreign minister (1959–66) before becoming chancellor. He retired when the Socialist party lost its majority.

Kreisler, Fritz (1875–1962) Austrian violinist. A child prodigy, he studied at the Vienna and Paris conservatories and toured the US in 1889, the beginning of a brilliant career. He frequently played his own compositions, written in the style of older composers and (until 1935) ascribed to them.

Kremenchug 49 03N 33 25E A city in Ukraine, on the Dnepr River. It has a large hydroelectric station and metallurgical and engineering industries. Population (1991 est): 241,000.

Kremlin The citadel of any Russian city, now referring usually to that of Moscow. Built in 1156 but continually extended, it contains the Cathedral of the

Assumption (1475–79), the Cathedral of the Annunciation (1484–89), the Great Kremlin Palace (1838–49), etc. Except for the period between 1712 and 1918 it has served continually as the seat of the Russian government and is now also a public museum of Russian architecture.

Kreutzer, Rodolphe (1766–1831) French violinist and composer, renowned for his violin studies. Beethoven's *Kreutzer Sonata* for violin and piano (1803) was dedicated to him.

Krewo, Union of (1385) The union of Poland and Lithuania under Jagiełło, Grand Duke of Lithuania (*see* Jagiellon), whose rule there was threatened by rivals in the ducal family and by the *Teutonic Knights. He agreed to marry the young Polish queen and to accept Christianity while Lithuania was to be annexed to Poland. The union was only made permanent by the Union of *Lublin (1569).

krill Shrimplike marine *crustaceans, 0.3–2.4 in (8–60 mm) long, of the order *Euphausiacea* (82 species). Periodically krill swarms occur in certain regions, for example the Arctic and Antarctic Oceans, to become an important source of food for fishes, birds, and especially baleen whales.

Krishna A popular Hindu deity, the eighth incarnation of *Vishnu and the subject of much devotional worship, art, and literature. In the *Bhagavadgita* he is revealed as the creator, sustainer, and destroyer of the universe (*see* Trimurti). Elsewhere he is worshiped as a fertility god, whose flute playing entrances all and whose erotic love for young maidens expresses God's love for man. He is commonly represented as a beautiful youth with bluish skin wearing a crown of peacock feathers.

Krishna Menon. *See* Menon, Krishna.

Kristiansand 58 08N 8 01E A major seaport in S Norway, on the *Skagerrak. Its numerous industries include shipbuilding, textiles, smelting, and food processing. Population (1986 est): 62,500.

Krivoi Rog 47 55N 33 24E A city in SE Ukraine. Founded by the Cossacks in the 17th century, it is now an important iron mining center. Population (1991 est): 724,000.

Krochmal, Nachman (1785–1840) Jewish philosopher and historian, born in Poland. His *Guide to the Perplexed of Our Time* (published posthumously in 1851) offers an original philosophy of Jewish history and marks a significant achievement in the early modern study of Jewish history and literature.

Kronstadt 60 00N 29 40E A port in Russia, on Kotlin Island in the Gulf of Finland. The *Kronstadt Rebellion (1921) of sailors was instrumental in the Soviet Government's decision to inaugurate the New Economic Policy. Kronstadt is still an important naval base. Population (1987 est): 176,000.

Kronstadt Rebellion (1921) An uprising among Soviet sailors in Kronstadt. The sailors, who had supported the Bolsheviks in the Russian Revolution, demanded economic reforms and an end to Bolshevik political domination. The Red Army crushed the rebels and Lenin's *New Economic Policy (1921) was introduced to relieve the privations that had given rise to the revolt.

Kropotkin, Peter, Prince (1842–1921) Russian anarchist. A noted geographer and geologist, Kropotkin joined the anarchist movement in the 1870s, was arrested, and escaped abroad. He settled in England in 1886 and later wrote his famous autobiography, *Memoirs of a Revolutionist* (1899). In 1917, Kropotkin returned to Russia but, unsympathetic to the authoritarianism of the Bolsheviks, retired from politics.

Kruger, (Stephanus Johannes) Paul(us) (1825–1904) Afrikaner states-man; president (1883–1902) of the South African Republic (Transvaal). A farmer of Dutch descent, Kruger settled with his parents in the Transvaal after taking part in the *Great Trek. He led the struggle to regain independence for the Transvaal from the British, achieved in 1881, after the first *Boer War. As president he resisted British immigrant demands for political equality with the Afrikaner, a policy that led to the second Boer War (1899–1902). In the course of the war he went to Europe to seek aid for the Afrikaner cause. Unsuccessful, he settled in Holland and then Switzerland, where he died.

PAUL KRUGER

Kruger National Park A game and plant reserve in NE South Africa, adjacent to the border with Mozambique. About 202 mi (325 km) long and 12–31 mi (20–50 km) wide, it serves to protect most species found in the area, including lions, leopards, zebras, and elephants. Area: about 8106 sq mi (21,000 sq km).

krugerrand A South African coin containing one troy ounce of gold, minted since 1967 for overseas issue and bought for investment purposes. It has never been a true currency coin and was minted to enable investors to escape restrictions on the private ownership of gold.

Krugersdorp 26 06S 27 46E A city in South Africa, in the S Transvaal. Founded in 1887, it is an important mining and industrial center producing gold, uranium, and manganese. Population (1980 est): 102,940.

Krum (d. 814 AD) Khan of the Bulgars (802–14). After defeating a Byzantine army in 811, Krum besieged Constantinople in 813 and 814, dying during the campaign. Krum introduced the basis of a state administrative system to Bulgaria.

Krupp A German family of arms manufacturers. Under **Arndt Krupp** (d. 1624), the family settled in Essen, where in 1811 **Friedrich Krupp** (1787–1826) established a steel factory. His son **Alfred Krupp** (1812–87) di-versified the family business into arms manufacture, contributing to Prussian victory in the *Franco-Prussian War (1870–71). Under Alfred's son-in-law **Gus-tav Krupp von Bohlen und Halbach** (1870–1950), the company developed

Big Bertha, the World War I artillery piece named for Gustav's wife **Bertha Krupp** (1886–1957). Their son **Alfried Krupp** (1907–67) developed Gustav's ties with the Nazis, using concentration-camp internees in his factories. After World War II he was imprisoned for war crimes and his property was confiscated until 1951, when he was granted an amnesty.

krypton (Kr) A noble gas discovered in 1898 by Sir William Ramsay and M. W. Travers (1872–1961), in the residue left after boiling liquid air. Compounds include the fluoride KrF_2 and some *clathrates. It is used for filling some fluorescent light bulbs and the *meter is defined in terms of the wavelength of a specified transition of one of its isotopes. At no 36; at wt 83.80; mp −248.9°F (−156.6°C); bp −241.9°F (−152.2°C).

Kuala Lumpur 3 10N 101 40E The capital of Malaysia, in central Peninsular Malaysia. It became capital of the Federated Malay States in 1895. Formerly also capital of the state of Selangor, it became a federal territory in 1974. The University of Malaya was founded in 1962 and the Technological University of Malaysia in 1972. It is a major commercial center serving an important tin mining and rubber-growing area. Population: 1,209,000.

Kuang-chou. *See* Canton.

Kuang-hsü. *See* Guang Xu.

Kuan Ti. *See* Guan Di.

Kuan Yin. *See* Guan Yin.

Kuban River A river in Georgia and Russia. Rising in the Caucasus Mountains, it flows mainly NW into a swampy delta that enters the Sea of Azov. Its main port is Krasnodar. Length: 563 mi (906 km).

Kubelik, Rafael (1914–) Czech conductor. His career in Prague ended in 1948, when he went to live first in Britain and subsequently in the US. He was music director of Britain's Royal Opera (1955–58), and of the New York Metropolitan Opera (1972–74). In 1973 he took Swiss citizenship. His father **Jan Kubelik** (1880–1940) was a famous violinist.

Kublai Khan (1215–94) Emperor of China (1279–94), who founded the Yuan dynasty. Genghis Khan's grandson, Kublai established himself (1259) as chief of the Mongols after years of conflict with his brother Mangu (d. 1259). The conqueror and acknowledged ruler of all China from 1279, he administered from Peking an empire extending from the Danube River to the East China Sea. More humane than his predecessors and much influenced by Chinese culture and civilization, he opened up trade and communications with Europe, largely through Marco *Polo. However, his preoccupation with China and attempts to conquer SE Asia weakened the rest of the empire.

Kubrick, Stanley (1928–) US film writer, director, and producer. His first major film, *Paths of Glory* (1957), which he wrote and directed, concerned an unjust court-martial. His subsequent films, mainly satirical and highly imaginative, include *Lolita* (1962), *Dr Strangelove* (1963), *2001: A Space Odyssey* (1968), *A Clockwork Orange* (1971), *Barry Lyndon* (1975), and *The Shining* (1980).

Kuching 1 32N 110 20E A port in Malaysia, the capital of Sarawak state on the Sarawak River. It exports rubber, sago, and pepper. It has Anglican and Roman Catholic cathedrals. Population (1980): 120,000.

kudu A large antelope, *Tragelaphus strepsiceros*, of African bush regions. About 52 in (130 cm) high at the shoulder, kudus are red-brown with thin white vertical stripes on the flanks. Males have long corkscrew-shaped horns, a fringe on the lower side of the neck, and a mane along the back.

The lesser kudu (*T. imberbis*) is smaller and found only in NE Africa.

kudzu A climbing vine, *Pueraria lobata*, with entire or lobed leaves and fragrant purple flowers. Native to E Asia, it has been introduced to North America for its edible tubers, fiber, and as a quick-growing ornamental along highways, etc. However, its extreme hardiness has made it difficult to contain or control. Family: *Leguminosae*.

Kufah A town 90 mi (145 km) S of Baghdad, in Iraq. Founded as an Arab garrison town in 638 AD, Kufah became one of the most important centers of Islam. From the 10th century it began to decline and it is now an archeological site. Its suburb of Najaf is the burial place of *Ali and a flourishing center of *Shiite Islam.

Kuibyshev (name until 1935: Samara) 53 10N 50 10E A port in Russia, on the Volga River. Oil refining is a major industrial activity and market gardening is also important. Population (1991 est): 1,257,000.

Kukai (774–835) Japanese Buddhist monk, famous as a scholar and artist. The founder of the Kongobuji monastery on Mount Koya, Kukai reputedly invented hiragana, the character system of *Japanese writing.

Ku Klux Klan (KKK) A US secret society committed to the racist philosophy of white supremacy. Founded in Tennessee soon after the *Civil War to deter newly-enfranchised African Americans from voting, the Klan adopted bizarre membership rituals and was headed by an officer called the Imperial Wizard. During the early *Reconstruction period, Klansmen in white cloaks and hoods, burning fiery crosses, terrorized and killed innocent African Americans and destroyed their property. Although the original Klan was disbanded in 1869, it was revived in 1915 as a white supremacist party preaching hatred against immigrants, Catholics, and Jews, as well as African Americans. Membership in the KKK dropped during the Depression, but opposition in the South to the *civil rights movement in the 1950s led to another revival. The House Un-American Activities Committee investigated the Klan leadership in 1965, after it had been implicated in the murder of a civil rights demonstrator. The present Klan membership is tiny, but it maintains its fanatical opposition to any form of racial integration.

kulaks Wealthy peasants in late imperial and early Soviet Russia. Before the Russian Revolution (1917) they were prominent in village affairs. After the Revolution, they were favored by the *New Economic Policy (1921) until 1927, when Stalin raised their taxes and then transformed their lands into *collective farms. The dekulakization program led to the exile of many kulaks to remote regions.

Kulturkampf (German: conflict of beliefs) The struggle between *Bismarck and the German Roman Catholic Church during the 1870s and 1880s. Bismarck opposed the church's involvement in politics and subordinated it to the state. However, opposition to the persecution of priests had forced Bismarck to restore the church's rights by 1887.

Kumamoto 32 50N 130 42E A city in Japan, in W Kyushu on the Shira River. One of the strongest centers in feudal Japan, it has a 17th-century castle. Its university was established in 1949. It is an agricultural center, with bamboo, pottery, and textile industries. Population (1990): 579,306.

Kumasi 6 45N 1 35W The second largest city in Ghana. Formerly the capital of Ashanti, it was taken by the British in 1874. It is the commercial and transportation center of Ghana's chief cocoa-growing area. The University of Science and Technology was founded here in 1961. Population (1988 est): 385,000.

Kumayry (name from 1840 until 1924: Aleksandropol; name until 1991: Leninakan) 40 47N 43 49E A city in NW Armenia. Its textile industries are of major importance. A devastating earthquake in December 1988, demolished the city, and much of the population was killed. Population (1990 est): 120,000.

kumquat A shrubby plant of the genus *Fortunella* (6 species), of E and SE Asia, with fruits resembling small oranges. They are acid-tasting and mainly used for pickling and preserves. Kumquats can be grown farther N than citrus trees. Family: *Rutaceae*.

Kun, Béla (1886–?1939) Hungarian revolutionary. Kun founded the Hungarian Communist Party in 1918 and led the Soviet Republic that succeeded *Károlyi's government in March 1919. The populace's reluctance to accept his nationalization program led to a reign of terror, which with his unsuccessful campaigns against Romania forced him to flee in August to Vienna and then to Russia. He reportedly died in Stalin's purges.

KUNG FU *A demonstration of this popular martial art in a city square.*

kung fu An ancient Chinese form of combat, mainly for self-defense. Among the other *martial arts it is most closely related to *karate, which possibly developed from it. In the second half of the 20th century the *wing chun* style (according to tradition devised as a means of self-defense for women) has become particularly well known, partly because of the publicity given it by Bruce *Lee. Like other martial arts, it embodies a philosophy as well as a method of combat.

Kunlun Mountains A mountain system in W China, separating Tibet from the Tarim Basin. It extends 1000 mi (1600 km) E–W, reaching 25,378 ft (7723 m) at Ulugh Muztagh.

Kunming 25 04N 102 41E A city in S China, the capital of Yunnan province. A major commercial and cultural center, it is noted for its Ming bronze temple and is the site of Yunnan University. Industries include iron and steel, engineering, and chemicals. Population (1990): 1,127,411.

Kuomintang. *See* Guomindang.

Kuo Mo-jo (1892–1978) Chinese man of letters, translator of many western classics. Born in Szechwan, he went to Japan in 1913, where in 1921 he founded the Creation Society, dedicated to the reform of Chinese language and literature. He produced a vast amount of work as a poet, novelist, playwright, and critic. He returned to China in 1937 a committed communist and held many major cultural posts under Mao.

Kura River A river in W Asia. Rising in NE Turkey, it flows N into Georgia and Azerbaijan to enter the Caspian Sea near Baku. It is used for hydroelectric power and irrigation. Length: 941 mi (1515 km).

Kurchatov, Igor Vasilievich (1903–60) Soviet physicist, who headed his country's research into nuclear fission during World War II. His team constructed a nuclear reactor in 1946 and built the Soviet Union's first atomic bomb in 1949 and its first hydrogen bomb in 1952. The element kurchatovium is named for him.

kurchatovium (Ku) An artificial transuranic element and the first transactinide. It was first detected by Soviet scientists in 1964 and named for I. V. *Kurchatov. The claim is disputed by scientists at Berkeley, US, who proposed the name **rutherfordium** (Rf) after Lord *Rutherford, following their independent synthesis. At no 104.

Kurdistan An area in the Middle East inhabited by *Kurds, comprising parts of SE Turkey, N Syria, N Iraq, and NW Iran, including the Iranian province of Kordestan. The Turkish part includes a plateau that supports some agriculture, the remainder being mainly mountainous; the chief towns are Diyarbakir (Turkey), Kirkuk (Iraq), and Kermanshah (Iran). The area was split between different countries on the dissolution of the Ottoman Empire at the end of World War I, and subsequent attempts to form a Kurdish state have been only partially or temporarily successful. The Kurds of Iraq tried to form an autonomous state after the 1991 Gulf War but were repressed by the government. Area: 74,600 sq mi (192,000 sq km).

Kurds The major population group in *Kurdistan. Their language, Kurdish, is one of the *Iranian languages and is written in either a modified Arabic or a modified Cyrillic script. The Kurds grow cereals and cotton and are now mostly detribalized but a few nomadic groups still exist. They are Muslims but do not restrict their women to the same extent as other Islamic peoples. Known from Assyrian records (6th century BC), the Kurds have never enjoyed political unity, and nationalistic aspirations issuing in rebellions in the 19th and 20th centuries have led to reprisals, especially in Turkey (1925) and Iraq, where the government employed almost genocidal methods in their repression during the late 1980s and early 1990s.

Kure 34 14N 132 32E A port in Japan, in SW Honshu on Hiroshima Bay. An important naval base since 1886, an enormous battleship, the *Yamato*, was built here during World War II. Other industries include engineering and steel. Population (1990): 216,723.

Kurgan 55 30N 65 20E A city in Russia, on the Tobol River. Machinery is produced and food processed. Population (1991 est): 370,000.

Kuria Muria Islands A group of five islands off the coast of Oman, in the Arabian Sea. Area: 28 sq mi (72 sq km).

Kuril Islands A chain of 56 islands extending 746 mi (1200 km) NE–SW between Kamchatka (Russia) and Hokkaido (Japan) and separating the Sea of Okhotsk and the main body of the Pacific Ocean. Discovered in 1634 by the

Dutch, the islands were Japanese until seized by the Soviet Union in 1945. The largest are Paramushir, Urup, Iturup, and Kunashir. There are hot springs and 38 active volcanoes. Parallel to the chain, about 124 sq mi (200 km) to the E, is the **Kuril Trench**, which has a maximum depth of 34,587 ft (10,542 m). Total area: about 6022 sq mi (15,600 sq km).

Kurosawa, Akira (1910–) Japanese film director. His best-known films are action costume dramas such as *Rashomon* (1950) and *Seven Samurai* (1954). Working often with the actor Toshiro Mifune, he has also made films on contemporary themes of social injustice and several literary adaptations, notably *Throne of Blood* (1957) from Shakespeare's *Macbeth*. Later films included *The Shadow Warrior* (1980) and *Ran* (1985). In 1990 he received an Academy Award for lifetime achievement.

kuroshio A warm ocean current forming part of the N Pacific circulation. Analogous to the Gulf Stream of the Atlantic, it flows NE along the Pacific coast of Japan, then veers across the N Pacific as the North Pacific Drift.

Kursk 51 45N 36 14E A Russian city. Food processing and metallurgy are important. Population (1991 est): 433,300.

Kusunoki Masashige (1294–1336) Japanese samurai. His steadfast loyalty to Emperor *Daigo II and heroic defense of Chihaya castle became one of the most famous examples of *bushido* (the way of the warriors).

Kutaisi 42 15N 42 44E A city in W Georgia on the Rioni River. It is a historic Transcaucasian city and the 11th-century Bagrati Cathedral survives. It is a major industrial center, producing especially consumer goods. Population (1991 est): 238,200.

Kutch, Rann of An area of salt waste in central W India, near the border with S Pakistan. It consists of the Great Rann in the N and the Little Rann in the SE. It was a navigable lake in the 4th century BC, but is now salt marsh in the wet season and salt desert in the dry. Total area: about 8878 sq mi (23,000 sq km).

Kutenai A North American Indian people of the plateau region between the Rocky and Cascade Mountains of British Columbia. They were a hunting and fishing people, occasionally moving on to the Plains to hunt buffalo. Their language is distantly related to the *Algonquian family.

Kutuzov, Mikhail Ilarionovich, Prince of Smolensk (1745–1813) Russian field marshal. After service in Poland, Austria, and against the Turks, he commanded the forces opposing Napoleon's invasion of Russia. When Napoleon withdrew from Moscow, Kutuzov's army harassed his retreat until barely 100,000 French soldiers remained.

Kuwait 29 20N 48 00E The capital of the sheikdom of Kuwait, on the Persian Gulf. It has a good natural harbor, and its livelihood was based on sea trade, fishing, and boatbuilding until oil became the major industry in the early 1950s and the traditional Islamic town began to develop into a metropolis with modern facilities including a university (1962). Population (1985): 44,300.

Kuwait, State of A country in the Middle East, in Arabia situated at the head of the Persian Gulf. The country is flat, sandy, and barren and has a harsh climate with extremes of temperature. The inhabitants are predominantly Arab, although about half are foreigners, and the Kuwaitis are mainly Sunnite or Shiite Muslim. *Economy*: Kuwait is one of the largest oil producers in the world and has one of the highest per capita incomes; oil revenues account for over half the gross national product and oil-related services for most of the remainder, as the country has almost no other natural resources. Kuwait is a member of OPEC. There are some manufacturing industries, such as plastics and fertilizers, and the traditional fishing (especially for shrimp) and the building of dhows (Arab sailing craft) continue. *History*: Kuwait was originally settled in the early 18th century by nomads from the Arabian interior, who established a sheikdom in 1756. In 1899, to counter German and Ottoman expansionism, Kuwait made an agreement giving Britain control over its foreign affairs and on the outbreak of World War I it became a British protectorate. Its borders were fixed in 1922–23, including those of a neutral zone, the oil revenues from which are shared by Saudi Arabia and Kuwait. Oil was discovered in 1938 but it was not exploited until after World War II, when it transformed the Kuwaiti economy. On gaining independence in 1961, Kuwait almost immediately had to request troops from Britain in order to avert the threatened annexation by Iraq but soon after became accepted as a sovereign state. Kuwait nationalized its oil industry in 1975. War between Iran and Iraq from 1980 raised the fear of Iranian aggression against the Arab states in the Persian Gulf region. In 1986 the ruling Sheik dissolved parliament. In 1990, Iraq, citing long-standing territorial and economic grievances, suddenly invaded Kuwait. The country was quickly overrun and "annexed" by Iraq. The US and other countries pushed the UN to condemn the invasion. UN resolutions against Iraq's actions were followed by the creation of a US-led multinational coalition to liberate Kuwait. Assembled in Saudi Arabia, the coalition launched *Operation Desert Storm in January 1991 and freed Kuwait by the end of February. Kuwait's rulers returned, promising democratic reforms and facing years of rebuilding to repair Iraqi destruction. Head of state: Sheik Jabir al-Ahmad al-Jabir as-Sabah. Prime minister: Sheik Saad as-Salim as-Sabah. Official language: Arabic. Official currency: Kuwait dinar of 1000 fils. Area: 9375 sq mi (24,286 sq km). Population (1990 est): 2,080,000. Capital: Kuwait.

Kuznets, Simon (1901–85) US economist, born in Russia. His theory of the *gross national product as a measure of economic output is contained in his major work *National Income and Its Composition (1919–1938)* (1941). Kuznets was awarded the Nobel Prize (1971).

Kwa A major division of the *Niger-Congo language family that includes many languages of West Africa, such as Yoruba, Igbo (*see* Ibo) *Ewe, Twi, and Anyi.

Kwajalein 9 15N 167 30E The largest atoll of the Marshall Islands, in the W Pacific Ocean. It was the first Pacific territory captured by US forces in World War II and is now a US military base.

Kwakiutl A North American Indian people of the coastal region of British Columbia. They speak a *Wakashan language. Their vigorous traditional culture was typical of the NW coast and characterized by extreme competition for status and rank through ostentatious disposal and even destruction of wealth (*see* potlatch). There was an elaborate religious and ceremonial life and a distinctive artistic tradition based upon carving of wooden totem poles, masks, and other objects. Their economy was based on an abundance of salmon and other fish, game, and wild fruits and agriculture was not practiced.

Kwangju 35 07N 126 52E A city in SW South Korea. An ancient commercial and administrative center, it has industries that include motor-vehicle manufacture. Its university was established in 1952. Population (1990): 1,144,695.

kwashiorkor Severe protein deficiency in children under five years. **Marasmus** is deficiency not only of protein but also of carbohydrate and fat. Kwashiorkor and marasmus often occur together in some combination. Kwashiorkor, which develops in babies soon after they are weaned, occurs in poor countries, especially parts of West Africa, where the diet does not contain sufficient protein (the name derives from a Ghanaian word). The children fail to grow, are apathetic, have swollen stomachs and ankles, sparse hair, diarrhea, and enlarged livers. The slightest infection is usually fatal but the children recover rapidly with a good diet.

KwaZulu. *See* Bantu Homelands.

Kyd, Thomas (1558–94) English dramatist. A friend of *Marlowe, Kyd inaugurated the genre of revenge tragedy with *The Spanish Tragedy* (1592). Among his probable works is a play about Hamlet, now lost, which influenced Shakespeare.

Kyoga, Lake (*or* Lake Kioga) A lake in central Uganda. Formed by the Victoria Nile River, it is shallow and reedy and has many arms. Length: c. 81 mi (130 km).

Kyoto 35 2N 135 45E A city in Japan, in S Honshu. It has been a leading cultural center since early times, when it was the Japanese capital (794–1192 AD) and the old imperial palace and ancient Buddhist temples still remain. Kyoto university was established in 1897. It is also the center of Japanese Buddhism. Situated within the Osaka-Kobe industrial complex, it is famed for its silk, porcelain, and handicrafts. Population (1990): 1,461,140.

Kyprianou, Spyros (1932–   ) Cypriot statesman; president (1977–88). When Cyprus became independent in 1960 he was appointed minister of justice and then foreign minister (1960–72). In 1976 he founded the Cyprus Democratic party.

Kyrgyzstan, Republic of (*or* Kyrgyzstan) A republic in central Asia, bordering on China, a constituent republic of the Soviet Union known as Kirgizia until 1991. The Kirgiz, a traditionally nomadic Turkic people, comprise over one-third of the population. Kyrgyzstan, which is mountainous, has important deposits of coal, lead, oil, mercury, and antimony, as well as oil and natural gas. Industries include the manufacture of machinery and building materials and food processing. Wheat, cotton, and tobacco are grown and livestock, especially cattle, sheep, horses, and yaks, are important. *History*: the Kirgiz came under Russian rule in the 19th century and fought the new Soviet Government after the Russian Revolution. As a result they suffered a famine in 1921–22, in which over 500,000 Kirgiz died. Kirgizia became an SSR in 1936. It became independent in 1991 with the collapse of the Soviet Union. Kyrgyzstan became a member of the Commonwealth of Independent States in 1991 and the United Nations in 1992. Area: 76,460 sq mi (198,500 sq km). Population (1992): 4,533,000. Capital: Frunze.

Kyushu The southernmost of the four main islands of Japan, separated from Korea by the Korea Strait and from Honshu by Shimonoseki Strait. Mountainous and volcanic, it has hot springs and a subtropical climate and is the most densely populated of the Japanese islands. There is a large rice-growing area in the NW, drained by the Chikugo River, while heavy industry is centered on the N coalfield. Other important products are silk, fish, timber, fruit, and vegetables. It is noted for its Satsuma and Hizen porcelain. Area: 13,768 sq mi (35,659 sq km). Population (1990): 14,518,257. Chief cities: Kitakyushu, Fukuoka, and Nagasaki.

Kyzyl Kum A desert in central Asia, lying between the Amu Darya and Syr Darya Rivers in Kazakhstan and Uzbekistan. Area: about 115,806 sq mi (300,000 sq km).

L

Laaland. *See* Lolland.

Labanotation. *See* illustration at ballet.

labeled compounds. *See* radioactive tracer.

Labiatae A family of herbaceous plants and shrubs (about 3500 species), widely distributed but particularly abundant in the Mediterranean region. They typically have square stems, hairy simple leaves, and clusters of tubular two-lipped flowers. Many of the plants are aromatic and yield useful oils (lavender, rosemary, etc.) and many are used as culinary herbs (marjoram, mint, sage, thyme, etc.).

Labiche, Eugène (1815–88) French dramatist. His numerous popular farcical comedies include *The Italian Straw Hat* (1851) and *The Journey of Mr Perrichon* (1860). They are characterized by intricate plots and the satirical portrayal of contemporary bourgeois conventions.

Labor Day The day on which the labor movement is celebrated. In 1889, the Second International declared an international labor holiday on *May Day, which has since been thus celebrated in many countries. It is celebrated in the US on the first Monday in September.

Labor, Department of US cabinet-level executive branch department that administers laws guaranteeing workers' rights regarding working conditions, wages, discrimination, and compensation insurance. It protects pension rights, provides for job training and employment, strengthens collective bargaining, and measures the nation's economy. Established in 1913, it was originally the Bureau of Labor under the Interior Department.

Labor Party The Australian democratic socialist party. It was formed in New South Wales in 1891 and first held federal office in 1904. World War I provoked a split in the party with the Labor prime minister W. M. *Hughes leading the proconscription majority out of the party to form the National party (1916). The Labor party did not regain power until 1929 and in 1931 policies in dealing with the Depression caused another split. In power from 1939–49, the party introduced important social legislation but in opposition in the 1950s another split occurred over attitudes to communism. Labor was again in power from 1972–75 under Gough *Whitlam and from 1983, when Robert *Hawke became prime minister.

labor relations. *See* industrial relations.

labor theory of value The economic theory that the value of a product can be determined by the amount of labor needed to produce it, e.g. a product needing twice as many man hours (of equal skill) to produce it as another is worth twice as much.

labor union An organization of employees joined together to present a collective front in negotiations with an employer and to provide a measure of security for its members. The origins of labor unions lie in the local clubs of skilled craftsmen in 18th-century Britain. The union movement in the US began in the early 19th century but did not gain much support until after the Civil War. Significant gains were made in the early 20th century despite continued opposition by employers and government authorities. Local unions are often affiliated with large national unions, which in turn are part of the *AFL-CIO.

Labour party The democratic socialist party in Britain. The party was formed in 1900 as the Labour Representation Committee, being renamed the Labour party in 1906. Its origins lie in the trade-union movement of the 19th century, and the trade unions continue to provide over three-quarters of its funds. The *Fabian Society was also a powerful influence on its formation and political beliefs. In 1922 the Labour party replaced the divided Liberal party as one of the two major British parties (*compare* Conservative party) and in 1924 and 1929–31 Labour formed a minority government under Ramsay *MacDonald. After World War II, under Clement *Attlee, the party won a huge majority in the general election of 1945. In office from 1945–1951, the Labour administration undertook widespread *nationalization and set up a comprehensive system of *social security. The party was in office again from 1964–1970 and from 1974–1979, under Harold *Wilson (1964–76) and then James *Callaghan. The increasing prominence of the extreme left caused splits within the party and in 1981 four members from the right defected to form the *Social Democratic party. Michael Foot was succeeded as party leader by Neil *Kinnock in 1983.

Labrador A district of NE Canada, on the Atlantic Ocean. Although the coast has belonged to Newfoundland for several centuries, the interior was finally awarded to Newfoundland in 1927 by a judicial decision, which is still not recognized by Quebec. Labrador is mostly a rolling swampy plateau within the Canadian Shield. Generally barren except for forested river valleys, it has vast reserves of high-grade iron ore, which are being mined. Its hydroelectric potential is enormous. Area: 99,685 sq mi (258,185 sq km). *See also* Churchill Falls.

Labrador Current A major ocean current of the N Atlantic, flowing S from the polar seas down the W coast of Greenland and past Newfoundland, until it meets the Gulf Stream and, being cold and dense, sinks beneath it. The Labrador Current carries icebergs S and is a cause of frequent fogs in the region of Newfoundland.

Labrador retriever A breed of dog originating in Newfoundland, Canada. It is solidly built with a tapering otterlike tail and a short dense water-resistant coat, usually black or yellow-brown. Height: 22.4–22.8 in (56–57 cm) (dogs); 21.6–22.4 in (54–56 cm) (bitches).

La Bruyère, Jean de (1645–96) French satirist. He studied law and then served in the Bourbon household of Louis II, prince of Condé. His single work, *Caractères de Théophraste, avec les caractères ou les moeurs de ce siècle* (1688), consisted chiefly of satirical portrait sketches (often of real persons under disguised names) and contemporary illustrations of vices; it achieved lasting popularity.

Labuan A Malaysian island in the South China Sea. It became part of the state of Sabah in 1946. Copra, rubber, and rice are produced. Area: 38 sq mi (98 sq km). 7200. Chief town: Victoria.

laburnum A tree of the genus *Laburnum*, especially *L. anagyroides*, which is native to mountainous regions of central Europe and widely grown for ornament. Up to 23 ft (7 m) high, it has smooth olive-green or brown bark and its leaves each consist of three dark-green leaflets. The bright-yellow flowers grow in hanging clusters, 4–12 in (10–30 cm) long, and produce slender brown pods. All parts of the plant are poisonous, especially the seeds. Family: *Leguminosae*.

labyrinth fish A small elongated laterally compressed fish of the family *Anabantidae* (about 70 species), found in fresh waters of tropical Asia and Africa. They have an accessory respiratory organ (labyrinth) with which they obtain oxygen from air gulped at the surface—of benefit in poorly oxygenated water. The males often build a floating nest of bubbles to protect the eggs. Some species are popular aquarium fish. Order: *Perciformes. See also* climbing perch; fighting fish; gourami.

Laccadive, Minicoy, and Amindivi Islands. *See* Lakshadweep.

lace An ornamental network of threads of silk, linen, etc., used mainly for dress collars, cuffs, altar cloths, etc. Needlepoint lace, originating in Italy in the early 16th century, is made with a needle on parchment or fabric. Pillow or bobbin lace, reputedly invented by Barbara Uttmann (b. 1514) in Saxony, is formed by twisting threads around pins stuck in a pillow. The best work was done in Italy, Flanders, France, and England in the 17th and 18th centuries, famous types of lace being Brussels, Valenciennes, Mechlin, and Honiton. Lace making as an art declined in the 19th century after machine manufacture was introduced.

LACE *An example of bobbin lace from Brussels made in the first half of the 18th century.*

La Ceiba 15 45N 86 45W A port in N Honduras, on the Gulf of Honduras. It is a major port exporting chiefly coconuts, abaca fiber, and oranges. Population: 64,000.

lacewing An insect belonging to one of several families of the suborder *Plannipennia.* Lacewings have delicate net-veined wings and are carnivorous, with biting mouthparts. Green lacewings (*Chrysopidae*), also called golden-eyed lacewings, are about 0.4 in (10 mm) long and occur worldwide near vegetation. Eggs are laid individually on hairlike stalks and the larvae feed on aphids, scale insects, etc. The brown lacewings (*Hemerobiidae*) are smaller and often have spotted wings. Order: **Neuroptera.* ☐insect.

Lachish An ancient city in **Canaan, W of Hebron (Israel), occupied from before 1580 BC. The Israelites held it from about 1220 until its destruction by the Babylonians (588). Inscriptions discovered here are important evidence for the early evolution of the alphabet.

Lachian River A river in SE Australia, in New South Wales. Rising in the Great Dividing Range it flows generally NW to join the Murrumbidgee River. Length: 922 mi (1483 km).

lac insect An insect of the family *Lacciferidae*, found mainly in tropical and subtropical regions. The legless females have globular bodies covered with a layer of hardened resin. In the Indian species, *Laccifer lacca*, the females become encrusted on twigs to form sticklac, from which **shellac is produced. Suborder: *Homoptera*; order: **Hemiptera.*

Laclos, Pierre Choderlos de (1741–1803) French novelist. He was a professional soldier and died while serving as a general under Napoleon in Italy. His novel, *Les Liaisons dangereuses* (1782), written in the form of letters between the main characters, concerned sexual corruption and intrigue in aristocratic society. The seducer Valmont, his accomplice Mme de Merteuil, and their victims are depicted with keen psychological insight.

La Condamine, Charles Marie de (1701–74) French geographer. After service in the army he traveled widely and joined a geographical expedition to Peru (1735–43). He later went down the Amazon River on a raft, studying the region, and brought the drug curare to Europe.

Laconia (modern Greek name: Lakonía) The SE region of the Peloponnese. Once a prosperous Mycenaean kingdom, Laconia was conquered by invading *Dorians about 1000 BC. Settling in *Sparta, the newcomers became rulers of Laconia, using the indigenous inhabitants as serf laborers, called *helots.

La Coruña (*or* Corunna) 43 22N 8 24W A port in NW Spain, in Galicia on the Atlantic Ocean. The Spanish Armada sailed from here on July 26, 1588, and in 1589 the city was sacked by Sir Francis Drake. During the Peninsular War, Sir John *Moore was mortally wounded here after ensuring a British victory against the French. An important fishing center, it also manufactures tobacco and linen. Population (1974 est): 193,443.

lacquer Colored and often opaque varnish applied to metal or wood for protection and decoration. In Chinese and Japanese artwork, the sap of the *lacquer tree is used as wood lacquer. Other types of lacquer consist of *shellac dissolved in alcohol, which dries to form a protective film.

lacquer tree A tree, *Rhus vernicifera*, of SE Asia, also called varnish tree. Up to 98 ft (30 m) tall, it has compound leaves each with up to nine pairs of leaflets, which turn red in autumn. Japanese *lacquer is obtained from the milky resin that oozes from cuts in the bark. Family: *Anacardiaceae*.

lacrosse A 10-a-side field game (12 in Canada and for women; 6 in the indoor version) played with a ball and a long-handled stick (the crosse), which has a triangular head with a rawhide strung pocket for catching, throwing, and picking up the ball. Of North American Indian origin, it is played mainly in the US, Canada, and Britain. The object is to score goals by running with the ball and passing it. Each team consists of a goalkeeper, three defensive players, three attackmen, and three midfielders, whose function is both offensive and defensive. Body checking and striking an opponent's stick to dislodge the ball are allowed, and protective clothing is worn. The game developed from the Indian game of bagataway, in which the field was not defined and the teams could number over 1000 players.

lactation The secretion of milk from the breasts or mammary glands. In women lactation is controlled by hormones released from the ovary, placenta, and pituitary gland (*see* prolactin) and starts shortly after childbirth, in response to the sucking action of the baby at the nipple; it will continue for as long as the baby is breast fed. A protein-rich fluid called colostrum is secreted in the first few days of lactation, before the milk has been produced. It contains antibodies that give the baby temporary immunity to disease.

lactic acid A carboxylic acid ($CH_3CH(OH)COOH$) that is the end product of *glycolysis in animal muscles and of *fermentations (such as the souring of milk) by certain bacteria. A commercial preparation is used as a flavoring and preservative in pickles and salad dressings and in tanning leather.

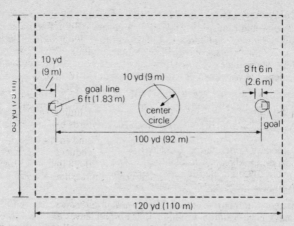

The optimum dimensions of the women's field, although the game is played with no boundaries.

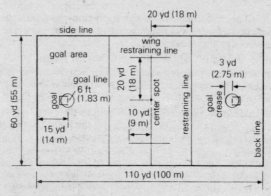

The dimensions of the men's field.

LACROSSE

lactose (*or* milk sugar) A disaccharide carbohydrate ($C_{12}H_{22}O_{11}$) consisting of one molecule of glucose linked to one of galactose. Lactose is found in the milk of all animals and is less sweet than sucrose.

Ladakh Range A mountain range mainly in NW India, extending about 230 mi (370 km) between the Karakoram Range and the Himalayas and rising to over 19,685 ft (6000 m).

Ladin A language spoken in the Dolomite region of Italy that belongs to the Rhaetian branch of the *Romance family. It is related to French and the Occitan dialects, to Romansh, and to Friulian, which is spoken around Udine in N Italy.

Ladino A *Romance language originally spoken by Sephardic Jews in Spain but taken by them after their exile in 1492 to the Balkans, the Near East, N Africa, Greece, and Turkey. It is an old form of Castilian Spanish mixed with Hebrew elements and written in Hebrew characters.

Ladoga, Lake A lake in NW Russia, the largest lake in Europe. It discharges via the Neva River into the Gulf of Finland. A canal forming part of the water route from the Gulf of Finland to the Volga River and the White Sea has been built parallel to its S shore to avoid the storms on the lake. *See also* Leningrad. Area: about 6836 sq mi (17,700 sq km).

ladybird beetle A small round beetle, 0.3–0.4 in (8–10 mm) long, that belongs to the widely distributed family *Coccinellidae* (5000 species). Most species are red or yellow with black spots and are of great benefit to man. Both the larvae and adults feed on a variety of plant pests, including aphids, scale insects, mealy-bugs, and whiteflies. When attacked, ladybirds exude a toxic fluid.

lady fern A delicate *fern, *Athyrium filix-femina*, found in moist shady temperate regions. It has a short stout scaly rhizome that produces a circular cluster of large light-green feathery branched fronds, usually 20–28 in (50–70 cm) long. The clusters of spore capsules (sori) are curved or horseshoe-shaped. Family: *Aspidiaceae*.

lady's slipper A terrestrial orchid, *Cypripedium calceolus*, native to N Europe and Asia. Up to 18 in (45 cm) high, it has broad leaves and the flowers are grouped singly or in twos and threes. Each flower has small twisted red-brown petals and an inflated yellow slipper-like lip. The lady's slipper is nearly extinct in Britain. *See also* slipper orchid.

lady's smock A perennial herb, *Cardamine pratensis*, also called cuckoo flower, found in damp meadows of N temperate regions; 6–12 in (15–60 cm) high, it has compound leaves and a tall spike of pink or violet four-petaled flowers on slender stalks. Family: *Cruciferae*.

Laënnec, René Théophile Hyacinth (1781–1826) French physician and inventor of the stethoscope. Laënnec listened to the chest sounds of his patients using a foot-long wooden cylinder, from which he was able to diagnose diseases of the heart and respiratory system.

Lafayette, Marie Joseph Gilbert Motier, Marquis de (1757–1834) French general and politician, prominent at the beginning of the French Revolution. His early career was distinguished by his military successes (1777–79, 1780–82) against the British in the *American Revolution. In France as a representative in the *States General, he presented the Declaration of the *Rights of Man (1789) and after the storming of the Bastille he became commander of the new National Guard. In 1792 the rising power of the radicals threatened his life and he gave himself up to France's enemy, Austria. Lafayette was also prominent in the July Revolution (1830), which overthrew Charles X.

La Fayette, Mme de (Marie Madeleine, Comtesse de L. F.; 1634–93) French novelist. She was a friend of *La Rochefoucauld and many other prominent writers. Her best-known novel is *La Princesse de Clèves* (1678), a study of the conflict between passion and duty in marriage.

Lafitte, Jean (also Laffite; ?1780–1825?) US privateer; born in France. He led smugglers that looted Spanish ships in the Gulf of Mexico and sold the stolen goods in New Orleans. He aided Andrew *Jackson's defense of New Orleans (1814–15) in the *War of 1812. Pardoned and proclaimed a hero, he returned to pirate life on an island in Galveston Bay until attacked by US ships (1820), after which he moved his activities to Central America.

La Follette, Robert Marion (1855–1925) US politician and lawyer. Born in Wisconsin, he practiced law there before serving as a Republicn in the US House of Representatives (1885–91), where he worked on the McKinley Tariff Act (1890). He was elected governor of Wisconsin (1900) on a progressive, anti-

Republican platform and by the end of his tenure (1906) had been able to institute many reforms in state government. He was a US senator (1906–25) during which time he founded the National Progressive Republican League (1909), instigated investigation of the Teapot Dome scandal (1921), and ran for president on the Progressive party ticket (1924).

Lafontaine, Henri-Marie (1854–1943) Belgian jurist and statesman. A senator (1894–1936) and president of the International Peace Bureau (1907–43), he is best known for his contribution to international law. He received the Nobel Peace Prize (1913).

La Fontaine, Jean de (1621–95) French poet. He was a friend of many prominent writers and patrons. His major work was the *Fables* (1668–94), sophisticated verse treatments of traditional fables from the collections of *Aesop, *Phaedrus, and later writers. His many other works included the bawdy verse tales, *Contes* (1664), which he is said to have repudiated after his religious conversion in 1692.

Laforgue, Jules (1860–87) French poet, one of the *Symbolists. He was born in Montevideo (Uruguay) and wrote most of his poetry in Berlin while serving as reader to the Empress Augusta (1858–1921). His ironic and slangy poetry in *vers libre* greatly influenced several later French and foreign poets, notably T. S. Eliot.

LAFTA. *See* Latin America.

Lagash A city of ancient *Sumer, N of *Ur, flourishing about 2500–2100 BC. *Cuneiform tablets found here bear witness to social, legal, and commercial conditions in Sumer.

Lagerkvist, Pär (Fabian) (1891–1974) Swedish novelist, poet, and dramatist. His early works were pessimistic in tone and influenced by expressionism. In the novels *Bödeln* (*The Hangman*; 1934) and *Dvärgen* (*The Dwarf*; 1944) he explored the problems of evil and human brutality. His best-known work is the novel *Barabbas* (1950), after which he achieved a worldwide reputation, winning the Nobel Prize (1951).

Lagerlöf, Selma Ottiliana Lovisa (1858–1940) Swedish novelist, who drew her inspiration from myth, legend, and her early life in Värmland. Her works include *Gösta Berlings Saga* (1891) and the children's storybook *The Wonderful Adventures of Nils* (1907). She was the first woman to be awarded the Nobel Prize (1909).

Lagomorpha An order of mammals (66 species) comprising *pikas, *rabbits, and *hares. Lagomorphs have teeth similar to rodents, with four continuously growing incisors. They are vegetarians and eat their own fecal pellets, thus obtaining the maximum value from their food. Lagomorphs are found all over the world except Antarctica.

Lagos 6 27N 3 28E The capital and main port of Nigeria, on Lagos Island on the Bight of Benin. First settled by Yoruba fishermen in the 17th century, it became the center of the Portuguese slave trade in West Africa and was ceded to Britain in 1861. Its university was founded in 1962. One of Africa's largest cities, it is an important commercial and industrial center. Exports include palm oil and kernels and groundnuts. Population (1992 est): 1,347,000.

Lagrange, Joseph Louis, Comte de (1736–1813) Mathematician and astronomer, born in Italy of French parents. In 1788, he published a book entitled *Mechanique analytique*, in which mechanics is developed algebraically and a wide variety of problems are solved by the application of general equations. In astronomy he solved the problem of predicting how two or more bodies move under each other's gravitational force and worked with *Laplace on planetary perturbations. Lagrange also headed the commission that produced the metric system of units in 1795.

La Guardia, Fiorello Henry (1882–1947) US politician; mayor of New York City (1933–45). As a lawyer and Congressman (1917–21, 1923–33) La Guardia helped initiate such laws as the Norris-La Guardia Act (1932), which allowed organized labor to strike, boycott, and picket. As mayor of New York he fought municipal corruption and supported action for civic improvement.

Lahore 31 34N 74 22E The second largest city in Pakistan, near the Ravi River. Traditionally the chief city of the Punjab, Lahore is situated close to the Indian border and has been the scene of much bloodshed and violence. It is a major railroad, commercial, and political center and the headquarters of the Muslim League. The famous Shalimar gardens lie to the E of the city. An important educational center, it is the site of the University of the Punjab (1882) and Pakistan University of Engineering and Technology (1961). *History*: founded about the 7th century AD, it fell to the Moguls in 1524 and in 1798 it became the seat of Ranjit Singh's Sikh empire. It came under British rule in 1849. Population (1981): 2,925,000.

Lahti 61 00N 25 40E A city in S Finland. A winter sports resort and growing industrial center, it has sawmills, furniture, and textile industries and is the site of Finland's main radio and television stations. Population (1988 est): 94,000.

Laing, R(onald) D(avid) (1927–89) British psychiatrist. He is best known for his explorations of the mind and madness, regarding schizophrenia as a defensive façade and madness as a journey of self-realization (*The Divided Self*, 1960). *The Politics of Experience* (1967) became influential among the radical movements of that period and his views on family life (*The Politics of the Family*, 1969) aroused controversy. His poetry includes *Knots* (1970).

laissez-faire The economic theory that governments should not interfere with market forces based on self-interest and the profit motive. The concept, originally proposed by the 18th-century French economists led by François *Quesnay (*see also* Physiocrats), was advocated by Adam *Smith and widely accepted until the beginning of the 19th century. By then the growth of capitalism had exposed its principal weaknesses: the rise of monopolies, the grossly inequitable distribution of wealth, and the exploitation of labor. In the 20th century, in western economies, laissez-faire policies have been largely abandoned for *mixed economies.

lake (landform) An extensive body of water occupying a hollow in the earth's surface. Rivers generally flow both into and out of lakes although some are landlocked with no outlet. An **oxbow lake** is crescent shaped and is formed when a river *meander is cut off by the river flow breaching its neck. The larger saline lakes form inland seas, such as the *Caspian Sea. Many lakes are man made, for water supply, hydroelectric-power generation, and irrigation; Lake *Kariba in S Africa is an example.

lake (pigment) An insoluble pigment formed by the combination of an organic dyestuff with a metallic compound (salt, oxide, or hydroxide). Lakes are used in paints and printing *inks.

Lake District (*or* Lakeland) An area in NW England, in Cumbria, a national park since 1951. It consists of a high dome incised by a radial system of glaciated valleys, many of which contain ribbon lakes. High mountains rise between the valleys. Its spectacular scenery, popularized by the Lakeland poets (notably Wordsworth), is now a major tourist attraction, together with facilities for hill walking, rock climbing, and water sports. Traditional occupations include farming, forestry, and quarrying. Area: about 700 sq mi (1813 sq km).

Lake Erie, Battle of (1813) US-British naval battle during the *War of 1812 that secured Lake Erie and the Northwest for the US. Oliver H. *Perry's fleet successfully engaged in victorious battle the British fleet under Capt. Robert H. Barclay that held Lake Erie. To report the victory, Perry wrote his famous message, "We have met the enemy and they are ours. . . ."

Lakeland terrier A breed of dog originating in the English Lake District and used to flush foxes from cover. It has a robust body and a long flat head with small folded triangular ears. The rough dense coat may be black or blue (with or without tan), red, or dark brown. Height: up to 14 in (36 cm).

Lake of the Woods A lake in S central Canada and N central Minnesota. About one third of the lake is in the US, where the Northwest Angle projects into Canada. In Canada it lies in SE Manitoba and SW Ontario. It is fed by the Rainy River and has almost 14,000 islands. Kenora, Ontario, on the N end of the lake, is the main resort town. Area: 1485 sq mi (3847 sq km).

Lakshadweep (name until 1973: Laccadive, Minicoy, and Amindivi Islands) A Union Territory of India comprising 27 islands in the Indian Ocean, 186 mi (300 km) W of Kerala. Ruled by Britain from 1792, it was handed over to India in 1956 and depends economically on fish, coconuts, grains, bananas, and vegetables. Area: 12 sq mi (32 sq km). Population (1991): 51,681. Administrative headquarters: Kavaratti Island.

Lakshmi In Hinduism, the goddess of wealth and happiness, the benign aspect of Shakti, the supreme goddess. As the wife of Vishnu she appears in various forms according to his several incarnations. Many festivals are held in her honor (*see* Diwali). Lakshmi is also revered by the Jains.

Lalande, Joseph-Jérôme Le Français de (1732–1807) French astronomer, who published (1801) the most complete catalogue of the stars then known. It listed some 47,000 stars, one of which was found by *Leverrier a hundred years later to be the planet Neptune.

La Línea 36 10N 5 21W A city in SW Spain, in Andalusia on the Strait of Gibraltar. It was long tied economically to the British military base on Gibraltar. Industries include textiles and cork. Population (1970): 52,127.

Lalique, René (1860–1945) French *Art Nouveau jeweler and glassmaker. His jewelry is usually asymmetric with motifs of plants, snakes, etc. He later designed glassware with frosted patterns in relief, establishing a factory at Wingen-sur-Moder (1920).

Lallans The dialect of the lowlands of Scotland, in which Robert *Burns wrote. A movement to reestablish it as a literary medium occurred after World War I.

Lally, Thomas, Comte de (1702–66) French general of Irish ancestry. He took part in the *Jacobite rebellion of 1745 and subsequently became commander in chief in the French East Indies (1756), coming into conflict with the British. Forced to surrender in 1761, his action was construed as treason and he was beheaded.

Lalo, (Victor Antoine) Édouard (1823–92) French composer of Spanish descent. He is best remembered for his *Symphonie espagnole* (for violin and orchestra; 1873), a cello concerto (1876), and the ballet *Namouna* (1882).

lamaism. *See* Tibetan Buddhism.

Lamar, Lucius Quintus Cincinnatus (1825–93) US lawyer and politician; Supreme Court associate justice (1888–91). He practiced law in Mississippi before serving in the US House of Representatives (1857–60) where he was in favor of states' rights. At the start of the Civil War he returned home to work with Jefferson *Davis on secession. After the war, he taught at the University of Mississippi and then again became a representative in the House (1873–77), a US senator (1877–85), and secretary of the interior (1885–88), constantly advocating the "new South." His few years on the Supreme Court were devoted to states' rights and restraint in judicial matters.

Lamarck, Jean-Baptiste de Monet, Chevalier de (1744–1829) French naturalist, noted for his speculations about the evolution of living things, particularly his theory of the inheritance of acquired characteristics (*see* Lamarckism). Lamarck studied botany under Bernard de *Jussieu and published a flora of France in 1778. In 1793 he became professor of invertebrate zoology at the Museum of Natural History, Paris. Here Lamarck worked on a system of classification for invertebrate animals, published in his *Histoire naturelle des animaux sans vertebres* (7 vols, 1815–22). In 1809 Lamarck published his theory of evolution (in *Philosophie zoologique*). Lamarckism has generally been rejected in favor of Charles *Darwin's theory of evolution by natural selection, although some attempts have been made to revive it, most notably by *Lysenko. Lamarck's speculations about the physical and natural world found little favor among his contemporaries and he died blind and poverty stricken.

Lamarckism The first theory of *evolution as proposed by Jean-Baptiste *Lamarck in 1809, based on his concept of the inheritance of acquired characteristics. He suggested that an organism develops structural changes during its lifetime as an adaptation to its particular environment and that these features are then inherited by successive generations through sexual reproduction. A classic example of these acquired characteristics are the forelegs and neck of a giraffe, which he believed became longer through its habit of browsing on tall trees. There is now little support for Lamarck's theory, although it was revived in a slightly modified form (neo-Lamarckism) by the Soviet geneticist T. D. *Lysenko.

Lamartine, Alphonse de (1790–1869) French poet, one of the major figures of the Romantic movement. He established his reputation with *Méditations poétiques* (1820), a volume of lyrical poetry inspired by an unsuccessful love affair. During the 1820s he served as a diplomat in Naples and Florence and in the 1830s he became an active political champion of republican ideals. He was briefly head of the provisional government after the Revolution of 1848. His other major works include the narrative poems *Jocelyn* (1836) and *La Chute d'un ange* (1836).

Lamb, Charles (1775–1834) British essayist and critic. He worked as a clerk for the East India Company, devoting his private life to caring for his sister Mary (1764–1847), who had killed their mother in 1796 during one of her recurrent fits of insanity. He collaborated with Mary on *Tales from Shakespeare* (1807), a children's book. He is best remembered for his *Essays of Elia* (1822).

Lambaréné 0 41S 10 13E A town in W Gabon, on an island in the River Ogooué. Its hospital (1913) was founded by the missionary Albert *Schweitzer. Industries include palm products.

lambert A unit of luminance equal to the luminance of a surface that emits one lumen per square centimeter. Named for J. H. *Lambert.

Lambert, Johann Heinrich (1728–77) German mathematician and astronomer, who first derived the *hyperbolic functions and proved that π is an irrational *number. As an astronomer he measured the luminosities of stars and planets and introduced the term *albedo; a unit of luminance (*see* lambert) is named for him.

lamb's lettuce. *See* corn salad.

Lamentations of Jeremiah An Old Testament book, a sequel to the Book of *Jeremiah and traditionally attributed to him, although it is more likely a work of the 5th century BC. It consists of a series of five dirgelike chapters concerned with the capture and destruction of Jerusalem and its Temple by the Babylonians in 586 BC. The event is graphically described, as are the accompanying slavery and famine. Jeremiah sees it as a divine judgment and closes with a prayer for mercy.

Lamerie, Paul de (1688–1751) English silversmith of French Huguenot parents. Establishing his shop in 1712, he progressed from an unornamented Queen Anne style to *rococo designs, for which he is most famous.

Lamian War (323–322 BC) The conflict that confirmed Macedon's supremacy in Greece after Alexander the Great's death. *Antipater, the Macedonian regent, was besieged in Lamia by rebellious Greek forces but eventually crushed the city states and reimposed his authority more firmly.

laminar flow Fluid flow in which the particles move in parallel layers. A fluid moving slowly along a horizontal straight pipe flows in this way. Above a certain velocity, given by the *Reynolds number, the layers no longer remain parallel and the flow becomes turbulent.

Laminaria A genus of large brown seaweeds (*see* kelp), also called oarweed, that occurs in abundance along British and Pacific coasts. *L. digitata* (tangle) is a fan-shaped seaweed that may grow to a length of 165 ft (50 m). *Laminaria* is a good source of alginic acid and alginates, used in the manufacture of ice cream, tires, etc.

lammergeier A large *vulture, *Gypaetus barbatus*, also called bearded vulture because of the long bristles on its chin. It is over 40 in (1 m) long with a wingspan of 10 ft (3 m) and occurs in mountainous regions of S Europe, central Asia, and E Africa. It is brown with tawny underparts and a black-and-white face. Lammergeiers feed on bones and other carrion.

Lampedusa, Giuseppe Tomasi di (1896–1957) Italian novelist. He lived an adventurous early life as a wealthy Sicilian aristocrat. During his last years he wrote *The Leopard* (1958), a panoramic historical novel concerning Sicily in the late 19th century.

lamprey A fishlike vertebrate belonging to a family (*Petromyzonidae*; about 22 species) of *cyclostomes; 6–40 in (15–100 cm) long, lampreys have an eel-like body with one or two dorsal fins and seven pairs of gill slits. They occur in fresh or salt water and many are parasitic on fish, attaching themselves with a circular sucking mouth and feeding on the blood and flesh. Sexually mature adults move into fresh water to breed and then die after the eggs are laid. The burrowing larvae (ammocoetes) feed on microorganisms and take three to seven years to grow before their metamorphosis into adults and return to the sea. □fish.

lamp shell. *See* Brachiopoda.

Lanai 20 50N 156 55W An island in central Hawaii, S of Molokai and W of Maui. Noted for its pineapple plantations, it has been developed by the Dole Corporation (since 1922), which has been responsible for most construction and settlement. Mt Palawi (3369 ft; 1027 m) is the island's highest point. Area: 141 sq mi (366 sq km).

Lanark 55 41N 3 48W A city in S central Scotland, in Strathclyde Region overlooking the middle Clyde Valley. Nearby New Lanark, founded as a cotton-spinning center in 1784 by David Dale and Richard Arkwright, is well known for the social experiments carried out there by Robert *Owen. Population (1981): 9800.

Lancashire A county of NW England, bordering on the Irish Sea. It consists of lowlands in the W rising to the high level plateaus in the E, with the chief river, the Ribble, flowing SW to the Irish Sea. The lowlands are important agricultural regions, especially for dairy farming. Industry is based chiefly on textiles, mining, and engineering. Tourism is important in the coastal towns of Blackpool, Southport, and Morecambe. With industrialization, exploitation of the coal fields accelerated and by the 19th century Lancashire had become the greatest cotton-manufacturing center in the world. Area: 8191 sq mi (3043 sq km). Population (1987 est): 1,380,000. Administrative center: Preston.

Lancaster 40 08N 76 18W A city in SE Pennsylvania. Settled by German Mennonites in the early 18th century, it developed as an armaments center during the American Revolution. Today it is an agricultural and industrial center, producing tobacco, grain, livestock, and electrical products. Population (1990): 55,551.

Lancaster A ruling dynasty of England descended from Edmund, the second son of Henry III, who was created Earl of Lancaster in 1267. In 1361 the title passed by marriage to the third son of Edward III, *John of Gaunt. His son seized the throne from Richard II and ruled (1399–1413) as Henry IV. He was succeeded by Henry V, whose son Henry VI led the Lancastrians against the Yorkists (*see* York) in the Wars of the □Roses (1455–85), in which their emblem was a red rose. Following Henry VI's death (1471) the royal dynasty came to an end.

lancelet. *See* amphioxus.

Lancelot In *Arthurian legend, a knight of the Round Table, the son of King Ban and Queen Helaine of Benoic. While a child he was kidnapped by the Lady of the Lake, who educated him and later sent him to serve King Arthur. He was a celebrated warrior but failed in the quest of the *Holy Grail because of his adulterous love for *Guinevere.

lancewood Dense strong straight-grained wood obtained from various trees of the family *Annonaceae*, especially *Oxandra lanceolata*, native to the West Indies and South America. It is used in whip handles, fishing rods, etc., for which an elastic wood is essential. Australian lancewood comes from several trees, including *Acacia doratoxylon*. Family: *Leguminosae*.

Lanchow. *See* Lanzhou.

Land. *See* Germany, Federal Republic of.

Land, Edwin Herbert (1909–91) US inventor of *Polaroid, who set up the Polaroid Corporation in 1937 for its manufacture. He also invented the Polaroid Land Camera in 1947, in which pictures are printed inside the camera.

Land Acts, Irish A series of laws passed between 1870 and 1903 to deal with Irish agrarian problems. The three Fs (freedom to sell, fixity of tenure, and fair rents) were obtained in Gladstone's acts of 1870 and 1881. Later acts (especially those of 1885 and 1903) provided means for the tenant to buy his holding and Ireland thus became a land of owner occupiers.

landau A four-wheeled coach drawn by two or four horses. Landaus, first made in Landau (Germany) in the late 18th century, have fully collapsible tops and are still used in European royal processions.

Landau, Lev Davidovich (1908–68) Soviet physicist, who pioneered the mathematical theory of magnetic domains (*see* ferromagnetism). Working with Peter *Kapitza on *superfluid helium he was able to explain its properties in terms of quantum theory. For this work on superfluidity he was awarded the Nobel Prize (1962).

land crab A large square-bodied *crab of the tropical family *Gecarcinidae*, specialized for a terrestrial existence. It feeds on plant and animal materials. *Cardiosoma guanhumi*, 4 in (11 cm) across the back, is found in the West Indies and S North America. It lives in fields, swamps, and mangroves, sometimes several miles inland. Tribe: *Brachyura*.

Landes An area of heath and marshland in SW France, bordering on the Bay of Biscay and consisting chiefly of the Landes department. It is bordered by a strip of sand dunes, many over 148 ft (45 m) high, that have been fixed by the planting of pine forests. Area: 5400 sq mi (14,000 sq km).

Land-Grant College US state or territory higher-education institution for agricultural and mechanical arts, funded by the sale of federal lands as provided in the *Morrill Land Grant Act of 1862. Depending upon the circumstances in the state or territory, the school was made a part of an existing college or university or was established separately. By 1890 the second Morrill Act provided for annual funding by Congress to support these institutions.

landing craft Amphibious craft used for military assaults on beaches. Developed mainly by the US Marine Corps in World War II, they were first used on a large scale in the Anglo-American invasion of Sicily (June 1943), and later were important in the D-Day invasion of Normandy (1944) and in the Pacific campaign for Guadalcanal onward.

Landis, Kenesaw Mountain (1866–1944) US jurist and commissioner of baseball (1920–44). Named for the mountain where his father was wounded during the Civil War, he practiced law in Chicago before being appointed a US district judge (1905–22). He presided over the court that tried Socialist and labor leaders for sedition (1917) during World War I, and ruled in the "Black Sox" case that banned several players for taking bribes during the 1919 World Series. As baseball commissioner he was respected for his fair, honest, and irreversible decisions.

Land League An Irish agrarian organization established by Michael *Davitt in 1879 to press for land reforms. Its most famous tactic was one of organized ostracism (boycotting; *see* Boycott, Charles). After Gladstone's 1881 Land Act, the League's immediate aims were achieved and it was forced to disband.

landlord and tenant relationship The relationship arising from a grant (lease) of absolute possession of an *estate by a landlord to a tenant for a fixed period and, usually, for a regular payment of rent. The relationship is defined by a *contract, express or implied, which is contained in the lease or, for short terms, in a tenancy agreement.

Landon, Alfred Mossman ("Alf"; 1887–1987) US politician; governor of Kansas (1933–37). By 1912 he owned his own oil company and had become interested in politics. After working behind the scenes for Kansas Republicans, he served as governor for two terms, which led to his nomination as the Republican presidential candidate (1936), an election he lost by a landslide to Franklin D. *Roosevelt. His daughter, **Nancy L. Kassebaum** (1932–), a Republican, is a US senator (1978–).

Landor, Walter Savage (1775–1864) British poet and prose writer. He lived for many years on the Continent, chiefly in Florence. He wrote poems and dramas based on classical models, and is best known for his *Imaginary Conversations of Literary Men and Statesmen* (1824–28).

Landowska, Wanda (1877–1959) Polish-born harpsichordist and authority on its technique and repertoire. She established a school for advanced performers in Paris and later lived in the US.

Landrace A breed of pig originating in Denmark, where it has been intensively developed as a producer of high-quality lean bacon. It has a relatively small head and neck with light shoulders and long flanks. It can also produce good-quality pork.

Landrum-Griffin Act (also called US Labor-Management Reporting and Disclosure Act; 1959) US law designed to protect labor union members from corruption within a union. Under this legislation union financial records are open, elections are monitored, criminals are prevented from holding office for five years after conviction, and unfair disciplinary practices are discouraged.

landscape gardening The theory and practice of designing and planting a pleasing garden or park. Landscape gardening was carried out in the ancient Middle East, Greece, and Rome. In Europe, geometric formality in rigidly organized enclosed spaces predominated until the mid-18th century, when the possibilities were demonstrated of large-scale remolding of the landscape to achieve a naturalistic impression. Apparently random planting of trees, strategic siting of focal points, and sinuous expanses of water are key components. An excellent example of landscape architecture is Frederick Law Olmsted's design (1856) for Central Park in New York City, which provided an open area in the urban center. With the 20th-century decline of the *country estate, landscape gardening principles (harmony, variety, etc.) have come to be applied on a smaller scale.

Land's End (Cornish name: Pednanlaaz) 50 03N 5 44W The extreme western point of England. A granite headland in Cornwall, it lies at a distance of 603 mi (970 km) from John o'Groats at the N tip of Scotland. The southernmost point of England is the Lizard nearby.

Landshut 48 31N 12 10E A city in S Germany, in Bavaria on the Isar River. It is an industrial center and the site of a 13th-century castle. The Bavarian university was sited here (1800–26). Population: 52,300.

landslide (*or* landslip) The sudden downward movement of a mass of rock or earth. This may be triggered by an earthquake, or be due to an increase in the weight borne by a steep slope as a result of water soaking into it. Landslides may also occur as a result of undercutting of a slope by water, as in a riverbank or sea cliff.

Landsteiner, Karl (1868–1943) Austrian immunologist, who (in 1900) discovered human *blood groups and devised the ABO system of classification. Landsteiner's discovery enabled safe blood transfusions: by matching the blood groups of donor and recipient the immunological rejection of "foreign" blood by the recipient was avoided. He also discovered, in 1940, the *rhesus (Rh) factor in blood and made valuable contributions to poliomyelitis research. He was awarded the Nobel Prize (1930).

Lanfranc (c. 1010–89) Italian churchman and theologian; Archbishop of Canterbury (1070–89). In about 1043 he founded and became prior of a Benedictine abbey at Bec in Normandy; under the direction of his pupil St Anselm, the abbey became one of the most famous medieval schools. As archbishop under William the Conqueror from 1070, he launched a program of Church reform, which included appointing Normans as abbots of English monasteries and enforcing celibacy among the clergy.

Lang, Fritz (1890–1976) German film director. The best known of a number of distinguished and influential silent films are *Dr Mabuse the Gambler* (1922), *Metropolis* (1926), a nightmare vision of the future, and *M* (1931), a study of a psychopathic murderer. He left Germany in 1933 and went to Hollywood, where he made many commercially successful thrillers and westerns.

Langley, Samuel Pierpont (1834–1906) US astronomer, whose pioneering work on aerodynamics contributed greatly to the design of early aircraft. Langley himself failed to build a working aircraft, in spite of a grant of $50,000 from the US Government.

Langmuir, Irving (1881–1957) US chemist, whose early work on gases and vapors led to the invention of the Langmuir condensation pump. He also developed gas-filled filament lamps. He was awarded the Nobel Prize (1932) for his extensive work on monomolecular layers and surface chemistry.

Langtry, Lillie (Emilie Charlotte le Breton; 1853–1929) British actress, known as the Jersey Lily. After marrying a wealthy husband and becoming well known in London society, she made her stage debut in 1881. She was the first woman in Britain to prove that high social position was not incompatible with an acting career, although her fame was based more on her beauty than her acting talents. She was an intimate friend of the Prince of Wales, later Edward VII.

language The chief means by which human beings communicate with one another. Among the features that distinguish human language from other animals' communication systems are that it is learned, not inborn; the connection between a word or expression and that to which it refers is in principle arbitrary; it can be used to talk about itself, about events, objects, etc., not immediately present, or about any novel or unforeseen situation; and it is organized in recognizable patterns on two levels: *grammar and phonology. The origins of language are unknown, but since it is unique to man and all speech organs have some other more basic physiological function it is probably of quite recent origin in evolutionary terms. It is estimated that there are some 4000 languages spoken in the world today; countless thousands of others have perished, generally without trace. *See also* dialect; linguistics.

languages, classification of The division of languages into groups. There are three methods of classification. The first method is that of geographical or political division, in which languages are grouped together according to the continent or country in which they occur. Examples of the former include *Indian languages and European languages. The latter is represented by the similar but politically distinct languages *Swedish, *Danish, and *Norwegian. Such divisions do not always follow the genetic relationships that exist between languages. This relationship forms the basis for the second method of classification, which maps the historical development from one form of the language to another, as in the relation between Old English and modern *English. Further back both these and other languages can be traced to their common *Indo-European ancestor. However, some languages, such as *Basque, have no discoverable ancestry or relations. The third possible method of classification is on typological evidence, which depends on the grammatical structure of the language. The original three classes were devised by W. von *Humboldt: analytic (or isolating), agglutinative, and inflecting languages. **Analytic languages** (e.g. English, Chinese) show little variation in the forms of words but rely on strict word order to express grammatical relations (compare "The speaker thanked the chairman" with "The chairman thanked the speaker"; the words are the same in both sentences and the subject-object relations are understood purely by the order). In **agglutinative languages** (e.g. Turkish) words have the capacity to be split up into individual components with separate grammatical roles (in Turkish *sev/mek* means "to love"; *sev/dir/il/mek* means "to be made to love"; *sev/ish/mek/* means "to love one another"; and *sev/ish/dir/il/mek* means "to be made to love one another"). In **inflecting languages** (e.g. Latin, Sanskrit) words are characteristically built up of a root plus a component (morpheme) that represents several different grammatical categories (the Latin word *lavo* (I wash) consists of the root *lav-* and a suffix *-o*, the suffix here indicating the distinct grammatical elements of first person, singular number, present tense, indicative mood, and active voice). No language is entirely in one or other of these categories and the system itself has been modified and expanded by 20th-century linguists, but it is possible, on the grounds of predominant characteristics, to make general classifications.

LILLIE LANGTRY *As Rosalind in* As You Like It, *one of her most successful roles.*

Languedoc A former province in S France, on the Gulf of Lions. Its name derived from *langue d'oc*, the language of its inhabitants (*see* Provençal). In the 10th–12th centuries it flourished as an important cultural center. It is now incorporated chiefly into the planning region of **Languedoc-Roussillon** and is an important wine-producing area. Area: 10,595 sq mi (27,447 sq km). Population (1981 est): 10,117,200.

langur A leaf-eating *Old World monkey of tropical Asia. Langurs have specially adapted stomachs to digest their food. The largest is the hanuman, or entellus langur (*Presbytis entellus*), 30 in (75 cm) long with a 37-in (95-cm) tail. The douc langur (*Pygathrix nemaeus*) of Vietnam is mainly gray with white forearms and is now an endangered species. Chief genera: *Presbytis* (14 species), *Rhinopithecus* (4 species).

Lanier, Sidney (1842–81) US poet. As a Confederate soldier in the Civil War he was imprisoned and contracted tuberculosis, from which he eventually died.

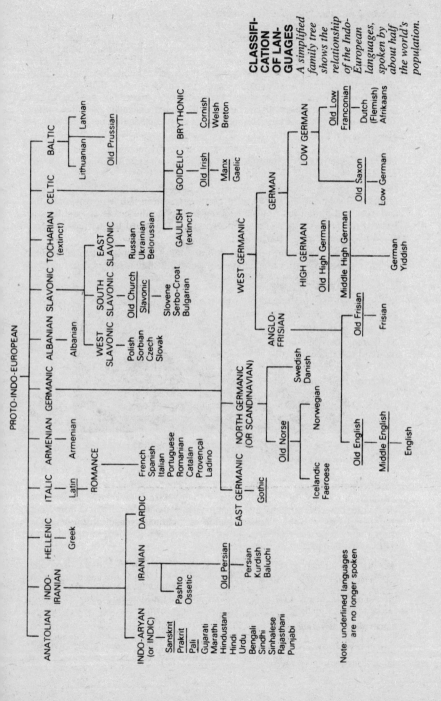

CLASSIFI-CATION OF LAN-GUAGES
A simplified family tree shows the relationship of the Indo-European languages, spoken by about half the world's population.

His poetry, notably "Corn" (1875), "The Symphony" (1875), and "The Marches of Glyn," was greatly influenced by his musical skills.

lanner falcon A large *falcon, *Falco biarmicus*, occurring in SE Europe and Africa. Up to 18 in (45 cm) long, it has a gray-brown back, white underparts flecked with black on the breast, a tawny head, and a black mustache. Lanner falcons feed chiefly on birds and are used in falconry.

lanolin A purified *wax extracted from wool. It is a mixture of cholesterol and other sterols, aliphatic alcohols, and esters. Because it is easily absorbed by the skin, lanolin is used as a base for creams, soaps, and other skin preparations.

Lansing 42 44N 85 34W The capital city of Michigan, on the Grand River. The site of the Michigan State University (1855), it contains part of the Detroit motor-vehicle industry, manufacturing car components. Population (1990): 127,321.

lantern fish A deepsea *bony fish belonging to the family *Myctophidae* (about 150 species). 1–6 in (2.5–15 cm) long, lantern fish have large mouths and eyes and numerous light-producing organs on the head, underside, and base of the tail. At night, many species migrate toward the surface. Order: *Myctophiformes*.

lanthanides (*or* rare-earth metals) A group of 15 *transition-metal elements, atomic numbers 57–71, which all have remarkably similar physical and chemical properties as a result of their electronic structures. They occur together in monazite and other minerals. They are used as catalysts in the petroleum industry, in iron alloys and permanent magnets, and in glass polishes. The **rare earths** are the oxides of these metals.

lanthanum (La) The first of the series of rare-earth metals (*see* lanthanides), all of which have similar chemical properties. It is used in *misch metal to make lighter flints. Its compounds include an oxide (La_2O_3) and a chloride ($LaCl_3$). At no 57; at wt 138.9055; mp 543°F (921°C); bp 1951°F (357°C).

Lanzhou (Lan-chou *or* Lanchow) 36 01N 103 45E A city in N China, the capital of Gansu province at the confluence of the Yellow and Wei Rivers. It is an ancient trade and communications center and the site of a university. Industries include oil refining, plutonium processing, and the manufacture of chemicals and machinery. Population (1990): 1,194,640.

Laocoon In Greek legend, a Trojan priest of Apollo who warned against accepting the Greek gift of the *Trojan Horse. He and his two sons were killed by sea serpents sent by Apollo, and the Trojans then opened their gates to the wooden horse.

Laodicea 37 46N 29 02E An ancient city of Asia Minor, near present-day Denizli (SW Turkey), founded by *Antiochus II about 250 BC. On an important trade route Laodicea soon prospered; early Christians condemned its worldliness. Under Diocletian it became Phyrgia's metropolis (mother city). Its Roman remains include theaters and an aqueduct.

Laoighis (*or* Leix; former name: Queen's County) A county in the E central Republic of Ireland, in Leinster. Predominantly low lying with bogs and drained chiefly by the Rivers Barrow and Nore, it rises to mountains in the NW. Agriculture is the main occupation with dairy farming and cattle rearing. Area: 664 sq mi (1719 sq km). Population (1979): 49,936. County town: Portlaoise.

Laon 49 34N 3 37E A city in N France, the capital of the Aisne department. A former leading town of the kingdom of the Franks, notable buildings include the cathedral (begun in the 12th century) and the bishop's palace. It has metallurgical and sugar-refining industries. Population (1982): 29,000.

Laos, People's Democratic Republic of A landlocked country in SE Asia, in the Indochina peninsula between Vietnam and Thailand. Except for the valley of the Mekong River along its W border, the country is mountainous and forested. Over half the population are Lao (descendants of the Thai) and there are minorities of Vietnamese, Chinese, and others. *Economy*: predominantly agricultural, the difficult terrain combined with recent political upheavals has hindered production and Laos remains the least developed of the nations of the Indochina peninsula. The main crops are rice, corn, coffee, cotton, tea, and tobacco. The valuable mineral resources (tin, iron ore, gold, and copper) have yet to be fully exploited. There is little industry. Hydroelectricity is an important source of power, especially since the opening of the Nan Ngum Dam in 1971. Communications are difficult; there are no railroads and river traffic is hindered by rapids and waterfalls. Meager exports include timber and tin. *History*: the origins of the area as a nation date from the rule of Fa Ngum in the 14th century. European contacts were initiated in the 17th century and in 1893 Laos became a French protectorate. It was occupied by the Japanese from 1941 to 1945, when the Lao Issara (Free Lao) proclaimed an independent government. This movement collapsed when the French returned in 1946 and a constitutional monarchy was formed in 1947. In 1949 Laos became independent within the French Union. In 1953 civil war, which was to last for 20 years, broke out between the government (supported by the US and by Thai mercenaries) and the communist-led Pathet Lao movement (supported by the North Vietnamese). In 1974 a provisional coalition government was formed but following the collapse of the South Vietnamese the Pathet Lao gained power (December 1975) and the People's Democratic Republic of Laos was formed with Prince Souphanouvong as president. Relations with Vietnam continued to be close and friction with Thailand eased somewhat. In 1980 the government announced its decision to adopt more liberal economic policies. Shortages of goods and a subsistence existence for many had led to an exodus of Laotians from their homeland. By the mid-1980s more goods and services were available to the Laotians although ordinary citizens were forced to make purchases with black market or smuggled money. Souphanouvong stepped down as president in 1986. Laos entered the 1990s seeking closer relations with the US, China, and Vietnam and trying to attract foreign investment. In 1991, prime minister Kaysone Phomvihan became the president and Khamtai Siphandon stepped into the prime ministership. Kaysone died in 1992 and was replaced by Nouhak Phoumsavan, a Communist party leader. Prime minister: Khamtai Siphandon. Official language: Laotian; French is widely spoken. Official currency: kip of 100 at. Area: 91,000 sq mi (235,700 sq km). Population (1990 est): 4,024,000. Capital: Vientiane.

Laotian A language of SE Asia belonging to the Thai language family. It is a tonal and monosyllabic language and written in an alphabet derived from *Khmer.

Lao Zi (*or* Lao Tzu; ?6th century BC) The founder of *Taoism. A shadowy, possibly legendary, figure, he was eventually deified. His purpose, propounded mainly in books compiled about 300 years after his likely date of death, was to reach harmony with the *Tao* (way) by dwelling on the beauty of nature, by being self-sufficient, and by desiring nothing.

La Paz 16 30S 68 00W The administrative capital of Bolivia, situated in the W of the country. At an altitude of 11,735 ft (3577 m), it is the world's highest capital. Founded by the Spanish in 1548, it became the seat of government in 1898. The University of San Andrés was founded here in 1830. Population (1989 est): 669,000. *See also* Sucre.

LA PAZ *Much of the city occupies the slopes of a steep-sided valley, below the high tableland of the Andean Altiplano.*

lapis lazuli A blue semiprecious stone composed mainly of a sulfur-rich variety of the mineral haüyne (a feldspathoid) called lazurite. It is formed by the metamorphism of limestone. It often contains specks or threads of yellow iron pyrites. Lapis lazuli has been mined in Afghanistan for over 6000 years. The pigment ultramarine was formerly made by grinding up lapis lazuli.

Laplace, Pierre Simon, Marquis de (1749–1827) French mathematician and astronomer. Laplace worked with *Lagrange on the effects, known as perturbations, of the small gravitational forces that planets exert on each other. (Newton's work considered only the gravitational force of the sun on the planets.) They deduced that the perturbations only cause small oscillations in the planets' motions and not any permanent movement, thus proving the stability of the solar system. Laplace published their results, without giving Lagrange credit, in a five-volume work, *Mécanique céleste* (1799–1825). At the end of the work, Laplace speculated that the solar system was formed from a condensing rotating cloud of gas.

Lapland (*or* Lappland) A vast region in N Europe, inhabited by the *Lapps and extending across northern parts of Norway, Sweden, Finland, and into the extreme NW of Russia. Lying mainly within the Arctic Circle, it consists of tundra in the N, mountains in the W, and forests in the S; there are many lakes and rivers. For many centuries the Lapps were reduced to virtual slavery by their more powerful neighbors. Subsistence farming, fishing, trapping, and hunting are the principal occupations and reindeer are a particularly important source of income. There are rich deposits of iron ore in Swedish Lapland. High unemployment, however, has led to considerable emigration S although there are plans to develop Lapland's fishing potential and to establish fur farms (especially the silver fox). Recent industrial successes include the new steel works at Tornio on the border between Finland and Sweden.

La Plata (name from 1952 until 1955: Eva Perón) 34 52S 57 55W A city in E Argentina, near the Río de la Plata. Its industries include meat packing and oil refining and it has a university (1884). Population (1991): 542,567.

Lapps A people of N Scandinavia and Russia's Kola peninsula. They speak a *Finno-Ugric language, which differs from the related Finnish and *Estonian mainly in its sound system. There are three major Lapp dialects, which are very different from one another. The mountain Lapps are nomadic reindeer herders who follow their herds on their seasonal migrations using them as pack animals or to pull sledges. Other Lapps are seminomadic hunters and fishers.

Laptev Sea A section of the Arctic Ocean off the coast of Russia, between the Taimyr Peninsula and the New Siberian Islands. Half of its supply of fresh water comes from the Lena River, and it is frozen for most of the year.

laptop computer A portable microcomputer that became popular with business executives and students in the early 1990s. The keyboard, screen, and disk or hard drive are incorporated in a single unit, usually weighing 15 lb (7 kg) or less and small enough to be held on a person's lap.

lapwing A Eurasian *plover, *Vanellus vanellus*, also called peewit and green plover. It occurs commonly on farmland, where it feeds on harmful insects, such as wireworms and leatherjackets; 11 in (28 cm) long, it has a greenish-black and white plumage, a long crest, short rounded wings, a short tail, and pink legs. In spring, lapwings perform acrobatic courtship displays.

Laramie 41 20N 105 38W A city in SE Wyoming, on the Laramie River. Founded in 1868 with the arrival of the Union Pacific Railroad, it is a commercial and industrial center for a timber, mining, and livestock region. The University of Wyoming was established here in 1886. Population (1990): 26,687.

larceny. *See* theft.

larch A deciduous conifer of the genus *Larix* (10 species), native to the cooler regions of the N hemisphere. Larches are graceful trees, with needles growing in bunches on short spurs and producing small woody cones. The common European larch (*L. decidua*), from the mountains of central Europe, is widely cultivated both for timber and ornament. It reaches a height of 130 ft (40 m) and its cones, 1–2 in (2–4 cm) long, ripen from pinkish-red to brown. The Japanese larch (*L. kaempferi*) is commonly grown on plantations. Family: *Pinaceae*. □tree.

Lardner, Ring (Ringgold Wilmer L.; 1885–1933) US short-story writer. He worked as a sports reporter and his early stories included in *You Know Me, Al* (1916) concern the life of a baseball player. His best-known stories are collected in *Gullible's Travels* (1917), *How to Write Short Stories* (1924), *What Of It?* (1925), and *The Love Nest and Other Stories* (1926). *The Story of a Wonder Man* (1927) was autobiographical.

Laredo 27 32N 99 22W A city in Texas, on the Rio Grande. Situated opposite Nuevo Laredo (Mexico), it was founded by the Spanish in 1755 and is a center for US and Mexican trade. It has a thriving tourist industry and is the commercial center for an oil-producing and agricultural region. Population (1990): 122,544.

Lares and Penates Roman household gods. The Lares were originally gods of cultivated land who were worshipped at crossroads and boundaries. The Penates were gods of the storeroom. Together with the *Manes, they were later worshipped in private homes as guardian spirits of the family, household, and state.

Large White A breed of pig originating in Yorkshire, England, also called the Yorkshire. Relatively large-framed, Large Whites are white-skinned with a sparse coat of fine hair. They are extensively used for bacon production. A smaller derivative breed, the Middle White, was formerly popular as a porker.

Lárisa (*or* Larissa) 39 38N 22 25E A city in E Greece, in Thessaly. It is a commercial center; products include silk cloth and tobacco. Population (1991): 113,426.

lark A slender long-winged songbird belonging to a family (*Alaudidae*; 75 species) found mainly in mudflats, marshes, grasslands, and deserts of the Old World and characterized by a beautiful song. Larks commonly have a brown or buff streaked plumage that often matches the local soil color. They have long slender bills and feed on seeds and insects. The only New World lark is the horned lark, or shorelark (*Eremophila alpestris*) of North America. *See also* skylark.

Larkin, Philip (1922–85) British poet. His poetry expresses a resigned but honest acceptance of the limitations of daily existence. His volumes include *The Whitsun Weddings* (1964) and *High Windows* (1974). He also edited *The Oxford Book of Twentieth Century English Verse* (1973) and published two novels and a volume of jazz criticism.

larkspur An annual herb of the genus *Consolida*, especially *C. ajacis, C. ambigua*, or *C. orientalis*, native to Eurasia but commonly grown for ornament. Larkspurs have feathery leaves and tall stems with branching spikes of white or blue spurred flowers. The name is also applied to species of the genus *Delphinium*. Family: *Ranunculaceae*.

La Rochefoucauld, François, Duc de (1613–80) French moralist. He was born into an ancient aristocratic family and played an active part in intrigues against Richelieu and in the *Fronde revolts against Mazarin (1648–53). Thereafter he lived in retirement, writing his *Mémoires* (1664) and compiling his celebrated *Maximes* (1665), a collection of cynical epigrammatic observations on human conduct.

La Rochelle 46 10N 1 10W A port in W France, the capital of the Charente-Maritime department on the Bay of Biscay. A major seaport (14th–16th centuries), it was a Huguenot stronghold until its capture by Richelieu in 1628. Industries include fishing, shipbuilding, fertilizers, and plastics. Population (1982): 102,000.

Larousse, Pierre (1817–75) French lexicographer, encyclopedist, and publisher. In 1852 he founded the publishing firm of Larousse, which specialized in dictionaries, encyclopedias, and other works of reference. His major work was the *Grand Dictionnaire universel du XIXe siècle* (15 vols, 1866–76). His firm continues as a major French publisher, with such reference works as the *Grand Larousse Encyclopédique* (1960–64).

Lars Porsena (*or* Porsenna; 6th century BC) Etruscan king of Clusium (now Chiusi, near Siena). According to legend, when *Tarquin the Proud, the last

Etruscan king of Rome, was deposed, Porsena successfully attacked Rome on his behalf. In another version of the story, Porsena made peace with the Romans from admiration of their bravery.

Lartet, Édouard Armand Isidore Hippolyte (1801–71) French archeologist, who was one of the founders of paleontology. Following his first discoveries of fossil remains in SW France, Lartet excavated many cave sites, finding important evidence for dating the various phases of human culture in the region.

larva The immature form of many animals, which hatches from the egg and often differs in appearance from the adult form. Larvae usually avoid competing for food, etc., with the adults by occupying a different habitat or adopting a different lifestyle. For example, adult barnacles, which are sessile, produce motile larvae, whose role is distribution of the species. Other larvae are responsible for gathering food reserves for the production of a fully formed adult, whose primary function is to breed. Caterpillars and maggots are types of insect larvae with this function. *See also* metamorphosis; tadpole.

laryngitis Inflammation of the larynx. Acute laryngitis is a common complication of colds and similar infections, particularly if the patient talks excessively or is exposed to irritants (such as smoke) in the atmosphere. The main symptoms are hoarseness and pain: sometimes the voice is lost completely. The best treatment is to rest the voice and remain in a warm humid atmosphere; steam inhalations ease the condition.

larynx An organ, situated at the front of the neck above the windpipe (*see* trachea), that contains the **vocal cords**, responsible for the production of vocal sounds. The larynx contains several cartilages (one of which—the thyroid cartilage—forms the Adam's apple) bound together by muscles and ligaments. Within are the two vocal cords: folds of tissue separated by a narrow slit (glottis). The vocal cords modify the flow of exhaled air through the glottis to produce the sounds of speech, song, etc.

La Salle, Robert Cavelier, Sieur de (1643–87) French explorer in North America. La Salle settled in Montreal in 1666 and in 1669 set out on his first expedition, exploring the Ohio region. From 1679 he concentrated on achieving his ambition to descend the Mississippi River to the Gulf of Mexico. In 1682, after two arduous years, he reached the Gulf and named the area watered by the Mississippi and its tributaries Louisiana, after Louis XIV of France. While attempting to found a permanent colony, he was murdered by mutineers.

La Scala (*or* Teatro alla Scala) The principal Italian opera house, opened in Milan in 1776. It is noted for its varied repertoire of new and classical works, and attained its highest reputation under Arturo *Toscanini, director (1898–1907; 1921–31).

Las Campanas Observatory. *See* Hale Observatories.

Las Casas, Bartolomé de (1474–1566) Spanish priest, known as the Apostle of the Indies. As a planter on Hispaniola, Las Casas was horrified by the treatment to which the Indians were subjected. He became a priest (1510) and entered the Dominican order, becoming the defender of the Indians at the Spanish court. His agitation included the publication of *The Brief Relation of the Destruction of the Indies* (1552) and bore fruit with the abolition of Indian slavery in 1542.

Las Cases, Emmanuel, Comte de (1776–1842) French writer. He held political office under Napoleon and shared his exile on St Helena. His *Mémorial de St Hélène* (1823) recorded Napoleon's final conversations and opinions on politics and religion and greatly influenced his posthumous reputation.

Lascaux Upper *Paleolithic cave site in the Dordogne (France), discovered in 1940. Lascaux contains rock paintings and engravings of horses, oxen, red deer, and other animals, dating from about 18,000 BC; traps and arrows depicted nearby suggest that the pictures had magical significance in a hunting ritual. Atmospheric changes resulting in deterioration of the paintings caused the cave to be closed again (1963).

laser (*l*ight *a*mplification by *s*timulated *e*mission of *r*adiation) A device that produces a beam of high-intensity coherent monochromatic radiation (light, infrared, or ultraviolet). Stimulated emission is the emission of a photon when an atomic electron falls from a higher energy level to a lower level as a result of being stimulated by another photon of the same frequency. In the laser large numbers of electrons are "pumped" into a higher energy level, an effect called population inversion, and then stimulated to produce a high-intensity beam. Laser beams have been produced from solids, liquids, and gases. The simplest type is the ruby laser, consisting of a cylinder of ruby, silvered at one end and partially silvered at the other. A flash lamp is used to excite chromium ions in the ruby to a high energy level. When the ions fall back to their ground state photons (wavelength 694.3 nanometers) are emitted. These photons collide with other excited ions producing radiation of the same wavelength (monochromatic) and the same phase (coherent), which is reflected up and down the ruby crystal and emerges as a narrow beam from the partially silvered end. Lasers are used in civil engineering to aid alignment, in eye surgery, in laser interferometers to measure very small displacements, in *holography, and in scientific research.

Lasker, Emanuel (1868–1941) German chess player, who became world champion in 1894 and remained champion until he conceded the title to *Capablanca in 1921. A Jew, he left Germany in 1933 to settle in the Soviet Union and finally the US.

Laski, Harold Joseph (1893–1950) British political theorist. Laski became professor of political science at the London School of Economics in 1926. A socialist, he was influenced by the theories of *Burke and *Mill but became progressively more Marxist in outlook. His writings include *Authority in the Modern State* (1919) and *Faith, Reason, Civilization* (1944).

Las Palmas 28 08N 15 27W The largest city in the Canary Islands, the capital of Las Palmas province in Gran Canaria. It is a popular resort noted for its palms and is a major fueling port between Europe and South America. Population (1991): 342,030.

La Spezia 44 07N 9 48E A port and resort in Italy, in Liguria on the Gulf of Spezia. It is a major naval base, with the largest harbor in Italy. Its industries include shipbuilding, textiles, and the manufacture of porcelain. Population (1988 est): 107,500.

Lassa fever A severe virus disease occurring in West Africa and first described in 1969 in Lassa, a village in Nigeria. It is a rare and often fatal disease that is transmitted to man by certain species of rat.

Lassalle, Ferdinand (1825–64) German socialist politician and theorist. Although deeply influenced by Karl Marx, Lassalle developed a distinctive theory of socialism, stressing the formation of workers' cooperatives as a peaceful way to socialism. He headed working-class opposition to Bismarck and helped to found the General German Workers' Association (1863), the precursor to the Social Democratic party. He was killed in a duel.

Lassen Volcanic National Park A national park in NE California, in the Cascade Ranges. The main feature of the park, established in 1916, is Lassen Peak (10,457 ft; 3188 m), an active volcano that erupted from 1914–21. Lava flows, lava plugs, other volcanoes, and boiling springs and lakes also attract tourists. Area: 167 sq mi (431 sq km).

ruby laser

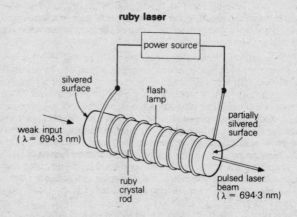

helium-neon gas laser

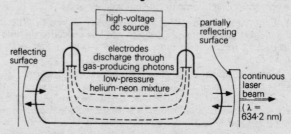

LASER *In the solid-state ruby laser, chromium ions are excited by an intense flash of light and then stimulated by weak light of one wavelength to emit a pulse of photons. In the helium-neon gas laser, a continuous laser beam is produced from an electrical discharge through low-pressure gas.*

Lassus, Roland de (Italian name: Orlando di Lasso; c. 1532–94) Flemish composer. He was born in Mons, where he became a chorister. He obtained appointments in Rome (choirmaster at St John Lateran), Antwerp, and with the Bavarian court in Munich. His madrigals, chansons, and motets exhibit great contrapuntal skill. He was afflicted with depression in later life.

Las Vegas 36 10N 115 12W A city in SE Nevada. Founded in 1855, it grew rapidly after construction of the nearby Hoover Dam. It is famous for its nightclubs and the Strip (a row of luxury hotels and gambling casinos). Population (1990): 258,295.

László I, Saint (1040–95) King of Hungary (1077–95). In 1091, László conquered Croatia, to which he introduced Roman Catholicism, founding the bishopric of Zagreb. He also reformed the criminal code, bringing peace and security to Hungary.

Latakia (Arabic name: Al Ladhiqiyah) 35 31N 35 47E A city in NW Syria, on the Mediterranean coast. It dates from Phoenician times and is now Syria's principal port. It is also famous for its tobacco. Population (1977 est): 191,329.

La Tène The second phase of the European Iron Age, succeeding *Hallstatt from the 5th century BC. Named for the site at La Tène (Switzerland), this recognizably Celtic culture spread throughout Europe, coming into contact with the civilizations of Greece and Rome. Aristocratic chariot burials replaced wagon burials and the geometric patterns of Hallstatt metalwork were superseded by the intricate curvilinear designs of *Celtic art. By the 1st century BC Roman expansionism effectively ended coherent La Tène culture. *See also* Celts.

latent heat The amount of heat absorbed or released by a substance when it undergoes a change of state. For example, a liquid absorbs heat (**latent heat of vaporization**) from its surroundings on evaporation, since energy is needed to overcome the forces of attraction between the molecules as the liquid expands into a gas. Similarly a solid absorbs heat (**latent heat of fusion**) when it melts. The heat absorbed or released per unit mass of substance is called the **specific latent heat**; per amount of substance it is the **molar latent heat**.

Lateran Councils Five ecumenical councils of the Roman Catholic Church convened in the Lateran Palace, Rome. **1.** (1123) The council that confirmed the settlement of the *investiture controversy. **2.** and **3.** (1139, 1179) The councils that were principally concerned with the papal-election procedure. **4.** (1215) The council, attended by most major European ecclesiastical and secular powers, that proclaimed the fifth Crusade (1217–21) and was enormously influential in its formulations of doctrine and Church organization and law. **5.** (1512–17) The council that endeavored to counteract hostility to papal power on the eve of the Reformation.

Lateran Treaty (1929) An agreement between the Italian government of Mussolini and the Vatican. The Vatican City state was created and the papacy abandoned its claim to the former *papal states.

laterite A deposit formed from the weathering of rocks in humid tropical conditions. It consists mostly of iron and aluminum oxides. It occurs either underground, where it is soft, or as a hardened reddish surface capping where the overlying material has been eroded. Most laterites developed in the Tertiary period.

latex A liquid, often milky, emulsion found in certain flowering plants. It has a complex composition and its function in the plant is not fully understood. The latex of the *rubber tree is used in rubber manufacture, while opium and morphine are obtained from the latex of the *opium poppy.

lathe A machine for turning wood, plastic, or metal into cylindrical or conical parts or for cutting holes or screw-threads in them. The piece to be worked is held in a rotating plate or chuck so that a cutting tool can be held against it. The **turret lathe** has a turret containing a set of cutting tools, which can be used independently or simultaneously. Automatic turret lathes perform a sequence of operations on the workpiece without manual interference and are extensively used in mass-production processes.

Latimer, Hugh (c. 1485–1555) Anglican reformer and martyr. While a university preacher, he was converted to Protestantism (1524). He became bishop of Worcester in 1535, but his opposition to Henry's Six Articles upholding Roman Catholic doctrine resulted in his resignation and imprisonment (1539). A popular preacher under Edward VI, he was arrested at Mary's accession, tried for heresy, and burned at the stake.

Latimeria. *See* coelacanth.

Latin America The countries of Central and South America lying S of the US-Mexican border, including those islands of the West Indies where a Romance language is spoken. Spanish is the most widely used language but Portuguese is spoken in Brazil, the largest country, and French in Haiti and French Guiana. The population is mainly mesitzo (people of mixed Indian and European—usually Spanish—parentage), with minorities of pure Indians and Europeans. The **Latin American Free Trade Association** (LAFTA) was formed in 1961 with the aim of removing all restrictions on trade among its member countries (Argentina, Brazil, Bolivia, Chile, Colombia, Ecuador, Mexico, Paraguay, Peru, Uruguay, and Venezuela).

Latin American Conferences A series of conferences held in Montevideo, Uruguay (1933); Buenos Aires, Argentina (1936); and Lima, Peru (1938). They discussed US-Latin American relations and inaugurated Pres. Franklin D. Roosevelt's *Good Neighbor Policy. As a result of these meetings, a policy of nonintervention in Latin America affairs was reaffirmed.

Latini, Brunetto (c. 1220–c. 1294) Florentine scholar and politician. A friend of *Dante, Latini contributed to the spread of French learning in Italy and wrote an encyclopedia entitled *Li Livres doue trésor.*

Latin language An Italic Indo-European language, the ancestor of modern Romance languages. First spoken on the plain of Latium near Rome, Latin spread throughout the Mediterranean world as Roman power expanded. An inflected and syntactically complex language, written Latin was gradually molded to express with equal power Cicero's rhetoric and philosophy, Martial's epigrams, and Virgil's subtle poetry. Educated conversational Latin developed contemporaneously with literary Latin, although, with its freer syntax and vocabulary, it remained less static than the formalized written language. Colloquial Vulgar Latin used prepositions and conjunctions freely to replace inflected forms and had a simpler word order; it became the Latin of the provinces, contributing to the early development of the Romance languages. As the western Roman Empire's official language, Latin was used in W Europe for religious, literary, and scholarly works until the middle ages and beyond, and remained the Roman Catholic Church's official language until the mid-20th century.

Latin literature The earliest Latin literature dates from after the conclusion of the first *Punic War (241 BC). Writers such as *Ennius, Naevius, and *Plautus (*see* Roman comedy) translated Greek epic, tragedy, and comedy and adapted them to Roman themes. Prose, particularly legal and historical writing, developed along more independent lines until the 1st century BC, when *Cicero conclusively established Latin as a mature literary medium. His contemporary *Lucretius perfected the Latin hexameter and, together with the lyric poet *Catullus, they inaugurated the *Golden Age of Latin literature. Their achievements were consolidated in the subsequent Augustan age (43 BC–18 AD), during which the emperor Augustus's adviser *Maecenas was patron to *Virgil, *Horace, and *Propertius. Among their important contemporaries were the poets *Ovid and *Tibullus and the historian *Livy. The spirit of the succeeding *Silver Age is encapsulated in *Seneca's highly rhetorical tragedies. *Juvenal and *Martial were the major poets and *Tacitus, *Suetonius, *Quintilian, and *Petronius contributed notable prose works. Imitations, anthologies, and commentaries later predominated over original work. In the 4th and 5th centuries the Latin Church Fathers set Latin on course for becoming the lingua franca of Christian intellectuals. As the literature of learning, Latin literature's characteristic products were encyclopedias and theological texts. Exceptions to this were the medieval Latin lyrics, which have the spontaneity of their vernacular counterparts. *See also* Latin language.

Latinus A legendary ancestor of the Romans, who gave his name to their language. *Aeneas arrived from Troy in his kingdom of Latium, an area S of Rome, and married his daughter Lavinia.

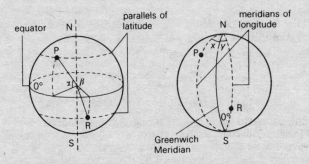

The latitude of P is given by the angle χ. In this case it would be χ°N. The latitude of R is β° S.

The longitude of P is given by the angle x. In this case it would be x° W. R has a longitude y° E.

LATITUDE AND LONGITUDE

latitude and longitude Imaginary lines on the earth's surface, enabling any point to be defined in terms of two angles. **Parallels of latitude** are circles drawn round the earth parallel to the equator; their diameters diminish as they approach the Poles. These parallels are specified by the angle subtended at the center of the earth by the arc formed between a point on the parallel and the equator. All points on the equator therefore have a latitude of 0°, while the North Pole has a latitude of 90°N and the South Pole of 90°S. Parallels of latitude 1° apart are separated on the earth's surface by about 63 mi (100 km).

Meridians of longitude are half great circles passing through both Poles; they cross parallels of latitude at right angles. In 1884 the meridian through Greenwich, London, England, was selected as the prime meridian and given the designation 0°. Other meridians are defined by the angle between the plane of the meridian and the plane of the prime meridian, specifying whether it is E or W of the prime meridian. At the equator meridians 1° apart are separated by about 70 mi (112 km).

Latium. *See* Lazio.

La Tour, Georges de (1593–1652) French painter, a native of Lorraine. He excelled in candlelit religious scenes, influenced by such Dutch followers of Caravaggio as *Honthorst. His works include *St Joseph the Carpenter* (Louvre) and *The Lamentation over St Sebastian* (Berlin). La Tour's reputation has only been reestablished in the 20th century.

La Tour, Maurice-Quentin de (1704–88) French portrait pastelist, born in Saint-Quentin. He settled in Paris, where he enjoyed an immense and lasting popularity. His sitters included Voltaire, Madame de Pompadour, and Louis XV.

Latrobe, Benjamin Henry (1764–1820) US architect and engineer; born in England. Educated as an architect, he came to the US in 1796 and by 1798 had designed the Greek Revival Bank of Pennsylvania building in Philadelphia. He redesigned part of the Capitol building in Washington, DC, in 1803 and rebuilt it (1815–17) after it was burned down. From 1805 until 1818 he worked on the Roman Catholic cathedral in Baltimore, Md.

Latter Day Saints, Reorganized Church of Jesus Christ of A splinter group of the *Mormons that separated from the main group in 1852 and refused to follow the leadership of Brigham Young, successor to Joseph *Smith. Headquarters for its almost 200,000 members is in Independence, Mo.

Latvia, Republic of A country in E Europe, on the Baltic Sea. It is a fertile lowland with extensive forests. Latvians, who comprise approximately 60% of the population, are mainly Lutheran Christians. Industries include shipbuilding, engineering, chemicals, and textiles. Fishing plays an important part in the economy and Riga, the capital, is an important seaport. *History*: the Latvians were conquered by the Livonian Knights (a German order of knighthood) in the 13th century, passing to Poland in the 16th century, to Sweden in the 17th century, and to Russia in the 18th century. Latvia gained independence in 1918, which was recognized by Soviet Russia in 1920. In 1940 it was incorporated into the Soviet Union as an SSR. It was occupied by Germany in World War II. With the disintegration of the Soviet Union in 1991, Latvia declared its independence. It was granted UN membership in 1991. Latvia, with Estonia and Lithuania, pursued policies that kept the Baltic republics distinct from other former Soviet republics. Area: 25,590 sq mi (63,700 sq km). Population (1989): 2,681,000. Capital: Riga.

Latvian A language belonging to the E division of the *Baltic languages division of the Indo-European family, spoken by about two million Latvians. Most live in Latvia, where Latvian is the official language. Also known as Lettish, it is closely related to *Lithuanian. It is written in a Latin alphabet and written texts date from the 16th century.

Laud, William (1573–1645) Anglican churchman and chief adviser to Charles I of Britain immediately before the *Civil War. As Archbishop of Canterbury (1633–45), he supported Charles I's personal rule and his attempt to enforce liturgical uniformity among both Roman Catholics and Puritans. His pressure on the Scots to accept the Book of Common Prayer paved the way for the Civil War and his own downfall. He was impeached for high treason in 1640 and eventually executed.

Laue, Max Theodor Felix von (1879–1960) German physicist, who became professor at the University of Berlin in 1919. His early investigations of X-rays led him to discover the technique of *X-ray crystallography, now widely used for determining crystal structures. For this work he won the Nobel Prize (1914). In 1943 he resigned his chair in protest against the Nazis. After the war he was appointed director of the Max Planck Institute for Physical Chemistry.

laughing owl A ground-nesting New Zealand *owl, *Sceloglaux albifacies*, probably now extinct due to the introduction of predatory mammals. It was 15 in (37 cm) long and had a speckled and barred brown plumage with whitish facial feathers.

Laughton, Charles (1899–1962) British actor. His international reputation was based on his numerous films, which included *The Private Life of Henry VIII* (1933), *Mutiny on the Bounty* (1935), *Rembrandt* (1936), and *Witness for the Prosecution* (1957). He was married to the actress Elsa Lanchester and lived for many years in Hollywood, but made several late appearances in the English theater, notably as King Lear in 1959.

CHARLES LAUGHTON *As Canon Chasuble with Elsa Lanchester as Miss Prism in Wilde's* The Importance of Being Earnest *(1934).*

Launceston 41 25S 147 07E A city and port in Australia, in N Tasmania situated at the confluence of the North and South Esk Rivers. It is an important commercial center; industries include aluminum smelting, heavy engineering, textiles, and sawmills. Population (1991): 66,286.

Laura The subject of Petrarch's love sonnets and other poems. She has been variously identified, traditionally as Laura de Noves (?1308–48), a married woman living in Avignon. The poems suggest that Petrarch's love for her was not returned.

Laurasia The supercontinent of the N hemisphere that is believed to have existed prior to 200 million years ago, when the drift of the continents to their present positions began. It probably consisted of Greenland, Europe, Asia (excluding India), and North America. *See also* Gondwanaland.

laurel One of several unrelated aromatic shrubs or small trees with attractive evergreen leaves. The so-called true laurels (genus *Laurus*) include the *bay tree. Other laurels include the ornamental *cherry laurels, the spotted laurels (genus *Aucuba*; family *Cornaceae*), and the mountain laurel (*Kalmia latifolia*; family *Ericaceae*). The spurge laurel is a species of *Daphne*.

Laurel and Hardy US film comedians. **Stan Laurel** (Arthur Stanley Jefferson; 1890–1965), the thin member of the team and originator of the gags, was born in Britain. He joined with **Oliver Hardy** (1892–1957), who played the pompous fat partner, in 1926. They made numerous outstanding two-reel and feature-length comedy films in the 1920s and 1930s, including *The Music Box* (1932), *Our Relations* (1936), and *Way Out West* (1937).

Laurentian Shield. *See* shield.

Laurier, Sir Wilfrid (1841–1919) Canadian statesman; the first French-Canadian prime minister of Canada (1896–1911). His Liberal government was notable for the settlement of the West and the defense of Canadian autonomy within the British Empire.

laurustinus An ornamental evergreen shrub, *Viburnum tinus*, native to the Mediterranean region and up to 10 ft (3 m) tall. It has pointed oval leaves, reddish twigs, and round heads of tiny five-petaled pink-and-white flowers, borne on red stalks and producing blue-black berries. It is often grown as a pot plant. Family: *Caprifoliaceae*.

Lausanne 46 32N 6 39E A city and resort in W Switzerland, on the N shore of Lake Geneva. A cultural and intellectual center, it has a notable cathedral (13th century) and a university (1891) founded as a college in the 16th century. Lausanne is the seat of the Swiss Supreme Court and the headquarters of the International Olympic Committee. Industries include chocolate, precision instruments, and clothing. Population (1991 est): 123,000.

Lausanne, Conferences of 1. (1922–23) A conference between the Allied Powers and Turkey that modified the post-World War I Treaty of Sèvres (1920), which had been unacceptable to Turkey. By the Treaty of Lausanne, Turkey regained territory from Greece and the Allies recognized Turkey's right to control its own affairs. **2.** (1932) A conference between the UK, France, Belgium, and Italy, which ended the payment by Germany of World War I reparations.

lava Magma that has reached the earth's surface through volcanic vents and from which the volatile material has escaped, either molten or cooled and solidified. Basic lavas tend to be liquid and flow over large areas, while acid lavas are viscous.

Laval 45 33N 73 43W A city in E Canada, in Quebec on the island next to *Montreal. Primarily a suburb, it has some industry, including electronics, paper, and metal goods. Population (1991): 314,398.

Laval, Pierre (1883–1945) French statesman, whose collaborations with Germany during the German occupation of France in World War II resulted in his execution as a traitor. A socialist, Laval was prime minister in 1930–32, and 1935–36 and foreign minister in 1934–36. In 1935, with Sir Samuel Hoare (1880–1959), the British foreign minister, he proposed an unsuccessful plan (the Hoare-Laval Plan) for the settlement of Mussolini's claims in Ethiopia. After the collapse of France (1940) he joined Marshal *Pétain's Vichy government. Increasingly powerful, he was dismissed and briefly imprisoned by Pétain (December 1940) but the support of Germany secured Laval the virtual leadership of the Vichy government in 1942. After the liberation of France (1944) he fled to Germany and then to Spain but later gave himself up for trial in France (July 1945).

La Vallière, Louise de Françoise de la Baume le Blanc, Duchesse de (1644–1710) The mistress of Louis XIV of France from 1661–1667, when she was replaced by Mme de Montespan. In 1674 she retired to a convent.

Lavalloisian A Middle *Paleolithic technique of making stone tools by flaking pieces away from a specially shaped lump (prepared core). It is often associated with *Mousterian sites.

lavender A small shrub of the genus *Lavandula* (about 8 species), especially *L. vera* and *L. angustifolia* (or *L. officinalis*); 12–31 in (30–80 cm) high, it has aromatic narrow gray-green leaves and long-stemmed spikes of small mauve or violet flowers. Native to the Mediterranean area, it is widely cultivated for its flowers, which retain their fragrance when dried, and for its oil, which is used in perfumes. Family: *Labiatae*.

laver An edible red *seaweed of the genus *Porphyra*, found growing at the high tide mark in both hemispheres. It has wide irregular membranous fronds, which are dried to provide an important food source in the Orient. In the British Isles it is fried and known as laverbread (*or* sloke).

Laver, Rod(ney George) (1938–   ) Australian tennis player. In 1962 he took all four major singles titles (Australian, French, US, and Wimbledon) as an amateur and repeated the feat as a professional in 1969.

Laveran, Charles Louis Alphonse (1845–1922) French physician, who (in 1880) first recognized the protozoan parasite responsible for malaria while stationed with the army in Algeria. Laveran investigated other diseases caused by protozoa, including trypanosomiasis and leishmaniasis. He was awarded the Nobel Prize (1907).

Lavoisier, Antoine Laurent (1743–94) French chemist, regarded as the founder of modern chemistry. Born into an aristocratic family, he became wealthy by investing his money in a private company hired by the government to collect taxes. With his wealth he built a large laboratory where he discovered in 1778 that air consists of a mixture of two gases, which he called oxygen and nitrogen. He then went on to study the role of oxygen in combustion, finally disposing of the *phlogiston theory. Lavoisier also discovered the law of conservation of mass and devised the modern method of naming compounds, which replaced the older nonsystematic method. Lavoisier was arrested during the French Revolution and tried for his involvement with the tax-collecting company. He was found guilty and guillotined.

law That which is laid down, ordained, or established. The body of rules include those that govern and regulate the relationship between one state and another (*see* international law), a state and its citizens (territorial or municipal law), and one person and another when the state is not directly involved (*see* civil law). Rules that must be obeyed and followed by citizens subject to sanctions or legal consequences is a law.

Law, (Andrew) Bonar (1858–1923) British statesman; Conservative prime minister (1922–23). While colonial secretary (1915–16), he fostered the revolt against *Asquith's coalition and in the subsequent coalition led by *Lloyd George became chancellor of the exchequer and leader of the House of Commons. He became prime minister after Lloyd George's resignation.

Lawrence, D(avid) H(erbert) (1885–1930) British novelist, poet, and painter. The son of a Nottinghamshire miner, he was encouraged by his mother to become a teacher; he published his first novel, *The White Peacock*, in 1911. The semiautobiographical *Sons and Lovers* (1913) established his reputation. In 1912 he eloped with Frieda Weekley, the German wife of a professor. Their extensive travels provided material for the novels *Kangaroo* (1923), reflecting a stay in Australia, and *The Plumed Serpent* (1926), set in Mexico. Lawrence explored marital and sexual relations in *The Rainbow* (1915) and *Women in Love* (1921); he treated this subject in more explicit detail in *Lady Chatterley's Lover* (privately printed, 1928). The novel was not published in its unexpurgated form for many years. Lawrence's collected poems were published in 1928. *Fantasia of the Unconscious* (1922) develops ideas that become increasingly prominent in the novels. A number of his critical writings are collected in *Selected Literary Criticism* (1955). He died of tuberculosis.

Lawrence, Ernest Orlando (1901–58) US physicist, who in 1930, at the University of California, designed and built the first *cyclotron, a type of particle *accelerator upon which almost all subsequent models have been based. For his invention he received the Nobel Prize (1939).

Lawrence, Gertrude (1898–1952) British actress and dancer. She performed in many revues and was especially successful in three productions by Noel *Coward, *Private Lives* (1930), *Tonight at 8:30* (1935–36), and *Lady in the Dark* (1941). She went to the US and made her final appearance in the musical *The King and I* in 1951. She also wrote her autobiography, *A Star Danced* (1945).

Lawrence, St (d. 258) Roman deacon martyred during the reign of Emperor Valerian. According to tradition he distributed ecclesiastical treasure to the poor and was condemned to death by being roasted on a gridiron, which has become his emblem. Feast day: Aug 10.

Lawrence, T(homas) E(dward) (1888–1935) British soldier and writer, known as Lawrence of Arabia. He learned Arabic while excavating Carchemish (1911–14) and after the outbreak of World War I worked for army intelligence in N Africa. In 1916 he joined the Arab revolt against the Turks, leading the Arab guerrillas triumphantly into Damascus in October 1918. His exploits, which brought him almost legendary fame, were recounted in his book *The Seven Pillars of Wisdom* (1926). Disillusioned by the failure of the Paris Peace Conference to establish Arab independence, in 1922 he joined the ranks of the Royal Air Force (RAF), assuming the name John Hume Ross, and then the Royal Tank Corps (1923), as T. E. Shaw. In 1925 he rejoined the RAF, where he worked as a mechanic. He died in a motorcycle accident.

Lawrence 38 58N 95 14W A city in NE Kansas, on the S banks of the Kansas River, NE of Topeka. The University of Kansas (1863) is there. Founded in 1854, the city was the scene in 1863 of a raid and massacre by William C. Quantrill and his guerrillas. Industries include food processing and the manufacture of greeting cards, chemicals, and paper products. Population (1990): 65,608.

lawrencium (Lr) A synthetic transuranic element discovered in 1961 and named for E. O. *Lawrence. Chemical tests on a few atoms suggest a dominantly trivalent chemistry. At no 103; at wt (257).

laxatives (*or* purgatives) Drugs used to treat constipation. Such laxatives as magnesium sulfate (Epsom salts) mix with the feces and cause them to retain water, which increases their bulk and makes them easier to pass. Irritant laxatives, such as castor oil, senna, and cascara, stimulate the bowel directly. Another group, which includes bran, both lubricates the feces and increases their bulk.

Laxness, Halldór (Kiljan) (1902–   ) Icelandic novelist and essayist. He spent much of his early life traveling in Europe, where he became a Roman Catholic. The novel *Vefarinn mikli frá Kasmir* (*The Great Weaver from Kashmir*; 1927) marked his abandonment of Catholicism and adoption of socialism, a theme of subsequent works written after his return to Iceland in 1930. These include *Salka Valka* (1934) and *Sjalfstaet folk* (*Independent People*; 1934–35). He was awarded the Nobel Prize (1955).

T. E. LAWRENCE *Drawing by Augustus John (1919).*

Layamon (early 13th century) English poet and priest. His alliterative verse chronicle *Brut*, based on the *Roman de Brut* by *Wace, relates the history of England from the arrival of Brutus (a legendary Trojan) to the defeat of the Britons by the Saxons in 689 AD and includes original detail in its treatment of *Arthurian legend.

Layard, Sir Austen Henry (1817–94) British archeologist and diplomat. As excavator of □Nimrud and *Nineveh (1845–51), Layard stimulated popular interest in Mesopotamian archeology by his book *Nineveh and Its Remains* (1848)—actually about Nimrud, as he had at first misidentified the site—and by his feat of transporting colossal statues of winged bulls to Britain.

Lazarists A Roman Catholic order of lay priests known more formally as the Congregation of the Mission. Established by St *Vincent de Paul at St Lazare Priory, Paris, in 1625, the Lazarists now have teaching and missionary communities all over the world.

Lazio (Latin name: Latium) A region in W central Italy. It consists of an extensive coastal plain in the W and mountains in the E, separated by volcanic hills. The majority of the population live in urban centers, such as Rome. Agriculture is important producing cereals, olives, wine, fruits, sheep, and cattle. Rome is an important center for manufacturing industries, such as food processing, chemicals, textiles, and paper; there is also a sizable service industry. Area: 6642 sq mi (17,204 sq km). Population (1991): 5,145,763. Capital: Rome.

L-dopa (*or* levodopa) A drug used to treat *parkinsonism, which is caused by a deficiency of dopamine (a chemical secreted at nerve endings when an impulse passes) in the brain. L-dopa is converted to this compound in the brain. It is taken by mouth, combined with carbidopa (Sinemet), which prevents its breakdown in the body.

Leacock, Stephen (Butler) (1869–1944) Canadian humorist, born in England. He was educated and taught economics and political science at Canadian universities. *Literary Lapses* (1910) and *Nonsense Novels* (1911) were the first of over 30 popular humorous books.

lead (Pb) A dense soft bluish-gray metal, known from prehistoric times. It occurs in nature chiefly as the sulfide *galena (PbS) but also as cerussite ($PbCO_3$), anglesite ($PbSO_4$), and occasionally as the native metal. The metal is very resistant to corrosion and some lead pipes installed by the Romans are still intact. Lead is used in plumbing (although it is now being replaced by plastics). It is also used to shield X-rays, as ammunition, as cable sheathing, in crystal glass (as lead oxide), and as an antiknock (as *tetraethyl lead; ($C_2H_5)_4Pb$). Other common compounds include the sulfate ($PbSO_4$), chromate ($PbCrO_4$), and the oxides red lead (Pb_3O_4) and litharge (PbO). These are colored white, yellow, red, and orange respectively and were formerly extensively used as paint pigments. Most lead salts are insoluble, with the exception of the nitrate, ($Pb(NO_3)_2$), and acetate ($Pb(CH_3COO)_2$). Acute lead poisoning causes diarrhea and vomiting, but poisoning is more often chronic and characterized by abdominal pain, muscle pains, anemia, and nerve and brain damage. Children are particularly vulnerable to excess lead levels from car exhaust fumes. At no 82; at wt 207.19; mp 214°F (327.50°C); bp 998°F (1740°C).

Leadbelly (Huddie Ledbetter; 1888–1949) US folksinger and songwriter, whose blues and work songs foreshadowed the folk revival of the 1960s.

Leadville 39 15N 106 20W A city in central Colorado, in the Rocky Mountains, NE of Aspen. Gold, lead, and silver deposits led to a large, thriving mining community by 1880. The town declined as silver prices fell and today is a large producer of molybdenum and a popular tourist attraction. Population (1990): 2629.

leaf An outgrowth from the stem of a □plant in which most of the green pigment chlorophyll, used for *photosynthesis, is concentrated. Foliage leaves are typically thin and flat, providing a large surface area for absorbing the maximum amount of light, and they contain pores (stomata) through which exchange of gases and water occurs. They may be simple or compound (composed of a number of leaflets) and with a branching vein system (in *dicotyledons) or parallel veins (in *monocotyledons). Other kinds of leaves include seed leaves (*see* cotyledon) and *bracts. The spines of cacti and the thorns of gorse are modified leaves.

leaf beetle A beetle belonging to a large family (*Chrysomelidae*; 26,000 species) occurring in tropical and temperate regions. Leaf beetles are generally small (less than 0.5 in [12 mm]) and brightly colored. Both the adults and larvae feed on leaves and flowers, although the larvae may also eat roots and stems. Leaf beetles have a wide range of habits: one group is aquatic; in others the larvae carry excrement on their backs (*see* tortoise beetle); and many are serious pests, including the notorious *Colorado potato beetle. □insect.

leafcutter ant An *ant, also called a parasol ant, belonging to the genus *Atta* and related genera and occurring in tropical and subtropical America. Armies of leafcutter ants damage crops by cutting pieces of leaf and carrying them to their large underground nests. The leaves are used as a medium on which the ants cultivate their diet of fungi. Subfamily: *Myrmicinae*.

leafcutter bee A solitary *bee, about 0.4 in (10 mm) long, belonging to a genus (*Megachile*) of the family *Megachilidae*. It nests in rotten wood and soil, lining the chamber and egg cells with pieces of leaf cut with its strong jaws. Leafcutters are similar to *honeybees in appearance and have pollen-carrying brushes on the underside of their abdomens.

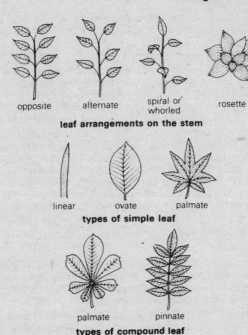

opposite　　　alternate　　　spiral or whorled　　　rosette

leaf arrangements on the stem

linear　　　ovate　　　palmate

types of simple leaf

palmate　　　pinnate

types of compound leaf

LEAF *The type and arrangement of the leaves are characteristic for a particular species of plant. For example, the pear has alternate ovate leaves; the horse chestnut has opposite palmate leaves.*

leaf hopper A small slender insect (up to 0.6 in [15 mm] long) belonging to the family *Cicadellidae*. Leaf hoppers are often brightly colored and are powerful jumpers. They feed by sucking plant juices and exude honeydew. Some species are serious pests of plants causing discoloration and weakening or spreading disease. Suborder: *Homoptera*; order: *Hemiptera*.

leaf insect A plant-eating insect, also called a walking leaf, belonging to the family *Phyllidae*. It is excellently camouflaged against foliage, having a broad leaflike body and wings and leaflike flaps on the legs. The female is much larger than the male and lacks hindwings. Order: *Phasmida*.

League of Nations An international organization created (1920) after World War I with the purpose of achieving world peace. The League's Covenant was incorporated into the postwar peace treaties and the failure of the US to ratify the Treaty of *Versailles meant its exclusion from the League. Before 1930 the League, from its Geneva headquarters, organized international conferences, settled minor disputes, and did much useful humanitarian work. However, it failed to deal effectively with the aggression during the 1930s of Japan in China, Italy in Ethiopia (in which the League's use of *sanctions was ineffectual), and Germany, which withdrew from the League in 1933. The UN superseded the League after World War II.

League of Women Voters US organization for women of voting age that keeps the public informed on voting laws and issues. Established in 1920, when women received the right to vote, it is nonpartisan and takes a stand on an issue only when a majority of the membership, after extensive study, indicates the need.

Leakey, Louis Seymour Bazett (1903–72) Kenyan paleontologist. His work at *Olduvai Gorge uncovered crucial evidence for man's early evolution, notably the *Zinjanthropus* skull dating from 1.75 million years ago. In 1974 his wife **Mary Leakey** (1913–   ) unearthed hominid remains at Laetolil (N Tanzania) dating back 3.75 million years. Their son **Richard Leakey** (1944–   ) has made significant fossil finds around Lake Turkana (formerly Lake Rudolf; N Kenya).

Lean, Sir David (1908–91) British film director. His early films in collaboration with Noël Coward include *In Which We Serve* (1942), *Blithe Spirit* (1945), and *Brief Encounter* (1946). Adaptations of Charles Dickens' *Great Expectations* (1946) and *Oliver Twist* (1947) were followed by the classic *The Bridge on the River Kwai* (1957). Later films include *Lawrence of Arabia* (1962) and *Dr Zhivago* (1965), and *A Passage to India* (1984). He received a knighthood in 1984.

Leander. *See* Hero and Leander.

leap year. *See* calendar.

Lear A legendary British king, probably invented by Geoffrey of Monmouth, who recounts the story of the old king's division of his kingdom among his three daughters. This story is the basis of Shakespeare's *King Lear* (c. 1605) and is referred to in other works of Elizabethan literature.

Lear, Edward (1812–88) British artist and poet. After 1837 he lived mainly abroad, working as a landscape painter and traveling extensively. He died in Italy. He showed great verbal inventiveness in his four books of nonsense verse for children, beginning with *The Book of Nonsense* (1846), and he popularized a form of the limerick.

leasing back An operation to raise liquid cash from a capital asset. The owner of a property, such as a house, sells it on the condition that the buyer leases it back to the seller for a fixed period for a specified rent.

leather Specially treated animal skin. Although any skin can be made into leather, that of domesticated animals, such as cows, sheep, goats, and pigs, is chiefly used. Animals killed exclusively for their skins, such as crocodiles and lizards, produce beautiful but very expensive leather. The skin is first stripped of the fleshy inner and hairy outer layers and then tanned by steeping it in tannin, a preservative. Various finishing processes include rubbing to bring out the grain, as in Morocco leather (goatskin); dyeing; oiling; lacquering for patent leather; and sueding to raise a nap. The uses of leather, which is strong, versatile, flexible, waterproof, and permeable to air, range from industrial parts and saddles to clothing and bookbindings. Synthetic leather has been made since about 1850; modern varieties are usually made from vinyl polymers. *See also* fur; parchment.

leatherback turtle The largest living turtle, *Dermochelys coriacea*, found worldwide. Up to 7 ft (2.1 m) long with a weight of 1200 lb (540 kg), it has no horny external shell and its bones are buried in a ridged leathery brown-black skin. It is a strong swimmer and feeds on marine invertebrates, especially large jellyfish. It is the sole member of its family, *Dermochelyidae*.

Leavis, F(rank) R(aymond) (1895–1978) British literary critic. The moral value of the study of literature was the primary conviction of his teaching at Cambridge University and of his critical journal *Scrutiny* (1932–53). His books include *The Great Tradition* (1948), *The Common Pursuit* (1952), and studies of D. H. *Lawrence (1955) and *Dickens (1970).

Lebanon A country in the Middle East, on the E coast of the Mediterranean Sea. It contains two mountain ranges (the Lebanon and Anti-Lebanon Mountains) extending N–S separated by the Beqaa Valley. The population is mixed, having Arab, Phoenician, Crusader, and Greek origins. Roughly half are Christian and half Muslim; political and official posts are rigorously divided between the two religions. *Economy*: Lebanon was once heavily forested and famous for its cedars, but much has been cleared and converted to arable use, which constitutes a significant part of the country's economy. The fertile Beqaa Valley is the main area of production but has suffered through fighting in the area. The extensive grazing of goats has also seriously depleted the forests and has caused widespread erosion. Industries include traditional crafts and there are two oil refineries, which process oil from Iraq and Saudi Arabia. Until the civil war of 1975–76, international trade, banking, and insurance were the major sources of income. *History*: Lebanon was an early convert to Christianity but in the 7th century broke away from the rest of the Church (*see* Maronite Church) and was invaded by Muslims. Crusaders received support from the Maronites in the 12th and 13th centuries, and Lebanon was held by the Mamelukes during the 14th and 15th centuries and by the Ottoman Turks from the early 16th century to 1918. France, having invaded Lebanon in 1861 to stop the massacres of Christians by Druzes, was given the mandate over Greater Lebanon after World War I. Lebanon became independent in 1941, although France retained control until 1945. In 1958, at the request of Pres. Camille Chamoun, US troops were sent to quell a rebellion against his pro-Western policies. Lebanon did not fight in the 1967 and 1973 Arab-Israeli Wars, but Israel has continually made raids across the border in retaliation for Lebanon's harboring of Palestinian guerrillas. In 1975, a civil war broke out between Christians and Muslims, which lasted 19 months and resulted in virtual religious partition. It was brought to an end by intervention from a Syrian-backed Arab Deterrent Force but unrest continued, especially in the S. In 1982 Israel again invaded S Lebanon, clashing with Syrian forces in the Beqaa Valley and, after besieging Beirut, forced the Palestine Liberation Organization to leave. Bashir Gemayel (1947–82), the president-elect, was killed in a bomb explosion and his brother, Amin Gamayel (1942–   ) succeeded him. Violence continued with US and French troops in the multinational peacekeeping forces suffering heavy casualties in separate terrorist bomb attacks (1983). Leader of the Maronite Christian minority, Gemayel sought to extend his government's authority over bitterly hostile Muslim and Druze factions supported by Syria. Israel withdrew its forces from the country in 1985. Gemayel stepped down as president in 1988; Gen. Michel Aouin formed an interim government. A new constitution in 1989 brought René Moawad to the presidency, but less than three weeks later he was assassinated. Elias Hrawi succeeded him. In 1990 the Syrian-backed Lebanese army drove the PLO from southern strongholds. Despite Middle East peace talks, Israeli-Lebanese clashes occurred in 1992–93. Official language: Arabic. Official currency: Lebanese pound of 100 piastres. Area: 3927 sq mi (10,173 sq km). Population (1990): 3,340,000. Capital: Beirut.

Le Brun, Charles (1619–90) French history and portrait painter and designer. During Louis XIV's reign he helped to make Paris the artistic center of Europe. He visited Rome (1642–46) with Poussin and was patronized by the finance minister Colbert and became First Painter to Louis XIV, for whom he decorated rooms in Versailles. He became director of the Gobelins tapestry works (1664) and of the French Academy (1683), which he had helped to found in 1648.

Le Carré, John (David Cornwell; 1931–   ) British novelist. He served in the foreign service in Germany (1961–64). His novels *The Spy Who Came in from the Cold* (1963), *Tinker, Tailor, Soldier, Spy* (1974), *Smiley's People* (1980), *Lit-*

tle Drummer Girl (1983), *The Russia House* (1989), *The Secret Pilgrim* (1991), and *The Night Manager* (1993), are realistic studies of the world of espionage.

Lecce 40 21N 18 11E A town in SE Italy, in Apulia. It has Roman remains, a 12th-century cathedral, and a university (1956). It has a wine industry. Population (1991): 102,344.

Lech River A river in central Europe. Rising in SW Austria, it flows mainly N through Germany and joins the Danube River. Length: 177 mi (285 km).

Le Châtelier, Henri-Louis (1850–1936) French chemist, who discovered (1888) **Le Châtelier's principle**, that a chemical system will react to a disturbance of its equilibrium by tending to compensate for the disturbance. He used this principle to assist in the foundation of chemical thermodynamics. He was also the first to use a thermocouple to measure high temperatures and invented an optical pyrometer.

Leconte de Lisle, Charles Marie René (1818–94) French poet. He was born on Réunion Island in the Indian Ocean and settled in Paris in 1846. His poetry, especially in *Poèmes antiques* (1852) and *Poèmes barbares* (1862), contains powerful descriptions of natural physical beauty. His disciples were known as the *Parnassians.

Lecoq de Boisbaudran, Paul-Émile (1838–1912) French chemist, who used the technique of spectroscopy, newly developed by *Bunsen and *Kirchhoff, to discover the element gallium (1874). He also discovered samarium (1879) and dysprosium (1886).

Le Corbusier (Charles-Édouard Jeanneret; 1887–1965) French architect, born in Switzerland, one of the most inventive artists of the 20th century. The influence of Le Corbusier's buildings and writings has been enormous. He trained under Auguste Perret (1874–1954) and *Behrens. His career falls into two parts. Until World War II he pioneered a rational, almost cubist, form of design, especially with his villas at Garches (1927) and Poissy (1929). Afterward he became more individual, for example at his extraordinary chapel at Ronchamp (1950; □architecture). He was also concerned with town planning (e.g. *Chandigarh, 1950s) and large-scale housing projects (L'Unité, Marseilles, 1945). As a member of the architectural panel, he also contributed much to the UN buildings in New York (1946).

Leda In Greek myth, the wife of Tyndareus, King of Sparta, and mother, either by her husband or by Zeus, of Clytemnestra, Helen, and Castor and Pollux. Helen was born from an egg after Zeus had visited Leda as a swan.

Lederberg, Joshua (1925–   ) US geneticist, who discovered the phenomenon of transduction in bacteria. Lederberg found that fragments of bacterial DNA could be transmitted from one bacterium to another by a virus. For this, together with his earlier work on bacterial sex factors, Lederberg shared a Nobel Prize (1958) with George *Beadle and Edward *Tatum.

Le Duc Tho (1911–   ) Vietnamese politician. He was a founding member of the Indochinese Communist Party (1930) and the Viet Minh (1945). His negotiations with Henry Kissinger toward the close of the *Vietnam War were instrumental in securing the ceasefire of 1973; the two men were jointly awarded the Nobel Peace Prize (1974) but Le Duc Tho refrained from accepting it.

Lee, Bruce (Lee Yuen Kam; 1940–73) US film actor and *kung fu expert, whose films include *Enter the Dragon*. He became famous for films made in Hong Kong, after only moderate success in Hollywood.

Lee, Francis Lightfoot (1734–97) US statesman; signer of the Declaration of Independence. A political leader in Virginia, he was a delegate to the Second

Continental Congress (1775–79) and was instrumental in Virginia's ratification of the Constitution. His brother **Richard Henry Lee** (1732–94) was a statesman and orator. He was a delegate to the first and second Continental Congress; his resolution leading to the Declaration of Independence was adopted in 1776. He served in Congress (1784–87) but was against ratification of the Constitution because it lacked a bill of rights and advocated strong federal government. As a US senator (1789–92), he fought for adoption of the Bill of Rights (1791).

LE CORBUSIER

Lee, Gypsy Rose (Rose Louise Hovick; 1914–70) US entertainer, who brought grace and sophistication to the art of striptease. She appeared in the Ziegfeld Follies in 1936 and in several films. A film and a musical were based on her autobiography, *Gypsy* (1957).

Lee, Robert E(dward) (1807–70) US military leader and commander of Confederate forces during the Civil War. He graduated from West Point in 1829 and joined the Corps of Engineers. After service in the *Mexican War, Lee was appointed superintendent of West Point (1852–53). He was later transferred to Texas to command the frontier cavalry (1855–61). During a leave in Virginia in 1859, he led the federal forces that suppressed the raid of John *Brown on Harper's Ferry. At the outbreak of the *Civil War, Lee was offered the command of the US army by Pres. Abraham Lincoln, but he declined that appointment to accept a commission as the head of Virginia's military forces. Lee saw his role as one of defending his native state, using superior mobility to defeat federal attacks in the Seven Days' battles, the second battle of Bull Run (1862), and Chancellorsville (1863). His subsequent loss at *Gettysburg, however, forced him to adopt a defensive strategy. Appointed general in chief of all Confederate armies in February 1865, he surrendered to US Gen. Ulysses S. *Grant at Appomattox Courthouse on Apr 9. With the end of the war Lee urged reconciliation between North and South and ended his military career to become president of Washington College, which was later renamed Washington and Lee University as a tribute to him. His father, **Henry Lee** ("Lighthorse Harry"; 1756–1818), was a US American Revolution soldier. He commanded a cavalry infantry unit during the Revolution (1775–83) and was responsible for the taking of the British fort at Paulus Hook, N.J., in 1779. He later served in the Carolina campaign and was at the surrender at Yorktown (1781). He returned to Virginia politics at the war's end and was governor of Virginia (1792–95) and in the US House of Representatives (1799–1801). His well-known words, "First in war, first in peace, and first in the hearts of his countrymen," eulogized George Washington.

ROBERT E. LEE *Confederate general who surrendered for the defeated Confederacy at Appomattox Court House in April 1865.*

Lee, Tsung-Dao (1926–) US physicist, born in China, who (working with his countryman Chen Ning *Yang) showed that parity is not conserved in *weak interactions. For this discovery the two shared the Nobel Prize (1957).

leech A carnivorous aquatic *annelid worm of the class *Hirudinea* (about 300 species). Leeches inhabit fresh and salt water throughout the world and also occur in wet soil and rain forests. They have one sucker around the mouth and a second at the rear. Leeches can move by "looping," using their suckers. Most feed on the blood of animals and man, using specialized piercing mouthparts, but some species feed on insect larvae and earthworms.

Leeds 53 50N 1 35W A city in N England, the largest city in West Yorkshire on the River Aire. Canal links with Liverpool and Goole and the local outcropping of coal assisted in promoting Leeds as an important industrial and commercial center. Its main industries are clothing, textiles, printing, engineering, chemicals, and leather goods. The university was founded in 1904. Population (1991 est): 675,000.

leek A hardy biennial plant, *Allium porrum*, native to SW Asia and E Mediterranean regions and widely grown in Europe as a vegetable. The bulb is hardly differentiated from the stem, which bears long broad leaves. Cultivated leeks are grown from seed and the stems and leaves are eaten in the first year, before flowering. They are set deep in the soil to ensure blanching. The leek is the national emblem of Wales.

Lee Kuan Yew (1923–) Singaporean statesman; prime minister (1959–90). As leader of the People's Action Party (PAP) from 1954, he advocated Singaporean self-government within the British Commonwealth and in 1958–59 helped to draft a constitution in preparation for independence. He agreed, in 1963, to lead Singapore into the Federation of Malaysia but constant dissensions led to Singapore's withdrawal in 1965. His government was authoritative and pro-Western.

Leeuwarden 53 12N 5 48E A city in the N Netherlands, the capital of Friesland province. An economic center with trade in cattle and dairy produce, its industries include engineering and glass production. It contains the notable Frisian museum. Population (1987 est): 85,000.

Leeuwenhoek, Antonie van (1632–1723) Dutch scientist, noted for his microscopic studies of living organisms. He was the first to describe protozoa, bacteria, and spermatozoa and he also made observations of yeasts, red blood cells, and blood capillaries. Among his many other achievements, Leeuwenhoek traced the life histories of various animals, including the flea, ant, and weevil; in so doing he refuted many popular misconceptions concerning their origin. Leeuwenhoek ground over 400 of his own lenses during his lifetime, achieving magnifications of up to 300 times with a single lens.

Leeward Islands 1. A West Indian group of islands in the Lesser Antilles, in the Caribbean Sea extending SE from Puerto Rico to the Windward Islands. 2. A former British colony in the West Indies (1871–1956), comprising Antigua, St Kitts-Nevis-Anguilla, Montserrat, and the British Virgin Islands. 3. A group of islands in the Netherlands Antilles, in the Caribbean Sea comprising St Eustatius, Saba, and part of St Martin. 4. A group of islands in French Polynesia, in the Society Islands in the S Pacific Ocean.

leg In human anatomy, the lower limb, which extends from the hip to the foot. The bone of the thigh (*see* femur) is connected by a ball-and-socket joint to the pelvis, permitting a wide range of movements. It forms a hinge joint at the knee with the bones of the lower leg—the shin bone (tibia) and the smaller fibula. This joint is overlain at the front by a bone (the patella, or kneecap) embedded in the tendon of the quadriceps muscle of the thigh.

Le Gallienne, Eva (1899–1991) US actress, producer, and director, born in England. She translated Henrik *Ibsen's works and played in many of them. Appearing on the New York stage from 1916, she starred in *Liliom* (1921) and in 1926 founded the Civic Repertory Theater, for which she produced many classical revivals; 20 years later, she founded the American Repertory Theater. She directed *The Cherry Orchard* (1968) on Broadway. Her well-known roles included leading parts in *Camille* (1931), *Royal Family* (1975), and *To Grandmother's House We Go* (1981).

Legendre, Adrien Marie (1752–1833) French mathematician, who made important contributions to number theory and mathematical physics. Due to the jealousy of *Laplace, then the foremost mathematician in France, Legendre never in his lifetime received the recognition that he deserved.

Léger, Fernand (1881–1955) French painter, born in Argentan. He settled in Paris (1900) where, associated with *cubism, he produced robotlike figure paintings, followed by an abstract series entitled *Contrasts of Forms* (1913), consisting of brightly colored tubes. His experiences in World War I inspired the machine imagery of such paintings as *The City* (1919; Philadelphia) but later he often returned to the human figure. Broad areas of bright colors are the most characteristic feature of his work. He also painted murals, designed ballet sets, and made the first non-narrative film, *Le Ballet mécanique* (1924).

Leghorn (bird) A breed of domestic fowl originating in Italy and widely used in breeding commercial hybrids for egg laying. It has a full rounded breast, a flat sloping back, a short stout beak, long wattles, and a prominent comb in the male. The plumage can be of various colors, including black, blue, reddish brown, white, and black and white. Weight: 7.5 lb (3.4 kg) (cocks); 5.5 lb (2.5 km) (hens).

Leghorn (port). *See* Livorno.

legionnaires' disease An acute severe pneumonia, caused by the bacterium *Legionella pneumophila*, first described in 1976 after an outbreak among US legionnaires in Philadelphia. There have since been other outbreaks, in the US and other countries. The disease has a mortality rate of less than 5%. The route of transmission is thought to be through air-conditioning systems contaminated by the bacteria.

Legion of Honor (French name: Légion d'Honneur) A French order of knighthood, established by Napoleon in 1802. Its five ranks, to which foreigners are admitted, are knight of the grand cross, grand officer, commander, officer, and chevalier. Its grand master is the president of France.

Leguminosae A worldwide family of herbs, shrubs, and trees (about 7000 species), which includes many important crop plants, such as peas, beans, clovers, and alfalfa. They all have compound leaves and the fruit is a pod containing a single row of seeds. Both pods and seeds are rich in protein. Most species possess root nodules that contain nitrogen-fixing bacteria and leguminous crops replenish nitrogen in the soil (*see* nitrogen cycle).

Lehár, Franz (Ferencz L.; 1870–1948) Hungarian composer. He studied at the Prague conservatory and after a period as a military band conductor (1894–99) turned to the composition of operettas, of which *The Merry Widow* (1905) was his greatest success. Others include *The Count of Luxembourg* (1911) and *Land of Smiles* (1923).

Le Havre 49 30N 0 06E A port in N France, in the Seine-Maritimes department on the English Channel at the mouth of the Seine River. Severely damaged in World War II, its harbor was subsequently rebuilt and now maintains an important transatlantic cargo service and a car-ferry service to England. Population (1975): 219,583.

Lehmann, Lilli (1848–1929) German operatic soprano. She was taught by her mother. During a long career she sang many roles, including Brünnhilde in *Die Walküre*, Isolde, Donna Anna in *Don Giovanni*, and Leonora in *Fidelio*.

Lehmann, Lotte (1885–1976) German soprano, a US citizen from 1938. She studied in Berlin with Mathilde Mallinger (1847–1920) and became one of the most renowned dramatic sopranos of her time; her most famous role was the Marschallin in Richard Strauss's opera *Der Rosenkavalier*.

LOTTE LEHMANN

Leibniz, Gottfried Wilhelm (1646–1716) German philosopher and mathematician. He put forward a coherent philosophy, which is summarized in his two philosophical books, *New Essays on the Human Understanding* (c. 1705) and *Theodicy* (1710), and numerous essays. Leibniz's best-known doctrine is that the universe consists of an infinite set of independent substances (monads) in each of which a life force is present. In creating the world, God took account of the wishes of monads and this led to a rational harmony in the "best of all possible worlds"—a view satirized in *Voltaire's Candide*. As a rationalist Leibniz founded the distinction between the logically necessary and the merely contingent truth. His claim to have invented the calculus was disputed by *Newton.

Leicester 52 38N 1 05W A city in central England, the administrative center of Leicestershire. Ancient Ratae Coritanorum on the Fosse Way, Leicester has many Roman remains including the Jewry Wall and sections of the forum and baths. Parts of the Norman castle also remain. The university was established in 1957. The principal industries are hosiery, knitwear, footwear, engineering, printing, plastics, and electronics. Population (1983 est): 283,000.

Leicester, Robert Dudley, Earl of (c. 1532–88) English courtier. Dudley's good looks attracted the attention of Elizabeth I, who made him Master of the Horse (1558) and then a privy councillor (1659). It was rumored that he might marry the queen after the death of his wife. His incompetent command (1685–87) of an English force against Spain led to his recall but he retained

Elizabeth's favor until his death. He was a strong supporter of the Protestant cause.

Leiden (English name: Leyden) 52 10N 4 30E A city in the W Netherlands, in South Holland province. In 1574 it survived a Spanish siege by cutting the dikes and flooding the countryside. Its famous university was founded in 1575 as a reward for this heroic defense. During the 17th and 18th centuries it was an artistic and educational center. The painters Rembrandt and Lucas van Leyden were born here. Industries include textiles and metallurgy. Population (1988 est): 108,000.

Leigh, Vivien (Vivien Hartley; 1913–67) British actress. In the theater, she played many leading Shakespearean roles, frequently appearing with Laurence *Olivier, her husband from 1937 to 1960. Her films include *Gone with the Wind* (1939), in which she played the heroine Scarlett O'Hara, and *A Streetcar Named Desire* (1951).

Leinster A province in the SE Republic of Ireland. It consists of the counties of Carlow, Dublin, Kildare, Kilkenny, Laoighis, Longford, Louth, Meath, Offaly, Westmeath, Wexford, and Wicklow. It incorporates the ancient kingdoms of Meath and Leinster. Area: 7580 sq mi (19,632 sq km). Population (1986): 1,853,000.

Leipzig 51 20N 12 21E A city in S Germany, near the confluence of the Elster, Pleisse, and Parthe Rivers. Important international trade fairs have been held in Leipzig since the middle ages. It was also the center of the German book and publishing industry until World War II. Notable buildings include the 15th-century Church of St Thomas and Auerbach's Keller, an inn that provided the setting for Goethe's *Faust*. A famous musical center, the city has associations with J. S. Bach and Mendelssohn. The university was founded in 1409 and renamed Karl Marx University in 1952. Leipzig is the country's second largest city and one of its chief industrial and commercial centers. Its industries include iron and steel, chemicals, printing, and textiles. Population (1991 est): 511,000.

Leipzig, Battle of (*or* Battle of the Nations; Oct 16–19, 1813) The battle in which Napoleon was defeated by an alliance including Prussia, Russia, and Austria. The engagement culminated in the allies driving the French into Leipzig and then storming the city. The French army was shattered and its remnants retreated westward across the Rhine, ending Napoleon's empire in Germany and Poland.

leishmaniasis A tropical disease caused by infection with parasitic protozoans of the genus *Leishmania* (*see* Flagellata), which are transmitted to man by the bite of sandflies. The disease may affect the skin, causing open sores or ulcers, or the internal organs, principally the liver and spleen (this form of leishmaniasis is called **kala-azar**). Treatment is by means of drugs that destroy the parasites.

leitmotif (German: leading theme) A short musical phrase characterizing an object, person, state of mind, event, etc. *Wagner developed the technique of constructing large-scale compositions from leitmotifs in his mature operas, such as the cycle *Der Ring des Nibelungen*.

Leitrim (Irish name: Contae Liathdroma) A county in the NW Republic of Ireland, in Connacht bordering on Donegal Bay. Mainly hilly, descending to lowlands in the S, it contains several lakes, notably Lough Allen. Agriculture consists chiefly of cattle and sheep rearing; potatoes and oats are also grown. Area: 589 sq mi (1525 sq km). Population (1986): 27,000. County town: Carrick-on-Shannon.

Leix. *See* Laoighis.

Lely, Sir Peter (Pieter van der Faes; 1618–80) Portrait painter, born in Germany of Dutch parents. He studied and worked in Haarlem before settling in London (1641), where he was patronized by Charles I and later Cromwell. As court painter to Charles II from 1661, he produced his best-known works.

Lemaître, Georges Édouard, Abbé (1894–1966) Belgian priest and astronomer, who originated the *big-bang theory of the universe (1927). Lemaître based his theory on *Hubble's suggestion that the universe is expanding; it went unnoticed until *Eddington drew attention to it.

Léman, Lac. *See* Geneva, Lake.

Le Mans 48 00N 0 12E A city in NW France, the capital of the Sarthe department. Its many historical buildings include the cathedral (11th–15th centuries) in which Queen Berengaria (died c. 1290), the wife of Richard the Lionheart, is buried. The Le Mans Grand Prix, a 24-hour motor race, is held here annually. Le Mans is an agricultural, industrial, and commercial center. Population (1982): 150,350.

Lemberg. *See* Lvov.

lemming A *rodent belonging to the subfamily *Microtini* (which also includes voles), found in northern regions of Asia, America, and Europe. They range from 3–6 in (7.5–15 cm) in length and have long thick fur. When their food of grass, berries, and roots is abundant, they breed at a great rate but when food is scarce they migrate southward, often in large swarms crossing swamps, rivers, and other obstacles. Although able to swim, they sometimes drown through exhaustion. (Contrary to popular belief, they do not deliberately drown themselves.) Chief genera: *Dicrostonyx* (collared lemmings; 4 species), *Lemmus* (true lemmings; 4 species). Family *Cricetidae*. □mammal.

Lemnos (Modern Greek name: Límnos) A Greek island in the N Aegean Sea. Remains of the most advanced Neolithic communities in the Aegean have been found here. Area: 184 sq mi (477 sq km).

lemon A small tree or shrub, *Citrus limon*, 10–20 ft (3–6 m) high, probably native to the E Mediterranean but widely cultivated in subtropical climates for its fruit. Its fragrant white flowers produce oval fruits with thick yellow skin and acid-tasting pulp rich in vitamin C. The juice is used as a flavoring in cookery and confectionery and as a drink. Family: *Rutaceae*.

lemon sole A *flatfish, *Microstomus kitt*, also called lemon dab, found in the NE Atlantic and North Sea. Up to 18 in (45 cm) long, its upper side is red-brown or yellow-brown with light or dark marbling. It is an important food fish. Family: *Pleuronectidae*.

lemur A small *prosimian primate belonging to the family *Lemuridae* (16 species), found only in Madagascar and neighboring islands. Lemurs are mostly arboreal and nocturnal and often live in groups, feeding mainly on fruit, shoots, leaves, and insects. The ring-tailed lemur (*Lemur catta*) is 28–37 in (70–95 cm) long including the tail (16–20 in [40–50 cm]) and is mainly terrestrial, sheltering among rocks and in caves. Dwarf lemurs (subfamily *Cheirogaleinae*) are only 10–20 in (25–50 cm) long including the tail (5–10 in [12–25 cm]).

Lemures In Roman religion, maleficent spirits of the dead. They haunted their former homes and were ritually appeased at the annual festival of the Lemuria, held in May.

Lena River A long river in Asiatic Russia. Rising in S Siberia, W of Lake Baikal, it flows mainly NE to the Laptev Sea. Its large delta, about 11,580 sq mi

(30,000 sq km) in area, is frozen for about nine months of the year. Length: 2653 mi (4271 km).

Le Nain A family of French painters, natives of Laon, who established a workshop together in Paris (c. 1680). The individual contributions of **Antoine** (c. 1588–1648), **Louis** (c. 1593–1648), and **Mathieu** (1607–77) are uncertain, since their works were not signed and some were probably joint efforts. Louis probably painted the dignified peasant scenes, such as *The Peasant's Meal* (Louvre); small-scale works on copper, often of family life, are credited to Antoine. All three became members of the newly established French Academy in 1648.

Lenclos, Ninon de (Anne de L.; 1620–1705) French courtesan, whose salon was the meeting place for many prominent literary and political figures of her day. She herself was much interested in Epicurean philosophy. Her lovers included *La Rochefoucauld and *Sévigné.

Lend-Lease Act (1941) Legislation introduced by President Roosevelt enabling Congress to lend or lease information, services, and defense items to any country vital to US defense. Britain and its World War II allies immediately received desperately needed planes, tanks, raw materials, and food.

L'Enfant, Pierre-Charles (1754–1825) French-born US architect and town planner. His principal achievement was his scheme for the design of Washington, DC (1791), which was a layout in a traditional French style, with long parallel avenues and dramatic focal points. The design was inspired by Versailles and a 16th-century plan of Rome. Due to the expense involved, the plan was long abandoned. It was not executed until 1901.

Lenglen, Suzanne (1899–1938) French tennis player. She first won the Wimbledon singles in 1919 and subsequently was only once beaten in singles until 1926, when she turned professional. Her accurate play, grace, and daring dress did much to make tennis a spectator sport.

Lenin, Vladimir Ilich (V. I. Ulyanov; 1870–1924) Russian revolutionary and first leader of communist Russia. Lenin became a Marxist after the execution (1887) of his brother Aleksandr for attempting to assassinate the tsar, Alexander III. In 1893 Lenin joined a revolutionary group in St Petersburg (subsequently renamed *Leningrad), where he practiced as a lawyer. In 1895 he was imprisoned and in 1897, exiled to Siberia, where he married (1898) Nadezhda Krupskaya, a fellow Marxist, with whom he worked closely throughout his career. In 1902 he published *What Is to Be Done?*, in which he emphasized the role of the party in effecting revolution. This emphasis led to a split in the Russian Social Democratic Workers' Party between the *Bolsheviks under Lenin and the *Mensheviks. After the failure of the *Revolution of 1905, Lenin again went into exile, settling in Zurich in 1914, where he wrote *Imperialism, the Highest Stage of Capitalism* (1917). In April 1917, after the outbreak of the *Russian Revolution, Lenin returned to Russia. Calling for the transfer of power from the Provisional Government to the soviets (workers' councils), he was forced into hiding and then to flee to Finland. Lenin returned in October to lead the Bolshevik revolution, which overthrew the Provisional Government and established the ruling Soviet of People's Commissars under Lenin's chairmanship. He made peace with Germany and then led the revolutionaries to victory against the Whites in the civil war (1918–20). He founded (1919) the Third *International and initiated far-reaching social reforms, including the redistribution of land to the peasants, but in response to the disastrous economic effects of the war he introduced the *New Economic Policy (1921), which permitted a modicum of free enterprise.

In 1918 Lenin was injured in an attempt on his life and a series of strokes from 1922 led to his premature death. *See also* Leninism.

LENIN *Sitting at the center, surrounded by his colleagues in the St Petersburg Union for the Struggle for the Liberation of the Working Class (1895).*

Leninabad. *See* Khudzhand.

Leninakan. *See* Kumayry.

Leningrad. *See* St Petersburg.

Leninism Developments in the theory of scientific socialism (*see* Marxism) by V. I. *Lenin. His theory of imperialism is an account of the final stage of capitalism, in which it dominates the entire world, decisive control resting with finance capital (banks) as opposed to industrial capital. Because of the worldwide nature of capitalism, socialist revolution becomes possible even in economically underdeveloped countries, the "weak link" of imperialism.

According to his theory of the revolutionary party, the most conscious element of the proletariat provides the leadership for the rest of the working class and the peasantry in organizing the overthrow of the capitalist class.

Lenin Peak 39 21N 73 01E The second highest mountain in the Trans-Altai range of Kyrgyzstan and Tajikistan. Height: 23,406 ft (7134 m).

Leninsk-Kuznetskii (name from 1864 until 1925: Kolchugino) 40 37N 72 15E A city in central S Russia in the Kuznetsk Basin. Coal mining has been the most important industrial activity since its foundation in 1864. Population (1991 est): 133,000.

Lenni-Lenape *See* Delaware.

Lennon, John (1940–80) British rock musician and founding member of the *Beatles. After the Beatles disbanded Lennon recorded solo albums, several of which featured his second wife, **Yoko Ono** (1933–   ). Music critics consider his most distinctive recording to be *Imagine* (1971). He was assassinated in 1980.

Le Nôtre, André (1613–1700) French landscape gardener. Le Nôtre perfected the French version of the formal garden with his use of imposing vistas and was imitated throughout Europe. His first complete garden was at Vaux-le-Vicomte (1656–61) but his largest and most perfect was for Louis XIV at *Versailles, on which he worked for nearly 30 years.

lens A piece of transparent material, usually glass, quartz, or plastic, used for directing and focusing beams of light. The surfaces of a lens have a constant curvature; if both sides curve outward at the middle the lens is called convex, if they curve inward it is concave. The image formed by a lens may be real, in which case the rays converge to the image point (a converging lens), or virtual, in which the rays diverge from the image point (a diverging lens). The focal length of a lens is the distance from the lens at which a parallel beam of light is brought to a focus. If the focal length of the lens is f, the rays from an object distance u from the lens are focused at a distance v from the lens, where $1/f = 1/u + 1/v$ and u, v, and f all obey certain sign conventions.

Lent The Christian period of fasting and penance preceding Easter. Beginning on *Ash Wednesday, the Lenten fast covers 40 days, in emulation of Christ's 40 days in the wilderness (Matthew 4.2). In the Middle Ages the fast was more or less strictly observed, especially with regard to the prohibition on eating meat, but since the Reformation the rules have been generally relaxed in both Roman Catholic and Protestant Churches.

lentil An annual herb, *Lens culinaris*, native to the Near East but widely cultivated. Each pod produces 1–2 flat round green or reddish seeds, which are rich in protein and can be dried and stored for use in soups, stews, etc. Family: *Leguminosae*.

Lenya, Lotte (Caroline Blamauer; 1900–81) Austrian singer and character actress, famous for her interpretations of the songs by her husband, the composer Kurt *Weill.

Lenz's law The direction of an induced current in a conductor is such as to oppose the cause of the induction. For example, a current induced by a conductor cutting the lines of flux of a magnetic field would produce a magnetic field of its own, which would oppose the original magnetic field. Named for Heinrich Lenz (1804–65).

Leo (Latin: Lion) A large conspicuous constellation in the N sky near Ursa Major, lying on the *zodiac between Virgo and Cancer. The brightest stars are the 1st-magnitude Regulus, which lies at the base of the **Sickle of Leo**, and the 2nd-magnitude Denebola and Algeiba.

Leo (I) the Great, St (d. 461 AD) Pope (440–61). One of the greatest medieval popes, St. Leo the Great was largely successful in his attempts to extend papal control in the West after the fall of the western Roman Empire, but Leo failed to find support in the East. His treaties with the invading *Huns (452) and *Vandals (455) protected Rome from their onslaughts. Leo's Christology, expressed in the *Epistola Dogmatica* (or *Tome of Leo*; 449), defined the doctrine of the Incarnation and was accepted at the Council of Chalcedon (451). Feast day: Apr 11.

Leo (III) the Isaurian (c. 675–741 AD) Byzantine emperor (717–41). He repulsed a Muslim attack on Constantinople in 718 and finally secured Asia Minor in 740 after a great victory over the Muslims at Acroïnon. In 730 he issued a decree that established the policy of *iconoclasm (the destruction of Christian images).

Leo III, St (d. 816 AD) Pope (795–816). After his election he was opposed by a Roman faction and was forced to flee to *Charlemagne, who supported his return to Rome. There, in 800, Leo crowned Charlemagne Emperor of the West—an act that marks the start of the Holy Roman Empire. His rule was noted for its munificent church building. He was canonized in 1673. Feast day: June 12.

Leo IX, St (Bruno of Egisheim; 1002–54) Pope (1049–54), the first of the great medieval reforming popes. At successive councils clerical marriage and simony were condemned and, assisted by Hildebrand (later *Gregory VII) and Humbert of Moyenmoutier (c. 1000–61), he attempted to free the papacy from imperial control. Rival claims with the Normans to gain control of S Italy resulted in Leo's defeat at the battle of Civitella (1053). His conflict with the Eastern Church led to the schism between Rome and Constantinople (1054; *see* Filioque). Feast day: Apr 19.

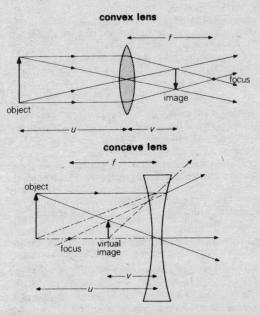

LENS *The lines representing light rays show how a convex lens gives a real inverted image and how a concave lens gives an upright virtual image.*

Leo X (Giovanni de' Medici; 1475–1521) Pope (1513–21), the second son of Lorenzo the Magnificent (*see* Medici), by whose influence Giovanni was made a cardinal in 1489. His pontificate was marked by political vacillation and financial disasters but lavish patronage of the arts. He negotiated the Concordat of Bologna (1516) with Francis I, giving the French crown almost total control over ecclesiastical appointments in France.

Leo XIII (Vincenzo Gioacchino Pecci; 1810–1903) Pope (1878–1903). Elected after a long career as a papal diplomat, Leo fostered relations between the papacy and European powers, the US, and Japan. He also encouraged learning, foreign missions, and lay piety. His encyclical *Rerum novarum* (*Of New Things*; 1891), while condemning socialism, emphasized the duty of the Church in matters of social justice.

León (*or* León de los Aldamas) 21 10N 101 42W A city in central Mexico. It is a commercial and distribution center; industries include the manufacture of footwear and leather goods. Population (1980): 593,002.

León 42 35N 5 34W A city in NW Spain, in León. Formerly capital of the kingdom of León, it declined after the 13th century. Medieval in atmosphere, it has a notable gothic cathedral. Population (1991): 144,137.

León 12 24N 86 52W A city in W Nicaragua. Moved to its present site after the original city near Lake Managua was destroyed by an earthquake in 1610, it was the capital of Nicaragua until 1855. It is the country's cultural center and has a university (1812). Industries include textiles, distilleries, tanneries, and food processing. Population (1985 est): 101,000.

Leonardo da Vinci (1452–1519) Italian artistic and scientific genius of the *Renaissance, born in Vinci, the illegitimate son of a notary. He trained in Florence under *Verrocchio and painted the *Adoration of the Magi* (Uffizi) for the monks of S Donato a Scopeto (1481). In 1482 he became painter, engineer, and designer to Duke Ludovico Sforza in Milan, where he painted the fresco of the *Last Supper* (Sta Maria delle Grazie) and the first version of the *Virgin of the Rocks* (Louvre). His promised equestrian sculpture glorifying the Duke was never cast but the studies of horses for the project have survived. After the French invasion of Milan (1499), he returned to Florence, becoming military engineer and architect (1502) to Cesare *Borgia. Paintings in this period include the *Battle of Anghiari* for the Palazzo Vecchio, *The Virgin and Child with St John the Baptist and St Anne* (painting, Louvre; cartoon, National Gallery, London) and the *Mona Lisa* (Louvre). Some of his paintings were left unfinished and others, because of his experimental techniques, failed to survive. After working again in Milan (1506–13) and in Rome (1513–15), he was invited by Francis I to France (1516), where he spent his last years in Cloux near Amboise. His notebooks reveal his wide range of interests, including anatomy, botany, geology, hydraulics, and mechanics.

Leoncavallo, Ruggiero (1858–1919) Italian composer of operas. Only *I Pagliacci* (1892) has met with continuing success, although he composed over 15.

Leonidas I (d. 480 BC) King of Sparta (?490–480). He was the hero of the battle of *Thermopylae.

Leonov, Leonid (1899–) Soviet novelist and playwright. His moral and psychological themes were most powerfully expressed in his early novels, notably *Barsuki* (*The Badgers*; 1924) and *Vor* (*The Thief*; 1927).

Leontief, Wasily (1906–) US economist, born in Russia. He won the Nobel Prize in economics (1973). His input-output theory explained the interaction of economic changes and became a forecasting tool. He wrote *The Structure of American Economy* (1919–29) and *Input-Output Economics* (1966).

leopard A large spotted *cat, *Panthera pardus*, found throughout Africa and most of Asia. Leopards are slender, up to 7 ft (2.1 m) long including the 35-in (90-cm) tail, having a yellow coat spotted with black rosettes. Color variations, such as the *panther, sometimes occur. Leopards are solitary and nocturnal, typically lying in wait in a tree for their prey.

Leopardi, Giacomo (1798–1837) Italian poet. He is best known for the intense lyric poetry of *I canti* (1831).

leopard lily A perennial herbaceous plant, *Belamcanda chinensis*, also called blackberry lily, native to E Asia and widely planted as a garden ornamental.

leopard seal A solitary Antarctic *seal, *Hydrurga leptonyx*, of the pack ice. Leopard seals are fast agile hunters, feeding mainly on penguins.

Leopold I (1640–1705) Holy Roman Emperor (1658–1705). Leopold was ultimately successful against the Turks, who had besieged Vienna in 1683, freeing most of Hungary from Turkish dominance by 1699.

LEONARDO DA VINCI *This head of an old man, drawn after 1515, is possibly a self-portrait of the artist.*

Leopold I (1790–1865) The first King of the Belgians (1831–65). He defended Belgium against William III of the Netherlands (1817–90; reigned 1849–90), who refused to recognize Belgian independence until 1838. A leading diplomat in Europe, at home he encouraged educational and economic reforms.

Leopold II (1797–1870) Grandduke of Tuscany (1824–59).

Leopold II (1835–1909) King of the Belgians (1865–1909), who sponsored Stanley's exploration of the Congo. In 1885 he obtained sovereignty over the Congo Free State, which was annexed as the Belgian Congo in 1908.

Leopold III (1901–83) King of the Belgians (1934–51). He surrendered to the Germans in *World War II, provoking opposition to his return to Belgium in 1945 and forcing his abdication in favor of his son *Baudouin.

Léopoldville. *See* Kinshasa.

Lepanto, Battle of (Oct 7, 1571) A naval battle off Lepanto, Greece, in which the *Holy League routed the Ottoman navy, which was threatening to dominate the Mediterranean.

Lepidodendron An extinct genus of treelike pteridophytes that, with *Cala-mites, were dominant forest trees of the Carboniferous period (370–280 million years ago), their fossilized remains forming coal seams.

Lepidoptera. *See* butterflies and moths.

Lepidus, Marcus Aemilius (died c. 13 BC) Roman protégé of Julius Caesar. In 36 Lepidus attempted to secure Sicily and was forced to retire.

leprosy A chronic disease, occurring almost entirely in tropical countries, caused by the bacterium *Mycobacterium leprae* (which is related to the tuberculosis bacillus). The incubation period is usually one to three years and, contrary to popular belief, leprosy is contracted only after close personal contact with an infected person. In the lepromatous form of the disease lumps appear on the skin, which, together with the nerves, becomes thickened and progressively destroyed, resulting in disfigurement and deformity. Eyes, bones, and muscles may also be affected. Tuberculoid leprosy usually produces only discolored patches on the skin associated with loss of sensation in the affected areas. There are now potent drugs—sulfones—available to cure the disease.

Leptis Magna An ancient trading center near present-day Homs (Libya). Founded by the Phoenicians (6th century BC) Leptis' importance increased during Roman imperial times; ruins of unusually splendid public buildings attest its former grandeur.

lepton A group of elementary particles, consisting of the *electron, *muon, *tau particle, *neutrinos, and their antiparticles. They take part only in the *weak and *electromagnetic interactions; together with *quarks and photons they are thought to be the only truly elementary particles. *See* particle physics.

Le Puy 45 03N 3 53E A city in S France, the capital of the Haute-Loire department. It has a 12th-century cathedral and is famous for its lace making. Population (1975): 29,024.

Lérida 41 37N 0 38E A city in NE Spain, in Catalonia. It possesses two cathedrals and a massive Moorish castle. An agricultural center, its industries include glass and silk. Population (1991): 111,880.

Lermontov, Mikhail (1814–41) Russian poet and novelist. His early Romantic poetry, published while he was a student at Moscow University, was greatly influenced by *Byron. As an army officer and an observer of high society he developed the cynical attitudes expressed in his novel *A Hero of Our Time* (1840). He was twice exiled to the Caucasus, the first time for a poem attacking the court, and was killed in a duel.

Lerner, Alan Jay (1918–1986) US lyricist and librettist, who collaborated with the composer Frederick *Loewe in the musicals *Brigadoon* (1947), *My Fair Lady* (1956), and *Camelot* (1960). Lerner also wrote the scripts for *An American in Paris* (1951) and *Gigi* (1958).

Lesage, Alain-René (1668–1747) French novelist. His best-known work is the picaresque novel *Gil Blas* (1715–35). He also made translations and satirical adaptations of Spanish plays as well as writing over 60 plays and librettos of his own.

lesbianism. *See* homosexuality.

Lesbos (Modern Greek name: Lésvos) A Greek island in the E Aegean Sea, situated close to the mainland of Turkey. Settled by Aeolians about 1000 BC, it is associated with the development of Greek lyric poetry (especially through the work of Alcaeus and Sappho). Lesbos was a member of the Delian League and the chief town, Mytilene, was made a free port in the era of Roman power.

Olives, grapes, and cereals are grown here and there is sardine fishing. Area: 629 sq mi (1630 sq km).

Leschetizky, Theodor (1830–1915) Polish pianist and piano teacher. His method influenced a generation of pianists, including Paderewski. He was a pupil of Czerny in Vienna and moved to St Petersburg in 1852, becoming head of the piano department at the conservatory.

Lesotho, Kingdom of (name until 1966: Basutoland) A small country in SE Africa, enclosed by South Africa. It is largely mountainous, rising to 11,000 ft (3350 m). Most of the inhabitants are *Sotho. *Economy*: chiefly agricultural, the main crops being maize, wheat, and sorghum. Livestock is important but soil erosion due to overgrazing is a serious problem. The main exports, along with diamonds, are cattle, wool, and mohair. Some industry, including tourism, is being developed, but a large proportion of the male population still works in South African mines. *History*: Originally inhabited by San (Bushmen), Lesotho received many refugees of tribal warfare in the 17th and 18th century, and in the 19th century the disparate inhabitants of the country were consolidated into the Basuto tribe by Chief Moshesh. In 1884, following warfare with the Orange Free State, Basutoland came under British protection on the request of Chief Moshesh to protect his people from Boer incursions. When the Union of South Africa was formed in 1910, Basutoland resisted incorporation, but was placed under the authority of the British High Commission in South Africa. In 1966 Lesotho became an independent kingdom within the Commonwealth under King Moshoeshoe II. A state of emergency existed from 1970 to 1973. Prime Minister Leabua Jonathan (1914–   ) was overthrown in a military coup in 1986. King Moshoeshoe was stripped of his powers, went into exile in Britain in 1990, and returned in 1992. Moshoeshoe's son, who took the name Letsie III, succeeded to the throne during his father's exile. Official languages: Sesotho and English. Official currency: South African rand of 100 cents. Area: 11,716 sq mi (30,340 sq km). Population (1990 est.): 1,757,000. Capital: Maseru.

LESOTHO *The architecture of this handcraft center at Maseru was inspired by the huts of the Sotho; the decorative top is based on the Mokorotla, the traditional head gear.*

Lesseps, Ferdinand de (1805–94) French diplomat, who supervised the construction of the Suez Canal, which was completed in 1869. A subsequent project to construct the Panama Canal ended in disaster when Lesseps was prosecuted for embezzling funds.

Lesser Antilles (former name: Caribbees) A West Indian group of islands, comprising a chain extending from Puerto Rico to the N coast of Venezuela. They include the Leeward and Windward Islands, Barbados, Trinidad and Tobago, and the Netherlands Antilles.

Lessing, Doris (1919–) British novelist. Born in Iran and brought up in Rhodesia, she came to England in 1949. Political and social themes predominate in her fiction, notably the sequence of five novels entitled *Children of Violence* (1952–69) and *The Golden Notebook* (1962). Later novels include *Memoirs of a Survivor* (1974). She began a series of futuristic science-fiction novels with *Shikasta* (1979) and followed with *Marriages Between Zones Three, Four and Five* (1980) and others. Other works include *The Good Terrorist* (1985) and *The Fifth Child* (1988).

Lessing, Gotthold Ephraim (1729–81) German dramatist and writer. His *Miss Sara Sampson* (1755) was the first successful German tragedy to reject the classical French model and to use middle-class protagonists, while his comedy *Minna von Barnhelm* (1767) demonstrates the *Enlightenment ideal of reason. In his influential essays, the *Hamburgische Dramaturgie* (1767–69), he developed his dramatic theories.

Le Tellier, Michel. *See* Louvois, Michel Le Tellier, Marquis de.

Lethbridge 49 43N 112 48W A city in W Canada, in S Alberta. Founded in 1870 as a coal mining center, it has become an agricultural, distribution, and research center, housing the University of Lethbridge (1967). Most industry is agriculturally based. Population (1991): 60,974.

Lethe In Greek and Roman mythology, a river in the underworld, the water of which caused those who drank it to forget their former lives.

Leto In Greek mythology, a daughter of the *Titans loved by Zeus. During her pregnancy she was not welcomed anywhere because of the fear of Hera and was forced to give birth to Apollo and Artemis on the barren island of Delos.

letter of credit A letter from a bank to a foreign bank authorizing the payment of a specified sum to the person or company named. They are widely used as a means of paying for goods in foreign trade. An **irrevocable letter of credit** cannot be cancelled by the purchaser or the issuing bank. A **confirmed letter of credit** guarantees payment to the beneficiary should the issuing bank fail to honor it. A confirmed irrevocable letter of credit opened at a first-class bank is a safe basis for trading, although it must be negotiated before its expiration date. Unconfirmed or revocable letters of credit do not have great value.

Lettish. *See* Latvian.

lettres de cachet (French: letters of the seal) Administrative and judicial orders issued by the Kings of France. They were much misused during the 17th and 18th centuries to authorize arrest and imprisonment without trial or appeal. As symbols of the monarchy's despotism they were abolished (1790) during the French Revolution.

lettuce An annual herb, *Lactuca sativa*, probably from the Near East and widely cultivated as a salad plant. It has a tight rosette of juicy leaves, rich in vitamin A, and is usually eaten fresh or cooked in soups. Family: *Compositae*.

Leucippus (5th century BC) Greek philosopher. He developed from the teachings of *Parmenides the theory that there are two ultimate realities: (1) an infinite number of tiny irreducible particles (atoms), randomly circulating in (2) empty space. This theory is remarkably close to modern *atomic theory. *See also* Democritus of Abdera.

leucite A feldspathoid mineral of composition $KAl(SiO_3)_2$, occurring as whitish or grayish crystals in some volcanic rocks deficient in silica. Where sufficiently concentrated it is a source of potash.

Leuckart, Karl Georg Friedrich Rudolph (1822–98) German zoologist, who founded the science of parasitology. Leuckart described the life cycles of tapeworms and the liver fluke and revealed the importance of wormlike parasites in causing diseases in man.

Leuctra, Battle of (371 BC) The battle in which the reorganized Theban army under *Epaminondas crushed the Spartan invasion of Boeotia in Sparta's first major defeat on land. Sparta's resultant loss of influence allowed Thebes a short-lived ascendency in Greece.

leukemia A disease in which the blood contains an abnormally large number of white blood cells (*see* leukocyte). Leukemia is a type of cancer of the blood-forming tissues, which undergo uncontrolled proliferation to produce many immature and abnormal white blood cells that do not function properly. Leukemias may be acute or chronic, depending on the rate of progression of the disease. They are also classified according to the type of white cell affected. For example acute lymphocytic leukemia (affecting the lymphocytes) occurs most commonly in children and young adults; it can now often be controlled by means of radiotherapy or *cytotoxic drugs. Chronic leukemias occur more often in old people and may not need any treatment.

leukocyte (*or* white blood cell) A colorless *blood cell, up to 0.008 in (0.02 mm) in diameter, of which there are normally 4000–11,000 per cubic millimeter of blood. There are several kinds, all involved in the body's defense mechanisms. Granulocytes (*or* polymorphs), which have granules in their cytoplasm, and monocytes ingest and feed on bacteria and other microorganisms that cause infection (*see also* phagocyte). The lymphocytes are involved with the production of *antibodies. Cancer of the white blood cells is called *leukemia.

leukotomy The surgical operation of interrupting the course of white nerve fibers within the brain. It is performed to relieve uncontrollable pain or emotional tension in very severe and intractable psychiatric illnesses, such as severe depression, chronic anxiety, and obsessional neurosis. The original form of the operation—prefrontal leukotomy (*or* lobotomy)—had the serious complication of epilepsy, apathy, and irresponsibility. Modern procedures make small and selective lesions and side effects are uncommon. *See also* psychosurgery.

Leuven. *See* Louvain.

Levant A former name for the lands on the E coast of the Mediterranean Sea, now within Turkey, Syria, Lebanon, and Israel. The French mandates (1920–46) of Syria and Lebanon were known as the Levant States.

Le Vau, Louis (1612–70) French *baroque architect. His first building, the Hôtel Lambert, Paris (1642), was remarkable for its ingenious room planning. As first architect to the crown from 1654, he completed the Louvre, built the Collège des Quatre Nations (begun 1661), and designed the first extension of *Versailles (1669), which was later obliterated by the work of *Hardouin-Mansart. His most famous building is Vaux-le-Vicomte (begun in 1657), a chateau outside Paris built for Nicolas Fouquet.

level 1. An instrument (also called a spirit level) for indicating whether or not a surface is level. It consists of a sealed glass tube containing spirit (alcohol) and a bubble of gas. The tube is mounted so that the wooden or metal frame supporting it is level when the bubble is in the center of the tube. **2.** An instrument for obtaining a horizontal line of sight. It consists of a telescope with cross hairs on both sights together with a parallel tubular spirit level, mounted on a tripod. Leveling is achieved by means of screw legs on the tripod table.

Levellers An extremist English Puritan sect, active 1647–49. Led by the pamphleteer John *Lilburne, they campaigned for a written constitution, radical extension of the franchise, and abolition of the monarchy and of other social distinctions. Oliver Cromwell's refusal to execute this program led to mutinies (1647, 1649). After suppression of the last of these, the Levellers lost their identity and influence. *See also* Diggers.

Leverkusen 51 02N 6 59E A city in NW Germany, in North Rhine-Westphalia on the Rhine River. It is the site of the large Bayer chemical works. Population (1991 est): 161,000.

Leverrier, Urbain Jean Joseph (1811–77) French astronomer, who predicted the existence of the planet *Neptune (1846) after investigating anomalies in the orbit of Uranus. John *Adams had made similar calculations but the planet was actually first observed by Johann Galle (1812–1910), the German astronomer, in 1846 on information supplied by Leverrier.

Lévesque, René (1922–87) French Canadian politician. An advocate of French separatism, in 1968 he founded the Parti Québecois and in 1976 became Quebec's prime minister. He is the author of *Option Quebec* (1968).

Leviathan An animal mentioned in several passages (Job, Isaiah, Psalms) of the Old Testament and variously interpreted as referring to the whale or crocodile. Leviathan was mythologically associated with evil and the devil.

Levine, James (1943–) US pianist and musical conductor and director. A child prodigy, he performed on the piano from six years old and played with the Cincinnati Symphony Orchestra in 1953. He studied conducting at the Juilliard School. He became principal conductor of the Metropolitan Opera (1972) and also its musical director (1976).

Lévi-Strauss, Claude (1908–) French anthropologist, famous as the founder of structural anthropology. After teaching in America, Lévi-Strauss became professor of ethnology at the University of Paris in 1948 and in 1959 professor of anthropology at the Collège de France. His works include *The Elementary Structures of Kinship* (1949), *Structural Anthropology* (1958), *The Savage Mind* (1962), and *From Honey to Ashes* (1967).

Levites In ancient Israel, the descendants of Levi, the son of Jacob and Leah, who formed one of the 12 *tribes of Israel and became the priestly caste. They were not allocated a specific territory in Palestine but only scattered settlements with grazing rights and they were partly supported by offerings. After the *Babylonian exile, the priesthood was confined to those Levites descended from Aaron.

Leviticus The third book of the Old Testament, attributed to Moses and concerned with religious and ceremonial law. Its purpose is to give instruction in the laws governing sacrifice and purification, in which the priestly caste of *Levites officiate. It also relates the laws governing diet, hygiene, the five annual national feasts, the use of land, and personal chastity.

Lewis, C. Day. *See* Day Lewis, C(ecil).

Lewis, C(live) S(taples) (1898–1963) British scholar and writer. He taught at Oxford University from 1925 to 1954 and at Cambridge University from 1954 to 1963. He wrote science-fiction novels, including *Out of the Silent Planet* (1938), children's books chronicling the land of Narnia, and works on religious and moral themes, notably *The Problem of Pain* (1940), *The Screwtape Letters* (1942) and *Mere Christianity* (1952).

Lewis, John L(lewellyn) (1880–1969) US labor leader; president of United Mine Workers of America (UMW) (1920–60) and *Congress of Industrial Organizations (CIO) (1935–40). He worked his way up in the ranks of the UMW, an affiliate of the American Federation of Labor (AFL). When he organized what became the Congress of Industrial Organizations for industrial workers in 1935, he and his union were expelled from the AFL. As president of the independent CIO he unionized the steel and automobile industries, often using violent methods. He withdrew the UMW from the CIO in 1942. His union practices were the impetus for the passage of the Smith-Connally Anti-Strike Act (1943) and the Taft-Hartley Act (1947), laws that restricted unions.

Lewis, (Harry) Sinclair (1885–1951) US novelist. He established his reputation with *Main Street* (1920), a satire on small-town materialism. His other social satires include *Babbitt* (1922), in which he portrayed the archetypal well-meaning but dehumanized businessman; *Arrowsmith* (1925), about an idealistic doctor; and *Elmer Gantry* (1927) a scathing portrait of an evangelical minister. He was the first US writer to win the Nobel Prize (1930). His later novels, such as *Cass Timberlane* (1945) and *Kingsblood Royal* (1947), were less successful.

Lewis, (Percy) Wyndham (1882–1957) British novelist and painter. After studying art in London and Paris, he helped found *vorticism, the manifestos of which were published in *Blast*, a journal he cofounded with Ezra Pound in 1914. In many polemical works and brilliant satirical novels, which include *The Apes of God* (1930) and the trilogy *The Human Age* (1928–55), he sustained a continual attack on the liberal cultural establishment.

Lewis and Clark expedition (1804–06) A journey of exploration across the American continent by Meriwether Lewis (1774–1809) and William Clark (1770–1838). Starting in the spring of 1804 they ascended the Missouri, reaching the area of Bismarck, N. Dak., by winter. The next year they crossed the Rockies, greatly aided by the Indian girl Sacajawea. Finally they descended the Columbia River to the Pacific, exploring the Yellowstone River on the return journey to Saint Louis, which they reached in September 1806. Promoted by Thomas Jefferson, the expedition established the US claim to the vast lands of the Louisiana Purchase.

lewisite (*or* chlorovinyl dichloroarsine; $ClCH:CHAsCl_2$) A colorless volatile liquid that causes blistering of the skin and is used as a war gas. It can be destroyed by oxidizing agents such as *bleaching powder. Named for the US chemist W. L. Lewis (1878–1943).

Lewis with Harris The largest island of the Outer Hebrides, separated from the coast of NW Scotland by the Minch. Often referred to as separate islands, Lewis in the N is linked with Harris by a narrow isthmus; its most northerly point is the Butt of Lewis. The main occupations are crofting, sheep farming, fishing, and the weaving of the famous Harris tweed. Area: 824 sq mi (2134 sq km). Population (1971): 23,188. Chief town: Stornoway.

lexicography The compilation of dictionaries. Dictionaries can be monolingual (dealing with only one language) or bi- or multilingual (giving equivalents of words in other languages). Both were known in antiquity. Monolingual dictionaries differ in the style and fullness of the definitions, in the audience for which they are intended (e.g. for native speakers or foreign learners), and the principles on which they are complied. Some are on historical principles (listing definitions of a word in historical order) while others take the language as it is at the time of compilation (listing definitions in order of current usage). Some dictionaries are prescriptive in that they set out to tell the user how the language should be used; most modern dictionaries tend to be only descriptive, recording without comment the way words are currently used. Almost all dictionaries contain information about spelling and meaning; many also offer guidance on pronunciation, usage, inflected forms of words, *etymology, etc.

The earliest English dictionary was *A Table Alphabeticall of Hard Words* (1604) by Robert Cawdrey; the most famous are Samuel *Johnson's *Dictionary* (1755), the *Oxford English Dictionary on Historical Principles* (1884–1928; chief editor, Sir James *Murray), and Noah *Webster's *American Dictionary of the English Language* (1828). Both the Oxford and Webster's have several updated and shortened modern versions.

Lexington 38 02N 84 37W A city in Kentucky. A major horse-breeding center, Lexington is the market and distribution center for E Kentucky's farm produce, oil, and coal. The University of Kentucky was established here in 1865. Population (1990): 225,366.

Lexington 37 47N 79 27W A city in W central Virginia, NE in the Shenandoah Valley. Virginia Military Institute (1839) and Washington and Lee University (1749) are here, as are the graves of Robert E. Lee and Stonewall Jackson. Population (1990): 6959.

Lexington and Concord, Battle of (Apr 19, 1775) The first battle in the *American Revolution. British troops led by Lt. Col. Francis Smith intending to destroy American supplies of gunpowder were attacked at Lexington by militiamen under Capt. John Parker alerted by Paul *Revere. Going on to Concord they destroyed the stores but were then attacked and forced to retreat to Boston, suffering many casualties.

Leyden. *See* Leiden.

Leyden jar An early form of *capacitor, consisting of a glass jar coated with tinfoil on part of its inner and outer surfaces. Named for Leiden (*or* Leyden), the town in the Netherlands in which it was invented.

Leyte Gulf, Battle of (Oct 23–26, 1944) The battle in World War II in which a US armada of 250,000 men commanded by General MacArthur defeated almost the entire Japanese navy. It initiated the reconquest of the Philippines and US command of the Pacific.

Lhasa 29 41N 91 10E A city in W China, the capital of Tibet, surrounded by mountains. As the traditional center of *Tibetan Buddhism, it is the site of many temples, monasteries, and of the Potala, the former palace of the Dalai Lama, the priest-ruler. Tibet's trading center, it has many traditional handicrafts and some light industry. *History*: the Tibetan capital since 1642, it was closed to foreigners in the 19th century. Before the Chinese occupation (1951) monks comprised half the population. Since then many Tibetans have fled, including the Dalai Lama following the 1959 uprising, while much Chinese immigration has taken place. Population (1990): 106,885.

Liaodong Peninsula (*or* Liaotung Peninsula) A mountainous peninsula in NE China, in Liaoning province. After rivalry with Russia (1895–1905; *see* Sino-Japanese War, Russo-Japanese War) Japan occupied its strategic S harbors (1905–45).

Liaoning A province in NE China, on the Yellow Sea in S Manchuria. The Japanese controlled it (1905–45) and developed its industry. Rich in coal and iron, it is an important industrial area. Area: 58,500 sq mi (150,000 sq km). Population (1990): 39,459,657. Capital: Shenyang.

Libau. *See* Liepaja.

Libby, Willard Frank (1908–80) US chemist, who was awarded the Nobel Prize (1960) for his discovery of *radiocarbon dating. He also perfected a similar technique in which water is dated from its tritium content.

libel. *See* defamation.

Liberal Party (Australia) A conservative political party, formed in 1944 from the *United Australia party, which had performed disastrously in the 1943 election. A Liberal-Country party (*see* National Country party) coalition won the election of 1949 and under the leadership successively of Robert *Menzies, Harold *Holt, John *Gorton, and William *McMahon held office until 1972. Under Malcolm *Fraser the Liberals were again in power (1975–83).

Liberal Party (UK) A political party that grew out of the *Whig party. The heyday of the party was from the mid-19th century in World War I, under the prime ministers *Gladstone, *Campbell-Bannerman, *Asquith, and *Lloyd George. Conflict between Asquith and Lloyd George led to a split in the party after World War I, and in 1922 the Labour party replaced the Liberals as the official opposition. The Liberals enjoyed a small revival in the 1960s and 1970s.

Liberal Republican Party US political party. Founded in 1872 for the purpose of opposing Republican Pres. Ulysses S. Grant's policies, it nominated Horace *Greeley for president. Its platform for reform of the civil service, local and federal government, and tariffs allied the party with the Democrats. When Grant won reelection, the party ceased to exist.

Liberec (German name: Reichenberg) 50 48N 15 05E A city in Czechoslovakia, in Bohemia on the Neisse River. In 1938 it was a center of the Sudeten-German movement. Population (1987 est): 103,000.

Liberia, Republic of A country in West Africa, on the Atlantic Ocean. Coastal plains rise to higher ground inland and to mountains in the N; much of the land is covered with tropical rain forests. Most of the population belongs to indigenous tribes, including the Kpelle, Bassa, and Kru, with a minority who are descended from American slaves. *Economy*: agriculture is extensive, the main food crops being rice and cassava. There have been considerable efforts to increase rice production, including the growing of swamp as well as hill rice and there has been large-scale development in the sugar industry with aid from China. The main cash crop is rubber, some of it grown under concession to US companies. Foreign investment in other areas includes the exploitation of Liberia's rich mineral resources, which form the basis of the country's economy, especially high-grade iron ore and diamonds. These, together with rubber and timber, are the main exports. Ships are easily registered in Liberia and, with many foreign vessels, its merchant fleet is the largest in the world. *History*: it was founded in 1822 by the American Colonization Society as a settlement for freed American slaves. In 1847 it became the Free and Independent Republic of Liberia with a constitution based on that of the US. It has had considerable US aid, and from the 1920s the Firestone Company, developing rubber resources, played an important part in the economy, as have many other foreign companies. Liberia also has close economic ties with Sierra Leone. In 1980 the president, Dr. William R. Tolbert, Jr. (1913–80), was assassinated in a military coup led by M. S. Samuel Doe. The constitution was suspended; a new one was not approved until 1984. Doe remained president after a 1985 civilian election. Civil war erupted in the late 1980s. In 1990 a West African coalition force was sent to Liberia in an attempt to end the fighting in which thousands had been killed.

Amid charges of corruption and oppression, Doe was executed by rebels in 1990. In 1991, Amos Sawyer was appointed to lead a coalition caretaker government, but rebels under Charles Taylor continued their opposition, threatening to take the capital in 1992. Official language: English. Official currency: Liberian dollar of 100 cents. Area: 43,000 sq mi (111,400 sq km). Population (1990 est): 2,644,000. Capital and main port: Monrovia.

Liberty Party (1840–48) US antislavery political party. It was established by northeastern abolitionists who disagreed with William Lloyd *Garrison over the political approach to abolition. It eventually merged (1848) with the *Free Soil Party.

libido The sexual drive. In *psychoanalysis the libido (like the death instinct) is a fundamental source of energy for all mental life, and changes in the normal course of psychosexual development are responsible for many distortions of the adult personality.

Libra (Latin: Scales) A constellation in the S sky, lying on the *zodiac between Scorpius and Virgo. The brightest star is of 2nd magnitude.

library A collection of books, recordings, photographic materials, etc., organized for private or public consultation or borrowing. In ancient Mesopotamia libraries were offshoots of royal archives (*see* Nineveh). Aristotle's teaching library at his *Lyceum inspired the Ptolemaic rulers of Egypt to found a library at Alexandria that became the cultural center of Hellenism. Sizable private libraries were assembled by Roman scholars, such as *Cicero, and Roman and Byzantine emperors founded large public libraries. With the growth of Christian literature it became customary to attach libraries to churches. Monastic libraries grew from the requirement of daily study of religious treatises, especially among the *Benedictines. Late medieval and Renaissance nonecclesiastical collections form the basis of many of today's great libraries, such as the *Bodleian, the Vatican (present building opened in 1571), the *Bibliothèque Nationale, the British Library, and the US *Library of Congress. In response to increasing literacy in the 19th century most European countries developed a municipal library network.

The explosion in the numbers both of items held by libraries and of library users has placed increasing demands on **library science**, a discipline that is concerned chiefly with the acquisition, classification, and cataloguing of items in a library. The acquisition of materials is dictated by a library's selection policy, which is influenced by its budget, storage space, and readers' requirements. The systems of classification of materials into subject fields that are most widely used today are the *Universal Decimal Classification, based on the *Dewey Decimal Classification, and the Library of Congress system. Catalogs, or lists, of holdings generally consist of an alphabetized author catalog and a subject catalog. The practice of printing catalogs, with regularly issued supplements, has been complemented since the late 19th century by card catalogs, which facilitate the incorporation of new items. More recent developments include the use of *microcopy systems for recording holdings and of automatic *data processing, which aid the centralization on a regional, national, or international scale of library information. Centralization demands standardization and all publications now bear an International Standard Book Number (ISBN) or an International Standard Serial Number (ISSN), by which an item may be quickly identified.

Formal training for libraries was pioneered by the American Library Association (founded 1876). The International Library Committee was set up in 1927 to try to achieve internationally accepted conventions in such matters as the transliteration of Cyrillic characters into the Roman alphabet, and UNESCO has a division concerned with libraries.

Library of Congress The national library of the US, founded in 1800. First housed in the Capitol, it was moved to its present site in Washington in 1897. It contains over 60 million items, and its system of classification is widely used in academic libraries.

Library of Congress Classification System A numerical system for classifying books by subject, initiated by the US Library of Congress in 1904. Within the system there are 41 subjects, which are, in turn, subdivided.

libretto (Italian: little book) The text of an opera or operetta. The most notable early librettists were the Italians Apostolo Zeno (1668–1750) and Pietro Metastasio (1698–1782), whose elevated style eventually provoked a reaction in favor of greater realism. Dramatists whose plays have been used as libretti include von *Hofmannsthal, *Maeterlinck, and Óscar *Wilde. *Wagner and *Berlioz wrote their own libretti. Notable partnerships between librettists and composers include Calzabigi (1714–95) and Gluck, da Ponte (1749–1838) and Mozart, Boito and Verdi, and Gilbert and Sullivan.

Libreville 0 25N 9 25E The capital of Gabon, a port in the NW on the Gabon Estuary. It was founded by the French in the 19th century, when freed slaves were sent there. The National University was established in 1970. Population (1987 est): 352,000.

Libya (official name: Popular Socialist Libyan Arab Jamahiriya) A country in N Africa, on the Mediterranean Sea. It consists chiefly of desert, with a narrow coastal plain, rising to the Tibesti Mountains along its southern border and is divided into the three main areas (provinces until 1963) of Cyrenaica, Tripolitania, and Fezzan. The population is mainly of Berber and Arabic origin. *Economy*: between 1955 and 1970 considerable prospecting for oil took place during which time major deposits were discovered, notably at Zelten (1959). Libya is now one of the world's major oil producers and oil constitutes about 95% of exports in value; liquefied natural gas is also exported. Subsistence agriculture is important, livestock farming of sheep, goats, and cattle being the main agricultural occupation, nomadic in the S. The aridity of the land restricts crop production to the narrow coastal areas and scattered oases; barley, wheat, and olives are grown here and esparto grass in semidesert areas. Recently programs have been implemented to improve agriculture, such as in the Fezzan. Manufacturing industry is based largely on traditional crafts. *History*: the area was important within the Roman Empire. During the 16th century it came under Turkish domination and in 1912 was annexed by Italy. It was the scene of heavy fighting in World War II; the French occupied Fezzan and the British occupied Cyrenaica and Tripolitania. In 1951 the United Kingdom of Libya was formed from the federation of these three areas and the Emir of Cyrenaica, Mohammed Idris Al-Senussi (1889–1983), became its first king. He was deposed in a military coup led by Col. Muammar al-*Gadafi in 1969 and Libya was proclaimed a republic. The Revolutionary Command Council was established to rule the country. In 1973 Gadafi introduced a cultural revolution, an attempt to govern the country according to Islamic principles. Since 1969 Libya has taken an active part in Arab affairs being firmly aligned against Israel. Libya's association with terrorism has led to extreme international criticism and in 1986 to U.S. bombing of targets in Libya. In 1991, Libya, opposed to the invasion of Kuwait by Iraq and against retaliation by UN coalition forces, sought for a way to settle matters diplomatically. When war did break out in the Persian Gulf, Gadafi, per an agreement with Egypt, supported the war. Relations with the US worsened in 1992 when Libya refused to extradite two suspects in the 1988 Lockerbie, Scotland, bombing of Pan American Flight 103. In 1992 the UN passed economic sanctions against Libya for this refusal and tightened the sanctions in 1993. Official language: Arabic; English and Italian are also spoken. Official currency: Libyan dinar of 1000 millemes. Area: 679,216 sq mi (1,759,540 sq km). Population (1990 est): 4,280,000. Capital: Tripoli.

lichee. *See* litchi.

lichens A large group of plants (*Lichenes*; about 15,000 species) consisting of two components, an alga and a fungus, in a mutually beneficial association. Millions of algal cells (the phycobiont) are interwoven with fungal filaments (the mycobiont) to form the lichen body (a thallus), which may be crusty, scaly, leafy, or stalked and shrublike in appearance. Lichens occur in almost all areas of the world, mainly on tree trunks, rocks, and soil, and can survive in extremely harsh conditions. They normally reproduce asexually by fragmentation, *budding, or by producing special structures (soredia), consisting of a few algal cells enmeshed with fungal threads. Lichens are an important source of food for browsing animals of tundra regions (*see* reindeer moss) and they are used by man for food, dyes, medicine, in perfume, and as pollution indicators. *See also* crottle; oak moss; orchil; rock tripe.

Lichtenstein, Roy (1923–   ) A leading US painter of *pop art. He taught at Ohio and New York Universities and in 1962 had an important one-man show of comic-strip paintings, which pioneered the use of mass-media techniques in the context of noncommercial art. His works include *Whaam* (1963).

licorice A perennial herb, *Glycyrrhiza glabra*, native to S Europe but cultivated throughout warm temperate regions. It bears clusters of blue flowers and long flat pods and its sweet roots, up to 3 ft (1 m) long, are a source of flavoring for confectionery, tobacco, and medicines. The thickened juice of the roots is made into licorice paste (*or* black sugar). Family: *Leguminosae*.

Lidice 50 03N 14 08E A small mining village in W Czech Republic. On June 10, 1942, it was destroyed by the Nazis in revenge for the assassination of Reinhard Heydrich, their local administrative head. The 400 or so inhabitants were either shot or deported to concentration camps. The site is now a memorial garden.

Lie, Trygve (Halvdan) (1896–1968) Norwegian Labor politician and international civil servant; the first secretary general of the UN (1946–52). At the UN he dealt with the first Arab-Israeli War and UN armed aid to South Korea in the *Korean War. Soviet opposition to his Korean policies resulted in his resignation.

Liebig, Justus, Baron von (1803–73) German chemist; one of the earliest investigators of organic compounds. His work on fulminates (1920) was followed by the development of a technique for measuring the proportion of carbon and hydrogen in a compound by burning it and determining the amount of carbon dioxide and water released (1831). His later work was concerned with biochemistry and agricultural chemistry. His name is also connected with the Liebig condenser, a much used piece of laboratory equipment.

Liebknecht, Wilhelm (1826–1900) German socialist. He participated in the *Revolution of 1848 and was forced to flee Germany, living in Britain, where he worked with Karl Marx. Returning to Germany in 1862, he was expelled from Prussia in 1865 for his socialist activities but in 1867 became a member of the North German Reichstag. His opposition to the Franco-Prussian War (1870–71) brought imprisonment but he subsequently became a leader of what became (1891) the Social Democratic Party. His son **Karl Liebknecht** (1871–1919) was among the few socialists who refused to support the war effort in 1914. In 1915 he helped to found the revolutionary *Spartacus League, which he led with Rosa *Luxemburg. They were both murdered following the unsuccessful communist revolt of 1919.

Liechtenstein, Principality of A small country in central Europe, between Switzerland and Austria. Mountains rise from the Rhine Valley to heights of over

8000 ft (2500 m). *Economy*: although there is still a considerable amount of farming, the balance of the economy has shifted since World War II to light industry, including textiles, ceramics, tools, instruments, and food processing. Tourism and the sale of postage stamps are also important sources of revenue. *History*: the principality was formed from the union of the countries of Vaduz and Schellenberg in 1719 and was part of the Holy Roman Empire until 1806. It formed a customs union with Switzerland in 1923. Until 1984 women were banned from voting in national elections. Head of state: Prince Hans Adam II. Head of government: Hans Brunhart. Official language: German. Official religion: Roman Catholic. Official currency: Swiss franc of 100 centimes (*or* Rappen). Area: 62 sq mi (160 sq km). Population (1990 est): 30,000. Capital: Vaduz.

lie detector. *See* polygraph.

Liège (Flemish name: Luik) 50 38N 5 35E A city in E Belgium, on the Meuse River. It has many old churches, including St Martin's (692 AD). Its university was founded in 1817. The center of a coal mining area, its industries include the manufacture of armaments, iron, textiles, and paper. Population (1988 est): 200,500.

Liegnitz. *See* Legnica.

Liepaja (German name: Libau) 56 30N 21 00E A port in Latvia on the Baltic Sea. It was founded by the Teutonic Knights (1263), passing to Russia in 1795. The independent Latvian Government met here in 1918. A naval base, it has shipbuilding and metallurgy industries. Population (1991 est):115,000.

Lif and Lifthrasir In Norse mythology, a man and woman destined to sleep during the destruction of the world (*see* Ragnarök), awaking afterward to found a new race.

Lifar, Serge (1905–86) Russian ballet dancer and choreographer. He joined Diaghilev's Ballets Russes in 1923 and from 1932 to 1958 was ballet master at the Paris Opéra Ballet, which he revitalized with his experimental choreography. His ballets include *Prométhée* (1929), *Icare* (1935), and *Phèdre* (1950).

life The property that enables a living organism to assimilate nonliving materials from its environment and use them to increase its size and complexity (the process of growth), to repair its existing tissues, and to produce new independent organisms that also possess the properties of life (the process of reproduction). *See also* animal; plant.

Life on earth is thought to have originated between 4500 and 3000 million years ago. The atmosphere then consisted chiefly of methane, hydrogen, ammonia, and water vapor, from which simple organic molecules (such as amino acids, proteins, and fatty acids) were formed as a result of energy supplied by solar radiation, lightning, and volcanic activity. The first "cells" may have arisen spontaneously as simple envelopes of protein and fat molecules. However, the crucial steps toward life would probably have been the inclusion in such a cell of both the enzyme molecules necessary to perform primitive fermentations and the nucleic acid molecules, such as RNA and DNA, capable of directing the metabolic processes of the cell and of self-replication, i.e. passing on this information to succeeding generations. These early cells are thought to have arisen in the sea, deriving their energy from the fermentation of simple organic molecules. In the course of time increasingly efficient biochemical pathways evolved, including the process of trapping light energy in cellular pigments, enabling the first simple green plants to develop the process of photosynthesis. This led to the gradual build-up of oxygen in the atmosphere, which started about 2000 million years ago; by about 400 million years ago the *ozone layer in the upper atmosphere was sufficiently dense to shield the land from harmful ultraviolet radiation, enabling plants and animals to survive. With increasing oxygen levels, aerobic respiration—the most efficient method of energy utilization—was adopted by most living organisms.

The factors involved in the origination of life on earth have prompted a search for similar conditions on other planets and in other solar systems, but so far no evidence of life elsewhere in the universe has been discovered. *See* astrobiology.

lifeboat A boat carried aboard a ship, used for accommodating passengers and crew if the ship has to be abandoned.

life cycle The progressive series of stages through which a species of organism passes from its *fertilization or production by asexual means to the same stage in the next generation. The simplest life cycles occur by asexual *reproduction, producing offspring similar to the parent. Life cycles involving sexual reproduction are much more complex and the young do not necessarily resemble the adults: marine crustaceans, for example, pass through several different larval stages before becoming adult. In many plants and animals there is a succession of individuals showing an alternation of sexual and asexual reproduction before completing the cycle (*see* alternation of generations).

Liffey River A river in the E Republic of Ireland, rising in the Wicklow Mountains and flowing mainly W and NE through Dublin to Dublin Bay. Length: 50 mi (80 km).

ligament A strong fibrous tissue that joins one bone to another at a *joint. Ligaments are flexible but inelastic; they increase the stability of the joint and limit its movements to certain directions. Unusual stresses on a joint often damage ("pull") a ligament, as occurs in a "twisted" ankle.

ligature Any material, such as silk, gut, cotton, or wire, used to tie a blood vessel (to stop bleeding) or the base of a tumor (to constrict it). Ligatures are widely used in surgery and are available in various thicknesses.

liger. *See* tigon.

Ligeti, György (1923–) Hungarian composer. He worked in the West German Radio's studio for electronic music in Cologne (1957–58) and settled in Vienna. His compositions are largely experimental, often involving indeterminacy of pitch and rhythm, and include *Volumina* (1961–62) for organ, a Requiem (1963–65), *Continuum* (1968) for harpsichord, and *Melodien* (1971) for orchestra.

light The form of *electromagnetic radiation to which the eye is sensitive. It forms the part of the electromagnetic spectrum from 740 nanometers (red light) to 400 nanometers (blue light), white light consisting of a mixture of all the colors of the visible spectrum. The nature of light has been in dispute from earliest times, *Newton supporting a corpuscular theory in which a luminous body was believed to emit particles of light. This theory adequately explained reflection and geometric optics but failed to explain *interference and *polarized light. The wave theory, supported in the 19th century by *Fresnel and *Foucault, adequately explains these phenomena and achieved a mathematical basis when *Maxwell showed that light is a form of electromagnetic radiation. The wave theory, however, does not explain the *photoelectric effect and *Einstein reverted to a form of the corpuscular theory in using the *quantum theory to postulate that in some cases light is best regarded as consisting of energy quanta called photons. The present view, expressing *Bohr's concept of complementarity, is that both electromagnetic theory and quantum theory are needed to explain this phenomenon. Light travels at a velocity of $2.997,925 \times 10^8$ m per second in free space, this being, according to the special *relativity, the highest attainable velocity in the universe.

light-emitting diode. *See* semiconductor diode.

lighthouse A tall structure, built on a coastal promontory or cape or on an island at sea, equipped with a powerful beacon, visible at some distance, to mark an obstruction or other hazard. Modern lighthouses are also equipped with radio beacons. Both light and radio signals are emitted in a unique pattern to enable vessels to identify the lighthouse producing them.

lightning An electrical discharge in the atmosphere caused by the build-up of electrical charges in a cloud by such methods as friction between the particles in the cloud. The potential difference causing the discharge may be as high as one thousand million volts. The electricity then discharges itself in a lightning flash, which may be between the cloud and the ground or, much more commonly, between two clouds or parts of a cloud. Thunder is the noise made by the discharge or its reverberations. *See also* ball lightning; thunderstorm.

lightning conductor A grounded conducting rod placed at the top of buildings, etc., to protect them from damage by lightning. It acts by providing a low-resistance path to earth for the lightning current.

lightship A vessel, anchored at sea, used as a lighthouse. In wide use until the mid-20th century, most lightships have now been replaced by fixed structures or, because of advances in sophisticated navigation devices, have been eliminated entirely.

light-year A unit of distance, used in astronomy, equal to the distance traveled by light in one year. One light-year = 5.88×10^{12} mi (9.46×10^{15} m).

lignin A complex chemical deposited in plant cell walls to add extra strength and support. It is the main constituent of *wood cells, allowing the trunk to support the heavy crown of leaves and branches.

lignum vitae Wood from trees of the genus *Guaiacum*, especially *G. officinale*, a tropical evergreen of the New World. Lignum vitae is hard, dense, greenish-brown, and rich in fat (making it waterproof). It is used for shafts, pulleys, and bowling balls. Lignum vitae was formerly thought to have medicinal properties: its name (from the Latin) means "wood of life." Family: *Zygophyllaceae*.

Liguria A region in NW Italy. It consists of a narrow strip of land between the Apennines and Maritime Alps in the N and the Gulf of Genoa in the S. It is an important industrial region, concentrating on engineering, shipbuilding, metals, petroleum products, and chemicals. Tourism is a major source of revenue, the region more or less corresponding to the Italian Riviera. Agricultural products include vegetables, olives, and flowers. Area: 2091 sq mi (5415 sq km). Population (1991): 1,701,788. Capital: Genoa.

Ligurian Sea A section of the NW Mediterranean Sea, between Italy (N of Elba) and Corsica.

Li Hong Zhang (or Li Hung-chang; 1823–1901) Chinese soldier and statesman of the *Qing dynasty. His armies helped suppress the *Taiping Rebellion in 1864 and, as the trusted adviser of the empress *Zi Xi, he encouraged commerce and industry, attempting to introduce modernizing projects, and conducted China's foreign affairs. He amassed a huge personal fortune.

Likasi (name until 1966: Jadotville) 10 58S 26 47E A city in SE Zaire. Founded in 1917, near the site of old copper workings, it is a major mineral-processing center refining copper and cobalt. Other industries include chemicals and brewing. Population (1991 est): 280,000.

lilac A deciduous bush or small tree of the genus *Syringa* (30 species), especially *S. vulgaris*, native to temperate Eurasia and often grown as a garden ornamental. It has heart-shaped leaves arranged in opposite pairs and dense terminal clusters of white, purple, or pink tubular fragrant flowers with four flaring lobes. The fruit is a leathery capsule. Family: *Oleaceae*.

Lilburne, John (c. 1614–57) English pamphleteer; leader of the radical Puritan sect called the *Levellers. He joined the parliamentarians in the Civil War but resigned from the army in 1645 to organize the Levellers. After 1645 he was frequently in prison and was twice tried and acquitted for treason.

Liliaceae A family of monocotyledonous plants (about 250 species) mostly herbaceous and native to temperate and subtropical regions. They usually grow from bulbs or rhizomes to produce six-lobed flowers and three-chambered capsular fruits. The family includes many popular garden plants, including the lilies, tulip, hyacinth, and lily-of-the-valley. A few are economically important, for example *Asparagus*. Some authorities enlarge this family to include related plants, such as the onion, leek, etc., (*see* Allium), *Agave*, and *Yucca*.

Lilienthal, Otto (1848–96) German aeronautical engineer, who pioneered the construction of gliders. A student of bird flight, Lilienthal demonstrated the superiority of a curved wing over a flat wing. He made some 2000 flights before being killed in a crash.

Lilith In Jewish folklore, a female demon, traditionally the first wife of Adam, who refused to recognize his authority over her. An amulet bearing the names of the three angels who tried to persuade her to return to Adam was worn as protection against her evil powers.

Liliuokalani (1838–1917) The only queen and last sovereign of Hawaii (1891–95). Hawaiian resistance to US attempts to annex the islands led to an insurrection after which she abdicated. She composed the song "Aloha Oe," as a farewell gift to her people.

Lille 50 39N 3 05E A city in N France, the capital of the Nord department on the Deûle River. The center of a large industrial and commercial complex, its industries include textiles, machinery, chemicals, distilling, and brewing. Notable buildings include the citadel (built by Vauban) and the university (1887). *History*: following a prosperous period under the Dukes of Burgundy (14th century), Lille later passed to Austria and then Spain before returning to France in 1668, and was badly damaged in both World Wars. General de Gaulle was born there. Population (1982): 174,000.

Lillehammer 61 08N 10 30E A town in S Norway 85 mi (135 km) N of Oslo, center of an agricultural region. It was the site of the 1994 Winter Olympics.

Lillie, Beatrice (Constance Sylvia Munston, Lady Peel; 1898–1989) British actress, born in Canada. The sophisticated comedy of her performances in revues and cabaret was successful in both London and New York. She also made several films, notably *Exit Smiling* (1926) and *On Approval* (1943).

Lilongwe 13 58S 33 49E The capital of Malawi. It replaced Zomba as the capital in 1975. Tobacco production is important. Population (1986): 292,000.

lily A perennial herbaceous plant of the genus *Lilium* (80–100 species), native to N temperate regions and widely grown for ornament. Lilies grow from bulbs to produce leafy stems with terminal clusters of showy flowers, usually with backward-curving petals. Some popular species are the tiger lily (*L. tigrinum*), from China and Japan, 24–48 in (60–120 cm) high with purple-spotted golden flowers; the Japanese golden ray lily (*L. auratum*), 35–71 in (90–180 cm) high, whose white flowers are marked with yellow and crimson; the Eurasian Madonna lily (*L. candida*), 24–48 in (60–120 cm) high with pure-white flowers;

and the turk's cap or martagon lily (*L. martagon*), also from Eurasia, 35–60 in (90–150 cm) high, the purplish-pink flowers of which are marked with darker spots. There are numerous varieties and hybrids of these and other species. Family: *Lilaceae*.

The name is also applied to numerous other unrelated plants, such as the *arum lily, *day lily, and *leopard lily.

lily-of-the-valley A fragrant perennial herbaceous plant, *Convallaria majalis*, native to Eurasia and E North America and a popular garden plant. Growing from creeping underground stems (rhizomes), it has a stem, 5–8 in (13–20 cm) long, bearing a cluster of white nodding bell-shaped flowers. Family: *Liliaceae*.

Lima 12 06S 77 03W The capital of Peru, situated in the E of the country near its Pacific port of Callao. Founded by Pizarro in 1535, it became the main base of Spanish power in Peru. Notable buildings include the 16th-century cathedral and the National University of San Marcos (1551). Lima has expanded rapidly in recent years and now has considerable industry; the main manufactures include motor vehicles, textiles, paper, paint, and food products. Approximately one-third of the population lives in the shanty-town settlements that surround the city. Population (1990 est): 6,115,000.

Lima bean A herb, *Phaseolus lunatus*, also called butter bean or Madagascar bean, native to South America but widely cultivated in the tropics and subtropics as a source of protein. It is easily stored when dry. Family: *Leguminosae*.

Limassol (modern Greek name: Lemesós; Turkish name: Limasol) 34 40N 33 03E A city in Cyprus, on the S coast. It is the island's second largest city and a major port, exporting notably wine and fruit. Population (1980 est): 105,200.

limbo In medieval Christian theology, the state of existence of souls that merit neither heavenly bliss nor the torments of hell after death. The two categories of souls destined for limbo were unbaptized babies and the patriarchs and prophets of the Old Testament.

Limburg 1. A former duchy in W Europe, divided in 1839 between Belgium and the Netherlands. 2. (French name: Limbourg) A province in NE Belgium, bordering on the Netherlands. In the N, the Kempen heath area has rich coalfields and industries include chemicals and glass. The S is chiefly agricultural (especially dairy farming). Area: 935 sq mi (2422 sq km). Population (1991): 999,646. Capital: Hasselt. 3. A province in the SE Netherlands. Its traditional coal mining industry has declined in recent years. Agriculture is varied producing cereals, fruit, vegetables, and sugar beet; cattle, pigs, and poultry are raised. Area: 852 sq mi (2208 sq km). Population (1990 est): 1,104,000. Capital: Maastricht.

Limburg, de (*or* de Limbourg) A family (active c. 1400–c. 1416) of manuscript illuminators comprising three brothers, Pol, Herman, and Jehanequin, born in Nijmegen (Netherlands), the sons of a sculptor. They worked for the Duke of Burgundy (1402–04) and later for the Duke of Berry, for whom they illuminated the *Très Riches Heures* (Chantilly, France), a fine example of the *international gothic style. They influenced the development of Flemish landscape painting.

lime (botany) 1. A large deciduous tree of the genus *Tilia* (about 30 species), also called linden. Growing to a height of 98 ft (30 m), it has toothed heart-shaped leaves and fragrant pale-yellow flowers that hang in small clusters on a long winged stalk. The small round fruits remain attached to the papery wing when shed. Family: *Tiliaceae*. 2. A tree, *Citrus aurantifolia*, growing to a height of about 13 ft (4 m) and cultivated in the tropics for its fruit. Lime fruits are pear-shaped, 2 in (4 cm) in diameter, with a thick greenish-yellow skin and acid-tasting pulp; the juice is used to flavor food and drinks.

lime (chemistry) Calcium oxide (*or* quicklime; CaO), calcium hydroxide (*or* slaked lime; Ca(OH)$_2$), or, loosely, calcium salts in general. Ca(OH)$_2$ is prepared by reacting CaO with water and is used in *cement. CaO is used in making paper, as a *flux in *steel manufacture, and in softening water.

limerick A short form of comic and usually bawdy verse having five lines of three or two feet and usually rhyming aabba, as in:

There was a young lady of Lynn

Who was so uncommonly thin

 That when she essayed

 To drink lemonade,

She slipped through the straw and fell in.

The form, the origin of which is uncertain, was popularized by Edward *Lear in the 19th century and practiced by several notable poets, but the best-known limericks are by anonymous authors. The name is said to have originated in the chorus of an Irish soldiers' song, "Will you come up to Limerick?"

Limerick (Irish name: Luimneach) 52 40N 8 38W A port in the Republic of Ireland, the county town of Co Limerick on the Shannon estuary. It was besieged by William III (1691). Notable buildings include two cathedrals. Its industries include flour milling, tanning, and brewing. Population (1991): 52,040.

Limerick (Irish name: Luimneach) A county in the SW Republic of Ireland, in Munster bordering on the River Shannon estuary. It consists chiefly of lowlands rising to hills in the S. Lying mainly in the fertile Golden Vale, it is important for dairy farming. Area: 1037 sq mi (2686 sq km). Population (1991): 161,856. County town: Limerick.

limestone A common sedimentary rock consisting largely of carbonates, especially calcium carbonate (calcite) or dolomite. Most limestones were deposited in the sea in warm clear water, but some limestones were formed in fresh water. Organic limestones, including *chalk, consist of fossil skeletal material. Precipitated limestones include evaporites and *oolites (spherically grained calcite). Clastic limestones consist of fragments of pre-existing limestones. Marble is metamorphosed limestone. Limestone is used as a building stone, in the manufacture of cement and glass, for agricultural lime, for roadbeds, and as a flux in smelting.

Limoges 45 50N 1 15E A city in W France, the capital of the Haute-Vienne department on the Vienne River. The center of the French porcelain industry, it has Roman remains, a cathedral (13th–16th centuries), and a university (1808). It is the birthplace of Pierre Auguste Renoir. Population (1975): 147,422.

limonite A naturally occurring mixture of hydrated iron oxides and iron hydroxides, both amorphous and cryptocrystalline, derived from the weathering of minerals containing iron. It ranges in color from yellow to brown to black and occurs in bog iron ore, in gossan, and in *laterite.

Limosin, Léonard (*or* Limousin; c. 1505–c. 1577) French artist, born in Limoges. As court painter to Francis I and later Henry II he was popular chiefly for his enamel portraits, although he also painted plates, vases, etc., and worked in oils.

Limousin A planning region and former province in central France, on the W Massif Central. It was in the possession of the English from 1152 until 1369. Area: 6536 sq mi (16,932 sq km). Population (1991 est): 721,700.

limpet A marine *gastropod mollusk with a flattened shell and powerful muscular foot for clinging to rocks and other surfaces. The true limpets (superfamily *Patellacea*; about 400 species) are oval-shaped and up to 4 in (10 cm) long whereas the keyhole limpets (superfamily *Fissurellacea*; several hundred species) have an opening in the shell for expelling wastes and tend to be smaller.

Limpopo River A river in SE Africa. Rising as the Crocodile River in the Witwatersrand, South Africa, it flows generally NE through Mozambique, to the Indian Ocean, forming part of the border between the Transvaal and Botswana. Length: 1100 mi (1770 km).

Lin Biao (*or* Lin Piao; 1908–71) Chinese communist soldier and statesman. Lin received military training under *Chiang Kai-shek at the Whampoa Military Academy. He became a Guomindang (Nationalist People's party) colonel but led his regiment to join the communist uprising in Nanchang. He became commander of the First Red Army Corps and played a major part in the communist victory against the Guomindang (1949). In 1959 he became defense minister and in 1969, vice chairman of the Chinese Communist party. Lin seemed destined to become Mao Tse-tung's successor but he was the fatal victim of a mysterious airplane crash in Outer Mongolia in 1971, when he may have been attempting to flee China after making an unsuccessful bid for power.

Lincoln 53 14N 0 33W A city in E central England, on the River Witham. The British settlement became Lindum Colonia under the Romans. The castle was begun in 1068 and the cathedral in 1075. The principal manufactures are machinery, radios, metal goods, vehicle components, and cattle feed. Population (1981): 76,660.

Lincoln 40 49N 96 41W The capital city of Nebraska. It is the industrial and commercial center of a region producing grain and livestock. The University of Nebraska was established there in 1869. Population (1990): 191,972.

Lincoln, Abraham (1809–65) US statesman; 16th President of the United States (1861–65). A self-educated man who was raised in rural Indiana, Lincoln settled in Illinois, where he became a storekeeper and served in the local militia during the *Black Hawk War (1832). After deciding on a career as a lawyer, he served as the postmaster for New Salem, Ill., (1833–36) while pursuing his legal studies. Admitted to the Illinois bar in 1836, Lincoln moved to Springfield, where he established a successful legal practice. Lincoln was active in Illinois politics and served as a Whig representative in the state legislature (1834–42) and later as a member of the US House of Representatives for a single term (1847–49). Holding longstanding convictions against slavery, he opposed its extension to the new western states as proposed in the *Kansas-Nebraska Act of 1854, sponsored by Illinois Sen. Stephen A. *Douglas. In 1856, Lincoln joined the newly formed *Republican Party and ran against Douglas in the senatorial campaign of 1858. Although Douglas won reelection, Lincoln gained a national reputation through his eloquent opposition to slavery in the *Lincoln-Douglas Debates.

In 1860, Lincoln received the Republican presidential nomination, and his election to that office precipitated the secession of the southern states from the Union and the outbreak of the *Civil War. Believing that the Union was indivisible, he supervised the military operations intended to force the dissolution of the *Confederate States of America. In 1863, Lincoln issued the *Emancipation Proclamation, liberating the slaves in the southern states, and later in the same year, he gave his famous *Gettysburg Address, reaffirming the principles of equality established by America's founding fathers. Winning reelection in 1864, he appointed Gen. Ulysses S. *Grant commander-in-chief of the Union forces and supported the 13th Amendment to the US Constitution, ratified in 1865, which prohibited slavery in the US. He also advocated a magnanimous *Reconstruction program for the readmission of the Confederate states into the Union after the war, but did not live to see that program carried out. He was assassinated by John Wilkes *Booth in Washington, a few days after the surrender of the South. His wife **Mary Todd Lincoln** (1818–82), whom he married in 1842, bore him four sons, only one of whom, Robert Todd (1843–1926) lived beyond 18 years of age. Her unstableness, due to her husband's assassination and the death of three sons, led to a court declaration of insanity in 1875, a decision that was overturned in 1876.

ABRAHAM LINCOLN *Civil War President (1861–65) who was known as "The Great Emancipator" and who delivered the Gettysburg Address.*

Lincoln-Douglas Debates (1858) A series of debates on the territorial slavery question during the 1858 Illinois campaign for the US Senate. Abraham *Lincoln and incumbent Sen. Stephen A. *Douglas debated at Ottawa, Freeport, Jonesboro, Charleston, Galesburg, Quincy, and Alton, Ill. Lincoln advocated complete abolition of slavery; Douglas furthered his "popular sovereignty" doctrine, that of the right of people to decide whether or not to allow slavery. Lincoln won the popular vote, but lost the election to Douglas due to a Democratic majority in the legislature.

Lincolnshire A county in E England, bordering on the North Sea. It is generally low lying, with the Lincolnshire Edge (a limestone escarpment) in the W and the Lincolnshire Wolds in the E. It is mainly agricultural producing arable crops and livestock; horticulture is also important. Industry is associated with agriculture. Area: 2272 sq mi (5885 sq km). Population (1981): 547,560. Administrative center: Lincoln.

Lincoln's Inn. *See* Inns of Court.

Lind, Jenny (1820–87) Swedish soprano, known as "the Swedish nightingale." Her brilliant career in opera and on the concert platform took her all over Europe. P. T. Barnum arranged her very successful tour of the US (1850–52).

Lindbergh, Charles A(ugustus) (1902–74) US aviator who made the first solo nonstop flight across the Atlantic Ocean, from New York to Paris (1927), in the monoplane *Spirit of St Louis*. The success of the flight brought him worldwide fame. After the kidnapping and murder of his two-year-old son in 1932 he and his wife moved to Europe to escape the ensuing publicity. He advocated US neutrality at the start of World War II but subsequently contributed to the Allied cause. His book *The Spirit of St Louis* (1953) won a Pulitzer Prize. His wife **Anne Morrow Lindbergh** (1906–) is an author. Her works include *North to the Orient* (1935), *Listen! The Wind* (1938), *Gift From the Sea* (1955), *The Unicorn and Other Poems* (1956), *Dearly Beloved* (1962), *Hour of Gold, Hour of Lead* (1974), and *War Within and Without* (1980).

CHARLES LINDBERGH *Aviator, known as "Lucky Lindy," who made the first transatlantic solo flight, from New York to Paris, in 1927.*

linden. *See* lime.

Lindisfarne. *See* Holy Island.

Lindsay, (Nicholas) Vachel (1879–1931) US poet. After an unsuccessful attempt to be a painter he became an itinerant poet, earning his living by reciting his poems. His best-known volumes, *General William Booth Enters into Heaven and Other Poems* (1913) and *The Congo and Other Poems* (1914), owe much to his interest in regional folklore and his mastery of balladlike verse.

Lindsey, Parts of. *See* Lincolnshire.

Linear A A syllabic script used (c. 1700–1450 BC) to write the lost language of the *Minoan civilization of Crete. It evolved from a pictographic script. Known from fewer than 400 inscriptions, it is still undeciphered, but, like its successor, *Linear B, was mainly used on clay tablets to record inventories.

linear accelerator An *accelerator in which charged elementary particles are repeatedly accelerated along a long straight tube by a radio-frequency electric field. In modern linear accelerators the field is supplied by the electric component of a traveling radio wave in a waveguide. The particles are confined in the tube by a series of magnetic lenses, which focus the beam. The maximum energy attained by a linear accelerator is about 10 GeV for electrons and 2 GeV for protons.

Linear B A syllabic script apparently adapted (c. 1450–1400 BC) from *Linear A by the invading Mycaeneans at *Knossos to write their own language (*see* Mycaenean civilization). In 1952 Michael *Ventris deciphered this language as an early form of *Greek. Several thousand Linear B clay tablets, mainly containing inventories, survive from Knossos, *Pylos, and elsewhere, dating between about 1400 and 1100 BC.

linear motor A form of electric induction motor in which the stator and the rotor are linear instead of cylindrical and parallel instead of coaxial. The development of linear motors as a method of traction for monorail intercity trains has been proposed by E. R. Laithwaite. In this arrangement one winding would be in the train and the other on the single rail, thus obviating the need for rotating parts.

Line Islands A chain of coral atolls in the W central Pacific Ocean. Of the N islands, Palmyra and Jarvis Islands are US territories while Washington, Fanning, and Christmas Islands, the only permanently inhabited ones, form part of Kiribati. Copra is produced.

linen A fabric manufactured from *flax (*Linum usitatissimum*). Probably the first textile of plant origin, specimens 4500 years old have been found in Egyptian tombs. Flax growing was brought to Britain by the Romans and in the 16th century a flourishing trade grew up, especially in Scotland and Northern Ireland. Greatly reduced by the 18th-century expansion of the cotton trade, and even more so by the advent of man-made fibers, these strong absorbent fibers now constitute less than 2% of the world fiber production, being reserved for luxury household fabrics and summer garments.

line of force. *See* field.

ling A deep-sea fish, belonging to a genus (*Molva*; 3 species) related to cod, that is cured and dried for food. The common ling (*M. molva*) has a long slim body, up to about 7 ft (2 m) long, mottled brown or green, a long chin barbel, and two dorsal fins.

lingua franca Any language that is used as a means of communication between speakers with different native languages. It may be a hybrid of other languages, such as *pidgin English, or it may refer to an already existing language, such as French, which was formerly the lingus franca of diplomacy. Lingua franca, meaning Frank language, was originally a pidgin used by Mediterranean traders in the middle ages (Frank being the Arabic word for European).

linguistics The scientific study of *language. The earliest recorded studies of particular languages include the Sanskrit grammar of *Panini (6th–4th century BC) and the Greek grammar of Dionysius Thrax of Alexandria (2nd century BC). In the 19th century the study of language (then called *philology) was mainly concerned with establishing the history and relationships of the *Indo-European languages. The chief influences in broadening the scope of linguistics to its present range were Ferdinand de *Saussure, Leonard *Bloomfield, and Noam *Chomsky. Modern linguistics has three main branches, corresponding to the three main components of language: *semantics, *grammar, and *phonetics. Many linguists at present see it as their task to contribute to the building of a formal model of language, in which the theoretical problems are resolved, the components and processes accurately identified, and the relationships among the components and between linguistic systems and other worlds are plausibly described. Other linguists believe that a coherent one-piece model is simply not possible.

Various specialized interests exist within the field of linguistics. **Comparative linguistics** compares languages either to establish the history of and relationships among related languages (e.g. the Indo-European family) or to test theories about linguistic universals by comparing unrelated languages (*see also* etymology). The main contribution of **structural linguistics**, which developed in the early 20th century, was to free linguistics from the historical and comparative approach, viewing language as a unique relational structure. **Sociolinguistics** deals with social aspects of language, including such matters as how language affects and reflects the role and status of individuals within the community, attitudes to dialect and "correctness," linguistic taboos and preferences, bilingualism, etc. **Psycholinguistics** is the comparatively recent branch of linguistics that deals with psychological aspects of language, including how children acquire language, how language is stored in and generated by the brain, the relationship between meaning and memory, etc. **Neurolinguistics**, a branch of psycholinguistics, is concerned with the relationship between language and the physiology of the brain, especially with speech disorders that arise from brain damage.

Linköping 58 25N 15 35E A town in SE Sweden. It has a notable romanesque cathedral and its university was established in 1970. Industries include railroad engineering and the manufacture of cars and textiles. Population (1992 est): 124,400.

Linnaeus, Carolus (Carl Linné; 1707–78) Swedish botanist, who established the principles for naming and classifying plants and animals. As a result of his botanical studies, Linnaeus proposed a system for classifying plants based on their flower parts. He published *Systema naturae* in 1735 followed by *Genera plantarum* (1737) and *Species plantarum* (1753). In his system, Linnaeus defined each type of plant by two names: a generic name and a specific name (*see* binomial nomenclature). Furthermore he grouped related genera into classes and combined related classes into orders. Linnaeus also applied his system to the animal kingdom. His was the first major attempt to bring systematic order to the great array of living things and provided a valuable framework that *Cuvier and others were able to modify and improve. Linnaeus's manuscripts and collections are kept at the Linnaean Society, London, which was founded in his honor in 1788.

linnet A small Eurasian *finch, *Acanthis cannabina*, occurring in dry open regions, where it feeds on the seeds of common weed plants. The female has a dull brown-streaked plumage; the male has a crimson crown and breast, a grayish head, and a red-brown back with darker wings and tail. Male linnets have a beautiful flutelike voice and were popular cagebirds in the 19th century.

LINNET *Nests are built in hedges and thickets and the young are cared for by both parents.*

linotype. *See* typesetting.

linsang A carnivorous mammal belonging to the genus *Prionodon* (2 species) of SE Asia. Linsangs are short-legged, about 30 in (75 cm) long including the tail (12–14 in [30–35 cm]), and have short velvety fur. Nocturnal, with large ears and eyes, they prey on lizards, small mammals, birds, frogs, and insects. Family: *Viverridae*.

linseed The flat oval seed of cultivated *flax, which is a source of linseed oil, used in paints, inks, varnishes, oilcloth, and sailcloth. The crushed seed residues form linseed meal, an important protein feed for ruminants and pigs.

Linz 48 19N 14 18E The third largest city in Austria, the capital of Upper Austria on the Danube River. Its many historical buildings include two 13th-century baroque churches and a cathedral (1862–1924). A cultural center, it has art galleries, libraries, and theaters. Its industries include iron and steel processing using local hydroelectric power. Population (1991): 202,855.

Lin Ze Xu (*or* Lin Tse-hsü; 1785–1850) Chinese statesman and scholar. Lin Ze Xu served as governor of several provinces. While imperial commissioner of Canton (1839–41) he confiscated opium and tried to put an end to its trafficking through British merchants, thus provoking the *Opium War (1839–42). He is also known for his efforts to introduce western defense techniques to China.

lion A large carnivorous □mammal *Panthera leo*, one of the big *cats. Lions are found mainly in Africa (there are a few in India). They are heavily built with sandy-colored coats: the shaggy-maned males grow to 9 ft (2.8 m) while females lack a mane and are more lightly built. Both sexes have a thin tail with a tuft at the end.

Lions inhabit grasslands, living in groups (prides) containing between 4–30 individuals dominated by a supreme male. They hunt mainly at twilight.

Lions, Gulf of (French name: Golfe du Lion) An inlet of the NW Mediterranean Sea, on the coast of central S France between Marseilles and the Spanish border.

Liouville, Joseph (1809–82) French mathematician, who proved that there exists a class of numbers, called transcendental numbers, that cannot be expressed as a solution of a polynomial equation (i.e. one of the form $a_0 + a_1x + \ldots + a_nx^n = 0$, where n and the a's are integers). Liouville could not identify any transcendental numbers, a feat first achieved by *Hermite.

Lipari Islands (*or* Aeolian Is; Italian name: Isole Eolie) An Italian group of seven volcanic islands in the Tyrrhenian Sea, off the N coast of Sicily. The largest is Lipari and the islands of Stromboli and Vulcano have active volcanoes. Exports include pumice stone, grapes, wine, and figs. Area: 44 sq mi (114 sq km). Chief town: Lipari, on Lipari.

lipase An enzyme that splits the glycerides of fats in food and fatty tissue into their component fatty acids and glycerol. Digestive lipases are secreted by the pancreas and small intestine.

Lipchitz, Jacques (1891–1973) Lithuanian cubist sculptor, who lived in Paris from 1909 and New York after 1941. Producing his first cubist sculpture in 1914, Lipchitz developed heavy angular forms in such characteristically cubist subjects as bathers and musicians. In 1925 he began experimenting with the use of voids in bronze sculptures, which he entitled "transparents." His later mythological and religious sculptures explored themes of love, evil, and conflict.

Lipetsk 52 37N 39 36E A city in E Russia on the Voronezh River. Industries include iron and steel and engineering. Its mud spa attracts health devotees. Population (1991 est): 460,000.

lipids A group of compounds, generally insoluble in water but soluble in organic solvents, that includes *fats, *oils, *waxes, phospholipids, sphingolipids, and *steroids. Fats and oils function as energy reserves in plants and animals and form a major source of dietary energy in animals. Phospholipids are important structural components of cell membranes, and sphingolipids are found predominantly in nerve tissues. Steroids have many important derivatives, including cholesterol, bile salts, and certain hormones. *Prostaglandins, *carotenoids, and *terpenes are also classified as lipids. Lipids often occur in association with proteins as lipoproteins.

Lipizzaner A breed of ☐horse long associated with the Spanish Riding School in Vienna, where they are trained for spectacular displays. It is named for the stud founded by Archduke Charles at Lipizza, near Trieste, in 1580. The Lipizzaner has a short back, strong hindquarters, a powerful neck, and a small head. Born black, they mature to a gray color. Height: 14½–15 hands (1.47–1.52 m).

Li Po (Li Bo *or* Li T'ai Po; 705–62) Chinese poet. Li Po and *Du Fu together are often considered China's greatest poets. Li Po's poetry is mostly light-hearted and romantic and has its stylistic origins in folk ballads and other old traditions. Legend has it that he drowned trying to embrace the reflection of the moon from a boat.

Lipmann, Fritz Albert (1899–1986) US biochemist, born in Germany. He won a Nobel prize in physiology and medicine (1953). He came to the US (1939) and conducted research at Massachusetts General Hospital (1941–49) where he discovered (1946–47) coenzyme A and its important intermediary role in metabolism and body energy. He taught at Harvard University (1949–57) and worked for Rockefeller Institute from 1957.

Lippe River A river in NW Germany, rising in the Teutoburger Wald (forest) and flowing generally W to join the Rhine River at Wesel. **The Lippe Canal** (1929), which runs parallel to the river, is the more important waterway. Length: 150 mi (240 km).

Lippershey, Hans (died c. 1619) Dutch lens grinder, who built the first *telescope. The Dutch Government tried to keep the invention a secret but news of it eventually reached *Galileo, who built his own telescope, which he used for astronomical observations.

Lippi, Fra Filippo (c. 1406–69) An early Renaissance Florentine painter, who was a Carmelite monk from 1421 to about 1432. During this time he probably trained under *Masaccio. He was frequently patronized by the Medici but his greatest works are his fresco decorations for the choir of Prato Cathedral (1452–64), showing scenes from the lives of St John the Baptist and St Stephen. He is also noted for his idealized Madonnas, e.g. *The Madonna and Child with Two Angels* (Uffizi). He abducted and later married a nun, Lucrezia Buti; their son, **Filippino Lippi** (1457–1504), was also a painter. Filippino trained under *Botticelli after his father's death and completed Masaccio's fresco cycle in the Brancacci Chapel. His paintings, such as *The Vision of St Bernard* (Badia, Florence), influenced the Florentine mannerists of the 16th century.

Lipscomb, William Nunn (1919–   ) US chemist, who won the Nobel Prize (1976) for his elucidation of the structure of *boranes. He discovered the arrangement of atoms inside borane molecules by means of X-ray diffraction and showed how groups of three such atoms are bonded by a single pair of electrons.

liquefaction of gases Gases are liquefied in several ways. If the temperature of the gas is below its critical temperature (*see* critical state), it can be liquefied simply by compressing it. If the critical temperature is too low for this, the cascade process can be used. In this a gas with a high critical temperature is first liquefied by compression and then allowed to cool by evaporation under reduced pressure. This gas cools a second gas below its critical temperature, so that it in turn can be liquefied, evaporated, and cooled still further. Thus the temperature is reduced in stages. Other methods include cooling by the *Joule-Kelvin effect, which is used industrially in the Linde process (named for Carl von Linde; 1842–1934), and by adiabatic expansion in which a compressed gas is cooled by performing external work. This is the basis of the Claude process (named for Georges Claude; 1870–1960).

Liquefied Petroleum Gas (LPG) Propane, propene, butane, butene, or a mixture of any of these. LPG is a product of *oil refining and is also produced from *natural gas. It is transported by pipeline or in specially built tankers by road, rail, or sea.

Most of the LPG produced is sold in low-pressure cylinders for heating or used as a raw material for chemical manufacture, although it is also used as engine fuel.

liqueurs Alcoholic *spirits flavored with herbs or other ingredients, usually heavily sweetened. Liqueurs are generally sipped, neat, from small glasses after dinner. Some liqueurs, such as Benedictine, were originated by monks; the yellow or green Chartreuse is still made by the Carthusians. Other liqueurs include Curaçao, Cointreau, and Grand Marnier, which are made with brandy and oranges; Kümmel made with cumin and caraway seeds; Maraschino made with marasca cherries; and Drambuie made with whisky and honey. Aged high-quality brandy and whisky, drunk neat, are sometimes described as liqueurs.

liquid crystal A substance exhibiting some liquid properties, especially fluidity, and some crystalline properties, in that large clusters of molecules are aligned in parallel formations. As liquid crystals change their reflectivity when an electric potential is applied to them, they are used in the digital display of electronic calculators, etc.

liquidity preference The proportion of an individual's total assets held in cash. Liquidity preference is determined chiefly by the general price level (if prices are high people need more cash to finance their purchases) and the rate of interest (if interest rates are high people will wish to invest their assets in interest-bearing bonds rather than in money). The concept was originated by J. M. *Keynes to explain the demand for money.

liquids A state of matter between that of *gases and the *solid state. Liquids assume the shape of the container in the same way as gases but being incompressible do not expand to fill the container. Intermolecular forces are considerably stronger than in gases but weaker than in solids. Molecules are only maintained in an orderly arrangement by intermolecular forces over relatively small groups of molecules. The theory of liquids is much less well established than that of gases and solids.

lira 1. Another name for the hurdy-gurdy. **2.** A bowed string instrument of the late Middle Ages. The **lira da braccio** (Italian: lyre for the arm) resembled the *violin but had a flatter body; it was held against the shoulder. The larger **lira da gamba** (Italian: lyre for the leg) was held like a *cello or viola da gamba. Both instruments had between 7 and 15 strings, some of which were sympathetic strings.

Lisbon (Portuguese name: Lisboa) 38 44N 9 08W The capital of Portugal, in the SW on the Tagus River. The country's chief seaport, it has one of the finest harbors in Europe; main exports include wine, olive oil, and cork. Lisbon is also a major industrial and commercial center. Historic buildings include the Tower of Belém and the Jerónimos Monastery; its university was founded in 1290. *History*: a settlement from very early times, it was an organized community under the Roman Empire but was later overrun by German tribes. Occupied by the Moors in the 8th century AD, it was captured by the Portuguese in the 12th century and became their capital in 1256. It flourished in the 15th and 16th centuries, the great age of Portuguese exploration and colonization, but later suffered a decline. In 1755 it was almost totally destroyed by an earthquake. It has expanded considerably in the 20th century and in 1966 one of the world's longest suspension bridges was opened across the Tagus River, linking Lisbon with Almada. Population (1991): 677,790.

Lisieux 49 09N 0 14E A city in N France, in the Calvados department. The shrine of St Thérèse (1873–1917) attracts large numbers of pilgrims to Lisieux. An agricultural trading center (especially in dairy products), its manufactures include textiles and car components. Population (1975): 26,674.

Lissajous figures Patterns arising from the addition of two *simple harmonic motions at right angles to each other, first studied by Jules Lissajous (1822–80). The shape of the pattern depends on the periods of the two motions and the initial conditions. If one of the two periods is an exact multiple of the other the curve is closed, otherwise the curve is open. Lissajous figures are displayed on a *cathode-ray oscilloscope when two sinusoidal signals control the vertical and horizontal motion of the electron beam.

Lissitzky, El (Eliezer L.; 1890–1941) Russian painter, typographer, designer, and architect, known particularly for his work in advertising and exhibition design. While teaching architecture at Vitebsk (1919–21) he painted his series of abstract geometrical paintings, *Proun*. Between 1922 and 1929 he lived in the West, where he was instrumental in spreading Russian ideas on design (*see* constructivism).

List, Friedrich (1789–1846) German economist, who was exiled in 1825 and emigrated to the US. In *Outlines of American Economy* (1827), he argued the need for tariffs to encourage the growth of industry, especially in a developing country. He also wrote *The National System of Political Economy* (1841).

Lister, Joseph, 1st Baron (1827–1912) British surgeon, who pioneered antiseptic techniques in surgery. In 1865, while surgeon at Glasgow Royal Infirmary, Lister realized the significance of *Pasteur's germ theory of disease in trying to prevent the infection of wounds following surgical operations. Lister devised a means of eliminating contamination and introduced carbolic acid as an antiseptic to dress wounds. Mortality arising from infected wounds declined sharply in Lister's ward and his antiseptic procedures eventually became standard practice in hospitals everywhere.

Liszt, Franz (Ferencz L.; 1811–86) Hungarian pianist and composer. He made his debut at the age of nine. After studying the piano with Czerny and studying composition he began a career as a virtuoso. From 1835 to 1839 he lived with the Comtesse d'Agoult (1805–76); their daughter Cosima married Wagner, of whose works Liszt was an early champion. From 1848 to 1861 Liszt lived with the Princess Sayn-Wittgenstein. In 1865 he took minor orders in the Roman Catholic Church; he spent most of the rest of his life in Weimar, Budapest, and Rome. As a pianist Liszt was considered the greatest performer of his time. As a composer he invented the symphonic poem and made use of advanced harmonies and original forms. His compositions include much piano music (including a sonata in B minor and operatic paraphrases), the *Faust Symphony* (1854–57) and *Dante Symphony* (1855–56), and the symphonic poem *Les Préludes* (1854).

litchi (lychee *or* lichee) A Chinese tree, *Litchi chinensis*, cultivated in the tropics and subtropics for its fruits. The fruit is almost globular, 1 in (2.5 cm) in diameter, with a warty deep-pink rind and is borne in branched clusters. The white translucent watery flesh has a sweet acid flavor and encloses a single large brown seed. The fruit is eaten fresh, canned, or dried as litchi nuts. Family: *Sapindacea*.

liter A unit of volume in the *metric system formerly defined as the volume of one kilogram of pure water under specified conditions. This definition still applies for most purposes but in *SI units the liter is a special name, not recommended for high-precision measurements, for the cubic decimeter.

litharge. *See* lead.

lithium (Li) The lightest metal (relative density 0.534), discovered by Arfvedson in 1817. It is an alkali metal and gives a crimson-red color to flames. It occurs in nature in lepidolite, spodumene ($LiAlSi_2O_6$), and other minerals; as well as in brine, from which it is extracted commercially by electrolysis of the molten chloride (LiCl). The metal has the highest specific heat capacity of any solid element. It is corrosive, combustible, and reacts with water. Because of its efficiency in reflecting neutrons, lithium has important applications as a blanketing material in both the hydrogen bomb and proposed *thermonuclear reactors. It forms salts, like the other alkali metals, and the hydride LiH. Lithium salts are used in the treatment of some forms of mental depression. At no 3; at wt 6.941; mp 132°F (180.54°C); bp 780°F (1347°C).

lithography. *See* printing.

Lithops A genus of succulent South African desert plants (about 50 species), with no stems and leaves partly buried in the soil. The tips of the leaves are smooth, with a deep cleft across the top, camouflaged to resemble pebbles. The daisy-like flowers are white or yellow. Family: *Aizoaceae*.

Lithuanian A language belonging to the E division of the Baltic languages division of the Indo-European family, spoken mainly by the Lithuanians of the Lithuanian SSR, where it is the official language. The total population of Lithuanian speakers, including those in America, is about 2,750,000. Lithuanian is closely related to *Latvian. It is written in a Latin alphabet and written texts date from the 16th century.

Lithuania, Republic of (*or* Lithuania) A country in N Europe on the Baltic Sea, a constituent republic of the Soviet Union until 1991. Most of Lithuania comprises a central lowland and is a particularly fertile region, with forests and peat reserves. The Lithuanians comprise about 80% of the population. Lithuania has large fertilizer, textile, and metalworking industries. Agriculture, especially livestock breeding, has been intensified in the postwar period. *History*: one of the largest states in medieval Europe, in the 14th century Lithuania united with Poland under the *Jagiellon dynasty, passing after the partition of Poland in the 18th century to Russia. It became independent in 1918 but was incorporated into the Soviet Union as an SSR in 1940. It was occupied by Germany during World War II, during which the large Jewish minority was virtually exterminated. It became independent in 1991 with the collapse of the Soviet Union. Lithuania became a member of the UN in 1991. Lithuania, with Estonia and Latvia, pursued policies that kept the Baltic republics distinct from other Soviet republics. Area: 25,170 sq mi (65,200 sq km). Population (1989): 3,690,000. Capital: Vilnius.

litmus A soluble compound obtained from certain lichens. Litmus turns red in an acid solution and blue in an alkaline solution. It is therefore used as an *indicator, often in the form of **litmus paper**, strips of paper impregnated with litmus.

Little America 78 11S 162 10W The main US Antarctic base, near the coast of Ross Dependency. It was established in 1928 as the headquarters for the polar expeditions of Richard *Byrd.

Little Belt (Danish name: Lille Bælt) A strait in SW Denmark, between the mainland and the island of Fyn. It links the Kattegat with the Baltic Sea and narrows to 0.6 mi (1 km).

Little Bighorn, Battle of the (June 25, 1876) The battle fought on the S bank of the Little Bighorn River in the Montana Territory, in which General *Custer and men of the 7th Cavalry were massacred by Sioux Indians led by *Crazy Horse and *Sitting Bull. The battle was also known as Custer's Last Stand. Custer's men were outnumbered nearly 10 to 1. The Indians were resisting incursions by whites into land that had been granted to them by treaty in 1868, but shortly after the battle would be driven from the area. The battlefield is now a national monument.

little owl A small *owl, *Athene noctua*, occurring in Eurasia and North Africa; 8 in (20 cm) long, it has a white-mottled brown plumage with heavily barred underparts, rounded wings, and bright-yellow eyes and hunts over open country at dawn and dusk, feeding on insects, worms, and occasionally mice.

Little Rock 34 42N 92 17W The capital city of Arkansas. In 1957, when African-American pupils entered the high school for the first time, it was the scene of major race riots protesting against desegregation. Population (1990): 175,795.

Little Turtle (1752–1812) Miami Indian chief. He successfully fought against Gen. Josiah Hormar (1790) and Gen. Arthur St Clair (1791) in their efforts to end Indian raids and to settle the Northwest Territory. In 1793 he was defeated by Gen. Anthony Wayne's forces at Fort Recovery and Fallen Timbers in present-day Ohio. He signed and honored the Treaty of Greenville (1795) and from then on advocated peace.

Litvinov, Maksim Maksimovich (1876–1951) Soviet diplomat; foreign minister (1930–39). Litvinov, who believed in cooperation between the Soviet Union and the West, obtained US recognition of his country in 1934. In the League of Nations he advocated action against the Axis powers and was dismissed shortly before the German-Soviet nonaggression treaty of 1939. After the German invasion of the Soviet Union, Litvinov was ambassador to the US (1941–43).

Liu Shao Qi (*or* Liu Shao-ch'i; 1898–1974) Chinese communist statesman. He joined the Communist Party in Moscow in 1921 and later became a leader of the trade union movement in the *Jiangxi Soviet. In 1959 he succeeded *Mao Tse-tung as chairman of the People's Republic of China but was condemned as a reactionary during the *Cultural Revolution and disappeared from public view.

liver A large glandular organ, weighing 2.6–3.5 lb (1.2–1.6 kg), situated in the upper right region of the abdomen, just below the diaphragm. The liver has many important functions concerned with the utilization of absorbed foods. It converts excess glucose into glycogen, which it stores and reconverts into glucose when required; it breaks down excess amino acids into *urea; and it stores and metabolizes fats. The liver forms and secretes *bile, which contains the breakdown products of worn-out red blood cells, and synthesizes blood-clotting factors, plasma proteins, and—in the fetus—red blood cells. It also breaks down (detoxifies) poisonous substances, including alcohol. *Cirrhosis of the liver is commonly caused by a combination of sensitivity to, and excess of, alcohol.

liver fluke A parasitic *flatworm that inhabits the bile duct of sheep, cattle, and man. The common liver fluke (*Fasciola hepatica*) passes its larval stages in a marshland snail before infecting grazing animals (or, rarely, man). The Chinese liver fluke (*Opisthorchus sinensis*), 0.4–0.8 in (1–2 cm) long, passes two larval stages in a freshwater snail and fish before maturing in a human host.

Liverpool 53 25N 2 55W A major city in NW England, on the estuary of the River Mersey. It is the UK's second most important port and the foremost for Atlantic trade. The most famous landmark is the Royal Liver Building (1910) at the Pier Head. Other notable buildings include St George's Hall (1854). There is a new Roman Catholic cathedral (constructed 1962–67). The Anglican cathedral (begun 1904) is the country's largest ecclesiastical building. Liverpool has one of the largest provincial universities in the UK (1903). Exports include all kinds of manufactured goods, especially textiles and machinery. The main imports are petroleum, grain, ores, nonferrous metals, sugar, wood, fruit, and cotton. These are reflected in some of Liverpool's industries: flour milling, electrical engineering, food processing, chemicals, soap, margarine, tanning, and motor vehicles. *History*: originally trading with Ireland, Liverpool grew rapidly in the 18th and 19th centuries, superseding Bristol as the chief west coast port as a result of trade with the Americas (sugar, tobacco, slaves, cotton). Population (1991): 448,300.

Liverpool, Robert Banks Jenkinson, 2nd Earl of (1770–1828) British statesman; Tory prime minister (1812–27). He became a member of Parliament in 1790 and held office almost continuously until 1827. He was foreign secretary (1801–04), home secretary (1807–09), and secretary for war and the colonies

(1809–12). As prime minister he is remembered for his unenlightened response to the unrest that followed the Napoleonic Wars (1803–15). He also opposed *Catholic emancipation but the last years of his government saw the development of Tory reform.

liverwort A *bryophyte plant of the class *Hepaticae* (10,000 species), found growing on moist soil, rocks, trees, etc. There are two groups: leafy liverworts, in which the plant body is differentiated into stems and leaves; and thallose liverworts, which have a flat lobed liverlike body (thallus). The liverwort plant is the gamete-producing phase (gametophyte) and gives rise to a capsule, the spore-producing phase (sporophyte), which is sometimes borne on a slender erect column (*see* hornwort).

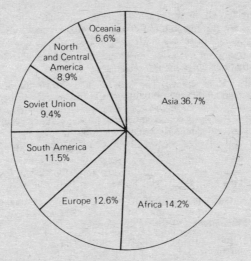

LIVESTOCK FARMING *Distribution of the world's livestock (cattle, sheep, pigs, horses, asses and mules) in the 1980s.*

livestock farming The maintenance and management of domesticated animals for the production of milk, meat, eggs, fibers, skins, etc. Farming methods vary widely throughout the world and modern improvements in livestock breeds and husbandry techniques have enabled dramatic increases to be made in productivity, nutrition and disease control being essential aspects of management.

Cattle produce milk (*see* dairy farming) and beef. The gestation period is about 9 months, followed by about 10 months of lactation and a 2-month dry period before calving again. A cow is known as a heifer until her second lactation. Heifers are reared either for beef or as dairy replacements and bull calves are generally castrated and reared for beef, being known as bullocks or steers. Age at slaughter depends on the breed and level of feeding but is generally about 18 months. Calves for veal are reared on a milk-based diet and are slaughtered at about 14 weeks.

Sheep are farmed worldwide for meat and wool (and in some countries for milk), often grazing on poor mountainous or arid pastures. One or two lambs per ewe are born in early spring. Males are castrated and reared for slaughter at weights of 44–99 lb (20–45 kg). Selected females are reared as replacement ewes. Each sheep yields 4–11 lb (2–5 kg) of wool.

Pigs have traditionally been kept outdoors, foraging for roots, seeds, etc. In modern intensive systems, they are housed under controlled conditions. Young females (gilts) are first mated at 7–8 months. Following the gestation period of 115 days, an average of 7–9 piglets are born per litter. Pork pigs are slaughtered at 88–110 lb (40–50 kg); those reared for bacon are slaughtered at 176–220 lb (80–100 kg).

Poultry are now kept indoors in an artificially controlled environment. Chicks are hatched artificially, the female birds starting to lay after about 20 weeks and producing about 250 eggs per year. Laying flocks are kept in "batteries" of cages with 3–5 birds per cage, feeding, cleaning, and egg collection being automatic. Table birds are fed ad lib and reach a weight of around 4 lb (2 kg) in 8–12 weeks. Turkeys are also reared for meat under intensive conditions.

Apart from producing food, many livestock, especially horses, mules, and donkeys, provide important means of transport and motive power. Goats provide milk in many traditional agricultural systems.

Livia Drusilla (58 BC–29 AD) The wife of Octavian (Emperor *Augustus) from 39 BC and the mother by her first husband of Emperor *Tiberius. As Augustus's consort Livia's image was one of matronly dignity and reports of her machinations on Tiberius's behalf are probably exaggerated. After Augustus's death (14 AD) she received the honorific name Julia Augusta.

living fossil A living organism whose closest relatives are all extinct, being known only as fossils. Such organisms were thought—before their discovery in modern times—to be extinct themselves. Examples of living fossils are the *coelacanth and the *dawn redwood, discovered in 1938 and 1941, respectively.

Livingstone (or Maramba) 17 50S 25 53E A city in S Zambia, on the Zambezi River. It was the former capital of Northern Rhodesia (1907–35). It is a tourist center for the nearby Victoria Falls. Population (1980 est): 80,000.

Livingstone, David (1813–73) Scottish missionary and explorer of Africa. A physician and missionary, in 1840 he set out for Bechuanaland (now Botswana). He traced long stretches of the Zambezi, Shire, and Rovuma Rivers, and discovered Lake Ngami (1849), the Victoria Falls (1855), and Lake Nyasa (now Malawi). During an attempt to trace the source of the Nile (1866–73) his famous encounter with Sir Henry Morton *Stanley occurred. He died near Lake Bangweulu.

Livingston, Robert R. (1746–1813) US lawyer and statesman; first secretary for foreign affairs (1781–83). Between service at the Continental Congress (1775–76; 1779–81; 1784–85), he helped to draft the Declaration of Independence (1776), served as chancellor of New York state (1777–1801), and became the first US secretary for foreign affairs, supervising the US delegation to the Paris Peace Conference (1782–83). He was appointed minister to France (1801–04) and, with James *Monroe, negotiated the Louisiana Purchase (1803). He spent the rest of his life promoting steamboating with Robert *Fulton.

Living Theater An experimental theater company founded in New York City in 1947 by Julian Beck (1925–) and Judith Malina (1926–). Their best-known productions include Jack Gelber's *The Connection* (1959), a play about drug addiction, and *Paradise Now* (1968), in which they developed controversial experiments in audience participation.

Livonian Knights (Livonian Brothers of the Sword) A German military and religious order of knighthood founded in 1202 to conquer and christianize the region, notably Livonia, around the Baltic Sea. They merged with the Teutonic Knights in 1237 and were disbanded in 1561.

DAVID LIVINGSTONE *"Found" by Stanley (on the right) at Ujiji.*

Livonian War (1558–83) A confrontation over Russian expansion toward the Baltic Sea. In 1558 *Ivan the Terrible invaded Livonia and defeated its rulers, the Livonian Knights, who placed Livonia under Lithuanian protection. Russia was eventually defeated by the Polish-Lithuanian commonwealth (*see* Lublin, Union of) and Sweden, losing its Livonian conquests and some border towns on the Gulf of Finland.

Livorno (English name: Leghorn) 43 33N 10 18E A port in central Italy, in Tuscany on the Ligurian Sea. It has a 16th-century cathedral. Its industries include shipbuilding, oil refining, and engineering. Straw (Leghorn) hats are produced. Olive oil, copper products, and marble are exported. Population (1991 est): 171,000.

Livy (Titus Livius; 59 BC–17 AD) Roman historian. He was born in Patavium (Padua) in N Italy and settled in Rome about 29 BC. His monumental history of Rome from its legendary foundation to the death of Drusus in 9 BC, written in an elevated style and emphasizing the moral examples of individual lives, was immediately popular. Only 35 of the original 142 books survive, covering the early history up to the 4th century BC, the second Punic War against Hannibal, and the wars against Macedonia up to 166 BC.

lizard A *reptile belonging to the suborder *Sauria* (3000 species), occurring worldwide but most abundant in tropical regions. They are mainly terrestrial with

Lizard Point

cylindrical or narrow scaly long-tailed bodies, some with limbs reduced or absent (*see* glass snake; skink), and often with crests, spines, and frills. They range in size from the smallest *geckos to the formidable *Komodo dragon. Lizards lay leathery-shelled eggs although certain species of colder regions and many skinks bear live young. The female builds a simple nest and may guard her eggs until the young hatch and disperse. Some lizards reproduce by parthenogenesis, i.e. unfertilized eggs develop into races of females. Lizards eat chiefly insects and vegetation and have been known to live for 25 years in captivity.

Lizard Point (*or* Lizard Head) 49 56N 5 13W The most southerly point of the British Isles, in SW Cornwall on the Atlantic Ocean. It possesses magnificent coastal scenery with distinctive green- and purple-colored serpentine rock.

Ljubljana (German name: Laibach) 46 04N 14 30E The capital city of Slovenia. Under foreign rule until 1918, it is the center of Slovene culture with a university (1595). It was largely destroyed by an earthquake in 1895. Population (1991): 323,291.

llama A hoofed mammal, *Lama glama*, of S and W South America. Up to 48 in (120 cm) high at the shoulder, llamas are sure-footed, nimble, and hardy, with thick warm coats. They are now only found in the domesticated state, being used for meat, wool, and as pack animals. Family: *Camelidae* (camels, etc.).

llanos The treeless grasslands of South America that cover about 220,000 sq mi (570,000 sq km) of central Venezuela and N Colombia. Drained by the Orinoco River and its tributaries, the llanos are traditionally a cattle-rearing region but the discovery of oil in he 1930s led to considerable population growth and economic development.

Llewellyn, Richard (R. D. V. L. Lloyd; 1907–83) Welsh novelist. After working in films and journalism, he achieved success with his novel about a Welsh mining village, *How Green Was My Valley* (1939). His other novels include the sequel *Up, Into the Singing Mountains* (1960).

Lloyd, Harold (1893–1971) US film comedian. He developed the character of the dogged little man in conventional suit and spectacles in numerous early silent comedies, most of them characterized by his use of dangerous stunts. His films include *Just Nuts* (1915), *Safety Last* (1923), and *The Freshman* (1925).

Lloyd George, David, 1st Earl (1863–1945) British statesman; Liberal prime minister (1914–22). He entered Parliament in 1890 and gained a reputation for radicalism as a Welsh nationalist. He was president of the Board of Trade (1905–08) and then chancellor of the exchequer (1908–15). In World War I he served as minister of munitions (1915–16) and secretary for war (1916) before succeeding Asquith as prime minister. After the war he continued to lead a coalition government increasingly dominated by the Conservatives. He was criticized for negotiating with Irish militants in the establishment of the Irish Free State (1921) and his government fell when Britain came close to war with the Turkish nationalists. Lloyd George never regained prominence in British politics, although he held his parliamentary seat until 1945.

Lloyd's An association of British insurance underwriters named for the 17th-century London coffee house, owned by Edward Lloyd, where underwriters used to meet. Lloyd's itself does not underwrite insurance business, which is undertaken by private underwriters, who are wholly responsible for losses.

Lloyd Webber, Andrew (1948–) British composer. His musicals, with lyrics by Tim Rice (1944–), include *Joseph and the Amazing Technicolor Dreamcoat* (1968), *Jesus Christ Superstar* (1970), and *Evita* (1978); later works include *Cats* (1981), *Song and Dance* (1982), *Starlight Express* (1984), *Requiem* (1985), and *Phantom of the Opera* (1986).

DAVID LLOYD GEORGE *Haig (left) and Joffre (center) argue a point with the British prime minister on the Western Front (1916).*

Llywelyn ap Gruffudd (d. 1282) The only native Prince of Wales (1258–82) to be recognized as such by England. He aided the English barons against Henry III (1263–67) and refused homage to Edward I (1276), who forced Llywelyn into submission but allowed him to remain Prince of Wales by title. Llywelyn was killed in another revolt.

Llywelyn ap Iorwerth (d. 1240) Prince of Gwynedd, N Wales (1194–1238), who achieved supremacy over most other Welsh princes. He supported the barons against his father-in-law King John of England (1215), obtaining recognition for Welsh rights in the Magna Carta.

loach A small elongated freshwater *bony fish of the family *Cobitidae* (over 200 species), found mainly in Asia, but also in Europe and N Africa. Loaches feed usually at night on bottom-dwelling invertebrates detected by the three to six pairs of barbels around the mouth. The intestine can serve as an accessory respiratory organ using swallowed air. Order: *Cypriniformes*.

loam A type of soil containing approximately equal proportions of sand, silt, and clay. It is an ideal soil for agriculture since it can retain some moisture and plant nutrients but is well aerated and drained and easily worked.

Lobachevski, Nikolai Ivanovich (1793–1856) Russian mathematician, who (in 1829) produced the first *non-Euclidean geometry. He achieved this by examining what is possible if the fifth axiom in Euclid's *Elements* is neglected. In Lobachevski's geometry the angles of a triangle always add up to less than 180°.

Lobelia A genus of annual and perennial herbs (about 250 species), found in most warm and temperate regions. The leaves are simple; flowers are tubular, with a two-lobed upper lip and a larger three-lobed lower lip, and are arranged in a terminal spike. Ornamental species, called cardinal flowers, are usually blue or red. Family: *Lobeliaceae*.

Lobengula (c. 1836–94) King (1870–94) of the Matabele (*or* Ndebele) kingdom in S Rhodesia. Son of *Mzilikazi, Lobengula granted land and mineral rights to the British South Africa Company but this was no protection against the conquest of his kingdom in 1893.

Lobito 12 20S 13 34E A port in W Angola, on the Atlantic coast. Its fine natural harbor has made it the country's busiest port. Population (1983): 150,000.

lobotomy. *See* leukotomy.

lobster A large marine *crustacean of the section *Macrura* that has a long abdomen ending in a tailfan. True lobsters (family *Homaridae*) have segmented bodies, a pair of pincers, four pairs of walking legs, and several pairs of swimming legs (swimmerets). They live on the ocean bottom and are mainly nocturnal, feeding on seaweed and animals. Eggs are carried on the swimmerets and hatch into free-swimming larvae that later descend to the bottom. Many species are commercially important as food, for example *Homarus vulgaris* and *H. americanus*. Order: *Decapoda*.

Local Group The small irregularly shaped cluster of *galaxies to which our *Galaxy belongs. Other members include the *Andromeda galaxy, the Triangulum Spiral, and both *Magellanic Clouds. There are 25 or more members.

Locarno (German name: Lugarrus) 46 10N 8 48E A city and health resort in S Switzerland, on Lake Locarno. Its church of Madonna del Sasso (1480) is a place of pilgrimage. The Pact of Locarno was signed here. Population (1970): 14,143.

Locarno Pact (1925) A series of treaties between Germany, France, Belgium, Poland, Czechoslovakia, the UK, and Italy. The most important was an agreement between France, Germany, and Belgium, guaranteed by the UK and Italy, to maintain the borders between Germany and France and Belgium respectively and the demilitarized zone of the Rhineland. The latter was violated by Hitler in 1936.

Lochner, Stefan (c. 1400–51) German painter of the Cologne School, born in Meersburg on Lake Constance. He probably trained in the Netherlands before settling in Cologne. His *Madonna of the Rose Bower* (Wallraf-Richartz Museum, Cologne) combines the delicacy of the *international gothic with the naturalism of Flemish painting.

lock A section of a canal or river, enclosed by gates, that is used to regulate the water level and raise or lower vessels wishing to navigate the waterway. The more common pound lock consists of two sets of mitered gates set a distance apart pointing into the downward force of the water. A vessel wishing to pass from the lower water level to the higher level enters the lock, the lower gates are closed behind it, and water from the upper level is allowed to flow into the lock through gaps in the upper gates. When the two levels are equal the upper gates are opened and the vessel leaves. The reverse procedure enables vessels to travel from the higher to the lower level.

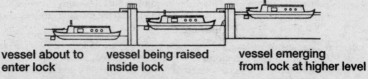

| vessel about to enter lock | vessel being raised inside lock | vessel emerging from lock at higher level |

Locke, John (1632–1704) English philosopher. His greatest work, the *Essay concerning Human Understanding* (1690), reveals him as a pioneer of *empiricism. It maintains, contrary to received tradition, that every one of our ideas comes from sense impressions; at birth the human mind is a *tabula rasa* (blank tablet). The *Essay* also attempts to sustain the distinction between primary qualities (found without exception in all bodies) and secondary qualities (originating in the impressions these bodies make on our senses). Locke's two works *Of Government* (1690) were enormously influential in molding modern concepts of liberal democracy. He dismissed any divine right to kingship and advocated liberal government, the function of which was, he thought, to preside over the exchange of "natural" for "civil" rights. He held that, in virtue of the occurrence of some form of *social contract in antiquity, political rulers were obliged to guarantee as civil rights any liberties that their subjects' ancestors might be supposed to have surrendered. There were, however, some inalienable rights that could never be given up to a citizen's ruler.

lockjaw. *See* tetanus.

lockout The closure of a workplace by an employer to prevent employees from working, in an attempt to persuade them to accept the employer's terms of employment. In the interests of good industrial relations, the measure is now rarely used.

Lockyer, Sir Joseph Norman (1836–1920) British astronomer, who in 1868 first recognized the existence of an unknown element, which he called helium, in the sun's spectrum. Terrestrial helium was eventually discovered nearly 40 years later by Sir William *Ramsay. Lockyer also founded the scientific journal *Nature*.

locomotive An engine that draws a train on a *railroad. The first locomotives, designed by *Trevithick and *Stephenson were driven by steam engines and steam dominated the railroads until the end of World War II. Even in the mid-1970s, it was estimated that over 25,000 steam locomotives were still in use throughout the world. However, the steam engine has a low efficiency (about 8% in a locomotive, which does not use a condenser), it takes a long time to become operational while steam is raised, it uses an awkward and dirty solid fuel (which it has to pull with it in a tender immediately behind the engine), and it creates pollution. For these reasons steam locomotives have largely been replaced in the industrial countries by electric, Diesel-electric, or Diesel trains, all of which have efficiencies of about 22%.

Where the traffic justifies the cost of installing overhead wires or a conductor rail, electric trains are usually preferred, as it is more efficient to generate electricity centrally than in the locomotive. Various configurations have been tried, but series-wound direct-current motors are the most widely used, with rectification in the locomotive when the supply is alternating current. In some cases a three-phase supply is used, with *thyristor control. For lines in which a permanent installation is not economic, Diesel engines are used as a prime mover. These are either coupled hydraulically to the wheels, using a hydraulic torque converter (or fluid flywheel) and a gearbox, or to an electric generator or alternator, which produces current to power electric motors that drive the wheels. The first Diesel-electric train was used in Sweden in 1912 and the first Diesel-hydraulic in Germany a year later. Because the Diesel provides a very low torque at low speeds, it cannot be used without a hydraulic coupling, but even these units are usually restricted to small trains.

The use of *gas turbines on the railroads began in 1934, when a turbine powered a Swedish experimental train. A gas turbine-electric train was first tried in Switzerland in 1941. Although the gas turbine is lighter than the Diesel, it is only efficient at high power, and most of the long runs that could utilize its smooth full-power output are already electrified. The outlook for gas turbines is therefore not regarded as very promising.

LOCOMOTIVES

Stephenson's "Rocket" *The first locomotive to combine a multitubular boiler and a blast pipe, the "Rocket" ran on the earliest public railroad, in NE England, between Stockton and Darlington, in 1829.*

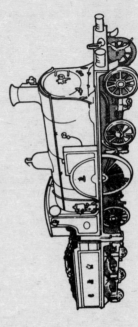

C.R. No. 123 *Caledonian Railway's famous locomotive ran the difficult 100.6 miles between Carlisle and Edinburgh, Scotland, in 102.5 minutes in 1888.*

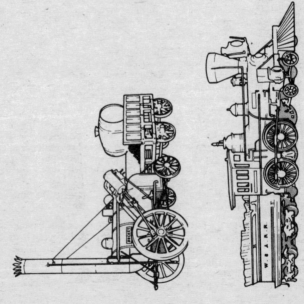

"General" *Typical of the most common type of US locomotive in the 19th century, the "General" was involved in a dramatic sabotage incident in 1862 during the Civil War. One of this class was the first to run at 100 mph (1893).*

LOCOMOTIVES

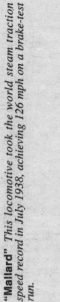

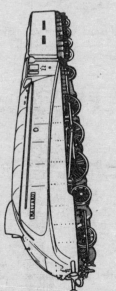

"Mallard" This locomotive took the world steam traction speed record in July 1938, achieving 126 mph on a brake-test run.

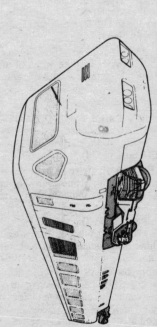

S.N.C.F. BB 9004 For many years France held the world rail speed record. In 1955, the electric BB 9004 reached a speed of 205.6 mph, hauling three carriages weighing 100 tons.

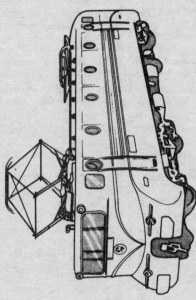

Advanced Passenger Train (APT) British Rail's prototype gas-turbine APT traveled at 152 mph in 1975. Production APTs are electrically powered.

Locri 38 14N 16 15E A city founded by Dorian Greek colonists about 700 BC on the E of the toe of Italy. Well governed by oligarchic rulers, Locri possessed in Zaleucus's legal code (c. 650 BC) Europe's earliest written laws. Its strategic position inevitably brought involvement in Rome's wars with Pyrrhus and Hannibal, and Scipio Africanus conquered it in 205 BC. Locri subsequently declined and was destroyed by Muslims in 915 AD. Excavations in 1889–1900 and the 1950s revealed a temple and many 5th-century terra-cotta plaques.

locus In mathematics, a set of points that satisfy certain conditions. For example, in two dimensions the set of points a fixed distance from a particular point is a circle.

locust (botany) An evergreen Mediterranean tree, *Ceratonia siliqua*, also called carob tree or St John's bread; 40–49 ft (12–15 m) in height, it has catkins of petalless flowers and produces leathery pods containing a sweet edible pulp and small flat beans. The black locust (*Robinia pseudoacacia*), also called false acacia, is a North American tree widely cultivated for ornament (it is common in streets and parks). Up to 78 ft (24 m) tall, it has deeply ridged dark-brown bark, paired pale-green leaves, hanging clusters of white flowers, and black pods. Family: **Leguminosae*.

locust (zoology) A *grasshopper that undergoes sporadic increases in population size to form huge swarms, which migrate long distances and devour all the crops and other vegetation on which they settle. When the population density is high, due to favorable environmental conditions, the nymphs (immature forms), called hoppers, are brightly colored and crowd together—the gregarious phase, maturing into gregarious swarming adults. Solitary-phase nymphs, whose coloration is that of their surroundings, mature in uncrowded conditions into solitary nonswarming adults. Economically important species include the migratory locust (*Locusta migratoria*), about 2 in (55 mm) long (all locusts are relatively large), found throughout Africa and S Eurasia and eastward to Australia and New Zealand; and the desert locust (*Schistocerca gregaria*), occurring from N Africa to the Punjab.

Lod (*or* Lydda) 31 57N 34 54E A city in central Israel, between Jerusalem and Tel Aviv-Yafo. Lydda was the scene of many biblical events. It fell to Israeli forces in 1948 during the war with the Arabs and is now the site of Israel's international airport. Population: 30,500.

lodestone. *See* magnetite.

Lodge, Henry Cabot (1850–1924) US Republican politician; a senator from 1893 to 1924. An isolationist, he led the group of Republican senators who rejected the Treaty of *Versailles (1919) and prevented US membership of the League of Nations (1920).

Lodi 45 19N 9 30E A city in Italy, in Lombardy on the Adda River. It has a 12th-century cathedral. Manufactures include iron, majolica, silk, and linen. Situated in a rich dairy-farming district, it has a large trade in cheese, especially Parmesan. Population: 44,422.

Łódź 51 49N 19 28E The second largest city in Poland. It developed rapidly during the 19th century and is now a leading industrial center specializing in textiles. Other manufactures include chemicals and electrical goods. Its university was founded in 1945. Population (1992 est): 847,000.

Loeb, Jacques (1859–1924) US zoologist, born in Germany, who demonstrated that unfertilized eggs of sea urchins and frogs could develop to maturity by means of controlled changes in their environment, which influenced cell division (*see* parthenogenesis). Loeb also worked on brain physiology, animal *tropisms (involuntary movements), and tissue regeneration.

Loeffler, Friedrich August Johannes (1852–1915) German bacteriologist, who (with Edwin *Klebs in 1884) first isolated the diphtheria bacillus (the Klebs-Loeffler bacillus). Loeffler also showed how some animals were immune to diphtheria, which helped *Behring to develop an antitoxin, and investigated several other animal diseases.

loess A deposit consisting of wind-born dust from desert or vegetation-free areas at the margins of ice sheets. Vast thick deposits occur in NW China; in Europe loess occurs in Germany (the Bördeland), Belgium, and NE France. Deep well-drained soils develop from loess.

Loewe, Frederick (1904–88) US composer of musical comedies, born in Austria. He is famous for such musicals as *Brigadoon* (1947), *Paint Your Wagon* (1950), *My Fair Lady* (1956), and *Camelot* (1960), written with the librettist Alan *Lerner. They also wrote the Academy Award–winning film *Gigi* (1958).

Loewi, Otto (1873–1961) US physiologist, who demonstrated that stimulation of nerves causes the release of a chemical transmitter that affects the muscle concerned. He identified this transmitter as *acetylcholine—a substance first isolated by Sir Henry *Dale, with whom Loewi shared the Nobel Prize (1936).

Lofoten Islands A large group of islands off the NW coast of Norway, within the Arctic Circle. There are rich cod and herring fisheries in the surrounding waters, to which many Norwegian fishermen come during spring. Area: about 1980 sq mi (5130 sq km).

log 1. A book containing a detailed record of the events occurring in and navigation of a vessel. **2.** A device, towed behind or fastened to a vessel, that records the speed of the vessel through the water. Its name comes from chip log, the device formerly used, which consisted of a chip tossed overboard, at the bow of a vessel; the time required to pass the chip and the distance covered were used to calculate the speed of the vessel.

Logan, Mount 60 31N 140 22W The highest mountain in Canada, in SW Yukon in the St Elias Mountains. Its huge mass towers 13,780 ft (4200 m) above glaciers. Height: 19,850 ft (6050 m).

loganberry A trailing bramble-like shrub that is a cross between a raspberry and a blackberry. It bears heads of juicy wine-red tart-tasting fleshy berries, which are used for preserves, puddings, and wine. It originated in California and is named for James H. Logan (1841–1928), who first grew it in 1881. Family: *Rosacea*.

logarithms A mathematical function used to facilitate multiplication and division. Based on the law that $a^x \times a^y = a^{x+y}$, two numbers p and q can be multiplied together by writing them in the form $p = a^x$ and $q = a^y$ and then adding together the values of x and y (the exponents). x is called the logarithm of p to the base a, i.e. $x = \log_a p$. Thus $p \times q$ is found by looking up their logarithms in books of tables, adding them together, and looking up the antilogarithm of the result. Division is carried out in a similar way using subtraction, based on the law $a^x \div a^y = a^{x-y}$. The base of common logarithms is 10 (i.e. $a = 10$); Naperian or natural logarithms use the base e. Pocket calculators have obviated the need for logarithms as a method of computation but they remain useful mathematical functions.

logic In the widest sense, the science of reasoned argument. As a mental discipline, it is concerned not so much with the application of argument in specific instances as with the general rules covering the construction of valid inferences. The dialogues of *Plato present *Socrates as pursuing wisdom through rational discourse, but *Aristotle was the first to make a systematic study of the principles governing such discourse (*see also* syllogism). His six logical treatises, known collectively as the *Organon*, were the sourcebooks for such medieval logicians as *Abelard. After the Renaissance philosophers became increasingly aware of limitations in the Aristotelian approach. *Leibniz, for instance, was worried by the difference between the logical and grammatical structure of sentences; two grammatically identical sentences may be very different logically. (Suppose, for example, that Jemima is a cat and compare the following two sentences: "Jemima is a cat; Jemima is mine; therefore Jemima is my cat." "Jemima is a mother; Jemima is mine; therefore Jemima is my mother.") Rules must therefore be found to formalize ordinary language in such a way as to make plain its underlying logical structure, before further rules for the construction of valid arguments can be drawn up. Since the 19th century formulation of such rules has become mainly the province of mathematicians. *Boole and *Frege were important pioneers in what is now called "mathematical logic" to differentiate it from the wider still current sense. *Russell, whose work had important repercussions for *set theory, called "logic . . . the youth of mathematics, and mathematics . . . the manhood of logic."

logical positivism A philosophical movement that arose from the *Vienna Circle in the 1920s. Influenced by *Mach and *Wittgenstein, it insisted that philosophy should be scientific, regarding it as an analytical (rather than a speculative) activity, the purpose of which was clarification of thought. Any assertion claiming to be factual has meaning only if its truth (or falsity) can be empirically tested. Metaphysical propositions and those of aesthetics and religion are consequently meaningless, since it is impossible to say how they can be verified. A secondary goal of logical positivism was the analysis and unification of scientific terminology. After the Nazi invasion of Austria, members of the Circle emigrated to Britain and the US, where the movement continued to be influential.

logos (Greek: word) A term with several different philosophical interpretations. *Heraclitus used it to mean the pervading rational underpinning of the universe. For the *Sophists logos could simply mean an argument. For the Stoics it was the kind of god from whom stems all the rationality in the universe. Students of St John's Gospel tend to interpret its occurrence there in the Stoic sense. *See also* Stoicism.

logwood A thorny tropical American tree, *Hematoxylon campechianum*, 30–48 ft (9–15 m) tall, with a short twisted trunk, compound leaves comprising many paired leaflets, and clusters of small yellow flowers. The blood-red heartwood yields the black to purple dye hematoxylin, used in the textile industry and as a biological stain. Family: *Leguminosae.*

Lohengrin In *Arthurian legend, the son of Percival (Parzival). He champions a young noblewoman, Elsa of Brabant, whom he agrees to marry on condition that she does not inquire into his origins. When her curiosity overcomes her, he is taken back by his swan guide to the castle of the *Holy Grail, whence he came. The story was adapted by *Wagner in the opera *Lohengrin* (1850).

Loire River The longest river in France. Rising in the Cévennes Mountains, it flows mainly W to the Bay of Biscay at St Nazaire, passing through Orléans, Tours, and Nantes. Its tributaries include the Allier, Vienne, and Maine and it drains an area of 40,000 sq mi (119,140 sq km), one-fifth of the area of France. The Loire Valley is renowned for its vineyards and chateaux (Amboise, Blois, Chambord, Chaumont, Chenonceaux). It is linked by canal with the Seine River. Length: 634 mi (1020 km).

Loki In Norse mythology, a mischief-making giant with the ability to change his shape and sex, who lived among the gods until imprisoned in a cave for the murder of Balder. His offspring—Hel, the goddess of death, Jörmungandr, the evil serpent surrounding the earth, and Fenris, the wolf—are among the forces of evil which he leads against the gods at doomsday (□Ragnarök).

Lolland (*or* Laaland) A Danish island in the Baltic Sea, S of Sjælland. Produce includes cereals, hops, apples, and sugar beet. Area: 480 sq mi (1240 sq km). Population (1970): 78,916. Chief town: Maribo.

Lollards The followers of the English reformer *Wycliffe. Until his retirement from Oxford in 1378, the preaching of his doctrines attacking the Church hierarchy and transubstantiation and advocating the primacy of Scripture was largely confined to the University. Thereafter his teachings were taken up by nonacademics, including merchants, lesser clergy, and a few members of Richard II's court. Henry IV's reign saw considerable repression of the Lollards culminating in the defeat of *Oldcastle's rebellion in 1414. The movement then went underground and became increasingly proletarian. Many of its tenets were adopted by the early Protestants.

Lomax, Alan (1915–   ) US compiler of folk songs. With his father **John Avery Lomax** (1867–1948), He traveled around the country, recording songs that had never been published. He compiled *American Ballads and Folk Songs* (1934), *Negro Folk Songs as Sung by Leadbelly* (1936), and *Our Singing Country* (1941).

Lombard League A confederacy of Lombard towns formed with papal support in 1167 against attempts by the Holy Roman Empire to weaken their communal liberties. These were confirmed by Frederick (I) Barbarossa at the Peace of Constance (1183). Renewed against the threat of Frederick II the League was disbanded after his death (1250).

Lombardo, Pietro (c. 1438–1515) Italian sculptor and architect. Lombardo worked mainly in Venice, where he was the leading sculptor of his generation. His works include the Pietro Mocenigo monument (c. 1476–81; SS Giovanni e Paolo) and the design and sculptural decoration of Sta Maria dei Miracoli (1481–89). He was frequently assisted by his two sons **Antonio Lombardo** (c. 1458–c. 1516) and **Tullio Lombardo** (c. 1460–1532).

Lombards (Latin name: Langobardi) A Germanic people who, under *Alboin, invaded Italy and established a kingdom centered on Pavia (572 AD). When *Aistulf and then Desiderius (reigned 756–74) threatened Rome, the pope sought Carolingian assistance and in 773–74 the Lombards lost their independence to Charlemagne.

Lombardy (Italian name: Lombardia) A region in N Italy, consisting mainly of mountains in the N and lowlands in the S. Italy's most industrialized region, its economic prosperity has attracted large numbers of immigrants from other parts of the country. The industrial area containing Milan is dominated by textile, chemical, and engineering industries; metal manufacture is also important. Agriculture is highly productive and the most mechanized in Italy, producing a wide range of foods. There are important natural-gas fields and hydroelectric plants. Area: 9191 sq mi (23,834 sq km). Population (1991): 8,940,594. Capital: Milan.

Lombok An Indonesian island in the Nusa Tenggara group. The N and S are mountainous, while on the central fertile plain intensive cultivation produces rice, coffee, and tobacco. Under Hindu-Buddhist rule until the 15th century, it resisted later Islamic influence and came under Dutch control in 1894. Area: 1826 sq mi (4730 sq km). Chief town: Mataram.

Lombroso, Cesare (1835–1909) Italian criminologist. His theories that some criminals are born as such and can be recognized by physical characteristics are no longer considered valid, but his major work, *L'uomo delinquente* (1876), initiated a new emphasis in criminology on the study of the criminal mind.

Lomé 6 10N 1 21E The capital and chief port of Togo, on the Gulf of Guinea. The Lomé Convention was signed here in 1975 between 46 African and Caribbean states providing for trade concessions into the EEC countries. It has a university (1970). Population (1983 est): 366,500.

Lomond, Loch The largest lake in Scotland, in E Strathclyde Region. It is a popular tourist area with picturesque scenery. Length: about 24 mi (38 km). Width: 5 mi (8 km).

Lomonosov, Mikhail Vasilievich (1711–65) Russian poet and scientist. The son of a fisherman, he did innovative work in the natural sciences and became a professor at the St Petersburg Academy. In 1755 he founded Moscow University. He also wrote classical poetry and works on grammar and rhetoric.

LONDON *Big Ben and the statue of Queen Boadicea, who sacked the city.*

London (Latin name: Londinium) 51 30N 0 10W The capital of the UK, in SE England on the River Thames.

London's financial hub is to be found in its original nucleus, the **City of London,** on the N bank of the Thames, with an area of 1 sq mi (2.6 sq km). London's **East End,** has long provided a home for successive immigrant groups and acquired in the 19th century a reputation for harboring criminals. The **West End** comprises the district around Oxford Street and is the city's shopping and entertainment center.

London's **cultural life** is outstanding. There are remarkable art collections housed in the *National Gallery, the National Portrait Gallery, the *Tate Gallery, and the *Courtauld Institute. Its museums include the *British Museum, the *Victoria and Albert Museum, and the *Imperial War Museum. Most of London's commercial theaters are in the West End.

Many industries have now moved from central London to the suburbs but a wide variety of light industries, including clothing, precision instruments, and printing and publishing, remain. Activities are often localized: for example, the newspaper industry is centered on Fleet Street, and Harley Street is synonymous with doctors.

History: the foundations of London Wall are the chief reminder of the City's origins under the Romans, who built London at the highest point at which the Thames could be forded and at the river's tidal limit. It was sacked by Boadicea in 61 AD and subsequently, on several occasions, by the Vikings. During the reign of William the Conqueror the famous White Tower (*see* Tower of London) was built, and as London prospered in the Middle Ages both the Church and the *guilds sponsored exceptional building programs. □Westminster Abbey dates from the 11th century. The early Stuart period witnessed the great work of Inigo Jones, notably the Queen's House and the Banqueting Hall (1619–22), its ceiling painted by Rubens. London's population was decimated by the Plague (1665) and much of the city's fabric was destroyed in the calamitous Fire of the following year. The greatest loss—Old St Paul's (□St Paul's Cathedral)—was replaced by Wren, who was responsible for much of the work of reconstruction. Many of London's finest squares were built in the late 17th and early 18th centuries. The 19th century produced the Palace of Westminster, the Law Courts, and the Byzantine-style Westminster Cathedral. London, especially the City and the East End, was seriously damaged by bomb attacks during World War II and subsequent rebuilding has consisted largely of high-rise offices and apartments. Area: 610 sq mi (1580 sq km). Population (1991): 6,377,900.

London 42 58N 81 15W A city in central Canada, in Ontario. Founded in 1826, it has become SW Ontario's center for transportation, manufacturing, finance, and education. London's industries include textiles, printing, food processing, chemicals, electrical and metal goods, motor vehicle parts, and engines. It houses the University of Western Ontario (1878). Population (1991): 303,165.

London, Jack (1876–1916) US novelist. After childhood poverty and imprisonment for vagrancy he embarked on a course of self-education from which he emerged as a committed socialist and best-selling author. *The Sea Wolf* (1904) grew out of his life aboard a sealing ship at 17. His best-known novels, *The Call of the Wild* (1903) and *White Fang* (1906), and many short stories were written after his experience of the Klondike gold rush in 1897. His other novels include *The Iron Heel* (1907) and the autobiographical *Martin Eden* (1909).

London Bridge A bridge spanning the River Thames from the SE region of the City of London to the borough of Southwark. Bridges on this site date back to Roman times but the most famous London Bridge was built in stone between 1176 and 1209. It was replaced by a new bridge in the 1820s. The present bridge was completed in 1973.

Londonderry (*or* Derry) 55 00N 7 19W A city and port in Northern Ireland, the county town of Co Londonderry on the River Foyle. The City of London Corporation was granted Londonderry and the Irish Society established (1610) to administer it. In a famous siege (1688–89) it held out for 105 days against the forces of James II. Industries include shirt manufacture, light engineering, and food processing. Population: 51,850.

Londonderry (*or* Derry) A historic county in N Northern Ireland, bordering on the Atlantic Ocean. It consists of central uplands bordered by lowlands with Low Neagh in the SE. It is drained by the Foyle, Bann, and Roe Rivers. Londonderry is predominantly agricultural producing flax, cereals, and dairy produce. Fishing is also an important source of income. Industries include textiles, chemicals, and light engineering. Area: 814 sq mi (2108 sq km). County town: Londonderry.

London Economic Conference (1933) A meeting of the US and League of Nations members in London to discuss financial and economic stability. Also known as the World Monetary and Economic Conference, it aimed at finding ways to equalize the international economy during the Depression, but failed because of disagreement over returning to the gold standard.

London Naval Conference (1930) A meeting of the US, UK, Japan, France, and Italy in London to discuss limitation of warships. The US, UK, and Japan were able to come to agreements regarding the number of submarines and construction of ships, but France and Italy did not agree and did not sign the treaty.

London pride A succulent herb, *Saxifraga umbrosa*, also called St Patrick's cabbage, native to Ireland and Portugal and widely grown as an ornamental. It has a basal rosette of fleshy leaves with wavy edges and small white or pinkish five-petaled flowers in branching clusters on slender stems, 12–20 in (30–50 cm) tall. The garden form is a hybrid, *S. × urbium.* Family: *Saxifragacea.*

Londrina 23 18S 51 13W A city in S Brazil, in Paraná state. Founded in 1930, it is the center of a coffee-growing area and has a university (1971). Population (1980 est): 258,000.

Long, Huey (Pierce) (1893–1935) US politician; nicknamed the "Kingfish." He was elected governor of Louisiana in 1928 and worked to revamp the state public works and welfare programs. He alienated the wealthy by financing his programs with new taxation. As a US senator (1932–35) he continued to run his state by making sure his supporters were in official positions. He proposed a national "Share-the-Wealth" program that would have limited the income of the rich and guaranteed an income and housing for the poor. He was assassinated by the relative of a long-time enemy.

Long Beach 33 47N 118 06W A city and port in California, on San Pedro Bay. It is a major tourist center, with a beach 8.5 mi (13.5 km) long. Other attractions include the former British liner *Queen Mary*, which has been converted into a hotel and conference center. Industries include the manufacture of aircraft and oil refining. Population (1990): 429,433.

longbow A bow of straight-grained yew used from about 1400 to about 1600. Originally Welsh, longbows were up to 6 ft (1.8 m) long and could fire a 37 in (110 cm) arrow capable of piercing chainmail and some plate armor at 200 yd (183 m) every 10 seconds.

Longfellow, Henry Wadsworth (1807–82) US poet. He traveled extensively in Europe and was professor of modern languages at Harvard (1834–54). He achieved enormous popularity with such narrative poems as *Evangeline* (1847), *The Song of Hiawatha* (1855), *The Courtship of Miles Standish* (1858), and *Paul Revere's Ride* (1861). He also produced an undistinguished translation of Dante's *Divine Comedy* (1865–67).

Longford (Irish name: Longphort) A county in the N central Republic of Ireland, in Leinster. Chiefly low-lying with areas of bog, it contains part of Low Ree in the SW. Agriculture consists of cattle and sheep rearing and the production of oats and potatoes. Area: 403 sq mi (1043 sq km). Population (1991): 30,293. County town: Longford.

Longhi, Pietro (Pietro Falca; 1702–85) Venetian painter, who specialized in historically interesting scenes of upper-class life. Small in scale, they are distinguished by their doll-like figures and humorous approach, notably in *Exhibition of a Rhinoceros* (National Gallery, London). His son **Alessandro Longhi** (1733–1813) was a portrait painter.

Longinus (1st century AD) Greek rhetorician, supposed author of *On the Sublime.* This treatise, a critical analysis of the quality of excellence in literature with illustrative quotations from numerous Greek writers, greatly influenced many later neoclassical writers, including Dryden, Pope, and Gibbon; it was first translated (1674) into a modern language by the French critic Boileau.

Long Island An island in New York state, separated from the mainland by Long Island Sound. Chiefly residential with many resorts, it contains the New York City boroughs of *Brooklyn and *Queens and the international John F. Kennedy Airport. Aircraft industries have long been a mainstay of the economy. Area: 1723 sq mi (4462 sq km).

longitude. *See* latitude and longitude.

long jump A field event in athletics. Competitors sprint up a runway and leap as far as possible into a sandpit from a take-off board. The competitor who makes the longest jump in three or six tries is the winner.

Long March (1934–35) The flight of the Chinese communists from the *Jiangxi Soviet, which they were forced by the *Guomindang to abandon, to Yan'an, a distance of 6000 mi (10,000 km). Over 100,000 people, led by Mao Tse-tung, took part in the heroic march but only about 30,000 reached Yan'an. The Long March established Mao as the leader of the Chinese Communist party.

LONG MARCH *Survivors of the Chinese communist flight from Jiangxi attend a rally in Yan'an.*

Long Parliament (1640–60) The Parliament that was summoned by Charles I of England following his defeat in the second *Bishop's War. In 1641 it expressed its grievances against Charles in the *Grand Remonstrance, and in 1642 it assumed control of the militia. Charles's rejection of its demands for reform (Nineteen Propositions) precipitated the outbreak of the Civil War. Its power declined as that of the *New Model Army increased, and in 1648 it was purged of its moderate members. The remaining Rump Parliament was dismissed in 1653 by Oliver □Cromwell, who established the *Protectorate. The Rump was reinstated in 1659 and the full membership of the Long Parliament was restored in 1660. Shortly afterward it dissolved itself, being replaced by the Convention Parliament, which effected the *Restoration.

longship A large sailing vessel equipped with a bank of oars on each side for use when there was no wind or when it blew adversely. Longships were used by Scandinavian maritime peoples until the mid-18th century. They had square sails and very high prows and were steered by a long tiller attached to a large rudder. Larger longships could carry about a hundred people and are said to have carried the Vikings from Scandinavia as far as Greenland and to the coast of North America.

Longstreet, James (1821–1904) US Confederate general. After graduating from West Point he served during the *Mexican War. At the outset of the Civil War he resigned from the army to join the Confederates at the first Battle of *Bull Run (1861). By 1862 he had partial command of the Army of Northern Virginia and fought at Bull Run, Antietam, and Fredericksburg. As a lieutenant general he commanded troops at Gettysburg (1863), Chickamauga (1863), Knoxville (1863), and the Battle of the Wilderness (1864) where he was wounded. After the war he became a Republican and served as minister to Turkey (1880–81).

long-tailed tit An acrobatic Eurasian tit, *Aegithalus caudatus*, about 6 in (14 cm) long, with a black, pink, and white plumage and a long (3 in; 7 cm) black-and-white tail. It feeds chiefly on insects and spiders and builds an elaborate domed nest from lichens, animal hair, cobwebs, and feathers.

loofah The fibrous skeleton of the fruit of the tropical dishcloth gourd, or vegetable sponge (genus *Luffa* (6 species), especially *L. cylindrica*). These vines produce cucumber-like straw-colored fruits, about 12 in (30 cm) long. When mature, the pulp and seeds are removed leaving a dense network of fibrous conducting tissue, which is used as a bath sponge, dish washer, and industrial filter. Family: *Cucurbitaceae*.

Lookout Mountain, Battle of (1863) Civil War battle in S Tennessee, part of the Chattanooga Campaign. Lookout Mountain, a ridge near Chattanooga, was held by the Confederate Army. Union troops, under Gen. Joseph *Hooker, advancing on Chattanooga, scaled the ridge under cloud-cover (from which the conflict's nickname of Battle Above the Clouds) and overwhelmed the weakened Confederates.

looper. *See* geometrid moth.

Loos, Adolph (1870–1933) Austrian architect. One of the pioneers of modern architecture, Loos was influenced by the styles of Otto *Wagner and Louis *Sullivan. His austere plain style, evident in the Steiner House, Vienna (1910), influenced *Gropius and the development of *functionalism. Later in his career, however, he became less dogmatic, designing buildings with classical motifs.

loosestrife Either of two perennial herbs occurring in marshes, ditches, and along river banks. Purple loosestrife, *Lythrum salicaria* (family *Lythraceae*), native to Eurasia, N Africa, and North America, grows to a height of 24–47 in (60–120 cm) and bears spikes of purple flowers. The Eurasian yellow loosestrife, *Lysimachia vulgaris* (family *Primulaceae*), grows to a height of 40 in (1 m) and forms branching terminal clusters of yellow flowers.

Lope de Vega. *See* Vega (Carpio), Lope Félix de.

López, Carlos Antonio (?1790–1862) Paraguayan statesman. As president (1844–62) he attempted to modernize the country and to end its isolation. He was succeeded by his son **Francisco Solano López** (1826–70), who led Paraguay into the disastrous War of the *Triple Alliance.

Lopez, Nancy (Marie) (1957–) US golfer. She began to play professional golf in 1977 and, in 1978, won nine tournaments, was named Player of the Year, and had total winnings of almost $190,000. She was again named Player of the Year in 1979 and was the leading money winner that year and in 1985.

López de Ayala, Pero (c. 1332–c. 1407) Spanish poet and chronicler, who became chancellor of Castile in 1399. His works include translations of Livy,

Boethius, and Boccaccio, as well as *Rimado de palacio*, a collection of satirical poetry, and *Crónicas de los reyes de Castilla.*

Lop Nor An area of salt marsh and shallow shifting lakes in NW China, in the *Tarim Basin. Nuclear tests have been carried out here. Formerly a large salt lake, its area now varies widely.

loquat A small evergreen tree *Eriobotrya japonica*, native to China and Japan but widely cultivated in Mediterranean countries; 20–30 ft (6–9 m) high, it bears fragrant white flowers in dense terminal clusters. The yellow or orange fruit is pear-shaped with a woolly skin; it is eaten fresh, in preserves, or in stews. Family: *Rosaceae.*

Lorca, Federico Garcia. *See* Garcia Lorca, Federico.

Lord Dunmore's War (1774) A conflict between Virginia colonials and the Shawnee Indians over lands in Kentucky and W Pennsylvania. John Murray, Earl of Dunmore and royal governor of Virginia, ordered the militia, under Andrew Lewis, to attack the hostile Indians. The battle at Point Pleasant was won by the militia, and by the Treaty of Camp Charlotte that followed the Indians gave up their hunting grounds.

Lords, House of. *See* Parliament.

Lorelei A rock in the Rhine River in western Germany noted for its echo and its association with a legend concerning a water nymph whose singing lured sailors to destruction. The legend first appears in the works of Clemens *Brentano.

Loren, Sophia (S. Scicoloni; 1934–   ) Italian film actress. From working as an extra and then as a supporting actress, she progressed to international stardom in such films as *Two Women* (for which she won an Academy Award in 1961), *The Millionairess* (1961), *Marriage Italian Style* (1964), *The Cassandra Crossing* (1977), and *Firepower* (1979). She married the Italian film producer Carlo Ponti in 1957.

Lorentz, Hendrick Antoon (1853–1928) Dutch physicist, who was awarded the Nobel Prize (1902), with his pupil *Zeeman, for their work on the relationship between magnetism and radiation. Independently of *Fitzgerald, he suggested that bodies become shorter as their velocity increases, in order to explain the negative result of the *Michelson-Morley experiment. This phenomenon, now known as the **Lorentz-Fitzgerald** contraction, was later incorporated into Einstein's theory of *relativity. The mathematical treatment for transforming a set of coordinates from one frame of reference to another was worked out by Lorentz (**Lorentz transformations**) and also formed part of Einstein's theory of relativity.

Lorenz, Konrad (1903–89) Austrian zoologist, who was one of the founders of modern ethology (the study of animal behavior). In the 1930s Lorenz identified the phenomenon of *imprinting in young chicks. He was concerned with determining the elements of behavior, how they were stimulated, their development in an individual, and their evolutionary significance. Lorenz has written several popular books about his work, including *King Solomon's Ring* (1949) and *Man Meets Dog* (1950). He has applied his theories of animal behavior to the human species, with controversial implications (*On Aggression*, 1963). He was awarded a Nobel Prize (1973) with Karl von *Frisch and Niko *Tinbergen.

Lorenzetti Two brothers, both Italian painters of the Sienese school, who were influenced by Giovanni *Pisano and *Giotto. They probably both died in the plague of 1348. **Pietro Lorenzetti** (c. 1280–1348?) was probably the pupil of *Duccio; he introduced a new humanity into his master's style in such works as *The Birth of the Virgin* (Duomo, Siena). His brother **Ambrogio Lorenzetti** (c. 1290–1348?) is renowned for his frescoes of *Good and Bad Government* (1337–39; Palazzo Pubblico, Siena). They are among the first Italian paintings to show scenes of contemporary life and are remarkable for their early mastery of perspective.

KONRAD LORENZ *A pioneer of the science of ethology (the behavior of animals in their natural surroundings). Lorenz is pictured here in 1973, the year he received a Nobel Prize.*

Lorenzo Monaco (Piero di Giovanni; c. 1370–1425) Italian painter, born in Siena. He settled in Florence, becoming a monk in 1391. Influenced by both the Sienese school and the Florentine tradition of *Giotto, his *Coronation of the Virgin* (Uffizi) is his major work.

Lorestan. *See* Luristan.

Loreto 43 26N 13 36E A small town in central Italy, in Marche. Pilgrims travel here to see the Santa Casa (Holy House), which is said to have been the home of the Virgin Mary in Nazareth and to have been brought to Loreto by angels in the 13th century.

Lorient 47 45N 3 21W A port in NW France, in the Morbihan department on the Bay of Biscay. Formerly the principal naval shipyard in France, it was badly destroyed in World War II. Today it has an important fishing industry and manufactures car components. Population (1983): 104,000.

loris A nocturnal Asian *prosimian primate belonging to the subfamily *Lorisine* (5 species). Lorises are 8–14 in (20–35 cm) long with almost no tail and very large dark eyes. They are generally slow-moving and arboreal, feeding on insects and fruit. Family: *Lorisidae*. *See also* angwantibo; potto.

Lorrain, Claude. *See* Claude Lorrain.

Lorraine (German name: Lothringen) A planning region and former province in NE France, bordering on Belgium, Luxembourg, and Germany. Its valuable iron-ore deposits are the largest in Europe outside Sweden and Russia. *History*: it was frequently the scene of conflict between France and Germany. In the 9th century AD it formed part of the kingdom of Lotharingia, later becoming a duchy under the Holy Roman Empire. Disputed between France and the Hapsburgs, it was finally incorporated into France, as a province, in 1766. Following the Franco-Prussian War (1871) part of Lorraine (now Moselle department) was lost to Germany and united with *Alsace to form the imperial territory of Alsace-Lorraine. Area: 9087 sq mi (23,540 sq km). Population (1991 est): 2,304,000.

Lorraine, Charles, Cardinal de. *See* Guise.

lory A small brightly colored *parrot belonging to the subfamily *Loriinae* (62 species), occurring in Australia, New Guinea, and Polynesia. Lories have a slender bill with a brush-tipped tongue and feed on pollen and nectar, particularly that of gum trees.

Los Alamos 28 54N 103 00W A city in New Mexico. Chosen by the US government (1942) for atomic research, the first atom bombs were made here during World War II. The H-bomb was later developed here by the scientific laboratory of the University of California, which now covers an area of 77 sq mi (199 sq km). Government control of Los Alamos ended in 1962. Population (1990): 18,115.

Los Angeles 34 00N 118 15W A city and seaport in S California on the Pacific coast. Founded in 1781 by Franciscan missionaries, it was made the capital of Mexican California in 1845 but was captured by US forces in the following year. Over the years it has incorporated many neighboring towns so that today it comprises a large industrial and urban complex, with the third largest population in the US. It is the center of the US film industry, which attracts many tourists to the city, and more recently several television studios have been established here. Other major industries include the manufacture of aircraft and oil refining. Industrial pollution, augmented by the high density of cars (Los Angeles is the only major US city without a comprehensive public system of transport), is a serious problem. An educational center, it is the site of several universities. In 1992 severe rioting in the wake of the acquittal of police officers in the beating of an African-American motorist left more than 50 dead. In 1994 the Los Angeles area was rocked by a major earthquake. Population (1990): 3,485,398.

Lost Generation A term applied to the expatriate US writers of the 1920s including Ernest *Hemingway, F. Scott *Fitzgerald, Henry *Miller, John *Dos Passos, and Ezra *Pound, whose works expressed their sense of spiritual alienation. The term derives from a remark attributed to Gertrude Stein and used as an epigraph to Hemingway's novel *The Sun Also Rises* (1926).

Lot River A river in S France, flowing mainly W through the departments of Lozère, Aveyron, Lot, and Lot-et-Garonne to the Garonne River. Length: 300 mi (483 km).

Lothair (c. 835–69 AD) King (855–69) of an area W of the Rhine, inherited from his father Lothair I, that came to be called Lotharingia. His attempts to divorce his childless wife Theutberga developed into a struggle with Pope Nicholas I.

Lothair I (795–855 AD) Coemperor of the West; eldest son of *Louis (I) the Pious, whose coemperor he became in 817. On Louis's death in 840 Lothair's position was challenged by his brothers Louis the German (d. 876) and Charles the Bald and in 843 the Frankish territories were divided between them.

Lothair II (1075–1137) Holy Roman Emperor (1133–37) and, as Lothair III, German king (1125–37). He became Duke of Saxony in 1106 in return for supporting Emperor Henry V against his father in 1104 but subsequently turned against Henry, defeating him at the battle of Welfesholz (1115). The Hohenstaufen family contested his election as king until 1135. As emperor, he tried to expel Roger II of Sicily from Italy.

Loti, Pierre (Julien Viaud; 1850–1923) French novelist. He served as a naval officer and wrote numerous novels of romance and adventure with exotic settings and several travel books. His best-known novels include three studies of Breton sailors, *Mon frère Yves* (1883), *Pêcheur d'Islande* (1886), and *Matelot* (1893).

Lotto, Lorenzo (c. 1480–1556) Venetian painter. He traveled extensively in Italy and his work is consequently marked by a number of influences; he frequently visited Venice but, unable to compete with Titian's success, worked chiefly in Bergamo. He is noted for his altarpieces, e.g. the *Crucifixion* (Monte San Giusto, Bergamo), and the psychological insight of such portraits as *A Young Man* (Kunsthistorisches Museum, Vienna), and *Andrea Odoni* (Hampton Court). He spent his last years in a monastery in Loreto.

lotus Any of several different water plants. The sacred lotus of ancient Egypt was probably *Nymphaea iotus*, a sweet-scented white night-flowering *water lily with broad petals, or *N. caerulea*, a blue-flowered species. The sacred Indian lotus, *Nelumbo nucifera* (family *Nelumbaceae*), has roselike pink flowers and its seeds, called lotus nuts, are eaten raw or in soups. The genus *Lotus* contains about 70 species of herbs, including the birdsfoot *trefoils.

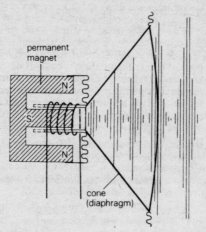

LOUDSPEAKER *A moving-coil loudspeaker with a pot-shaped permanent magnet.*

loudspeaker A device for converting electrical signals into sound. It usually consists of a small coil fixed to the center of a movable diaphragm or cone. The coil is in an annular gap between the poles of a strong *magnet. An audio-frequency electrical signal fed to the coil creates a varying magnetic field, which interacts with the steady field in the gap. This causes the coil, and the attached cone, to vibrate and produce sound waves of the same frequencies as the electrical signal. Generally, larger cones give a better response at low frequencies and the smaller cones are best at high frequencies; for the best results two or more different-sized cones are therefore used, either in the same or in separate cabinets. The loudspeaker cabinet is also an important part of the system since it can act as a sound baffle and improve the frequency response.

Louis (I) the Pious (778–840 AD) Emperor of the West (813–40); son of Charlemagne. He fostered Christianity but imperial unity was undermined by his rebellious sons and after his death the Empire was partitioned.

Louis (I) the Great (1326–82) King of Hungary (1342–82) and Poland (1370–82). Louis encouraged commerce and the arts and in 1367 he founded Hungary's first university at Pécs. His campaigns against Venice had brought Hungary most of Dalmatia by 1381.

Louis II (1845–86) King of Bavaria (1864–86) renowned for his extravagant castles, especially Neuschwanstein, and patronage of the composer Richard Wagner. His hopes for Bavaria in the newly founded German empire (1871) were disappointed and he subsequently withdrew from politics. In 1886 he was pronounced mad and shortly afterward drowned himself.

Louis (IV) the Bavarian (?1283–1347) German king and Holy Roman Emperor (1314–47; crowned 1328). In 1324 Pope John XXII excommunicated Louis in support of Frederick III of Austria (c. 1286–1330), who contested the German throne. Louis deposed John in 1327 and in 1328 was crowned emperor by the antipope Nicholas V. From 1294 Louis was Duke of Bavaria, for which he devised a legal code (c. 1335).

Louis (V) le Fainéant (967–87AD) The last Carolingian King of France (986–87), whose frivolity (his nickname means "feckless") helped to discredit the dynasty, bringing the Capetian *Hugh Capet to power.

Louis (VII) le Jeune (c. 1120–80) King of France (1137–80). He was engaged in a bitter struggle with Henry II of England between 1152, when Henry acquired Aquitaine through his marriage to Louis's former wife *Eleanor of Aquitaine, until 1174.

Louis VIII (1187–1226) King of France (1223–26), known as the Lionheart. He was offered the English throne by King John's baronial opponents but his invasion of England was defeated in 1217. He gained Toulouse and Languedoc for the French crown and in 1226 launched a crusade against the *Albigensians.

Louis IX, St (1214–70) King of France (1226–70), regarded as the model medieval Christian king. After defeating Henry III of England (1242) he set out as leader of the sixth *Crusade (1248), during which he was captured by the Egyptians. On his return to France he introduced administrative reforms and fostered learning and the arts. He died on a Crusade in Tunisia and was canonized in 1297.

Louis XI (1423–83) King of France (1461–83), who united most of France under his rule. In 1447 his father, Charles VII, exiled him to Dauphiné for his part in a conspiracy. After becoming king Louis overcame the aristocratic opposition of the League of the Public Weal (1465) and in 1477 finally defeated Charles the Bold of Burgundy. He extended royal authority over the church and encouraged commerce, gaining the support of the middle classes.

Louis XII (1462–1515) King of France (1498–1515). His reign was dominated by the wars that his father Charles VIII had initiated in Italy, and Louis suffered major defeats (1511–13) on several fronts at the hands of the Holy League.

Louis XIII (1601–43) King of France (1610–43), whose reign was dominated by his chief minister Cardinal de *Richelieu. He was the son of the assassinated Henry IV and of *Marie de' Medici, who was regent during his minority. In 1617 he exiled Marie from court and she raised two revolts against him but mother and son were later reconciled by Richelieu, her adviser, who in 1624 became Louis's chief minister. The king defeated two *Huguenot uprisings (1622, 1628), taking their fortress of La Rochelle in 1628.

LOUIS XIV *The Sun King portrayed in all his glory.*

Louis XIV (1638–1715) King of France (1643–1715), known as the Sun King because of the splendor of his reign. His minority was dominated by Cardinal *Mazarin, after whose death in 1661 Louis allowed no single minister to dominate. He was ably served by such men as *Colbert, who revived French trade, industry, and agriculture, and *Louvois, who with his father made France's army the best in Europe, but insisted that *L'état c'est moi* ("I am the state"). He was a firm advocate of the *divine right of kings and subdued the aristocrats, whose rebellion known as the *Fronde had threatened the crown during his minority, by providing diversions at his great palaces—outstandingly *Versailles. His patronage of artists, including the writers Molière and Racine, further enhanced the magnificence of his court. In 1660 he married Maria Theresa (1638–83), the daughter of Philip IV of Spain (1605–65; reigned 1621–65). His mistresses included Mme de *Montespan and then Mme de *Maintenon, whom he secretly married after Maria Theresa's death. Abroad, France became the dominant power in Europe during Louis's reign. His ambitions in the Spanish Netherlands sparked off the War of *Devolution (1667–68) and were renewed by a second invasion in 1672. From this, the third *Dutch War, France emerged (1678) at the pinnacle of its power, a position Louis was unable to retain through the subsequent Wars of the *Grand Alliance (1689–97) and *Spanish Succession (1701–14). France was further weakened by Louis's revocation (1685) of the Edict of Nantes, ending toleration of Protestants and driving many of France's most productive citizens into exile. He left a country weakened by the economic demands of his wars and a monarchy that was to prove unequal to the enormous demands placed on it by his personal rule. His reign was nevertheless one of incomparable brilliance.

The **Louis Quartorze style** of late 17th century interior design was developed in a deliberate attempt by Louis XIV and his designers to establish a French national idiom. The formal baroque furniture made in the new royal workshops derived from Italian antiquity and was sumptuously gilded or veneered for such regal settings as *Versailles. The most resplendent items were made of cast silver.

Louis XV (1710–74) King of France (1715–74), whose weak rule discredited the crown and contributed to the outbreak of the French Revolution of 1789. His early reign was dominated by *Fleury, after whose death in 1744 Louis's indecisiveness and the influence of his mistresses, especially Mme de *Pompadour and, later, Mme *Du Barry, fostered faction and intrigue. The loss of almost all France's colonies in the *Seven Years' War (1756–63) increased his unpopularity, which hasty judicial and financial reforms at the end of his reign did nothing to alleviate.

The **Louis Quinze style** of French interior decoration and furnishing lasted from about 1723 until Louis's death. A sophisticated and informal style, it was a reaction to the formal baroque pomp of Louis XIV's court. The rococo, with its lighthearted use of eccentric scrolls, replaced symmetrical antique and Renaissance motifs. Chairs, formerly ranged around the walls of large rooms, were designed and arranged for ease of conversation in the new, smaller, and more intimate rooms.

Louis XVI (1754–93) King of France (1774–93), who was guillotined during the *French Revolution. The opposition of Louis's wife *Marie Antoinette and the aristocracy thwarted the attempted reforms of his ministers *Turgot and *Necker. The consequent economic crisis forced the king to summon (1789) the States General; the disaffected Third Estate of which precipitated revolution. The royal family was confined to the Tuileries Palace from which they attempted to flee in 1791, reaching Varennes. Brought back to the Tuileries, Louis was deposed after it had been stormed by the Paris mob. In 1793 he was guillotined and was followed to the scaffold by his wife.

The **Louis Seize style**, a neoclassical French style of furnishing, came into fashion after Louis XVI's accession. It was characterized by rejection of the rococo with straight lines replacing curves and a continuing tendency toward lightness and utility. The predominant idiom was restrained classicism (key patterns, caryatids, garlands, trophies). After the French Revolution (1789–99) this style remained in vogue for some time.

Louis XVII (1785–95) King of France in name (1793–95) following the execution of his father Louis XVI during the French Revolution. He died in prison.

Louis XVIII (1755–1824) King of France, in name from 1795, following the death in prison of his nephew *Louis XVII, and in fact from 1814, following the overthrow of Napoleon. He fled Paris when Napoleon returned from Elba, being restored with diminished prestige after Waterloo "in the baggage train of the allied armies." His attempts to be a moderate constitutional monarch were thwarted by the ultraroyalists.

Louis, Joe (Joseph Louis Barrow; 1914–81) US boxer, called the Brown Bomber, who was world heavyweight champion from 1937 to 1948, when he retired. He defended his title 25 times and has been regarded as the world's greatest boxer.

Louisiana A state on the Gulf of Mexico in the S central US. Mississippi lies to the E, with the Mississippi River forming about half the boundary between the two states. The Gulf of Mexico forms its S shore. Texas lies to the W and Arkansas to the N. Chiefly low lying, Louisiana is crossed by the Mississippi River, the delta of which dominates the coastal lowlands in the S. The bayous, shallow, swampy rivers, and languid steamy atmosphere of the Mississippi delta lend a distinctive flavor to the region. The main upland area in the state is found in the NW along the Red River Valley. The increasingly urban population (60%) lives mainly in the S. The state produces chemicals and petrochemicals, paper, and food products. Oil is exploited throughout the state and there are major deposits of natural gas, sulfur, and salt. New Orleans and Baton Rouge are important ports and tourism is a growing industry. Its favorable climate and fertile soils make it an important agricultural state; the chief products are beef cattle, rice, soybeans, dairy products, sugar cane, and cotton. It is an important cultural region, famous for its jazz music centered on New Orleans. Distinctive ethnic groups include Creoles (descendants of the original French and Spanish settlers) and Cajuns (descendants of French-speaking Acadians who were expelled from Nova Scotia). *History*: although discovered by the Spanish, it was claimed for France and named for Louis XIV in 1682. It was ceded to Spain (1762) but was restored to France (1800). It was acquired by the US as part of the Louisiana Purchase (1803), becoming a state in 1812. It was a supporter of the Confederate cause in the Civil War. Discoveries of oil and natural gas in the 20th century transformed the economy, and since World War II industrial development has increased substantially. Area: 48,523 sq mi (125,675 sq km). Population (1990): 4,219,973. Capital: Baton Rouge.

Louisiana Purchase (1803) The acquisition by the US government of approximately 828,000 sq mi (2,144,250 sq km) of territory between the Mississippi River and the Rocky Mountains. Concerned by the potential threat to the US posed by extensive French possessions in North America, Pres. Thomas *Jefferson dispatched James *Monroe to Paris in 1801 to negotiate with the French government for the purchase of its American territories. As a result of the negotiations, the US agreed to pay approximately $15 million for the sovereign rights to a huge and largely unexplored tract of land, which doubled the size of the US and established US dominance in North America. Its initial exploration was undertaken by the *Lewis and Clark Expedition in 1804–06.

Louisbourg 45 55N 59 58W A town in NE Nova Scotia, Canada, on E Cape Breton Island. Originally the French fort Fort Louisbourg (1720–45), and now a national historic park, the fort was taken by British forces in 1745, returned to France in 1748, and recaptured by the British under Jeffrey Amherst and James Wolfe in 1758, when it was destroyed. Restoration began in 1961.

Louis of Nassau (1538–74) A leader of the *Revolt of the Netherlands against Spain. His opposition to the Spanish led to his exile in 1567 but, after gaining support in Germany and France, he invaded the Netherlands with a Protestant army (1568). The campaign was indecisive and in the second invasion, in 1574, Louis and his younger brother were killed.

Louis Philippe (1773–1850) King of the French (1830–48), the son of the Duke of *Orléans. He supported the *French Revolution until 1793, when he deserted to the Austrians, living abroad until 1814. He joined the liberal opposition to the restored Louis XVIII and came to the throne after the July Revolution had ousted Louis's successor Charles X. Styled King of the French rather than of France and described by Thiers as the Citizen King, Louis Philippe relied on the support of the middle class. His initial moderation turned to repression in the face of the many rebellions against his rule and he abdicated in the Revolution of 1848. He retired to England, dying at Claremont, in Surrey.

Louisville 38 13N 85 48W A city and port in N Kentucky, on the Ohio River. The state's largest city, it has many historical buildings and is the site of the University of Louisville (1798). The American Printing House for the Blind is situated here. Since 1875 the famous Kentucky Derby has been held in Louisville at the Churchill Downs racetrack. Industries include tobacco manufacture, whiskey distilling, milling, and chemicals. Population (1990): 269,063.

Lourdes 43 06N 0 02W A town in SW France, in the Hautes-Pyrénées department situated at the foot of the Pyrenees. It is a major pilgrimage center for the Roman Catholics (*see* Bernadette of Lourdes). Population (1982): 17,700.

Lourenço Marques. *See* Maputo.

louse A wingless □insect parasitic on warm-blooded animals. The sucking lice (order *Anoplura*; 225 species) suck the blood of mammals. They have hairy flattened bodies, 0.01–0.24 in (0.5–6 mm) long, and claws for attachment to the host. The eyes are often reduced or absent. One of the most important species is the human louse (*Pediculus humanus*), of which there are two varieties—the head louse (*P. humanus capitis*) and the body louse (*P. humanus humanus*). Both are transmitted by direct contact and lay their eggs ("nits") on hair or clothing. Body lice are carriers of typhus and related diseases. Biting lice (order *Mallophaga*; 2600 species) resemble sucking lice but have biting mouthparts for feeding on the skin, feathers, etc., of birds—their principal hosts.

Louth (Irish name: Contae Lughbhaidh) The smallest county in the Republic of Ireland, in Leinster bordering on the Irish Sea. It is chiefly low lying. Agriculture is important with cattle rearing and arable farming producing oats and potatoes. Area: 317 sq mi (821 sq km). Population (1991): 90,707. County town: Dundalk.

Louvain (Flemish name: Leuven) 50 53N 04 42E A city in central Belgium. It was a center of the cloth trade in the middle ages and the capital of the duchy of Brabant. It possesses a gothic town hall and a university (1426). Much of the town was destroyed in World War I. Industries include leather and chemicals. Population (1988 est): 84,500.

Louvois, Michel Le Tellier, Marquis de (1641–91) French statesman; minister for war (1666–77). With his father **Michel Le Tellier** (1603–85), war minister (1643–66), he reorganized the French army. Their success was demonstrated by Louis XIV's many military victories. Louvois was the king's chief minister after 1683.

Louvre The national museum of France containing the art collection of the French kings and housed in the former royal palace and Tuileries palace in Paris. It was opened to the public in 1793. Napoleon exhibited his war loot here, of which the celebrated Venus de Milo still remains. Other highlights are Leonardo da Vinci's *Mona Lisa* and a collection of impressionist paintings, housed separately in the Jeu de Paumes in the Tuileries gardens.

lovage A perennial herb, *Ligusticum scoticum*, that grows 6–35 in (15–90 cm) high and has large compound leaves with pairs of divided toothed leaflets and clusters of greenish-white flowers. It is native to Europe and used as a pot herb and salad plant. Family: *Umbelliferae*.

lovebird A small brightly colored *parrot belonging to a genus (*Agapornis*; 9 species) occurring in Africa and Madagascar; 4–6 in (10–16 cm) long, lovebirds typically have a short tail, a red bill, and a prominent eye ring. Lovebirds often feed in large flocks and may damage crops. They are popular cagebirds because they are long-lived, can be taught tricks, and appear to have great affection for each other.

Lovecraft, H(oward) P(hilips) (1890–1937) US novelist and short-story writer. He lived virtually as a recluse and wrote science-fiction stories and tales of macabre fantasy, such as *The Case of Charles Dexter Ward* (1928) and *At the Mountains of Madness* (1931).

love-in-a-mist An annual herb, *Nigella damascena*, also called fennel flower, native to S Europe and grown as an ornamental in temperate regions. It has fern-like leaves and blue or white flowers, 1.6 in (4 cm) across, with many clawed petals surrounded by the leaves. The fruit is a globular head of capsules. Family: *Ranunculaceae*.

Lovelace, Richard (1618–57) English Cavalier poet. During the Civil War, although he was not actively involved, he was committed to and spent nearly all his fortune in the royalist cause, and was twice imprisoned. In prison he wrote one of his best-known poems, "To Althea, from Prison." *Lucasta* (1649) contains most of his best lyrics.

Lovell, Sir Bernard (1913–   ) British astronomer. After working on radar during World War II he became interested in *radio astronomy and supervised the construction of a 250-foot radio telescope at *Jodrell Bank Experimental Station, a part of Manchester University. His books include *The Exploration of Outer Space* (1961) and *Out of the Zenith* (1973).

Low Countries The Netherlands, Belgium, and Luxembourg. The Low Countries originally comprised numerous small states, controlled by major powers. In 1568 the N Protestant states revolted against Spanish rule, becoming the independent United Provinces of the Netherlands (*see* Revolt of the Netherlands). Belgium and Luxembourg gained independence in 1830 and 1867 respectively.

Lowell 42 38N 71 19W A city in NE Massachusetts, at the confluence of the Concord and Merrimack Rivers. Its growth began with the establishment of textile mills here in 1822 and it became one of the most famous textile centers in the US. Population (1990): 103,439.

Lowell, Amy (1874–1925) US poet, and critic and biographer. After meeting Ezra *Pound in London in 1913, she became the leading propagandist for *Imagism. The volume *What's O'Clock* (1925) was awarded a Pulitzer Prize. Her *Collected Poetical Works* was published in 1955. She also wrote criticism including *Six French Poets* (1915) and *Tendencies in Modern Poetry* (1917), and a biography of *John Keats* (1925).

Lowell, Francis Cabot (1775–1817) US industrialist; founder of the first complete textile factory. He observed power looms in England (1810–12) and then established the Boston Manufacturing Company (1812) in Waltham, Mass. His factory was the first in the world to process cotton from beginning to end— from just-harvested cotton to finished material. It was long used as a model for other manufacturers. The city of Lowell, Mass., was named in his honor.

Lowell, James Russell (1819–91) US poet, critic, and diplomat. He published literary criticism, political works, and poetry ranging from the satirical *Fable for Critics* (1848) to the dialect *Biglow Papers* (1848, 1867). He edited the *Atlantic Monthly* (1857–61). He served as minister to Spain (1877–80) and Britain (1880–85).

Lowell, Percival (1855–1916) US astronomer, who first predicted the existence of the planet *Pluto, because of certain irregularities in the orbit of Uranus. Lowell never discovered Pluto despite intense searching and it was not found until 14 years after his death. He also made a detailed study of the "canals" on Mars.

Lowell, Robert (1917–77) US poet. In 1943 he was imprisoned as a conscientious objector. *Life Studies* (1959) marked a change from his complex and allusive early poetry, such as *Lord Weary's Castle* (1946), to a looser, more personal style. His left-wing political involvement during the 1960s is reflected in *For the Union Dead* (1964). He also published free translations, collected in *Imitations* (1962), and verse dramas. His last book was *Day by Day* (1977).

Lower California (Spanish name: Baja California) A peninsula in NW Mexico, between the Gulf of California and the Pacific Ocean. It is chiefly mountainous and arid. Within irrigated areas, especially in the N near the US border, cotton, fruit, vegetables, and vines are grown. There are important mineral deposits; these include copper, silver, and lead. Length: 760 mi (1223 km).

Lower Hutt 41 12S 174 54E A city in New Zealand, in S North Island on Port Nicholson (an inlet of Cook Strait). An important industrial center, it has meat freezing, engineering, and textile industries. Population (1981): 94,700.

Lower Saxony (German name: Niedersachsen) A *Land* in N Germany, bordering on the North Sea and the Netherlands. Formed in 1946 from four former states, it lies on the N German plain, with mountains in the S. It is chiefly agricultural but some minerals are extracted, including oil and iron ore. Area: 18,301 sq mi (47,430 sq km). Population (1991 est): 7,387,000. Capital: Hanover.

lowest common denominator The smallest common multiple of the denominators of two or more fractions. For example, the group $\frac{2}{3}$, $\frac{1}{6}$, $\frac{5}{8}$ have the lowest common denominator 24.

Lowry, L(awrence) S(tephen) (1887–1976) British painter, born in Manchester. He worked as a clerk until his retirement at 65, using his spare time for art lessons and painting. He exhibited regularly in Manchester from the 1920s, when he began his most characteristic works, bleak industrial landscapes and towns dotted with matchstick figures. These first attracted serious attention in the 1940s. A large retrospective exhibition was held in 1976.

Lowry, (Clarence) Malcolm (1909–57) British novelist. His first novel *Ultramarine* (1933), was based on his experience as a deckhand on a voyage to China. After studying at Cambridge he lived in Paris before going to Mexico, the setting of his novel *Under the Volcano* (1947), the semiautobiographical account of the self-destruction of an alcoholic ex-consul. He lived in Canada from 1940 to 1954. Further stories and fragments were published posthumously.

Loyalists. *See* United Empire Loyalists.

Lo-yang. *See* Luoyang.

Lozi A Bantu-speaking people of Zambia, also known as Barotse. They are cereal cultivators on the fertile flood plain of the upper Zambezi, but hunting and animal husbandry are also important. Political authority is vested in a divine king and subordinate queen who rule from separate northern and southern capitals with a council of ministers and regional chiefs drawn from the aristocracy. There is an elaborate system of taxation, centralization, and redistribution of reserves.

LPG. *See* Liquefied Petroleum Gas.

LSD (lysergic acid diethylamide) A drug that, in very small doses, produces hallucinations, altered sensory perception, and a sense of happiness and relaxation or, in some people, fear and anxiety. Long-term use of LSD can cause a schizophrenia-like illness and, if taken by pregnant women, may produce deformities in the developing fetus.

Lualaba River A river in SE Zaïre, the headstream of the Zaïre River. Rising in the Shaba region, it flows N to join the Luvua River and becomes the Zaïre River at the Boyoma Falls. Length: 1100 mi (1800 km).

Luanda 8 58S 13 09E The capital of Angola, a port in the NW on the Atlantic Ocean. Founded by the Portuguese in 1575, it became a center of the slave trade to Brazil. Oil was discovered nearby in 1955 and a refinery was established; main exports include coffee, cotton, diamonds, iron, and salt. The University of Luanda was established in 1963. Population (1990 est): 1,544,000.

Lubbock 33 35N 101 53W A city in NW Texas. Settled by Quakers in 1879, it is an important market center for cotton, grain, cattle, and poultry. Population (1990): 186,206.

Lübeck 53 52N 10 40E A city in N Germany, in Schleswig-Holstein on the Trave estuary. A leading city of the Hanseatic League, it has a cathedral (1173) and city hall (13th–15th centuries), both restored after World War II. Buxtehude lived here (1668–1707) and it is the birthplace of Thomas and Heinrich Mann. Germany's largest Baltic port, its industries include shipbuilding and metal founding. Population (1991 est): 215,000.

Lubitsch, Ernst (1892–1947) US film director, born in Germany. Following the success of *Madame Dubarry* (1919), a historical romance, he went to Hollywood, where he made a series of sophisticated comedies during the 1920s and 1930s. These include *Forbidden Paradise* (1924), *Bluebeard's Eighth Wife* (1938), and *Ninotchka* (1939).

Lublin 51 18N 22 31E A city in E Poland. The Union of *Lublin, between Poland and Lithuania, was signed here in 1569. Notable buildings include the 16th-century cathedral; its university was founded in 1944. It is an important commercial and industrial center; manufactures include farm machinery, motor vehicles, and beer. Population (1992 est): 352,000.

Lublin, Union of (1569) The act that created a Polish-Lithuanian commonwealth. Poland and Lithuania were to share a common monarch and diet (Parliament) but each maintained its own laws, administration, treasury, and army.

Lubumbashi (name until 1966: Elizabethville) 11 30S 27 31E A city in SE Zaïre. Founded in 1910 as a copper-mining settlement, it is the industrial center of an important mining area. It has a cathedral and a campus (1955) of the Université Nationale du Zaïre. Population (1991 est): 739,000.

Lucan (Marcus Annaeus Lucanus; 39–65 AD) Roman poet, nephew of the Stoic philosopher Seneca. He was born in Spain. The *Pharsalia*, his single surviving work, is an epic poem in ten books concerning the civil war between Caesar and Pompey. He committed suicide after the discovery of his involvement in a conspiracy against the emperor Nero.

Lucas, George (1944–   ) US film director, producer, and writer; creator of *Star Wars* (1977). He produced *American Graffiti* (1973) before the science fiction, fairy-tale trilogy including *Star Wars*, *The Empire Strikes Back* (1980), and *Return of the Jedi* (1983). He also produced the trilogy *Raiders of the Lost Ark* (1981), *Indiana Jones and the Temple of Doom* (1984), and *Indiana Jones and the Last Crusade* (1989). His other films include *Willow* (1988).

Lucas, van Leyden (Lucas Hugensz *or* Jacobsz; c. 1494–1533) Northern Renaissance artist. His early paintings include everyday subjects, notably *The Chess Players* (Berlin), but he mainly painted religious works, his masterpiece being the triptych of *The Last Judgment* (Leiden). Best known as an engraver, he was influenced by Dürer, whom he met in Antwerp (1521). He was probably the first to etch on copper rather than iron and to combine *etching with *engraving; his portrait of Emperor Maximilian I (1521) uses these techniques.

Lucca 43 50N 10 30E A city in NW Italy, in Tuscany on the Serchio River. It has Roman remains, an 8th-century church, and a cathedral (11th–15th centuries). Industries include chemicals, engineering, and food processing. It is the birthplace of Puccini. Population (1981): 91,000.

Luce, Henry R(obinson) (1898–1967) US publisher, who was a cofounder of the magazine *Time* (1923), which he edited and published. He founded *Fortune* in 1930, *Life* in 1936, and *Sports Illustrated* in 1954. Over the years he used his position and power to influence US politics. He retired from publishing in 1964. His wife **Clare Booth Luce** (1903–87), a playwright, whom he married in 1935, wrote the satire *Kiss the Boys Goodbye* (1938). She sat in the US House of Representatives (1943–47) and was subsequently ambassador to Italy (1953–56) and Brazil (1959).

lucerne. *See* alfalfa.

Lucerne (German name: Luzern) 47 03N 8 17E A city in central Switzerland, on Lake Lucerne. The Lion of Lucerne, a monument to the Swiss guards who fell in Paris (1792), is a notable feature and Lucerne also has a 17th-century cathedral. It is a major tourist center. Population (1987): 161,000.

Lucerne, Lake (German name: Vierwaldstättersee) A lake in N central Switzerland. It has four arms formed from deep winding glaciated valleys. Area: 44 sq mi (114 sq km).

Lucian (c. 120–c. 180 AD) Greek rhetorician. He was born in Syria and traveled during his early life as a public lecturer in Asia Minor, Greece, Italy, and Gaul (France). He eventually settled in Athens but also held an administrative post in Alexandria. His many lively satirical works attacking contemporary superstitions and religious fanaticism include *Dialogues of the Dead* and *Dialogues of Courtesans.*

Lucifer In Christian tradition, the leader of the angels expelled from heaven for rebelling against God. Known thereafter as Satan (Hebrew: adversary) or the Devil, he presides over the souls condemned to torment in *hell. He is identified with the serpent that tempted Eve (Genesis 3.1–6) and the great red dragon cast out of heaven by Michael (Revelation 12.3–9). The exact nature of Lucifer's sin was much debated; the commonest view is that his sin was pride.

Lucknow 26 50N 80 54E A city in India, the capital of Uttar Pradesh. Capital of the nawabs of Oudh (1775–1856), it has many notable buildings including the Great Imambara (1784), which is a Muslim meeting place, and the British Residency (1800), which was besieged in 1857 during the Indian Mutiny. The University of Lucknow was established here in 1921. An agricultural trading center, its industries include food processing, railroad engineering, and the manufacture of chemicals, carpets, and copper and brass products. Population (1991): 1,592,010.

Lucretia A legendary Roman heroine, wife of Tarquinius Collatinus. After being raped by Sextus, son of Tarquinius Superbus, the Etruscan King of Rome, she committed suicide. Junius Brutus then led a rebellion that expelled the Tarquins and established the Roman Republic.

Lucretius (Titus Lucretius Carus; c. 95–c. 55 BC) Roman philosopher and poet. The biographical records are unreliable, including St Jerome's statements that he became insane but in moments of sanity wrote books that were edited by Cicero and that he committed suicide. His single work, *De rerum natura*, consists of six books that give the most complete exposition of the philosophy of *Epicurus, including his atomic theory of phenomena and the belief that the soul was material (and mortal). His style blends moral intention with poetic sensitivity to the physical world.

Lucullus, Lucius Licinius (died c. 57 BC) Roman general. After service with *Sulla, he successfully conducted the third war against *Mithridates until his troops mutinied and Pompey took command in 67. Lucullus retired to private life and luxury; the splendors of "Lucullan" feasts became proverbial.

Lüda (or Lü-ta) 38 53N 121 37E A port complex in NE China, at the end of the *Liaodong Peninsula. It comprises the two cities **Lüshun** (English name: Port Arthur) and **Dalian** (or Ta-lien; English name: Darien). Industries include shipbuilding, railroad engineering, and fishing. *History*: Lüshun, a major naval base from 1878, was the base of the Russian Pacific fleet during the Russian occupation (1898–1905). The Russians began the construction of the commercial port at Dalian, completed under Japanese occupation (1905–45). Population (1988 est): 2,330,000.

Luddites A group of Nottingham frameworkers, named for their probably mythical leader, Ned Ludd, who destroyed labor-saving machinery in 1811 when the industrial revolution brought unemployment. Luddism, which spread to other parts of industrial England, showed the hostility of the handicraftsmen to the new machines that were taking their livelihood from them. They were severely repressed.

Ludendorff, Erich (1865–1937) German general in World War I. He became chief of staff under *Hindenburg in 1914 and was largely responsible for the German victory at *Tannenberg. After being appointed quartermaster general (1916) Ludendorff exerted considerable political as well as military influence, forcing the resignation of *Bethmann-Hollwegg. He himself resigned after the German defeat and from 1924 to 1928 sat in the Reichstag as a Nazi.

Ludhiana 30 56N 75 52E A city in India, in Punjab. An important grain market, its manufactures include textiles, machinery, and agricultural tools. It is the site of Punjab Agricultural University (1962). Population (1991): 1,012,000.

Ludwigshafen 49 29N 8 27E A city in SW Germany, in Rhineland-Palatinate on the Rhine River. It is a transshipment point and center of the chemical industry. Population (1991 est): 161,000.

Luftwaffe The German air force. The Luftwaffe, which fought in World War I, was reorganized by Göring in the 1930s. In *World War II, countries destined for Nazi invasion were first hit by aerial bombardment (see Blitzkreig) but the Luftwaffe's failure in the battle of Britain was disastrous to German plans to invade Britain.

Lugano 46 01N 8 57E A city in S Switzerland, on Lake Lugano. Noted for the beauty of its scenery, it is a popular tourist center. It is also a center of international finance. Population: 22,280.

Lugansk. *See* Voroshilovgrad.

Luger pistol A German automatic *pistol developed from a Borchard design by George Luger in 1902. The Parabellum 9-mm model was the standard sidearm of the German navy (1904) and army (1908) until 1938.

Lugus One of the principal Celtic gods. In Ireland he was called Lug and was skilled in many fields, being a warrior, poet, musician, craftsman, magician, etc. His Welsh counterpart was Lleu Llaw Gyffes (skillful hand). Many European placenames, notably, Lyon, Laon, and Leiden, derive from his name.

lugworm A burrowing *annelid worm, *Arenicola marina*, of Atlantic shores, also known as the lobworm. Up to 16 in (40 cm) long, lugworms have about 20 segments, with tufts of red gills on all but the last few. They feed on organic material in the mud, leaving casts of egested mud on the surface. Class: *Polychaeta.*

Lu Hsün (*or* Chou Shu-jen; 1881–1936) Chinese writer, famous for his short stories criticizing traditional Chinese thought and government. Among the best known are *The True Story of Ah Q* (1921) and those collected in *Call to Arms* (1923) and *Wandering* (1924–25). Although he never joined the Communist party, the Chinese regard him as a revolutionary hero.

Luik. *See* Liège.

Lukacs, Giorgi (1885–1971) Hungarian Marxist philosopher. Having shown the resemblance between the philosophies of *Hegel and the young *Marx in *History and Class Consciousness* (1923), he disowned the book, which was also condemned by Soviet orthodoxy. For Lukacs, a cultural relativist, the dynamic of all art is the historical movement of its time; in the 20th century this is socialist realism.

Luke, St A New Testament evangelist, traditionally the author of the third Gospel and of the Acts of the Apostles. Although information about him is scarce, he seems to have been a Gentile doctor and to have accompanied *Paul on numerous missions, notably to Greece, Macedonia, and Jerusalem. He is the patron saint of doctors and artists. Feast day: Oct 18.

The Gospel according to St Luke was written in the latter part of the 1st century AD. It was written in idiomatic Greek and with Gentile readers in mind. It contains the most complete account of the life of Jesus. Many historic hymns, such as the *Ave Maria, Magnificat, Benedictus, Gloria in Excelsis*, and *Nunc Dimittis*, are taken from it.

Luleå 65 35N 22 10E A seaport in N Sweden, on the Gulf of Bothnia. Icebound in the winter it exports iron ore from *Gällivare and *Kiruna during the rest of the year. Its university was established in 1971. Population: 66,834.

Lull, Ramón (English name: Raymond Lully; c. 1235–c. 1315) Catalan mystic and poet. After an early secular career, he became a Franciscan and devoted himself to missionary work among the Muslims. His mystical writings foreshadow those of St *Teresa and St *John of the Cross. His important theological work *Ars magna*, was condemned by Pope Gregory XI in 1376 for its attempt to show that the mysteries of faith could be proved by reason. According to tradition, he was stoned to death in N Africa.

Lully, Jean Baptiste (Giovanni Battista Lulli; 1632–87) French composer of Italian birth. The son of a miller, he worked as a scullion in an aristocratic French household but subsequently became composer, violinist, and dancer to Louis XIV. He composed ballets, incidental music to Molière's plays, and operas, being granted a monopoly of operatic production in 1684. He died from gangrene as a result of striking his foot with a pointed stick while conducting.

Luluabourg. *See* Kananga.

lumbago Chronic backache. Almost everybody experiences backache at some time and many biologists regard it as the price man pays for walking upright. More serious backache may be caused by arthritis, a slipped disk, muscle strain, or strained ligaments.

lumbar puncture A procedure in which *cerebrospinal fluid is withdrawn using a hypodermic needle inserted through the spine and into the spinal cord in the region of the lower back. Examination of the fluid assists in the diagnosis of various conditions, for example the presence of blood may indicate a brain hemorrhage.

Lumbini A park and Buddhist shrine in the modern village of Rummindei, in S Nepal. According to legend, the Buddha was born here in about 563 BC.

lumen (lm) The *SI unit of luminous flux equal to the light emitted per second in a cone of one steradian solid angle by a point source of one candela.

Lumière, Auguste (1862–1954) French photographer, who, with his brother **Louis Lumière** (1864–1948), manufactured photographic equipment and made innovations in the techniques of photography, especially in motion pictures. In 1895 they invented the *cinématographe*, which had a camera and projector combined into one. In the same year they used their invention to film and show the first motion picture, *La Sortie des usines lumière*, which was an immediate success. They went on to make a great number of short films, especially comedies. They also greatly improved existing methods of color photography.

luminance The *luminous intensity of a surface in a given direction per unit of orthogonally projected area of that surface. It is measured in candela per square meter.

luminescence The emission of light by a substance for any reason except high temperature. It occurs as a result of the emission of a *photon by an atom of the substance when it decays from an excited state to its ground state. The atom may be excited by absorbing a photon (photoluminescence), colliding with an electron (electroluminescence), etc. If the luminescence stops as soon as the exciting source is removed, it is known as fluorescence; if it persists for longer than 10^{-8} second it is called phosphorescence. The photons emitted may have a different energy (in visible light, a different color) from the absorbed energy. Fluorescent dyes in washing powders make clothes look brighter. Luminous paint is phosphorescent. Other examples of luminescence include triboluminescence, caused by friction, chemiluminescence, caused by chemical reaction. Bioluminescence, which is seen in glow worms, seaweeds, and other organisms, is a form of chemiluminescence. Radioluminescence is caused by radioactive decay.

luminosity The intrinsic brightness of an object, such as a star, equal to the total energy radiated per second from the object. A star's luminosity increases both with surface temperature and with surface area: the hotter and larger a star, the greater its luminosity. Stellar luminosity is related (logarithmically) to absolute *magnitude.

luminous flux The rate of flow of light energy, taking into account the sensitivity of the observer or detector to the different wavelengths. For example, the human eye is most sensitive to the color green. Luminous flux is measured in *lumens.

luminous intensity The amount of light emitted per second by a point source per unit solid angle in a specified direction. It is measured in *candela.

lumpsucker A slow-moving carnivorous *bony fish, also called lumpfish, belonging to the family *Cyciopteridae*, found in cold northern seas. They have a thickset body, sometimes studded with bony tubercles, a cleft dorsal fin, and a ventral sucking disk formed from fused pelvic fins. *Cyclopterus lumpus* is the largest species, reaching 24 in (60 cm) long. The roe is used as a substitute for caviar. Order: *Scorpaeniformes*.

Lumumba, Patrice (Hemery) (1925–61) Congolese statesman; prime minister (1960–61) of the Congo (now Zaïre). Mission-educated, Lumumba was active in labor unionism before entering national politics. He became prime minister of the newly independent Congo under president *Kasavubu in 1960 and opposed the secession of Katanga province under *Tshombe. The following year he was deposed and murdered.

luna moth A large North American saturniid moth, *Actias luna*. It is pale green with a long "tail" on each hindwing, moonlike markings on the forewings, and a wingspan of about 6 in (150 mm). The pale-green larvae feed on trees.

Lund 55 42N 13 10E A town in S Sweden, near Malmö. It has a university (1668) and an 11th-century cathedral. Its varied industries include printing, publishing, and sugar refining. Population (1986): 83,500.

Lunda A group of Central Bantu tribes speaking languages of the Benne-Congo division of the *Niger-Congo family. Historically they were united under a paramount chief but their customs and culture vary considerably. Cultivation, hunting and gathering, and trade are all important economic factors.

Lüneburg 53 15N 10 24E A spa in N Germany, in Lower Saxony. There are many fine medieval buildings. **Lüneburg Heath** was the site of the surrender of German troops to Britain's *Montgomery in 1945 at the end of World War II. Population (1985): 61,000.

lungfish A freshwater *bony fish belonging to the formerly abundant order *Dipnoi*, now reduced to six species including *Lepidosiren paradoxa* of South America, *Protopterus annectens* of Africa, and the Australian *Neoceratodus forsteri*. Up to 7 ft (2 m) long, lungfish have slender bodies, narrow paired fins, and tapering tails. Their swim bladders are modified for breathing air, an adaptation for droughts, when some make burrows in the bottom mud, leaving air vents above the mouth. They reemerge in the rainy season to feed on bottom-dwelling fish, snails, mussels, etc., and to spawn. Subclass: *Sarcopterygii*. ▢fish.

lungs The respiratory organs of many air-breathing animals and man. The human lungs are situated within the rib cage on either side of the heart. Each lung is enclosed by a smooth moist membrane (the pleura), which permits it to expand without friction, and contains many tiny thin-walled air sacs (alveoli), through which exchange of oxygen and carbon dioxide takes place during breathing (*see* respiration). Air to the lungs passes through the *trachea (windpipe) to the two main airways (bronchi), which subdivide into progressively smaller branches that terminate (as respiratory bronchioles) in the alveoli.

Diseases most commonly affecting the lungs and airways are virus infections and bronchitis; cancer and tuberculosis are less common.

lungworm One of several species of parasitic *nematodes that inhabit the lungs and bronchial passages of cattle, pigs, deer, sheep, and other animals. They damage lung tissue, causing coughing, distress, and debilitation, and may act as reservoirs of such diseases as swine influenza.

lungwort A perennial herb of the genus *Pulmonaria* (about 10 species), especially *P. officinalis*, native to woods of Eurasia. The leaves are heart-shaped or oval, often white-spotted, and the tubular five-lobed flowers, borne in drooping terminal clusters, are pink when young, turning blue later. The plant grows to a height of 12 in (30 cm). Family: *Boraginaceae*.

Lunt, Alfred (1892–1977) US actor, who worked with **Lynne Fontanne** (1887–1983) after their marriage in 1922. They were most successful in sophisticated comedies, such as Noel Coward's *Design for Living* (1933) and Terence Rattigan's *Love in Idleness* (1944), but they also performed more serious productions, notably Dürrenmatt's *The Visit* (1959).

Luo A Nilotic people of N Uganda and Kenya, who moved into this area from the SE Sudan after about 1500. They speak a Sudanic language. The Luo cultivate cereal crops and herd cattle. For lakeside groups fishing is important. They lack centralized political institutions or chiefs.

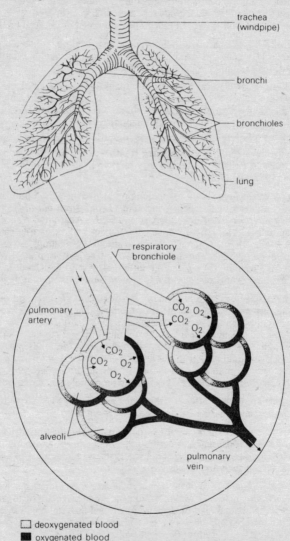

LUNGS *The air passages in the lungs terminate in millions of tiny air sacs (alveoli), into which blood from the pulmonary artery releases its carbon dioxide. Inhaled oxygen in the alveoli is absorbed by the blood, which is carried back to the heart by the pulmonary vein.*

Luoyang (*or* Lo-yang) 34 47N 112 26E A city in E central China, in Henan province. A commercial and cultural center, it was the Tang dynastic capital. Manufactures include machinery and ball bearings. Population (1990): 759,752.

Lupercalia An ancient Roman festival of purification and fertility held annually on February 15. After performing sacrifices, priests carrying whips of goat hide made a circuit of the Palatine. Women struck by their whips were ensured fertility. The ceremony was suppressed in 494 AD by Pope Gelasius.

lupin An annual or perennial herb of the genus *Lupinus* (about 200 species), native to the N hemisphere and widely cultivated for ornament. They grow 12–47 in (30–120 cm) high and have compound leaves with up to 18 radiating leaflets. Lupins produce dense spikes of blue, purple, white, pink, or yellow flowers. Family: **Leguminosae*.

lupus A skin disease of which there are two forms. Used alone, the term usually refers to **lupus vulgaris**, which is a tuberculous infection of the skin. Without treatment the infection will progress to erode the face (hence the name, which is Latin for wolf, implying a gnawing disease), but it is now readily cured by drugs. **Lupus erythematosus** (LE) is a disease in which inflammation of tissues is brought about by the body's own antibodies. Discoid LE is a chronic condition of scaling and scarring of the skin. Systemic LE affects the connective tissues and so can have serious effects in almost any part of the body, particularly the joints, skin, kidneys, heart, lungs, and brain. LE can be controlled with steroid drugs.

Lurçat, Jean (1892–1966) French tapestry designer. A painter in the cubist style until 1936, he established a tapestry factory at Aubusson in 1939, where he played a major part in the 20th-century revival of tapestry weaving and design.

Luria, Isaac (1534–72) Jewish mystic of Safed (Galilee); the founder of an important school of *kabbalah. He attracted a large band of disciples who, after his early death in an epidemic, collected and developed his teachings, which became extremely influential, especially later in *Hasidism.

Luria, Salvador E(dward) (1912–91) US molecular biologist, born in Italy. He won a Nobel Prize in physiology or medicine (1969). He came to the US (1940) and worked with Max *Delbruck on the study of the structure and reproduction of bacterial viruses.

Luristan (*or* Lorestan) A province in W Iran, comprising part of a larger historical region in which many important archeological finds have been made since 1929.

Lusaka 15 03S 28 30E The capital of Zambia, lying on the Tanzam Railroad. It became the capital of Northern Rhodesia in 1935 and of Zambia on independence in 1964. The University of Zambia was founded here in 1965. The center of an important agricultural region, it has expanded rapidly and industries include food processing, paint, clothing, and plastics. Population (1990): 982,362.

Lüshun. *See* Lüda.

Lusitania A British liner that, although unarmed, was sunk by a German submarine off the Irish coast on May 7, 1915, during World War I. Of the 1195 lives lost, some 128 were Americans and the incident contributed to the anti-German feeling in the US that ultimately brought the country into the war.

Lü-ta. *See* Lüda.

lute A plucked stringed instrument of Moorish origin; the name derives from the Arabic *al'lud*. The European lute, popular during the 15th, 16th, and 17th centuries, had a body in the shape of a half pear, six or more courses of double strings and a fretted fingerboard. The round sound hole was often intricately carved. Music for the lute was written in tablature, a system of notation using letters or numbers to indicate the position of the fingers. The lute was used chiefly as a solo instrument and to accompany singers; it has been revived in the 20th century.

luteinizing hormone. *See* gonàdotrophin.

lutetium (Lu) The heaviest *lanthanide element, separated from ytterbium by G. Urbain (1872–1938) in 1907 and named for Paris (Latin name: *Lutetia*), his native city. It was also discovered independently by C. A. von Welsbach, who called it **cassiopeium**, a name used until the 1950s, especially in Germany. It is present in small amounts in monazite ($CePO_4$) and extracted by reduction of $LuCl_3$ or LuF_3 by alkali metals (e.g. sodium). It is separated from the other lanthanides by ion-exchange techniques. At no 71; at wt 174.97; mp 3028°F (1663°C); bp 6149°F (3395°C).

Luther, Martin (1483–1546) German Protestant reformer, founder of *Lutheranism. An Augustinian monk and from 1507 a priest, he became professor of theology at Wittenberg University in 1511. After experiencing a personal revelation he came to believe that salvation could be attained by faith alone. Several visits to Rome convinced him of the corruption of the papacy, the Dominican monk *Tetzel, who sold *indulgences on behalf of papal funds, being a particular target for his hostility. In 1517 he nailed his 95 theses against this practice to the church door at Wittenberg. He disobeyed the papal summons to Rome (1518) and further attacked the papal system in such writings as *On the Babylonian Captivity of the Church of God* (1520). His public burning of a papal bull condemning his theses and writings resulted in his excommunication in 1521. He appeared before Charles V's imperial diet (legislative assembly) at Worms but refused to recant and was declared an outlaw. While in hiding at Wartburg, under the protection of the Elector of Saxony, he completed a German translation of the New Testament. In 1522 he returned openly to Wittenberg, where he led the reform of its church and in 1525 married the former nun Catherina van Bora (1499–1552). At the same time he lost much popular support because of his opposition to the Peasants' Revolt (1524–25). His contention that human will was incapable of following the good resulted in his rift with *Erasmus and in 1529 he also broke with *Zwingli, maintaining his belief in *consubstantiation. His original intention was reform not schism, but with the *Augsburg Confession (1530) a separate Protestant church emerged. Subsequently the leadership of the German Reformation was gradually taken over by *Melanchthon.

Lutheranism The belief and practice of the Protestant Churches that derive from the teaching of Martin *Luther, especially as formulated in the *Augsburg Confession (1530). There is a wide divergence in matters of belief among Lutherans. Essentially Scripture is taken to be the only rule of faith and conservative Lutherans accept Luther's basic doctrine of justification by faith alone, i.e. that redemption is only through faith in Christ. Lutheranism is the national faith in all Scandinavian countries, where there are some 19 million Lutherans. It is the principal Protestant Church in Germany (about 40 million adherents) and is also strong in North America (over 8 million). The Lutheran World Federation, the largest Protestant organization, is based in Geneva and claims authority over Lutherans world wide.

Luton 51 53N 0 25W A city in SE England, the largest in Bedfordshire. It has an important motor-vehicle industry and also manufactures household appliances, engineering components, and chemicals. A straw-plaiting industry has survived from the 17th century. Population (1985): 165,000.

Lutoslawski, Witold (1913–   ) Polish composer. His early works, such as his first symphony, were influenced by Bartók. From the orchestral *Venetian Games* (1961) onward—most of his works contain *aleatoric sections. They include a second symphony (1967), a cello concerto (1970), and *Preludes and Fugue for 13 Solo Strings* (1972).

Lutuli, Albert (John Mvumbi) (1898–1967) South African black leader, whose advocacy of nonviolent opposition to racial discrimination won him the Nobel Peace Prize (1960). A Zulu chief, in 1952 he became president of the African National Congress, formed in 1912 to further the black cause in South Africa. In 1956 he was arrested for treason and although acquitted in 1957 continued to suffer social and political restrictions.

Lutyens, Sir Edwin Landseer (1869–1944) British architect, known as the last English designer of country houses, a notable example of which is Middlefield, Cambridgeshire (1908). His most spectacular commission was the layout and viceregal palace of New Delhi, India (1912–30).

Lutzen, Battles of 1. (Nov 16, 1632) The battle in the *Thirty Years' War in which the Swedes under Gustavus II Adolphus clashed with imperial forces in a costly and indecisive battle. Gustavus Adolphus was killed. **2.** (May 1813) A battle in which Russian and Prussian forces were defeated by Napoleon.

lux (lx) The *SI unit of intensity of illumination equal to the illumination resulting from a flux of one lumen falling on an area of one square meter. Former name: meter candle.

Luxembourg A province in SE Belgium, bordering on the Grand Duchy of Luxembourg and France. The *Ardennes is an important tourist area. Area: 1705 sq mi (4416 sq km). Population (1991): 232,813. Capital: Arlon.

Luxembourg, Grand Duchy of A small country in W Europe, between Belgium, France, and Germany. The generally undulating S with its wide valleys rises to the rugged uplands of the Ardennes Plateau in the N. *Economy*: predominantly industrial, the manufacture of iron and steel is especially important although considerable economic diversification has taken place (e.g. chemicals, rubber, and synthetic fibers). Agriculture remains important, especially livestock raising, and wine is produced from the vineyards of the Moselle Valley. The city of Luxembourg is an important international center with the headquarters of the European Parliament and the European Coal and Steel Community, as well as many international companies. *History*: with the Netherlands and Belgium it formed part of the so-called Low Countries. It became a duchy in 1354 and passed to Burgundy in 1443 and to the Hapsburgs in 1482. It became a grand duchy in 1815 under the Dutch crown. In 1830 it joined the Belgium revolt against the Netherlands, W Luxembourg joining independent Belgium and the E forming part of the Netherlands until obtaining independence in 1867. It was occupied by the Germans in both World Wars. In 1921 it formed an economic union with Belgium and in 1948 both joined with the Netherlands to form the *Benelux Economic Union. Luxembourg is now a member of the EEC. Head of state: Grand Duke Jean. Head of Government: Jacques Santer. Official languages: Luxemburgish, French, and German. Official currency: Luxembourg franc of 100 centimes. Area: 999 sq mi (2597 sq km). Population (1990): 369,000. Capital: Luxembourg.

Luxemburg, Rosa (1871–1919) German revolutionary, born in Poland. She was converted to communism in 1890, helped to found the Polish Social Democratic party (later the Communist party), and from 1898 was a leader of the left wing of the German Social Democratic party. Upon the outbreak of World War I she broke with the majority of German socialists and formed, with

Karl *Liebknecht, the *Spartacus League. She spent most of the war in prison and after her release participated in the abortive uprising of 1919, following which she and Liebknecht were murdered.

Luxor (*or* El Aksur) 25 40N 32 38E A city in central Egypt, on the Nile River. It occupies the S part of the ancient city of *Thebes. Its numerous ruins and tombs include the temple built by Amenhotep III to the god Ammon. It is a winter resort. Population (1986 est): 148,000.

Luzern. *See* Lucerne.

Luzon A volcanic island in the N Philippines, the largest and most important. Largely mountainous, its central fertile plain is a major grain growing area with rice terraces to the N. Other products include sugar cane, hemp, timber, and minerals, notably chromite. Most industry is concentrated around Manila. *History*: power struggles for the Philippines have been centered here, including the Japanese invasion during World War II (*see* Corregidor). Area: 41,845 sq mi (108,378 sq km). Population: 17,900,000. Chief town: Quezon City.

Lviv (name until 1991: Lvov; German name: Lemberg) 49 50N 24 00E A city in Ukraine. A major industrial and cultural center of W Ukraine, Lviv supports machine building, food processing, and chemical and textile industries, and has a notable university (1661). *History*: founded in the 13th century, it subsequently passed to Poland, Turkey, and then Sweden. Under Austrian rule from 1772, it became the capital of Galicia. It was ceded to Poland after World War I and to the Soviet Union in 1939. It was occupied by the Germans in World War II. Population (1991 est): 802,000.

Lvov, Georgi Yevgenievich, Prince (1861–1925) Russian statesman. Lvov was the first leader of the provisional government in the *Russian Revolution. His unrealistic policies led to the Petrograd uprising in July 1917, and he resigned. He emigrated to Paris, where he died.

Lyallpur *See* Faisalabad.

Lyautey, Louis Hubert Gonzalve (1854–1934) French marshal and colonial administrator. He served in Indochina and then in Madagascar, where he reformed the colonial government. In 1912 he became resident general of the French protectorate of Morocco, where he again reorganized the administration, maintaining the French position there during World War I. He was briefly war minister (1917–18).

Lyceum The gardens and gymnasium in ancient Athens in which *Aristotle lectured and which gave their name to the school and research foundation that he established there in about 335 BC. The name is now applied particularly to Aristotle's philosophical doctrines.

Lycurgus A legendary Spartan statesman credited with establishing the constitution and military regime of Sparta after a slave rebellion in the 7th century BC. He is mentioned by *Herodotus and his biography was written by *Plutarch. The name refers to several other figures in Greek legend, notably a king of Thrace who opposed the cult of *Dionysus and was subsequently blinded or driven mad.

Lydda *See* Lod.

Lydgate, John (c. 1370–c. 1450) English poet. He lived at the monastery of Bury St Edmunds. A prolific writer, his major works include the long narrative poems *The Troy Book* (1412–21), written at the request of Henry V, and *The Fall of Princes* (1431–38).

Lydia In antiquity, a region of W Asia Minor with its capital at *Sardis. Its last native king, *Croesus (ruled 560–546 BC), enriched by Lydia's alluvial gold, controlled Anatolia eastward to the Halys River, until his defeat by *Cyrus the Great. The Lydians invented coined money (c. 700 BC).

Lyell, Sir Charles (1797–1875) British geologist, who was mainly responsible for the acceptance of the view that rocks are formed by slow continual processes, such as heat and erosion. Lyell popularized this theory in his *The Principles of Geology* (3 vols, 1830–33). Lyell's work had a great influence on Charles *Darwin and, in turn, Lyell became one of the earliest supporters of Darwin's theory of natural selection.

lymph A clear colorless fluid, consisting of water and dissolved substances, that is contained in a network of vessels called the **lymphatic system**. It is derived from blood and bathes the cells, supplying them with nutrients and absorbing their waste products, before passing into the lymphatic vessels. Here the lymph passes through a series of small swellings called **lymph nodes**, which filter out bacteria and other foreign particles, before draining into the main lymphatic vessels—the thoracic duct and the right lymphatic duct—in the neck. These two vessels are connected to veins in the neck and so drain the lymph back into the bloodstream. The lymph nodes, which also produce lymphocytes (a type of white blood cell), sometimes become enlarged during infections. The lymphatic system is one of the routes by which cancer is spread.

lymphocyte. *See* leukocyte.

lymphoma Cancer of the lymph nodes, which is one of the commonest cancers of young people. There are several different types but the most common is Hodgkin's disease, which can now often be controlled by chemotherapy.

Lynch, Jack (1917–   ) Irish statesman; prime minister (1966–73, 1977–79). A former hurling star, in 1948 he was first elected as a member of Parliament from Cork, enjoying enormous popular support in that city.

Lynd, Robert Staughton (1892–1970) US sociologist. Lynd taught at Columbia University from 1931 to 1961. He collaborated with his wife **Helen Lynd** (1896–1982) on the field study of Muncie, Ind., their findings being published in *Middletown: A Study in Contemporary American Culture* (1929) and *Middletown in Transition* (1937).

Lynn 42 29N 70 57W A city in Massachusetts. A long-established industrial center, it was the site of the first ironworks (1643) and the first fire engine (1654) in the US. A shoe-manufacturing center since 1636, Lynn also manufactures jet engines and marine turbines. Population (1990): 81,245.

lynx A short-tailed *cat, *Felis lynx*, that inhabits forests of Eurasia and North America. Lynxes are about 40 in (1 m) long with faintly spotted yellow-brown thick fur; their ears are tipped with black tufts. The rare Spanish race has especially bright spots.

Lynxes hunt at night, usually for small mammals (such as lemmings) but sometimes catching moose or reindeer, especially in deep snow. □mammal.

Lyon 45 46N 4 50E The third largest city in France, the capital of the Rhône department at the confluence of the Rhône and Saône Rivers. Notable buildings include the cathedral (12th–15th centuries) and the *hôtel de ville* and Palais des Arts (both 17th century). The university was founded in 1808. A *métro* (underground railroad) was opened here in 1978. The focal point of road and rail routes, Lyon is an important financial center and has been a leading textile center since the 15th century. Manufactures include synthetic fibers, cars, chemicals, and hosiery. Population (1990): 415,487.

Lyons, Joseph Aloysius (1879–1939) Australian statesman; prime minister (1931–39). At first a Labor politician, he resigned over financial policy in 1931 and with the Nationalist party formed the *United Australia party. He died in office.

Lyra (Latin: Lyre) A constellation in the N sky near Cygnus. The brightest star is *Vega. The constellation contains the **Ring nebula** (a *planetary nebula) and the *variable stars **RR Lyrae** (a pulsating variable) and **Beta Lyrae** (an eclipsing binary).

lyre An ancient plucked string instrument. It consists of a sound box with two symmetrical arms supporting a cross piece from which strings are stretched to a bridge on the belly. Greek vases often show players holding a lyre in the left hand and a large plectrum in the right.

LYREBIRD *The underside of the tail of the male superb lyrebird forms a silvery shimmering veil during display.*

lyrebird A primitive ground-dwelling passerine bird belonging to a family (*Menuridae*; 2 species) restricted to forests of E Australia. The male superb lyrebird (*Menura superba*), about 51 in (130 cm) long, is brown with gray underparts. Its magnificent tail is spread out into a lyre shape during the courtship display, which is performed on a mound of mud and debris. The smaller Prince Albert's lyrebird (*M. alberti*) does not build display mounds and has a smaller tail. All lyrebirds sing loudly and are excellent mimics.

Lysander (d. 395 BC) Spartan general and politician. He commanded the fleets that defeated the Athenians at Notium (407) and Aegospotami (405) toward the end of the *Peloponnesian War. His plot to make the Spartan throne elective rather than hereditary was thwarted by the government but Lysander escaped punishment. He was subsequently killed in action in Boeotia.

Lysenko, Trofim Denisovich (1898–1976) Soviet biologist, who achieved notoriety for his maverick ideas and damaging influence on Soviet biology. He claimed that changes induced in wheat by his vernalization experiments could be inherited, thus endorsing *Lamarck's discredited theory of evolution through inheritance of acquired characteristics. This led him to attack Mendelian genetics and the chromosome theory of inheritance, which, in the 1930s, were widely accepted elsewhere. With the backing of Stalin, Lysenko's influence grew. In 1939 he attacked the Soviet geneticist *Vavilov, who was later exiled to Siberia, and by 1948, Soviet scientific opposition to his views had been stifled. Lysenko's influence was eclipsed after Stalin's death although he retained his post as director of the Institute of Genetics until 1965, after the fall of Khrushchev.

lysergic acid diethylamide. *See* LSD.

Lysias (c. 459–c. 380 BC) Greek orator. He escaped from Athens during the reign of terror of the Thirty Tyrants (404 BC), but returned to prosecute one of them in his speech "Against Eratosthenes." About 35 of his legal speeches in plain unadorned style survive. He and his family are portrayed in Plato's *Republic*.

Lysippus (4th century BC) The court sculptor of Alexander the Great. Long-lived, original, and prolific, Lysippus worked in bronze and was noted for his portraiture and new system of proportions for human figures. Surviving copies of his works (e.g. the Vatican statue of the athlete scraping oil from his arm) indicate his naturalism.

lysosome A membrane-bounded structure occurring in large numbers in nearly all animal ☐cells and containing enzymes responsible for the breakdown of materials both within and outside the cell. Functions of lysosomes include the destruction of bacteria in white blood cells, the digestion of food by protozoa, and the breakdown of cellular material after death.

lysozyme An enzyme, present in tears, nasal secretions, and egg white, that destroys bacteria by breaking down their cell walls. It was one of the first enzymes whose molecular structure and mode of action were analyzed by X-ray diffraction techniques.

Lytton, Edward George Earle Bulwer-Lytton, 1st Baron (1803–73) British novelist and politician. His long career in Parliament as a Liberal and then a Tory culminated in his peerage in 1866. The best known of his many popular volumes of fiction, verse, and drama are his historical novels, which include *The Last Days of Pompeii* (1834). His son **(Edward) Robert Bulwer-Lytton, 1st Earl of Lytton** (1831–91) was viceroy of India (1876–80), initiating the second Afghan War (1878–80).

M

Maas River. *See* Meuse River.

Maastricht 50 51N 5 42E A city in the SE Netherlands, the capital of Limburg province on the Meuse River. It has the Netherlands' oldest church (founded in the 6th century AD) and is a cultural center. Industries include pottery and textiles. Population (1991 est): 117,417.

Maastricht Treaty (1993) Pact among European Community countries (Belgium, Denmark, France, Great Britain, Germany, Greece, Ireland, Italy, Luxembourg, the Netherlands, Portugal, Spain) that was drawn up in Maastricht, the Netherlands, in December 1991 and ratified in October 1993. It created a closer union among its member nations and, among other unifying measures, granted member citizens the right to petition the European Parliament and the right to file complaints with the parliament.

McAdam, John Loudon (1756–1836) British inventor of the macadam road surface. It consisted of rocks interspersed with small chips, bound together with slag or gravel and raised to facilitate drainage. In 1823 McAdam's methods were adopted by the British government and in 1827 he became general surveyor of roads.

Macadamia A genus of bushy evergreen trees, 30–49 ft (9–15 m) tall, native to Australia and often grown as ornamentals. *M. ternifolia* has long stiff leaves and slender clusters of small white or lilac flowers. The round hard-shelled fruit contains a single edible seed. These seeds—called macadamia or Queensland nuts—are used as dessert nuts. Family: *Proteaceae.*

Macao (Portuguese name: Macáu; Chinese name: Aomen) 22 13N 113 36E A Portuguese province and free port in S China, across the Zhu estuary from Hong Kong. Although the population is mainly Chinese, there are Portuguese buildings and cultural traditions. Chief industries are textiles and fishing; tourism, and gambling are also important. *History*: it was a major trading center until the 19th century. Immigration of refugees from Communist China was stopped after procommunist riots (1966–67). Area: 6 sq mi (16 sq km). Population (1986 est): 367,000.

macaque An *Old World monkey belonging to the genus *Macaca* (12 species), found mainly in the forests of S Asia; 14–31 in (35–78 cm) long (the tail is absent or up to 35 in [90 cm] long), macaques have short legs and areas of hard bare skin on the rump. Intelligent and sociable, they are mainly terrestrial, feeding on plant and animal matter. *See also* Barbary ape; rhesus monkey.

MacArthur, Douglas (1880–1964) US general. A graduate of West Point (1903), he had an outstanding combat record in World War I and then returned to West Point as superintendent (1919–22). Following duty in the Philippines, MacArthur served as US Army chief of staff (1930–35). After reorganizing the Philippine Army (1937–41), he was named supreme commander of Allied forces in the SW Pacific during *World War II (1942–45). As one of the outstanding strategists of the war, he directed the recapture of occupied territories, was named general of the army, and as supreme commander accepted Japan's unconditional surrender in August 1945. MacArthur later headed the military occupation of Japan (1945–51) and was named commander of UN forces in the *Korean War. Despite his initial military success in that conflict, MacArthur developed a serious disagreement with President Truman over the conduct of the war. He was relieved of his command in 1951.

DOUGLAS MACARTHUR *General who commanded US troops in the Pacific during World War II and in Korea during the Korean War.*

Macassar. *See* Ujung Padang.

Macaulay, Thomas Babington, 1st Baron (1800–59) British essayist and historian. From 1825 he was a leading contributor to the *Edinburgh Review*. He had a long career in Parliament (1830–34, 1839–47, 1852–56) and worked in India from 1834 to 1838. His Whig sympathies are clearly evident in his immensely successful *History of England* (5 vols, 1849–61).

macaw A large brightly colored *parrot belonging to one of two genera (*Ara* and *Anodorhynchos*), ranging from Mexico to Paraguay. Up to 40 in (100 cm) long, macaws have a characteristically long loose tail and a huge hooked bill that is used to crack open large nuts.

Macbeth (d. 1058) King of Scots (1040–58), after killing Duncan I in battle at Bothnagowan. He was killed by Duncan's son Malcolm.

MacBride, Seán (1904–88) Irish diplomat. The son of the nationalist Maud Gonne (1866–1953), he belonged to the IRA before becoming a member of the Irish assembly (1947). He was chairman of Amnesty International (1961–75) and UN commissioner for Namibia (1973–77). He shared the Nobel Peace Prize in 1974.

Maccabees The name applied loosely to the Hasmonean dynasty, founded in Jerusalem by Judas Maccabee (d. 161 BC) after a revolt against Syrian (Seleucid) rule. It continued until the capture of Jerusalem by the Romans in 63 BC. In Christian usage it is applied to seven young brothers martyred during the revolt. In 1895 it was revived in the name of a Jewish athletics organization, Maccabi, the World Union of which was formed in 1921.

The **Books of Maccabees** are four books of the *Apocrypha. I and II Maccabees record the revolt (168 BC) of the Maccabees against the Seleucid king Antiochus Epiphanes and the establishment of an independent Jewish kingdom. They date from the late second century BC. III and IV Maccabees are unrelated works, written probably at the beginning of the Christian era. III Maccabees describes a (probably imaginary) persecution of Jews by Ptolemy IV, Philopator of Egypt (late 3rd century BC), while IV Maccabees is a philosophical treatise, with a Stoic flavor, on the superiority of intellect over passions.

McCarran-Walter Act (Immigration and Nationality Act; 1952) US legislation on immigration policies. It retained most of the quotas established in 1924, but lifted the ban on Asiatic and Pacific immigrants, gave priority to higher educated immigrants with necessary skills, and defined admittance and deportation policies regarding aliens considered national security risks.

McCarthy, Eugene Joseph (1916–) US political leader and author. He served in the US House of Representatives (1949–59) and the Senate (1959–71) as a Democrat from Minnesota. An opponent of the Vietnam War, he ran for the Democratic presidential nomination in 1968 and again as an independent in 1976, but was unsuccessful both times.

McCarthy, Joseph R(aymond) (1908–57) US Republican senator (1947–57) from Wisconsin, who led Senate investigations of supposed communists during the Cold War. His claim in 1950 to have the names of communist infiltrators into the state department created a sensation but was not proved. In 1954, televised hearings into alleged communism in the army discredited him; he was censured by the Senate, and his anticommunist witchhunt—commonly known as McCarthyism—came to an end.

McCarthy, Mary (1912–89) US novelist and critic. Her novels are sensitive to and often satirical of aspects of American society and include *The Groves of Academe* (1952), *The Group* (1963), *Birds of America* (1971), and *Cannibals and Missionaries* (1979). She published criticism, travel books, the autobiographical *Memories of a Catholic Girlhood* (1957), and *How I Grew* (1987) and, journalism, notably *Vietnam* (1967), concerning US involvement in Vietnam.

McCartney, Paul (1942–) British rock musician, formerly a member of the *Beatles. His solo career was launched with the hit "Maybe I'm Amazed" (1970). With his wife **Linda McCartney** (1942–) he formed Wings (1971), the band with which he recorded such albums as *Band on the Run* (1973) and made world tours.

McClellan, George B(rinton) (1826–85) Union general in the *Civil War. An 1842 graduate of West Point, he served in the Mexican War and later entered civilian life as a railroad executive. He rejoined the regular army in 1861. His 1861 campaign preserved Kentucky and separated W Virginia from the Confederacy. In the *Peninsular Campaign that followed, he fortified Washington, rebuilding the Federal forces there, and in 1862 he was defeated before Richmond. Despite superior strength he did not press *Lee's retreating forces at Antietam and President *Lincoln dismissed him (1862). He ran unsuccessfully as the Democratic candidate against Lincoln in 1864 and later served as governor of New Jersey (1878–81).

McClintock, Barbara (1902–92) US geneticist, who was awarded a Nobel Prize in physiology or medicine (1983). She was educated at Cornell University (1919–27) and taught there (1927–31). In 1942 she joined Cold Spring Harbor Laboratory where she conducted experiments on the corn plant and discovered that genes in chromosomes "jump" and cause mutations (1951), opening up new avenues in the fields of antibiotic and cancer research. Her theories were so far ahead of the times that it was not until the 1970s that others understood and took her work seriously.

McClure, Sir Robert John Le Mesurier (1807–73) Irish naval officer and explorer. In 1850, in search of Sir John *Franklin, missing in the Arctic, McClure entered the Beaufort Sea from the Pacific and was marooned in the strait named for him. He was rescued, returning home via the Atlantic (1854), and was thus the first to traverse the *Northwest Passage.

McCormack, John William (1891–1980) US politician; speaker of the House (1962–70). He served in the Massachusetts legislature (1920–26) before representing Massachusetts as a Democrat in the US House of Representatives (1928–70). He was majority leader (1940–47; 1949–51; 1955–61) and minority leader (1947–49; 1953–55). He succeeded Sam Rayburn as the Speaker, a post he held until his retirement.

McCormick, Cyrus Hall (1809–84) US inventor and industrialist. He invented (1831), patented (1834), and manufactured and marketed (from 1844) the mechanical reaper. A project started by his inventor father, the reaper did not do well in the hilly East, and it was not until McCormick moved his business to Chicago (1847) to take advantage of the flat Midwest farmlands that he prospered. He founded McCormick Theological Seminary.

McCullers, Carson (1917–67) US novelist and playwright. Her novels, which include *The Heart Is a Lonely Hunter* (1940), *Reflections in a Golden Eye* (1941), and *A Member of the Wedding* (1946), are set in her native South and describe a grotesque and violent world. Other works include *The Ballad of the Sad Cafe* (1951), *The Square Root of Wonderful* (1958), and *Clock Without Hands* (1961).

McCulloch v. Maryland (1819) US Supreme Court decision that upheld the right of the federal government to establish federal banks in states and not be subject to the banking laws of the specific states. The state of Maryland had challenged the power of the Bank of the United States to issue banknotes from its Baltimore branch without affixing state tax stamps.

Macdonald, Sir John (Alexander) (1815–91) Canadian statesman; prime minister (1857–58, 1864, 1867–73, 1878–91). Macdonald helped to establish Canada's dominion status within the British Empire (1867) and served as the first prime minister of the Dominion of Canada. He promoted the expansion of Canada to include Manitoba, British Columbia, and Prince Edward Island.

MacDonald, (James) Ramsay (1866–1937) British statesman; the first Labour prime minister (1924, 1929–31, 1931–35). Elected to Parliament (1906) he became leader of the *Labour party (1911) but resigned in opposition to World War I (1914) and lost his seat in the 1918 election. Reelected to Parliament in 1922 he again led the Labour party, becoming prime minister briefly in 1924. His 1929–31 government, failing to deal with current economic problems, was broadened into a coalition (1931–35) that was increasingly dominated by the Conservatives and he was replaced by Baldwin in 1935.

Macdonnell Ranges A system of mountain ranges in Australia. They extend for about 40 mi (65 km) E and 200 mi (320 km) W of Alice Springs, across S Northern Territory reaching 4955 ft (1510 m) at Mount Ziel.

MacDowell, Edward (Alexander) (1861–1908) US composer and pianist. He studied music in New York City, France, and Germany. Returning to the US in 1888, he composed and also developed and headed a music department (1896–1904) at Columbia University. His works include *Second Piano Concerto in D Minor* (1889), *The Saracens* (1891), *Indian Suite* (1892), *Woodland Sketches* (1896), *Sea Pieces* (1898), *Keltic* (1901), and *New England Idylls* (1902).

mace. *See* nutmeg.

Macedonia Independent nation in SE Europe, bordered by Yugoslavia (N), Bulgaria (E), Greece (S), and Albania (W); formerly a constituent republic of Yugoslavia. Landlocked and mountainous, Macedonia is traversed by the Vardar River, which links central Europe with the Aegean Sea. Other prominent features include lakes Prespa and Ohrid. The people are primarily Macedonian, with substantial populations of Albanians and Serbs. Economically, the country is poor in resources and relatively undeveloped. Part of the historic region of Macedonia, the current country evolved as a separate republic within Yugoslavia as World War II ended. As ethnic tensions mounted in Yugoslavia after the death of Tito in 1980, Macedonian nationalism intensified. Fearing domination by Serbia in a reduced Yugoslavia, Macedonia proclaimed its independence in 1991. Full international recognition was delayed by Greece's insistence on its right to the use of the name "Macedonia," but this obstacle was largely overcome in 1993, and Macedonia joined the UN. Area: 9925 sq mi (25,705 sq km). Population (1992 est): 2,000,000. Capital: Skopje.

Macedonia The central region of the Balkans. Inhabited from Neolithic times, Macedonia was settled by many migrating northern tribes. About 640 BC Perdiccas I became the first ruler of the kingdom of Macedon. *Philip II (359–336 BC) quelled the warlike tribes and founded Macedon's military and economic power, which under his son *Alexander the Great was extended to the East. Alexander's successors were harassed by rebellious uprisings and, after defeat (168 BC) in the *Macedonian Wars, Macedonia became a Roman province (146), losing its independence but remaining a center of Hellenistic culture. The region is now divided between the country of Macedonia (formerly a constituent republic of Yugoslavia), N Greece, and SW Bulgaria.

Macedonian Wars The three campaigns that secured Roman control of the kingdom of Macedon. The first Macedonian War (214–205 BC) coincided with the intervention of Philip V of Macedon (237–179; reigned 220–179) against Rome in the second *Punic War. The second Macedonian War (200–196) ended with the Roman victory at Cynoscephalae, in Thessaly. Rome instigated the third Macedonian War (171–168) against Philip's son Perseus (reigned 179–168) and finally crushed the Macedonians at the battle of Pydna.

Maceió 9 40S 35 44W A city in NE Brazil, the capital of Alagoas state. It contains many colonial buildings and has sugar-refining, distilling, sawmilling, and textile industries. Population (1991): 628,210.

McEnroe, John (Patrick, Jr) (1959–) US tennis player. He won the US singles title in 1979, 1980, 1981, and 1984 and Wimbledon in 1981, 1983, and 1984. An intense competitor noted for his tempestuous court behavior, he was one of the world's finest doubles players.

Macgillicuddy's Reeks A mountain range in the Republic of Ireland, in Co Kerry. It extends W of the Lakes of Killarney, reaching 3414 ft (1041 m) at Carrantuohill.

McGovern, George S(tanley) (1922–   ) US political leader. He served in the House of Representatives (1957–61) and the Senate (1963–81) as a Democrat from South Dakota. Opposed to the Vietnam War, he was the Democratic presidential nominee (1972) and was overwhelmingly defeated by incumbent Richard M. *Nixon.

McGraw, John J(oseph) (1873–1934) US baseball player and manager. He played third base for the Baltimore Orioles (1891–99). As manager of the National League's New York Giants (1902–32), he won 10 pennants and 3 World Series. He was elected to the Baseball Hall of Fame in 1937.

McGuffey, William Holmes (1800–73) US educator; author of *McGuffey's Readers*, the standard elementary school textbooks throughout the Midwest during the 1800s and early 1900s. Self-educated, he began teaching at the age of 13 in frontier Ohio. He graduated (1826) from Washington College and taught (1826–36) at Miami University. In 1836 the first and second McGuffey's school readers were published; they were followed by several other editions. He also served as president of Cincinnati College (1836–39) and Ohio University at Athens (1839–43), and he chaired the moral philosophy department at the University of Virginia (1845–73).

Mach, Ernst (1838–1916) Austrian physicist and philosopher, after whom the *Mach number is named in recognition of his researches into airflow and his observation that as the velocity of sound is reached the airflow changes. Philosophically he was a positivist and as such argued strongly against the concept of atoms, which he regarded as mystical entities since their existence could not be detected but only inferred. *See also* logical positivism.

Machaut, Guillaume de (c. 1300–77) French poet and composer, who held a number of court and ecclesiastical appointments in Bohemia and France before becoming canon of Rheims in 1337. He wrote a number of allegorical poems and developed the *ballade* and *rondeau*. He was one of the leading composers of the *ars nova* style and was the first composer to write a complete musical setting of the mass.

Machel, Samora Moïses (1933–86) Mozambique statesman; president (1975–86). Machel, who trained as a male nurse, led the FRELIMO (Front for the Liberation of Mozambique) forces in the struggle for independence against Portugal (1966–74) and on independence became Mozambique's first president.

Machiavelli, Niccolò (1469–1527) Italian political theorist. He served the Florentine republic as statesman and diplomat from 1498 to 1512, when the restoration of the Medici family forced him into exile. In *The Prince* (1532), written in 1513, he argued that all means are permissible in the realization of a secure and stable state, and in the *Discorsi* (written 1513–19) he used the example of the ancient Roman Republic to reinforce his arguments. The adjective Machiavellian is used to describe the view, or a supporter of the view, that opportunist or amoral means justify politically desirable ends.

machine gun A *small arm that fires repeatedly without reloading. The first was a rotating cylinder flintlock (1718). By 1862 the Gatling, named for Richard Jordan Gatling (1818–1903), was firing six rounds in a second by means of its several barrels and a hand-rotated breech. Modern weapons are derived from the recoil-operated belt-fed water-cooled weapons designed by Sir Hiram *Maxim toward the end of the 19th century, some of which are still in service. Ammunition from pan, box, belt, or drum is loaded, fired, extracted, and reloaded automatically by recoil or in later models by gas and piston. Classes are: light machine gun (LMG), developed from the rifle; medium machine gun (MMG), normally having a two-man crew and using belt-fed rifle ammunition; and heavy machine gun (HMG), with calibers up to 20 mm (0.8 in). *Submachine guns using pistol ammunition are light derivatives.

machine tools Power-driven mechanical tools used to turn, form, drill, mill, shape, or plane metal or other materials. In *lathes the material to be worked (workpiece) is rotated and the tool is applied to it, whereas in other types of machine tool the workpiece is held stationary and a rotating cutter (milling machine), drill (drilling machine), or reciprocating cutter (shaping machine) is applied to it. In a planing machine the workpiece is reciprocated past the tool. In mass-production techniques a number of operations are carried out on the workpiece without human intervention, often by using a transfer machine to convey it from one machine tool to another. Computer-controlled machine tools are a further step in the automation of production lines.

Mach number The ratio of the velocity of a body in a fluid to the velocity of sound in that fluid. The velocity is said to be supersonic if the Mach number is greater than one. If it exceeds five the velocity is said to be hypersonic. Named for Ernst *Mach.

MACHU PICCHU *The real name of this fortified Inca retreat is unknown, Machu Picchu being the name of the mountain that rises above it.*

Machu Picchu A well-preserved *Inca town in the Urubamba valley (Peru), discovered in 1911. Dramatically sited on a precipitous ridge, Machu Picchu is flanked by extensive agricultural terraces. A typical Inca city, it contains a central plaza, royal palace, and sun temple, all built of polygonal dressed stone blocks.

Macías Nguema. *See* Equatorial Guinea, Republic of.

McKay, Donald (1810–80) US clipper shipbuilder born in Canada. By 1845 he owned his own shipyard in Boston and soon gained fame as the builder of the fastest and the largest clipper ships. The *Flying Cloud* set a speed record from Boston to San Francisco in 1852; the *Great Republic* was the largest clipper ship ever built. The popularity of iron steam-powered ships and a slump in the economy led to the end of the clipper ship business, and the yard closed in 1873.

Macke, August (1887–1914) German painter. During visits to France he was successively influenced by *impressionism, *fauvism, and *cubism. A member of Der *Blaue Reiter group, he became known for his lighthearted subjects, particularly parks and zoos, although his best works were watercolors painted in Tunis (1914), shortly before his death in World War I.

McKenna, Siobhán (1923–86) Irish actress. She acted at the Abbey Theater, Dublin, from 1943 to 1946 and made her London debut in 1947. She was particularly successful in the roles of St Joan in G. B. Shaw's play and of Pegeen in Synge's *The Playboy of the Western World*, a role she also played in the film (1962).

Mackenzie A district of N Canada, the westernmost district of the *Northwest Territories. Mountains straddle the W border with the Yukon, the *Mackenzie River valley runs N through the center, and barren plains cover the E. The Territories' most populous district, it produces zinc, lead, gold, and oil. Area: 527,490 sq mi (1,366,199 sq km).

Mackenzie, Sir Alexander (?1764–1820) Canadian explorer; born in Scotland. He traveled from Montreal to establish Ft. Chipewyan (1788) on Lake Athabasca in NE Alberta, for the North West Company. Then he traveled along the Mackenzie River NW to its delta at the Beaufort Sea in the Arctic (1789) and, in his next expedition, went S and W across the Rocky Mountains to the Pacific coast of British Columbia (1793). These explorations constituted the first transcontinental crossing N of Mexico. He wrote *Voyage from Montreal on the River St Lawrence, Through the Continent of North America, to the Frozen and Pacific Oceans, in the Years 1789 and 1793* (1801).

Mackenzie, Alexander (1822–92) Canadian statesman and prime minister (1873–78), born in Scotland. A mason and building contractor, he settled in Ontario in 1842; by 1852 he had become editor of a Liberal newspaper, *Lambton Shield*, and in 1861 served in the provincial parliament as a Liberal. After confederation in 1867, he first led the minority Liberals in the House of Commons and then became prime minister in 1873. His five years were spent unsuccessfully trying to change the Conservative policies that had preceded him.

Mackenzie, Sir (Edward Montague) Compton (1883–1972) British novelist. His early novels include the semiautobiographical *Sinister Street* (1913). He served at Gallipoli in World War I and later settled on a Hebridean island. All of his later work is in a lighter vein and includes several volumes of memoirs and many humorous novels, notably *Whisky Galore* (1947).

Mackenzie, William Lyon (1795–1861) Canadian journalist, politician, and reformer; born in Scotland. He used his newspapers (*Colonial Advocate*, 1824; *Constitution*, 1836) to oppose majority Tories in the York (now Ontario) Parliament. Six times elected to the province's parliament, he was ejected each time by the Tories because of his attacks on and his grievances about colonial rule. Attempts to organize a rebellion for independence failed, and he fled to the US (1837), where he was jailed briefly for breaking neutrality laws. Pardoned, he returned to Canada in 1849, was elected to Parliament as a Radical, and continued to fight for independence and agrarian democracy.

Mackenzie Mountains A mountain range in NW Canada that runs N and S straddling the border between Yukon and Northwest Territories, part of the Rocky Mountains. Keele Peak (9750 ft; 2972 m) is the highest point.

Mackenzie River The longest river in Canada, flowing from Great Slave Lake in the Northwest Territories W and NNW through sparsely settled country to an extensive delta on the Beaufort Sea. Navigable in summer, it carries oil and minerals from the Arctic Ocean to S Canada. Its tributaries generate cheap hydroelectricity. Length: 1065 mi (1705 km).

mackerel An important food and game fish belonging to the genus *Scomber*, related to tuna. Mackerels live in shoals in tropical and temperate oceans, feeding on fish and invertebrates. They have a streamlined body, two dorsal fins, and a series of finlets running in front of the forked tail. The common Atlantic mackerel (*S. scombrus*), about 1 ft (30 cm) long, is marked with black and green bands above and is silvery-white below.

mackerel shark A medium to large carnivorous oceanic *shark of the family *Isuridae*, which includes the *porbeagle and the *white shark. They are heavy bodied and have large keels along both sides of the crescent-shaped tail for stability during fast swimming.

McKinley, Mount A mountain in the US, in S central Alaska in the Alaska Range; also known as Denali. The highest peak in North America, it was first successfully climbed in 1913 by the US explorer Hudson Stuck (1863–1920). Denali (McKinley, 1917–80) National Park surrounds it. Height: 20,320 ft (6194 m).

McKinley, William (1843–1901) US statesman; 25th president of the US (1897–1901). After serving in the Union army during the Civil War, McKinley became a lawyer and began his political career as a member of the US House of Representatives (1884–91). As an advocate of economic protectionism, he introduced the McKinley Tariff Act of 1890. McKinley later served two terms as governor of Ohio (1892–96) and waged a successful campaign as the Republican presidential nominee in 1896. As president, McKinley continued to support high tariffs and encouraged the expansion of US economic interests abroad. During his administration, the US became increasingly involved in foreign affairs, gaining territories in the Pacific as a result of the *Spanish–American War (1898) and intervening in China in the suppression of the *Boxer Rebellion (1900). McKinley was reelected in 1900 but was assassinated in 1901 at the Buffalo Pan-American Exposition by an anarchist, Leon Czolgosz.

Mackintosh, Charles Rennie (1868–1928) Scottish architect and designer. One of the most brilliant exponents of *Art Nouveau, Mackintosh evolved an austere version of the style, which was highly influential throughout Europe, though less so in Britain. All his best work was in Glasgow, in particular the School of Art (1897–1909) and four tearooms (1897–1912), for which he also designed the furniture. In 1923 he moved to London, where his practice collapsed, resulting in his retirement soon afterward.

Macleish, Archibald (1892–1982) US poet. He lived among the expatriate writers in France during the 1920s and later worked in the US government service. Much of the verse in his *Collected Poems* (1952) and *New and Collected Poems 1917–1976* (1976) was influenced by his liberal political principles. He also wrote verse dramas, including *Panic* (1935) and *J. B.* (1958), for which he was awarded a Pulitzer Prize, and a collection, *Six Plays* (1980).

Macleod, John James Rickard (1876–1935) British physiologist, noted for his work on carbohydrate metabolism. He was professor of physiology at Toronto University (1919–28), where F. G. *Banting and C. H. *Best first isolated the hormone insulin. Macleod was awarded the 1923 Nobel Prize with Banting.

McLeod gauge An instrument that uses *Boyle's law to measure the pressure of a near vacuum. A sample of the vacuum is compressed into a small volume thus raising its pressure, which may then be measured. It is accurate down to about 10^{-6} millimeter of mercury.

Mac Liammóir, Micheál (1899–1978) Irish actor, scenic artist, and dramatist. In 1928 he was a founder of the Gate Theater in Dublin, a home for international drama and a platform for young Irish dramatists. As an actor, he is best known for his one-man show, *The Importance of Being Oscar* (1960–61), based on the works of Oscar Wilde.

McLuhan, (Herbert) Marshall (1911–81) Canadian writer and educator. He taught at universities in the US and Canada from 1936 until 1979. An observer of the effects of mass media technology on the human condition, he concentrated on electricity as an extension of the human nervous system. He felt that the media—television, computers, etc.—had the most influence while the impact of print media was fast disappearing. His works include *The Mechanical Bride: Folklore of Industrial Man* (1951), *The Gutenberg Galaxy: The Making of Typographic Man* (1962), *Understanding Media: The Extensions of Man* (1964), *The Medium is the Message* (1967), and *The City as Classroom* (1977).

MacMahon, Marie Edme Patrice Maurice, Comte de (1808–93) French marshal and statesman; president (1873–79). He came to prominence in the Crimean War (1854–56) and in Italy, where his victory at Magenta (1859) brought him the title Duc de Magenta. He helped to suppress the Commune of Paris (1871) succeeding Thiers as president; he attempted to break the influence of the republican party by appointing a royalist cabinet in defiance of the chamber of deputies. The chamber's successful resistance to this move forced MacMahon to resign.

McMahon, William (1908–88) Australian statesman, prime minister (1971–72) of a coalition of Liberal and Country parties. He became Liberal deputy leader in 1966 and minister for foreign affairs in 1969.

McMillan, Edwin Mattison (1907–91) US physicist, who shared the 1951 Nobel Prize with Glenn *Seaborg for their discovery of transuranic elements. The first such element, *neptunium, was discovered by McMillan in 1940 by bombarding uranium with neutrons.

Macmillan, (Maurice) Harold (1894–1986) British statesman; Conservative prime minister (1957–63). He was a member of Parliament from 1924 to 1929 and again from 1931. During World War II he held office under Churchill. He became minister of defense (1954), foreign secretary (1955), and chancellor of the exchequer (1955–57). He succeeded Sir Anthony Eden as prime minister. His "wind of change" speech in Africa in 1958 marked his government's support of independence for African states. His second ministry failed to deal effectively with inflation and suffered a major blow when de Gaulle frustrated Britain's attempt to join the EEC (1963). However, he improved relations with the US and helped to achieve the *Nuclear Test-Ban Treaty (1963). He entered the House of Lords in 1984 as Lord Stockton.

McNamara, Robert (Strange) (1916–   ) US executive and public official. An executive of the Ford Motor Co., he served as its president briefly (1960–61) before being appointed secretary of defense (1961–68). He was responsible for revamping the Pentagon and overseeing much of the Vietnam War. Convinced that peace would be achieved through economic stability, not arms, he resigned his position (1967) and took over leadership of the World Bank (1968–81).

HAROLD MACMILLAN *While prime minister (1957–63) he supported independence for British colonies in Africa but in Europe was frustrated in attempts to join the EEC.*

MacNeice, Louis (1907–63) Irish-born British poet. A friend of *Auden, *Spender, and *Day-Lewis at Oxford in the 1930s, he published his first volume of poetry, *Blind Fireworks*, in 1929. Among his other volumes are *Autumn Journal* (1939), *The Burning Perch* (1963), and a distinguished collection of plays for radio, *The Dark Tower* (1947).

Macon 32 49N 83 37W A city in Georgia, on the Ocmulgee River. It is the industrial center of a large agricultural area. Population (1990): 106,612.

Mâcon 46 18N 4 50E A city in E France, the capital of the Saône-et-Loire department on the Saône River. An important trading center for Burgundy wines, its manufactures include textiles, vats, and agricultural machinery. Population (1983): 39,000.

McPherson, Aimee Semple (1890–1944) US evangelist; born in Canada. After traveling with her first husband, a Pentecostal evangelist, she started her "Foursquare Gospel" movement and opened Angelus Temple in Los Angeles in 1923, from which she ran a Bible school and radio station. She incorporated the International Church of the Foursquare Gospel in 1927. After a disappearance—supposedly a kidnapping—in 1926, she discontinued public appearances and devoted her time to writing and the business of running her church.

Macquarie Island A subantarctic volcanic island in the S Pacific Ocean, in the Australian Antarctic Territory. The site of a meteorological research station, it is the only known breeding ground of the royal penguin. Area: about 65 sq mi (168 sq km).

McQueen, Steve (1930–80) US film actor. Following his success in *The Magnificent Seven* (1960) he was usually associated with the roles of tough laconic heroes. His later films include *The Cincinnati Kid* (1965) and *Bullitt* (1968), *Papillon* (1973), and *An Enemy of the People* (1976).

Macready, William Charles (1793–1873) British actor and theater manager. One of the most distinguished of 19th-century tragedians, he was particularly successful in the roles of Lear, Hamlet, and Macbeth, and was regarded as the chief rival of Edmund *Kean. He reformed production standards and advocated fidelity to the original texts of Shakespeare.

Madagascar, Democratic Republic of (name until 1975: Malagasy Republic) An island country in the Indian Ocean, off the SE coast of Africa. A narrow coastal plain in the E and a broader one in the W rise to central highlands, reaching heights of over 9000 ft (2800 m). Most of the inhabitants are Merina, Betsimisaraka, and Betsileo, all speaking *Austronesian dialects. *Economy*: chiefly agricultural, now developed on a cooperative basis. Livestock is important and the main crops include manioc as well as coffee, sugar, and spices, which are the main exports. A declining agricultural sector has forced Madagascar to import rice, once a major export. Nonetheless, agricultural products account for 80% of exports. Forests produce not only timber, but also gums, resins, and dyes. Clearing of the forests has, however, seriously depleted the unique indigenous fauna, especially the lemurs. Minerals include graphite, chrome, and ilmenite. Industry, previously based mainly on food processing and tobacco, now includes metals, plastics, paper, and oil refining. *History*: settled by Indonesians from the 1st century AD and by Muslim traders from Africa from the 8th century; the Portuguese visited the island in the 16th century. It remained a native kingdom until the late 19th century, when the French laid claim to Madagascar and, after much bloodshed, established a protectorate (1896). It became a French overseas territory in 1946 and a republic within the French Community in 1958, gaining full independence in 1960. A military government took over in 1972 but was overthrown in 1975. A new socialist constitution was then approved by a referendum and Madagascar became a democratic republic, with Capt. Didier Ratsiraka as its first president. Supporting huge foreign indebtedness, Madagascar was forced to impose economic austerity measures on its people. Political unrest prevailed through the 1980s. Labor strikes and antigovernment demonstrations forced a promise for democratic reform in the early 1990s. Multiparty politics was announced in 1990, but in 1991 opposition parties still were demanding concrete reforms. Ratsiraka relinquished power in mid-1991, and after a period of transitional government, Albert Zafy was elected president in 1993. Official languages: Malagasy and French. Official currency: Malagasy franc of 100 centimes. Area: 229,233 sq mi (587,041 sq km). Population (1990 est): 11,802,000. Capital: Antananarivo. Main port: Tamatave.

Madariaga y Rojo, Salvador de (1886–1978) Spanish historian and diplomat, who was ambassador to the US (1931) and to France (1932–34). His historical writings include *The Rise and Fall of the Spanish American Empire* (1947) and *Bolívar* (1952).

madder A perennial herb of the genus *Rubia* (about 38 species), especially *R. tinctorum*, native to Eurasia. It has trailing stems with whorls of narrow leaves, clusters of small yellow flowers, and blackish berrylike fruits. A red dye is extracted from the roots. Family: *Rubiaceae*.

Madeira, Rio A river in W Brazil, formed by the union of the Ríos Beni and Mamoré and flowing generally NE to join the Amazon River. Length: 2013 mi (3241 km).

Madeira Islands (*or* Funchal Islands) A Portuguese archipelago in the Atlantic Ocean, about 398 mi (640 km) off the coast of Morocco. It comprises the inhabited islands of Madeira and Porto Santo and two uninhabited island groups. Madeira, the largest and most important island, is densely vegetated and its mild climate attracts vacationers. Its products include basketwork, fruit (such as mangoes), sugar, and the famous Madeira wine. Area: 300 sq mi (777 sq km). Population (1986): 269,000. Capital: Funchal.

Maderna, Carlo (1556–1629) Roman architect. A precursor of the Roman *baroque style of architecture, Maderna's vigorous style first gained full expression in the façade of Sta Susanna (1597–1603). His major work was the completion of St Peter's Basilica, adding the nave and façade to Michelangelo's design.

Madhya Pradesh A state in central India, stretching N over highlands to the S edge of the Ganges plain. The largest state, it is predominantly agricultural, producing grains, cotton, and sugar cane. Its huge hydroelectric potential is harnessed for a few industries, including steel, aluminum, and cement. Coal, iron ore, and other minerals are mined. *History*: under Islamic (11th–18th centuries) and Maratha (18th–19th centuries) rule until Britain established control, Madhaya Pradesh became a state in 1956. Area: 170,937 sq mi (442,841 sq km). Population (1991): 66,135,862. Capital: Bhopal.

Madison, Dolley (Payne Todd) (1768–1849) US first lady; wife of James *Madison, fourth president. She married Madison in 1794 after losing her first husband, John Todd, and one of their two sons to yellow fever in 1793. She helped as hostess at the White House during widower Thomas *Jefferson's administration, gaining experience for her husband's two terms (1809–17). During Madison's tenure she was well known for her hospitality.

Madison, James (1751–1836) US statesman; fourth president of the US (1809–17). An influential advocate of a strong federal system for the newly created US, Madison played an important role in the drafting of the US *Constitution in 1787. He later urged its ratification and defended federal powers over *states' rights in the *Federalist Papers, a series of essays he published in collaboration with Alexander *Hamilton and John *Jay. After service in the US House of Representatives (1789–97), Madison was appointed secretary of state in the administration of Thomas *Jefferson (1801–09) and was instrumental in the negotiations leading to the *Louisiana Purchase (1803). In 1809, Madison succeeded Jefferson as president. During Madison's first term in office, US relations with Great Britain deteriorated to the point of open war. The *War of 1812 was initially a military disaster for the Americans, who suffered a blockade of the ports of the eastern seaboard. In 1814, British troops occupied Washington, DC, forcing a temporary evacuation by the American government. The war ended in 1815 with the ratification of the Treaty of Ghent. After leaving office, Madison spent his later years at Montpelier, his estate in Virginia.

Madison 43 04N 89 22W The capital city of Wisconsin, situated on an isthmus between Lakes Mendota and Monona. The commercial and industrial center of a rich agricultural region, it is the site of the University of Wisconsin (1848). Population (1990): 191,262.

Madonna (M. Ciccone; 1958–) US entertainer and actress. A flamboyant performer, she enjoyed great commercial success with her first album, *Madonna* (1983), and followed it with numerous other hit recordings. She also acted in movies including *Dick Tracy* (1990), *A League of Their Own* (1992), and *Body of Evidence* (1993). Her rebellious personal style, both in dress and actions, appealed to young female fans, who imitated her clothes and makeup. Highly publicized concert tours, including the "Blonde Ambition" tour of 1990, and music videos noted for their sexual content contributed to her image. Her 1992 book *Sex* was published as her album *Erotica* was released.

Madras 13 05N 80 18N A city and major seaport in India, the capital of Tamil Nadu on the Coromandel Coast. Founded (1639) by the British East India Company, the city developed around the small fort, Fort St George, which now contains state government offices and is the site of the first English church built in India (1678–80). The University of Madras was established here in 1857. An important industrial center, Madras manufactures cars, bicycles, and cement and its chief exports are leather, iron ore, and cotton textiles. Population (1981 est): 4,276,635.

Madras. *See* Tamil Nadu.

Madrid 40 27N 3 42W The capital of Spain, situated on a high plateau in the center of the country on the Manzanares River. Madrid is the focal point of rail, road, and air routes and is the financial center of Spain. Its industries include the manufacture of leather goods, textiles, chemicals, engineering, glassware, and porcelain and the processing of agricultural products. A cultural center, Madrid possesses a university (transferred from Alcalá de Henares in 1836), notable art galleries (especially the *Prado), and the national library (founded in 1712). Fine buildings include the former royal palace, the parliament, many churches, and the 17th-century cathedral. *History*: Madrid was captured from the Moors in 1083 by Alfonso VI. Philip II established it as the capital in 1561. The citizens' uprising against Napoleon's army of occupation in 1808 provided inspiration for the rest of Spain. In the Spanish Civil War Madrid was a Republican stronghold until it fell to the Nationalists in March 1939, after being besieged for over two years. Population (1991): 2,909,792.

madrigal A secular polyphonic composition (*see* polyphony) for voices, often a setting of a love poem. Its first flowering was in 14th-century Florence, where Landini wrote madrigals in two and three parts for voices and instruments. The Italian madrigal of the 16th and 17th centuries developed as an aristocratic art form of great expressiveness in the complex and often chromatic compositions of Marenzio, Monteverdi, and Gesualdo. The English school (Byrd, Morley, Weelkes, etc.) wrote in a simpler but idiomatic style; many sets of madrigals were composed in praise of Elizabeth I.

Madura An Indonesian island in the Java Sea, off NE Java. Largely infertile, its chief industries are cattle rearing and fish farming. It is known for its bull races. The population is Muslim and there is a notable mosque at Bangkalan. Area: 2113 sq mi (5472 sq km). Chief town: Pamekasan.

Madurai 9 55N 78 07E A city in India, in Tamil Nadu. Capital of the Pandya kings (4th–11th centuries AD), it is the site of a large Hindu temple (rebuilt 16th–17th centuries). Its university was established in 1966. Industries include brassware and textiles. Population (1991): 951,696.

Maeander River. *See* Menderes River.

Maecenas, Gaius (d. 8 BC) Roman statesman, who was a close adviser of Emperor *Augustus. Also noted as a literary patron, Maecenas included in his circle the three most important Augustan poets, Virgil, Horace, and Propertius.

Maelstrom A violent whirlpool in a channel in the Norwegian Lofoten Islands, a notorious shipping hazard. The word (uncapitalized) is also used for any whirlpool, particularly one of tidal origin occurring in a narrow irregular channel, as between islands.

Maes, Nicolas (*or* N. Maas; 1634–93) Dutch painter of domestic scenes and portraits, born in Dordrecht. Initially influenced by his teacher *Rembrandt, in such paintings as *Girl at the Window* (c. 1655; Rijksmuseum, Amsterdam), he later adopted the style of Flemish portraiture, after visiting Antwerp in the 1660s.

Maeterlinck, Maurice (1862–1949) Belgian poet and dramatist. Having established his reputation as a poet he became the leading dramatist of the *Symbolist movement with such plays as *Pelléas et Mélisande* (1892), on which Debussy based his opera of the same name, and *L'Oiseau bleu* (1908). He also wrote several philosophical and mystical prose works. From 1890 he lived mostly in France. He won the Nobel Prize in 1911.

Mafeking (*or* Mafikeng) 25 53S 25 39E A town in South Africa, in Bophutha Tswana. It was besieged for 217 days by Boers during the second Boer War (1899–1902) but was held by Colonel *Baden-Powell until relieved. Although outside the territory, it was the capital of the protectorate of Bechuanaland (now Botswana) until 1965. The town was officially surrendered to Bophutha Tswana by South Africa in 1980.

Mafia A criminal organization that originated as a secret society in 13th-century Sicily. The word (meaning "swank") was coined in the 19th century, when the Mafia was employed by the great landowners of Sicily to manage their estates. By extortion, "protection," ransom, and blackmail, the Mafia formed an organization so powerful that it virtually ruled Sicily. Repeated attempts to end its power, including the almost successful efforts of the fascists, have been hampered by the code of absolute silence enforced by reprisals. Italian emigrants took the Mafia to the US in the early 20th century, where as Cosa Nostra (Our Affair), it has flourished despite repeated attempts by federal and local authorities to curtail organized crime.

Magadha An ancient kingdom in NE India, now absorbed by Bihar state. Its early kings included Bimbisara (reigned c. 543–c. 491 BC) and Ajataśatru (reigned c. 491–c. 459). Under *Chandragupta Maurya, *Aśoka, and later the *Gupta kings, Magadha, and its capital Pataliputra, became a great cultural and political center.

Magdalena, Río A river in Colombia, rising in the SW of the country and flowing generally N to enter the Caribbean Sea near Barranquilla. Length: 956 mi (1540 km).

Magdalenian A culture of the Upper *Paleolithic, succeeding the *Solutrean in W Europe. Named for La Madeleine cave in the Dordogne (SW France), the Magdalenian is marked by an abundance of bone and antler tools, notably barbed harpoons and spear throwers, both new additions to man's toolkit. Dating from about 15,000 to 10,000 BC, it was the heyday of prehistoric art with magnificent cave paintings (e.g. at *Altamira) and carved and engraved decoration on bone artifacts.

Magdeburg 52 8N 11 35E A city in W Germany, on the *Elbe River. It achieved fame in the Middle Ages for its judicial system, the "Magdeburg Law," which was used as a model by many other European cities. It was also a leading member of the Hanseatic League. Bombs destroyed much of the city during World War II, including the town hall (1691), but the cathedral (begun in the 13th century) survived. An important inland port, its industries include iron, oil and sugar refining, chemicals, and textiles. Population (1991 est): 278,807.

Magellan, Ferdinand (c. 1480–1521) Portuguese explorer. He undertook many expeditions to India and Africa for Portugal between 1505 and 1516. In 1519, under Spanish patronage, he set off to seek a passage W to the Moluccas. The expedition of five ships—Magellan's flagship *Trinidad* with *San Antonio, Concepción, Victoria*, and *Santiago*—crossed the Pacific and late in 1520 sailed through the strait that was named for him. In the spring of 1521, after severe privations, they reached the East Indies, where Magellan was killed. Only the *Victoria* returned to Spain, thus completing under del *Cano the first circumnavigation of the world. *See also* Magellanic Clouds.

Magellan, Strait of A channel separating the mainland of South America from Tierra del Fuego. Discovered in 1520 by the Portuguese explorer Magellan, it is an important passage between the S Atlantic and the S Pacific Oceans. Length: 370 mi (600 km). Maximum width: 20 mi (32 km).

Magellanic Clouds Two relatively small irregular *galaxies, the Small and Large Magellanic Clouds are close neighbors of our *Galaxy. They can be seen, by eye, from the S hemisphere and were first recorded by Ferdinand *Magellan in 1519.

Magendie, François (1783–1855) French physiologist, noted for his work on the nervous system. He investigated the finding, first made by the anatomist Sir Charles Bell (1774–1842), that the anterior roots of the spinal cord carry motor nerves and the posterior roots carry sensory nerves. Magendie also experimented on nutritional requirements and studied the effects of drugs on the body.

Magenta 43 28N 8 52E A city in N Italy, in Lombardy. A decisive battle in the struggle for Italian national independence was fought here in 1859, in which the French and Sardinians defeated the Austrians; Magenta dye was named in honor of the event. Population: 23,890.

Maggiore, Lake (Latin name: Lacus Verbanus) A long narrow lake in Italy and Switzerland. Sheltered from the N by the Alps, it enjoys a mild climate: the holiday resorts at its edge include Locarno, in Switzerland. Area: 82 sq mi (212 sq km).

maggot The legless soft-bodied larva of many two-winged flies, such as the *blowfly and *housefly. Rat-tailed maggots are the aquatic larvae of certain *hoverflies, so called because of their long respiratory siphons.

Maghrib (*or* Maghreb; Arabic: west) The area in NW Africa occupied by the states of Morocco, Algeria, Tunisia, and Libya, so called on account of its geographical position in the Arab world. It formerly included Moorish Spain. Its inhabitants are of mixed *Arab and *Berber stock. Although the peoples of the Maghrib have their own distinctive customs and Arabic and Berber dialects they have always formed an integral part of the Arabic cultural tradition. *Compare* Mashriq.

Magi **1.** In antiquity, the priests of Zoroaster, renowned for their astronomical knowledge (*see* Zoroastrianism). **2.** The sages who came from the East, following a star, to worship the infant Christ at Bethlehem (Matthew 2.1–12). Early Christian tradition embroidered the New Testament account, giving them the title of kings and the names of Caspar, Melchior, and Balthazar. Symbolic significance was ascribed to their gifts: gold (kingship), frankincense (divinity), and myrrh (death). Honored as saints during the Middle Ages, they became the patron saints of *Cologne, and their adoration of Christ was a favorite theme in Christian art.

magic A system of beliefs and practices by which it is believed that man may control the natural and supernatural forces that affect his life. Generally regarded as "superstition" in industrial societies, magic still lingers in such popular rituals as touching wood to avert ill luck. In many preindustrial societies, magic plays an important social role. Its practitioners may rank next to the chief in prestige and authority, being credited with the ability to communicate with good and evil spirits to ensure success in war and hunting and the fertility of land and livestock. Some primitive rituals, such as pouring water on the ground to bring rain, are purely magical. They differ from religious rituals (praying for rain) because they rely on the naive belief that the poured water can in some way directly affect the mechanics of precipitation.

Maginot line Fortifications built (1929–38) to protect the E frontier of France. They were named for André Maginot (1877–1932), French minister of war (1929–32), who authorized its construction. Outflanked in World War II by the invading Germans (1940), the line was never tested.

Maglemosian A *Mesolithic culture of N Europe, dating from about 8000 to 5000 BC. Named for a site at Mullerup on Sjaelland (Denmark), the Maglemosian extended from E England to NW Russia. Hunters of forest game and fishers in the lakes by which they preferred to live, the Maglemosians used wood, stone, antler, and bone artifacts, including dugout canoes, but lacked domestic animals (apart from dogs), cultivated crops, and pottery.

magma Molten rock lying beneath the earth's surface, either in the crust or upper mantle. It may rise to the surface through volcanic fissures and be extruded as lava; if it solidifies underground it forms intrusive *igneous rock. Magma is a hot largely silicate liquid, containing dissolved gases and sometimes suspended crystals.

Magna Carta (1215) The Great Charter that was sealed at Runnymede by King John of England in response to the baronial unrest that resulted from his disastrous foreign policy and arbitrary government. The charter defined the baron's feudal obligations to the monarch, opposed his arbitrary application of justice, and confirmed the liberties of the English Church; its enforcement was to be supervised by 25 men elected by the barons. Although it failed to avert the outbreak of the first *Barons' War and was annulled by the pope, it was reissued, with some changes, in 1216, 1217, and 1225. The charter was subsequently upheld, especially by the Parliamentarians in the 17th century, as a statement of fundamental civil rights.

Magnani, Anna (1908–73) Italian film actress, born in Egypt. She began her career as a nightclub singer in Rome. She appeared in Rossellini's *Rome, Open City* (1945), Renoir's *The Golden Coach* (1953), and, after she went to Hollywood, *The Rose Tattoo* (1955).

magnesite A white or colorless mineral consisting of magnesium carbonate. It results from the alteration of magnesium-rich rocks, as in the veins of magnesite in serpentine, and as replacement deposits in limestone and dolomite. It is an important ore of magnesium and is used in the manufacture of refractory material, fertilizers, abrasives, etc.

magnesium (Mg) A light silvery-white reactive metal, first isolated by Sir Humphry Davy in 1808. Magnesium is the eighth most common element in the earth's crust and is a major constituent of the earth's mantle as the minerals olivine (Mg_2SiO_4) and enstatite ($MgSiO_3$). It is extracted by electrolysis of lead chloride ($MgCl_2$), which is obtained from sea water and is responsible for the stickiness of unrefined table salt, since magnesium chloride is deliquescent. Magnesium forms many other ionic salts, such as the sulfate ($MgSO_4$; Epsom salts), the oxide (MgO), the nitrate ($Mg(NO_3)_2$), and the hydroxide ($Mg(OH)_2$; milk of magnesia). It also plays a central role in plant life, occurring in *chlorophyll. It has important commercial uses when alloyed with aluminum to make the strong light alloys used in aircraft construction. It is also used in flares, incendiary bombs, and as magnesium oxide in refractory furnace linings. At no 12; at wt 24.305; mp 1201°F (648.8°C); bp 1996°F (1090°C).

magnet A body that has an appreciable external *magnetic field (*see also* magnetism). Every magnet has two distinct areas around which the field is greatest—these areas are called the north and south poles. If two magnets are brought together, the like poles repel each other and the opposite poles attract each other. Ferromagnetic materials (*see* ferromagnetism) are attracted to magnets because the magnet induces a field in the material in line with its own field.

Permanent magnets are made of ferromagnetic materials and retain their magnetism unless they are heated above a certain temperature or are demagnetized by a strong opposing field. **Electromagnets** only function when an electric current flows through their coils. The field strength along the axis of the coil is proportional to the number of turns of the coil and the current flowing through it.

magnetic bottle An arrangement of magnetic fields designed to contain a *plasma. Usually the fields are linear with strong magnetic fields called **magnetic mirrors** at both ends so that the plasma is confined within a cylinder. They are used in experimental *thermonuclear reactors.

magnetic constant (μ_0) A constant frequently occurring in magnetic equations in SI units. Also known as the *permeability of free space, its value is $4\pi \times 10^{-7}$ henry per meter. It is related to the *electric constant (ϵ_0) by $\mu_0\epsilon_0 = 1/c^2$, where c is the velocity of light.

magnetic declination The angle between geographical north and the horizontal component of the *geomagnetic field at the same point. It is also known as the magnetic variation.

magnetic dip The angle formed between the horizon and a compass allowed to swing freely in the vertical plane. It thus indicates the direction of the vertical component of the *geomagnetic field. It is measured with a **dip circle**, a vertically mounted magnetic needle surrounded by a circular scale.

magnetic domain. *See* ferromagnetism.

magnetic field The concept, devised by *Faraday, to explain the action-at-a-distance forces produced by a *magnet. The magnet is thought of as being surrounded by a field of force, within which its magnetic properties are effective. The strength and direction of the field is indicated by the lines of force that join the magnet's north and south poles. These lines of force can be seen if a card is laid over a magnet and iron filings sprinkled onto the card; when the card is tapped, the filings congregate along the lines of force. A wire carrying an electric current is also surrounded by a magnetic field, with concentric lines of force. An electromagnet usually consists of a coil of wire, in which the lines of force run through the center of the coil and around its circumference. The strength of the field at the center of the coil is proportional to the current and the number of turns, and inversely proportional to the radius of the coil. *See also* electromagnetic field.

magnetic flux A measure of the current-inducing properties of a magnetic field (*see* flux). It is measured in *webers.

magnetic moment A measure of the strength of a *magnet in terms of the torque or twisting force it experiences in a uniform magnetic field. It is equal to the product of the strength of a magnet's poles and the distance between them.

magnetic monopole A hypothetical particle that would carry a magnetic charge equivalent to either a north pole or a south pole. Such particles would be analogous to charged elementary particles and would provide a complete symmetry between electricity and magnetism. Unlike an electrically charged particle, a stationary magnetic monopole would give rise to a magnetic field and, when moving, an additional electric field. No monopole has ever been discovered.

magnetic tape. *See* cassette; tape recorder.

magnetism A phenomenon in which one body can exert a force on another body with which it is not in contact (action at a distance). The space in which such a force exists is called a *magnetic field. Stationary charged particles are surrounded by an *electric field; when these charged particles move or spin, an associated effect, the magnetic field, is created. Thus, an electric current, consisting of a flow of electrons, produces a magnetic field around the conductor carrying the current. The behavior of materials when placed in such a field depends on how the spinning electrons inside its atoms align themselves to reinforce or oppose the external field. *See also* antiferromagnetism; diamagnetism; ferrimagnetism; ferromagnetism; paramagnetism.

magnetite (*or* lodestone) A black magnetic material, a form of iron oxide (Fe_3O_4). It often has distinct north and south magnetic poles and was known around 500 BC for its use as a compass. It is one of the ores from which iron is extracted.

magneto An alternating-current *electric generator that uses a permanent *magnet, rather than an electromagnet, to create the magnetic field. It usually consists of one or more conducting coils rotating between a number of pairs of *magnetic poles. The induced voltage has a frequency equal to the number of magnets times the speed of rotation of the coils. It is used in some small internal-combustion engines to produce the ignition spark, often combined with the flywheel.

magnetohydrodynamics (MHD) A method of generating electricity in which current carriers in a fluid are forced by an external magnetic field to flow between electrodes placed in the fluid. Usually the fluid is a hot ionized gas or plasma in which the current carriers are electrons. The electron concentration is increased by adding substances of low ionization potential (e.g. sodium or potassium salts) to the flame. The method has been used to increase the efficiency of generation of a gas turbine, the exhaust flame of which is used for MHD generation.

magnetomotive force (mmf) A measure of the magnetic effect of an electric current in a coil. It is analogous to *electromotive force and is measured in ampere-turns, being dependent on the number of turns in the coil.

magnetosphere A region surrounding a planet in which charged particles are controlled by the magnetic field of the planet rather than by the interplanetary magnetic field carried by the *solar wind; beyond a magnetosphere, solar-wind particles flow undisturbed. Its shape arises from the interaction between solar wind and planetary magnetic field. The earth's magnetosphere, which includes the *Van Allen radiation belts, extends 37,000 mi (60,000 km) from the sunward side of the planet but is drawn out to a much greater extent on the opposite side.

magnetostriction The mechanical deformation of a ferromagnetic material (*see* ferromagnetism) when it is subjected to a magnetic field. The effect is the result of internal mechanical stress that arises because the energy required to magnetize the crystal domains varies with their orientation in the field. The converse effect, mechanical stress causing a change in magnetization, also occurs. Magnetostriction is used in *echo-sounding oscillators to produce the ultrasonic sound wave.

magnetron An electronic device used to generate and amplify *microwaves. It consists of a sealed evacuated tube containing a central cylindrical cathode (source of electrons) inside a cylindrical anode to which electrons are drawn by an electrostatic field. A steady magnetic field applied along the axis of the tube deflects the electrons from their radial path and, if strong enough, will cause them to rotate around the cathode setting up microwave-frequency oscillations. It is widely used in radar generators.

magnification In optical systems, the ratio of the width of an object is the width of its image, both being measured perpendicular to the axis of the system. For a single lens this reduces to the ratio of the distances of the image and the object from the lens when the image is in focus. For optical instruments the magnification is defined as the ratio of the size of the image on the retina produced by an object with and without the instrument.

Magnitogorsk 53 28N 59 06E A city in Russia, on the Ural River. It is an important metallurgy center and also possesses the largest iron and steel plant in the country. Population (1987): 430,000.

magnitude A measure of the brightness of stars and other astronomical objects. An object's **apparent magnitude** is its brightness as observed from earth and depends primarily on its *luminosity and its distance. An object's **absolute magnitude** is its apparent magnitude if it lay at a distance of 10 parsecs (32.616 light years). Both apparent and absolute magnitude are measured at various specific wavebands in the visible, ultraviolet, and infrared regions of the electromagnetic spectrum.

Magnitude value ranges from about +25 for the faintest objects so far detected through zero to negative values for the brightest objects. One star 5 magnitudes less than another is 100 times brighter; a difference of one magnitude thus denotes a brightness ratio of $\sqrt[5]{100}$, i.e. 2.512.

Magnolia A genus of evergreen or deciduous shrubs and ☐trees (35 species), native to North America and Asia and widely grown as ornamentals. Up to 148 ft (45 m) high, they have large simple leaves and big showy flowers, with a whorl of white, yellow, greenish, or pink petals and many stamens. These produce papery conelike structures containing winged fruits. A popular ornamental magnolia is the Chinese hybrid *M. × soulangeana*, which has pink-tinged flowers. Family: *Magnoliaceae. See also* umbrella tree.

magpie A noisy black-and-white crow, *Pica pica*, occurring in Eurasia, NW Africa, and W North America; 17 in (44 cm) long, it has a long wedge-shaped tail and an iridescent blue sheen on the wings. Magpies are omnivorous and notorious predators of eggs and nestlings; they are also attracted to bright objects.

The name is also given to Australian songbirds of the family *Cracticidae*, which includes the *currawongs.

Magritte, René (1898–1967) Belgian surrealist painter. Initially a wallpaper designer and commercial artist, he became associated with the Paris surrealists (*see* surrealism) in the late 1920s. Using a realistic but deadpan technique, he made everyday images appear menacing by the use of unusual juxtapositions.

Magyars The largest ethnic group in Hungary. There are substantial Magyar minorities in neighboring countries. They originated from mixed Ugric and Turkic stock, who migrated from Siberia during the 5th century and eventually reached their present location during the late 9th century. They subjugated the local *Slavs and *Huns and for 50 years raided far into Europe causing widespread disruption and fear. Today they are predominantly peasant farmers. *See also* Hungarian.

Mahabharata (Sanskrit: great epic of the Bharatas) A Hindu epic poem in 18 books. Probably composed about 300 BC, it may record actual events of a thousand years earlier. The main story relates the feud between the Pandava and Kaurava clans and is interwoven with many myths and other episodes, including the *Bhagavadgita* in the sixth book. The *Mahabharata* and *Ramayana* form the two great classics of Sanskrit literature.

Mahalla el-Kubra 30 59N 31 10E A city in N Egypt, on the Nile Delta. In a region producing rice, cereal, and cotton, it is an important cotton-manufacturing center. Population (1986 est): 385,000.

Mahan, Alfred Thayer (1840–1914) US sailor and historian. The son of a West Point professor, he went to the Naval Academy (1859). After serving in the

Civil War, he devoted his time to writing and lecturing, formulating the role of a strong navy in a nation and profoundly influencing naval planning internationally. He wrote *The Influence of Sea Power upon History, 1660–1783* (1890) and *The Influence of Sea Power upon the French Revolution and Empire, 1793–1812* (2 vols., 1892). He came out of retirement in 1898 to serve on the operations board during the *Spanish–American War.

Maharashtra A state in W central India, on the Arabian Sea. Rising from its coastal plain eastward over the Western *Ghats, it lies mostly on the *Deccan plateau. Cotton, millet, wheat, and rice are farmed. The second most industrialized state, it produces cotton textiles, chemicals, machinery, and oil products. Bauxite, manganese, and iron ore are mined. *History*: conquered by Muslims (1307), the Marathas regained their freedom (16th century) and maintained it until Britain established control (19th century). Maharashtra became a state in 1960. Area: 118,796 sq mi (307,762 sq km). Population (1991): 78,748,215. Capital: Bombay.

Mahavira, title of **Vardhamana** (?599–527 BC) The 24th and final *Tirthankara and founder of *Jainism. Born a member of the warrior caste, at the age of 30 he left his family to become an ascetic, following the teaching of the previous Tirthankara. After 12 years of austere self-mortification, he gained the spiritual knowledge he sought. He devoted the rest of his life to teaching Jaina doctrine.

Mahayana (Sanskrit: Great Vehicle) The school of Buddhism dominant in Tibet, Mongolia, China, Korea, and Japan. More evolved, adaptable, and less conservative and academic than the rival school, the *Theravada, the Mahayana teaching differs from it primarily in promulgating the ideal of the *Bodhisattva—the one who, having gained enlightenment, remains in the world in order to help other beings to their release.

Mahdi, al- (Arabic: the guided one) In Islamic tradition, a messianic leader who will appear shortly before the end of the world and, for a few years, restore justice and religion. According to some *Shiite Muslims, the 12th *imam (9th century AD), who is now hidden, will return as the Mahdi. Of a number of claimants to the title, the best known was the Sudanese leader **Muhammad Ahmad** (1844–85). After a religious experience, he proclaimed himself the Mahdi and led an uprising against the Egyptian government. In 1884 he attacked Khartoum, which was defended by General *Gordon, and captured it in January 1885, after a 10-months' siege. He died at Omdurman, near Khartoum, in June 1885, probably of typhus. His rule was continued by *Abd Allah, the Khalifa.

Mahfouz, Naguib (1911–) Egyptian author, recipient of the 1988 Nobel Prize for Literature. His early work centered on short stories and screenplays. His first novels had historical settings, but he then turned to contemporary themes. These included his well-known *Cairo Trilogy* (1956–57), *The Thief and the Dogs* (1961), and *Miramar* (1967).

mahjong An ancient Chinese game. It is usually played by four people using two dice and 136 tiles of bone, ivory, or plastic; 108 of the tiles are arranged in three suits: circles, bamboos, and characters. Each suit comprises tiles numbered one to nine, with four of each type of tile. There are also four each of red, white, and green dragons and four each of east, south, west, and north winds. Many sets have eight additional tiles, the flowers and seasons. The tiles are built into a square of four walls, symbolizing a walled city. Players score by collecting sequences of tiles according to complex rules.

Mahler, Gustav (1860–1911) Austrian composer and conductor. He studied at the Vienna conservatory and directed the Viennese Court Opera from

1897–1907, where he acquired a brilliant reputation. In 1909 he became conductor of the New York Philharmonic Society, but met resistance to his advocacy of modern music. He died of pneumonia at the age of 50. His nine large-scale symphonies (and uncompleted tenth) were written during brief vacations. The second (*Resurrection Symphony*), third, fourth, and eighth (*Symphony of a Thousand*) employ vocal soloists. He also wrote the song cycles *Kindertotenlieder* (1901–04) and *Das Lied von der Erde* (1907–10).

Mahmud II (1785–1839) Sultan of the Ottoman Empire (1808–39). He continued and increased the modernization and Westernization of the Empire that had begun under Selim III (1761–1808; reigned 1789–1807). He destroyed the *Janissaries in 1826 and in 1829 was forced to recognize Greek independence (*see* Greek Independence, War of).

Mahmud of Ghazna (971–1030) The third sultan (997–1030) of the Ghaznavid dynasty, which ruled a kingdom comprising modern Afghanistan. During his reign Mahmud led about 17 expeditions into India, conquering Kashmir and the Punjab, and also expanded his state in Iran. He is regarded as the greatest of his dynasty.

mahogany An evergreen tree of the genus *Swietenia* (7 species), native to tropical America and the West Indies and widely cultivated for timber. Up to about 65 ft (20 m) high, it has large compound leaves with 2–6 pairs of leaflets, greenish-yellow flower clusters, and fruit capsules containing winged seeds. *S. macrophylla* and *S. mahagoni* are the most important species: their hard red-brown wood is highly valued for furniture. Similar wood is obtained from members of other genera (*Khaya, Trichilia*, etc.). Family: *Meliaceae. See also* jarrah.

Mahonia A genus of evergreen shrubs (70 species), native to N temperate regions and South American mountains and often grown as ornamentals. They have leaves with paired, sometimes spiky, leaflets, and bunches of yellow or orange flowers that produce berries; only those of the Oregon grape (*M. aquifolium*) are edible. Family: *Berberidaceae*.

Maiden Castle The 115-acre site on Fordington Hill, near Dorchester, England of a prehistoric fortress that may date back to 2000 BC. Excavations provided evidence that an Iron Age fortified village occupied the site in the 4th century BC. It was captured by the Romans in 43 AD and abandoned in about 70.

maidenhair fern An ornamental *fern of the genus *Adiantum* (about 200 species), especially *A. capillus-veneris*, found worldwide in moist warm places. From a creeping rhizome arise delicate brown or black stalks, about 0.98–12 in (2.5–30 cm) high, bearing fan-shaped green leaflets. Clusters of spore capsules (sori) are situated on the leaf margins, which are folded onto the underside. Famly: *Adiantaceae*.

maidenhair tree. *See* ginkgo.

Maidstone 51 17N 0 32E A city in SE England, the administrative center of Kent on the Medway River. It is an ancient city and the center of an important fruit- and hop-growing region. There are brewing, paper, cement, confectionery, and engineering industries. Population (1986): 133,700.

Maiduguri (*or* Yerwa) 11 53N 13 16E A city in NE Nigeria. It comprises the towns of Yerwa and Maiduguri. It mainly exports livestock, hides, crocodile skins, and leather goods. It has a university (1960). Population (1992 est): 289,100.

Maikop 44 37N 40 48E A city in SW Russia, the capital of the Adygei autonomous region. It is the center of an oil-producing region and is also important for timber and food processing. Population (1985): 140,000.

Mailer, Norman (1923–) US novelist and journalist. He established his reputation with the World War II novel *The Naked and the Dead* (1948). His concern with American society, which provided the themes for novels such as *An American Dream* (1965), is more directly expressed in later works, such as *The Armies of the Night* (1968), concerned with a protest march on the Pentagon, and *Executioner's Song* (1979), about a convicted murderer, in which he attempted to transcend the conventional distinctions between fiction and journalism. Both were awarded Pulitzer Prizes. Other works include *The Deer Park* (1955), *Pieces and Pontifications* (1982), *Ancient Evenings* (1983), *Tough Guys Don't Dance* (1984), and *Harlot's Ghost* (1991).

Maillol, Aristide (1861–1944) French sculptor. Originally a painter and tapestry designer influenced by the *Nabis and *Gauguin, Maillol turned to sculpture in 1896. He made his name in the early 1900s with his monumental female nudes, the best known being *Mediterranean* (c. 1901; New York) and *Night* (1902; Paris). Although influenced by classical Greek models, their extreme simplicity anticipated modern abstract sculpture. Maillol's later works include war memorials and monuments to Cézanne and Debussy.

mail-order business A method of retail trading in which members of the public purchase goods (clothes, household goods, etc.) direct from mail-order houses through the mail, either in response to individual advertisements or from large highly illustrated catalogues. As no retailers' mark-up has to be paid, items can usually be purchased by mail order more cheaply than they can in stores. The customer, however, usually has to pay a delivery or postage charge. This method of trading was pioneered in the US in the 19th century, being especially appropriate to people living in remote areas.

Maimonides, Moses (Mosheh ben Maymun; 1135–1204) Jewish philosopher and physician. He was born in Córdoba (Spain), then under Moorish rule. After the fall of that city to the *Almohads and the subsequent religious persecution of Jews, Maimonides and his family left Spain. They settled in Cairo about 1165, where he later became physician to the Egyptian court. Maimonides' medical theories were advanced for his time. His celebrated philosophical work, *The Guide of the Perplexed*, which attempts to reconcile faith with reason, led to bitter controversy between orthodox Judaism and science.

Main River A river in W Germany, flowing generally W through Frankfurt to join the Rhine River at Mainz. It is linked by canal with the Danube River. Length: 320 mi (515 km).

Maine A coastal state in the extreme NE. Maine is the largest of the New England states. It is bordered by New Hampshire on the W, the Canadian provinces of Quebec and New Brunswick to the NW and NE, and the Atlantic Ocean to S and SE. It consists of uplands in the W and NW and lowlands along the deeply indented coast in the E. Four-fifths of the state is forested although the famous white pine is now almost extinct. It is the most sparsely populated state E of the Mississippi, most of its inhabitants living in the original settlements along the coast and river valleys. Manufacturing is most important and the major products are paper and pulp, leather goods, food, timber, and textiles. An area of considerable mineral wealth, limestone, building stone, and sand and gravel are exploited. The state's major agricultural products are potatoes, poultry, dairy, apples, and beef. *History*: It is thought that the Vikings visited Maine between the 9th and 11th centuries. When white explorers first arrived, the Abnaki Indians inhabited coastal and inland villages. The English also founded an unsuccessful colony in 1607 on the present site of Phippsburg. In 1613 a new French colony and mission was formed on Mt Desert Island but was expelled by English settlers under Sir Samuel Argall. In 1620, Captain John Mason and Fernando

Gorges were granted the region, and permanent settlements were soon made. Maine came under the jurisdiction of the Massachusetts Bay Colony in 1653. Succeeding struggles among the British, French, and Indians retarded settlement. In 1691, Massachusetts's control of Maine was settled but Indian rampages threatened expansion; the Queen Anne's War virtually ended Indian raids against the whites in the state. Lumbering, fisheries, and shipbuilding flourished under Massachusetts's administration. Maine entered the Union as part of Massachusetts (1788) and later became a separate state (1820). In the 1970s migration to the S was encouraged by the construction of highways and expanded transportation. In the 1980s a longstanding land claim by Indians in the state was settled with advantageous results for Maine through investments in business and property by the Indians. Area: 33,215 sq mi (86,027 sq km). Population (1990): 1,227,928. Capital: Augusta.

Maine A former province in NW France, approximating to the modern departments of Mayenne and Sarthe. United with Anjou in 1126, Maine became English territory in 1154. It was reconquered by Philip II Augustus in 1204 and was a province from about 1600 until divided into departments in 1789.

Mainland 1. (*or* Pomona) The largest of the Orkney Islands, divided into two main parts by Kirkwall Bay and *Scapa Flow. Area: 190 sq mi (492 sq km). Chief town: Kirkwall. **2.** The largest of the Shetland Islands. Area: about 225 sq mi (583 sq km). Chief town: Lerwick.

main sequence. *See* Hertzsprung-Russell diagram.

Maintenon, Mme de (Françoise d'Aubigné, Marquise de M.; c. 1635–1719) The second wife of Louis XIV of France. In 1652 she married the writer Paul *Scarron and after his death became the governess of Louis's illegitimate children (1669) and the king's mistress. She became his wife secretly after the death of Queen Marie Thérèse (1683).

Mainz (French name: Mayence) 50 00N 8 16E A city and port in S Germany, the capital of Rhineland-Palatinate at the confluence of the Rhine and Main Rivers. Originally a Celtic settlement, it was the first German archbishopric and in the 15th century Gutenberg set up his printing press there. Its cathedral was founded in 975 AD and its university in 1477 (discontinued 1816–1946). It is a wine-trading center with varied industries. Population (1991 est): 179,500.

Maistre, Joseph de (1753–1821) French monarchist. Settling in Lausanne, he became prominent as an opponent of Revolutionary France with his advocacy of absolutist government, faith in the divine right of kings, and belief, expounded in *Du pape* (1819), that an infallible pope can depose rulers who disregard the laws of God.

maize. *See* corn.

majolica Italian pottery originating in the 15th century. Made from calcareous clay, the soft buff body is coated with white tin glaze and brilliantly painted in luster and rainbow colors. Motifs include narrative pictures, botanical and zoological subjects, grotesques, arabesques, and armorial designs. Items made include tableware, drug jars, and display ornaments. Principal centers of manufacture were Gubbio (famous for lusters by Maestro Giorgio), Deruta (yellow and blue designs on orange backgrounds), Faenza (*see* faience), and *Caffaggiolo. The manufactures of the first quarter of the 16th century, which are sought after and valuable, were often financed by noble patronage. Imitations and forgeries abound.

Majorca (Spanish name: Mallorca) A Spanish island in the Mediterranean Sea, the largest of the Balearic Islands. The chief occupations are agriculture and tourism; cereals, legumes, oranges, olives, and figs are produced and marble is quarried. Area: 1465 sq mi (3639 sq km). Capital: Palma.

MAJOLICA *An enameled earthenware dish, made in Savona in the 17th century.*

Majuba Hill A mountain in South Africa, on the border between the Transvaal and Natal in the Drakensberg range. In 1881 it was the scene of a Boer victory over the British. Height: 6500 ft (1981 m).

Makarios III (Mikhail Khristodolou Mouskos; 1913–77) Cypriot churchman and statesman; archbishop of the Orthodox Church of Cyprus (1950–77) and president of Cyprus (1960–74, 1974–77). In 1956 he was deported to the Seychelles by the British because of his support for Greek-Cypriot union (*see* EOKA). He subsequently abandoned this aim, thus facilitating the attainment of Cypriot independence. In 1974 he was deposed in a coup that was backed by the Greek military regime but resumed the presidency before the end of the year.

Makassar. *See* Ujung Padang.

Makeevka (*or* Makeyevka) 48 01N 38 00E A city in SE Ukraine, in the Donets Basin. Its industry is based on coal mining and metallurgy. Population (1981 est): 442,000.

Makhachkala (name until 1921: Petrovsk) 42 59N 47 30E A port in SE Russia, the capital of the Dagestan republic on the Caspian Sea. It has oil-refining, engineering (especially aircraft), and textile industries. Population (1981 est): 269,000.

Malabar Coast (*or* Malabar) The W coast of India from Goa in the N to Cape Comorin in the S. In 1498 Vasco da Gama landed here, making it the first part of India to be brought into contact with Europe. The shore is fringed by sand dunes and coconut palms, while further inland there are long shallow lagoons and paddy fields.

Malabo (name until 1973: Santa Isabel) 3 45W 8 48E The capital of Equatorial Guinea, a port in the N of the island of Bioko (formerly Macías Nguema), founded by the British in 1827. Population (1983): 31,630.

Malacca 02 14N 102 14E A historic port in W Peninsular Malaysia, the capital of Malacca state. It was colonized successively by the Portuguese, Dutch, and British after 1511; many Portuguese and Dutch buildings remain. Population (1980): 88,073.

Malacca A state in W Peninsular Malaysia, on the Strait of Malacca. Consisting chiefly of a low-lying coastal plain, it produces rice, rubber, copra, tin, and bauxite. Area: 637 sq mi (1650 sq km). Population (1990): 583,500. Capital: Malacca.

Malacca, Strait of A channel between Sumatra and Peninsular Malaysia, linking the Indian Ocean with the Pacific Ocean. It is one of the world's most important shipping lanes. Length: about 500 mi (800 km).

Malachi An Old Testament prophet who rebuked religious hypocrites and the various social evils of the time, predicted a day of judgment, and urged the people to observe the Law of Moses. **The Book of Malachi** is the last book of the Old Testament.

malachite An ore of copper consisting of hydrated copper carbonate, $Cu_2(OH)_2CO_3$. It is bright green and is found in the oxidized zone of deposits of copper minerals. It occurs in massive form, often with a smooth surface.

malachite green (aniline green *or* China green; $C_{23}H_{25}ClN_2$) A dye that occurs as lustrous green crystals and is soluble in alcohol. It is used medicinally in dilute solution as an antiseptic and in fish breeding to kill fungus and bacteria. It is also used to dye leather and natural fabrics.

Malachy, St (1094–1148) Irish prelate, whose Church reforms initiated a religious revival in Ireland. He became bishop of Connor in 1124 and archbishop of Armagh in 1132. On his way to Rome (1139) he visited St *Bernard of Clairvaux, with whose encouragement he founded the first Cistercian abbey in Ireland, at Mellifont (1142). Feast day: Nov 3.

Málaga 36 43N 4 25W A city in S Spain, in Andalusia on the Mediterranean Sea. Founded by the Phoenicians (12th century BC), it passed successively to the Romans, the Visigoths, and the Moors, before falling to Ferdinand and Isabella in 1487. It has a cathedral (begun 16th century) and is the birthplace of the painter Picasso. A major tourist center and port, it exports olives, almonds, and dried fruits. Population (1991 est): 512,166.

Malagasy A language of the *Austronesian family, related to Malay, spoken in Madagascar. The standard form, written in Roman characters, is based on the Merina dialect. It has been influenced by Swahili and Arabic.

Malagasy Republic. *See* Madagascar, Democratic Republic of.

Malamud, Bernard (1914–86) US writer. With witty and ironic short stories and parables and such novels as *The Assistant* (1957) and *A New Life* (1961) he established his reputation as a skillful chronicler of Jewish characters and themes. His other works include the story collections *The Magic Barrel* (1958) and *Pictures of Fidelman* (1969) and the novels *The Fixer* (1966), *The Tenants* (1971), *Dubin's Lives* (1979), and *God's Grace* (1982).

Malan, Daniel F(rançois) (1874–1959) South African politician; prime minister (1948–54). Founder in 1939 with *Hertzog of the Nationalist party, which won the 1948 elections, Malan instituted *apartheid in South Africa. A minister of the Dutch Reformed Church, he was a right-wing Afrikaner nationalist.

Malang 07 59S 112 45E A city in Indonesia, in E Java. It is the site of ancient ruined royal palaces and Indonesian army and air-force bases. Its university was established in 1961. An agricultural center, it has soap, ceramics, and cigarette industries. Population (1980): 511,780.

Malaparte, Curzio (Kurt Erich Suckert; 1898–1957) Italian political journalist, novelist, and dramatist. He was an active but unorthodox adherent of fascism from the 1920s to the 1940s. His best-known novels are *Kaputt* (1944) and *The Skin* (1949), which drew on his experience as a war correspondent on the Russian front and as a liaison officer with the Allies in Naples during World War II.

malaria An infectious disease caused by protozoa of the genus *Plasmodium*. Malaria is transmitted by the female *Anopheles* mosquito, which lives only in the tropics. There are four species of *Plasmodium* that infect man and cause different types of malaria. Malignant tertian malaria (caused by *P. falciparum*) is the most severe; benign tertian malaria (caused by *P. vivax*) is less often fatal but there are repeated attacks. The parasites invade the red blood cells and cause them to burst. There is always fever but, depending on the type of parasite and the number of cells affected, there may also be fits, diarrhea, shock, and jaundice. Chronic infection causes enlargement of the liver and spleen. There are drugs (such as chloroquine) to treat the disease and these can also be taken to prevent it. Attempts by the World Health Organization to limit malaria, which is a major cause of death and illness in the tropics, by destroying the mosquito have not yet achieved complete success.

Malatesta A family that ruled Rimini (Italy) from 1295 to 1500. **Malatesta da Verrucchio** (d. 1312) led the local Guelf (papal) faction and came to power in 1295 after ousting the Ghibellines (imperial party; *see* Guelfs and Ghibellines). In the 15th century the family lost papal support and its most famous member, **Sigismondo Pandolfo Malatesta** (1417–68), was expelled from Rimini by Pope Pius II (1461). The family's temporary recovery of Rimini (1469–1500) ended when it was taken by Cesare *Borgia.

Malatya 38 22N 38 18E A city in SE central Turkey dating from 1838. It is in a fertile area producing cotton, tobacco, apricots, and grapes and has a university (1975). Population (1990): 281,776.

Malawi, Lake (former name: Lake Nyasa) A lake in Malawi, Tanzania, and Mozambique. Discovered for Europeans by Livingstone in 1859, it is 370 mi (595 km) long and is drained by the Shiré River S into the Zambezi River. Area: about 11,966 sq mi (31,000 sq km).

Malawi, Republic of (name until 1963: Nyasaland) A country in SE Africa, between Tanzania, Zambia, and Mozambique. Lake Malawi lies at its E border and the land consists mainly of high plateaus reaching heights of over 9800 ft (3000 m). The majority of the population is Bantu. *Economy*: chiefly agricultural. The main subsistence crop is maize, and cash crops include tobacco, tea, sugar, and groundnuts, which are the chief exports. Mineral resources are sparse and most power comes from hydroelectric sources, which are now being intensively developed. *History*: the area was visited by the Portuguese in the 17th century and, after Livingstone's exploration, became a British protectorate in 1891. In 1953, in spite of African opposition, it was joined with Northern and Southern Rhodesia to form the Federation of *Rhodesia and Nyasaland. This was dissolved in 1963 and Nyasaland gained internal self-government, becoming independent in 1964. In 1966 it became a republic within the British Commonwealth with Dr Hastings *Banda as its first president. The Malawi Congress

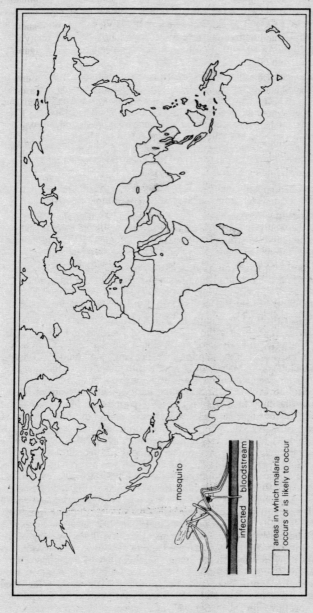

MALARIA *Despite eradication programs, malaria is still endemic in many parts of the tropics. By sucking the blood of an infected person, the female Anopheles mosquito can transmit the malarial parasite to an uninfected person.*

party is the only political party. Despite Banda's claims of self-sufficiency in Malawi, there were reports in the early 1990s of extreme malnutrition, especially among children, and of extensive human rights violations. Official language: English. Official currency, since 1971: kwacha of 199 tambala. Area: 36,324 sq mi (94,079 sq km). Population (1989 est): 8,515,000. Capital: Lilongwe.

Malay A language of the Indonesian branch of the *Austronesian family spoken in SE Asia and Indonesia. The dialect of the S Malay peninsula is the basis of standard Malay. It can be written in Roman or Arabic script. The Malay people probably migrated to this area from China between 2500 and 1500 BC. They became great seafarers, colonizing as far as Madagascar. Predominantly village dwellers, they live in nuclear families in houses raised on piling. Rice and rubber are the main crops. Distinction between noble and commoner social groups is important. Since the 15th century Islam has been the accepted religion, but vestiges of former Hinduism survive.

Malayalam A *Dravidian language of SW India. It is the official language of Kerala. It is related to Tamil from which its script, Koleluttu, is derived.

Malay Archipelago (former name: East Indies) An island group in SE Asia, the largest in the world. It lies between the Pacific and Indian Oceans and between the Asian and Australian continents. It comprises the Indonesian, Malaysian, and Philippine islands; New Guinea is sometimes included.

Malay Peninsula (*or* Kra Peninsula) A narrow peninsula in SE Asia, between the Andaman Sea and the South China Sea and separated from Sumatra by the Strait of Malacca. Politically it comprises SW Thailand, Peninsular Malaysia, and Singapore. Length: about 200 mi (320 km). *See also* Malaysia, Federation of.

Malaysia, Federation of A country in SE Asia, consisting of the 11 states of Peninsular Malaysia (formerly the Federation of Malaya) and the states of *Sabah and *Sarawak in N Borneo. Peninsular Malaysia consists of coastal plains rising to mountains in the interior, reaching heights of 7000 ft (2100 m). Most of the inhabitants are Malays and Chinese with minorities of Indians, Pakistanis, and others. *Economy*: Malaysia is a major exporter of rubber, tin, and palm oil. Agriculture is the chief occupation; besides the cash crops of rubber and palms, rice (the chief food crop) is extensively produced. Much of the land area is under dense forest producing considerable quantities of timber; fishing is also important. Other than tin, minerals exploited include iron ore, bauxite, ilmenite, and gold. The tourist industry is expanding, an added attraction being Malaysia's ethnic cultures. *History*: from the 9th to the 14th centuries the Srivijaya empire dominated the area. In the 14th century it was overrun by Hindu Javanese from the Majapahit kingdom and in about 1400 Malacca was established as an Islamic center. The spice trade flourished, centered on Malacca, attracting the attention of Europeans. In 1511 the port was taken by the Portuguese and in 1641 by the Dutch. British interest in the Malay states began in the 18th century; the East India Company established stations on Penang, Malacca, and Singapore Island, which became the Straits Settlements (1826). With the opening of the Suez Canal, British trade interests increased and in 1909 British protection was extended over the Federated Malay States (Selangor, Negri Sembilan, Perak, and Pahang) and the remaining five unfederated states. Following occupation by the Japanese during World War II, the Federation of Malaya was established (1948). Malaya became independent in 1957 and in 1963 part of the federal state of Malaysia, together with Sabah, Sarawak, and Singapore (which left the federation in 1965). There was considerable unrest through the years, caused mainly by Chinese resentment of Malay dominance in the government. A resurgence of communist guerrilla activities led to strong measures against communism. In foreign policy Malaysia has moved away from its previous pro-Western stand to a more neutral position. Supreme head of state: Sultan Azlan Muhibbuddin Shah. Prime minister: Datuk Seri Mahathir Muhammed. Official language: Bahasa Malaysia. Official religion: Islam. Official currency: Malaysian dollar of 100 cents. Area: 127,289 sq mi (329,749 sq km). Population (1990 est): 17,053,000. Capital: Kuala Lumpur. Main port: Georgetown.

Malcolm III (c. 1031–93) King of the Scots (1057–93). He became king after killing *Macbeth, the murderer of his father Duncan I (d. 1040; reigned 1034–40). Malcolm married St *Margaret. He became a vassal of William the Conqueror (1072) and was murdered during the last of frequent raids into N England.

Malcolm X (M. Little; 1925–65) US militant African-American leader. Formerly a member of the *Black Muslims, he founded the rival militant Organization of Afro-American Unity (1964), which supported violent means of achieving racial equality. He was assassinated while addressing a rally.

Maldives, Republic of (Divehi name: Divehi Raajje; name until 1969: Maldive Islands) A small country in the Indian Ocean, to the SW of Sri Lanka. It consists of a large number of small coral islands, grouped in atolls, of which just over 200 are inhabited. Most of the population is of mixed Indian, Sinhalese, and Arabic descent. *Economy*: the islands are covered with coconut palms; coconuts, along with fish, are the main export. Other sources of revenue are shipping, tourism, and copra production. *History*: adherents of Islam since the 12th century, the islands were ruled by a sultan. Formerly a dependency of Ceylon, they were officially under British protection from 1887 to 1965. They were ruled by an elected sultan until 1968, when they became a republic. The Republic of Maldives became a special member of the Commonwealth of Nations in 1982. Head of state: President Maumoon Abdul Gayoom. Official language: Divehi. Official religion: Islam. Official currency: Maldivian rupee of 100 larees. Area: 115 sq mi (298 sq km). Population (1990 est): 219,000. Capital and main port: Malé.

Malebo Pool (former name: Stanley Pool) 4 15S 15 25E A broad section of the Zaïre River in West Africa, on the Congo–Zaïre border. It contains the island of Bamu, which divides the river channel into N and S branches. Area: 174 sq mi (450 sq km).

Malebranche, Nicolas (1638–1715) French philosopher and theologian. Like *Descartes, whose work he publicized, Malebranche was concerned with the mind-body relation. In *De la recherche de la vérité* (1674) he held that the two could not interact causally. God brought about all events, including bodily movements, by direct intervention, a doctrine known as occasionalism.

maleic acid (or *cis*-butenedioic acid; $C_4H_4O_4$) A colorless crystalline toxic *fatty acid. It is an *isomer of **fumaric acid** (*trans*-butenedioic acid) and both are used in making dyes and synthetic resins.

Malenkov, Georgi Maksimilianovich (1901–88) Soviet statesman; prime minister (1953–55). A close associate of Stalin, Malenkov became first secretary of the Soviet Communist party and prime minister after Stalin's death. Shortly afterward, he was replaced in the former post by Khrushchev but continued as prime minister until forced to resign, owing to agricultural failures. He was expelled from the Communist party in 1961.

Malesherbes, Chrétien Guillaume de Lamoignon de (1721–94) French statesman, a leading figure of the prerevolutionary era of reform in France. In 1750 he became director of censorship and gained a reputation for his liberal attitude, permitting, for example, the *Philosophes to publish their work. Criticism of the monarchy led to his banishment from court in 1771 but he was executed as a Royalist during the French Revolution.

Malevich, Kazimir (1878–1935) Russian painter and art theorist, born in Kiev. He worked in most modern styles before exhibiting (1915) his *Black Square on White Ground*, which launched the art movement called *suprematism and made a significant contribution to *abstract art.

Malherbe, François de (1555–1628) French poet and critic. In 1605 he became court poet to Henry IV. In his criticism, mostly contained in letters and commentaries, he anticipated classicism by advocating principles of harmony, regularity, and propriety. His poetry consisted chiefly of conventional verses on political and religious themes.

Mali, Republic of (name until 1959: French Sudan) A large landlocked country in West Africa. It consists largely of desert, extending into the Sahara in the N, and is crossed by the Niger River, the flood plains of which provide most of the fertile land. The majority of the population are Bambara, Fulani, and Senufo. *Economy*: chiefly subsistence agriculture, especially livestock, including cattle, camels, and sheep. The main crops are rice, millet, cassava, cotton, and groundnuts, but all agriculture is often affected by droughts. River fishing is important and dried and smoked fish, together with cattle and groundnuts, are the main exports. Industry is based mainly on the processing of food and hides and skin. Mineral reserves of bauxite, uranium, and oil are present but only salt and small quantities of gold are exploited. Tourism is being developed, the main attractions being hunting, fishing, and the ancient city of Timbuktu. *History*: from the 4th century AD the area was occupied by successive empires, including those of Ghana, Mali (the most famous ruler of which was Mansu Musa), and Gao. In the late 19th century it was conquered by the French and, as French Sudan, it became part of French West Africa. It achieved internal self-government as part of the French Community in 1958. It briefly formed with Senegal the Federation of Mali in 1959, becoming a separate and fully independent republic in 1960. It broke away from the French Community but, because of economic problems, rejoined the franc zone in 1967. In 1968 the government was overthrown in a military coup led by Lt. Moussa Traoré, who became president in 1969 and was reelected in 1979 and 1985. Plans for a union or a confederation of Guinea and Mali were entertained in the mid-1980s, despite little public support. Traoré was overthrown in 1991. The transitional government, headed by Lt. Col. Amadou Toumani Toure, gave way to the elected government of Alpha Koware in mid-1992. Official language: French. Official currency: Mali franc of 100 centimes. Area: 464,752 sq mi (1,204,021 sq km). Population (1990 est): 9,182,000. Capital: Bamako.

malic acid A dicarboxylic acid ($C_4H_6O_5$) that occurs widely in fruits (including apples, plums, and grapes) as the free acid or its salts. The anion malate is an intermediate compound in the *Krebs cycle.

Malik-Shah (1055–92) The last of the three great Seljuq sultans of Turkey (1073–92), succeeding his father *Alp Arslan. Malik-Shah, a noted patron of science and the arts, built the famous mosques of Isfahan (his capital) and sponsored the poet *Omar Khayyam. His government owed its distinction to the work of the vizier *Nizam al-Mulk.

Malines. *See* Mechelen.

Malinke A people of West Africa, also known as Mandingo, who speak a language of the Mande division of the *Niger-Congo family. During the 7th century AD one group founded a state with its capital at Kangaba. This spread to become the empire of Mali, which flourished from about 1250 to 1500. The

Malinke are agriculturalists, who live in villages of round huts. Descent follows the patrilineal principle.

Malinowski, Bronisław (1884–1942) Polish anthropologist, regarded as the founder of social anthropology. Between 1914 and 1918 Malinowski lived among the natives of New Guinea and the Trobriand Islands, making a detailed study of their culture. A professor at London University from 1927, he became famous for his functional theory of anthropology, which saw every ritual and belief of a society as fulfilling a particular function. Malinowski's published work includes *The Natives of Mailu* (1915) and *The Father in Primitive Psychology* (1927).

Malipiero, Gian Francesco (1882–1973) Italian composer and teacher. His style owes much to the study of 17th- and 18th-century Venetian composers; his works include operas and orchestral, vocal, and chamber music. He published an edition of the works of Monteverdi.

mallard A *dabbling duck, *Anas platyrhynchos*, common on ponds and lakes in the N hemisphere. About 22 in (55 cm) long, females are mottled brown and males grayish with a green head, white collar, reddish breast, black rump, and a curly tail. Both sexes have a broad yellow bill and a purple wing speculum. The mallard is the ancestor of most domestic breeds of duck.

Mallarmé, Stéphane (1842–98) French poet. He visited England frequently and until 1871 taught English in schools in the French provinces and in Paris. Influenced by Baudelaire and Poe, he became a major figure of the *symbolist movement, believing that the function of poetry was to evoke the ideal essences that lay behind the world of actual appearances. His best-known works include *Hérodiade* (1864), *L'Après-Midi d'un faun* (1865), and his obscure final poem, *Un Coup de dés jamais n'abolira le hasard* (1897).

mallee Scrubland vegetation of the coastal regions of S Australia, dominated by small trees and shrubs of the genus *Eucalyptus*. Most are 7–10 ft (2–3 m) high, with leathery gray-green leaves and many thick roots that store water.

mallee fowl A white-spotted light-brown bird, *Leipoa ocellata*, occurring in semiarid interior regions of Australia; 25.5 in (65 cm) long, it feeds on seeds and flowers and builds a large nest mound of fermenting plant material and sand, which may reach 15 ft (4.5 m) across. Throughout the incubation period the male maintains the mound at a constant temperature by adding and taking away sand as necessary. Family: *Megapodidae* (megapodes).

Mallorca. *See* Majorca.

mallow A herbaceous plant of the genus *Malva* (30 species), native to N temperate regions. Mallows, which may be creeping or erect, grow up to 35 in (90 cm) tall. They have hairy lobed leaves and five-petaled flowers, which are usually purple, pink, or white and 0.6–2.4 in (1.5–6 cm) across. The name is also given to other plants of the same family. The tree mallow (*Lavatera arborea*) is a shrublike biennial, up to 10 ft (3 m) high, with rose-purple flowers. Family: *Malvaceae*. *See also* marsh mallow.

Malmédy. *See* Eupen-et-Malmédy.

Malmö 55 38N 12 57E A city and port in S Sweden, on the *Sound opposite Copenhagen. It was a prominent trade and shipping center in the Middle Ages. Malmö's varied industries include shipbuilding, textiles, and food processing. Population (1992 est): 234,796.

malnutrition Ill health resulting from an inadequate diet, usually associated with poverty. The body needs certain amounts of protein, carbohydrate, fat, vitamins, and minerals. Insufficient protein causes *kwashiorkor in children, and a diet deficient in all nutrients causes marasmus. Lack of vitamins causes a wide variety of diseases, including *scurvy, *rickets, *beriberi, and *pellagra. *Obesity can be considered as a form of malnutrition resulting from overeating.

Malory, Sir Thomas (?1400–1471) English writer. He was the author of *Morte d'Arthur* (c. 1469), a narrative in 21 books of the legendary court of King Arthur, drawn mostly from French sources. Malory's identity remains uncertain, but he was probably a Warwickshire knight who had fought in France, became a member of Parliament in 1445, and was several times imprisoned.

Malpighi, Marcello (1628–94) Italian anatomist, whose microscopical studies of living organisms provided new insights into their function. In 1661 he discovered the fine capillaries that connect arteries with veins, substantiating William *Harvey's theory of blood circulation. Malpighi made numerous studies of body organs—the kidney glomeruli (Malpighian corpuscles) and a layer of skin tissue (Malpighian layer) are named for him. He also made valuable early studies of embryology and comparative plant anatomy.

Malplaquet, Battle of (Sept. 11, 1709) A battle in the War of the *Spanish Succession in which the French faced the armies, under Marlborough and Prince Eugene of Savoy, of Britain, the Netherlands, and Austria, fought 10 mi (16 km) S of Mons. By a strategic retreat the French inflicted severe casualties upon the allies, who, although victorious, were checked in their advance upon Paris.

Malraux, André (1901–76) French novelist and essayist. His career included active service with communist revolutionaries in China in the 1920s, with the Republican forces in the Spanish Civil War, and with the French Resistance in World War II. His novels, which are notably objective treatments of the issues involved in these conflicts, include *Man's Estate* (1933) and *Days of Hope* (1938). He was minister for cultural affairs under de Gaulle from 1959 to 1969. He also wrote on art, notably in *Voices of Silence* (1953) and *Museum without Walls* (1967), and a volume of memoirs, *Antimémoires* (1967).

malt Barley or other grain prepared for brewing or distilling. The grain is softened by soaking in water, then either heaped on the malting floor and turned by hand or put in revolving drums to encourage germination. Germ growth is stopped by drying the malt by heat, after which it is ready for brewing. Alternatively, after eight to 10 days' germ growth the malt may be used for malt *whisky.

Malta, Republic of A small country in the Mediterranean Sea, to the S of Sicily comprising the two main islands of Malta and Gozo and several islets. *Economy*: previously heavily dependent on foreign military bases, Malta has made efforts to diversify the economy in recent years. The naval dockyards have been converted to commercial use and port facilities are being developed to encourage the use of Malta as a transit center for Mediterranean shipping. Shipbuilding and repair are important and the development of other varied industries is aided by foreign investment (especially from Libya, Algeria, and Saudi Arabia). There is some agriculture, both crops and livestock, and fishing. Tourism is an important source of revenue. Exports include clothing, textiles, machinery, and food. *History*: occupied successively by the Phoenicians, Greeks, Carthaginians, and Romans, the island was conquered by the Arabs in 870 AD. In 1090 it was united with Sicily and in 1530 was granted to the Knights Hospitallers. In 1798 the island was occupied by the French and then by the British, to whom it was formally ceded in 1814. As a crown colony it became an important naval and air base. In World War II Malta's heroic resistance to German attack (1940–42) gained it the George Cross. In 1947 and 1961 it acquired increasing self-government, becoming fully independent in 1964. In 1974 it became a republic within the British Commonwealth. During the 1970s and 1980s, Malta maintained close ties with Libya. US president Bush and Soviet president Gorbachev held an informal summit meeting at sea off the Malta coast in 1989. President: Vincent Tabone. Prime minister: Eddie Fenech Adami. Official languages: Maltese and English; Italian is widely spoken. Official religion: Roman Catholic. Official currency: Maltese pound of 100 cents and 1000 mils. Area: 122 sq mi (316 sq km). Population (1990): 373,000. Capital and main port: Valletta.

Malthus, Thomas Robert (1766–1834) British clergyman and economist, famous for his population theories. In his *Essay on the Principle of Population* (*First Essay*, 1798; *Second Essay*, 1803) Malthus argued that mankind is doomed to remain at near-starvation level as growth in food production, which increases at an arithmetical rate, is negated by the geometrical increase in population. Elaborating ideas from Plato, Aristotle, and Hume, Malthus called for positive efforts to cut the birth rate, preferably by sexual restraint but, failing that, by birth control.

Maluku. *See* Moluccas.

Malvinas, Islas. *See* Falkland Islands.

mamba A large agile highly venomous snake belonging to the African genus *Dendroaspis* (4–5 species). The aggressive black mamba (*D. polylepis*) is 14 ft (4.3 m) long, lives in open rocky regions, and preys on birds and small mammals. The smaller arboreal green mamba (*D. angusticeps*) reaches a length of 9 ft (2.7 m) and is much less aggressive. Mambas are egg-laying snakes. Family: *Elapidae* (cobras, mambas, coral snakes).

Mamelukes (Arabic: *mamluk*, slave) The rulers of Egypt and Syria (1250–1517). The Mamelukes were slave soldiers who seized power and then provided a succession of rulers from their own ranks. They drove back the Mongols and finally expelled the Crusaders from Syria. In 1517 the Ottoman Turks conquered Syria and Egypt but the Mamelukes survived as a class and were frequently the effective rulers of Egypt until destroyed by *Mehemet Ali in 1811.

mammal A warm-blooded animal belonging to the class *Mammalia* (about 4250 species). The evolution of mammals from reptiles involved the development of a temperature-regulation system with an insulating layer of fur and sweat glands in the skin for cooling. This enabled mammals to become highly active, with well-developed sense organs and brains, and to colonize cold climates. The survival of the young was improved by the evolution of milk-secreting *mammary glands, and in placental mammals a specialized nourishing membrane (the *placenta) in the uterus (womb) enabled the young to be born at an advanced stage of development. The stages involved in this evolution can still be seen in such primitive mammals as the egg-laying *monotremes and the *marsupials, which produce young at an early developmental stage.

The majority of modern mammalian species are terrestrial, ranging in size from tiny shrews to the elephant. However, bats are flying mammals and whales have adapted to a wholly marine existence.

mammary gland The gland in female mammals that secretes milk. Believed to have evolved from sweat glands, there are one or more pairs on the ventral (under) side of the body. The number of glands is related to the number of young produced at one birth; for example, rats and mice have five or six pairs; whales and humans have one pair. Each gland consists of branching ducts leading from milk-secreting cells and opening to the exterior through a nipple. In the most primitive mammals (*Monotremata*) there are no nipples and the milk is secreted directly onto the body surface. The secretion of milk (*see* lactation) is under hormonal control. *See also* breast.

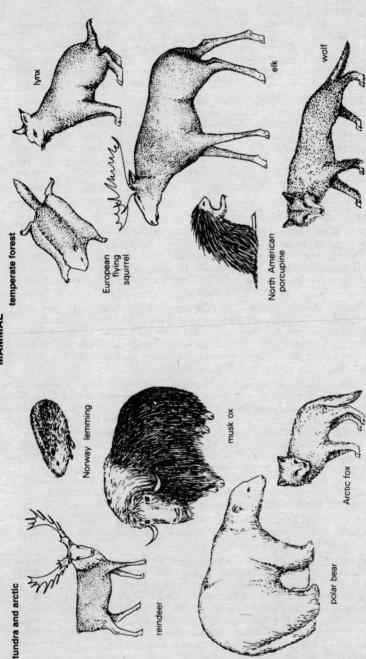

MAMMAL *This large and diverse group of animals has succeeded in colonizing almost every available habitat on earth, even the most inhospitable. Representative mammals are shown from eight of the world's major habitats (the animals depicted in each habitat are not necessarily from the same geographical region).*

MAMMAL

temperate forest

lynx

European flying squirrel

elk

North American porcupine

wolf

tundra and arctic

Norway lemming

reindeer

musk ox

polar bear

Arctic fox

MAMMAL

tropical forest

common opossum

fruit bat

bongo

clouded leopard

colobus monkey

Philippine tarsier

tropical grassland

chacma baboon

lion

spotted hyena

springbok

African mongoose

MAMMAL

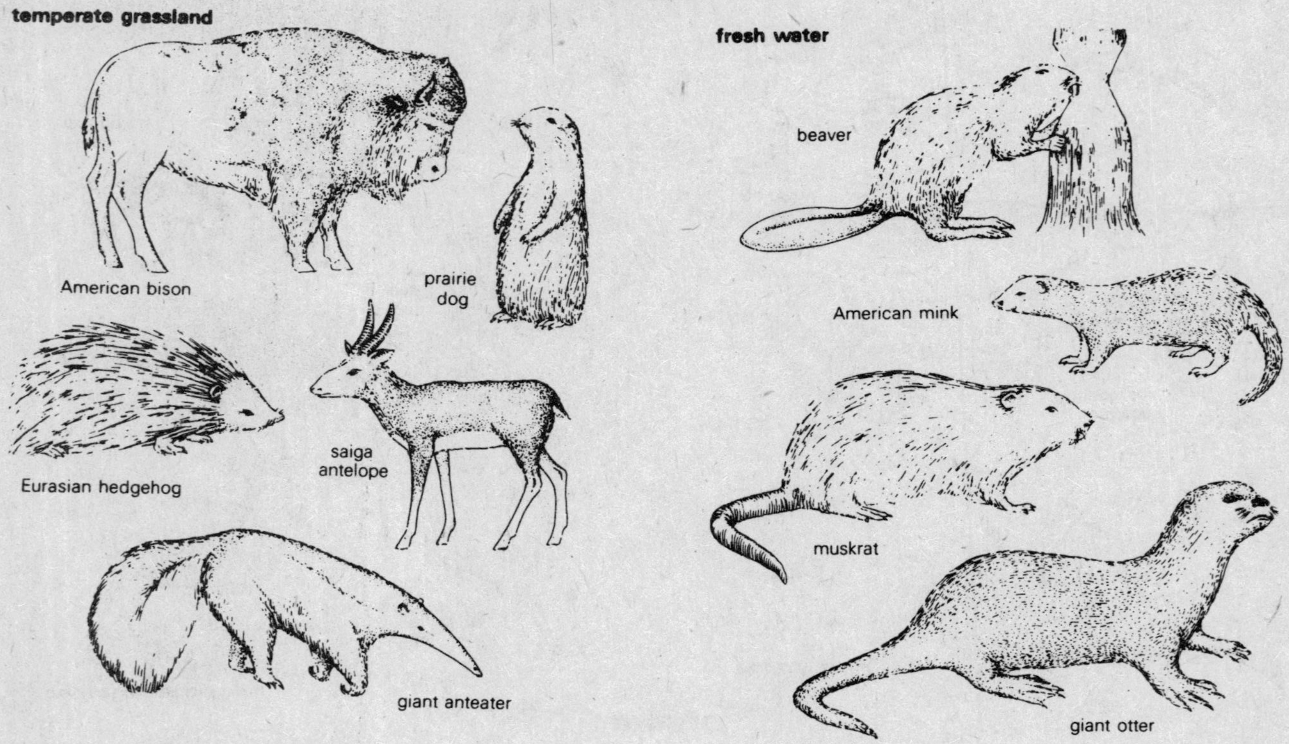

fresh water

beaver

American mink

muskrat

giant otter

temperate grassland

prairie dog

saiga antelope

American bison

Eurasian hedgehog

giant anteater

MAMMAL

salt water

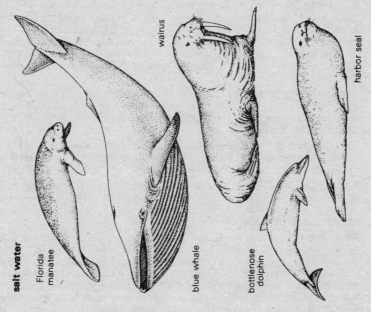

Florida
manatee

walrus

blue whale

bottlenose
dolphin

harbor seal

desert

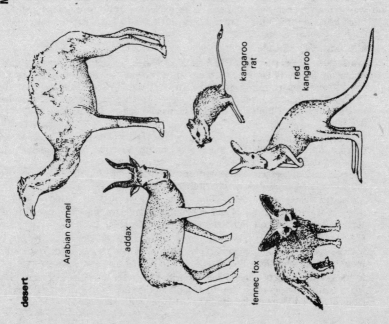

Arabian camel

kangaroo
rat

red
kangaroo

addax

fennec fox

mammoth An extinct elephant belonging to the genus *Mammuthus*, whose remains have been found in India, Europe, and North America. Of the four types known, the imperial mammoth (*M. imperator*) was the largest, 15 ft (4.5 m) at the shoulder. The woolly mammoth (*M. primigenius*) had thick body hair and tusks up to 8 ft (2.5 m) long. The well-preserved remains of woolly mammoths, which died out about 10,000 years ago, have been found frozen in the permafrost of Siberia. □fossil.

Mammoth Cave A large cavern in W central Kentucky, in the Mammoth Cave National Park. It consists of a series of limestone caves with spectacular stalactites and stalagmites. The largest cave reaches 125 ft (38 m) in height and a width of 300 ft (91 m).

Mamoré, Río A river in South America, rising in the Andes in central Bolivia and flowing generally N. It forms part of the Bolivia–Brazil border before joining the Río Bení to become the Rio Madeira. Length: about 930 sq mi (1500 km).

Ma'mun, al- (786–833 AD) The seventh *caliph (813–833) of the 'Abbasid dynasty. A son of Harun ar-Rashid, al-Ma'mun seized the caliphate from his half-brother al-Amin (c. 785–813). As caliph he was inclined toward Shiite ideas and encouraged philosophical and scientific work.

Man, Isle of An island in the Irish Sea, between England and Ireland. It has been a possession of the British crown since 1828, but is virtually self-governing with its own parliament. It consists of central hills rising to 2034 ft (620 m), with lowlands in the N and S. Tourism is the main source of revenue; attractions include its mild climate, scenery, and the annual motorcycle races. The island's low taxation levels encourage a steady influx of retired people. Its agriculture is varied; sheep and cattle are raised and produce includes cereals, turnips, and potatoes. Some manufacturing industry exists including light engineering. *History*: originally inhabited by Celts, the derivative Manx language survived in common usage until the 19th century. The island became a dependency of Norway in the 9th century AD and was ceded to Scotland (1266), coming under English control after 1406. Area: 227 sq mi (588 sq km). Population (1986): 64,300. Capital: Douglas.

Manado. *See* Menado.

Managua 12 06N 86 18W The capital of Nicaragua, on the S shore of Lake Managua. Formerly an Indian settlement, it became the capital in 1857. It suffered severe damage from earthquakes in 1931 and 1972 and from the civil war (1979). The Nicaragua campus of the Central American University was founded in 1961. It is the country's principal industrial center. Population (1985 est): 682,000.

manakin A small stocky bird belonging to a family (*Pipridae*; 59 species) occurring in tropical forests of South and Central America. Male manakins are generally dark with bright patches and decorative crests and tail feathers; the females are usually green. Males perform elaborate courtship displays, either on the ground in specially cleared territories or in the trees.

Manama (Arabic name: Al Manamah) 26 12N 50 38E The capital of Bahrain since 1971, situated at the N end of Bahrain Island. An important free port, its economy is based on oil. Population (1988 est): 150,000.

Manassas 38 45N 72 48W A city in N Virginia, SW of Alexandria. Nearby is Manassas National Battlefield Park, which commemorates two Civil War battles fought in 1861 and 1862. Population (1990): 27,957.

Manasseh, tribe of One of the 12 *tribes of Israel. It claimed descent from Manasseh, King of Judah, son of Joseph and grandson of Jacob. Manasseh's lands lay E and W of Jordan, midway between Galilee and the Dead Sea.

Manasseh ben Israel (Manoel Dias Soeiro; 1604–57) Rabbi of Amsterdam. His *Hope of Israel* (1650) dealt with the supposed discovery of the 10 lost tribes in South America. Encouraged by English mystics, he presented a petition to Oliver *Cromwell (1655), asking for the readmission of the Jews to England (they had been expelled in 1290). He died before he could witness the success of his mission.

manatee A herbivorous aquatic □mammal belonging to the genus *Trichechus* (3 species), of warm Atlantic waters and coastal rivers of Africa and America. Up to 15 ft (4.5 m) long, manatees have a rounded body with tail fin and flippers and a squarish snout. The American manatee (*T. manatus*) of Florida feeds mainly at night. Slow and placid, it rests on the bottom during the day, rising regularly to breathe. Family: *Trichechidae*; order: *Sirenia. See also* dugong.

Manaus (*or* Manáos) 3 06S 60 00W A city in NW Brazil, the capital of Amazonas state on the Rio Negro. Founded in 1660, it became the center of the rubber boom (1890–1920). It remains the chief inland port of the Amazon basin and is accessible to oceangoing steamers. Exports include rubber, Brazil nuts, timber, and other forest products. Notable buildings include the Teatro Amazonas (the opera house, 1896) and the University of Amazonas (1965). Population (1980): 613,098.

Manawatu River A river in New Zealand, in SW North Island flowing generally W and SW to the Tasman Sea NE of Wellington. The surrounding plain is one of New Zealand's most productive farming areas. Length: 113 mi (182 km).

Mancha, La An area and former province in Spain. It consists of an extensive sparsely populated arid plateau. Windmills, used to pump water from underground, are a distinctive feature. It became famous as the setting of Cervantes's *Don Quixote de la Mancha.*

Manchester 53 30N 2 15W A city in NW England, situated on the Irwell River and forming part of a large conurbation. Linked with the Mersey estuary by the Manchester Ship Canal (opened 1894), it is an important port as well as England's second largest commercial center (banking, insurance). Long the center of Lancashire's traditional cotton industry, its other industries include chemicals, engineering, clothing, printing, publishing, paper, rubber, food products, and electrical goods. *History*: the Roman fort of Mancunium, Manchester developed as a regional wool marketplace. From the mid-18th century onward a number of factors, such as new technology, the humid climate, and the availability of labor, combined to make it the world's main cotton-manufacturing town. It became the center of a network of roads, canals, and railroads but its rapid growth led to industrial discontent and political agitation (*see* Peterloo Massacre). Population (1991): 397,400,

Manchester 42 59N 71 28W A city in S New Hampshire, on the W bank of the Merrimack River. It is New Hampshire's largest city and a major distribution center for the surrounding area. Industries include electronics, leather and food processing, wood and paper products, and textiles. Population (1990): 99,567.

Manchu A nomadic people of Manchuria who conquered China during the 16th and 17th centuries and established the *Qing dynasty.

Manchukuo A puppet state set up by the Japanese in Manchuria in 1932 in a bid to occupy all China. It was administered by Chinese with the last Chinese emperor, Henry P'u-i (1906–67), as ruler, and lasted until Japan's defeat in 1945.

Manchuria A region in NE China bordering on Russia, roughly comprising the provinces of Heilongjiang, Jilin, and Liaoning. It is mountainous in the E and W with a large central fertile plain. The densely populated plain is a major industrial and agricultural area. Products include timber, minerals such as coal and iron, and fish. *History*: the area was for centuries inhabited and fought over by the Manchu, Mongols, and Chinese. Their power struggles resulted in empires established over China by the Mongols (1279–1368; *see* Yuan) and Manchus (1644–1912; *see* Qing). Although the S had long been colonized by the Chinese, immigration into the whole area increased greatly under the Qing because of land hunger in China. In the late 19th century this fertile area was dominated by Russia (1898–1904) and then by Japan (1905–45), which developed industrial centers in the region. In 1931, following the Mukden Incident (*see* Shenyang), Japanese forces invaded Manchuria and established a puppet state (*see* Manchukuo). After 1945 the area, staunchly communist, received much aid from the Soviet Union until the 1960s, when the break between China and the Soviet Union took place. Area: about 500,000 sq mi (1,300,000 sq km).

Manchu-Tungus A group of languages of the *Altaic language family, related to *Mongolian and *Turkic. It comprises only a few languages, of which only the almost extinct Manchu has any literary tradition.

Mandaeanism A Gnostic sect surviving in S Iraq and SW Iran (*see* Gnosticism). It originated in the 1st or 2nd century AD, but its place of origin and its relationship to Christianity, Judaism, and indigenous Iranian religions, on all of which it draws, are disputed. Mandaeans are hostile to Christ but revere John the Baptist. Their most important rite is frequent baptism. The sacred *Ginza* describes their cosmology, which envisages a universe in which hostile spirits (*archons*) endeavor to prevent the soul's ascent to God.

mandala A Buddhist painted or sometimes metal-wrought symbol used in meditation and other religious practices and particularly associated with Tibetan and Japanese Buddhism. It usually consists of a series of concentric circles, representing universal harmony and containing religious figures, the Buddha being represented in the center.

Mandalay 21 57N 96 04E A city in Myanmar (formerly Burma), on the Irrawaddy River. The last capital of the Burmese kingdom, it fell to the British in 1885. It has numerous monasteries, temples, and pagodas and is the site of a university (1964). Mandalay is the principal commercial center of Myanmar. Population (1983 est): 530,000.

Mandan North American Siouan-speaking Indian tribe, found in North Dakota, near the Missouri River. The Mandan, whose name means "river people," were basically hunters, weavers, farmers, and traders, who traveled in round bullboats. Smallpox, brought by white traders, devastated the tribe in 1837; today, about 350 descendants of the Mandan live on Fort Berthold Reservation in North Dakota.

mandarin (fruit). *See* tangerine.

mandarin (official) A Chinese bureaucrat, whose appointment to salaried posts in the civil service was, from early Han times until the 1911 revolution, by examination. Mandarins occupied a privileged position in society, wore special embroidered robes, and spoke the Mandarin dialect of *Chinese, which in its standard, Beijing (Peking), form is now spoken by 70% of the population.

mandarin duck A brilliantly colored *duck, *Aix galericulata*, native to China—where it was the symbol of marital fidelity—and widespread as an ornamental bird. It is 17 in (43 cm) long. The female is gray-brown with a bluish head, a white eye stripe, and a black bill; the male has a red bill, black-and-white head, purple breast, white underparts, and distinctive chestnut wing fans and whiskers at the sides of the face.

mandate The system whereby former German colonies and Turkish territories were entrusted by the League of Nations to the principal Allied powers after World War I. The powers were to be responsible for their administration, welfare, and development until the mandatories were ready for self-government. After the establishment of the UN those that remained became *trust territories.

Mandela, Nelson Rolihahla (1918–) South African nationalist and political leader. The son of a tribal chief, he became a lawyer and helped to found (1944) the Youth League of the African National Congress (ANC), the black African organization opposed to rule by whites in South Africa. In 1964 he was sent to prison for treason. Despite harsh treatment, he eventually became a symbol of opposition to white rule. Released in 1990, he immediately began to lead negotiations for greater black political power. With President F. W. de Klerk, Mandela supported a 1992 national referendum for greater political power for blacks. In 1993 he shared the Nobel Peace Prize with de Klerk.

Mandelstam, Osip (1891–1938?) Russian poet. He was a friend of Akhmatova and a leading poet of *acmeism. His second volume, *Tristia* (1922), contains poems noted for their classical form and spiritual intensity. He was arrested in 1934 and 1938, and is presumed to have died in a labor camp.

mandolin A plucked musical instrument, generally having four double courses of wire strings tuned in the same way as the violin. It is played with a plectrum, using a tremolo effect to sustain longer notes. It is used in informal music making and more rarely as a solo or orchestral instrument.

mandrake A herb of the genus *Mandragora*, especially *M. officinarum*, native to Europe. It has large simple leaves, white flowers, and a thick forked root, which resembles the human form and was formerly believed to have healing and aphrodisiac properties. Family: *Solanaceae*.

mandrill A large *Old World monkey, *Mandrillus sphinx*, of West African coastal forests. They are 26–33 in (66–84 cm) long including the tail (2–3 in; 5–7.5 cm), with red and blue muzzle and buttocks and shaggy yellow-brown hair. They live in small family groups and forage for plants and insects, sometimes climbing for berries. *See also* drill.

Manet, Edouard (1832–83) French painter, born in Paris. After overcoming parental opposition, he trained under the classical painter Thomas Couture (1815–79) between 1850 and 1856. By 1860 he was painting contemporary scenes, but throughout his career he remained indebted to the Old Masters, particularly to Velázquez and Hals. He exhibited mainly at the Paris Salon, where such paintings as *Olympia* and *Déjeuner sur l'herbe* (both Louvre) became targets for considerable scorn and derision. However, his friend Émile *Zola spiritedly defended his work in an article published in 1867. In the 1870s he adopted the technique of the impressionists, although he refused to participate in their exhibitions (*see* impressionism).

mangabey A large long-tailed *Old World monkey belonging to the genus *Cercocebus* (4 species), of central African forests. Mangabeys are 31–65 in (80–165 cm) long including the tail (17–30 in; 43–75 cm) and have long limbs and muscular bodies. They live in troops, feeding on fruit high in the trees.

Mangalore 12 54N 74 51E A port in India, in Karnataka on the Malabar Coast. Its manufactures include textiles and tiles. Population (1991): 272,819.

manganese (Mn) A hard gray brittle transition element that resembles iron, first isolated in 1774 by J. G. Gahn (1745–1818). It occurs in nature in many minerals, especially pyrolusite (MnO_2) and rhodochrosite ($MnCO_3$), in addition to the extensive deposits of manganese nodules discovered on the deep ocean floors. It is extracted by reduction of the oxide, with magnesium or aluminum, or by electrolysis. The metal is used in many alloys, particularly in steel, in which manganese improves the strength and hardness. Manganese forms compounds in a number of different *valence states: for example MnO, Mn_3O_4, MnO_2. The permanganate ion (MnO_4^-) is a well-known oxidizing agent. At no 25; at wt 54.9380; mp 2273°F (1244°C); bp 3567°F (1962°C).

mange A contagious skin disease, caused by mites, that can affect domestic livestock, pets, and man (*see* scabies). The parasites bite or burrow into the skin causing hair loss, scaly dry skin, pimples, blisters, and intense itching. Treatment is with a suitable insecticide, such as gamma benzene hexachloride.

mangel-wurzel. *See* beet.

mango A large evergreen tropical tree, *Mangifera indica*, native to SE Asia but cultivated throughout the tropics for its fruit. Growing 49–59 ft (15–18 m) high, it has long narrow leaves and large clusters of pinkish flowers. The oblong fruit, up to 5 lb (2.3 kg) in weight, has a green, yellow, or reddish skin and contains a stony seed, surrounded by juicy orange edible flesh that has a spicy flavor. Mangos are eaten fresh and used in preserves or for canning. Family: *Anacardiaceae*.

mangosteen A tropical fruit tree, *Garcinia mangostana*, native to SE Asia and reaching a height of 31 ft (9.5 m). The round or oval fruit, up to 3 in (8 cm) in diameter, has a thick hard purple rind and contains a few seeds surrounded by juicy white edible flesh, which is divided into separate segments and has a slightly sharp taste. Family: *Guttiferae*.

mangroves Shrubs and trees forming dense thickets and low forests on coastal mudflats, salt marshes, and estuaries throughout the tropics. Many are evergreen, with shiny leathery leaves, aerial supporting (prop) roots, and breathing roots with "knees" that protrude above the water or mud. The main species are the common or red mangrove (*Rhizophora mangle*), the black mangrove (*Avicennia nitida*), and *Sonneratia* species.

mangrove snake A mildly venomous snake belonging to the genus *Boiga* (30 species) occurring in mangrove swamps and lowland forests of Africa, Asia, Australia, and Polynesia. They live on the ground or in trees and prey on frogs, birds, lizards, crabs, fish, etc. The black-and-yellow mangrove snake (*B. dendrophila*) of E Asia can reach a length of 8 ft (2.5 m). Family: *Colubridae*.

Manhattan An island situated at the N end of New York Bay, between the Hudson, East, and Harlem Rivers, comprising one of the five boroughs of New York City. It is a major commercial and financial center focused on Wall Street. Other notable features include the famous Broadway theater district, *Greenwich Village, the United Nations, and its many skyscrapers, including the Empire State Building (1931) and the twin towers of the World Trade Center (1973). Area: 22 sq mi (47 sq km). Population (1990): 1,487,536.

Manhattan Project The code name for a project set up in 1942 to develop an atomic bomb. Research culminated in the construction of the bombs at Los Alamos, N.M. In 1945 a uranium bomb and a plutonium bomb were dropped on Hiroshima and Nagasaki respectively (*see* World War II; nuclear weapons).

manic-depressive psychosis A severe mental illness causing repeated episodes of severe *depression, mania (excessive euphoria, overactivity, irritability, and impaired judgment), or both. These episodes can be precipitated by upsetting events but are out of proportion to them. There is a genetically inherited predisposition to this psychosis; long-term treatment with lithium salts can prevent or reduce the frequency and severity of attacks.

Manichaeism A religion influenced by both *Gnosticism and Christianity. It originated in Persia (c. 230 AD), spread throughout Asia and the Roman Empire, and survived in Chinese Turkistan until the 13th century. It influenced several dualistic medieval heresies (*see* Cathari). Its founder, Mani (c. 216–c. 276), was martyred by the adherents of *Zoroastrianism. Fundamental to his creed was the belief that matter is entirely evil, but within each individual is imprisoned a soul, which is a spark of the divine light. By strict abstinence and prayer man can recover consciousness of the light and be liberated at death from material entanglement. Mani's followers were divided into the elect, teachers who lived in poverty and celibacy, and the hearers, who cared for the elect's material needs and could only achieve salvation after a cycle of reincarnation.

MANGROVES *A young specimen of* Rhizophora stilosa *with conspicuous prop roots, growing in Singapore.*

"Manifest Destiny" A phrase applied to US territorial expansion during the 1800s, implying that fate and divine will sanctioned the growth of the country. Coined (1845) by John L. O'Sullivan, editor of *United States Magazine and Democratic Review*, it was meant to justify the US annexation of Texas (1845) and was used afterward regarding annexations in Mexico, Oregon, the Caribbean, Hawaii, Alaska, and Guam.

Manila 14 30N 121 12E The capital and main port of the Philippines, on Manila Bay in Luzon. Founded by the Spanish in 1571, it suffered several foreign occupations over the centuries and the old town was destroyed in World War II. The official capital was transferred to Quezon City on the outskirts (1948–76). An educational center, it has over 20 universities, including the University of Santo Tomas founded in 1611. It has one of the finest harbors in the world and is also an important industrial center; its industries include textiles, pharmaceuticals, and food processing. Manila suffers from severe traffic congestion. Population (1990): 1,587,000.

Manila Bay An inlet of the South China Sea, in the Philippines in SW Luzon. One of the world's finest natural harbors, it was important before the ports of Manila and Cavite were founded. In the battle of Manila Bay in 1898 the US navy defeated the Spanish fleet, and there was again bitter fighting here during World War II. Area: 770 sq mi (1994 sq km).

Manila hemp A strong fiber obtained from a treelike herb, the *abaca, grown in the Philippines. It is largely used to make rope, matting, and strong paper. Finer grades are made into hats and local fabrics.

Manin, Daniele (1804–57) Italian patriot, born in Venice. His opposition to Austrian rule of Venice resulted in his imprisonment in 1847. He was released on the outbreak of the Revolution of 1848, appointed president of the newly restored Venetian Republic, and led a courageous defense of Venice against an Austrian siege. On its surrender (August 1849) he went into exile in Paris.

manioc. *See* cassava.

Manipur A state in NE India, on the hilly Myanmar border. Its largely Mongoloid inhabitants speak many languages. Rice, fruits, sugar cane, and mustard are grown. There is some silk weaving. The jungles yield bamboo and teak. *History*: Burmese threats caused the raja to seek British aid (1824), which became British rule (1891). Manipur became a state in 1972. Area: 8629 sq mi (22,356 sq km). Population (1981 est): 1,433,691. Capital: Imphal.

Manisa (ancient name: Magnesia) 38 36N 27 29E A city in W Turkey. Founded in the 12th century BC, Manisa is a commercial town with trade in such crops as tobacco, olives, and raisins. The Romans defeated Antiochus the Great here in 190 BC. Population (1990): 158,928.

Manitoba A province of W Canada, in the center of North America. Although it is one of the *Prairie Provinces, only the SW is true prairie. Further to the NE lies the *Red River Valley and three large lakes (Winnipeg, Winnipegosis, and Manitoba) with extensive forests in the N and tundra near Hudson Bay. Manitoba's economy is based on large mechanized farms producing grains and livestock. Forests, fisheries, and hydroelectricity are also important. Manitoba produces copper, gold, zinc, silver, nickel, and oil. Manufacturing is based on natural resources and agriculture. The province boasts a rich cultural life centered around Greater *Winnipeg, which contains over half the population. *History*: originally exploited for furs, Manitoba (then known simply as the Red River Settlement) first attracted dispossessed Scots Highlanders as settlers (1812). Acquisition of the area by Canada (1869) provoked the Riel Rebellion (1869–70), an uprising of French-speaking halfbreeds (Métis). Manitoba became a province in 1870. The transcontinental railroad (1882) and steady immigration (especially 1900–14) brought a prosperity that has been interrupted only between the World Wars. Area: 211,774 sq mi (548,495 sq km). Population (1991): 1,100,000. Capital: Winnipeg.

Manitoulin Islands A group of Canadian islands in N Lake *Huron. Timber, farming, and tourism are economically important. The main island, Manitoulin Island, is the largest freshwater lake island in the world. Area (Manitoulin Island): 1068 sq mi (2766 sq km).

Manizales 5 03N 75 32W A city in central Colombia, in the Central Cordillera. It is the commercial center of the country's chief coffee-growing area. Manufactures include textiles, chemicals, and leather products and it has a university (1943). Population (1985): 325,000.

Manley, Michael (1924–) Jamaican statesman, who, as leader of the People's National party, was elected prime minister of Jamaica in 1972 and reelected in 1976. His socialist policies included nationalizing 51% of the bauxite industry, developing close ties with Cuba, and speaking out for the Third World. He was defeated in the 1980 elections, but ran again and was elected in 1988. In 1992 he retired because of poor health.

Mann, Horace (1796–1859) US educator and politician. Largely self-taught, he studied at college and law school and served in the Massachusetts state legislature. In Massachusetts he was secretary of the nation's first state board of education (1837–48). Here, he formulated his educational philosophy and put it to practical use. Under his guidance the Massachusetts public school system became a model for the rest of the country. He was a US senator (1848–53) and the first president of Antioch College (1853–59).

Mann, Thomas (1875–1955) German novelist. Born into a wealthy merchant family, he chose a similar family as the subject of his first novel, *Buddenbrooks* (1901). Art and the artist are his main themes, however, in the novella *Death in Venice* (1912), *The Magic Mountain* (1924), in which a sanatorium is a microcosm of society, and *Doctor Faustus* (1947), a novel about a modern composer of genius. His other works include *Joseph and His Brothers* (1933–44), a series of four novels based on the biblical story of Joseph, and the picaresque *Felix Krull* (1954). Mann opposed nazism and was forced to emigrate to the US in the 1930s. He was awarded a Nobel Prize in 1929. His brother **Heinrich Mann** (1871–1950), also a novelist and opponent of fascism, is best known for his novel *Professor Unrat* (1905; filmed as *The Blue Angel*, 1928).

manna 1. In the Bible, the miraculous food that fell with the dew to sustain the Israelites in the wilderness (Exodus 16.14–15). This phenomenon has been variously identified as an exudation from the tamarisk tree or a form of lichen. **2.** A sugary substance obtained from the ash tree and used in medicine.

Mann Act (1910) US law that prohibited the transportation of women across state lines for immoral purposes. Sponsored by US Representative James Robert Mann of Illinois, it was also known as the White Slave Traffic Act.

Mannerheim, Carl Gustaf Emil, Baron von (1867–1951) Finnish general and statesman. He led the antisocialist forces to victory against the Finnish Bolsheviks in 1918 and then retired until 1931. In 1939, at the outbreak of the *Russo-Finnish War, he became commander in chief and, although defeated, was able to obtain good terms for Finland (1941). He reembarked on war with the Soviet Union (June 1941) and as president (1944–46) negotiated peace.

mannerism An art movement dominant in Italy from about 1520 to 1600. Mannerism developed out of the *Renaissance style, some of its characteristics being evident in the late work of *Raphael and *Michelangelo. It aimed to surpass the Renaissance style in virtuosity and emotional impact. In architecture this resulted in a clever and playful misuse of the rules of classical architecture, notably in the buildings of *Giulio Romano. In painting it led to a distortion of scale, an elongation of form, and dissonance of color, which frequently resulted in an effect of tension. Leading mannerist painters were *Pontormo, *Parmigianino, *Vasari, and *Bronzino. Features of mannerism also appeared in the work of *Tintoretto and *El Greco. Although largely confined to Italy, it appeared in France in the art of the school of *Fontainebleau and in Bohemia in the paintings of *Arcimboldo and Bartholomeus Spranger (1546–1611).

Mannheim 49 30N 8 28E A city in SW Germany, in Baden-Württemberg at the confluence of the Rhine and Neckar Rivers. It was the seat of the Electors Palatine (1720–98) and has a notable baroque castle. It is a major port with an oil refinery and its manufactures include motor vehicles and agricultural machinery. Population (1988): 295,000.

MANNERISM The Madonna with the Long Neck *(1532–40; Palazzo Pitti, Florence) by Parmigianino. The elongated proportions of the Madonna's neck and fingers, the angel's leg, and the child's body are typical of the reaction against naturalism.*

mannikin A *waxbill of the genus *Lonchura* (30 species) occurring in Africa, S Asia, and Australasia. Mannikins are typically small (about 4 in [11 cm] long) and brown or black with paler underparts. The chestnut mannikin (*L. ferruginosa*) of the Philippines has become so abundant that it is now a pest to rice growers.

Manolete (Manuel Laureano Rodriguez Sánchez; 1917–47) Spanish matador, who became a professional at 17 and achieved a reputation as a bullfighter of great style. He died of injuries received in the ring.

manometer An instrument for measuring pressure differences. The simplest form consists of a U-shaped tube containing a liquid (often mercury), one arm of which is connected to a source of pressure and the other left open to the atmosphere. The difference between the height of the liquid in the two arms is a measure of the pressure difference.

manor The most common unit of agrarian organization in medieval Europe, introduced into England by the Normans. The manor was essentially the lord's landed estate, usually consisting of the lord's own farm (the demesne), and land let out to peasant tenants, chiefly *villeins, who provided the labor for the demesne and were legally dependent upon their lord.

Mansart, François (*or* Mansard; 1596–1666) French classical architect. His first major achievement, the north wing of the chateau at Blois (1635–38) featured the double-angled (Mansard) roof. He built or remodeled several town houses in Paris, notably the Hôtel de la Vrillière (1635) but his most perfect building was Maisons-Laffitte near Paris (1642). He also designed the church of Val-de-Grâce, Paris (1645), but as with many other commissions, his arrogance, reputed dishonesty, and extravagance resulted in his dismissal.

Mansfield, Katherine (Kathleen Mansfield Beauchamp; 1888–1923) New Zealand short-story writer. She came to Europe in 1908, published her first collection of stories in 1811, and in 1918 married John Middleton *Murry. *Bliss* (1920) and *The Garden Party* (1922) contain her best-known stories, often compared in stylistic subtlety to those of Chekhov. She died of tuberculosis in France.

Mansfield, Mike (Michael Joseph M.; 1903–   ) US politician; majority leader of the Senate (1961–77). A Democrat from Montana, he served in the House of Representatives (1943–53) and was elected to the Senate in 1952. He succeeded Lyndon B. *Johnson as Senate majority leader and held the position for a record 16 years. Upon retirement from the Senate, he was appointed US ambassador to Japan (1977) by Pres. Jimmy Carter and served in that post until 1988.

manslaughter The crime of killing a person either (1) accidentally by an unlawful act or by culpable negligence or (2) in the heat of passion, after provocation. The second case is closely related to murder, and a verdict of manslaughter is possible only if there is no evidence of premeditation.

Mansur, Abu Ja'far al- (c. 712–75 AD) The second *caliph (754–75) of the 'Abbasid dynasty. He built Baghdad (begun 762) and made it the 'Abbasid capital. Influenced by Persian ideas, he developed the bureaucracy and is reckoned the real founder of the 'Abbasid caliphate.

Mansura, El (*or* al-Mansurah) 31 03N 31 23E A city in N Egypt, on the Nile Delta. In 1250 it was occupied by Crusaders under Louis IX (St Louis) of France, who was taken and held for ransom by Muslim forces. A market center, industries include cotton gins and flour mills. Population (1986): 316,870.

manta ray A *ray fish, also called devil ray or devil fish, of the family *Mobulidae*; 24–260 in (60–660 cm) long, they swim near the surface of warm-temperate and tropical waters, feeding on plankton and small animals swept into the mouth by hornlike feeding fins projecting from the front of the head.

Mantegna, Andrea (c. 1431–1506) Italian Renaissance painter and engraver, born near Vicenza. He was trained in Padua by his adopted father Francesco Squarcione, an artist and archeologist. His marriage (1453) to the daughter of Jacopo *Bellini connected him with the Venetian school. As court painter to the Duke of Mantua from 1459, he painted nine panels depicting *The Triumph of Caesar* (Hampton Court, London). His fresco decorations for the bridal chamber of the ducal palace include portraits of members of the Mantuan court and an illusionistic ceiling, which anticipates the *baroque.

mantis An insect belonging to the family *Mantidae* (2000 species), found in tropical and warm temperate regions. Up to 5 in (125 mm) long, mantids blend with the surrounding vegetation and are voracious carnivores, using their forelegs to capture insects and other small animals. The "praying" position held by the forelegs at rest accounts for the name praying mantis, applied in particular to *Mantis religiosa* but also to all other mantids. Eggs are laid in capsules (oothecae) on rocks and plants. Order: *Dictyoptera*. □insect.

mantis shrimp A marine *crustacean of the widely distributed order *Stomatopoda* (over 250 species), especially the genus *Squilla*; 0.04–12 in (1–300 mm) long, it has a short carapace and stalked eyes and the second pair of legs form large pincers for catching prey. Mantis shrimps live in sand burrows or crevices in coastal waters up to depths of 4265 ft (1300 m).

Mantua (Italian name: Mantova) 45 10N 10 47E A city in N Italy, in Lombardy on the Mincio River. Its history dates from Etruscan and Roman times and from 1328 to 1708 it was ruled by the Gonzaga family. It has several notable buildings, including a cathedral (10th–18th centuries), the 15th-century church of S Andrea (designed by Alberti), a 14th-century castle, and a ducal palace. The poet Virgil was born nearby. An important tourist center, Mantua's industries also include tanning, printing, and sugar refining. Population (1981): 60,866.

Manu In Hindu mythology, the ancestor of mankind. Like the biblical *Noah, he survives a flood because supernatural intervention warns him in time to build an ark. He is the reputed author of a Sanskrit code of laws, the *Manusmriti*, probably compiled between 500 and 300 BC.

Manuel I (1469–1521) King of Portugal (1495–1521) during the great period of Portuguese overseas exploration. The crown was greatly enriched by the voyages of Vasco da *Gama and *Cabral, which opened up Eastern markets to Portugal. Manuel's reign also saw a revision of the legal code and the expulsion of the Jews (1497–98).

Manukau 37 03S 174 32E A city in New Zealand, in N North Island on Manukau Harbor (an inlet of the Tasman Sea). It serves as the W coast harbor for *Auckland. Population (1991): 225,928.

Manutius, Aldus (Aldo Manucci *or* A. Manuzio; 1449–1515) Italian printer and classical scholar, who founded the famous Aldine Press in Venice in about 1490. He specialized in inexpensive compact editions of the Greek and Latin classics, many of them first printed editions. His edition of *Virgil* (1501) was the first book in italic type. After his death the Press was carried on by his brothers-in-law and later by his son **Paulus Manutius** (1512–74) and grandson **Aldus Manutius the Younger** (1547–97).

Manx An extinct language of the Goidelic branch of the *Celtic family. An offshoot of Irish Gaelic, it was spoken on the Isle of Man until the 19th century.

Manx cat A breed of short-haired tailless cat originating from the Isle of Man. The Manx has a short body with deep flanks and a large head. The soft coat has a thick undercoat and may be of any color.

Manzoni, Alessandro (1785–1873) Italian poet and novelist. After living in France from 1805 to 1810 he returned to Italy and established his reputation with the Catholic poems *Inni sacri* (1815), an ode to Napoleon, and two verse dramas. His patriotism and religious convictions are most fully expressed in his masterpiece, *The Betrothed* (1821–27), a historical novel set in 17th-century Milan during the Spanish occupation.

Maoism The theories developed by *Mao Tse-tung. Mao's strategy for revolution in China gave central importance to peasant armies rather than to the action of the industrial working class in urban centers. Similarly, on a world scale, he believed that socialist revolutions would develop first in underdeveloped countries rather than in advanced capitalist countries (*compare* Marxism). Mao laid great stress on moral exhortation, indoctrination, and willpower in overcoming objective obstacles and problems in socialist construction. Like Stalin, Mao defended the system of one-party rule and the view that socialism could be constructed in a single country.

Maori A Polynesian people of New Zealand, who make up about 10% of the population. They trace their origins to migrants, probably from the Cook Islands, who came in canoes around 1350. They were an agricultural people who lived mainly in the North Island in large fortified villages of timber dwellings. Descent was counted in both lines, and a person could attach himself to either his mother's or father's descent group (*hapu*) to obtain rights to land and residence. The traditional arts of wood carving and dancing still survive but urbanization and Christianization have largely destroyed the Maoris' way of life.

Maori Wars The wars between the colonial government of New Zealand and the Maoris, fought intermittently between 1845 and 1848 and between 1860 and 1872. They were caused by the enforced sale of Maori lands in infringement of the Treaty of *Waitangi. They resulted in the loss of much Maori land to European settlers.

Mao Tse-tung (*or* Mao Ze Dong; 1893–1976) Chinese communist statesman. Born into a peasant family in Hunan province, he was a Marxist by 1920 and helped to form the Chinese Communist party (CCP) in 1921. In the late 1920s he became a guerrilla leader against the *Guomindang (Nationalist party) and in 1931 he became chairman of the *Jiangxi Soviet. Forced to evacuate Jiangxi in 1934, Mao led the communist forces on the *Long March with a price of $250,000 on his head. His arrival in Yan'an in 1935 marked his emergence as a leader of the CCP. Following the defeat of Japan in the *Sino-Japanese War of 1937–45, in which the communists and Guomindang joined forces, civil war was resumed, ending in communist victory. In 1949 Mao, as chairman of the Communist party, proclaimed the establishment of the People's Republic of China. Mao's political writings formed the theoretical basis of the new government and led to the founding of communes and the *Great Leap Forward. He stepped down as chairman in 1958, purportedly due to ill health, but reappeared with greater standing during the *Cultural Revolution. Following his death, his third wife (from 1939) *Jiang Qing attempted unsuccessfully to seize power and Mao was succeeded by *Hua Guo Feng. *See also* Maoism.

maple A shrub or tree of the genus *Acer* (over 200 species), widespread in N temperate regions and often grown for timber and ornament. Growing 20–115 ft (6–35 m) high, maples usually bear lobed leaves, which turn yellow, orange, or red in autumn, and small yellow or greenish flowers, which give rise to paired winged fruits (samaras). Popular ornamental species are the *sycamore, *Japanese maple, and *box elder. The sugar maple (*A. saccharum*) of E North America is the source of maple sugar (obtained from the sap). Family: *Aceraceae*.

map projection The representation of the curved surface of the earth on a plane surface. The parallels of latitude and meridians of longitude (*see* latitude and longitude) are represented on the plane surface as a network or graticule of intersecting lines. It is not possible to produce a projection of the earth's surface without some distortion of area, shape, or direction and a compromise between these has to be reached. The basic map projections include conical, cylindrical, and azimuthal (*or* zenithal) projections. In the conical form the globe is projected onto a cone with its point above either the North or the South Pole. In the cylindrical projection the globe is projected onto a cylinder touching the equator; the *Mercator projection is of this type. Part of the globe is projected upon a plane from any point of vision in the azimuthal projection; all points have their true compass bearings. Many variations of the basic map projections are in use.

MAO TSE-TUNG *The cult of Mao finds expression in a portrait on silk measuring 12 ft (3.6 m) by 20 ft (6 m).*

Mapp v. Ohio (1961) US Supreme Court decision that upheld the 4th Amendment. The court ruled that illegally obtained evidence could not be used in state trials.

Maputo (name until 1975: Lourenço Marques) 25 58S 32 35E The capital and chief port of Mozambique, on Delagoe Bay. It became the capital of Portuguese East Africa in 1907. It has a university (1962). A major East African port, its exports include minerals from South Africa, Swaziland, and Zimbabwe. Population (1991 est.): 931,591.

Maquis Groups of provincial guerrillas of the French resistance to the Germans in World War II, as distinct from the urban underground groups. The maquisards took their name from the scrubland (French word: *maquis*) in which they hid. Their operations were usually limited to attacks upon enemy patrols and depots.

marabou A large African *stork, *Leptoptilus crumeniferus*. It is 60 in (150 cm) tall with a wingspan of 8.5 ft (2.6 m) and has a gray-and-white plumage, a bare black-spotted pink head and neck with a pendulous inflatable throat pouch, and a huge straight pointed bill. It feeds chiefly on carrion.

maraca A percussion instrument originating in Latin America, consisting of a dried gourd filled with beads, shot, or dried seeds. Maracas are usually played in pairs, chiefly in jazz bands. □musical instruments.

Maracaibo 10 44N 71 37W The second largest city in Venezuela, a port on the NW shore of Lake Maracaibo. Its economic importance is based on oil production; industries include petrochemicals. The University of Zulia was founded here in 1891. Population (1990 est): 1,207,513.

Maracaibo, Lake A lake in NW Venezuela. Oil is drilled both in and around the lake, providing about 70% of Venezuela's total oil production. It is connected with the Gulf of Venezuela by a waterway (completed in 1956). Area: about 5000 sq mi (13,000 sq km).

MAP PROJECTION

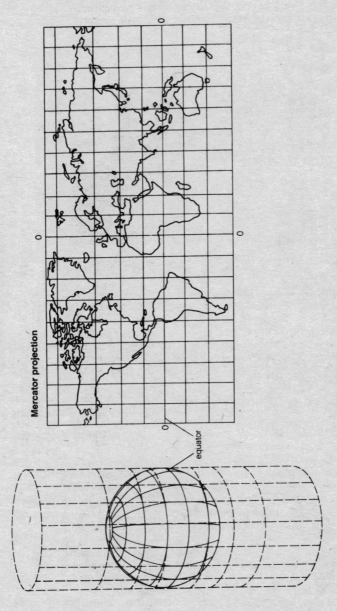

Mercator projection

equator

cylindrical *The globe is projected onto a cylinder, the Mercator projection being the best known.*

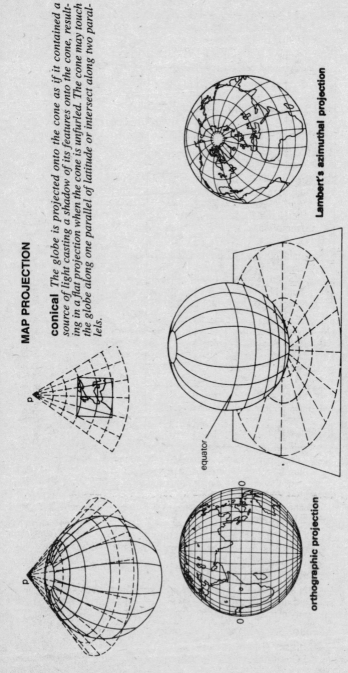

MAP PROJECTION

conical *The globe is projected onto the cone as if it contained a source of light casting a shadow of its features onto the cone, resulting in a flat projection when the cone is unfurled. The cone may touch the globe along one parallel of latitude or intersect along two parallels.*

Lambert's azimuthal projection

azimuthal *(or zenithal) The globe is pictured as a flattened disc. It may be projected as if it were seen from a point in the center of the earth (gnomonic), from a point on the far side of the earth (stereographic), or from a point in space (orthographic).*

equator

orthographic projection

Maracay 10 20N 67 28W A city in N Venezuela, NE of Lake Valencia. It is a military center with two airfields. The chief industry is the manufacture of textiles. Population (1990 est): 354,428.

Marajó Island (Portuguese: Ilka de Marajó) The world's largest fluvial island, in NE Brazil in the Amazon delta. Area: 15,444 sq mi (38,610 sq km).

Marañón, Río The headstream of the Amazon River, in South America. Rising in the Peruvian Andes, it flows generally NE forming the Amazon at its confluence with the Río Ucayali. Length: 900 mi (1450 km).

Maraş 37 34N 36 54E A city in central S Turkey. It dates from Hittite times and used to manufacture guns and swords but now exports carpets and embroidery. Population (1980): 178,557.

marasmus. *See* kwashiorkor.

Marat, Jean-Paul (1743–93) French politician, journalist, and physician, who devoted himself to radical journalism during the French Revolution. He became editor of *L'Ami du peuple*, supporting the *Jacobin cause of radical reform. Elected to the National Convention in 1792, he was murdered by Charlotte *Corday, a member of the *Girondins, whom Marat had helped to overthrow (1793).

Maratha (*or* Mahratta) A people of India, who live mainly in Maharashtra and speak the *Indo-Aryan Marathi language. More strictly the term applies to the high-ranking castes of this region, who are cultivators, landowners, and warriors of considerable repute. During the 17th century there was a Maratha kingdom in the area and a confederacy of Maratha leaders intermittently resisted the British between 1775 and 1818.

marathon A long-distance running race in athletics over 26 mi 385 yd (42 km 195 m). The marathon derives its name from the story of *Phidippides, who ran from the battlefield of Marathon to Sparta. As different courses vary, there is no official world record. In the Olympic Games there are marathon races for both men and women.

Marathon, Battle of (490 BC) The battle during the *Greek-Persian Wars in which the Athenians under *Miltiades defeated the Persians. *Phidippides was sent to summon Spartan help but the Athenians triumphantly routed the Persians before the Spartans arrived.

marble A rock consisting of metamorphosed limestone, although the term is often used of any rock, particularly limestone, that can be cut and polished for ornamental use. Pure marble is white recrystallized calcite, but impurities, such as dolomite, silica, or clay minerals result in variations of color. Certain quarries in Greece and Italy have been producing large quantities of marble since pre-Christian times. The flawless white marble from Carrara in Tuscany, Italy, is particularly prized by sculptors.

Marblehead 42 30N 70 51W A city in NE Massachusetts, on the NW shore of Massachusetts Bay, NE of Boston. Because of its excellent harbor it was long important in US commerce. Now a resort and boating center, most of its industries concentrate on yachting. Population (1990): 19,971.

Marburg 50 49N 8 36E A city in Germany, in Hessen on the Lahn River. It has a gothic castle and an important library and is the site of the country's first Protestant university (1527). Population (1984): 77,300.

Marburg disease. *See* green monkey disease.

Marbury v. Madison (1803) US Supreme Court decision that reinforced the supremacy of the Constitution over Congress and established the interpretative role of the Supreme Court. Marbury, appointed a justice of the peace by outgoing Pres. John Adams, was refused his commission by newly elected President Madison. The court ruled that the Judiciary Act of 1789, under which Marbury was suing, exceeded the judiciary powers outlined in the Constitution and declared it unconstitutional.

Marc, Franz (1880–1916) German expressionist painter, born in Munich. A member of *Neue Künstlervereinigung and a founder of Der *Blaue Reiter art group, Marc is known for his symbolic animal paintings, such as *Blue Horses* (1911; Walker Art Center, Minneapolis). He was killed in World War I.

marcasite A pale bronze mineral form of *pyrite. It occurs as nodules in sedimentary rocks as a replacement mineral, particularly in chalk. Marcasite jewelry is sometimes pyrite but more often polished steel or white metal.

Marceau, Marcel (1923–) French mime. He left conventional acting and began to study mime in 1946, gradually developing the original character Bip, a white-faced clown derived from the traditional pantomime figure of Pierrot. As well as giving solo performances, he formed his own company to produce complete mime plays.

Marcellus, Marcus Claudius (d. 208 BC) Roman general in the second *Punic War. After Roman defeats at Trasimene and Cannae, he was chosen, for his valor, to check Hannibal's advance through Italy. After capturing Syracuse, he harassed the Carthaginian armies in S Italy until his death.

March Third month of the year. Named for the Roman god Mars, it has 31 days. The zodiac signs for March are Pisces and Aries; the flowers are jonquils and daffodils, and the birthstones are aquamarine and bloodstone. St Patrick's Day falls on Mar 17.

Marchard, Jean Baptiste (1863–1934) French soldier and explorer. After exploring the Niger, W Sudan, and the Ivory Coast, he narrowly avoided causing a war with the British by occupying Fashoda (*see* Fashoda incident).

Marche (*or* the Marches) A region in central Italy, consisting of a narrow undulating coastal plain and a large hilly or mountainous interior. Primarily an agricultural region, it produces wheat, maize, wine, fruit, vegetables, and cattle. Area: 3742 sq mi (9692 sq km). Population (1991): 1,446,751. Capital: Ancona.

Marches The border areas of England and Wales, conquered between about 1067 and 1238 by vassals of the English kings. The so-called **marcher lords** enjoyed enormous powers in their lordships until the union of Wales and England in the 1530s.

March on Rome (1922) The display of armed strength by Mussolini's *Blackshirts that established fascist government in Italy. Using threats of violence to support his demands for representation in the government, Mussolini organized the Blackshirts in a march against Rome. They entered unopposed by government or army and Mussolini was asked by Victor Emmanuel III to form a cabinet.

Marciano, Rocky (Rocco Francis Marchegiano; 1923–69) US boxer, world heavyweight champion (1952–56). He became a professional fighter in 1947 and by 1952 had beaten Jersey Joe Walcott for the world title. Known as the Brockton Blockbuster, he defended his title six times before retiring undefeated.

Marconi, Guglielmo (1874–1937) Italian electrical engineer, who invented, independently of *Popov, communication by radio. On reading about the discovery of radio waves, Marconi built a device that would convert them into electrical signals. He then experimented with transmitting and receiving radio waves over increasing distances until, in 1901, he succeeded in transmitting a signal across the Atlantic Ocean. For this work he shared the Nobel Prize in physics in 1909.

Marcos, Ferdinand E(dralin) (1917–89) Philippine statesman; president (1965–86). In 1972 he declared martial law and assumed dictatorial powers. Although these controls were ostensibly relaxed in the early 1980s, the murder of opposition leader Benigno Aquino, Jr., probably with government complicity, in 1983 increased opposition to Marcos's extravagant rule. Opposed by Aquino's widow Corazon in 1986 presidential elections, Marcos left the Philippines for exile in Hawaii after demonstrations showed that most people believed that Aquino had won the disputed election.

Marcus Aurelius (121–80 AD) Roman emperor (161–80), in association with Lucius Verus (130–69) from 161 and alone from 169. Although he is known as the philosopher emperor on account of his *Meditations* (12 books of aphorisms in the Stoic tradition), his rule was active: from 170 he fought on the Danube frontier, dying during the campaign.

Marcuse, Herbert (1898–1979) German-born US thinker. His radical anti-authoritarian philosophy evolved from the Frankfurt School of social research. Marcuse attacked both Western positivism and orthodox Marxism, the former because it led to analysis rather than action, the latter because it lacked relevance to 20th-century conditions. His books include *The Ethics of Revolution* (1966) and *Counter-Revolution and Revolt* (1973).

Mar del Plata 38 00S 57 32W A resort in E Argentina, on the Atlantic Ocean. It possesses extensive beaches, hotels, and a casino. The National University of Mar del Plata was founded in 1961. Population (1975 est): 302,282.

Marduk The supreme god in Babylonian mythology. He created order out of the universe after defeating the sea dragon Tiamat and the forces of chaos. This victory, recounted in the Babylonian and Assyrian creation myth, *Enuma Elish*, was celebrated in a festival at the beginning of each year.

Marengo, Battle of (June 14, 1800) A battle, fought 3 mi (5 km) SE of Alessandria, in Napoleon's Italian campaign (*see* Revolutionary and Napoleonic Wars). Napoleon was surprised by the Austrians and only the timely arrival of reinforcements made French victory possible.

Marenzio, Luca (1553–99) Italian composer, noted for his nine volumes of madrigals containing over 200 works. Some, published in London, influenced English madrigalists.

mare's tail An aquatic perennial herb, *Hippuris vulgaris*, found in lakes and ponds throughout N temperate regions. It resembles the unrelated *horsetails in having stems, rising up to 12 in (30 cm) above the water surface, bearing whorls of small slender leaves with minute greenish flowers at their bases. Family: *Hippuridaceae*.

Margaret (1353–1412) Queen of Denmark, Norway, and Sweden. Daughter of Valdemar IV Atterdag of Denmark, in 1363 she married Haakon VI of Norway (1339–80; reigned 1355–80). Their son Olaf (1370–87) succeeded Valdemar in Denmark (1375) and Haakon in Norway and following Olaf's death Margaret became queen of both countries, which remained united until 1814. In 1388 she was proclaimed queen of Sweden by discontented Swedish nobles. The union of the three countries was formalized in 1397, when her heir Erik of Pomerania (1382–1459) was crowned at Kalmar. Margaret remained effective ruler until her death.

Margaret (Rose) (1930–   ) Princess of the United Kingdom. She is the younger daugher of George VI and sister of Elizabeth II. In 1960 she married Antony Armstrong-Jones (later Lord *Snowdon); they were divorced in 1978.

Margaret, Maid of Norway (?1282–90) Queen of the Scots (1286–90), succeeding her grandfather *Alexander III; she was the daughter of Eric II of Norway (reigned 1280–99). Betrothed to the future Edward II of England, she died while traveling to England and Edward I promptly declared himself overlord of Scotland.

Margaret, St (1045–93) The wife of *Malcolm III of Scotland and the sister of *Edgar the Aetheling. She was noted for her piety and reform of the Scottish Church in accordance with Gregorian principles, for which she was canonized in 1250.

Margaret of Angoulême (1492–1549) An outstanding patron of Renaissance artists and writers; wife of Henry II of Navarre (1503–55). Her own writings include a collection of tales (*Heptaméron*, 1558) and of poetry (*Miroir de l'âme pécheresse,* 1531).

Margaret of Anjou (1430–82) The wife (1445–71) of Henry VI of England; their marriage constituted an attempt to cement peace between England and France during the Wars of the *Roses, in which she was one of the most formidable Lancastrian leaders. She was captured and imprisoned after the Lancastrian defeat in the battle of *Tewkesbury (1471), in which her son Edward was killed. Her husband died, probably murdered, shortly afterward and she returned to France (1476) after Louis XI had paid a ransom for her release.

Margaret of Valois (1553–1615) The wife of Henry IV of France, famous for her *Mémoires* (1628). Daughter of Henry II and Catherine de' Medici, her marriage, which took place in 1572, was dissolved in 1599 to enable Henry to marry Marie de Médicis.

Margaret Tudor (1489–1541) Regent of Scotland (1513–14) for her son James V. The elder daughter of Henry VII of England and the wife of James IV of the Scots (d. 1513), she was ousted from the regency by the English but continued to play an active role in politics until 1534. Her great-grandson, James VI of the Scots, succeeded to the English throne as James I in 1603.

margarine A butter substitute that does not contain dairy-product fat. A type of margarine was first produced in France in 1869 from beef tallow. However, vegetable oils were only able to be used extensively after 1910, when a hydrogenation process was developed to solidify the liquid vegetable oils by adding hydrogen to saturate some of the unsaturated fatty-acid residues in the oils. In modern margarine, pasteurized fat-free milk powder is emulsified with water and such refined vegetable oils as soybean oil, peanut oil, and palm oil. Vitamins A and D are also added. The resulting emulsion is cooled, solidified, and kneaded to remove air. Soft margarines contain only lightly hydrogenated oils, retaining a large part of their unsaturated nature to comply with medical opinion that they are less likely to form damaging *cholesterol in the blood than saturated fats.

Margarita Island A Venezuelan island in the S Caribbean Sea. Pearl and deep-sea fishing are of importance. Area: 444 sq mi (1150 sq km). Capital: La Asunsión.

Margate 51 24N 1 24E A resort in SE England, on the N Kent coast, including the resorts of Westgate-on-Sea and Cliftonville. It developed as a resort in the late 18th century, when the bathing machine was invented. Population (1981): 53,280.

margay A spotted *cat, *Felis wiedi* of Central and South America. It is 35 in (90 cm) long including the tail (12 in [30 cm]), found in forests and brush, hunting small mammals and reptiles in trees and on the ground.

Margrethe II (1940–) Queen of Denmark (1972–), who succeeded her father Frederick IX after the Danish constitution had been altered to permit the accession of a woman to the throne.

marguerite A perennial herb, *Chrysanthemum frutescens*, also called Paris daisy, native to the Canary Isles. Each stem bears a single large daisylike flower. The name is also applied to the similar *oxeye daisy. *See also* Chrysanthemum.

Mari An ancient city on the middle Euphrates River in Syria. Commanding major trade routes, Mari throve during the early Sumerian period (*see* Sumer) and under the rule of *Akkad (c. 2300 BC). Excavated buildings of Mari's final period of prosperity include the palace of the last king, Zimrilim, killed when *Hammurabi destroyed the city (c. 1763). Its archive of 25,000 cuneiform tablets throws light on contemporary diplomacy, administration, and trade.

maria (Latin: seas) Dark expanses of iron-rich basaltic lava that erupted onto the moon's surface (primarily on the nearside) some 3000–3900 million years ago. The lava flooded the immense basins produced by earlier impacts of bodies from space, creating both circular and irregularly shaped maria.

Mariana Islands (*or* Ladrone Islands) A group of mountainous islands in the W Pacific Ocean, comprising the US unincorporated territory of *Guam and the US commonwealth territory of the Northern Marianas. Strategically important, they include the islands of Tinian and *Saipan. Discovered in 1521, the islands were colonized by Spanish Jesuits after 1668. Guam was ceded to the US after the Spanish-American War, while the Northern Marianas were sold to Germany (1899) and occupied by Japan (1914–44) until taken by the US. They voted in 1975 to leave the UN Trust Territory of the *Pacific Islands. Sugarcane, coffee, and coconuts are produced. Area: 370 sq mi (958 sq km). Administrative center: Garapan, on Saipan.

Marianas Trench A deep trench in the earth's crust in the W Pacific; it is the greatest known ocean depth (36,198 ft; 11,033 m). It marks the site of a plate margin (*see* plate tectonics), where one plate is being submerged beneath another.

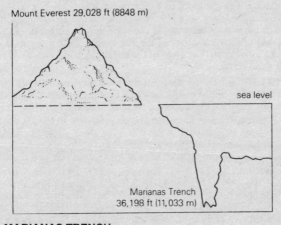

Mount Everest 29,028 ft (8848 m)

sea level

Marianas Trench
36,198 ft (11,033 m)

MARIANAS TRENCH

Mariánské Lázně (German name: Marienbad) 49 59N 12 40E A city in the Czech Republic, in W Bohemia. During the 18th and 19th centuries it was a popular spa, patronized by such famous people as Edward VII of the UK and the composer Richard Wagner. Population (1981): 18,000.

Maria Theresa (1717–80) Archduchess of Austria (1740–80). Her father Emperor Charles VI issued the *Pragmatic Sanction (1713) to enable Maria Theresa, as a woman, to succeed to his Austrian territories. Her accession nevertheless precipitated the War of the *Austrian Succession (1740–48), with European powers, especially Prussia, which seized Silesia, hoping to expand their possessions at her expense. In 1745 her husband Francis (whom she married in 1736) became Holy Roman Emperor. Under the influence of *Kaunitz, and determined to regain Silesia, Maria Theresa substituted her English alliance with a French coalition but in the subsequent *Seven Years' War (1756–63) Austria suffered resounding defeat. At home she combined absolutism with a measure of reform, anticipating the Enlightened Despotism (*see* Enlightenment) of her son and successor, Emperor Joseph.

Mari Autonomous Republic An administrative division in W central Russia. It is heavily forested. The Mari people, who speak a Finno-Ugric language, are known for their wood and stone carving and embroidery; they came under Russian rule in the 16th century and the region became an autonomous republic in 1936. Industries include machine building, metalworking, timber, paper and food processing; agriculture comprises mainly cereal production. Area: 8955 sq mi (23,200 sq km). Population (1985): 725,000. Capital: Yoshkar-Ola.

Maribor (German name: Marburg) 46 35N 15 40E A city in Slovenia on the Drava River. A former Hapsburg trading center, it is now a large industrial center. Its university was established in 1975. Population (1981): 185,000.

Marie (1875–1938) The wife of *Ferdinand of Romania. Marie was instrumental in affiliating Romania with the Allies in World War I. A granddaughter of Queen Victoria, Marie wrote several books in English, including an autobiography (1934–35).

Marie Antoinette (1755–93) The wife of Louis XVI of France, whose uncompromising attitude to the *French Revolution contributed to the overthrow of the monarchy. The daughter of Emperor Francis I and Maria Theresa, she married the dauphin Louis in 1770. Her extravagance and alleged immorality contributed to the unpopularity of the crown. After the outbreak of the Revolution she is said to have remarked of the Paris mob: "If they have no bread, let them eat cake." After the overthrow of the monarchy and Louis's execution, she was herself guillotined.

Marie Byrd Land (*or* Byrd Land) An area in Antarctica, between the Ross Ice Shelf and Ellsworth Land. The US, although laying no claim to it, has long been active in the area and has established a research station.

Marie de France (12th century AD) French poet. Her identity is uncertain, although it has been suggested that she was a daughter of Geoffrey Plantagenet and half-sister of Henry II of England. Her works include several *lais,* verse narratives based on traditional Celtic stories of love, adventure, and the marvelous.

Marie de Médicis (1573–1642) The wife (1600–10) of Henry IV of France and regent (1610–14) for her son Louis XIII. Banished by Louis from court in 1617 she raised two revolts (1619, 1620) and was readmitted to the king's council in 1622. She persuaded Louis to make her protégé Richelieu chief minister in 1624 but she subsequently tried to oust him and in 1631 fled to Brussels. She built the Luxembourg Palace in Paris, the galleries of which were decorated by Rubens (1622–24).

Marie Louise (1791–1847) The second wife of Napoleon Bonaparte, who married her (1810) following the dissolution of his marriage to Empress

Josephine. Their son, his longed-for heir, was entitled King of Rome (*see* Napoleon II). After her husband's fall she became duchess of Parma (1816).

Marienbad. *See* Mariánské Lázně.

marigold One of several annual herbaceous plants of the family **Compositae*, popular as garden ornamentals. The pot marigold (*Calendula officinalis*), native to S Europe, bears orange or yellow flowers, which can be eaten in salads. The African and French marigolds (genus *Tagetes*), native to Mexico, have single or double flowers with large outer florets; there are several dwarf varieties. Cape marigolds (genus *Dimorphotheca*) are more daisylike. *See also* marsh marigold.

marijuana. *See* cannabis.

marine biology The study of the organisms that live in the sea and on shore and the features of the environment that influence them. Marine biology is of great economic importance to man in view of his dependence upon the oceans for food, in the form of fish and shellfish, and the effects of pollution upon these organisms. *See also* fishing industry.

Marine Corps, United States Branch of military service whose members are trained in amphibious warfare, within the Department of the Navy, but separate from the navy. It is directed by the commandant of the Marine Corps, who is a full member of the joint chiefs of staff, and consists of three active divisions, three active aircraft wings, and three force service support groups. Its primary mission is to provide fleet marine forces with supporting air force and land forces in defense of naval bases and in any land operations essential to a naval campaign. Established in 1775 as part of the Navy, the Marine Corps became a separate service in 1947.

marine insurance *Insurance against the perils of the sea, including storm, collision, theft, stranding, fire, and piracy. Marine insurance falls into three categories: hull, cargo, and freight. Hull insurance provides cover against losses arising from the perils of the sea as well as accidents caused by the crew, faulty machinery, etc., to the ship itself. Cargo insurance is arranged for each cargo and for each voyage. Freight insurance is the form of marine insurance enabling a buyer or a seller to cover himself against loss for sums paid out in chartering a ship or hiring cargo space.

Mariner probes A series of highly successful US *planetary probes. Mariners 2 and 5 approached Venus in 1962 and 1967, while Mariner 10 flew past Venus in 1974 and then three times past Mercury in 1974–75. Mariners 4 (1964), 6 and 7 (1969), and 9 (1971–72) investigated Mars, with Mariner 9 going into Martian orbit. Mariners 11 and 12 were renamed the *Voyager probes. Mariners 1, 3, and 8 did not achieve their missions.

Marinetti, Filippo Tommaso (1876–1944) Italian poet and novelist. His manifesto published in Paris in 1909 calling for the destruction of traditional literary goals and the creation of new means of expression inaugurated the literary and artistic movement of futurism. His glorification of warfare and technology resulted in his commitment to fascism, which he defended in *Futurism and Fascism* (1924).

Marini, Marino (1901–80) Italian sculptor, born in Pistoia. Originally a painter, he turned to sculpture in the late 1920s, becoming professor of sculpture at the Brera Academy, Milan, in 1940. Marini, under the influence of ancient Etruscan and Roman sculpture, continued the figural tradition of European art with his bronze horse-and-rider and dancer series.

Marion, Francis (?1732–95) US soldier in the American Revolution. Nicknamed the "Swamp Fox" because of his guerrilla band attacks on the British from the swamps of South Carolina, he was instrumental in US victories throughout South Carolina.

Maritain, Jacques (1882–1973) French Roman Catholic thinker. He was interested in applying St Thomas *Aquinas's methods to contemporary social problems. *Les Degrés du savoir* (1932) treats mystical, metaphysical, and scientific knowledge as complementary. When the metaphysical pretensions of the sciences are abandoned, Maritain thought they would not conflict with Christian faith. He was for a time associated with the reactionary group Action Française.

Maritime Alps (French name: Alpes Maritimes) A range of mountains in SE France and NW Italy, running about 81 mi (130 km) along the border and constituting the southernmost arm of the Alps. It reaches 10,817 ft (3297 m) at Punta Argentera.

maritime law The branch of law relating to ships and shipping. It evolved from the local customs of certain dominant ports. The Romans, borrowing from the customs of Rhodes, imposed a code in the Mediterranean that was international and uniform in character. This uniformity was preserved until 17th-century nationalism gave rise to various individual codes. The French *Code de Commerce* (1807) treated maritime law as a branch of commercial law and has been widely adopted by other European countries. Outside the Mediterranean the most important early code was the 12th-century Rolls of Oléron (an island off the W cost of France), which codified the customary laws of the Atlantic ports and formed the basis of the maritime law of England, Scotland, France, Flanders, and other countries. The laws of Wisby, the seat until 1361 of the Hanseatic League, were also important and contained the mercantile code of the Baltic. In the US, maritime law is subject to federal regulation and is primarily under the jurisdiction of federal courts.

Maritime Provinces (Maritimes *or* Atlantic Provinces) The easternmost provinces of Canada, on the Atlantic coast and the Gulf of St Lawrence. They consist of *New Brunswick, *Nova Scotia, *Prince Edward Island, and usually *Newfoundland and lie in the Appalachian Highlands.

Maritsa River A river in SE Europe. Rising in the Rila Mountains in W Bulgaria, it flows E then S forming part of the Greek-Turkish border, before entering the Aegean Sea. Length: 300 mi (483 km).

Mariupol. *See* Zhdanov.

Marius, Gaius (c. 157–86 BC) Roman general; an opponent of *Sulla. Military ability outweighing his undistinguished origins and educational deficiencies, he entered Roman politics after campaigns in Numantia, becoming associated with the popular party. After reorganizing the Roman army, he quelled *Jugurtha and crushed Gallic uprisings. In competition with Sulla for the command against *Mithridates, he was forced to flee Italy but in 87 returned with *Cinna and captured Rome, massacring his political opponents. He died shortly afterward.

Marivaux, Pierre Carlet de Chamblain de (1688–1763) French dramatist. His popular comedies, mostly witty and sophisticated treatments of romantic themes, include *La Surprise de l'amour* (1722) and *Le Jeu de l'amour et du hasard* (1730). He also wrote two unfinished novels and much literary journalism.

marjoram One of several aromatic perennial herbs or small shrubs of the Eurasian genera *Origanum* (about 13 species) or *Majorana* (about 4 species). Wild marjoram (*O. vulgaris*), is a hairy plant, 12–31 in (30–80 cm) tall, bearing clusters of small tubular pinkish-purple flowers. Sweet marjoram (*M. hortensis*), is widely cultivated for its aromatic leaves and flowers, which are used as culinary flavoring. Family: *Labiatae*.

Mark, St A New Testament evangelist, traditionally the author of the second Gospel. A cousin of *Barnabas, he went with him and Paul on their first mission. Subsequently he seems to have assisted Paul in Rome, where he also acted as interpreter for Peter. He was believed to have founded the Church in Alexandria and is also associated with Venice, of which he is patron saint. Feast day: Apr 25.

The Gospel according to St Mark is the earliest of the Gospels and is thought to have been written about 65–70 AD. It is a brief record of the life of Jesus and is believed to have been used by Matthew and Luke in the compiling of their Gospels.

Mark Antony (Marcus Antonius; c. 83–31 BC) Roman general and statesman. Antony fought under Julius *Caesar in Gaul (54–50) and held command in Caesar's civil-war victory at *Pharsalus (48). Following Caesar's assassination, Antony came into conflict with Octavian (*see* Augustus) but they were later reconciled and formed the second *Triumvirate with Lepidus (43). In 42 Antony defeated his opponents Brutus and Cassius at *Philippi. In 41 he met *Cleopatra for the first time; not until 37 did Antony abandon his wife Octavia (Octavian's sister) to live with Cleopatra in Egypt. His strained relations with Octavian were finally severed in about 33. In the following year the Senate declared war on Egypt and Antony was defeated at *Actium. Both he and Cleopatra committed suicide.

market forces. *See* supply and demand.

markhor A large wild *goat, *Capra falconeri,* of the Himalayas. Over 40 in (100 cm) tall at the shoulder, markhors are red-brown in summer and gray in winter and have massive corkscrew-like horns. The species is subdivided into four geographical races, which show variations in the horns.

Markiewicz, Constance, Countess of (?1868–1927) Irish nationalist, who married a Polish count. She fought in the 1916 Easter rising and was imprisoned. She was the first woman to be elected to the British Parliament (1918) but did not take her seat.

Markov, Andrei Andreevich (1856–1922) Russian mathematician, who did important work in probability theory, notably on the type of event series known as the Markov chain. In such series the probability of an event occurring depends upon previous events. His work led to the theory of *stochastic processes.

Markova, Dame Alicia (Lilian Alicia Marks; 1910–   ) British ballet dancer. She joined Diaghilev's Ballets Russes in 1925 and the Vic-Wells Ballet in 1931. Her dancing was noted for its lightness and delicacy, particularly evident in her performances in *Giselle, Swan Lake,* and *Les Sylphides.* She retired in 1962.

marl A calcareous clay that is soft and plastic when wet; consolidated marl is usually called marlstone. Marls are deposited in water, either fresh or marine. The word is also used for any friable clayey soil. Marls and marlstones are used in the manufacture of cement.

Marlborough, John Churchill, 1st Duke of (1650–1722) British general. He suppressed *Monmouth's rebellion against James II (1685) but subsequently supported the *Glorious Revolution (1688) against James. In 1691 he lost favor when suspected of Jacobite sympathies but was reinstated (1701) at the beginning of the War of the *Spanish Succession. As commander in chief under Queen Anne, he won the great victories of *Blenheim (1704), Ramilies (1706), Oudenaarde (1708), and Malplaquet (1709). A *Whig, his political importance owed much to the influence of his wife **Sarah Churchill** (1660–1744), a confidante of Anne. Following Sarah's fall from favor, he was charged with embezzlement and dismissed (1711), living in Holland until 1714.

marlin A large game fish, also called spearfish, belonging to the genus *Tetrapturus* (or *Makaira*). It has an elongated body, up to 8 ft (2.5 m) long, a cylindrical spearlike snout, and a long rigid dorsal fin, which extends forward to form a crest. Marlins are fast swimmers, occurring in all seas and hunting shoals of small fish. Family: *Istiophoridae*; order: *Perciformes*.

Marlowe, Christopher (1564–93) English dramatist and poet. His involvement in secret political activity while a student at Cambridge may have had some bearing on his death in a tavern fight in Deptford. His development of blank verse and dramatic characterization in his plays *Tamburlaine the Great* (written about 1587), *The Jew of Malta* (about 1590), *Faustus* (probably 1592), and *Edward II* (1592), prepared the way for the achievements of Shakespeare. His poetry included lyrics, translations, and the narrative *Hero and Leander* (unfinished; completed by Chapman, 1598).

Marmara, Sea of A sea lying between European and Asian Turkey and between the Bosporus and the Dardanelles. In it lies the island of Marmara, where marble (from which comes the name Marmara) and granite have long been quarried. Area: 4429 sq mi (11,474 sq km).

marmoset A small South American monkey belonging to the genus *Callithrix* (9 species), with claws instead of fingernails. Marmosets are 8–35 in (20–90 cm) long including the tail (4–15 in [10–38 cm]) and have silky fur, often strikingly colored and marked, and long balancing tails. They feed on fruit, insects, eggs, and small birds and have a twittering call. Family: *Callithricidae*.

marmot A large *ground squirrel belonging to the genus *Marmota* (8 species), also called groundhog, of Europe, Asia, and North America. Marmots are 12–24 in (30–60 cm) long and inhabit mountainous or hilly country, feeding on vegetation during the day and living in burrows at night. The woodchuck (*M. monax*) lives in North American woodlands. Marmots live in colonies; at any sign of danger, the whole colony will flee underground.

Marne River A river in NE France. Rising on the Plateau de Langres, it flows N and W to join the Seine River near Paris. Linked by canal to the Rhine, Rhône, and Aisne Rivers, it was the scene of two unsuccessful German offensives during *World War I (1914, 1918). Length: 326 mi (525 km).

Maronite Church A Lebanese Christian *uniat church named for St Maro (died c. 410). The Maronites apparently originated in a Syrian Orthodox Church group that embraced *Monothelite doctrines in the 7th century and were consequently excommunicated. In the 12th century Crusader influences caused them to enter into full communion with the Roman Catholic Church and in 1584 a Maronite college was established at Rome. Although Catholic in doctrine, the Maronites retain their own Syriac liturgy and church hierarchy.

Maros River. *See* Mureş River.

Marot, Clément (1496–1544) French poet. He served in the households of Marguerite of Navarre and of her brother Francis II. Suspected of being a Lutheran, he took refuge several times in Italy and died in Turin. He is best known for his metrical translations of the *Psalms* (1539–43), which received the encouragement of John Calvin. He was one of the first French poets to adopt the sonnet. His work marks the transition from the Middle Ages to the Renaissance and reflects the elegance and style of the new era.

Marquand, J(ohn) P(hillips) (1893–1960) US novelist. His best-known novels are satirical studies of upper-middle-class New England families adrift in an era of social change. These include *The Late George Apley* (1937), *Wickford Point* (1939), and *H. M. Pulham Esq* (1941). He was also the creator of Mr Moto, the Japanese detective who appeared in several novels.

Marquesas Islands A group of 12 volcanic islands in the S Pacific Ocean, in French Polynesia (annexed 1842). Nuku Hiva is the largest and Hiva Oa, where Gauguin is buried, the second largest. Since the 1850s European diseases have reduced the population by 75%. Mountainous and fertile, the islands export copra, cotton, and vanilla. Area: 497 sq mi (1287 sq km). Population (1977): 5419. Capital: Atuona on Hiva Oa.

marquetry A technique of veneering furniture with different woods, ivory, tortoiseshell, and metals cut into interlocking shapes, which form ornamental or pictorial compositions. It is frequently used on European 17th- and 18th-century fine furniture. *See also* parquetry.

Marquette, Jacques (1637–75) French explorer. A Jesuit, he worked among the Indians in Canada from 1666 and in 1673, with **Louis Jolliet** (1645–1700), he descended the Mississippi River as far as the mouth of the Arkansas River, establishing that it flows into the Gulf of Mexico rather than the Gulf of California.

Marrakech (*or* Marrakesh) 31 49N 8 00W The second largest city in Morocco. Founded in 1062, it was for a time the capital of the Moorish kingdom of Morocco. Its notable buildings include the 12th-century Kotubai Mosque. It is an important commercial center, producing carpets and leather goods, and it is also a tourist center. Population (1982): 439,728.

marram grass A coarse perennial *grass of the genus *Ammophila* (2 species), also called beach grass or sand reed, which grows on sandy coasts of temperate Europe, North America, and N Africa. About 40 in (1 m) high, it has spikelike leaves and tough scaly underground stems, which can spread over large areas. It is used to stabilize sand dunes.

marriage The socially, and sometimes legally, acknowledged union between a man or men and a woman or women, such that the resulting children are recognized as legitimate offspring of the parents. Although societies vary greatly in the rules that govern marriage, such legitimacy is always important in determining rights to property, position, rank, group membership, etc. Monogamy, in which each spouse may have only one partner, is general in Christianized societies. Most churches treat marriage as an important rite and in the Roman Catholic and Greek Orthodox Churches it is accounted a *sacrament. Polygyny, in which a man may be married to more than one woman simultaneously, is widespread and sanctioned by Islam. A few societies allow polyandry, in which a group of men, usually brothers, have a wife between them, as in traditional Nayar communities in India. Polygyny and polyandry are collectively known as polygamy. Many societies proscribe certain unions (*see* incest). Others insist on marriage within a particular group (endogamy) or outside it (exogamy). In most countries, social customs and tax laws presuppose some form of marriage as the basis of family life. However, in industrialized societies there has been a marked decline in both the insistence upon strict monogamy and the penalization of unmarried cohabiting couples. Furthermore, changes in the educational and economic status of women, the widespread use of *contraception, and the need for more than one income to support a family have combined to alter the economic structure of marriage. *See also* divorce.

marrow (botany). *See* squash.

marrow (zoology) The soft tissue contained in the central cavities of bones. In early life the marrow of all bones is engaged in the manufacture of blood cells: it is called red marrow. In adult life the marrow of the limb bones becomes filled with fat cells and ceases to function: this is yellow marrow.

Marryat, Captain Frederick (1792–1848) British novelist. His novels based on his long naval career include *Mr Midshipman Easy* (1836) and *Masterman*

Ready (1841). He also wrote children's books, notably *The Children of the New Forest* (1847).

Mars (astronomy) The fourth planet from the sun, orbiting the sun every 687 days at a mean distance of 141.5 million mi (227.9 million km). Its diameter is 4129 mi (6794 km) and its period of axial rotation 24 hours 37 minutes 23 seconds. It has two small *satellites. The Martian atmosphere is 95% carbon dioxide and is very thin (surface pressure 7 millibars). The dry reddish dust-covered surface is heavily cratered in the S hemisphere while N regions show signs of earlier volcanic activity: there are several immense volcanoes, the largest being **Olympus Mons** (15 mi [25 km] high), and extensive lava plains. Huge canyons and smaller valleys occur in equatorial regions; the valleys are evidence of running water in the past. *See also* planetary probe.

Mars (mythology) The Roman war god, the son of Juno. He was identified with the Greek *Ares and is usually portrayed as an armed warrior. Originally a god of agriculture, he was later worshiped at Rome as a major deity and protector of the city. The temple of Mars Ultor (Mars the Avenger) was erected by Augustus after the battle of *Philippi and dedicated in 2 BC.

Marsala (ancient name: Lilybaeum) 37 48N 12 27E A port in Italy, in W Sicily. Founded in 397 BC as a Carthaginian stronghold, it has ancient remains and a baroque cathedral. Marsala wine, grain, and salt are exported. Population: 79,920.

Marseillaise, La The French national anthem, written in April 1792, by *Rouget de l'Isle. It was originally a patriotic song entitled "Le Chant de guerre de l'armée du Rhin." It was taken up by a group of republican soldiers from Marseille, who were prominent in the storming of the Tuileries, and became the revolutionary anthem.

Marseilles (Marseille) 43 18N 5 22E The principal seaport in France, the capital of the Bouches-du-Rhône department. Flanked on three sides by limestone hills, it stands on a bay overlooking the Gulf of Lions. Founded about 600 BC, it was destroyed by the Arabs in the 9th century AD, redeveloped during the Crusades, and came under the French crown in 1481. Most industry is associated with its large world trade and includes oil refining at Fos, which lies to the W and is being developed as an industrial center. The city has few ancient buildings but is noted for Le Corbusier's L'Unité (multiple dwellings). A *métro* (underground railroad) was opened in 1978. Population (1990): 807, 726.

Marsh, Ngaio (1899–1981) New Zealand detective-story writer. She came to England in 1928. Her detective novels, which feature Roderick Alleyn of Scotland Yard and often draw on her experience of art and the theater, include *Final Curtain* (1947) and *Last Ditch* (1977).

Marshall, George C(atlett) (1880–1959) US general and statesman. As army chief of staff (1939–45), and Pres. Franklin Roosevelt's strategic adviser, he organized the build-up of US forces, ensuring that recruitment, training, weapons, and strength allocations conformed. He thus contributed greatly to the Allied victory. As secretary of state (1947–49) he devised the **Marshall Plan**, or European Recovery Program, in which the US undertook to provide economic aid to Europe after World War II. For this he won a Nobel Peace Prize (1953).

Marshall, John (1755–1835) US jurist. After serving in the Revolutionary War, Marshall began his political career as a member of the Virginia House of Burgesses (1782–88). He was a strong advocate of the ratification of the US *Constitution and was appointed US minister to France by Pres. John *Adams in 1797. He gained national recognition in the *XYZ Affair for his refusal to authorize American payments to France in return for diplomatic concessions. Returning to the US, Marshall served a single term in the US House of Representatives (1799–1800). He was named secretary of state in the last year of the Adams administration (1800–01) and shortly before the inauguration of Thomas *Jefferson, President Adams appointed him chief justice of the US Supreme Court. Marshall was instrumental in defining the legal relationship between the federal government and the states and in interpreting their constitutional powers. Among his most important opinions were the cases of *Marbury* v. *Madison* (1803), in which he firmly established the right of the Supreme Court to review the constitutionality of federal and state laws; *McCulloch* v. *Maryland* (1819), in which he ruled that Congress may utilize powers implied but not specifically mentioned in the Constitution; and *Gibbons* v. *Ogden* (1824), in which he established the precedent that the federal government has exclusive jurisdiction over interstate trade. Marshall held the office of chief justice until his death.

Marshall, Thurgood (1908–93) US jurist and civil rights advocate; associate justice of the US Supreme Court (1967–91). A special counsel for the NAACP (1938–40) and head of legal services (1940–61), he was instrumental in securing and effecting much of modern civil rights legislation. He served on the US Court of Appeals (1961–65) and was US solicitor general (1965–67) before becoming the first African American to be appointed to the Supreme Court.

Marshall Islands A republic and an archipelago of low-lying atolls in the central Pacific Ocean, in the UN Trust Territory of the *Pacific Islands. It consists of the Ralik (W) and Ratak (E) chains; the chief islands are Kwajalein, Majuro, and Jaluit. Self-government was achieved in 1979 and the voters approved a free association compact, in which the US is responsible for defense, in 1983. It was put into effect in 1986, and the trusteeship formally came to an end in 1990. The Marshall Islands became a member of the UN in 1991. Area: 61 sq mi (158 sq km). Population (1988): 41,000.

Marshall Plan US aid program for the recovery of Europe after World War II. Proposed by secretary of state George C. *Marshall in 1947, it was activated by the Economic Cooperation Act (1948) and spent $13.15 billion in aid to 16 countries.

marsh gas. *See* methane.

marsh harrier A temperate Eurasian *hawk, *Circus aeruginosus,* that hunts low over reedbeds and marshes, preying chiefly on water voles, waterbirds, and frogs. It is 21 in (53 cm) long and its plumage is dark brown; the male has a paler streaked breast, bluish wing patches, and a gray tail and the female has a pale head and throat.

marsh mallow A stout perennial herb, *Althaea officinalis*, of marshy coastal areas of Eurasia. Its velvety stems, 24–35 in (60–90 cm) high, bear lobed leaves and clusters of flesh-colored flowers, 2 in (5 cm) in diameter. The fleshy roots yield a mucilage that was formerly used to make marshmallows. Family: *Malvaceae.*

marsh marigold A stout perennial herb, *Caltha palustris*, also called kingcup, growing in marshes and wet woods throughout arctic and temperate Eurasia and North America. It has erect or prostrate stems, up to 31 in (80 cm) long, bearing round leaves and bright golden flowers, 0.8–2 in (2–5 cm) across. Family: *Ranunculaceae.*

Marsilius of Padua (c. 1280–1342) Italian critic of papal imperialism. Marsilius argued in his *Defensor Pacis* (1324) that since the Church is concerned entirely with faith through revelation, and not reason, which belongs to the secular world, it should be regulated by the civil power and should not interfere with government.

Mars-la-Tour and Gravelotte, Battles of (Aug 16–18, 1870) Successive battles in the *Franco-Prussian War in which the French were defeated. These engagements led to the encirclement of the French in Metz, allowing Prussian forces to march on Paris.

Marston, John (1576–1634) English dramatist. Initially a verse satirist, he was involved in a literary feud with Ben *Jonson until they collaborated (with *Chapman) on the satirical comedy *Eastward Ho!* (1605), for which they were both imprisoned. His best-known play is *The Malcontent* (1604). He was ordained priest in 1609.

Marston Moor, Battle of (July 2, 1644) The battle in the English *Civil War in which the Parliamentarians and the Scots decisively defeated the Royalists at Marston Moor, W of York. The parliamentary victory, which owed much to Oliver Cromwell's cavalry, destroyed the king's hold on N England.

marsupial A primitive *mammal belonging to the order *Marsupialia* (176 species). Most marsupials are found in Australia and New Guinea and include the *kangaroos, *wallabies, *marsupial moles, *dasyures, *bandicoots, and *phalangers. The only New World marsupials are the *opossums.

Marsupials have relatively small brains and they lack a placenta (through which—in other mammals—the embryos are nourished). Young marsupials, which are born in a very immature state, complete their development in a pouch of skin on the mother's belly surrounding the teat, from which they are fed until fully formed. In general, the pouch of herbivorous marsupials opens forward and that of carnivorous ones opens to the rear.

MARSUPIAL *The newly born young of all marsupials are incapable of independent existence. After a gestation period of only 12½ days, newly born opossums, the size of bees, climb into their mother's pouch, where they remain for 9–10 weeks feeding on milk from the nipples.*

marsupial mole An insectivorous burrowing *marsupial, *Notoryctes typhlops*, of Australia. It is molelike and has short velvety golden fur, powerful forelimbs with digging feet, tiny eyes, a sensitive nose, and a cylindrical body. Family: *Notoryctidae*.

Marsyas In Greek mythology a Phrygian satyr who discovered the flute that Athena had invented and discarded, and challenged Apollo, who played the lyre, to a musical contest. He lost and was bound and flayed alive by Apollo for his presumption.

Martello towers Fortifications containing cannon built in S Britain, Ireland, and Guernsey from 1804 to 1812. The towers were intended to check the potential invasion of Britain by Napoleon—which never materialized. Their construction was proposed after observation of the single tower mounting cannon at Mortella Point, Corsica, whence the term Martello was derived.

marten A carnivorous mammal belonging to the genus *Martes* (8 species), of Eurasian and North American forests. Up to 35 in (90 cm) long including the tail (6–12 in [15–30 cm]), martens are agile arboreal hunters with dark lustrous fur: they prey largely on squirrels but also take sitting birds and their eggs. The two European species are the *pine marten and the smaller stone marten (*M. foina*). The fur of the American marten (*M. americana*) is called American *sable. Family: *Mustelidae. See also* fisher.

martensite The hard brittle form of *steel produced after rapid quenching in *heat treatment. When steel is heated to red heat (1396°F [750°C]), the carbon in it forms a solid solution in the iron. On quenching the carbon is frozen into this configuration and the crystal structure of the steel has internal strains, which cause its hardness. Named for Adolph Martens (1850–1914).

Martha's Vineyard An island off the coast of SE Massachusetts. A former whaling and fishing center, it is now known chiefly as a summer resort. Area: about 100 sq mi (260 sq km).

Martí, José Julián (1853–95) Cuban poet and patriot. He worked for Cuban independence as a journalist in France, Mexico, Venezuela, and the US and died during a military expedition to Cuba. He published many essays on social and literary topics and several volumes of poetry, notably *Versos sencillos* (1891) and *Versos libres* (1913).

Martial (Marcus Valerius Martialis; c. 40–c. 104 AD) Roman poet. Born in Spain, he went to Rome in about 64 AD and gained the patronage of his fellow Spaniards Seneca and Lucan. His best-known works are his 12 books of epigrams, comprising about 1500 short poems describing the contemporary social scene with concise satirical wit and occasional lyricism. Shortly before his death he returned to Spain.

martial arts Styles of armed and unarmed combat developed in the East. The Japanese forms, such as *karate, *judo, *aikido, kendo, and sumo, derive largely from the fighting skills of the *samurai. Since the late 19th century they have become forms of sport, some popular worldwide, as has the Chinese style, *kung fu. They are closely associated with Eastern philosophies, especially Zen Buddhism. *See also* Bushido.

martin A bird belonging to the *swallow family (*Hirundidae*; 78 species). The purple martin (*Progne subis*), about 8 in (20 cm) long, is found from S Canada to the Caribbean and Mexico. It nests in natural holes or martin houses and is valued for the enormous number of insects it eats. The brown sand martin (*Riparia riparia*) is about 5 in (12 cm) long and has white underparts with a brown breast band. It nests in colonies in tunnels excavated in sand or clay banks. The black-and-white Old World house martin (*Delichon urbica*), about 5 in (13 cm) long, commonly nests beneath the eaves of houses.

Martin V (Oddone Colonna; 1368–1431) Pope (1417–31), whose election at the Council of *Constance ended the *Great Schism. He attempted to increase papal power by condemning the view that Church councils have supreme authority and by limiting the power of the national Churches. His attempts to suppress the *Hussites were largely unsuccessful.

Martin, Archer John Porter (1910–) British biochemist, who shared the 1952 Nobel Prize with Richard Synge (1914–) for their development of the technique of paper *chromatography (1944), which they used for separating amino acids. Martin went on to develop gas chromatography in 1953.

Martin, John (1789–1854) British painter. His large and grandiose paintings, often on biblical themes, including *The Fall of Babylon* (1819), *Belchazzar's Feast* (1826), and *The Deluge* (1834), brought him fame throughout Europe.

Martin, Pierre-Émile (1824–1915) French engineer, who invented the Siemens-Martin process of producing steel. In this process Martin employed the open-hearth furnace developed in 1856 by Sir William *Siemens but adopted his own steel-producing process, which utilized pig iron and scrap steel. The Siemens and the Siemens-Martin processes largely replaced the *Bessemer process but the Siemens-Martin eventually became the more widespread.

Martin, St (c. 316–97 AD) A patron saint of France; bishop of Tours (372–97). A soldier in the imperial army, he later settled at Poitiers and nearby founded the first monastery in Gaul. After becoming bishop of Tours, he continued to live as a monk at a monastery that he established outside Tours. His military cloak, part of which he reputedly gave to a naked beggar, has become a symbol of charity. Feast day: Nov 11.

Martin du Gard, Roger (1881–1958) French novelist. After active service in World War I he devoted his life entirely to writing. His major work was *Les Thibault* (1922–40), a cycle of novels analyzing contemporary society through family relationships. His other works include the outspoken *Notes sur André Gide* (1951). He won the Nobel Prize in 1937.

Martineau, Harriet (1802–76) British writer. Despite deafness and ill health, she was a leading figure in intellectual life. Her work includes novels, books on religion and economics, and the influential *History of England during the Thirty Years' Peace, 1816–46* (1849).

Martini, Simone (c. 1284–1344) Italian painter, born in Siena and probably the pupil of *Duccio. In 1317 he worked for Robert of Anjou (reigned 1309–43) in Naples, where he was influenced by French gothic art. His *Guidoriccio da Fogliano* (1328), commissioned for the town hall of Siena, is probably the first commemorative equestrian portrait in European art. The *Annunciation* (1333; Uffizi) is the best example of his decorative style and graceful use of line. In about 1340 he moved to Avignon (France), where he worked for the papal court.

Martinique A French overseas region in the West Indies, in the Windward Islands of the Lesser Antilles. It consists of a mountainous island of volcanic origin. Agriculture is of importance, the chief exports being sugar, bananas, and rum. Tourism is important. *History*: colonized by the French in 1635, it became a French overseas department in 1946. The volcanic eruption of Mont Pelée (1902) destroyed the town of St-Pierre. Area: 420 sq mi (1090 sq km). Population (1992): 369,000. Capital: Fort-de-France.

Martinmas The feast of St *Martin (Nov 11), traditionally the date for slaughtering livestock to be salted as winter food. Fairs, at which servants could be hired, were also held at Martinmas.

Martins, Peter (1946–) US ballet dancer and choreographer; born in Denmark. He danced for the Royal Danish Ballet before joining the New York City Ballet (1969–83) and becoming its ballet master-in-chief (1983). He danced the classical ballets, such as *Swan Lake, Firebird,* and *Serenade,* for the New York City Ballet and choreographed his own works, including *Calcium Light Night* (1978).

Martinů, Bohuslav (1890–1959) Czech composer. He was largely self-taught apart from a period of study with Roussel in Paris from 1923. During World War II he settled in the US. He composed many works, including symphonies, concertos, the ballet *La Revue de cuisine* (1927), the opera *Julietta* (1936–37), and a concerto for double string orchestra and timpani (1938).

Martin v. Hunter's Lessee (1816) US Supreme Court decision that interpreted federal jurisdiction over state courts. Martin, inheritor of Loyalist land confiscated by Virginia and given to Hunter during the American Revolution, sued the state for return of land under the terms of US-British treaties. The state refused, and Martin appealed to the Supreme Court, which ruled that the lands were to be returned to Martin and that the Supreme Court does have jurisdiction over local matters, as determined in the Constitution.

Marvell, Andrew (1621–78) English poet. He was employed as tutor by Cromwell and as secretary by Milton. From 1659 until his death he served as a member of Parliament. He published several satires and pamphlets attacking religious intolerance and government corruption. His poetry, most of which was published posthumously, is noted for its combination of intelligent argument and lyricism. Among his best known poems are "To His Coy Mistress" and "The Garden."

marvel of Peru. *See* four o'clock plant.

KARL MARX *Photographed (c. 1880) towards the end of his life.*

Marx, Karl (Heinrich) (1818–83) German philosopher, economist, and revolutionary. While studying at the University of Berlin, Marx became a member of the

Young Hegelians, an antireligious radical group. Unable to obtain a university post because of his radical views, Marx turned to journalism, becoming the editor of a radical paper in 1842. After its suppression Marx left Germany and spent the rest of his life in exile. He stayed first in Paris (until his expulsion in 1845), where he met several leading socialists including Friedrich *Engels, who later collaborated in many of Marx's writings and provided him with substantial financial support. While in Brussels, Marx's association with a group of German handicraftsmen led to the writing of *The Communist Manifesto* (1848). In 1849 Marx moved to London, where he remained for the rest of his life, publishing *The Class Struggles in France* (1850), *The Eighteenth Brumaire of Louis Bonaparte* (1852), and *A Contribution to the Critique of Political Economy* (1859). Following the establishment of the International Working Men's Association in 1864, Marx devoted many years to the affairs of the First *International, gaining wide recognition among socialists. The first volume of *Das Kapital* was published in 1867 but the rest of his work did not appear until after his death. *See also* Marxism.

Marx brothers A US family of comic film actors: **Chico** (Leonard M.; 1891–1961), **Harpo** (Adolph M.; 1893–1964), **Groucho** (Julius M.; 1895–1977), and, until 1933, **Zeppo** (Herbert M.; 1900–79). Their original vaudeville act also included **Gummo** (Milton M.; 1901–77). Their film comedies, characterized by irreverent comic interplay between the fast-talking Groucho, the incompetent Chico, and the dumb harp-playing Harpo, included *Horse Feathers* (1932), *Duck Soup* (1933), and *A Night at the Opera* (1935). The team disbanded in 1949.

Marxism The theory of scientific socialism introduced by Marx and Engels, which explains the origin, historical development, and demise of the capitalist economic system. It relies heavily on the philosophy of Hegel, in particular Hegel's thesis that change has to be explained in terms of contradiction (*see* dialectical materialism). Class analysis, the central component of Marxism, is not peculiar to Marx but was shared by contemporary political economists, such as Adam Smith and Ricardo. Marxism is distinct in that it developed the theory of proletarian revolution. The transition to a socialist and eventually a classless society would not be a gradual evolution but would involve the violent overthrow of the state power (army, police, bureaucracy, etc.) of the bourgeois class. The working class would have to establish its own state power, which would be more democratic because it would be the rule of the majority of the population, the working class. As classes gradually disappeared, however, state power would also wither away since the state was fundamentally an instrument by which one class ruled over other classes. The classless society of the future would allow the fullest developments of individuals through social cooperation. Since World War I many different versions of Marxism have been expounded (*see also* Leninism; Maoism; communism).

Mary 37 42N 61 54E A city in Turkmenistan. Located in a cotton-growing oasis of the Kara Kum Desert, it has important textile industries. Population (1985): 85,000.

Mary I (1516–58) Queen of England and Ireland (1553–58), succeeding her younger half-brother *Edward VI. The daughter of Henry VIII and Catherine of Aragon, Mary's life after her parents' divorce in 1533 was one of extreme uncertainty until her rehabilitation in the line of succession in 1544. She became queen after the failure of a conspiracy to place Lady Jane *Grey on the throne. Her single-minded aim was to restore Roman Catholicism in England: Edward's Protestant legislation was repealed and in 1554 the heresy laws were reintroduced, resulting in almost 300 deaths at the stake and the queen's nickname, Bloody Mary. Her marriage (1554) to Philip II of Spain, the announcement of which had incited the unsuccessful rebellion (1553) of Sir Thomas *Wyatt, led to England's entanglement in Philip's foreign policy and the loss in 1558 of its last possession on the Continent, Calais. This disaster, coupled with a series of false pregnancies, hastened Mary's death.

Mary II (1662–94) Queen of England, Scotland, and Ireland (1689–94), joint monarch with her husband William III. Daughter of James II, she was brought up as a Protestant and came to the throne after the enforced abdication of her Roman Catholic father during the *Glorious Revolution. She was a popular ruler, governing during William's absences abroad, and died prematurely of smallpox.

Mary, Queen of Scots (1542–87) Scottish queen. The daughter of James V, she succeeded to the throne shortly after her birth. From 1547 Mary, a Roman Catholic, lived at the French court, where in 1558 she married the dauphin (later Francis II). After Francis's death (1561) Mary returned to Scotland and in 1565 married her cousin Lord *Darnley. In 1566 Mary gave birth to the future James VI (James I of England). In 1567 Darnley was murdered by *Bothwell, who then married her. A rebellion of Scottish nobles defeated Mary and Bothwell at Carberry Hill (1567) and Mary was forced to abdicate in favor of her son. She then raised an army that was defeated at Langside (1568). Fleeing to England, where her claim to the English succession had long been an embarrassment to Elizabeth I, she was held prisoner for the rest of her life. She became the focus of a series of plots against Elizabeth and was finally tried for conspiracy and executed.

Mary, the Virgin In the New Testament, the mother of *Jesus Christ. The fullest accounts of Mary are contained in the birth stories in *Luke and *Matthew. *John (19.25) reports that she was present at the crucifixion, and she appears to have been present at the growth of the early Church in Jerusalem (Acts 1.14). Luke records the Annunciation (the announcement by the Angel Gabriel that she was to conceive the Son of God by the Holy Spirit); her betrothal to *Joseph; her meeting with her cousin Elizabeth; and her song of praise (the Magnificat) when Elizabeth had greeted her as the mother of the Lord. The Gospels also state that she was and remained a virgin. Mary's *Immaculate Conception has been recognized as a dogma of the Roman Catholic Church since 1854 and the belief that she was taken up bodily into heaven (the Bodily Assumption) was defined as doctrine in 1950. In the Orthodox and Roman Catholic Churches Mary is venerated as having a secondary mediating role between God and man.

Mary Magdalene, St In the New Testament, the first person to see Jesus after the resurrection. Jesus cured her of possession by evil spirits. She aided his work in Galilee and was present at the crucifixion and burial. Medieval scholars associated her with the repentant sinner who anointed Jesus' feet, mentioned in Luke's Gospel. Feast day: July 22. Emblem: an ointment jar.

Maryborough (Ireland). *See* Portlaoise.

Maryland A state on the E seaboard of the US, one of the mid-Atlantic states. Delaware and the Atlantic Ocean lie to the E, Washington, DC, to the S, Virginia and West Virginia to the S and W, and Pennsylvania to the N. It consists of two physical regions: the Atlantic Coastal Plain, which is split by Chesapeake Bay into a low flat plain in the E and uplands in the W; and an area of higher ground, part of the Alleghenies, in the N and W. The Susquehanna and Potomac Rivers empty into Chesapeake Bay. Most of the population (85%) lives in the Baltimore metropolitan area, which is contiguous with the urban area surrounding Washington, DC. Manufacturing is the most important sector of the economy (primary metals, metal products, food processing, transportation and electrical equipment, printing and publishing, and textiles). There is an important service sector and government is the major employer. The state's farmers produce livestock, poultry, and dairy products as well as some corn, tobacco, soybeans, and vegetables. *History*: one of the 13 original colonies, it was first settled by the English. It was granted (1632) to Cecilius Calvert, 2nd Baron Baltimore, by Charles I and named for Charles's wife, Henrietta Maria. Under the Calvert family the colony became a refuge for Roman Catholics persecuted in England. A border state, Maryland was divided on the slavery issue during the Civil War and was placed under military control to ensure loyalty to the Union. The construction of the Chesapeake Bay Bridge and other transportation improvements after World War II helped spur industrialization of the rural E shore. Area: 10,577 sq mi (27,394 sq km). Population (1990): 4,781,468. Capital: Annapolis. Chief port: Baltimore.

Mary Rose A Tudor warship (Henry VIII's flagship), which sank in 1545 in Portsmouth Harbor while sailing into battle. A search for the wreck was begun in 1965 by underwater archeologists and it was positively identified in 1971. The ship's contents, most of which were remarkably preserved, were raised during the following 10 years and the hull itself was lifted in 1982 and placed in a dry-dock at Portsmouth. The Mary Rose Trust, of which the Prince of Wales is president, was formed in 1979.

Masaccio (Tommaso di Giovanni di Simone Guidi; 1401–28) Florentine painter of the early Renaissance. He collaborated with *Masolino on the *Madonna and Child with St Anne* (Uffizi) and on the fresco cycle in the Brancacci Chapel in Sta Maria del Carmine. His independent paintings include the *Trinity* (Sta Maria Novella, Florence). Influenced by *Giotto and the innovations of *Brunelleschi and *Donatello, Masaccio initiated the use of linear perspective and a single light source in painting.

Masada 31 19N 35 21E A precipitous rocky hilltop near the W shore of the Dead Sea, in S Israel. The site of one of *Herod the Great's fortified palaces, it was later a center of the *Essene sect and a stronghold of the Jews in their revolt against Rome (66 AD). In the last action of the war (73 AD), after a siege lasting almost two years, the defenders, on the eve of the final assault by the Roman besiegers, committed mass suicide rather than surrender. The site is an Israeli national monument.

Masai A Nilotic people of Kenya and Tanzania who speak a Sudanic language. They are nomads with little centralized political organization. Age sets are the basis of social organization, with three principal stages for every male: boy, warrior, and elder. This system allowed the Masai to form large raiding parties to increase their stock of cattle, which are the basis of their economy. Milk and blood from cattle form an important part of their diet, the blood being drawn from a vein in the animal's neck without killing it. Tall and active, the Masai highly value courage in their warriors.

Masaryk, Tomáš (Garrigue) (1850–1937) Czechoslovak statesman, who was one of the founders of Czechoslovakia. In Paris, during World War II, he and *Beneš founded the Czechoslovak National Council, which the Allies recognized in 1918. When Austria-Hungary fell in November 1918, Masaryk was elected Czechoslovakia's first president; he was reelected in 1920, 1927, and 1934. His administration was marked by a major land reform. He resigned, owing to his age, in 1935. His son **Jan (Garrigue) Masaryk** (1886–1948), a diplomat, was Czechoslovak minister to Britain (1925–38) and foreign minister in Czechoslovakia's provisional government in London (1940–45). Following

World War II he returned to Prague but after the communists came to power in 1948 he died in a fall from a window, allegedly a suicide.

MASADA *Glass plates found in the Cave of Letters inside the fortress.*

Mascagni, Pietro (1863–1945) Italian opera composer. His fame rests chiefly on his one-act opera *Cavalleria Rusticana* (1889), written as an entry for a competition in which it won first prize. He wrote many other operas, including *L'amico Fritz* (1891).

Mascarene Islands (French name: Îles Mascareignes) The heavily populated islands of Mauritius, Réunion, and Rodrigues in the W Indian Ocean. Discovered by the Portuguese in the early 16th century, they were known earlier to the Arabs.

mascons Disk-shaped masses that are located beneath the lunar surface in the younger *maria and are denser than their surroundings. They were discovered when lunar-satellite orbits were found to be slightly perturbed as a result of the higher gravitational attraction over these regions.

Masefield, John (1878–1967) British poet. Having served briefly in the merchant navy, he captured the fascination of the sea in his first volume, *Salt-Water Ballads* (1902). He also wrote narrative poems, such as *Reynard the Fox* (1919), and several adventure novels, including *Sard Harker* (1924) and *Odtaa* (1926). He became poet laureate in 1930.

maser (*m*icrowave *a*mplification by *s*timulated *e*mission of *r*adiation) A device that works on the same principle as the *laser, the radiation produced being in the *microwave region instead of in the visible spectrum. Masers are used as oscillators (e.g. the *ammonia clock) and amplifiers.

Maseru 29 19S 27 29E The capital of Lesotho, near the South African border. It was founded in 1869. The University of Botswana, Lesotho, and Swaziland was established nearby in 1966. Population (1986): 109,932.

Mashhad (*or* Meshed) 36 16N 59 34E A city in NE Iran, close to the Afghan and Soviet borders. It is a pilgrimage center for Shiite Muslims; the shrine of the *imam* 'Ali ar-Rida is a magnificent structure. Mashhad is famous for carpets and turquoise; its university was founded in 1956. Population (1986): 1,463,508.

Mashonaland An area in central and NE Zimbabwe, inhabited by the Shona, a Bantu people. Mashonaland was administered by the British South Africa Company from 1889 to 1923, when it became a part of the new colony of Southern Rhodesia.

Mashriq (Arabic: east) The Arab countries of SW Asia (the Middle East) as compared with the *Maghrib countries of N Africa. Egypt and the Sudan are included in the Mashriq.

Masinissa (c. 240–148 BC) Ruler of Numidia in North Africa. With the support of Rome, whom he had helped against Carthage in the second Punic War (208–201), he established a strong state among the diverse Numidian tribes.

masochism Sexual pleasure derived from the experience of pain. The condition is named for an Austrian writer, Leopold von Sacher-Masoch (1835–95), whose novels depict it. It is often associated with a pathologically strong need to be humiliated by and submissive to one's sexual partner. Frequently, masochistic and sadistic desires are combined in the same individual.

Masolino (Tommaso di Cristoforo Fini; 1383–1447?) Italian painter, born in Pannicale but active mainly in Florence. He was strongly influenced by *Masaccio, particularly while working with him on the fresco cycle in the Brancacci Chapel, Florence. Later he painted in the *international gothic style. Independent works include *The Miracle of the Snow* (Sta Maria Maggiore, Rome).

Mason, George (1725–92) US politician and patriot. After inheriting a large plantation in Virginia, he became a prominent planter, businessman, and political leader. He was responsible for writing Virginia's constitution and Bill of Rights (1776) upon which Thomas *Jefferson modeled parts of the Declaration of Independence. A delegate to the Continental Congress in 1787, he strongly objected to the slave trade compromise and felt that the proposed constitution leaned too heavily toward central government. He worked actively against its ratification in Virginia, complying only after the Bill of Rights had been added.

mason bee A solitary *bee belonging to the genus *Osmia* and related genera, occurring in Europe, Africa, and elsewhere. It builds nests of soil cemented together with saliva in hollows in wood or stones. Family: *Megachilidae*.

Mason-Dixon line A line drawn in 1767 by two surveyors, Charles Mason and Jeremiah Dixon, to settle the conflict over borders between Pennsylvania and Maryland. Until the Civil War it also represented the division between southern proslavery and northern free states. It has remained a symbolic boundary between the North and South.

masoretes Transmitters of the textual tradition (*masorah*) of the Hebrew Bible. The textual study of the Bible goes back to antiquity (*see* scribes); in the gaonic period (*see* gaon) various schools of masoretes labored to establish a correct text and to mark the pronunciation with the help of accents. The text of Aaron ben Asher (930 AD) was recognized as authoritative by *Maimonides. The masoretic text is the basis of all Hebrew Bibles printed today.

masque A form of dramatic court entertainment popular in England during the late 16th and early 17th centuries. It consisted of a combination of verse, dance, and music, usually with a slight dramatic plot based on a mythological theme. The form was perfected in the collaborations of Ben *Jonson and Inigo *Jones, whose elaborate costumes and scenery were vastly expensive. Other writers of masques include Sir Philip *Sidney and Samuel *Daniel.

mass (physics). *See* mass and weight.

mass (religion). *See* Eucharist.

Massachusetts A state on the NE coast of the US, in New England. It is bordered by New York on the W, Vermont and New Hampshire on the N, the Atlantic Ocean on the E, and Rhode Island and Connecticut on the S. The uplands in the W, which are cut N–S by the Connecticut River, are separated from the lowlands of the Atlantic Coastal Plain and Cape Cod Peninsula by the rolling country of central Massachusetts. The mainly urban population is concentrated along the coast and river valleys. A major manufacturing state, its industries produce electrical and communications equipment, high-quality instruments, chemicals, textiles, and metal and food products. Boston is an important financial and service center. Its farmers produce dairy products, eggs, poultry, cranberries, and horticultural goods. Massachusetts is an important center in US educational and cultural life. *History*: Massachusetts was one of the 13 original colonies. The arrival of the Pilgrim Fathers on the *Mayflower* (1620) heralded major settlement with the formation of the Plymouth Colony. After early hardships, the colony took hold and was followed (1630) by the Massachusetts Bay Colony. The early Puritan government was quasi-theocratic and the perpetuation of Puritan ideas of representative government formed the basis of democracy. By the 1750s Massachusetts was a thriving center for trafficking of molasses, rum, and black slaves (known as the "triangular trade"). It was a center for opposition to British colonial policy, including such demonstrations as the Boston Tea Party. The American Revolution began in Massachusetts with fighting at Lexington and Concord (1775). Massachusetts retained its prominence through the early years of independence, sending several presidents to the White House. With the arrival of the industrial revolution a flourishing textile industry grew up. Boston became a center for many liberal religious and philosophical groups during the 19th century, including transcendentalism, unitarianism, and abolitionism. Labor disputes dominated the early 20th century. After World War II the decline of textile and shoe manufacturing was offset by the growth of computer- and defense-related industries. Area: 8257 sq mi (21,386 sq km). Population (1990): 6,016,425. Capital: Boston.

Massachusetts Bay Company A colony of English Puritans established at Salem, Mass., in 1628. The main body of colonists arrived in 1630 under the leadership of John *Winthrop. The Company's charter was withdrawn in 1684.

Massachusetts Government Act (1774). *See* Intolerable Acts.

Massachusetts Institute of Technology (MIT) A university in Cambridge, Mass. Founded in 1861 at Boston, it moved to its present site in 1916. It is world famous for scientific education and research.

mass action, law of The rate of a chemical reaction for a uniform system at constant temperature varies as the concentration of each reacting substance, raised to the power equal to the number of molecules of the substance appearing in the balanced equation. Thus, for the reaction $2H_2 + O_2 = 2H_2O$ the speed of the forward reaction is proportional to the concentration of O_2 (written $[O_2]$) and to $[H_2]^2$; the reverse reaction depends on $[H_2O]^2$. The law is thus useful for calculation of equilibrium concentrations when reaction speeds are known, and vice versa. It was first proposed in the period 1864–79 by two Norwegian scientists, C. M. Guldberg (1836–1902) and P. Waage (1833–1900).

massage Manipulation of the soft tissues of the body for therapeutic purposes. This includes rhythmic stroking (effleurage), kneading (petrissage), and repeated tapping (tapotement); it is used to relieve muscular spasm and pain, improve blood circulation in the skin, and reduce swelling due to accumulation of fluid in the tissues. *See also* physiotherapy.

mass and weight Two physical quantities used to express the extent to which a substance is present; they are sometimes confused. The mass of a body was defined by *Newton as the ratio of a force applied to the body to the acceleration it produces. This is now called the **inertial mass**, as it is a measure of the extent to which a body resists a change in its motion. **Gravitational mass** is defined in terms of the gravitational force between two bodies in accordance with Newton's law of gravitation. Lóránt Eotvos (1848–1919) showed experimentally that inertial mass and gravitational mass are equal, a result used by Einstein in his general theory of relativity.

Mass was also shown by Einstein, in his special theory of relativity, to be a form of energy, according to the relationship $E = mc^2$ (where c is the velocity of light). The total of the mass and the energy of a closed system remains unchanged under all circumstances (the law of the conservation of mass and energy).

Weight is proportional to gravitational mass, being the force by which an object is attracted to the earth. It is therefore equal to the product of the mass and the *acceleration of free fall (i.e. $W = mg$). Thus, the weight of a body may vary according to its position; the mass is a constant. In common usage mass and weight are used synonymously, but in scientific terms they are different, mass being expressed in units of mass (e.g. kilograms) and weight being expressed in units of force (e.g. newtons). *See also* amount of substance.

Massasoit (?1580–1661) American Indian chief; also called Wawmegin ("yellow feather"). Chief of the Wampanoag tribe in Massachusetts and Rhode Island, he made peace with the Pilgrims (1621) in Plymouth Colony and shared the first Thanksgiving with them. He also negotiated a peace treaty (1635) with Rhode Island colonists under Roger *Williams. Although peace reigned under Massasoit, his son Metacomet (King *Philip) warred against the colonists.

Massawa (*or* Mitsiwa) 15 37N 39 28E A port in Eritrea on the Red Sea. It was occupied (1885) by the Italians, who used it as a base for their offensive against Ethiopia in 1935. With good communications to Asmara, 40 mi (64 km) WSW, Massawa is an important outlet for Ethiopia's exports and has a naval base. Population: 19,820.

mass defect The difference between the total mass of the constituent protons and neutrons in an atomic nucleus and the mass of the nucleus. This defect is equal to the *binding energy of the nucleus.

Masséna, André (?1756–1817) French marshal. He fought in Napoleon's Italian campaign, winning an important victory at Rivoli (1797). He subsequently defeated the Russians in Switzerland (1799), fought again in Italy, and, outstandingly, against the Austrians (1809–10). In 1810–11 he was defeated by Wellington in the *Peninsular War and lost his command.

mass-energy equation. *See* relativity.

Massenet, Jules (1842–1912) French composer. He studied at the Paris conservatory and won the Prix de Rome in 1863. Massenet catered to the Parisian musical taste of his day, writing 27 operas, of which *Manon Lescaut* (1884) and *Werther* (1892) are still performed today.

Massey, Raymond (1896–1983) Canadian actor. He first acted on the stage in 1922 and thereafter appeared in a number of films, including *The Scarlet Pimpernel* (1934), *Abe Lincoln in Illinois* (1939), *Arsenic and Old Lace* (1944), and

East of Eden (1955). He also appeared in the television series *Dr Kildare* (1961–65).

Massey, (Charles) Vincent (1887–1967) Canadian statesman; governor-general of Canada (1952–59); brother of Raymond *Massey. He held various positions in Canada's governor's cabinet before becoming minister to the US (1926–30) and Canada's high commissioner in Great Britain (1935–46). He also headed the University of Toronto (1947–53). He was the first native Canadian to attain the governor-general's post.

Massey, William Ferguson (1856–1925) New Zealand statesman; prime minister (1912–25). He entered Parliament in 1894 and became (1903) leader of the Conservative opposition, which in 1909 he named the Reform party. His administration, in coalition (1915–19) with the Liberals during World War I, is noted for its support of agrarian interests.

Massif Central A plateau area in S central France. Generally considered to be that area over 984 ft (300 m) high, it rises to 6188 ft (1885 m) at Puy de Sancy. The central N area is also known as the Auvergne and the SE rim as the Cévennes. There is dairy and arable farming as well as heavy industry. Area: about 34,742 sq mi (90,000 sq km).

Massine, Léonide (Leonid Miassin; 1896–1979) Russian ballet dancer and choreographer. He joined Diaghilev's company in Paris in 1914 and choreographed his first ballet, *Soleil de nuit*, in 1915. He choreographed for many companies, notably the Ballet Russe de Monte Carlo. His most controversial ballets were the innovative symphonic ballets *Les Présages* (1933), *Choreartium* (1933), and *Symphonie Fantastique* (1936).

Massinger, Philip (1583–1640) English dramatist. He collaborated with several other writers before succeeding John *Fletcher in 1625 as chief dramatist for the leading theatrical company, the King's Men. His best-known plays are the satirical comedies *A New Way to Pay Old Debts* (1621) and *The City Madam* (1632).

mass number (*or* nucleon number) The total number of protons and neutrons in the *nucleus of an atom.

Massys, Quentin (*or* Matsys, Messys, Metsys; c. 1466–1530) Flemish painter, born in Louvain but active in Antwerp. He was influenced by Italian Renaissance artists, particularly *Leonardo. In portraits such as *Erasmus* (Galleria Nazionale, Rome), he anticipated *Holbein by depicting his sitter at work. He also painted scenes of daily life, notably *The Banker and His Wife* (Louvre).

mastectomy Surgical removal of a breast, usually for the treatment of breast cancer. There are several varieties of the operation. In a partial mastectomy (or lumpectomy) only the tumor is removed, while in a total mastectomy the entire breast is removed. A radical mastectomy includes removal of the breast together with the lymph nodes in the armpit and the chest muscles associated with it.

Masters, Edgar Lee (1868–1950) US poet. His best-known work is *Spoon River Anthology* (1915), a collection of free-verse epitaphs spoken as monologues by the inhabitants of a small provincial town. A successful stage version was produced in 1963.

Masters, William Howell (1915–   ) US physician, noted for his studies of human sexual behavior using volunteer subjects under laboratory conditions. Masters and his colleague, the psychologist **Virginia Eshelman Johnson** (1925–   ), measured physiological changes associated with sex and published their findings in *Human Sexual Responses* (1966). Although criticized, their work established a body of knowledge that is useful in such areas as marriage counseling.

Masterson, Bat (William Barclay M.; 1853–1921) US frontier law enforcer. He was deputy marshal of Dodge City, Kans., while in his early 20s and sheriff of Ford County, Kans., in 1877. In 1880 he was assistant to Wyatt Earp, the federal marshal in Tombstone, Ariz. He became a sportswriter for the *New York Morning Telegraph* in 1902 and eventually became an executive on the paper.

mastic An evergreen shrub, *Pistacia lentiscus,* up to 6 ft (1.8 m) high, native to the Mediterranean region. An aromatic yellowish-green resin is obtained from the bark and used to make varnishes for coating metals and paintings and as an adhesive. Family: *Anacardiaceae.* The name is also applied to other resin-yielding trees, including the related American mastic (*Schinus molle*) and *Sideroxylon mastichodendron* (family: *Sapotaceae*).

mastiff An ancient Eurasian breed of large dog long used as a guard dog and for bull- and bear-baiting. It is powerfully built with a large head and a short deep muzzle. The short smooth coat may be apricot, silver, or fawn; the muzzle, ears, and nose are black. Height: 30 in (76 cm) (dogs); 27 in (69 cm) (bitches). *See also* bull mastiff.

mastodon An extinct elephant that originated in Africa 34 million years ago and spread throughout Europe, Asia, and America. Early mastodons were small and had two pairs of tusks; later forms were larger and more elephant-like. The American mastodons survived until about 8000 years ago and were painted in hunting scenes by early man.

mastoid bone A nipple-shaped process of the temporal bone of the skull, situated behind the ear and containing many air spaces. Infection of the middle ear may spread through these spaces to affect the mastoid bone. Formerly treated surgically, this infection is now readily cured with antibiotics.

Mastroianni, Marcello (1924–) Italian actor. He became one of the best-known international film stars of the 1960s, a representative European leading man. He appeared in Visconti's *White Nights* (1957), Fellini's *La dolce vita* (1960), *8½* (1963), and *Ginger and Fred* (1985), and Antonioni's *La notte* (1961).

Matabeleland An area in W Zimbabwe, between the Limpopo and Zambezi Rivers. It was named for the Ndebele, a tribe that was driven across the Limpopo by the Voortrekkers in 1837. Consisting chiefly of extensive plains, the area has important gold deposits. Area: 70,118 sq mi (181,605 sq km).

Matadi 5 50S 13 32E The chief port in Zaïre, on the Zaïre River. It was founded in 1879 by *Stanley. It has one of central Africa's largest harbors and is accessible to oceangoing vessels. Population (1985): 145,000.

Mata Hari (Margaretha Geertruida Zelle; 1876–1917) Dutch courtesan and secret agent. She lived in Indonesia with her husband, a Dutch colonial officer, from 1897 to 1902. She became a professional dancer in Paris in 1905 and probably worked for both French and German intelligence services. She was executed by the French in 1917.

matamata. *See* snake-necked turtle.

Matamoros 25 50N 97 31W A city in N Mexico, on the Rio Grande on the US border. It is the manufacturing center for a region producing cotton and sugar cane and is an important point of entry for US tourists. Population (1980): 188,745.

Matanzas 23 04N 81 35W A port in Cuba, on Mantanzas Bay on the N coast. Its chief export is sugar. It is also a popular tourist center. Population (1986): 105,000.

Matapan, Cape (Modern Greek name: Ákra Taínaron) 36 23N 22 29E The southernmost point of mainland Greece, off which (March 1941) the British Mediterranean fleet scored a decisive victory over the Italians during World War II.

matches Small lengths of wood, cardboard, etc., tipped with an ignitable substance. The friction match was invented in 1816 (by Dérosne). Modern strike-anywhere matches are usually tipped with phosphorus sesquisulfide, potassium chlorate, and zinc oxide. Safety matches, invented in 1844, have their ignitable substances divided between the tip and a special striking surface. Usually the surface contains red phosphorus and the tip a mixture of antimony sulfide and such oxidizing agents as potassium chlorate and manganese dioxide.

matchlock. *See* musket.

maté The dried leaves of a *holly shrub or tree, *Ilex paraguariensis*, native to Paraguay and Brazil. They are roasted, powdered, and infused with water to make the stimulating greenish tealike beverage, popular in many South American countries.

materialism In classical metaphysics, materialism is the doctrine of *Democritus and *Leucippus that everything in the universe is matter or stuff. All events were explicable in terms of the movements and alterations initiated by this matter. By contrast *Plato sought to establish the existence of some incorporeal objects, called by him Forms. *Aristotle also did not confine himself to a completely materialist explanation of the world, believing that the soul was immaterial. His doctrines nevertheless led to more refined materialistic views than those of the pre-Socratics, but *Hobbes's uncompromising materialism owed nothing to Aristotle. *Marx's economic materialism, whereby human actions and beliefs are explained solely in terms of economic forces, was developed by *Lenin in *dialectical materialism. Some recent materialist philosophers studying the body-mind relationship have reduced thought to (physical) neural processes. In all these senses materialism is a metaphysical doctrine. More popularly, the term has also been used to signify worldly outlooks and behavior.

mathematics The logical study of numerical and spatial relationships. It is usually divided into pure and applied mathematics. In pure mathematics the general theoretical principles are studied, often in abstract. Its branches are *arithmetic, *algebra, *calculus, *geometry, and *trigonometry. Some form of mathematical calculation is an indispensable part of all financial transactions and all measurements. The ancient Egyptians, Sumerians, and Chinese were all using a form of *abacus to carry out these calculations for thousands of years before the Christian era. But it was not until the 9th century AD that *al-Khwarizmi introduced the idea of writing down calculations instead of carrying them out on an abacus. The Venetian mathematicians of the 11th and 12th centuries were largely responsible for the introduction of these methods to the West; indeed it was they who showed that commercial calculations based on algorisms (a word derived from Al-Khwarizmi's name) were superior to those performed on an abacus. However, the application of mathematics to the physical sciences (including astronomy) was largely a 16th-century development inspired by *Galileo. It was from this development that applied mathematics grew. It is now largely concerned with *mechanics and *statistics. *See also* new math.

Mather, Increase (1639–1723) US churchman and author. Minister of Second Church in Boston (1664–1723) and president of Harvard University

(1685–1701), he traveled to England in 1688 to appeal for a new colonial charter and governor. Partially successful, he returned with a new governor, but the colonists' dissatisfaction caused a decline in Mather's popularity. He was a driving force in ending the mushrooming witchcraft trials in Salem (1692) with the publication of *Cases of Conscience Concerning Evil Spirits* (1692). His son **Cotton Mather** (1663–1728) was also a churchman and author. A Puritan, he served (1685–1728) at Boston's Second Church, where his father was long the minister. He was active in the movement to remove Sir Edmund Andros, royal colonial governor, from office. His *Memorable Providences Relating to Witchcrafts and Possessions* (1689) contributed to the panic that incited the Salem witch trials in 1692. Among his more than 400 works were *The Ecclesiastical History of New England* (1702) and *The Christian Philosopher* (1721). He was a member of the Royal Society of London and a founding father of Yale University.

Mathewson, Christopher ("Christy"; 1880–1925) US baseball player. Also called "Matty" and "Big Six," he was pitcher for the New York Giants (1900–16) and the Cincinnati Reds (1916–18). During his career he won 373 games and in 1936 was one of the first players elected to the Baseball Hall of Fame.

Mathura 27 30N 77 42E A city in India, in Uttar Pradesh on the Jumna River. A pilgrimage center, it is the traditional birthplace of the Hindu god, Krishna. Population (1971): 132,028.

Matilda (*or* Maud; 1102–67) The daughter of Henry I of England, who designated her his heir. On his death (1135), his nephew Stephen seized the throne and Matilda invaded England (1139) inaugurating a period of inconclusive civil war. She and her second husband Geoffrey, duke of Anjou (1113–51), captured Normandy and in 1152 the Treaty of Wallingford recognized her son Henry as Stephen's heir. Her first husband was Emperor *Henry V (d. 1125).

Matisse, Henri (1869–1954) French painter and sculptor. Having abandoned his legal studies he became a pupil of the painter Gustave *Moreau in the 1890s. Matisse initiated *fauvism in the early 1900s with his boldly patterned and vibrantly colored still lifes, portraits, and nudes, notably the controversial *Woman with the Hat* (1905). He was the only artist to continue fauvist principles after the development of *cubism. He was also inspired by Islamic art. By 1909 he had achieved worldwide recognition and he remained inventive until his death, a stained glass design for the Dominican chapel at Vence (S France) being among his last works.

Mato Grosso A plateau area in SW central Brazil. It extends across the states of Mato Grosso and Goias, separating the Amazon and Plata River systems. Its height varies between about 328 ft (100 m) and 2953 ft (900 m). It is an important cattle-raising area.

Matopo Hills A range of hills in SW Zimbabwe, S of Bulawayo. Cecil Rhodes is buried here at a point named World's View.

matrix A set of numbers, called elements, arranged in rows and columns to form a rectangular array. It is used to assist in the solution of certain mathematical problems. The *commutative, *associative, and *distributive laws of matrix arithmetic and algebra are different from those of ordinary arithmetic. The **determinant** of a square matrix is a number, or algebraic expression, that is obtained by multiplication and addition of the elements in a specified way. It has properties that are useful for simplifying and solving sets of simultaneous equations. Single column matrices may represent *vectors, enabling them to be handled algebraically and processed by computer.

Ma-tsu. *See* Mazu.

$$\begin{pmatrix} a & b \\ c & d \\ e & f \end{pmatrix} + \begin{pmatrix} p & q \\ r & s \\ t & u \end{pmatrix} = \begin{pmatrix} a+p & b+q \\ c+r & d+s \\ e+t & f+u \end{pmatrix} \quad \text{addition}$$

$$k \times \begin{pmatrix} a & b \\ c & d \\ e & f \end{pmatrix} = \begin{pmatrix} ka & kb \\ kc & kd \\ ke & kf \end{pmatrix} \quad \text{multiplication by a constant}$$

$$\begin{pmatrix} a & b \\ c & d \\ e & f \end{pmatrix} \times \begin{pmatrix} p & q & r \\ s & t & u \end{pmatrix} = \quad \text{matrix multiplication}$$

$$\begin{pmatrix} (ap+bs) & (aq+bt) & (ar+bu) \\ (cp+ds) & (cq+dt) & (cr+du) \\ (ep+fs) & (eq+ft) & (er+fu) \end{pmatrix}$$

$$\text{the } \textbf{determinant} \text{ of } \begin{pmatrix} a & b \\ c & d \end{pmatrix} = \begin{vmatrix} a & b \\ c & d \end{vmatrix} = ad - bc$$

MATRIX *Examples of matrix algebra.*

Matsuo Basho (Matsuo Munefusa; 1644–94) Japanese poet. Born near Kyoto, he moved to Edo (Tokyo) in 1667 and in 1680 became a recluse. He transformed the traditional 17-syllable lyric verse form, the haiku, introducing the characteristic concentrated elliptical imagery and the philosophical spirit of *Zen Buddhism. He also wrote travel diaries, of which *The Narrow Road to the Deep North* (1694) is outstanding.

Matsuyama 33 50N 132 47E A port in Japan, in NW Shikoku on the Inland Sea. It is an agricultural and industrial center, with a university (1949). Population (1980): 402,000.

Matteotti, Giacomo (1885–1924) Italian Socialist politician, who was assassinated by fascists after denouncing their party in the Chamber of Deputies. His murder almost brought the fall of Mussolini's government. Three of his assassins were imprisoned following the reopening of the case after World War II.

Matterhorn (French name: Mont Cervin; Italian name: Monte Cervino) 45 59N 7 39E A mountain in Europe, on the Swiss-Italian border in the Alps near Zermatt. First climbed in 1865 by the British mountaineer Edward Whymper, it is conspicuous because of its striking pyramidal shape. Height: 14,692 ft (4478 m).

Matthew, St In the New Testament, one of the 12 *Apostles. He was a tax collector until he became a follower of Jesus. According to tradition, he preached in Judea, Ethiopia, and Persia and suffered martyrdom. Feast day: 21 Sept. Emblem: a man with wings. **The Gospel according to St Matthew** is generally believed to have been written sometime after St Mark's Gospel, from which it drew material. It is a narrative of the life and ministry of Jesus that seeks to convince the Jews that he is the Messiah predicted by the Old Testament. It contains the Sermon on the Mount (chapters 5–7).

Matthew Paris (c. 1200–59) English chronicler. He became a monk of the Benedictine abbey of St Albans in 1217 and was a member of the court of Henry III. His careful coverage of the years 1235–59 form the second part of his major work, the *Chronica majora,* a history of the world from the Creation to 1259.

Matthias (1557–1619) Holy Roman Emperor (1612–19). He became king of Hungary (1608) and of Bohemia (1611) following revolts against his brother Rudolph II and was in turn forced to cede these crowns to Ferdinand of Styria (later Ferdinand II) in 1618 and 1617 respectively. Matthias then tried unsuccessfully to moderate Ferdinand's harsh policies against the Bohemian Protestants.

Matthias I Corvinus (?1443–90) King of Hungary (1458–90). The son of János Hunyadi, Matthias brought Hungary to a peak of greatness before its fall in 1526 to the Turks. His reforms embraced administration, law, and the army. He also imposed high taxes, which greatly benefited the treasury but precipitated revolts. His foreign policy was dominated by conflict with Emperor *Frederick III and in 1485 Matthias occupied Vienna. He also added Bosnia, Moravia, and Silesia to his domains but failed in his efforts to take Bohemia. A great patron of Renaissance art and scholarship, Matthias founded the great Corvina library.

Mauchly, John W. *See* Eckert, John Presper.

Maud. *See* Matilda.

Maugham, W(illiam) Somerset (1874–1965) British novelist and dramatist. Born in Paris, he studied and qualified in medicine but abandoned it after the success of his first novel, *Liza of Lambeth* (1896). His later fiction includes *Of Human Bondage* (1915), *The Moon and Sixpence* (1919), *Cakes and Ale* (1930), and *The Razor's Edge* (1944). He wrote popular comedies of manners, such as *The Circle* (1921), and many short stories with Far Eastern or other exotic settings. From 1928 he lived in the South of France. His nephew **Robin Maugham** (1916–81) became famous with a controversial first novel, *The Servant* (1948), which was filmed in 1965. His later novels, often with homosexual themes, include *The Last Encounter* (1972) and *Lovers in Exile* (1977).

Maui 20 45N 156 15W An island in E central Hawaii, NW of Hawaii Island and E of Lanai and Kahoolawe islands. Mountains dominate each end of the island, with a flat isthmus, used for agriculture, joining them. The highest point Haleakala Crater (10,025 ft; 3056 m), in the E, is part of Haleakala National Park. Pineapple and sugar cane crops are the basis of the economy, and tourism is important. Area: 728 sq mi (1886 sq km).

Mau Mau A secret organization among the Kikuyu people of Kenya, which led a revolt (1952–57) against the British colonial government. Secret oaths were administered to participants, who committed appalling atrocities against whites and uncooperating blacks. Jomo *Kenyatta was thought to be a Mau Mau leader and was imprisoned from 1953 to 1961.

Mauna Loa 19 29N 155 36W An active volcano in SE Hawaii, on S central Hawaii Island, part of Hawaii Volcanoes National Park. Standing 13,677 ft (4169 m) high, Mauna Loa's central crater, Mokuaweoweo, and Kilauea, on its S side, have erupted in modern times, including 1950 and 1984.

Maundy Thursday The Thursday before *Good Friday. Its name derives from Latin *mandatum,* commandment, and its traditional foot-washing and almsgiving ceremonies originated at the Last Supper, when Christ washed the disciples' feet and commanded them to follow his example (John 13). The British sovereign's distribution of special Maundy money in Westminster Abbey is a survival of these rites.

Maupassant, Guy de (1850–93) French short-story writer and novelist. He was introduced into literary circles by Flaubert, his literary mentor, met Zola, and joined his group of naturalist writers (*see* naturalism). Following the phenomenal success of the first story he published under his own name, "Boule de Suif" (1880), he wrote about 300 short stories and six novels, including *Une Vie* (1883) and *Bel-Ami* (1885). He suffered from syphilis, which eventually resulted in mental disorder, and he died in an asylum.

Maupertuis, Pierre Louis Moreau de (1698–1759) French mathematician, best known for his principle of least action, by which the paths of moving bodies, rays of light, etc., are such that the action (momentum multiplied by distance) is a minimum. A quarrelsome and dislikeable man, Maupertuis argued with *Voltaire over his principle and became involved with the controversy between *Newton and *Leibniz over who first discovered the calculus.

Mauretania The coastal area N of the Atlas Mountains in ancient N Africa. Inhabited by Moorish tribes, who retained their independence while permitting settlements of Phoenician traders and later Italian colonists, Mauretania remained rebellious after incorporation in the Roman Empire in 40 AD. It was conquered by the Muslims in the 7th century. *See also* Moors.

Mauriac, François (1885–1970) French novelist. He was born into a middle-class Roman Catholic family near Bordeaux. His novels, which include *Le Désert de l'amour* (1925), *Thérèse Desqueyroux* (1927), and *Le Noeud de vipères* (1933), characteristically portray the conflict between worldly passions and religion in provincial marital and family relationships. He also wrote plays and polemical criticism and journalism. He won the Nobel Prize in 1952.

Maurice of Nassau (1567–1625) Stadtholder (chief magistrate) of the United Provinces of the Netherlands (1584–1625), succeeding his father William the Silent. A great military leader and a master of siege warfare, Maurice instituted army reforms that enabled the United Provinces to withstand Spanish attempts to destroy the newly established Protestant republic (*see* Revolt of the Netherlands). He failed to draw the Roman Catholic provinces of the S into the union and was forced to negotiate a 12-year truce with Spain in 1609. His career was marred by the arrest and execution of his colleague *Oldenbarnevelt in 1619.

Mauritania, Islamic Republic of (French name: Mauritanie; Arabic name: Muritaniyah) A country in West Africa, with a coastline on the Atlantic Ocean. The N part is desert while the S is mainly fertile. Most of the inhabitants are Arabs and Berbers with an African population, mainly Fulani, in the S. *Economy*: chiefly agricultural. Livestock, especially cattle, are particularly important and the main crops are millet, sorghum, beans, and rice. All agriculture was severely affected by the droughts of the late 1960s and early 1970s. Fishing is important and fish processing is one of the main industries. Iron ore and copper are exploited and, together with dried and salt fish, are now the main exports. *History*: dominated by Muslim Berber tribes from about 100 AD, the coast was visited by the Portuguese in the 15th century and by the Dutch, English, and French in the 17th century. The area became a French protectorate in 1903 and a colony in 1920. It achieved internal self-government within the French Community in 1958 and became fully independent in 1960 with Mokhtar Ould Daddah as its first president. It moved from French to Arab ties in international relations, joining the Arab League and the Arab Common Market. In 1976, with Morocco, it took over Western Sahara, part of the former Spanish Sahara territories, resistance to which led to considerable unrest, including guerrilla attacks from the Polisario, the Western Saharan independence movement. In 1979 Mauritania withdrew from almost all of Western Sahara. In 1978 Daddah was overthrown in a bloodless coup and Lt. Col. Mustapha Ould Mohamed Salek became president until his resignation in 1979. He was succeeded as head of state by Lt. Col. Khouna Ould Kaydalla. Mauritania continued to occupy La Guera at the S tip of Western Sahara, fearing for its security if either the Polisario or Morocco gained control. It nonetheless sought to remain neutral in the conflict. Its neutrality was threatened, however, when the military base at La Guera was shelled by what were thought to be Moroccan ships in 1983. President Kaydalla was deposed in a coup in 1984 and was replaced by a military committee headed by former prime minister Moauya Ould Sidi-Ahmad Taya. Often accused of human rights violations, Taya promised political reform. In 1991, reforms were made in an effort to improve Mauritania's international image. In 1992, Taya was elected president. Official language: French; Arabic, known as Hassaniya, is widely spoken. Official religion: Islam. Official currency: ougiya of 5 khoums. Area: 397,850 sq mi (1,030,700 sq km). Population (1990 est): 2,038,000. Capital and main port: Nouakchott.

Mauritius, State of An island country in the Indian Ocean, about 500 mi (800 km) to the E of Madagascar. It is mainly hilly and subject to tropical cyclones, which cause severe damage. Dependencies are the Agalega and St Brandon Islands. The majority of the population are of Indian descent, with European, African, and mixed minorities. *Economy*: it is dependent primarily on sugar production, sugar accounting for 90% of its total exports. Fishing is being developed and industry encouraged, as well as subsistence agriculture and tourism, in an effort to reduce unemployment. *History*: visited by the Arabs in the 10th century and by the Portuguese in the 16th century, the island was settled by the Dutch in 1598. In 1715 it came under French rule as Île de France and in 1814 it was ceded to Britain. After riots in 1968 it became independent within the British Commonwealth, with Dr Sir Seewoosagur Ramgoolam as its first prime minister. In the 1970s there was considerable political unrest. Rangoolam was ousted in the 1982 elections. In 1992, Mauritius became a republic within the Commonwealth of Nations. Official languages: English and French; Creole is widely spoken. Official currency: Mauritius rupee of 100 cents. Area: 720 sq mi (1843 sq km). Population (1990 est): 1,141,900. Capital and main port: Port Louis.

Maurois, André (Émile Herzog; 1885–1967) French biographer, novelist, and critic. He served in the British army in World War I and had a lifelong affection for English culture. He wrote several novels and short stories but is best known for his biographical studies of Shelley (*Ariel*, 1923), Disraeli (1927), Byron (1930), Voltaire (1935), Chateaubriand (1937), Proust (1949), and Hugo (1954).

Maurras, Charles (1868–1952) French political theorist and essayist. In 1899 he helped found L'Action Française, a political group dedicated to extreme monarchist, anti-Semitic, and Roman Catholic principles (although condemned and excommunicated by the Church). *Au signe de Flore* (1931) contains his memoirs of his political activities. After World War II, during which he supported the government of Pétain, he was condemned to life imprisonment, but was released because of ill health shortly before his death.

Mauser rifle The first successful metallic-cartridge breech-loading rifle, designed by Paul von Mauser (1838–1914) in 1868. The Model-98 rifle and Model-98a/b carbine were standard in the German infantry in World War I; the Model-98k (1938) was standard in World War II.

Mausoleum of Halicarnassus An ancient Greek tomb built (363–361 BC) as a monument to Mausolus of Caria by his widow. The building, designed by Pythius, was probably a standard temple form with adorning sculptures, fragments of which are in the British Museum, but raised on a high base and with a stepped pyramid-like roof. It was one of the *Seven Wonders of the World.

Maw, Nicholas (1935–) British composer. He studied with Lennox Berkeley and Nadia Boulanger. His works include *Scenes and Arias* (1962) for voices and orchestra and the opera *The Rising of the Moon* (1970).

Maxim, Sir Hiram Stevens (1840–1916) British inventor, born in the US, who in 1884 invented the first fully automatic *machine gun. The Maxim gun led him to discover cordite, which being smokeless increased the gun's efficiency. He also discovered a method of manufacturing carbon filaments, which were then being used in light bulbs.

Maximilian (1832–67) Emperor of Mexico (1864–67). Maximilian, the brother of Emperor Franz Josef I, was the archduke of Austria. He was offered the Mexican crown by France following its invasion of Mexico in 1863. He had no popular support and when in 1867 the French army withdrew under US pressure Maximilian was captured by the forces of Benito *Juarez and executed.

Maximilian I (1459–1519) Holy Roman Emperor (1493–1519). His ambition to rule an empire of all W Europe led him into ultimately unsuccessful wars, especially with France. However, his marriage (1477) to Mary of Burgundy (1457–82), and that of his son Philip the Handsome to Joanna the Mad of Castile, provided his grandson *Charles V with a vast empire.

Maximilian I (1756–1825) King of Bavaria (1806–25); formerly Elector of Bavaria (1799–1806) as Maximilian IV Joseph. In 1799 he joined the second coalition against France (*see* Revolutionary and Napoleonic Wars) but in 1801 negotiated peace. Until abandoning the French alliance in 1813 Maximilian gave military aid to Napoleon, acquiring in return extensive new territories. His government was noted for its liberalism.

maxwell The unit of magnetic flux in the *c.g.s. system equal to the flux through one square centimeter perpendicular to a field of one gauss. Named for James Clerk *Maxwell.

Maxwell, James Clerk (1831–79) Scottish physicist, who was responsible for one of the greatest achievements of the 19th century, the unification of electricity, magnetism, and light into one set of equations (known as **Maxwell's equations**). These equations, first published in their final form in 1873, enabled Faraday's lines of force to be treated mathematically by introducing the concept of the electromagnetic field. Maxwell observed that the field radiated outward from an oscillating electric charge at the speed of light, which led him to identify light as a form of electromagnetic radiation. Maxwell also made important advances in the kinetic theory of gases, by introducing the statistical approach known as Maxwell-Boltzmann statistics (since it was developed independently by *Boltzmann). *See also* Maxwell's demon.

Maxwell's demon A hypothetical creature, postulated by *Maxwell in 1871 as a theoretical construct to disprove the second law of *thermodynamics. The demon was visualized as being able to separate a gas into a hot region and a cold region by opening and closing a shutter to allow only fast-moving molecules to enter the hot region. No violation of the second law on these or any other grounds has ever been observed.

may. *See* hawthorn.

May Fifth month of the year. Named in honor of the Roman goddess Maia, who signified spring, it has 31 days. The zodiac signs for May are Taurus and Gemini; the flowers are lily of the valley and hawthorn, and the birthstone is the emerald. Memorial Day, honoring US military veterans, is celebrated on the last Monday in May.

maya (Sanskrit: illusion) In the Vedas maya is the magic power of a god or spirit. In the *Upanishads, maya is illusion or the mundane world, which is ultimately unreal because of its impermanence. Elsewhere maya is seen as the play of *Brahma, who splits himself into innumerable parts, thereby forgetting himself.

Maya An American Indian people of Yucatán (Mexico), Guatemala, and Belize. There are a number of languages in the Totonac-Mayan language family (see Mesoamerican languages). Today the Maya live mainly in farming villages and are nominally Roman Catholic, but between 300 and 900 AD they had established an advanced civilization. They developed hieroglyphic writing and had considerable knowledge of astronomy and mathematics. They devised a precise calendar, which regulated an elaborate ritual and ceremonial life centered on such sites as *Chichén Itzá, *Tikal, Copan, and Palenque, where large pyramid temples were constructed for the worship of the sun, moon, and rain gods. After 900 the influence of the *Toltecs led to a mixed Toltec-Maya culture in cities such as Mayapan.

Mayagüez 18 13N 67 09W A port in W Puerto Rico, in the West Indies. It has an important needlework industry; other manufactures include beer, rum, and soap. An experimental station operated here by the US Department of Agriculture has possibly the largest tropical-plant collection in the W hemisphere. Population (1990): 100,371.

Mayakovskii, Vladimir (1893–1930) Russian poet. He was a leading member of the futurist movement (see futurism) and a prolific propagandist for Bolshevism. Revolutionary politics and his frustrated private life are the main themes of his poetry, which is characterized by aggressive vitality and experimentalism. He also wrote two satirical dramas, *The Bedbug* (1929) and *The Bath-House* (1930). He committed suicide.

May Day May 1, traditionally a festival associated with spring fertility rites, celebrated by such customs as dancing around the maypole. In communist countries May Day is celebrated as International Worker's Day, often the occasion for a display of military technology.

Mayence. *See* Mainz.

Mayer, Julius Robert von (1814–78) German physicist, who (in 1842) was the first to calculate the mechanical equivalent of heat and formulated a form of the law of conservation of energy. However, his work went virtually unrecognized; *Joule received credit for the first achievement and *Helmholtz for the second.

Mayer, Louis B. (1885–1957) US film producer, born in Russia. He helped to create the Hollywood star system. With Samuel *Goldwyn in 1924 he founded the Metro-Goldwyn-Mayer (MGM) production company, whose films were largely determined by his personal taste for lavish but uncontroversial entertainment. He retired in 1951.

Mayfair A fashionable residential district in the Greater London borough of the City of Westminster. It was named for the annual fair held from the 16th century until 1809.

Mayflower The ship that carried the *Pilgrim Fathers to America. They had intended to settle in Virginia but the *Mayflower* was blown off course and reached Plymouth (Massachusetts) in December 1620. There, the Pilgrims drew up the **Mayflower Compact**, which based their government on the will of the colonists rather than the English crown.

MAYA *The Temple of the Sorcerer at Uxmal in Yucatán (Mexico).*

mayfly A slender ☐insect of the order *Ephemeroptera* (1500 species), found near fresh water. Up to 1.5 in (40 mm) long, mayflies are usually brown or yellow with two unequal pairs of membranous wings. The adults do not feed and only live long enough to mate and lay eggs. The aquatic nymphs feed on plant debris and algae.

May Fourth Movement (1917–21) A Chinese movement for social and intellectual reform that culminated in a student demonstration in Peking on May 4, 1919, against government acceptance of the allocation of Chinese territory to Japan by the Paris Peace Conference following World War I. The movement aimed to throw off foreign dominance and to build a new modern China.

Mayhew, Henry (1812–87) British journalist. His best-known work is *London Labour and the London Poor* (4 vols, 1851–62), a combination of vivid reportage and amateur social and economic analysis. He was a founder of *Punch* in 1841 and the author of many plays and novels.

Mayo (Irish name: Contae Mhuigheo) A county in the W Republic of Ireland, in Connacht bordering on the Atlantic Ocean. Mountainous in the W it contains several large lakes. Cattle, sheep, and pigs are raised and potatoes and oats are grown. Area: 2084 sq mi (5397 sq km). Population (1991): 110,696. County town: Castlebar.

Mayo A family of US physicians, who pioneered the concept of group practice and established the Mayo Clinic in Rochester, Minn., along these lines. The family included **William Worrall Mayo** (1819–1911), his sons **William James Mayo** (1861–1939) and **Charles Horace Mayo** (1865–1939), and Charles's son **Charles William Mayo** (1898–1968). The Mayos also made a number of contributions to medical research.

mayor of the palace An officer of the royal household and later a viceroy appointed by the Merovingian kings of the early Middle Ages. The most famous were *Pepin of Herstel and his grandson *Pepin the Short, who overthrew the Merovingians and founded the Carolingian dynasty.

Mayotte An island in the W Indian Ocean, in the Comoro Islands group. After the other islands declared independence from France (1975), Mayotte decided by a referendum to remain a French territory. Area: 144 sq mi (374 sq km). Population (1992 est): 97,400. Chief town: Dzaoudzi.

maypole dance A folk dance of ancient origin, traditionally performed on May 1 as part of the May Day festival. Participants circle around a tall pole, often adorned with ribbons, which they weave into patterns.

Mays, Willie (Howard, Jr.) (1931–) US baseball player. Nicknamed the "Say Hey Kid," he fielded for the New York (later San Francisco) Giants (1950–52; 1954–72) and the New York Mets (1972–73). He hit 660 career home runs and compiled 3283 hits during his career. He was elected to the Baseball Hall of Fame (1979).

Mazarin, Jules, Cardinal (1602–61) French statesman. A papal diplomat, he rose to prominence as a protégé of Cardinal de Richelieu and shortly after Richelieu's death (1642) became chief adviser to the regent Anne of Austria, Louis XIV's mother. The era of Mazarin witnessed a great expansion in the power of the monarchy, achieved largely through his suppression of rebellious aristocrats during the *Fronde. Abroad, he enhanced French supremacy in Europe by the Treaties of *Westphalia (1648) and the *Pyrenees (1659).

Mazatlán 23 11N 106 25W A port and resort in W Mexico, on the Gulf of California. The chief industries are textiles manufacture and sugar refining; exports include tobacco and minerals. Population (1980): 199,830.

Mazu (*or* Ma-tsu) 26 10N 119 59E A Taiwanese island in the East China Sea. It is near the Chinese mainland, from which it was bombed in 1958, causing an international incident. Area: 17 sq mi (44 sq km).

Mazurian Lakes Several hundred lakes in NE Poland, around which Germany inflicted two heavy defeats on the Russians in 1914 and 1915.

Mazzini, Giuseppe (1805–72) Italian patriot, who was a leader of the movement for Italian unification (*see* Risorgimento). Forced to live mostly in exile in France, Switzerland, and England, he planned with his *Young Italy movement a rising in Piedmont and an invasion of Savoy in the 1830s but both failed. Mazzini was in Italy during the Revolutions of 1848 in Milan, Piedmont, Tuscany, and Rome, where he became head of a short-lived Roman republic. Although a united kingdom of Italy was finally established in 1861, he never realized his ideal of an Italian republic.

Mbabane 26 30S 31 30E The capital of Swaziland, in the Mdimba Mountains. It was founded in the late 19th century. Tourism is important and nearby is a large iron mine. Population (1986): 38,290.

Mbini. *See* Equatorial Guinea, Republic of.

Mboya, Tom (1930–69) Kenyan politician. Mboya was from the Luo tribe and was an active trade unionist and general secretary of the Kenyan Federation of Labor. He was a founding member and the general secretary (1960–64) of the Kenya African National Union and after the achievement of independence became, under Kenyatta, minister of justice (1963) and later minister of economic planning and development (1964–69). He was assassinated.

Mbuji-Mayi (name until 1966: Bakwanga) 6 10S 23 39E A city in central Zaïre. Diamonds were discovered here in 1909 and the region now produces about 75% of the world's industrial diamonds. Population (1991 est): 613,027.

Mc–. Names beginning Mc are listed under Mac.

mead An alcoholic drink of fermented honey and water. The honey is dissolved in water and boiled with spices. When cool, after brewer's yeast has been added, the mead ferments in a barrel. It should be stored in a bottle for at least six months before serving. It was drunk in Anglo-Saxon England, and, called hydromel, by the ancient Romans.

Mead, Margaret (1901–78) US anthropologist. Margaret Mead's anthropological work centers on the study of child rearing and the family. Her field work was done in New Guinea, Polynesia, and other Pacific islands. Her books include *Coming of Age in Samoa* (1929), *Sex and Temperament in Three Primitive Societies* (1935), and *Male and Female* (1949). She also wrote on education, science, and culture. A significant amount of her work was in the field of mental health.

Meade, George Gordon (1815–72) US Union general born in Spain of American parents. He graduated from West Point and participated in the Seminole campaign (1835–36) and the *Mexican War. During the Civil War he led troops in the Peninsular Campaign and at *Bull Run (1862), Antietam, and Fredericksburg. In 1863 he became head of the Army of the Potomac and was victorious at Gettysburg.

meadowsweet A perennial herb, *Filipendula* (or *Spiraea*) *ulmaria*, common in damp places throughout temperate Eurasia; 24–47 in (60–120 cm) high, it has large compound leaves, with 8–20 pairs of toothed leaflets and fluffy terminal clusters of small, creamy-white fragrant flowers, with long stamens. An oil distilled from the flower buds is used in perfumes. Family: *Rosaceae*.

mealworm. *See* darkling beetle.

mealybug An insect of the worldwide family *Pseudococcidae*, closely related to the *scale insects. The female is covered with a white sticky powder, which may be extended into filaments. The species *Pseudococcus citri* is a serious pest of citrus trees in America.

mean. *See* average.

meander A sinuous curve in a river. The velocity of flow in a meandering river is highest on the outside of the meander bends; erosion is concentrated here with deposition occurring on the inside of the bend. The meander will become increasingly looped until the river eventually breaks through its narrow neck creating an oxbow *lake.

mean free path The average distance traveled by a molecule between successive collisions with other molecules. According to the *kinetic theory, the mean free path is directly proportional to the viscosity of the substance and inversely proportional to the average velocity of the molecules.

mean life (*or* lifetime) The average time for which a radioactive isotope, elementary particle, or other unstable state exists before decaying. *See* radioactivity.

Meany, George (1894–1980) US labor leader. He served as secretary-treasurer of the *American Federation of Labor (AFL) (1939–52) and then as president (1952–55). During this time he was largely responsible for the merger of the AFL and the *Congress of Industrial Organizations (CIO) in 1955, serving as president of the combination (1955–79). He was known for his reforms regarding corrupt union methods and financial practices and was a driving force in the expulsion of the Teamsters Union from the AFL-CIO in 1957.

measles A highly infectious viral disease, which usually affects children. After an incubation period of about two weeks the child becomes irritable and fevered and has a running nose and inflamed eyes. Two or three days later a rash appears on the head and face and spreads over the body. Usually the child recovers after a week, but sometimes pneumonia or encephalitis may develop. There is no specific treatment, but vaccine has reduced the incidence of the disease. *Compare* German measles.

Meath (Irish name: Contae na Midhe) A county in the E Republic of Ireland, in Leinster bordering on the Irish Sea. Consisting chiefly of fertile glacial drifts it is important for agriculture; cattle are fattened and oats and potatoes grown. Area: 903 sq mi (2338 sq km). Population (1991): 105,540. County town: Trim.

Meaux 48 58N 2 54E A city in N France, in the Seine-et-Marne department on the Marne River. The commercial and industrial center of the Brie region, it supplies Paris with agricultural produce. Population: 43,110.

Mecca (Arabic name: Makkah) 21 26N 39 49E A city in W Saudi Arabia, in a narrow valley surrounded by barren hills. Mecca and Riyadh are joint capitals of the kingdom, but it is famous as the holiest Muslim city, which every Muslim is expected to visit at least once in his lifetime; nonbelievers are not allowed to enter the city. It has been a holy city since ancient times, but was also the birthplace of Mohammed (c. 570). Inside the court of the al-Haram Mosque in the center of the city are located the chief shrines: the Kabaa (a small windowless building) and the secred well of Zamzam. In November 1979, the al-Haram Mosque was seized by armed militants, who held a number of worshipers hostage before being overpowered by the military forces. Population: 366,801.

mechanical advantage The ratio of the force output of a machine to the force input, i.e. the ratio of load to effort. It is useful only as an analysis of simple machines, such as levers, pulleys, jacks, etc., as no account of friction is taken. The **velocity ratio** of the machine is the distance moved by the effort divided by the distance moved by the load; the **mechanical efficiency** of a machine is the ratio of its mechanical advantage to its velocity ratio.

mechanical engineering The branch of *engineering concerned with the application of scientific knowledge to dynamical structures and systems, rather than the static structures of civil engineering. This branch encompasses the design, manufacture, and maintenance of machines of all kinds, engines, vehicles, and many aspects of industrial manufacturing. The subject has numerous specialized subdivisions, including *aeronautics, motor engineering, machine-tool design, etc.

mechanics The study of the motion of bodies and systems and the forces acting on them. The subject is traditionally divided into statics, the study of bodies in equilibrium, and dynamics, the study of forces that affect the motion of bodies. Dynamics is further divided into kinetics, the effects of forces and their moments on motion, and kinematics, the study of velocity, acceleration, etc., without regard to the forces causing them. Aristotelian (*see* Aristotle) mechanics was based on the erroneous concept that a force is required to maintain motion. *Newtonian mechanics recognizes that once a body is moving a force is required to stop it but no force is needed to keep it moving. Newtonian mechanics is the mechanics of classical systems, i.e. large-scale systems moving at relatively low velocities. The more general relativistic mechanics is also applicable to systems moving at speeds comparable to that of light (it reduces to Newtonian mechanics at velocities that are small compared to that of light). *Fluid mechanics is the application of mechanical principles to fluids, both stationary (hydrostatics) and flowing (hydrodynamics).

MECCA *The chief problems in the administration of the city (the second largest in Saudi Arabia) arise in providing sufficient water and other services for the pilgrims, who are its main source of revenue.*

Mechelen (French name: Malines; English name: Mechlin) 51 02N 4 29E A city in N Belgium, on the Ryle River. Its 12th-century cathedral contains an altarpiece by Van Eyck and there are Rubens masterpieces in two other churches. Once famous for Mechlin lace, industries now include textiles and canned vegetables. Population (1988 est): 76,000.

Mecklenberg A former German state on the SW Baltic Sea coast, now the Rostock, Schwerin, and Neubrandenburg districts of Germany. Thinly populated, with many lakes and forests, Mecklenberg was frequently partitioned until its permanent division in 1701 into the Duchies of Mecklenberg-Schwerin and Mecklenberg-Strelitz. After the Congress of Vienna in 1815, both duchies formed part of the German Confederation under Austria's leadership, but in 1866 joined Prussia's North German Confederation; thereafter Mecklenberg's history is linked with Prussia's.

medals Pieces of metal fashioned as coins or crosses to commemorate individuals or special occasions, or awarded in recognition of service to a state or institution. During the Renaissance personal medals, usually bearing a portrait of the owner with an emblem and motto on the reverse, achieved high artistic standards. *Pisanello, *Dürer, and *Cellini were notable medalists. Military medals multiplied in the 18th and 19th centuries. They usually portray a sovereign's head or insignia of the awarding body, bear a commemorative legend, and are worn suspended on a special ribbon. Many are individual rewards for bravery, such as France's Croix de Guerre and Britain's *Victoria Cross but some are general medals to commemorate campaigns and state occasions, such as coronations. In the US, the highest award for gallantry, the Congressional Medal of Honor, was first presented in 1863.

Medan 03 35N 98 39E A city in Indonesia, in N Sumatra. Its state and Islamic universities were established in 1952. An agricultural and trade center that grew around tobacco plantations, it has a seaport (Belawan). Population (1980): 1,379,000.

Medawar, Sir Peter Brian (1915–87) British immunologist, noted for his investigation of the development of the immune system in embryonic and young animals, including the phenomenon of acquired immunological tolerance to foreign tissue grafts. He also showed how genetically determined "markers" (antigens) enable the immune system to discriminate between host cells and foreign cells. Medawar shared the 1960 Nobel Prize with Sir Macfarlane *Burnet.

Medea In Greek legend, a sorceress, the daughter of King Aeetes of Colchis and niece of *Circe. She helped *Jason steal the *Golden Fleece and fled with him to Iolcus. When Jason deserted her for Glauce, daughter of the Corinthian King Creon, she killed Glauce, Creon, and her own two children and fled to Athens.

Medellin 6 15N 75 36W The second largest city in Colombia, in the Central Cordillera. It is the country's leading industrial center; steel processing and the manufacture of textiles are especially important. Its university was founded in 1822. Population (1985): 1,418,554.

Media An ancient region SW of the Caspian Sea settled by seminomadic tribes of Medes. Between the 8th and 6th centuries BC they began to unite against Assyria and in 612 under their sovereign Cyaxares (625–585) destroyed Nineveh with the help of Chaldea and overthrew the Assyrian empire. But in 550 the Medes were amalgamated with the Persians in Cyrus the Great's expanding empire.

median **1.** The line joining the vertex of a triangle to the midpoint of the opposite side. **2.** The middle value of a set of numbers arranged in order of magnitude. For example, the median of {2, 3, 3, 4, 5} $\neq\leq$ 3.

Medicaid US federal and state health-care assistance-insurance plan for the needy. Established in 1965, it is administered by the states under guidelines established by the federal Welfare Administration. It covers such services as hospital and nursing home care, x-rays, physicians' and dentists' fees, laboratory fees, and medicines.

Medicare US national health insurance program for the aged and severely disabled. It was established in 1966 and is administered by the Social Security Administration of the Department of Health and Human Services. Participants pay nominal premiums and are partially, but almost completely, covered for certain hospital and nursing home care and for physician's services.

Medici A family that dominated Florence from 1434 to 1494, from 1512 to 1527, and from 1530 to 1737 (as grand dukes from 1532). The Medici, who were merchants and bankers, dominated the government of Florence in the 15th century by manipulating elections to the key magistracies. The family's power was established by **Cosimo de' Medici** (1389–1464), entitled Pater Patriae (Father of His Country), who also initiated the Medici tradition of artistic patronage: Brunelleschi, Ghiberti, and Donatello, among others, were employed by Cosimo. His son **Piero de' Medici** (1416–69) succeeded to his position, which then passed to **Lorenzo the Magnificent** (1449–92). Following the *Pazzi conspiracy (1478), in which his brother **Giuliano de' Medici** (1453–78) died, Lorenzo's political prestige was greatly enhanced. An outstanding patron of Renaissance artists (Botticelli, Ghirlandaio, Michelangelo) and scholars (Ficino, Pico della Mirandola, Politian), Lorenzo tended to neglect the family business, which declined in the late 15th century. He was succeeded by his son **Piero de' Medici** (1472–1503), who was forced to flee Florence in a revolt incited by *Savonarola. Piero's brother **Giovanni de' Medici** (1475–1521) was restored to Florence in 1512, a year before he became Pope *Leo X. The Medici were again ousted, in 1527, but the combined efforts of Emperor Charles V and Pope

Clement VII (previously Giulio de' Medici, the illegitimate son of Lorenzo's brother Giuliano) established Clement's illegitimate son **Alessandro de' Medici** (1511–37) as the first duke of Florence. Subsequent grand dukes included **Cosimo I** (1519–74), **Francesco I** (1541–87), and **Ferdinando I** (1549–1609).

medicine The science and practice of preventing, diagnosing, and treating disease. The term is also used specifically for the management of disease by nonsurgical methods, for example by drugs, diet, etc. (*compare* surgery). Medicine involves study of the anatomy, physiology, and biochemistry of the body in health as well as the changes that occur in disease (pathology). It is closely connected with pharmacology (the study of drugs).

Medicine has its origins in ancient Greece. The medical school at Cnidos, established in the 7th century BC, was concerned purely with the description of symptoms, whereas that founded later by *Hippocrates considered the causes of symptoms in relation to the patient and the environment. In the Alexandrian school the emphasis was on the effects of disease rather than the causes. All existing knowledge of medicine was coordinated and supplemented in the 2nd century AD, by *Galen, whose influence prevailed until the Renaissance. Landmarks in the development of modern medicine were the publication of *Vesalius's major work on anatomy (1543) and of William Harvey's discovery of the circulation of the blood (1628). The nature, treatment, and prevention of infectious diseases were illuminated by the researches of *Pasteur, *Koch, and *Klebs in the 19th century; their work directed *Lister to the discovery of antiseptics, by means of which wound healing and hospital sanitation were greatly improved. Chemotherapy (the treatment of disease by chemical agents) was revolutionized in 1911, when *Ehrlich introduced salvarsan for treating syphilis. The late 1930s saw the development of the sulfonamides—the first powerful general antibacterial drugs—and World War II provided the stimulus for the widespread production and use of antibiotics (the first of which was penicillin). Together these drugs have enabled most infectious diseases to be cured. Viruses, however, do not succumb to antibiotics and the control of viral diseases has relied on immunological methods derived from *Jenner's discovery of vaccination in 1798. With infectious diseases under control, medical research since World War II has concentrated on the organic diseases, especially coronary artery disease, strokes, etc., and cancer. The emphasis has also been on preventive medicine, with the establishment of the *World Health Organization in 1948, campaigns to eradicate epidemic diseases, and the establishment of pre- and ante-natal clinics, medical inspections for schoolchildren, dental clinics, welfare centers, etc., in many parts of the world.

medick An annual or perennial herb of the genus *Medicago* (about 120 species), native to Eurasia and N Africa. The stems are creeping or erect, 2–35 in (5–90 cm) tall, bearing compound leaves with three toothed leaflets, dense yellow or purple flower heads, and curved or spirally twisted pods. Family: *Leguminosae.*

Medina (Arabic name: Al Madinah) 24 30N 39 35E A city in W Saudi Arabia, N of Mecca. The tomb of Mohammed is in the mosque at Medina, the second most holy Muslim city after Mecca. Husayn ibn Ali, with the assistance of T. E. *Lawrence, expelled the Turks during World War I by putting the railroad from Damascus out of commission. Date-packing supplements the city's income from pilgrims, and the Islamic University was founded in 1961. Population (1974): 198,186.

Mediterranean Sea An almost landlocked sea extending between Africa and Europe to Asia. It connects with the Atlantic Ocean at Gibraltar, the Black Sea via the Sea of Marmara, and the Red Sea via the Suez Canal. It loses twice as

much water through evaporation as it receives from rivers and thus is fed continuously by the Atlantic and to a lesser extent by the Black Sea. Although its waters return to the Atlantic in a 10-year cycle, it is saltier and warmer than the
oceans; pollution is a serious problem because of the large quantities of waste
discharged into its waters. Tidal variation is insignificant.

medlar A thorny shrub or tree, *Mespilus germanica*, native to SE Europe and
central Asia and cultivated for its fruit. Growing to a height of 20 ft (6 m), it
bears oblong toothed leaves, 6 in (15 cm) long, and white five-petaled flowers.
The globular brownish fruit, 2–2.4 in (5–6 cm) across, has an opening at the top,
surrounded by the remains of the sepals, through which the five seed chambers
can be seen. Medlars are eaten when partly decayed and have a pleasant acid
taste; they can also be made into jelly. Family: *Rosaceae*.

Médoc An area in SW France, bordering on the left bank of the Gironde estuary. Producing some of France's finest red wines, it contains some famous vineyards including Château Latour.

medulla oblongata. *See* brain.

medusa The free-swimming sexual form that occurs during the life cycle of
many animals of the phylum *Coelenterata*. Medusae resemble small *jellyfish
and have separate sexes, releasing eggs and sperm into the water. The ciliated
larvae settle and develop into the sedentary asexual forms (*see* polyp). *See also*
coelenterate.

Medusa In Greek mythology, the only mortal *Gorgon. Athena, angered by
her love affair with Poseidon, made her hair into serpents and her face so ugly
that all who saw it were turned to stone. She later sent *Perseus to behead her.
From her blood sprang *Pegasus and Chrysaor, her children by Poseidon.

Medway River A river in SE England. Rising in Sussex, it flows N and E
through Kent to join the Thames River by a long estuary. In 43 AD, near
Rochester, the invading Romans defeated the British under Caractacus in the
battle of the Medway. Length: 70 mi (113 km).

Meegeren, Hans van (1889–1947) Dutch painter, notorious for his *Vermeer forgeries. He successfully misled the art world, notably with works such as
Christ at Emmaus, bought by the Boymans Museum, Rotterdam, as an early
Vermeer painting. In 1945 he was arrested as a Nazi collaborator, confessed his
deceptions, was imprisoned, and died in poverty.

meerkat A small carnivorous mammal, *Suricata suricata*, also called suricate,
of South African grasslands. It is about 24 in (60 cm) long including the tail
(7–10 in; 17–25 cm), and lives in large colonies of shallow burrows, emerging
to sunbathe in the early morning. Meerkats stay close to home, feeding on insects, grubs, reptiles, birds, and small mammals. Family: *Viverridae*.

meerschaum A white mineral consisting of hydrated magnesium silicate,
$H_4Mg_2Si_3O_{10}$, found in some magnesium-rich rocks, such as serpentine. Turkey
has famous deposits of meerschaum; it also occurs in East and S Africa. It is
used for making tobacco pipes.

Meerut 29 00N 77 42E A city in India, in Uttar Pradesh. The scene of the first
uprising (1857) of the Indian Mutiny, Meerut is an important army headquarters
and has diverse industries. Population (1991): 752,078.

megalith (Greek: large stone) A large stone particularly favored for building
monuments in the *Neolithic and *Bronze Age (about 3500 BC to 1500 BC),
Megaliths could be placed singly or in lines, or in simple or complex circles as
at *Stonehenge. Megaliths were also used for tombs and temples in Malta,

Egypt, and elsewhere. Stones weighing many tons were set up using simple tackle of timbers and ropes.

Megaloceros. *See* Irish elk.

megapode A bird belonging to a family (*Megapodiidae*; 12 species) ranging from Australia to the Peninsular Malaysia; 19–27 in (48–68 cm) long, megapodes are fowl-like and ground-dwelling with brownish plumage and build a large nest mound in which the eggs are incubated by the heat of fermenting plant material, the sun's rays, or volcanic heat. Order: *Galliformes* (pheasants, turkeys, etc.). *See also* brush turkey; mallee fowl.

Mégara 38 00N 23 20E A city in E central Greece. It was an important city-state from the 8th century BC fostering many colonies, including *Chalcedon and Byzantium, before its decline in the 5th century BC. Population: 17,260.

Megatherium A genus of extinct giant ground sloths that lived in North and South America about a million years ago. *Megatherium* was about the size of a modern elephant and probably ate leaves. Giant mammals like this were common in South America before the Panama isthmus closed at the end of the Ice Age, when most of them—including *Megatherium*—became extinct.

megaton A measure of the explosive power of a nuclear weapon. It is equivalent to an explosion of one million tons of trinitroluene (TNT).

Meghalaya A state in NE India, NE of Bangladesh on a beautiful plateau falling N to the Brahmaputra Valley. One of the world's wettest areas, it has rich forests but little industry. Rice, potatoes, cotton, and fruits are grown. Meghalaya was separated from Assam in 1972. Area: 8681 sq mi (22,489 sq km). Population (1981 est): 1,327,824. Capital: Shillong.

Megiddo An ancient site in N Israel. Continuously occupied between about 3000 and 350 BC, Megiddo was strategically positioned on the route between Egypt and Syria and was the scene of many battles. Excavations (1925–39) unearthed hundreds of Phoenician ivories (13th–12th centuries BC) and stabling for about 450 horses, built probably by King Solomon. Megiddo is identified with the biblical Armageddon, where, according to St John the Divine (Revelation 16.16), the last battle will be fought.

Mehemet Ali (1769–1849) Viceroy of Egypt for the Ottoman Empire (1805–48). An Albanian in the Ottoman army, he was recognized as viceroy after he had seized power in Cairo. His important military, agricultural, and educational reforms have led some to see him as the founder of modern Egypt. In 1840 the Ottomans recognized him as hereditary ruler of Egypt and he was succeeded by his son *Ibrahim Pasha. His dynasty survived until 1952.

Meiji. *See* Mutsuhito.

meiosis The process by which the nucleus of a germ cell divides prior to the formation of gametes (such as sperm, pollen, or eggs). Meiosis consists of two successive divisions during which one cell with the normal duplicate (diploid) set of chromosomes gives rise to four cells each with only one chromosome of each type (haploid). Meiosis differs from *mitosis in that the chromosomes of each pair become closely associated, enabling the interchange of genetic material between maternal and paternal chromosomes. There is no duplication of chromosomes between the two divisions of meiosis.

Meir, Golda (1898–1978) Israeli stateswoman, born in Russia; prime minister (1969–74). Brought up in the US (1906–21), she emigrated to Palestine in 1921. A founder member of the Israeli Workers' party (Mapai) she was its secretary general (1966–68). She was minister of labor (1949–56) and minister of foreign affairs (1956–66) before becoming prime minister. She was committed to the establishment of peace in the Middle East and resigned after Israel had been surprised by the Arab attack in the 1973 *Arab-Israeli War.

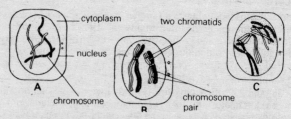

prophase I *The four chromosomes appear as thin threads (A), which form pairs (B). Each chromosome divides into two chromatids and exchange of genetic material occurs between the chromatids of each pair (C).*

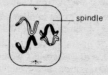

metaphase I *The chromosomes of each pair separate from each other and move to opposite poles of the spindle.*

metaphase II *The new spindles form and the chromatids of each group separate from each other.*

telophase II *Four new nuclei form, each containing two chromosomes.*

MEIOSIS *The formation of four egg or sperm cells from one parent cell takes place in two divisions, each of which is divided into several phases. Only four phases are shown here.*

Meissen 51 11N 13 23E A city in E Germany, on the Elbe River. Meissen is famous for porcelain manufacture, moved here from Dresden in 1710. The process of production of the porcelain (known as Dresden china) was discovered here. Population: 43,920.

Meissen porcelain The first hard-paste porcelain made in Europe following discovery (1710) of the technique by the alchemist J. F. Böttger (1682–1719) under the patronage of the Elector of Saxony. Initially, the Elector's oriental collection at Dresden was copied. There followed extensive ranges of domestic ware, figures (shepherdesses, monkey bands, Italian comedy, etc.), chinoiseries, small boxes, seals, and ornaments painted with landscapes, flowers, and insects. The styles were extensively copied by all 18th-century factories.

Meissonier, Jean-Louis-Ernest (1815–91) French painter, born in Lyons. He achieved great success at the Paris Salon exhibitions from the 1840s onward with his small, minutely detailed history and military paintings, particularly of Napoleonic battles, for example *Campagne de France, 1814* (1864).

Meistersingers (German: master singers) German singing guilds, which flourished from the 14th to the 17th centuries. As the *Minnesingers declined in Germany, song guilds developed in the artisan class, the first being established in Mainz in 1311. They flourished in most German towns; their contests were regulated by a superabundance of rules, as depicted by Wagner in his opera *The Mastersingers of Nuremberg*.

Meitner, Lise (1878–1968) Austrian physicist. After studying in Vienna under *Boltzmann, she worked with Otto *Hahn in Berlin (1907–38) until expelled by the Nazis. Together they discovered protactinium (1918) and caused the first fission of a uranium atom by neutron bombardment (1934). Hahn did not publish the results of this work and it was first published by Meitner from Stockholm in 1939. In Stockholm she worked with Karl Manne Georg Siegbahn (1886–1978), becoming a Swedish citizen in 1949.

Meknès 33 53N 5 37W A city in N Morocco. It became known as the "Moroccan Versailles" under Mawlay Isma'il (?1645–1727; reigned 1672–1727), when several palaces were built. It is a trade center for agricultural produce and carpets. Population (1982): 319,783.

Mekong River A major SE Asian river, rising in Tibet and flowing generally SE through China, Laos, Kampuchea, and Vietnam to the South China Sea. It is navigable for about 340 mi (550 km). The extensive delta is one of the greatest Asian rice-growing areas. Length: about 2500 mi (4025 km).

Melanchthon, Philip (P. Schwarzerd; 1497–1560) German Protestant reformer, who succeeded Martin *Luther as leader of the German Reformation movement. Professor of Greek at the University of Wittenberg, Melanchthon was a convinced humanist, influenced by *Erasmus, and a supporter of Luther in public confrontations, including the debate with *Zwingli over the Eucharist. He was largely responsible for the *Augsburg Confession (1530), the main Lutheran statement of belief.

Melanesia A division of Oceania in the SW Pacific Ocean, consisting of an arc of volcanic and coral islands NE of Australia. It includes the Bismarck Archipelago, the Solomon, Admiralty, and D'Entrecasteaux Islands, Vanuata Republic, New Caledonia, and Fiji. *See also* Micronesia; Polynesia.

Melanesians The people of the Melanesian islands. The term also covers similar peoples of New Guinea, though these are also often known as Papuan. They are of Oceanic Negroid race and speak languages of the *Austronesian family. There are a great many very different languages mostly spoken by only small numbers. The Melanesians cultivate yams, taro, and sweet potatoes and live in small, usually dispersed, homesteads. In coastal areas fishing is important. Pigs play a major role in the economy, being used in the ceremonial exchanges of valuables to establish status that are a common cultural trait. Social organization varies greatly among the different groups.

melanin A pigment, varying from brown-black to yellow, that occurs in hair, skin, feathers, and scales. Derived from the amino acid tyrosine, its presence in the skin helps protect underlying tissues from damage by sunlight. Melanin is also responsible for coloring the iris of the eye.

Melba, Dame Nellie (Helen Porter Armstrong; 1859–1931) Australian soprano, whose professional name was derived from her native city, Melbourne. She studied in Paris, making her debut in 1887 as Gilda in Verdi's opera *Rigoletto*. Her worldwide career culminated in a number of farewell performances in 1926.

Melbourne 37 45S 144 58E The second largest city in Australia, the capital of Victoria on Port Phillip Bay. It is a major commercial center and contains about two-thirds of the state's population. Port Melbourne is sited 2.5 mi (4 km) away, on the mouth of the Yarra River; exports include wool, scrap metal, and dairy products. The chief industries are heavy engineering, food processing, and the manufacture of textiles and clothes. A cultural center, Melbourne possesses three universities (including the University of Melbourne founded in 1853), and the new Arts Center of Victoria. Other notable buildings include the State Parliament House and the Anglican and Roman Catholic cathedrals. *History*: founded in 1835, it developed rapidly following the 1851 gold rush. It was the capital of the Commonwealth of Australia from 1901 until 1927. Population (1991 est): 3,153,500.

Melbourne, William Lamb, 2nd Viscount (1779–1848) British statesman; Whig prime minister (1834, 1835–41), who exerted an early influence on Queen Victoria. He was chief secretary for Ireland (1827–28) and then home secretary (1830–34), when he dealt harshly with the *Tolpuddle Martyrs.

Melchior, Lauritz (1890–1973) Danish tenor. He studied at the Royal Opera School in Copenhagen and made his debut in 1913. His performances in the roles of Tristan and Siegfried marked him as the leading Wagnerian tenor of the 20th century.

Melchites Christians of the Orthodox Churches in Syria and Egypt who, during the 5th-century *Monophysite controversy, adhered to the anti-Monophysite doctrine supported by the Byzantine emperor. Their name was therefore derived from a Syriac word meaning "imperial."

Meleager In Greek legend, the son of Oeneus, King of Calydon. He killed the Calydonian boar, sent by Artemis because Oeneus had neglected to sacrifice to her.

Melilla 35 17N 2 57W A Spanish port forming an enclave on the Mediterranean coast of N Morocco. Iron ore is the principal export. Population (1986): 55,600.

melilot An herb belonging to the genus *Melilotus* (25 species), also called sweet clover, occurring in temperate and subtropical Eurasia. The leaves consist of three leaflets and the small yellow or white flowers grow in clusters along the stems. The biennial common melilot (*M. officinalis*) has yellow flowers and grows to a height of 51 in (130 cm). Family: *Leguminosae*.

Melitopol 46 51N 35 22E A city in SE Ukraine. The center of a fruit-growing region, it has food-processing industries. Nearby is the site of ancient Merv, an Islamic center at its height under the Seljuq Turks in the 12th century. Population (1981 est): 165,000.

Mellon, Andrew William (1855–1937) US financier and philanthropist. As secretary of the treasury (1921–32) he played a major role in the government's postwar tax reforms. He was ambassador to Great Britain (1932–33). An art collector, he donated both his collection and $15 million to the construction of the National Gallery of Art in Washington, DC.

melon An annual trailing vine, *Cucumis melo*, native to tropical Africa but widely cultivated for its edible fruits. Melon plants have coarse-haired five- to seven-lobed leaves, yellow or orange cup-shaped flowers, and round or oval fruits, up to 9 lb (4 kg) in weight, with tough skins and sweet juicy flesh surrounding a core of seeds. There are several varieties including the muskmelon, with a net-veined skin and pinkish orange flesh; the honeydew melon, with smooth whitish or greenish skin and light-green flesh; the canteloupe, with rough warty skin and orange flesh; and a newer variety produced in Israel with a green skin and sweet green flesh. Melons are usually eaten fresh. Family: *Cucurbitaceae*. *See also* watermelon.

Melos (*or* Mílos) A Greek island in the Aegean Sea, one of the Cyclades. Successive Minoan cities have been excavated here and the famous statue *Venus de Milo* was discovered here in 1820. Area: 58 sq mi (150 sq km).

Melpomene In Greek religion, one of the nine Muses, the patron of tragedy and lyre playing. She was the mother of the *Sirens.

melting point The temperature at which the solid form of a substance becomes a liquid, usually at atmospheric pressure.

Mélusine (*or* Melusina) In French legend, a fairy who was punished for imprisoning her father in a mountain by being changed into a serpent from the waist down every Saturday. When her husband, Count Raymond of Lusignan, broke his promise not to see her on Saturdays, she vanished but her cries were heard at Lusignan castle shortly before the death of each of her descendants.

Melville, Herman (1819–91) US novelist. In 1841 he joined the crew of a whaler; his experiences in the South Seas form the raw material of *Typee* (1846), *Omoo* (1847), *Mardi* (1849), *Redburn* (1849), and *White Jacket* (1850). His masterpiece, *Moby Dick* (1851), is a narrative about whaling with an underlying philosophical theme on the nature of evil. After the failure of *Pierre* (1852), Melville abandoned professional writing. *Billy Budd*, published in 1924 after his death, formed the basis of a libretto for an opera by Benjamin Britten.

Memel. *See* Klaipeda.

Memling, Hans (*or* Memlinc; c. 1430–1494) Painter of portraits and religious subjects, born in Seligenstadt (Germany). He settled in the Netherlands, where he probably studied under Rogier van der *Weyden, the strongest influence on his painting. About 1465 he moved to Bruges, where his best-known works, *The Shrine of St Ursula* and *The Mystic Marriage of St Catherine*, were painted for the Hospital of St John.

memory The recollection of experiences from the past. Three processes are required: registration, in which an experience is received into the mind; retention, in which a permanent memory trace, or engram, is preserved in the brain, probably in the form of a chemical molecule; and recall, in which a particular memory is brought back into consciousness. Short-term memories are vivid but are forgotten with the passage of time unless they are registered in the long-term memory. Once in the long-term memory, they remain available unless they are interfered with by a similar memory.

Failure of memory (*see* amnesia) is a common consequence of diseases of the brain, especially those caused by *alcoholism and those affecting the part of the *brain called the hippocampus. An abnormally good memory (hypermnesia) can sometimes be produced by hypnosis and is sometimes found in *autism.

memory, computer The part of a computer that stores information. It usually refers to the computer's internal store, in which the programs and data needed to run the computer are held; this is under the direct control of the central process-

HANS MEMLING *Triptych: The Virgin and Child with Saints and Donors (c. 1477). The figures on the extreme left and right are St John the Baptist and St John the Evangelist.*

ing unit. In large computers, a high-speed buffer store holds information in active use by the central processing unit, while longer-term storage is provided by the slower main store.

Solid-state electronic memory devices operate at very high speeds and are used for the internal memory. Magnetic tapes and disks form the external memory, which is available to the computer through peripheral devices. The external memory contains information that is not needed frequently.

Memphis 35 10N 90 00W A city and port in Tennessee situated above the Mississippi River. Founded in 1819, it was so called because of the similarity of its riverside position to that of the ancient Egyptian city of Memphis. It is a major cotton, timber, and livestock market and its manufactures include textiles and chemicals. Memphis is associated with W. C. Handy, the composer of the blues. Memphis State University was established in 1912. Population (1990): 610,337.

Memphis An ancient city of Lower Egypt, S of modern Cairo. A center for *Ptah worship, Memphis was founded as the capital of all Egypt after its unification by *Menes (c. 3100 BC), remaining the capital until supplanted by *Thebes (c. 1570 BC). The necropolis of *Saqqarah and the *pyramids and sphinx at Giza formed part of its extensive complex of monuments.

Menado (*or* Manado) 01 32N 124 55E A port in Indonesia, in N Sulawesi on the Celebes Sea. A trading center, it exports copra, coffee, and spices. Its university was established in 1961. Population (1980): 217,200.

Menander (c. 341–c. 290 BC) Greek dramatist. The most celebrated dramatist of the *New Comedy, he wrote sophisticated comedies on romantic and domestic themes with strongly individualized characters. His single surviving complete play is the *Dyscolus*, recovered from an Egyptian papyrus in 1958, but many of his other plays are known from their adaptations by the Roman dramatists Plautus and Terence.

Menander (c. 160–c. 20 BC) Greek king of the Punjab and one of the heirs to *Alexander the Great's conquests. His capital was at Sakala (probably present-day Sialkot, Pakistan) and he commanded an extensive empire over NW India. He became a devout Buddhist.

menarche. *See* puberty.

Mencius (Mengzi *or* Meng-tzu; 371–289 BC) Chinese moral philosopher. He was taught by pupils of *Confucius and produced the *Mencius*, an exposition of Confucian thought read by Chinese schoolchildren until the 20th century. For Mencius, moral thinking was superior to theorizing and he made benevolence (*ren* or *jen*) the keynote of his political philosophy. He traveled extensively, advocating that rulers should treat their subjects humanely.

Mencken, H(enry) L(ouis) (1880–1956) US journalist and critic. As editor of *The Smart Set* (1914–23) and *American Mercury* (1924–33), he boldly attacked both the political and the literary establishments and championed many young novelists. His miscellaneous essays were collected in *Prejudices* (6 vols, 1919–27). In *The American Language* (1919) he surveyed the development of English in America. *Newspaper Days 1899–1908* (1914) and *Heathen Days (1890–1936)* (1943) are autobiographical.

Mendel, Gregor Johann (1822–84) Austrian botanist, who discovered the fundamental principles governing the inheritance of characters in living things (*see* genetics). Mendel was a monk with a scientific education and an interest in botany. In 1856 in the monastery garden at Brünn, Moravia, he began to inbreed lines of pea plants by means of repeated self-pollination. All the dwarf plants produced dwarf offspring only, but of tall plants, only about one-third were true-breeding. The majority each produced both tall plants and dwarf plants in the ratio 3:1. Mendel then crossed purebred tall and dwarf plants and found that all the resulting hybrids were tall. Crossing these hybrids resulted in a mixture of purebred dwarf, hybrid tall, and purebred tall plants in the ratio 1:2:1. From these and similar experiments Mendel concluded that such characteristics were determined by factors of inheritance that were contributed equally by both parents and that sorted themselves among the offspring according to simple statistical rules. He summarized these findings in two principles (now known as *Mendel's laws of inheritance). Mendel reported his findings in 1865 but met with little response. The importance of his achievement was not appreciated until the rediscovery of his work by C. E. *Correns, Hugo *de Vries and E. von Tschermak (1871–1962) in 1900.

mendelevium (Md) A synthetic element, first produced in 1955 by Ghiorso and others, by bombarding einsteinium with helium ions; it is named for the chemist Mendeleyev. At no 101; at wt 256.

Mendeleyev, Dimitrii Ivanovich (1834–1907) Russian chemist, who was professor at St Petersburg (now Leningrad) from 1866 to 1890. He became interested in the subject of atomic weights after hearing *Cannizzaro lecture on the subject and, in 1869, succeeded in arranging the elements in order of increasing atomic weights so that those with similar properties were grouped together (*see* periodic table). Mendeleyev succeeded where others had failed, by recognizing that the rows of the table were not all of equal length and that there were gaps in the table, representing undiscovered elements.

Mendel's laws The basic principles governing the inheritance of characters, first proposed by Gregor *Mendel in 1865. His first law, the Law of Independent Segregation, states that the factors of inheritance (now called *alleles of the gene) that determine a particular characteristic segregate into separate sex cells. His second law, the Law of Independent Assortment, states that the segregation of factors for one character occurs independently of that for any other character. (This is true except for alleles of genes located on the same chromosome, which have a tendency to be segregated together.)

Mendelssohn, Felix (Jacob Ludwig Felix Mendelssohn-Bartholdy; 1809–47) German composer; the grandson of Moses Mendelssohn. A child prodigy, his education was strictly supervised by his father. His string octet (1825) and the overture to *A Midsummer Night's Dream* (1826) demonstrated his precocious brilliance. In 1836 he became conductor of the Leipzig Gewandhaus orchestra and subsequently founded the Leipzig conservatory. His music was popular in Britain and he was entertained by Queen Victoria. His compositions include five symphonies, overtures, the oratorios *St Paul* (1836) and *Elijah* (1846), chamber music, and piano music. He revived Bach's *St Matthew Passion* in 1829.

Mendelssohn, Moses (1729–86) German Jewish philosopher and literary critic. He was admired by *Kant and *Lessing and did much to improve the position of the Jews, for whom he sought civil rights. He also advocated the separation of church and state. Mendelssohn is known for his proofs of the immortality of the soul, in *Phaedon* (1767), and the existence of a personal God, in *Morgenstunden* (1785).

Menderes, Adnan (1899–1961) Turkish statesman; prime minister (1950–60). His repressive policies led to an army coup in 1960 and his execution.

Menderes River (ancient name: R. Maeander; Turkish name: Büyük Menderes) A river in W Turkey, flowing generally WSW into the Aegean Sea.

The ancient name of this winding river gave rise to the term *meander. Length: 249 mi (400 km).

Mendès-France, Pierre (1907–82) French statesman; prime minister (1954–55). A radical socialist, Mendès-France was forced to resign because of his unpopular policies, which aimed to restore the failing Fourth Republic; these included strengthening the executive, ending the war in Indochina, and granting independence to Tunisia.

Mendip Hills (*or* Mendips) A range of limestone hills in SW England, in Somerset. It extends NW–SE between Axbridge and the Frome Valley, reaching 1068 ft (325 m) at Blackdown.

Mendoza 32 48S 68 52W A city in W Argentina. It is the commercial center of an irrigated area specializing in wine production and has a university (1939). Population (1991): 121,696.

Mendoza, Antonio de (?1490–1552) Spanish colonial adminstrator. Mendoza was the first viceroy (1535–50) of New Spain (Mexico), where he fostered economic development and education, bringing the first printing press to the New World. He subsequently became viceroy of Peru (1551–52), where he died.

Menelaus A legendary Spartan king and husband of *Helen. He served under his brother Agamemnon in the *Trojan War and after the fall of Troy was reunited with Helen.

Menelik II (1844–1913) Emperor of Ethiopia (1889–1913). He greatly expanded Ethiopia and carried out important reforms, limiting the power of the nobility and modernizing the administration. In 1896 he was able to repel an Italian invasion.

Menes The first ruler of a united Egypt (c. 3100 BC); the founder of the 1st dynasty. Perhaps a legendary figure, he was said to have founded *Memphis.

Mengelberg, William (1871–1951) Dutch conductor. He studied at the Cologne conservatory and was conductor of the Amsterdam Concertgebouw Orchestra from 1895 to 1941. He was famous for his performances of Beethoven.

Mengs, Anton Raphael (1728–79) German painter, born in Aussig, Bohemia. An early exponent of *neoclassicism, he achieved a high reputation particularly in Rome, where he settled (1755), and in Spain, where he worked for Charles III. Apart from numerous portraits, his best-known work is the *Parnassus* fresco (1761; Villa Albani, Rome).

menhir (Breton: long stone) A prehistoric *megalith set upright either by itself or with others in circles (e.g. *Stonehenge) or alignments (e.g. *Carnac).

Ménière's disease A disease of the inner ear causing progressive deafness, tinnitus (ringing in the ear), and vertigo. The disease normally occurs in the later years and treatment (medical or surgical) is not altogether successful.

Menindee Lakes A series of lakes and reservoirs in Australia. They lie in SW New South Wales, forming part of the Darling River Conservation Scheme, and provide water for irrigation and industrial and domestic purposes.

meningitis Inflammation of the meninges—the membranes that surround the brain. This is usually caused by bacteria or viruses and occurs most commonly in children. Symptoms include headache, vomiting, stiff neck, intolerance to light, tiredness, irritability, and fits. Treatment for bacterial meningitis is with antibiotics and the patient usually recovers rapidly. Viral meningitis is often mild but may have serious effects. Tuberculous meningitis comes on more slowly and—before modern drugs were developed—was always fatal. Complications such as mental handicap, deafness, and weak limbs may occasionally occur.

Menlo Park 37 28N 122 13W An unincorporated community in E central New Jersey, part of the town of Edison. Many of Thomas Alva Edison's experiments, including the invention of the incandescent lightbulb (1879), took place in his laboratory here. A state park houses memorabilia and commemorates the inventor.

Mennonites A Christian sect that originated in Holland and adjacent areas in the 16th century. Their name derives from Menno Simons, who reorganized persecuted *Anabaptist groups after 1536. There are sizable Mennonite communities in Holland and in North America, where the first colony settled in 1683. Common ground between the doctrinally diverse Mennonite groups is their rejection of hierarchical Church organization and of infant baptism. In secular life Mennonites are pacifists and avoid public office.

Menno Simons (c. 1496–1561) Dutch Anabaptist leader. A former Roman Catholic priest, Menno became the traveling shepherd of scattered *Anabaptist groups in N Europe, persecuted by both Roman Catholics and Reformers. His preaching of total pacifism became the mark of the *Mennonites, one section of the Anabaptist movement.

Menon, Krishna (Vengalil Krishnan Krishna Menon; 1896–1974) Indian diplomat. He was secretary of the India League from 1929 and a major figure in the campaign for Indian independence. After this was achieved in 1947 he was high commissioner for India to the UK (1947–52) before becoming a member of the Indian legislature; he was a delegate at the UN (1952–62) and defense minister (1957–62).

menopause The cessation of menstruation. It is the time in a woman's life when the menstrual periods become irregular and finally cease because egg cells are no longer produced by the ovaries. The menopause can occur at any age between the late 30s and late 50s. Some women may experience physical and emotional symptoms, including flushing, palpitations, and irritability, due to reduced secretion of estrogens.

Menorca. *See* Minorca.

Menotti, Gian Carlo (1911–) Italian-born US composer. Living in the US since 1928, he studied and later taught at the Curtis Institute, Philadelphia. Among his compositions are the operas *The Medium* (1946) and *The Saint of Bleeker Street* (1954), both of which received Pulitzer Prizes, *The Consul* (1950) and the television opera *Amahl and the Night Visitors* (1951). In 1958 he founded the Spoleto Festival.

Mensheviks One of the two factions into which the Russian Social Democratic Workers' party split in 1903 in London. Unlike the rival *Bolsheviks, the Mensheviks (meaning those in the minority) believed in a large and loosely organized party. They supported Russia's participation in World War I and were prominent in the Russian Revolution until the Bolsheviks seized power in October 1917. They were finally suppressed in 1922.

menstruation The monthly discharge of blood and fragments of womb lining from the vagina. This is part of the **menstrual cycle**—the sequence of events, occurring in women from puberty to menopause, by which an egg cell is released from the ovary. Menstruation is the stage at which the egg cell (with blood, etc.) is expelled from the womb if conception has not occurred. Ovulation occurs at around the middle of the cycle; it may be associated with abdominal pain. Depression and irritability are common shortly before menstruation (premenstrual syndrome, or tension).

mental retardation A state of arrested or incomplete development of the intellect. Mildly retarded people (with an IQ of approximately 50–70) usually make a good adjustment to life after special help with education; their condition is usually caused by inherited disorders or psychological disturbances. Severely retarded people (with an IQ of less than 50) usually require permanent help from other people and may need care in a special home or a hospital. Severe retardation is nearly always caused by physical diseases affecting the brain, but good education improves the outcome. *See also* intelligence.

menthol ($C_{10}H_{20}O$) A white crystalline solid. It is a constituent of peppermint oil and is responsible for the characteristic smell of the mint plant, but can also be prepared synthetically. Menthol is used as an analgesic in medicine (in skin creams, throat pastilles, and inhalers) as well as in flavoring for sweets and cigarettes.

Menton 43 47N 7 30E A city in SE France, in the Alpes-Maritimes department on the French Riviera near the Italian border. A popular holiday resort, it produces fruit and flowers. Population: 25,314.

Menuhin, Yehudi (1916–   ) US violinist, living in England. A pupil of Georges Enesco, he became famous in boyhood; Elgar coached him for performances of the composer's violin concerto. From 1959 to 1968 Menuhin was director of the Bath (England) Festival, where he also participated as a conductor. He founded the Yehudi Menuhin School for musically gifted children in 1963. He was frequently partnered in recitals by his sister, the pianist **Hephzibah Menuhin** (1920–81). □Stern, Isaac.

Menzies, Sir Robert Gordon (1894–1978) Australian prime minister. Elected to the federal Parliament in 1934, he was attorney general (1934–39) before becoming prime minister as leader of the United Australian party. He resigned in 1941 and formed the Liberal party in 1944. As Liberal prime minister he increased US influence in Australian affairs and was strongly anticommunist. He encouraged immigration from Europe and developed the Australian universities.

Merca 1 45N 44 47E A city in Somalia, on the Indian Ocean. Merca has a deepwater harbor and exports agricultural produce, especially bananas. Population (1980 est): 60,000.

mercantilism An economic doctrine that flourished in the 17th and 18th centuries. Primarily concerned with international trade, mercantilism attempted to maximize national wealth, which it identified with a nation's bullion reserves. To this end, tariffs were applied to imports in the hope of creating a *balance-of-trade surplus and adding to bullion reserves. Mercantilism was replaced by *free trade, after *Hume and Adam *Smith had shown that mercantilism merely served the self-interest of the merchant classes.

Mercator, Gerardus (Gerhard Kremer; 1512–94) Flemish geographer, best known for his method of mapping the earth's surface, known as the *Mercator projection. He worked at Louvain, but was prosecuted for heresy in 1544 and emigrated to Protestant Germany in 1552, where he was appointed cartographer to the duke of Cleves. In later life he prepared a book of maps, which, since it had a picture of Atlas supporting the earth on its cover, became known as an atlas.

Mercator projection A cylindrical □map projection, originally used (1569) by Gerardus Mercator. The parallels of latitude are represented as being straight lines of equal length to the equator. The meridians are equally spaced and intersect at right angles. The correct ratio between latitude and longitude is maintained by increasing the distance between the parallels away from the equator causing increased distortion toward the Poles. Compass bearings are accurately shown and the projection is commonly used for navigation charts. The **Transverse Mercator projection** is a development of the Mercator projection but in this case the cylinder is tangential to a meridian rather than to the equator. It is used chiefly for small areas with a N–S orientation and is used in all British *Ordnance Survey maps.

SIR ROBERT MENZIES *The Australian Parliament listens to the prime minister speaking on his Communist Party Dissolution Bill (1950). After its enactment it was declared invalid (1951) by the Australian courts.*

mercerization A finishing process for cotton fabrics and yarns. Named for John Mercer (1791–1866), who investigated the process (1844), mercerization involves treating the cotton by immersion, while under tension, in a caustic soda solution, later neutralized by acid. This process causes the fibers to swell permanently; cotton thus treated dyes better and is stronger and more lustrous.

Merchant Marine Academy, United States Training institution for US Merchant Marine officers. It trains students in nautical and naval science and in ship management. The program offers a bachelor of science degree and a naval reserve commission. It was established in 1943 at Kings Point, N.Y., on Long Island.

Merchants Adventurers An English trading company, incorporated in 1407, which controlled the export of cloth to continental Europe. Its center was at Bruges until 1446, when it moved to Antwerp; in 1567 it transferred to Hamburg but returned to a series of Dutch marts after 1580. The Adventurers, which rivaled the *Hanseatic League, were criticized for furthering their own interests at the expense of the English economy and lost their charter in 1689.

Merchant Staplers English merchants who controlled the export and sale of wool from the late 13th to late 16th centuries. Exports were sold at one market (the staple), which from 1363 was Calais. At its height in the 15th century, the company declined with the growth of English manufacturing.

Mercia A kingdom of Anglo-Saxon England. The Mercians were *Angles and their territory embraced most of central England S of the Humber between Wales and East Anglia. Mercia became a formidable power under *Penda (c. 634–55) and achieved preeminence under *Offa (757–96), who controlled all England S of the Humber. Thereafter it declined and was merged in the 9th century into a united England under Wessex.

Mercouri, Melina (1925–94) Greek actress and politician; minister of culture and science (1981–94). Her best-known films were made with the US director Jules Dassin (1911–), whom she married, and include *Never on Sunday* (1960) and *Topkapi* (1964). She campaigned in exile against the military junta (1967–74) and returned to Greece when civilian government was restored.

mercury (botany) An annual or perennial herb of the genus *Mercurialis* (8 species), native to Eurasia and N Africa. The perennial dog's mercury (*M. perennis*) of woodland areas has an evil smell and is poisonous to grazing animals. Growing 6–16 in (15–40 cm) high, it has large toothed leaves arranged in pairs and clusters of small green male and female flowers borne on separate plants. The annual mercury (*M. annua*) occurs on wasteland and as a garden weed. Family: *Euphorbiaceae*.

mercury (Hg) The only common metal that is liquid at room temperature (it has a high relative density of 13.546). It occurs chiefly as the sulfide cinnabar (HgS), from which mercury is obtained simply by heating in a current of air. The element was known in ancient Egypt, India, and China and occurs rarely in nature in the metallic state. It is used in thermometers, barometers, and batteries and as an amalgam in dentistry. Compounds include the oxide (HgO), mercurous and mercuric chlorides ((Hg$_2$Cl$_2$, HgCl$_2$), and the explosive mercury fulminate (Hg(ONC)$_2$), which is widely used as a detonator. Mercury and its compounds are highly poisonous and are only slowly excreted by the human body. Organo-mercury compounds, such as dimethyl mercury, (CH$_3$)$_2$Hg, are particularly toxic (*see* Minimata disease). At no 80; at wt 200.59; mp $-38.03°F$ ($-38.87°C$); bp 674°F (356.58°C).

Mercury (astronomy) The innermost and second smallest (3030 mi [4880 km] diameter) planet, orbiting the sun every 88 days at a mean distance of 36 million mi (57.9 million km). Its long period of axial rotation, 58.6 days, is two thirds of its orbital period. Mercury can only be seen low in the twilight and early morning sky and, like the moon, exhibits *phases. Its surface is heavily cratered, with intervening lava-flooded plains. It has only a very tenuous atmosphere, mainly helium and argon. *See also* planetary probe.

Mercury (mythology) The Roman god of merchants and commerce and patron of astronomy. He is usually portrayed as holding a purse, and also with a cap, winged sandals, and staff, the attributes of the Greek *Hermes, with whom he was identified.

Meredith, George (1828–1909) British poet and novelist. Educated in Germany, he returned to England to study law but embarked on a literary career instead. For many years he was dependent on literary hackwork. His long poem *Modern Love* (1862) was partly based on his unhappy marriage to Mary Ellen Nicholls, daughter of Thomas Love *Peacock. With his novels, including *The Egoist* (1879) and *The Tragic Comedians* (1880), he achieved critical acclaim and financial security.

Meredith, Owen. *See* Lytton, Edward George Earle Bulwer-Lytton, 1st Baron.

merganser A *duck belonging to a genus (*Mergus*) of the N hemisphere, also called sawbill. It occurs on inland lakes in summer and coastal regions in winter.

16–22 in (40–57 cm) long, mergansers have a long serrated bill for feeding on worms, fish, and eels. Males have a dark-green double-crested head, a chestnut breast, and a gray-and-white back; females are brown with a white wing bar. *See also* goosander.

merger The amalgamation of two or more companies to form one new company; usually the shareholders of the old companies exchange their old shares for shares in the new company. **Vertical mergers** involve the amalgamation of companies specializing in different parts of the production process (e.g. a car manufacturer and a steelmaker); **horizontal mergers** involve the amalgamation of related product manufacturers (e.g. car and truck manufacturers); and **conglomerate mergers** are between firms unrelated in production. Mergers usually require government approval, as they can lead to *monopolies.

Mérida (Latin name: Augusta Emerita) 38 55N 06 20W A city in W Spain, in Estremadura on the Guadiana River. Founded by the Romans in 25 BC, it has numerous Roman remains, including an aqueduct, temples, two bridges, and a triumphal arch. Population (1970): 40,059.

Mérida 20 59N 89 39W A city in E Mexico. It is the commercial and industrial center for an agricultural area specializing in henequen (a fiber) production. It has a 16th-century cathedral and is the site of the University of Yucatán (refounded 1922). Population (1978 est): 263,186.

meridian. *See* latitude and longitude.

meridian circle An instrument for determining very accurately the position of a celestial body by measuring the body's altitude and the time as it crosses the observer's meridian (which passes through the observer's zenith and N and S celestrial poles). It consists of a telescope pivoted on a horizontal E–W axis so that the telescope's line of sight follows the meridian plane.

Mérimée, Prosper (1803–70) French novelist. His first published works were fake translations of plays and ballads that deceived many leading scholars. His best-known works are his short novels, especially *Columba* (1841) and *Carmen* (1843), the source of Bizet's opera. He was also a distinguished historian and archeologist, and a friend of the empress Eugénie.

Merino A breed of sheep originating from Spain and noted for its long thick high-quality white fleece. Merinos are well adapted to hot arid climates and have been exported to many parts of the world, especially Australia, where the Australian Merino has been developed for its superior fleece.

Merionethshire A former county of NW Wales. Under local government reorganization in 1974 it became part of *Clwyd and *Gwynedd.

meristem An area of actively dividing plant cells responsible for growth in the plant. The main meristematic regions in dicotyledon plants are the shoot tip and root tip (apical meristems) and the *cambium (lateral meristem). A damaged meristem produces distorted growth, but it can be used for plant propagation.

Merleau-Ponty, Maurice (1908–61) French philospher. He was interested in the nature of human consciousness and its interaction with matter, problems that he examined in *Le Structure du comportement* (1942) and *Phénoménologie de perception* (1945). In his eyes, causal and behavioristic theories misinterpreted consciousness, as did dualism, and he accepted the Marxist view of the dependence of consciousness upon material conditions.

merlin A small *falcon, *Falco columbarius*, occurring in moorland and heathland regions of the N hemisphere. The female is 12.5 in (32 cm) long and is dark brown with heavily streaked underparts; the male is 10 in (26 cm) long and has a gray-blue back and tail. Merlins feed chiefly on small birds, which are caught in flight.

Merlin In *Arthurian legend, the wizard who counsels and assists Arthur and his father, Uther Pendragon. There are various accounts of Merlin's life in *Geoffrey of Monmouth and later writers. He helped Uther to win Igraine, Arthur's mother, made the Round Table, cared for Arthur as a child, and gave him, or arranged for him to be given, the sword Excalibur. In old age Merlin fell in love with Nimue (*or* Vivien), who tricked him into a cave or hollow tree and left him there forever imprisoned by a spell.

mermaid A lengendary creature whose form is that of a beautiful woman above the waist and a fish below. A mermaid's male counterpart is called a **merman**. They are generally represented as malicious to man. Such aquatic mammals as dugongs may account for mermaid stories in mythology and folklore.

Merneptah King of Egypt (c. 1236–1223 BC) of the 19th dynasty. His father *Ramses II had neglected frontier defense in his old age and Merneptah faced the aggression of Libya and the Sea Peoples, against whom he scored a victory in 1232.

Meroë The capital of an ancient Nubian kingdom in the area that is now the Sudan. After ruling Egypt (c. 730–670 BC), Nubian kings established Meroë in about 600 BC. Its temples and pyramids show Egyptian influence. Before its abandonment (7th century AD), Meroë may have been the route by which iron technology reached sub-Saharan Africa.

Merovingians The first Frankish ruling dynasty (*see* Franks). It was founded by Merovech, king of the Salian Franks, in the mid-5th century AD. His grandson *Clovis (reigned 481–511) greatly extended Merovingian possessions and the kingdom reached its zenith in the mid-6th century. The last Merovingian king, Childeric III, was deposed in 751 by the *Carolingian Pepin the Short.

Merrill, Robert (1919–   ) US singer. A baritone, he first sang at the Metropolitan Opera House (1945) in *La Traviata*. With the Met since then, he is known for his roles in such operas as *Carmen, Otello, A Masked Ball*, and *La Forza del Destino*. He wrote *Once More from the Beginning* (1965) and *Between Acts* (1977).

Merseburg 51 22N 12 0E A city in S Germany, on the Saale River just S of Halle. Founded in 800 AD, there is a 15th-century castle and a 13th-century cathedral. Industries include tanning, brewing, engineering, lignite mining, and the manufacture of machinery and paper. Population (1988 est): 57,000.

Mersey River A river in NW England. Formed by the confluence of the Goyt and Tame Rivers at Stockport, it flows W to enter the Irish Sea by way of a 16 mi (26 km) long estuary, with the ocean ports of *Liverpool and Birkenhead on its banks. Length: 70 mi (113 km).

Mersin 36 47N 34 37E A port in central S Turkey, the major port on the S coast. It has an oil refinery and exports wool, cotton, and agricultural produce. Population (1985): 314,100.

Meru, Mount In Hindu mythology, the cosmic mountain at the center of the universe. It is symbolized in the massive pyramidal towers of Hindu shrines.

mesa An isolated flat-topped hill occurring in areas of long-continued erosion of horizontally bedded strata, usually in semiarid climates. The upper slopes are steep, and gentler lower slopes merge into the surrounding plain. The cap rock is of resistant material. Further erosion may reduce the mesa to a *butte.

Mesa Verde A high plateau, in SW Colorado. It contains the remains of numerous cliff dwellings, spanning four archeological periods.

mescaline A hallucinogenic drug obtained from the *peyote cactus of Mexico, where it was once widely used in religious ceremonies. The effect of mescaline varies from individual to individual; it does not cause serious dependence and the hallucinations are mostly visual.

Mesembryanthemum. *See* fig marigold.

Meshed. *See* Mashhad.

Mesmer, Franz Anton (1734–1815) German physician, who claimed to cure diseases by correcting the flow of "animal magnetism" in his patients' bodies during séance-like group sessions. Investigation of "mesmerism" by a commission of his contemporaries concluded that any cures were due to the powers of suggestion. Mesmer's claims stimulated serious study of hypnosis by such men as James *Braid.

Mesoamerican languages A geographical classification of the languages spoken by the American Indian peoples of Mexico, Guatemala, Honduras, Belize, El Salvador, and Nicaragua. It includes around 70 languages belonging to a number of families. The main families are: the Totonac-Mayan (e.g. Mayan); Uto-Aztecan (e.g. *Nahuatl); the Otomangean (e.g. Mixtec); the Hokan-Coahuiltecan; and Tarascan.

Mesolithic The middle division of the *Stone Age, especially in N Europe, where a distinct cultural stage, the *Maglemosian, intervened between the last ice age and the evolution of farming communities. Generally, the Mesolithic is characterized by production of microliths (very minute stone tools), which were hafted into wooden, bone, or other handles. The dog was the only domesticated animal. Outside Europe the Mesolithic distinction is less useful: for example, the Middle Eastern transition between *Paleolithic and *Neolithic was more rapid and less definable and in Japan pottery, a Neolithic characteristic, coexisted with microlith manufacture.

mesons A group of unstable elementary particles (lifetimes between 10^{-8} and 10^{-15} second) that are classified as hadrons; each meson is believed to consist of a quark-antiquark pair (*see* particle physics). The muon was originally called the mu-meson as it was thought to be a meson but is now classified as a lepton.

Mesopotamia The region between the Tigris and Euphrates Rivers, "the land between two rivers." The Sumerians (*see* Sumer) settled in S Mesopotamia about 4000 BC to cultivate the alluvial land left by flooding. They established the world's first civilization and founded city states, such as *Ur, *Kish, and *Uruk. *Babylon became Mesopotamia's capital under *Hammurabi, whose code of laws shows the development of civilized conduct and government. After his death Mesopotamia, overrun successively by Kassites, Assyrians, and Persians, was no longer the most advanced civilization, being overtaken by Egypt.

Mesosaurus A small slender freshwater reptile of the late Carboniferous and early Permian periods (around 280 million years ago). It was 40 in (1 m) long and had a long narrow skull with numerous teeth for straining crustaceans from water.

Mesozoic era The geological era following the Paleozoic and preceding the Cenozoic. It contains the Triassic, Jurassic, and Cretaceous periods, and lasted from about 240 to 65 million years ago. The reptiles were at their greatest development during this era but became extinct before the end of it. The Alpine orogeny began at the end of the Mesozoic.

mesquite A spiny shrub or small tree, of the genus *Prosopis,* with deep penetrating roots, native to the SW US and Mexico. Up to 49 ft (15 m) tall, it has compound leaves, with many narrow leaflets, and creamy flower catkins producing long narrow pods, which are used as cattlefeed. The hard wood is sometimes used in furniture. Family: **Leguminosae.*

Messager, André (Charles Prosper) (1853–1929) French composer and conductor. His compositions include the operetta *Véronique* (1898) and the ballet *Les Deux Pigeons* (1886). He directed the first performance of Debussy's *Pelléas et Mélisande* in 1902.

Messalina, Valeria (c. 26–48 AD) The third wife of Emperor Claudius and mother of Britannicus (41–55) and Octavia (the wife of Nero). Messalina was notorious for her promiscuity and, according to Roman scandal, contracted a bigamous and treacherous marriage to the senator Gaius Silius, for which they were both executed.

Messerschmitt, Willy (1898–1978) German □aircraft designer. He is best known for his World War II military planes, particularly the Me-109 fighter (1935) and the Me-262, the first jet fighter. In 1927 he was appointed chief designer at the Bayerische Flugzeugwerke, which was later renamed Messerschmitt-Aktien-Gesellschaft.

Messiaen, Oliver (1908–92) French composer, organist, and teacher. Messiaen was a pupil of Paul Dukas and Marcel Dupré. In 1931 he was appointed organist of La Trinité in Paris. His music has been heavily influenced by Catholic mysticism and the rhythms of Eastern music; he has also made use of bird song in his later compositions. His works include *La Nativité du Seigneur* (for organ; 1935), the symphony *Turangalîla* (1948), the *Quatuor pour la fin du temps* (for violin, cello, clarinet, and piano; 1941), and *La Transfiguration* (for chorus and orchestra; 1965–69).

Messier, Charles (1730–1817) French astronomer. In 1760 he began making a list of what he thought were nebulae. The result was the **Messier catalogue,** which listed 109 bright nonstellar celestial objects and was published in 1784–86. The objects were given a number preceded by the letter M, as in M31—the Andromeda galaxy. They are mainly galaxies and star clusters together with some nebulae.

Messina 38 13N 15 33E A port in Italy, in NE Sicily on the Strait of Messina. Originally known as Zancle, after the sickle shape of its harbor, it was successively occupied by Greeks, Carthaginians, Mamertines, Romans, Saracens, Normans, and Spaniards. In 1860 it became the last city in Sicily to be made part of a united Italy. Most of its old buildings were destroyed by severe earthquakes in 1783 and 1903. It has a university (1549) and its manufactures include macaroni, chemicals, and soap. Population (1991 est): 274,846.

Messina, Strait of A channel in the central Mediterranean Sea, between Italy and Sicily and narrowing to 2 mi (3 km). The rocks on the Italian side and the whirlpool on the Sicilian are possibly the origin of the myth of *Scylla and Charybdis.

Meštrovič, Ivan (1883–1962) Yugoslav-born US sculptor. Trained at the Vienna Academy, Meštrovič enjoyed an international reputation with his religious and portrait sculptures. His sitters included Herbert Hoover, Pope Pius XI, and Sir Thomas Beecham. Moving to the US (1947), he became a citizen in 1954.

metabolism The sum of the processes and chemical reactions that occur in living organisms in order to maintain life. It can be divided into two components. **Anabolism** involves building up the tissues and organs of the body using simple substances, such as amino acids, simple sugars, etc., to construct the proteins, carbohydrates, and fats of which they are made. These processes require energy, which is provided by the oxidation of nutrients or the body's own food reserves. Oxidation and all other processes involving the chemical breakdown of substances with the production of waste products are known collectively as **catabolism**. Basal metabolism is the energy required to maintain vital functions (e.g. respiration, circulation) with the body at rest. It is measured by estimating the amount of heat produced by the body and is controlled by hormones from the thyroid gland.

metal An element that is usually a hard crystalline solid, opaque, malleable, a good conductor of heat and electricity, and forms a salt and hydrogen when reacted with an acid and a salt and water when reacted with an alkali. Not all metals have all these properties, however: mercury is a liquid at normal temperatures, sodium is soft, and antimony is brittle. Of the 70-odd metals known, the most important are the heavy metals (iron, copper, lead, and zinc) used in engineering and the rarer heavy metals (nickel, chromium, tungsten, etc.) used in *alloys. Other commercially important metals are the *noble metals (gold, silver, platinum, and mercury) and the light metals (aluminum and magnesium). Chemically important metals include the *alkali metals (sodium, potassium, and lithium), the *alkaline-earth metals (calcium, barium, etc.), and the rare-earth metals (*see* lanthanides). Uranium is an important metal in the nuclear power industry (*see* nuclear energy).

Most metals occur in the earth's crust in the combined state and have to be mined (*see* mining and quarrying) before being extracted from their ores (*see* metallurgy). The extracted metal is then usually formed into an alloy (*see also* steel) before being ready for use.

metal fatigue The deterioration of metal caused by repeated stresses. Fatigue, which eventually leads to failure, occurs in vibrating parts of machinery, but only when the stresses are above a critical value, known as the endurance limit. It is an important consideration in the design of aircraft, where high engine speeds and high stresses are unavoidable.

metallography The study of the crystalline structure of metals. It includes various techniques and is used to test the quality of steel after *heat treatment. Usually a small sample is taken from a batch and polished before being examined under a microscope for cracks, impurities, or holes. The polished surface may also be treated chemically to show up the different constituents of an alloy or to highlight cracks. In 1911 Max von *Laue used X-rays to show that the atoms in metals are arranged in a regular geometrical fashion, i.e. they are crystalline. His technique of *X-ray diffraction is still used to examine metallic crystals.

metalloids Elements displaying the physical and chemical properties both of *metals and nonmetals. Examples of metalloids are arsenic and germanium, which both have metallic and nonmetallic allotropes. Chemically, their behavior is intermediate between metals and nonmetals in that they may form positive ions as well as covalently bonded compounds. The metalloid elements are often *semiconductors.

metallurgy The science and technology of producing metals. It includes the extraction of metals from their ores, alloying to form materials with specific properties, and *heat treatment to improve their properties. The art of working metals was known as early as 3500 BC, when copper, lead, tin, gold, and silver were in use in various parts of the world. Modern metallurgy is concerned with all metals, but primarily with those, such as iron, that are abundant and useful (*see* steel). Metallurgy originally developed by finding new *alloys and treatments by trial and error. Techniques, such as *metallography, have reduced the element of chance by identifying the factors in the microscopic structure of metals that contribute to hardness, strength, and ductility.

metamorphic rock One of the three major rock categories (*compare* igneous rock; sedimentary rock) consisting of rocks produced by the alteration (in the solid state) of existing rocks by heat, pressure, and chemically active fluids. Contact (*or* thermal) metamorphism occurs around igneous intrusions and results from heat alone. Regional metamorphism, extending over large areas, results from the heat and pressure created by crustal deformation. Dislocation metamorphism results from localized mechanical deformation, as along fault planes. Metamorphic rocks tend to be resistant to denudation and often form upland masses. Marble is a metamorphic rock formed from recrystallized limestone.

metamorphosis The process in animals by which a *larva changes into an adult. This radical change of internal and external body structures may be gradual or abrupt. Certain insects, such as dragonflies, undergo incomplete metamorphosis, during which successive stages (known as nymphs) become increasingly like the adult through a series of molts. In complete metamorphosis, seen in such insects as butterflies and houseflies, the larva passes into a quiescent pupal stage, during which the adult tissues are developed. Metamorphosis also occurs in amphibians (*see* frog). The process in insects and amphibians is controlled by hormones.

metaphor A figure of speech in which one thing is described in terms of another. The comparison is implicit, lacking such words as *like* or *as* (*see* simile). The metaphor is a common feature of ordinary language, as in such phrases as "time flies" and "to lose one's head," and is a fundamental poetic device. This example is from Shakespeare's *Macbeth* (act 5, scene 3):

Life's but a walking shadow, a poor player

That struts and frets his hour upon the stage.

metaphysical painting A style of painting practiced by Carlo Carrà (1881–1966) and Giorgio de *Chirico in the second decade of the 20th century. Together they established a school in Ferrara in 1917. They illustrated the mystery behind everyday reality by depicting dreamlike illusions, characterized by hallucinatory lighting with stark shadows, incongruous juxtapositions of objects, sharply plunging perspectives of empty streets, and the use of mannequins rather than people. *Surrealism adopted many of their ideas and devices.

metaphysical poets A group of 17th-century English poets whose work was characterized by intellectual wit and ingenuity, especially in their use of elaborate figures of speech. The leading poet was John *Donne, and his successors included George *Herbert, Henry Vaughan, Andrew *Marvell, and Abraham Cowley. They frequently employed colloquial speech rhythms in both their secular and their religious verse. The influential criticism of T. S. Eliot, who praised their union of intellect and emotion, helped to establish their high reputation in the 20th century.

metaphysics The study of existence or being in general. The term derives from the title given to a group of Aristotle's writings by the philosopher Andronicus of Rhodes (1st century BC). The status of metaphysics has been much debated; *Kant thought this kind of investigation impossible because our minds can only cope with the phenomenal world or the world of appearances and *Ayer used the word in *Language, Truth and Logic* (1936) as a pejorative term to indicate the meaninglessness of much traditional philosophy. However, with *ethics and *epistemology, metaphysics is still held to be one of the main divisions of philosophy.

Metastasio, Pietro (Pietro Antonio Domenico Trapassi; 1698–1782) Italian poet and librettist. In 1730 he was appointed court poet in Vienna, where he wrote numerous classical libretti. These include *L'Adriano* (1731) and *La clemenza di Tito* (1732), which has been set to music by many composers.

Metaxas, Ioannis (1871–1941) Greek general; dictator (1936–41). After the monarchy was reestablished in 1935, he became premier and then, with George II's support, dictator. He led Greek resistance to the Italian invasion in World War II.

metayage A type of land tenure in which rent is paid in kind. Metayage, a French word (from Latin *medietas*, half), was at one time the dominant form of tenure in S France, involving payment of approximately half the tenant's output to the landowner.

Metazoa A subkingdom of animals whose bodies consist of many cells differentiated and coordinated to perform specialized functions. The Metazoa includes all animals except the single-celled *Protozoa and the Parazoa (*see* sponge).

Metchnikov, Ilya Ilich (*or* I. I. Mechnikov; 1845–1916) Russian zoologist, who discovered that certain cells in animals could surround and engulf foreign particles, such as disease-causing bacteria. He called these cells *phagocytes and was awarded, with Paul *Ehrlich, the 1908 Nobel Prize.

metempsychosis. *See* reincarnation.

meteor A streak of light seen in the night sky when a **meteoroid**—an interplanetary rock or dust particle, usually with a mass from 10^{-7} to 10^{-3} gram but sometimes weighing over 22 lb (10 kg)—enters and burns up in the earth's atmosphere. A decaying *comet gradually produces a **meteor stream** of meteoroids around its orbit. When the earth passes through a meteor stream, an often spectacular **meteor shower** is observed, usually at the same time each year. The August Perseids and December Geminids are examples. A **meteorite** is a large piece of interplanetary debris that falls to the earth's surface, usually breaking up in the process. It produces a brilliant meteor. Meteorite composition is either principally iron or stone, or an intermediate mixture. Meteorites were formed early in the history of the solar system and most are believed to be fragments of minor planets. The rare fragile stony carbonaceous chondrites are possibly cometary fragments.

meteorology The study of the physics, chemistry, and movements of the *atmosphere and its interactions with the ground surface. The troposphere and stratosphere, the lower layers of the atmosphere in which most weather phenomena occur, are the chief focuses of meteorology and much attention has been paid to the explanation of surface weather and to weather forecasting. **Weather** is the state of atmospheric conditions (including temperature, sunshine, wind, clouds, and precipitation) at a particular place and time. A **weather forecast** is a prediction of what weather conditions will be over a stated future period; it is made by studying weather maps, especially those obtained from satellites (often feeding the observations into a computer). Short-term forecasts are made usually for a period of 24 hours (less for specialized uses) and long-range forecasts may be made for a month ahead although they are considerably less accurate. Weather forecasts are essential to shipping and aviation and are of use to many other bodies, including power authorities (predicting cold spells) and transport authorities (predicting snow, ice, and fog), as well as to farmers. Attempts have been made to modify weather, including cloud seeding, hurricane steering, and fog clearance, but success has been limited. *See also* climate.

weather conditions

• rain	✳ snow	⌒ dew
۹ drizzle	▲ hail	≡ fog
▽ showers	◬ ice pellets	⊺ thunderstorm

weather map *The numbers at the stations show temperature (0°C). Isobars show atmospheric pressure in millibars.*

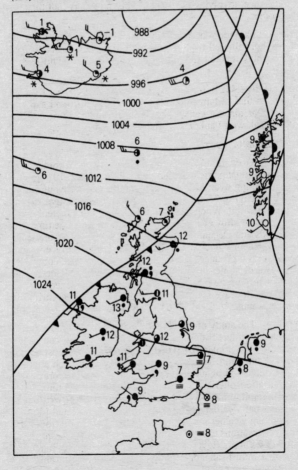

METEOROLOGY *Internationally agreed symbols are used throughout the world by meteorological stations to represent current weather conditions. These are plotted on weather maps from which forecasts can be made.*

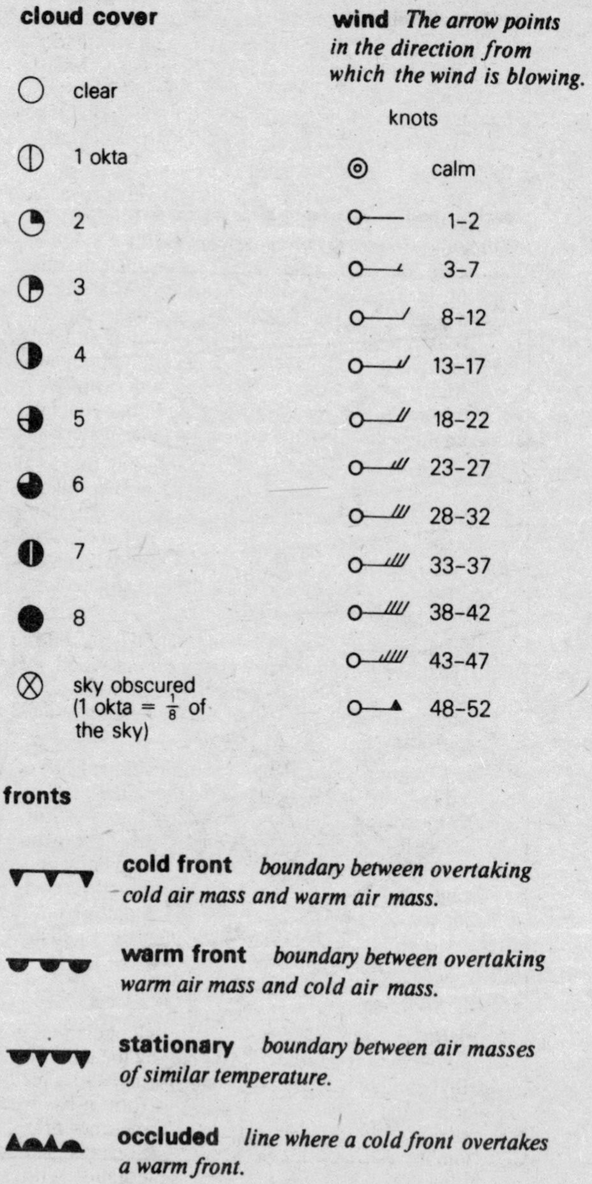

cloud cover

○ clear

◐ 1 okta

◕ 2

◕ 3

◑ 4

◓ 5

◕ 6

◐ 7

● 8

⊗ sky obscured
(1 okta = $\frac{1}{8}$ of
the sky)

wind *The arrow points in the direction from which the wind is blowing.*

knots

⊙   calm

○——   1–2

○——   3–7

○——   8–12

○——   13–17

○——   18–22

○——   23–27

○——   28–32

○——   33–37

○——   38–42

○——   43–47

○——▲   48–52

fronts

▼▼▼ **cold front**   *boundary between overtaking cold air mass and warm air mass.*

●●● **warm front**   *boundary between overtaking warm air mass and cold air mass.*

▼●▼● **stationary**   *boundary between air masses of similar temperature.*

▲●▲● **occluded**   *line where a cold front overtakes a warm front.*

METEOROLOGY *Internationally agreed symbols are used throughout the world by meteorological stations to represent current weather conditions. These are plotted on weather maps from which forecasts can be made.*

meter (m) The unit of length of the metric system. Originally defined in 1791 as one ten-millionth of the length of the quadrant of the earth's meridian through Paris, it was redefined in 1927 as the distance between two marks on a platinum-iridium bar kept at the International Bureau of Weights and Measures near Paris. It is now defined (General Conference on Weights and Measures, 1983) as the length of the path traveled by light in a vacuum in 1/299,792,458 second, which replaced the 1960 definition based on the wavelength of the emission of a krypton·lamp.

meter (poetry) The rhythmic pattern of a line of verse measured in terms of basic metrical units or feet. In accentual verse, as in English, a foot consists of various arrangements of stressed (´) and unstressed (˘) syllables. In classical Greek and Latin verse, the quantity or length rather than the stress of syllables determines the foot. In English the most common feet are the *iamb (˘´), the trochee (´˘), the anapaest (˘˘´), the dactyl (´˘˘), and the spondee (´ ´). A typical line of *blank verse consisting of five iambs is known as an iambic pentameter. Most traditional poetic forms, such as the *sonnet, are written according to strict metrical patterns. Many poets of the late 19th and 20th centuries have written in free verse, which has no regular meter or line length, or syllabic verse, in which each line has a fixed number of syllables but no regular pattern of stress.

methane (CH_4) A colorless odorless flammable gas that is the main constituent of *natural gas. It is the simplest member of the *alkane series and is used as a fuel and a source of other chemicals. Methane is produced in nature by the decay of vegetable matter under water, rising in bubbles from marshes as **marsh gas**. Coal gas also contains methane and is found in coal mines. Recently the generation of methane from sewage has been investigated as an *alternative energy source. It burns with a clear blue flame.

methanol (methyl alcohol *or* wood alcohol; CH_3OH) A colorless poisonous flammable liquid. Originally produced by distillation of wood, it is now usually made from hydrogen and carbon monoxide by high-pressure *catalysis. It is used as a solvent, antifreeze, and a raw material for making other chemicals. *See also* methylated spirits.

Methodism The Christian denomination that developed out of the religious practices advocated by John Wesley and his brother Charles. Although not conceived initially as an institution separate from the Church of England, to which it is very close in doctrinal matters, Methodism evolved its own church organization during the 1790s. The supreme decision-making body is the Conference; local societies (congregations) are highly organized, and pastoral and missionary work are major concerns. Methodism in the US dates from the 1780s. It is the second largest US Protestant denomination (after the Baptists).

Methodius, St. *See* Cyril, St.

methyl alcohol. *See* methanol.

methylated spirits A form of *ethanol (ethyl alcohol) that has been made unsuitable for drinking (and is therefore duty free) by the addition of about 9.5% of methanol (methyl alcohol), about 0.5% of pyridine, and a methyl violet dye (as a warning that it is dangerous to drink). In this form it has many household uses, especially as a fuel for spirit burners. It is sometimes drunk by desperate alcoholics, in whom it can cause blindness and other serious medical conditions. Industrial methylated spirits (IMS) consist of ethanol with about 5% of methanol and no pyridine. It is used as a solvent for varnishes, etc.

metric system A system of measurement based on the decimal system. First suggested in 1585 by Simon Stevin (1548–1620), an inspector of dikes in the Low Countries, it was not given formal acceptance until 1795, when a French law provided definitions for the *meter, *are, *stere, *liter, and gram. In 1799 a subsequent law established legal standards, made of platinum, for the meter and the kilogram. However, this form of the metric system was not widely used, even in France, until the third decade of the 19th century; during this period it was also adopted by most European countries. The metric system is not widely used in the US and Great Britain, except by the scientific community.

For scientific purposes, former metric systems (such as the *c.g.s. system and the *m.k.s. system) have been replaced by *SI units, a coherent system of metric units.

metrology The science of measurement. The scientific method is based on making accurate measurements, i.e. of expressing the magnitude of a physical quantity (say, length) in terms of a number and a unit (say, meters). Metrologists study methods of making these accurate measurements and of deciding what units should be used and how they should be defined. Modern metrology is based on *SI units and the methods of defining the system's seven basic units. The decision to adopt this system was taken in 1960 by metrologists from 30 nations meeting at the Conférence Générale des Poids et Mesures.

metronome A device consisting of a pendulum and a small sliding weight, which can be regulated to make the pendulum beat at a desired number of beats per minute. The most common type is the clockwork metronome invented by J. N. Maelzel (1770–1838); electric metronomes also exist. Metronome markings are often given in musical scores to indicate the exact speed of the music.

Metropolitan Museum of Art The largest art museum in the US and one of the most important in the world. Founded in 1870, it was opened in its present premises in New York City's Central Park in 1880. Its enormous collection comprises paintings, drawings, sculptures, ceramics, furniture, etc., from many periods and countries, including China, ancient Egypt, Greece, and Rome as well as an extensive American collection. Since 1938 its collection of medieval art has been housed in the Cloisters, built in Fort Tryon Park, Manhattan, from fragments of medieval monasteries and churches.

Metropolitan Opera Association The principal US opera company, founded in New York City in 1883. *Caruso sang regularly with the company from 1904 to 1921. The general manager from 1950 to 1972 was Sir Rudolph *Bing. The company occupied the Metropolitan Opera House until 1966, when it moved into the Lincoln Center for the Performing Arts, the original building being demolished.

Metsu, Gabriel (1629–67) Dutch painter, who was born in Leyden but lived in Amsterdam from about 1650. His early subjects were often religious but he is better known for his interiors showing middle-class life in such paintings as *The Duet* (National Gallery, London).

Metternich, Klemens Wenzel Nepomuk Lothar, Fürst von (1773–1859) Austrian statesman, the leading figure in European diplomacy from the fall of Napoleon (1815) until the Revolutions of 1848. As foreign minister (1809–48) he sought to maintain the balance of power in Europe, supporting dynastic monarchies and suppressing liberalism. His policies dominated the great Congresses of *Vienna (1814–15), *Aix-la-Chapelle (1818), Troppau (1820), Laibach (1821), and Verona (1822). The Revolution of 1848 forced him to seek refuge in Britain, the constitutional monarchy that he had always condemned.

Metz (Latin name: Divodorum) 49 07N 6 11E A city in NE France, the capital of the Moselle department on the Moselle River. The center of the Lorraine coal and metal industries, it trades in wine and agricultural products and has varied manufacturing industries. It has a fine cathedral (13th–16th centuries) and a university (1971). *History*: part of the Holy Roman Empire until seized by France

(1552), it fell to Germany (1871) but returned to France after World War I. Population (1990): 123,920.

Meuse River (Dutch and Flemish name: Maas) A river in W Europe. Rising in NE France and flowing mainly N past Liège in Belgium and Maastricht in the S Netherlands, it enters the North Sea at the Rhine Delta. It was the scene of heavy fighting in World War I (1914) and World War II (1940). Its lower course is an important commercial waterway. Length: 575 mi (926 km).

Mewar. *See* Udaipur.

Mexicali 32 36N 115 30W A city in the extreme NW of Mexico, on the US border. It is the commercial center for a rich irrigated agricultural area. Population (1980): 341,559.

Mexican Border Campaign (1916–17) US expedition into Mexico to quell attacks on New Mexico and Texas by Mexican revolutionary Pancho *Villa. Led by Gen. John J. *Pershing, US cavalry chased Villa 300–400 mi (480–640 km) into Mexico, but never captured him.

Mexican War (1846–48) A territorial conflict between Mexico and the US arising from a dispute over the S border of Texas. Hostilities began when Mexican forces crossed the Rio Grande to attack a detachment of the US Army commanded by Gen. Zachary *Taylor. Taylor repulsed the attackers and pursued them into Mexico, winning a crucial victory at *Buena Vista. At the same time, Gen. Stephen *Kearny was ordered to capture the territories of New Mexico and California. The end of the war came with an invasion of Mexico commanded by Gen. Winfield *Scott, during which American forces captured Mexico City. By the Treaty of Guadalupe Hidalgo, the Mexicans ceded the disputed territory in Texas as well as New Mexico and California for a payment of $15 million by the US government. The border between the US and Mexico was finalized with the *Gadsden Purchase in 1853.

Mexico, Gulf of An arm of the Atlantic Ocean that is bounded by the S United States and E Mexico. Its outlets are via the Straits of Florida and the Yucatan Channel-Caribbean Sea to the Atlantic Ocean. Waters warmed in the gulf flow through the Straits of Florida to create the warming Gulf Stream. Large rivers, including the Mississippi in the United States and the Rio Grande that forms the US–Mexican border, flow into the gulf. The average depth is about 4700 ft (1433 m), with a maximum depth of 17,070 ft (5200 m). It yields major quantities of oil, natural gas, and fish and has substantial tourist industries along its coast. Area: 596,000 sq mi (1,540,000 sq km).

Mexico, United States of A country in Central America between the Gulf of Mexico and the Pacific Ocean. Narrow coastal plains rise to high mountain ranges in the interior, which include the volcano Popocatépetl. Much of the N is arid with tropical forest in the S, especially in the Yucatán Peninsula in the SE (the only extensive low-lying area). Most of the population is of mixed Indian and Spanish descent. *Economy*: Mexico now ranks among the world's main oil-producing countries following substantial finds in several areas, the most recent being along the E coastline of the states of Tamaulipas and Veracruz. Mexico also has large reserves of natural gas and there are substantial deposits of uranium. Other minerals extracted include iron ore, zinc, sulfur, silver, and copper, and Mexico is the world's largest producer of fluorite and graphite. Agriculture remains relatively underdeveloped and during the mid-1970s a program to collectivize small farms was launched in an effort to increase food production. Corn is the main food crop; cash crops include cotton, sugar, coffee, and fruit and vegetables, as well as sisal in Yucatán. Fishing has been developed considerably in recent years and important catches include sardines, shrimps, and oysters. Tourism is an important source of foreign currency. *History*: Mexico was the site of the Mayan civilization from the 2nd to the 13th centuries AD, and between the 8th and 12th centuries the *Toltecs flourished. The 14th century saw the rise of the *Aztecs, whose capital was at Tenochtitlán, the site of present-day Mexico City. The Aztecs were conquered by the Spanish under Cortés in 1521 and Mexico became part of the viceroyalty of New Spain. The struggle for independence from Spain began in 1810 and was achieved in 1821. A turbulent period dominated by *Santa Anna was followed by the *Mexican War (1846–48), in which territory was lost to the US. In 1864 *Maximilian, archduke of Austria, was installed as emperor by the French, but in 1867 he was shot in the successful anti-French revolution led by Benito Juárez. In 1911 the long dictatorship of Porfirio Díaz ended in an uprising under Francisco Madera. The Mexican Revolution culminated in the constitution of 1917, the democratic goals of which have been the declared aims of subsequent governments. Mexico is now a one-party state dominated by the Party of Institutionalized Revolution (PRI), against which serious demonstrations have occurred. Mexico faced perhaps the worst crisis in its history in the 1980s with drastic economic ills brought on by a reduction of exports and a flight of capital from Mexican to US banks. Corruption in previous governments contributed to the dangerous conditions, as did the recession of 1980–82. Higher prices of US exports, a reduction of Mexican imports by the US, and increased interest rates on its debts forced further borrowing. By the end of 1982 the inflation rate had soared to over 100%. Mexico responded by devaluing the peso three times in 1982, nationalizing private banks, and imposing severe austerity measures. By the end of 1983 the government held more than 80% of the country's economic resources. The importance of a healthy Mexican economy to global economic stability (Mexico is a major US trading partner) induced a rescheduling of debts by the International Monetary Fund and further loans by foreign nations. Economic problems continued into the late 1980s, complicated by strained US relations caused in part by illegal Mexican emigration to the US. A 1985 earthquake that killed more than 7000 people and a 1988 hurricane that left almost 200,000 homeless further strained the economy. In the early 1990s, President Salinas worked to improve his country's economy by encouraging international trade and privatization of business. Negotiations in 1991 with the US led to the North American Free Trade Agreement (*NAFTA) in 1993. An uprising in S Mexico in early 1994 showed that dissatisfaction among Mexico's peasants remained high. Mexico is a member of the OAS. President: Carlos Salinas de Gortari. Official language: Spanish. Official currency: Mexican peso of 100 centavos. Area: 761,530 sq mi (1,967,183 sq km). Population (1992 est): 88,335,000. Capital: Mexico City. Main port: Veracruz.

Mexico City (Spanish name: Ciudad de México) 19 25N 99 10W The capital of Mexico, in the S of the high central plateau at a height of 7800 ft (2380 m), surrounded by mountains. The 14th-century Aztec city of Tenochtitlán (built on a lake, since filled in) had a population of almost half a million when it was destroyed by Cortés in 1521. A new Spanish city was built on the site and it rapidly became the most important in the New World. It was captured by the US and then by France in the 19th century and in the 20th century was the center of several revolutions. It has seen rapid growth in recent years and now has considerable industry. It was severely damaged by a 1985 earthquake. A cultural center, it is the site of the National Autonomous University of Mexico (founded in 1551), the national library, a famous school of mining engineering, the museum (containing the Aztec Calendar Stone), and the Palace of Fine Arts Theater. Other famous landmarks include the fine cathedral (16th–19th centuries) and the 17th-century Palacio National. Population (1986 est): 18,750,000.

Meyerbeer, Giacomo (Jacob Liebmann Beer; 1791–1864) German composer and pianist. A child prodigy, he studied the piano with Clementi and composition with Abbé Vogler (1749–1814). His early German operas failed while those in the more superficial Italian style were more successful. It was in Paris that he composed the spectacular works by which he is remembered: *Robert le Diable* (1831), *Les Huguenots* (1836), and *L'Africaine* (performed posthumously; 1865).

Meyerhof, Otto Fritz (1884–1951) US biochemist, born in Germany, who showed that glycogen in muscles is broken down anaerobically into lactic acid when the muscle is working. He shared the 1922 Nobel Prize with Archibald *Hill for this discovery.

Meyerhold, Vsevolod Emilievich (1874–1943?) Russian theater director. He joined the Moscow Art Theater in 1898, but eventually rejected the naturalism of *Stanislavsky and experimented with a symbolic and abstract drama in which the actor's individual role was reduced to a minimum. He supported the Revolution and joined the Bolshevik Party in 1918. In the 1920s he was the first director to specialize in producing Soviet plays, but fell out of favor with the government in the 1930s. He most likely died in a Soviet labor camp.

Mezzogiorno (Italian: midday) Southern Italy; the name refers to the heat of the region, which is economically, socially, and politically backward. After the unification of Italy in the 19th century the development of the N received greater attention from the central government than the S, where local government was ineffectual, the *Mafia flourished, and the gulf between landowners and peasants was considerable. Despite special government aid during the 20th century, the problems are still largely unsolved.

mezzotint A technique of printing tonal areas (as opposed to lines), invented by a German officer, Ludwig von Sieger (1609–1680?). It was thus particularly suitable for reproducing paintings, being popular in 18th- and 19th-century England for printing Reynolds's portraits, Constable's landscapes, etc. The technique involves roughening and indenting a copper or steel plate with a serrated edged tool (rocker). Some of the roughened parts are then scraped away before the plate's surface is coated with ink. The indentations create the dark tones of the print, while the polished parts produce the lighter accents. Mezzotint is often combined with *etching and line engraving.

Mfecane (1818–28) A period of wars and upheaval among Bantu peoples of S Africa. The Zulu, under their warrior king *Shaka, turned on neighboring tribes, causing them to abandon their cattle and grain stores and to flee into the territory of other tribes. This movement of peoples radically altered tribal groupings and led to the formation of new groupings, such as the Swazi, Basuto, Kololo, and Ndebele.

Miami 25 45N 80 15W A city and port in □Florida, on Biscayne Bay. A major tourist resort and retirement center, it grew during the Florida land boom of the 1920s and includes Coral Gables (site of the University of Miami, established in 1925) and Miami Beach. It is famous for its citrus fruit and winter vegetables. Industries include aircraft repairing, clothing, and concrete. Population (1990): 358,548.

Miami Beach 25 47N 80 08W A resort city in SE Florida, on islands across Biscayne Bay from Miami. Causeways connect it to the mainland. It was created in the early 1900s from sandy swampy land. It is a major US tourist center in the winter. Population (1990): 92,639.

Miami River, or Great Miami River A river that flows from W central Ohio SW to join the Ohio River at the Indiana border W of Cincinnati. Length: 160 mi (258 km).

Micah (8th century BC) An Old Testament prophet of Judah and contemporary of Isaiah. **The Book of Micah** records his condemnation of a number of specific sins in the corrupt nation and predicts the fall of Jerusalem, the renewal of the people, and the coming of a Messiah.

micas A group of common rock-forming silicate minerals that have a layered structure and complex composition. Muscovite, $K_2Al_4(Si_6Al_2)O_{20}(OH,F)_4$, is a white mica and economically the most important; it occurs in granitic rocks (often pegmatites), gneisses, and schists. The other principal micas are *phlogopite (amber), biotite (dark), paragonite, margarite, zinnwaldite, and lepidolite (a source of lithium). Their perfect cleavage is reflected in the layered structure. In its commercial form it is sold in blocks (sheets), books (flakes resembling the pages of a book), and splittings (loose flakes). Since it is a good insulator and can withstand high temperatures, mica has many electrical uses and is used for furnace windows. Splittings bonded together with shellac or synthetic resins are used to make Micanite.

Michael (1596–1645) Tsar of Russia (1613–45) and founder of the *Romanov dynasty. Michael's election as tsar ended the *Time of Troubles. Michael was a weak ruler, relying upon his father Patriarch Philaret (c. 1553–1633). Serfdom was intensified during his reign.

Michael (1921–   ) King of Romania (1927–30, 1940–47). Michael succeeded his grandfather in 1927 but lost the crown in 1930, when his father *Carol II returned from exile. After Carol's abdication in 1940, Michael again became king. In 1944 he overthrew the dictatorship of Ion Antonescu and declared war on Germany. He abdicated in 1947.

Michael. *See* archangels.

Michael VIII Palaeologus (1224–82 AD) Byzantine emperor (1259–82), who founded the Palaeologan (the last Byzantine) dynasty (1259–1453). In 1261 Michael captured Constantinople from the Latins and reestablished the Byzantine empire there after a 57-year absence. His subsequent policies were determined by the fear of another attack from the west. An alliance with the papacy against Charles I of Naples and Sicily led to the union (1274) of the Greek and Roman Churches, for which he was vilified after his death.

Michaelmas daisy. *See* Aster.

Michelangelo Buonarroti (1475–1564) Italian sculptor, painter, architect, and poet, born at Caprese, in Tuscany. Michelangelo was trained in Florence under the painter *Ghirlandaio and in the school in the Medici gardens, under the patronage of Lorenzo de' Medici. Working in Rome from 1496 until 1501, he produced his first major sculptures, notably the *Pietà* (St Peter's, Rome). This was followed (1501–05) by his work in Florence, including *David* (Accademia, Florence), the painting of the *Holy Family* (Uffizi), and the influential cartoon of the *Battle of Cascina*. The last was commissioned as a fresco for the Palazzo Vecchio but was never finished and was painted over by Vasari. Michelangelo's productive but stormy association with Pope Julius II began in 1505, when the pope commissioned Michelangelo to produce his tomb. Although this proved to be his most checkered and lengthy project, it resulted in such masterpieces as the *Slaves* (Accademia, Florence). The celebrated Sistine Chapel ceiling (1508–12), in the Vatican, established his reputation as the greatest painter of his day. Returning to Florence (1516), Michelangelo became the architect and sculptor of the Medici funerary chapel (1520–34) in S Lorenzo and he also designed the Laurentian Library. These architectural projects and the fresco of the *Last Judgment* (1534–41) for the Sistine Chapel were his first major works in the new mannerist style (*see* mannerism). In his last years he worked mainly as an architect, becoming in 1547 chief architect of St Peter's, Rome, in which capacity he designed its great dome. His last sculptures included the *Rondanini Pietà* (Milan, Castello).

Michelet, Jules (1798–1874) French historian. He established his academic reputation while still young and was appointed Keeper of the National Archives in 1831. His *Histoire de France* (6 vols, 1833–43; 11 vols, 1855–67) and *La Révolution française* (7 vols, 1847–53) were unashamedly nationalist works, written with romantic imagination. During the Second Empire (1852–70) he retired from public life and wrote works on natural science.

Michelin, André (1853–1931) French tire manufacturer, who founded, with his brother **Édouard Michelin** (1859–1940), the Michelin Tire Co. (1888). In 1895 they became the first to demonstrate the feasibility of using pneumatic tires on motor cars. The company is now also famous for its maps and guidebooks.

Michelozzo di Bartolommeo (1396–1472) Florentine *Renaissance sculptor and architect. As a sculptor he collaborated first with *Ghiberti and then with *Donatello, but after 1433 he turned to architecture. He designed several buildings for the Medici, including the Palazzo Medici (1444–59), which was the first Renaissance palace.

Michelson, Albert Abraham (1852–1931) US physicist, born in Germany. He designed a highly accurate interferometer known as the Michelson interferometer and used it to measure precisely the speed of light. He also used it in an attempt to measure the velocity of the earth through the ether. This work, carried out in conjunction with Edward *Morley and known as the *Michelson-Morley experiment, eventually led *Einstein to his theory of relativity. Michelson received the Nobel Prize in 1907.

Michelson-Morley experiment An experiment performed by A. A. *Michelson and E. W. *Morley in 1881 in an attempt to demonstrate the existence of the luminiferous ether by measuring the earth's velocity relative to it. They used a Michelson interferometer to obtain interference fringes and then rotated the apparatus through 90° expecting to find a shift in the fringes, since the velocity of light would be different in the two directions. This difference would result from the earth's motion through the ether. However, no shift was detected. This negative result led to the downfall of the ether theory and was explained by Einstein's theory of *relativity in 1905 (*see also* Lorentz, Hendrick Antoon).

Michener, James A(lbert) (1907–   ) US author. After serving in the navy, he wrote *Tales of the South Pacific* (Pulitzer Prize; 1947), short stories about his experiences during World War II. *The Bridges at Toko-Ri* (1953) and *Sayonara* (1954) had Oriental themes, while *The Bridge at Andau* (1957) told of the aftermath of the Hungarian Revolution. *Hawaii* (1959) began Michener's epics that covered thousands of years. He followed with *The Source* (1965), *Iberia* (1968), *Centennial* (1974), *Chesapeake* (1978), *The Covenant* (1980), *Space* (1982), *Poland* (1983), *Texas* (1985), *Legacy* (1987), *Alaska* (1988), and *Caribbean* (1989).

Michigan A state in the N central US, bordered largely by water (Lakes Superior, Huron, Michigan, Erie, and St Clair). It has land borders with Ohio and Indiana in the S, Wisconsin in the NW, and the Canadian province of Ontario in the E. Michigan is divided by the Straits of Mackinac into the Lower Peninsula (with Lake Michigan on the W and Lakes Huron and Erie on the E) and the Upper Peninsula (with Lake Michigan on the S and Lake Superior on the W). The Lower Peninsula consists of lowlands where most of the state's population and industry are concentrated. The sparsely populated Upper Peninsula, with lowlands in the E and uplands in the W, contains Isle Royale National Park. Michigan is highly industrialized, and its manufacturing sector contributes significantly to US revenues. Especially important is the production of motor vehicles at Detroit; other industries include machinery, iron and steel, and chemicals. The state exploits its large mineral reserves of gypsum, calcium, magnesium compounds, natural gas, and oil. Tourism is the state's second largest industry. It is also an important agricultural state, producing corn, beans, other vegetables, fruit, and livestock. *History*: first explored by the French in the 17th century. The region at the time of the arrival of the first whites was inhabited principally by Ojibwa, Ottawa, and Potawatomi Indians. It remained under French control until it was acquired by the British (1763) as part of Canada. Pontiac's Rebellion erupted in the same year, ending with the signing of a peace treaty with the Indians. Michigan came under US control in 1796, although Britain held the area during the War of 1812. The opening of the Erie Canal (1825) between Lake Erie and the Hudson River provided a link from the central states to the Atlantic Ocean, bringing new settlers to the area. The rise of the lumber industry after 1850 resulted in the destruction of huge stands of forest. The state's industrial base was established with the founding of the Ford Motor Co. by Henry Ford, who adapted the assembly line to automobile manufacturing. Michigan's economy suffered with the decline in the US automobile industry in the 1970s and early 1980s but prospects for diversifying the economy brightened with the discovery of oil in Grant Traverse Bay in Lake Michigan. Area: 58,216 sq mi (150,779 sq km). Population (1990): 9,295,297. Capital: Lansing.

Michigan, Lake The third largest of the Great Lakes in North America, the only one wholly in the US. It is linked with Lake Huron via the Straits of Mackinac; the city of Chicago is on its S bank. Area: 22,400 sq mi (58,000 sq km).

Mickiewicz, Adam (1798–1855) Polish poet. His early poetry was strongly influenced by the romantics, especially Byron. In 1823 he was arrested with other students of Vilna University and deported to Russia, where he became a friend of Pushkin. He left Russia in 1829 and settled in Paris in 1832. His works include the romantic drama *Dziadzy* (1823–32) and the epic poem *Pan Tadeusz* (1832–34).

microbiology The study of microorganisms, or microbes—organisms that are invisible to the naked eye, including bacteria, small fungi (e.g. yeasts and molds), algae, protozoa, and viruses. Microorganisms, which are abundant everywhere, are of immense importance to all living things. They bring about *decomposition and the recycling of nutrients. They are vital to numerous industries, including brewing, baking, dairying, and food processing, and they have revolutionized medical treatment with the discovery of antibiotics. Some microorganisms, however, are parasites that cause disease in plants, animals, and man (*see* infection).

microcomputers Small sophisticated *computers designed for a single user and often for a specific application. The central processing unit, called a *microprocessor, is extremely small. Microcomputers were introduced in the 1970s for a wide range of industrial, commercial, and even domestic applications. They have had a considerable impact in speeding the process of automation.

ers can rapidly wind the film to the correct page. **Microfiche** is a similar system on cards holding a single film negative, with even greater reduction of the pictures. The viewers often have a printer attached to reproduce paper copies. Microfiche is widely used in data-processing systems as an alternative to paper computer printout, and in libraries to store periodicals, etc.

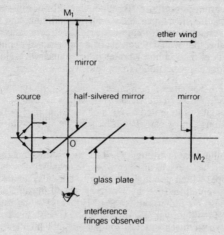

Michelson interferometer

MICHELSON-MORLEY EXPERIMENT *The Michelson interferometer was used in an attempt to detect changes in the velocity of light of the earth's motion through the ether. Distances OM_1 and OM_2 are equal. The glass plate compensates for the thickness of the half-silvered mirror.*

micrometer An instrument for measuring small lengths with great accuracy. The object to be measured is held between the jaws of a C-shaped metal piece, one jaw of which can be adjusted by a screw. The screw is turned by rotating a drum with a *vernier scale marked on it, from which the required dimension can be read. Micrometer is also the name for one-millionth of a meter.

micron (μm) An obsolete name for one-millionth of a meter. The correct name is now the **micrometer** (*see* SI units).

Micronesia A division of Oceania in the W Pacific Ocean, consisting of an arc of islands E of the Philippines. It includes the Belau, Kiribati, Mariana, Caroline, and Marshall archipelagos. *See also* Melanesia; Polynesia.

Micronesia, Federated States of An island group within the UN Trust Territory of the *Pacific Islands, comprising Truk, Yap, Ponape, and Yosrae. Self-government was achieved in 1979. Population (1992 est): 114,000.

microphone A device that converts sound into electrical signals. It acts like a *loudspeaker in reverse and some microphones may also be used as loudspeakers. Most consist of a thin diaphragm, the mechanical vibration of which is converted to an electrical signal proportional to the sound pressure. A telephone mouthpiece usually consists of a carbon microphone in which the sound waves exert a varying pressure on carbon granules, so varying their electrical resis-

ers. Most consist of a thin diaphragm, the mechanical vibration of which is converted to an electrical signal proportional to the sound pressure. A telephone mouthpiece usually consists of a carbon microphone in which the sound waves exert a varying pressure on carbon granules, so varying their electrical resistance. In capacitor microphones, once the most commonly used in music recording, the diaphragm forms one plate of a capacitor, across which the sound waves produce a fluctuating potential difference. Crystal microphones rely on the *piezoelectric effect. Other types use magnetic induction, and less commonly magnetostriction or other electromagnetic effects. Ribbon microphones have a highly directional response. They consist of a thin strip of aluminum alloy in a strong magnetic field. The ribbon vibrates in the sound waves, inducing in itself an electromotive force proportional to its velocity.

microprocessor The central processing unit of a *microcomputer. Its development was made possible in the 1970s by advances in solid-state electronics, in particular the design of integrated circuits of such complexity that all the main calculating functions can be carried out by a single silicon chip (*see* integrated circuit).

microscope An optical instrument used for producing a magnified image of a small object. There are several distinct types, the most common being the compound microscope, which contains an objective lens system and an eyepiece system. It was invented in 1609 by Dutch spectacle maker Zacharias Janssen (1580–c. 1638) and his father, but Robert *Hooke gave the first extensive description of its use in biology in his *Micrographia* (1665). In a compound microscope the objective produces a real magnified image, which is further magnified by the eyepiece. At low *magnifications the system is illuminated by a source the light of which is reflected through the specimen by a mirror. At high magnifications special illuminating systems are needed. The magnification, which may be up to a thousand, is limited by the *resolving power of the lenses; the smallest detail capable of resolution by an optical microscope is about 0.2 micrometer. This can be increased by using an *oil-immersion lens (*see also* ultramicroscope). Still higher magnifications are obtained by using shorter wavelength radiations as in the *electron microscope.

A **photomicrograph** is a photograph of the image obtained using a microscope. This enables a permanent record to be kept and also enables ultraviolet radiation to be used for illumination of the specimen.

microwave background radiation. *See* big-bang theory; cosmology.

microwaves Electromagnetic radiation with wavelengths between 1 and 300 millimeters, lying between infrared rays and radio waves in the electromagnetic spectrum. They are used in *radar and **microwave heating**. This method is used in the rapid cooking of food as the radiation penetrates to the interior of the food. The microwave photon is the same order of magnitude as the vibrational energy of atoms and molecules and therefore heats the interior directly, rather than by conduction from the surface. It is also used in sterilization and in drying wood, etc. Microwaves are generated by such devices as *magnetrons and *klystrons.

Midas In Greek legend, a king of Phrygia whose wish that everything he touched be turned to gold was granted by Dionysus in gratitude for his hospitality to the satyr *Silenus. Because he was therefore unable to eat or drink, he was released from this handicap by bathing in the Pactolus River. In another legend, Midas was asked to judge between the music of Pan and Apollo and chose the former. Apollo punished his tactlessness by changing his ears into those of an ass.

Mid-Atlantic Ridge The submarine ridge extending N–S through the Atlantic Ocean. It forms part of the mid-ocean ridge system that crosses all the major oceans. Much of it is over 621 mi (1000 km) wide and rises to between 0.6 and 1.9 mi (1–3 km) above the ocean basin, in places rising above sea level to form islands. Along the crest are rift mountains and a fractured plateau. *See* plate tectonics.

Middle Ages The period of European history that is generally regarded as commencing in the 5th century with the fall of the western Roman Empire and ending with the Renaissance. This period begins with the creation of the barbarian kingdoms, which developed into the nation states of W Europe. In Church history, the period covers the rise to supremacy of the Roman Catholic Church, centered on Rome, and the development of the papacy as an international religious and political power. Socially and economically the period saw the rising power of the great landed magnates and the creation of a feudal society, while urban growth and the development of trade reached unprecedented heights. The period can be said to end with the fall of Constantinople to the Turks (1453), the discovery of America (1492), and the successful challenge to the papacy by national reform movements.

Middleback Range A range of hills in S South Australia. It extends N–S for 40 mi (64 km) in the Eyre Peninsula and possesses rich deposits of iron ore; these are worked at Iron Knob, Iron Monarch, and Iron Baron.

Middle Comedy The transitional period of Greek comic drama, lasting from about 400 BC to about 320 BC. Its characteristics are evident in the last two plays of Aristophanes, *Ecclesiazusae* (392) and *Plutus* (388). A more oblique humor replaced the exuberant and scurrilous wit of earlier comedy, perhaps reflecting the Athenians' loss of confidence in themselves after their defeat (404) in the Peloponnesian War. *See also* Old Comedy; New Comedy.

Middle East The area comprising Iran and the countries of the Arabian peninsula and the Mediterranean seaboard. The Middle East, sometimes called the cradle of civilization, is the birthplace of three major world religions, Judaism, Christianity, and Islam, and their attendant cultures. A world crossroads, its troubled history has been dominated at different times by the Jews, Assyrians, Babylonians, Romans, Tatars, Turks, and Arabs. The present unrest derives from the conflict between superpowers to influence an area that produces 40% of the world's oil, by conflict between Arab countries and Israel (exacerbated by the displaced Palestinians), and by differing politico-religious objectives.

Middlesbrough 54 35N 1 14W A city in NE England, on the Tees estuary. Local iron ore and coke gave Middlesbrough early industrial advantages. Iron and steel, chemicals, constructional engineering, and shipbuilding are the major industries and almost all the traffic through the port is related to the steel and chemical industries. Population (1983): 148,500.

Middletown 41 33N 72 39W A city in central Connecticut, on the W bank of the Connecticut River, SE of Hartford. Wesleyan University (1831) is there. A 19th-century port and ship building center, it now houses banking and insurance firms and produces skis, marine accessories, airplane parts, and electronics. Population (1990): 42,762.

Middle West, the. *See* Midwest, the.

Midgard In Norse mythology, the earth, which lies between Hel or Nifleheim, the land of ice, and Muspelheim, the land of fire, and is reached from *Asgard (the home of the gods) by Bifrost, the rainbow bridge. It was formed by the gods from the dead body of the giant Aurgelmir, his flesh being the land, his blood the oceans, etc.

midge A small fly, also called a nonbiting midge, belonging to the family *Chironomidae* (over 2000 species). It resembles a mosquito but is harmless. Midges are found near fresh water, often in large swarms. The wormlike aquatic larvae are often red (*see* bloodworm) and live in gelatinous or sand tubes, feeding on algae.

The term is also applied loosely to similar but unrelated flies, including the biting or bloodsucking midges (family *Ceratopogonidae*) and the *gall midges.

Midland 32 00N 102 05W A city in W central Texas, S of Lubbock. It is an administrative center for Texas's oil industry. Originally a 19th-century cattle-shipping center, it still processes the area's agricultural products; other manufactures include aircraft, chemicals, and tools. Population (1990): 89,443.

Midlands A collective term for the central counties of England. The area includes the counties of Derbyshire, Leicestershire, Northamptonshire, Nottinghamshire, Staffordshire, Warwickshire, Hereford and Worcester, and the metropolitan county of West Midlands.

midnight sun The sun when it is seen on or above the horizon at midnight at places within the Arctic or Antarctic circles. At the polar circles it is seen only at the summer *solstice. At the Poles it is seen for the six months between the summer and winter solstices.

Midrash (Hebrew: inquiry, exposition) Exposition of the Bible, and more particularly a book consisting of such exposition. There are many Midrashim, mostly dating from the early Middle Ages, and they are a valuable source for the religious ideas of the Jews of the time. The *Talmuds also contain a great deal of Midrash.

midshipman A fish, also called singing fish, belonging to a genus (*Porichthys*) of *toadfishes. It is able to produce a whistling sound and has rows of light-producing organs on its underside.

Midway Islands 28 15N 177 25W A small group of US islands in the central Pacific Ocean. A military base, they are unpopulated apart from US military personnel. The sea and air battle that took place here (June 3–6, 1942) resulted in a major Allied victory. Area: 2 sq mi (5 sq km).

Midwest, the (*or* Middle West) An area in the N central US. Its boundaries are indefinite but it is generally accepted to be N of the Ohio River, W of Lake Erie, and E of the Great Plains. One of the world's most fertile agricultural areas, it produces chiefly corn and wheat.

midwifery The nursing specialty concerned with the care of women during pregnancy and childbirth. Midwives assist in monitoring the health of the mother and baby during labor and deliver the baby in the absence of complications. Midwives undergo extensive training beyond basic nursing training.

midwife toad A *toad, *Alytes obstetricans*, found in W Europe up to 7218 ft (2200 m) above sea level. Pale gray and slow-moving, it has an unusual breeding habit. As the eggs are laid, the male winds the two egg strings around his hind legs. He keeps the eggs for about a month, frequently moistening them with dew and finally takes them to hatch in a pool.

Mies van der Rohe, Ludwig (1886–1969) German architect. A pioneering architect of the 1920s and 1930s, Mies first achieved fame with his glass sky-scrapers (1919–21). However, his most influential building was the glass, steel, and marble German pavilion at the Barcelona international exhibition (1929; *furniture). After a short period running the *Bauhaus, he moved (1937) to the US, where he designed such buildings as the Illinois Institute of Technology (1939) and the Seagram building, New York (1958; □architecture).

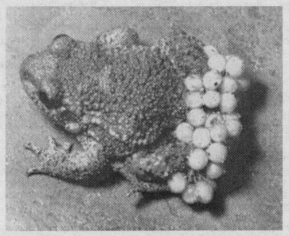

MIDWIFE TOAD *Mating takes place on land. Soon after fertilization the male twists the eggs around his legs and carries them around, thus protecting them from the predators they would otherwise encounter if laid in water.*

mignonette A bushy annual herb, *Reseda odorata*, native to N Africa and widely grown as an ornamental. Up to 24 in (60 cm) high, it bears dense terminal clusters of tiny yellow or white flowers, which have a musky fragrance and are used in perfumery. The name is also applied to other species of *Reseda*. Family: *Resedaceae*.

migraine Recurrent headaches, usually affecting one side of the head and thought to be caused by contraction and then dilation of the arteries in the brain. The attacks are often preceded by certain symptoms, usually visual—blurring of vision and flickering lights (called an aura). During the headache itself vomiting commonly occurs. There are some drugs that can reduce the incidence of attacks and others that relieve the severity of an attack.

migration, animal The periodic movement of animal populations between one region and another, usually associated with seasonal climatic changes or breeding cycles. Migration is best known among birds. Many European species travel to S Africa to avoid the harsh winter weather and the Arctic tern makes a spectacular migration of 11,000 mi (17,600 km) between its breeding grounds in the Arctic and the Antarctic. The phenomenon is seen in many other animals, including fish (notably salmon), which return each year from the sea to spawn in the same river where they themselves were spawned, butterflies, bats, lemmings, and whales.

The mechanism of navigation and homing is not completely understood. In birds it seems to involve sighting of visible landmarks, such as mountains and vegetation, as well as a compass sense, using the sun or the stars as bearings. Other animals are thought to use similar methods. Land mammals may lay scent trails for local direction finding.

migration, human The movement of groups of people from one country to another in which they intend to settle. Religious persecution has led many (e.g. the *Pilgrim Fathers, the French *Huguenots following the revocation of the Edict of *Nantes, and the Jews) to flee their homelands and settle elsewhere. The 19th century was a period of migration on a large scale, often prompted by severe population pressures, rural unemployment, the economic opportunities in the country of destination, or racial persecution. Many of the major countries such as the US, Australia, and South Africa, able to absorb large numbers of immigrants, have had historic policies favoring Europeans. Even European immigration in these countries was severely restricted by legislation in the 1920s. Since World War I governments have been more active in controlling migration. War and political upheaval in the late 20th century have prompted many people to flee their native countries in recent years. Such groups include Vietnamese, Cambodians, Cubans, and Haitians.

Mihajlović, Draža (*or* D. Mihailović; 1893–1946) Yugoslav general. After Germany occupied Yugoslavia in World War II he organized the *Chetniks. In 1943 he was appointed minister of war by Peter II (1923–70; reigned 1934–45) but lost the king's confidence and Allied support, which was given to *Tito. After the liberation he was convicted of treason and shot.

Mikonos (*or* Mykonos) A Greek island in the S Aegean Sea, one of the Cyclades. It is popular with tourists and is noted for having a large number of churches. Area: 35 sq mi (90 sq km).

Milan (Italian name: Milano; Latin name: Mediolanum) 45 28N 9 12E A city in N Italy, the capital of Lombardy on the Olona River. Milan is the focal point of rail and road routes and is the chief commercial and industrial center of Italy. Its manufactures include motor vehicles, machinery, silk and other textiles, and chemicals and it is a major publishing center. Milan has a gothic cathedral (duomo), two universities (both founded in the 1920s), the Brera Palace (containing the city's chief art collection), a library, and the opera house of *La Scala. The convent of Sta Maria delle Grazie contains Leonardo da Vinci's fresco *The Last Supper*. *History*: founded by the Gauls about 600 BC, it was captured by the Romans in 222. Later devastated by the Huns and the Goths, it was involved in much warfare until the 12th century, after which time it enjoyed considerable economic prosperity. It was ruled by the Visconti family from 1310 until 1447, after which it passed to the Sforza family, who ruled almost continuously until the fall of Milan to Spain (1535). It was under Austrian rule (1713–96) and in 1797 Napoleon made it capital of the Cisalpine Republic (1797) and the kingdom of Italy (1805–14). It grew in industrial importance after its unification (1861) with Italy. Population (1991 est): 1,432,184.

mildew Any fungus that grows as dense filaments forming visible white patches. Many fungal diseases of plants are called mildews; powdery mildews are infestations by fungi of the order *Peronosporales*, while downy mildews are due to infection by fungi of the family *Erysiphaceae*.

mile A unit of length traditionally used in the US. A statute mile is equal to 1760 yards. The unit is based on the Roman mile of 1000 paces.

Miles Gloriosus (Latin: boastful soldier) A stock character in comic drama who boasts of brave deeds yet is easily shown to be a fool or coward. The term derives from the title of a play by *Plautus.

Miletus An ancient Greek city in *Ionia, founded about 1000 BC. Center of the wool trade, early colonizer of the Black Sea area, and commercially active from Italy to Egypt, Miletus exemplified Ionian energy and enterprise. Milesians were prominent among the 6th-century Ionian thinkers, and even after destruction by Persia (494 BC) Miletus recovered, remaining commercially important until its harbors silted up.

milfoil. *See* yarrow.

Milhaud, Darius (1892–1974) French composer, a member of Les *Six. He made use of polytonality in many of his compositions, some of which were influenced by jazz. In collaboration with Jean Cocteau he wrote the ballets *Le Boeuf sur le toit* (1919) and *Le Train bleu* (1924); with Paul Claudel he wrote the opera *Christophe Colomb* (1928). His numerous other works include 12 symphonies, 15 string quartets (the last 2 of which can be played simultaneously as an octet), concertos, and Jewish liturgical music.

Military Reconstruction Act (1867) US law that, after the Civil War, redistricted the South. Because every southern state except Tennessee refused to ratify the 14th Amendment, Congress divided the South into 5 districts, subject to martial law. The act required the states to call constitutional conventions that would establish governments that would ratify the 14th Amendment before the states could be readmitted to the Union.

militia A military force composed of reservists enlisted in emergencies to reinforce a standing army. The militia is descended from the Anglo-Saxon *fyrd*, to which all free men were compulsorily recruited for short-term local service.

milk A fluid secreted by the *mammary glands of mammals to feed their young. Cows' milk consists typically of about 87% water, 3.6% fat, 3.3% protein, 4.7% lactose (milk sugar), small quantities of minerals (mainly calcium and phosphorus), and vitamins (mainly vitamins A and B). (Human milk, in contrast, contains less protein and more lactose.) Although its composition depends on the breed of animal, its diet, and the season, milk forms a well-balanced and highly nutritious food.

Milk River A river that flows from NW Montana NE through Alberta, Canada, and then SE to NE Montana where it joins the Missouri River. Used mainly for irrigation, the river is dotted with hydroelectric dams. Length: 625 mi (1007 km).

milk of magnesia A suspension of magnesium hydroxide ($Mg(OH)_2$) in water. It is a white milky fluid used as an antacid and a mild laxative.

milkweed An herb of the genus *Asclepias* (120 species), native to North America and often grown in the tropics and subtropics for ornament. Up to 4 ft (1.2 m) high, it bears umbrella-shaped clusters of orange, purple, pink, or red flowers and yields a milky latex. The seeds have long silky hairs ("vegetable silk"), often used in water-safety equipment, in upholstery padding, or as insulation. Family: *Asclepiadaceae*.

milkweed butterfly A butterfly belonging to the widely distributed mainly tropical family *Danaidae*. The adults are typically large and colorful and may fly long distances (*see* monarch). The caterpillars feed on milkweed and other plants, which makes them taste unpleasant to predators.

milkwort A perennial herb or small shrub of the genus *Polygala* (500–600 species), native to Europe and North America. The common European milkwort (*P. vulgaris*) has slender branching stems, 2.8–10 in (7–25 cm) long, and spikes of irregular flowers, white, pink, or blue in color. Family: *Polygalaceae*.

Milky Way The diffuse band of light that is seen, on a clear moonless night, stretching across the sky. It is composed of innumerable stars that are too faint to be seen individually. They lie around the sun in the flattened and densely populated disk of our *Galaxy.

Mill, James (1773–1836) Scottish writer, historian, and philosophical radical. In the course of a busy journalistic career he met *Bentham (1808), whose enthusiastic disciple he became. Mill's *History of India* (1818) secured him an official post at India House for the remainder of his life. His *Elements of Political Economy* (1821) influenced *Marx and his philosophical stance is reflected by his son **John Stuart Mill** (1806–73), one of the greatest 19th-century thinkers. In economics, J. S. Mill was influenced by the theories of Adam *Smith, *Ricardo, and *Malthus, and his *Principles of Political Economy* (1848) is little more than a restatement of their ideas. He was also the last of the English philosophers in the empirical tradition of Locke. He was a proponent of *utilitarianism, publishing a book under that title (1863). *On Liberty* (1859) shows that he was concerned for the rights of the individual, yet sympathetic to the ideas of contemporary socialists. He believed strongly in the equality of the sexes, publishing his views in *Subjection of Women* (1869).

Millais, Sir John Everett (1829–96) British painter. He was one of the founders of the *Pre-Raphaelite Brotherhood, the principles of which he applied to his best paintings, notably the controversial *Christ in the House of His Parents* (1850) and *Ophelia* (1852). After abandoning Pre-Raphaelitism in the 1860s, he painted more popular and sentimental works, such as *Bubbles* (1886), a portrait of his grandson.

Millay, Edna St Vincent (1892–1950) US poet. The rebellious bohemianism of her early lyrical poetry matured into a more profound disillusion, expressed with great technical skill especially in *The Buck in the Snow* (1928) and *Fatal Interview* (1931), a sonnet sequence. *The Harp Weaver and Other Poems* (1923) was awarded the Pulitzer Prize.

millenarianism A belief, widespread among early Christians and sporadically revived since, that Christ will soon return to reign on earth with his elect for a period of a thousand years preceding the Last Judgment. The idea was fostered by literal interpretations of the Book of Revelation (especially chapter 20) but was rejected by *Origen, whose views on the matter became generally accepted. At the Reformation, millenarianism flourished among persecuted minorities, such as the *Anabaptists. Puritan millenarian sects, notably the *Fifth Monarchy Men, proliferated in the mid-17th-century turmoils in England. The political frustrations of colonial rule, combined with fundamentalist biblical teaching, fostered millenarianism among the indigenous peoples of Africa and Polynesia, where it sometimes took the form of *cargo cults. Contemporary millenarian groups include the *Adventists and *Mormons.

Miller, Arthur (1915–   ) US dramatist. As a Jewish liberal intellectual, he has played an active role in political life, and one of the main themes of his plays is social responsibility. His plays include *All My Sons* (1947); *Death of a Salesman* (1947), which won a Pulitzer Prize; *The Crucible* (1953), concerning the Salem witch trials of the 1690s; *A View From the Bridge* (1955); and *After the Fall* (1964), which is in part a portrait of his late wife Marilyn □Monroe. *Playing for Time* (1980) was produced on television.

Miller, Glenn (1904–44) US jazz trombonist, band leader, and composer of the popular songs "Moonlight Serenade" and "In the Mood." Miller's band, assembled in 1938, recorded many hit swing tunes and entertained the troops during World War II. He died on a routine flight between England and France; the plane and the bodies of the passengers were never recovered.

Miller, Henry (1891–1980) US novelist. During the 1930s he lived in Paris, where he became a close friend of Lawrence *Durrell; he lived in California from 1944. He first gained notoriety with the sexually explicit novels *Tropic of Cancer* (1934) and *Tropic of Capricorn* (1939), which were banned in the US until 1961. His works, which are mostly autobiographical, are anarchic celebrations of life and liberty. Other works include *The Rosy Crucifixion* (1949–60) and *My Life and Times* (1972).

miller's thumb. *See* bullhead.

millet One of various *grasses or their seeds, cultivated in Asia and Africa as a cereal crop and in parts of Europe and North America chiefly as a pasture grass and fodder crop. It grows 12–51 in (30–130 cm) high and the flowers form spikes or branched clusters. Common or broomcorn millet (*Panicum miliaceum*) is used for poultry feed or flour milling. Pearl millet (*Pennisetum glaucum*) is grown in arid and infertile soils as a food grain; Italian millet (*Setaria italica*) has been cultivated as a grain crop in Asia since ancient times; and Japanese millet (*Echinochloa crus-galli* var. *frumentacea*) is grown mainly for fodder. A variety of sorghum (*see* durra) is also known as millet.

Millet, Jean François (1814–75) French painter of peasant origin, famous for his peasant subjects. He studied in Cherbourg and in Paris under *Delaroche, achieving acclaim in 1844, although his works were later criticized for expressing socialist ideas. After settling in Barbizon (1849), he became associated with the *Barbizon school and painted melancholy and sometimes sentimental agricultural scenes, notably *The Gleaners* (1857) and *The Angelus* (1859; both Louvre).

millibar. *See* bar.

Millikan, Robert Andrews (1868–1953) US physicist, who first measured the charge on the electron. For this and other work, he was awarded the Nobel Prize in 1932. In **Millikan's oil-drop experiment**, he balanced the effects of an upward electromagnetic attraction and the downward pull of gravity on an electrically charged droplet. As changes in the drop's charge (caused by bombardment with X-rays) occur in whole numbers of units of electronic charge, the size of the unit can be calculated from the movement of the drop. Millikan also studied cosmic rays. He was deeply religious and was actively concerned to reconcile religion and science.

millipede A slow-moving *arthropod of the widely distributed class *Diplopoda* (about 8000 species). Its slender cylindrical body, 0.08–11 in (2–280 mm) long, is covered by a calcareous cuticle and consists of 20–100 segments, most of which bear two pairs of legs (*compare* centipede). Millipedes live in dark humid places—under stones, rotting logs, or in soil—as scavengers of dead plant and animal materials. In defense they secrete a toxic fluid containing cyanide and iodine. Eggs are usually sheltered in a nest of excrement.

Mills, Sir John (1908–) British actor. He appeared in the roles of quiet but gallant heroes in *This Happy Breed* (1944) and other war films and later in character roles, as in *Ryan's Daughter* (1971). His daughters **Hayley Mills** (1946–) and **Juliet Mills** (1941–) are both actresses.

Mills, C(harles) Wright (1916–62) US sociologist. He was professor of sociology at Columbia University (1946–62) and concentrated on the theories of German sociologists Karl *Marx and Max *Weber. His works include *From Max Weber* (1946), *White Collar* (1951), *The Power Elite* (1956), *The Sociological Imagination* (1959), *Listen Yankee* (1960), and *The Marxists* (1962).

Milne, A(lan) A(lexander) (1882–1956) British novelist and dramatist. He contributed to *Punch* and wrote several popular comedies, but is best known for his books for and about his son Christopher Robin. These include *When We Were Very Young* (1924), a collection of verse, and two books about toy animals, *Winnie-the-Pooh* (1926) and *The House at Pooh Corner* (1928).

Milo (late 6th century BC) Greek wrestler of legendary strength, who won six Olympic prizes. He is said to have carried a calf on his shoulders once every day from its birth and eventually to have carried the grown cow round the Olympic stadium.

Miloš (1780–1860) Prince of Serbia (1815–39, 1858–60), who led a successful revolt against the Ottoman Empire (1815) and founded the *Obrenović dynasty. Miloš was the alleged assassin of *Karageorge. He was forced to abdicate in 1839 but was recalled in 1858.

Milstein, Nathan (1904–) US violinist, born in Russia, resident in the US since 1929. A pupil of Leopold Auer (1843–1930) and Eugène Ysaÿe (1858–1931), Milstein gave recitals with Vladimir Horowitz in Russia before establishing a European reputation in 1925. He has published a number of violin transcriptions.

Miltiades (c. 550–489 BC) Athenian general and statesman. Sent to govern the Thracian peninsula in Athenian interests, he ruled as tyrant and fought with *Darius I of Persia in Scythia. Later, after joining the Ionian cities' unsuccessful revolt against the Persians, he had to flee to Athens (493) but escaped punishment. Appointed a general in 490, he devised the strategy by which the Greeks decisively defeated the Persians at the battle of *Marathon.

Milton, John (1608–74) English poet. After leaving Cambridge University he studied privately at his father's house, where he wrote the poems *L'Allegro* and *Il Penseroso* (1632), the masque *Comus* (1633), and the elegy *Lycidas* (1637). In 1638 he traveled in France and Italy. During the 1640s and 1650s he actively supported the Puritan revolution and wrote many polemical pamphlets, notably *Areopagitica* (1644), a defense of free speech. He also wrote a series of pamphlets justifying divorce in cases of incompatibility, a position reflecting his own unhappy marriage (1642) to Mary Powell. In 1649 he was appointed Latin Secretary to the Council of State, but his eyesight began to fail and he had become totally blind by 1652. After the Restoration he retired from public life to write his great epic poem *Paradise Lost* (1667), its sequel *Paradise Regained* (1677), and the dramatic poem *Samson Agonistes* (1671).

Milton Keynes 52 02N 0 42W A city in S England, in Buckinghamshire. Developed since 1967 as a new town, it is the headquarters of the Open University (1969) and has varied light industries. Population (1981): 106,974.

Milwaukee 43 03N 87 56W A city and port in Wisconsin, on Lake Michigan. Originally a fur-trading post, it grew after an influx of German refugees in 1848. The German immigrants established the city's famous brewing industries. The state's largest city and a major shipping center, Milwaukee is a leading producer of heavy machinery, electrical equipment, and diesel and gasoline engines. Population (1990): 628,088.

WEBSTER'S
FAMILY
ENCYCLOPEDIA

WEBSTER'S FAMILY ENCYCLOPEDIA

VOLUME 7

1995 Edition

Exclusively distributed by
Archer Worldwide, Inc.
Great Neck, New York, USA

Abbreviations Used in Webster's Family Encyclopedia

AD	After Christ	ht	height	N.M.	New Mexico
Adm.	Admiral	i.e.	that is	NNE	north-northeast
Ala.	Alabama	in	inches	NNW	north-northwest
Apr	April	Ind.	Indiana	Nov	November
AR	Autonomous Republic	Ill.	Illinois	NW	northwest
		Jan	January	N.Y.	New York
at no	atomic number	K	Kelvin	OAS	Organization of American States
at wt	atomic weight	Kans.	Kansas		
Aug	August	kg	kilograms	Oct	October
b.	born	km	kilometers	Okla.	Oklahoma
BC	Before Christ	kph	kilometers per hour	OPEC	Organization of Petroleum Exporting Countries
bp	boiling point				
C	Celsius, Centigrade	kW	kilowatts		
		lb	pounds	Pa.	Pennsylvania
c.	circa	Lt.	Lieutenant	PLO	Palestine Liberation Organization
Calif.	California	Lt. Gen.	Lieutenant General		
Capt.	Captain			Pres.	President
CIS	Commonwealth of Independent States	m	meters	R.I.	Rhode Island
		M. Sgt.	Master Sergeant	S	south, southern
		Mar	March	S.C.	South Carolina
cm	centimeters	Mass.	Massachusetts	SE	southeast
Co.	Company	Md.	Maryland	Sen.	Senator
Col.	Colonel	mi	miles	Sept	September
Conn.	Connecticut	Mich.	Michigan	Sgt.	Sergeant
d.	died	Minn.	Minnesota	sq mi	square miles
Dec	December	Miss.	Mississippi	SSE	south-southeast
Del.	Delaware	mm	millimeters	SSW	south-southwest
E	east, eastern	Mo.	Missouri	SW	southwest
EC	European Community	MP	Member of Parliament	Tenn.	Tennessee
				Tex.	Texas
e.g.	for example	mp	melting point	UN	United Nations
est	estimated	mph	miles per hour	US	United States
F	Fahrenheit	N	north, northern	USSR	Union of Soviet Socialist Republics
Feb	February	NATO	North Atlantic Treaty Organization		
Fl. Lt.	Flight Lieutenant			Va.	Virginia
Fla.	Florida	NE	northeast	Vt.	Vermont
ft	feet	Neb.	Nebraska	W	west, western
Ga.	Georgia	N.H.	New Hampshire	wt	weight
Gen.	General	N.J.	New Jersey		
Gov.	Governor				

mime Acting without words by physical gestures alone. It was practiced in ancient Greek and Roman drama and was an important constituent of the *commedia dell'arte in the 16th century. Modern mime was developed during the early 19th century in France by *Debureau and was revived in the 1920s by Etienne Decroux, whose pupils included Jean-Louis *Barrault and Marcel *Marceau.

MIME *Marcel Marceau in the role of Bip, at the Theâtre des Champs-Élysées, Paris.*

mimesis (Greek: imitation) A philosophical concept introduced by *Aristotle in the *Poetics*. He argues that imitation is the basis of all the arts but they differ as to the means they use and the objects they imitate. Thus, drama is the imitation of an action and the dramatic genres, tragedy and comedy, may be differentiated by their characters, who are either better (in tragedy) or worse (in comedy) than average humanity. Imitation in the arts does not refer to a simple realistic rendering of detail but to the poet's (or artist's) ability to select and present his material so as to express essential truth.

mimicry The phenomenon of two or more organisms (commonly different species) resembling each other closely, which confers an advantage—usually protection—to one or both of them. In **Batesian mimicry**, named for H. W. *Bates, a poisonous or inedible species (the model) has a conspicuous coloration, which acts as a warning to predators. This coloration is adopted by a harmless edible species (the mimic), which derives protection against the same predators. In **Müllerian mimicry**, first described by the German naturalist Fritz Müller (1821–97), two or more species—all inedible—have the same warning coloration. After a predator has associated this pattern with an inedible species it will learn not to select similarly colored species, resulting in a reduction in total mortality.

Mimosa A genus of trees, shrubs, and herbs (450–500 species), mostly native to tropical and subtropical America. They have feathery compound leaves and fluffy round catkins of yellow flowers. The genus includes the sensitive plants, *M. pudica* and *M. sensitiva*, of which the leaflets fold upward and the leafstalks droop at the slightest touch. Florists' mimosas are species of *Acacia* (*see* wattle). Family: **Leguminosae*.

Mina Hassan Tani. *See* Kenitra.

Minamoto Yoritomo (1147–99) Japanese military leader descended from a 9th-century emperor, who as the first **shogun (military overlord, 1192–99), laid the foundations of feudal government in Japan. After the defeat (1185) of the dominant **Taira clan, Yoritomo built up an extensive vassal network based on Kamakura, near modern Yokohama. In 1192 he obtained the title of shogun from the emperor and his administrative organization gradually moved from co-existence with the imperial government to dominance over it. His half-brother **Minamoto Yoshitsune** (1159–89) was a warrior whose flair and valor contributed greatly to the Minamoto triumph against the Taira but who subsequently incurred the suspicion or jealousy of Minamoto Yoritomo. His adventures before he was finally hunted down and committed suicide have captured the imagination of succeeding generations.

minaret A tall slender tower attached to a mosque from which the muezzin calls Muslims to prayer five times a day.

mind A philosophical term for whatever it is in a person that thinks, feels, wills, etc. Whether it is immaterial or not is controversial. **Materialism denies its existence as an incorporeal entity. For **Aristotle mind was *nous* (intellect), the only part of the soul to survive death. For **Descartes it is his starting point, an incorporeal mental substance by virtue of whose activity (thought) he knew he existed (*cogito ergo sum*—I think therefore I am). Until recently it has been usual to suppose that nonhuman animals do not have minds, the possession of mind being perhaps a defining characteristic of human beings. A more modern view identifies mental attitudes with brain states (*see* behaviorism).

Mindanao An island in the S Philippines, the second largest. Volcanic and rugged, soil erosion caused by indiscriminate tree felling is a serious problem. Hemp, maize, pineapples, timber, nickel, and gold are the chief products. *History*: the Muslim population has resisted Spanish, US, and now Philippine rule. Separatism, aggravated by rapid economic development in the 1960s, resulted in heavy fighting in 1975. A tribe with a Stone Age culture was discovered here in 1971. Area: 39,351 sq mi (101,919 sq km). Population (1990 est): 10,900,000. Chief towns: Davao and Zamboanga.

Minden 52 18N 8 54E A city in NW Germany, in North Rhine-Westphalia on the Weser River. In 1759 the English and Hanoverians defeated the French here. Its cathedral (11th–13th centuries) was rebuilt after World War II. Its varied manufactures include chemicals and glass. Population (1985): 80,000.

Mindoro A mountainous island in the central Philippines, S of Luzon. The chief products are timber and coal. Area: 3952 sq mi (10,236 sq km). Population (1980): 500,000. Chief town: Calapan.

Mindszenty, József, Cardinal (J. Pehm; 1892–1975) Hungarian Roman Catholic churchman. He was a vehement opponent of the Nazis and later the Communists, who imprisoned him in 1948. Released by the insurgents in the 1956 Hungarian Revolution, he gained asylum at the US legation in Budapest and eventually settled in Rome in 1971.

minerals Naturally occurring substances of definite chemical composition (although this may vary within limits). Some consist of a single element but most are compounds of at least two. Strictly defined, minerals are solid (except native mercury) and are inorganically formed, although the constituents of organic limestones, for instance, are considered minerals. The term is used loosely for any naturally occurring material that is of economic value, especially if it is obtained by mining, and the fossil fuels (of organic origin) are in this broader sense minerals. Almost all true minerals are crystalline; a few, such as opal, are amorphous. Minerals are identified by the following properties: crystal system (e.g. cubic) and habit or form (e.g. fibrous), hardness (*see* Mohs' scale), relative density, luster (e.g. metallic), color, streak (color when finely divided), *cleavage, and fracture. *Rocks are composed of mixtures of minerals. If a rock contains an economically extractable quantity of a mineral of commercial value, it constitutes a mineral deposit (*see* mining and quarrying). **Mineralogy** is the study of minerals (in the strict sense): their identification, classification, and formation.

Minerva A Roman goddess originally of the arts and the crafts of wisdom, later identified with the Greek *Athena. As goddess of war her importance almost equaled that of Mars. Her annual festival was the Quinquatrus, held in March.

minesweeper A powerful fast vessel equipped to cut the cables of floating mines. Partially submerged cables, attached to paravanes that keep them taut and at a desired angle to the boat, are towed through a minefield so that the cable, passing under the mines, cuts their anchor chains, allowing the mines to float so that they can be detonated by gunfire.

Ming (1368–1644) A native Chinese dynasty, which succeeded the Mongol Yüan dynasty. It was founded by *Hong Wu, the first of 17 Ming emperors. The Ming provided an era of stable government personally controlled by the emperor. The examination system to select bureaucrats was restored and overseas expeditions were encouraged. Painting and pottery, especially blue and white porcelain, flourished under the Ming, who built the Forbidden City in Peking in the 15th century.

Mingus, Charlie (1922–79) US African-American jazz musician, who experimented with atonality and dissonance in jazz. A double-bass player, he played with Louis Armstrong, Lionel Hampton, and others. He also led his own band and appeared in films.

Minho River. *See* Miño River.

miniature painting The art of painting on a very small scale, using watercolor on a vellum, card, or (from the 18th century) ivory base. The medieval Persian and Indian miniatures are the first great examples of the art. In Europe it flourished in the form of oval, circular, and occasionally rectangular portraits from the 16th to mid-19th centuries. There it developed from the medieval art of manuscript illumination (sometimes also called miniature painting) and *Renaissance portrait medals. Although *Holbein the Younger produced some miniatures, Nicholas *Hilliard in England was the first major specialist of the art. His portraits were often worn as jewelry. Other famous miniaturists were the Frenchmen Jean Clovet and Jean Fouquet in the 16th century, and the 17th- and 18th-century Englishmen Isaac Oliver, Samuel Cooper, and Richard Cosway. The Venetian Rosalba Carriera painted on ivory in the late 17th century. In the US, James Peale was the foremost miniaturist in the late 18th century.

Minicoy Islands. *See* Lakshadweep.

minimal art An abstract style of painting and sculpture developed in New York in the late 1960s. In reaction against the personal character of *action painting, it aims to eliminate artistic self-expression by reducing creativity to a minimum. This has been achieved by using simple hard-edged geometrical shapes and unmodulated vibrant colors. Leading minimalists include the painters Kenneth Noland (1924–) and Frank Stella (1936–) and the sculptor Carl André (1935–).

Minimata disease A form of mercury poisoning that killed 43 people in the Japanese town of Minimata between 1953 and 1956. The disease was contracted by eating fish contaminated with dimethyl mercury, derived from an effluent from a local PVC factory. The symptoms of mercury poisoning include tremors, paralysis, severe anemia, and bone deformities.

mining and quarrying The extraction of useful minerals from the earth's crust. Quarrying is usually regarded as the extraction of stone, sand, gravel, etc., from surface workings. Mining is the extraction by opencast or underground workings of ores producing metals (gold, silver, zinc, copper, lead, tin, iron, and uranium) and other valuable minerals (coal, limestone, asbestos, salt, precious stones, etc.); mining also includes the extraction of oil from wells and the extraction of alluvial deposits. Some 70% of mineral ores come from surface workings, which, using modern equipment, can reach down to depths of 1640 ft (500 m). After the overburden of rock or sand has been removed, the underlying mineral is blasted by explosives or broken up by machinery and excavated by power shovels, which load it onto conveyors or trucks. To comply with environmental requirements the overburden is often backfilled (deposited behind the current working face). In underground workings many factors have to be taken into account, such as the size, shape, and hardness of the deposit, the nature of the surrounding rock and the surface terrain, and the risk of subsidence. Ores are loosened and excavated by blasting, drilling, and mechanical shoveling. The waste material after the valuable ore has been extracted is often fed back into the mine (sometimes hydraulically, as a slurry) to reduce the risk of subsidence. *See also* coal mining; oil.

minivet An Asian songbird of the genus *Pericrocotus* (10 species), occurring in forests, where it hunts for insects in small flocks. Male minivets, about 7 in (17 cm) long, have a black-and-red plumage; the females are yellowish gray. Family: *Campephagidae* (cuckoo-shrikes and minivets).

mink A small carnivorous ☐mammal belonging to the genus *Mustela* (weasels, stoats, etc.), prized for its fur. The American mink (*M. vison*) is the largest species (about 27.5 in [70 cm] long) and has the most valuable fur. It is bred in captivity in many parts of the world, and escaped animals readily adapt to life in the wild. They are nocturnal, semi-aquatic, and efficient hunters both on land and in water, preying on fish, rodents, and waterfowl. Family: **Mustelidae*.

Minneapolis 45 00N 93 15W A city in Minnesota, on the Mississippi River. Adjacent to St Paul, the Twin Cities comprise the commercial, industrial, and financial center of a large grain and cattle area; flour milling is the main industry. Minneapolis is noted for its wide streets, many lakes, and parks. The University of Minnesota was established in 1851. Population (1990): 368,383.

Minnelli, Liza. *See* Garland, Judy.

Minnesingers (German: singers of love) Aristocratic German singing guilds that flourished in the 12th and 13th centuries; the German equivalent of the French *troubadours. Their decline coincided with the rise of the *Meistersingers.

Minnesota A midwestern US state bounded by Lake Superior and the states of Wisconsin on the E, Iowa on the S, South Dakota and North Dakota on the W, and Manitoba and Ontario, Canada, on the N. It consists of rolling prairies rising to the heavily forested, mineral-rich Superior Highlands in the N. Prehistoric glacial activity has left numerous lakes, the largest being the Lake of the Woods. Boulders, also remnants of the glacial age, strew the N hilly regions, giving way to the prairies in the S. Manufacturing industries (especially food processing) now form the most important sector of the economy. The high-grade iron ores, of which it was a major source, are virtually exhausted but mining remains important following new finds of copper and nickel. Agriculture, concentrated chiefly in the S, produces corn and soybeans. Tourism is an important source of revenue. *History*: first explored by the French in the mid-17th century. The Ojibwa and Sioux Indians inhabited the region at the time. Minnesota formed part of the Louisiana Purchase (1803). Settlers began to arrive in the 1820s; it became a state in 1858. Toward the end of the century many Scandinavian immigrants established homes in Minnesota, becoming a dominant influence in the development of the state. Agrarian reform groups took readily in rural Minnesota, where the Granger Movement was founded. The Populist party (which held that federal economic policy prejudiced agrarian interests) and the Farmer-Labor party (uniting farmers and organized labor) received widespread support in Minnesota. In 1944 the Farmer-Labor party merged with the Democratic party. Such national political leaders as Hubert Humphrey and Walter Mondale grew out of this political climate. Area: 84,068 sq mi (217,736 sq km). Population (1990): 4,375,099. Capital: St Paul.

MINK *An American mink. This species occurs naturally throughout North America (except in the arid US SW) and is also bred on farms.*

Minnesota River A river that flows from Big Stone Lake on the NE South Dakota–W central Minnesota border SE to Mankato, Minn., and NE to the St Paul area, where it joins the Mississippi River. It was once an important exploration and trading route. Length: 332 mi (535 km).

minnow One of several fish of the family *Cyprinidae*, especially *Phoxinus phoxinus*, found in clear fresh waters of Europe and N Asia. Its slim body is usually about 3 in (7.5 cm) long, has small scales, and ranges in color from gold to green. Order: *Cypriniformes*.

The name is also applied to various other small fish, including mudminnows (family *Umbridae*; order *Salmoniformes*) and *killifish.

Miño River (Portuguese name: Minho) A river in SW Europe. Rising in NW Spain, it flows mainly SSW, forming part of the border between Spain and Portugal, to the Atlantic Ocean. Length: 210 mi (338 km).

Minoan civilization The civilization of Bronze Age Crete, named by Sir Arthur *Evans after the legendary King *Minos. The most advanced Aegean civilization, the Minoan arose after 2500 BC. It is conventionally divided into three phases; Early (2500–2000), Middle (2000–1700), and Late (1700–1400). During the Middle Minoan period, palace building at *Knossos, Mallia, and Phaistos attests Crete's growing wealth. Around 1700 these structures were destroyed and replaced by grander ones, the centers of power in a marine empire covering the S Aegean. A catastrophic eruption on *Thera (c. 1450) ended Minoan prosperity as the sterile volcanic fallout temporarily ruined Crete's agriculture. Subsequent occupation levels show increasing Mycenaean influence (*see* Mycenaean civilization).

Excavated frescoes and artifacts show that Minoan material culture was highly sophisticated; craftsmen included skilled architects, potters, painters, stone cutters, goldsmiths, and jewelers. Three scripts were used: hieroglyphics (c. 1900–1700), *Linear A (c. 1700–1450), and *Linear B (c. 1450–1400). A prominent deity was a snake goddess; religious symbols of bulls' horns suggest ritual significance for the famous bull sports.

Minorca (Spanish name: Menorca) A Spanish island in the Mediterranean Sea, the second largest of the Balearic Islands. It is generally low lying and dry and agriculture is limited to livestock raising. Shoe manufacture is important and it has an expanding tourist industry. Area: 271 sq mi (702 sq km). Population (1985 est): 55,500. Chief town: Mahón.

minor planet. *See* asteroid.

Minos A legendary king of Crete, son of Zeus and Europa. His wife was Pasiphae, by whom he had two daughters, *Ariadne and *Phaedra. Although usually regarded as a good ruler, the Athenians portrayed him as a tyrant, who exacted an annual tribute of seven youths and seven maidens who were fed to the *Minotaur. According to Herodotus, he was killed in Sicily while pursuing *Daedalus after his escape from Crete. He is, with Rhadamanthus and Aeacus, one of the judges of the dead in Hades.

Minotaur In Greek legend, a Cretan monster with a bull's head and a man's body. It was the offspring of Pasiphae, wife of *Minos, and a bull with which Poseidon had caused her to become enamored. It was kept in the labyrinth built by *Daedalus and fed on Athenian youths and maidens sent in tribute to Minos. *Theseus killed it with the help of Ariadne.

Minsk 53 51N 27 30E The capital city of Belarus. Dating from at least the 11th century, it came under Lithuanian and then Polish rule; it was restored to Russia in 1793. It was virtually destroyed in World War II, and its large Jewish population exterminated during the German occupation. Its varied industries include machine and vehicle manufacturing, textiles, and food processing. It boasts a lively cultural life. Population (1991 est): 1,633,600.

mint An aromatic perennial herb of the genus *Mentha* (about 25 species), native to Eurasia and Australia and widely distributed throughout temperate and subtropical regions. It has creeping roots from which arise square stems, bearing simple toothed leaves and terminal clusters of purple, pink, or white flowers. Many species are grown in gardens for their fragrance or as culinary herbs, especially *peppermint and *spearmint: their leaves are used fresh or dried as flavoring. An oil extracted from mint stems and leaves is used in perfumes and medicines. Family: *Labiatae.

Mint Act (1792) US law that authorized the creation of the first official US mint. It provided for a mint in Philadelphia for gold and silver coinage and set ratio values on the metal content.

Mintoff, Dom(inic) (1916–) Maltese statesman; Labor prime minister (1955–58, 1971–85). He was an active proponent of Maltese independence from British rule, which was achieved in 1964.

Minton, Sherman (1890–1965) US jurist and politician; associate justice of the US Supreme Court (1949–56). He practiced law in Indiana (1916–25) and Florida (1925–29). He went on to become counselor of the Indiana Public Service Commission (1933–34), a Democratic US senator (1935–41), and US Circuit Court of Appeals judge (1941–49). He was primarily a conservative on the Supreme Court.

Minton ware Porcelain produced at the pottery founded (1796) by Thomas Minton (1765–1836) at Stoke (England). Famous for artistic and technical innovation, the Minton works still make fine porcelain. Remarkable products included imitation *majolica, tiles, and Parian (imitation marble) statuary.

minuet A court dance of the 17th and 18th centuries in triple time. Of rustic origin, it was often included in the instrumental suite and became part of the sonata and symphony in the works of Haydn, Mozart, etc. The first statement of the minuet was followed by a second minuet in a related key (called a trio), after which the first minuet was repeated.

Minya, El 28 06N 30 45E A port in N central Egypt, on the Nile River. It is an important link between the left bank of the Nile and the Bahr Yusuf Canal and trade includes cotton and flour. Population (1986): 179,136.

Miocene epoch. *See* Tertiary period.

Miquelon Island. *See* St Pierre et Miquelon.

Mirabeau, Honoré Gabriel Riquetti, Comte de (1749–91) French statesman. In the years before the *French Revolution he gained notoriety as a libertine and profligate. In 1789 he was elected to the States General, championing the cause of the Third Estate at the outbreak of the Revolution. However, he was out of sympathy with the growing republicanism, advocating the establishment of a constitutional monarchy on the British model. By 1790 he was coming under increasing attack from the *Jacobins but died of natural causes before a crisis was reached.

Mira Ceti A *red giant in the equatorial constellation Cetus that is a *variable star with a mean period of 331 days. Long known to vary considerably in brightness (by 5–6 magnitudes on average), it is the prototype of the **Mira stars**, which are all long-period pulsating variables.

miracle plays Medieval European dramas based on religious themes. In England, they flourished particularly in the 14th and early 15th centuries. A distinction between mystery plays (based on episodes in the Bible) and miracle plays (based on the lives of saints) is often made with regard to French examples of the genre, but in England the plays were almost invariably based on scriptural stories. They were originally performed in churches on religious holidays, especially Corpus Christi and Whitsuntide. They became increasingly secular in form and content and were eventually performed on mobile stages by trade guilds in public marketplaces. Almost complete cycles of plays from York, Coventry, Wakefield, and Chester have survived.

mirage An optical illusion sometimes observed on hot days. It is caused by the air near the ground being considerably hotter than the air above, causing refraction of light rays from the sky, since the refractive index of air depends on its density and therefore on its temperature. Thus rays near the horizon can be bent upward sufficiently to appear to be coming from the ground, creating the illusion of a lake.

Miranda v. Arizona (1966) US Supreme Court decision that upheld the rights of alleged criminals. It ruled that a suspect must be informed of right to counsel and that any statements obtained may be used as evidence for prosecution. It expanded the conditions set forth in *Escobedo* v. *Illinois*.

Miró, Joan (1893–1983) Surrealist painter, born in Barcelona. He moved to Paris (1919), where he participated in the first surrealist exhibition (1925) and began painting in a childlike style under the influence of dreams and poetry. The gaiety of his painting disappeared in the late 1930s with his "savage" paintings, expressing the horrors of the Spanish Civil War; it reappeared, however, in his *Constellations*, painted (during World War II) with his characteristic amebic shapes intertwined with threadlike lines. He is also known for his ballet sets, murals, and sculptures.

mirrors Devices for reflecting light, usually consisting of a sheet of glass with one surface silvered. A plane mirror, in which the sheet is flat, forms a laterally inverted virtual image. Spherical mirrors, concave or convex, magnify or reduce the image. If the distances of the object and image from the mirror surface are u and v, then $1/u + 1/v = 1/f$, where f is the focal length of the mirror, taking all distances as positive in front of the mirror and negative behind it. To avoid spherical aberration, parabolic mirrors are used in reflecting *telescopes.

miscarriage. *See* abortion.

misch metal An *alloy of between 15% and 40% iron with cerium and other rare metals. When rubbed with an abrasive it produces sparks and it is used for flints in cigarette lighters. The name comes from the German *Mischmetall*, mixed metal.

misdemeanor. *See* felony.

Mishima, Yukio (Kimitake Hiraoka; 1925–70) Japanese novelist and playwright of international fame. He also acted in several films. His novels, which include *Confessions of a Mask* (1948) and *Sun and Steel* (1970), dealt with homosexuality, death, suicide, and the importance of traditional Japanese military values. He organized his own military group, the Shield Society, and in 1970 shocked the world by committing harakiri as a protest against the weakness of postwar Japan.

Mishnah (Hebrew: instruction) An early code of Jewish law. Written in Hebrew, it is traditionally thought to have been based on earlier compilations and edited in Palestine by the ethnarch Judah I in the early 3rd century AD. It consists of *halakhah on a wide range of subjects, derived partly from biblical law as interpreted by the early rabbis (called *Tannaim*) and partly from customs that had grown up over a long period of time. *See also* Talmud.

Miskolc 48 07N 20 47E A city in NE Hungary. It has much fine architecture including a 13th-century gothic church and the National Theater. The Technical University of Heavy Industry was established in 1949. A major industrial center, its manufactures include iron, steel, and chemicals. Population (1991 est): 194,033.

missiles. *See* antiballistic missiles; ballistic missiles; guided missiles; Polaris missile.

Missionary Ridge, Battle of (1863) US Civil War battle in S Tennessee, part of the Chattanooga Campaign. After the Battle of *Lookout Mountain, the Union troops under Generals Joseph *Hooker, William T. *Sherman, and George H. Thomas assaulted Missionary Ridge, broke the Confederate hold, and gained complete control of Chattanooga for the Union.

missions, Christian Enterprises to spread the Christian faith among those who profess other religions or none. The missionary journeys of St *Paul and the Apostles set an example that Christian individuals and organizations have followed ever since. St *Patrick, St *Columba, and St *Augustine of Canterbury were outstanding early missionaries in the British Isles. Isolated medieval missions reached as far as China, but concentrated activity began only with the discovery of the Americas and the sea route around Africa in the late 15th century. Roman Catholic orders, such as the *Dominicans, *Franciscans, and *Jesuits, made substantial conversions, especially in the 17th century, but Protestant denominations, with the exception of the *Moravian Brethren, did not enter the field in force until the 1790s. The 19th century was the peak period of activity with mission stations being established in even the most inaccessible regions. Developing countries frequently recognize the value of this work, which generally includes training in literary, practical, and medical skills, and allow missions to remain in the postcolonial period, although sometimes in conditions of great hardship and danger. Missionary attempts are now felt, ironically, to be necessary against the indifference and materialism of the Western world.

Mississippi A state in the S central US, on the Gulf of Mexico. Located in the Deep South, Mississippi is bordered by Alabama to the E, the Gulf of Mexico to the S, Arkansas and Louisiana to the W (with the Mississippi River forming most of the boundary), and Tennessee to the N. Mainly low lying, it consists of the cotton-producing alluvial plain of the Mississippi River (the Mississippi Delta) in the W, an area of extensive swamps in the SW, and a generally infertile region of low hills in the E and NE. The predominantly rural population (only one-fourth of the population lives in urban areas) has a large African-American community (35% of the total population), giving Mississippi the highest proportion of African Americans to whites of any state. Still an important agricultural state, its main products are cotton and soybeans, which have superseded cotton in importance. Manufacturing has grown steadily, and in 1965 surpassed agriculture in contribution to revenue. Ship construction and repair is the main industry, with timber and paper products, textiles, chemicals, and food processing also major sources of income. Petroleum is the chief mineral; natural gas, clay, and sand and gravel are also exploited. Mississippi remains, however, one of the country's poorest states. *History*: first visited by De Soto for Spain. Upon his arrival, the indigenous inhabitants were Choctaw, Chickasaw, and Natchez Indians. The French claimed Mississippi and established the first permanent settlement (1690). In 1763, England received Mississippi along with most of the French territory E of the Mississippi River by the Treaty of Paris. Traffic along the Natchez Trace brought settlers to Mississippi. As a cotton state based on slave holdings, Mississippi joined the southern cause in the Civil War. Jefferson Davis, a native son, became president of the Confederacy. After the Civil War, Mississippi enacted the notorious "Jim Crow" laws, which in effect disenfranchised its African-American population. The civil rights movement of the 1960s drew world attention to Mississippi, one of the most segregated states in the US. Gov. Ross Barnett gained notoriety when he attempted to block the entrance of an African-American student into the University of Mississippi. By the 1980s the African-American vote had become significant, and African Americans occupied state office in substantial numbers. Area: 47,716 sq mi (123,584 sq km). Population (1990): 2,573,216. Capital: Jackson.

Mississippian period. *See* Carboniferous period.

Mississippi River A river in the central US, the second longest river in North America. Rising in N Minnesota, it flows generally S into the Gulf of Mexico, through several channels (known as the Passes). Together with its chief tributary, the Missouri River, it forms the third longest river system in the world, at 3759 mi (6050 km) long with the world's third-largest drainage basin, covering 1,243,753 sq mi (3,222,000 sq km). Because of the danger of flooding, the lower course has high artificial embankments (levees), many of which overflowed in 1993 floods. Famous for its steamboats, celebrated by Mark Twain, it is now one of the world's busiest commercial waterways, with major ports at St Louis and New Orleans. Length: 3780 km (2348 mi).

Missolonghi (Modern Greek name: Mesolóngion) A town in W Greece, on the Gulf of Patras. It is famous for its defense against the Turks during the War of Greek Independence (1821–29). Lord Byron died here in 1824. Population: 11,614.

Missouri A midwestern state in the central US, lying immediately W of the Mississippi River. It is bounded by Illinois, Kentucky, and Tennessee in the E (where the Mississippi River forms the boundary); Arkansas on the S; Oklahoma, Kansas, and Nebraska on the W; and Iowa on the N. It is divided by the Missouri River (which joins the Mississippi at St Louis) into fertile prairies and rolling hills in the N and W and the hills of the Ozark plateau in the S. Highly urbanized, much of its population lives in the two main cities of St Louis and Kansas City. Manufacturing dominates the economy, with transport and aerospace equipment, food processing, chemicals, and printing and publishing. The leading lead producer in the US, it also exploits barite, iron ore, and zinc deposits. Agriculture is diversified, producing livestock, dairy products, soybeans, corn, wheat, cotton, and sorghum grains. *History*: claimed by La Salle for France in 1682; at the time the Osage and Missouri Indians inhabited the region. It was ceded to Spain (1783) before returning to France in 1800. It formed part of the Louisiana Purchase (1803). St Louis, because of its strategic position, became the gateway to the west, experiencing enormous growth with the advent of steamboat traffic on its two great rivers. The question of Missouri's admittance to the US as a state became the focus of the slavery debate in 1820–21. Missouri's entrance as a slave state (most of the inhabitants were southerners) would have balanced slave and free states. Legislative attempts to emancipate the slaves in Missouri met with sharp opposition, and prolonged controversy over the issue greatly increased sectionalism. The ultimate solution, the *Missouri Compromise, authorized Missouri to adopt a constitution with no restrictions on slavery but prohibited any curtailment of the rights of any US citizens. Missouri was admitted to the Union as a slave state in 1821. The arrival of the railroads and subsequent immigration (most notably thousands of Germans in the 1840s and 1850s) expanded settlement. Missouri fought with the Union during the Civil War. The guerrilla warfare that had characterized fighting in Missouri led to the proliferation of gangs of outlaws after the war, among them the notorious Jesse and Frank James. Industry gradually came to surpass the agrarian sector in importance, particularly with the rise of the automobile industry. Area: 69,686 sq mi (180,486 sq km). Population (1990): 5,117,073. Capital: Jefferson City.

Missouri Compromise (1820) US laws that admitted Missouri as a slave state and Maine as a free state to the Union in order to maintain a balance in the

Senate. Guided through Congress by Henry *Clay, the compromise also prohibited slavery north of 36° 30" in the Louisiana Purchase territory, with the exception of Missouri.

Missouri River A river in the central US, the longest river in North America and chief tributary of the Mississippi River. Rising in the Rocky Mountains, it flows N and E through Montana, then SE across North and South Dakota before joining the Mississippi at St Louis. A series of dams provides irrigation and has considerably reduced the danger of flooding along its lower course. Length: 2714 mi (4367 km).

Mistinguett (Jeanne-Marie Bourgeois; 1875–1956) French singer and comedienne. She was a leading star of the Moulin Rouge, the Folies-Bergère, and other Paris music halls between the wars. She performed with elaborate costumes and settings, often in company with Maurice *Chevalier.

mistle thrush A heavily built thrush, *Turdus viscivorus*, of Eurasia and NW Africa. It is about 11 in (28 cm) long and has a grayish-brown upper plumage with a thickly speckled yellowish breast and white underwings. It feeds on berries (especially mistletoe—hence its name), snails, and worms.

mistletoe A semiparasitic evergreen shrub of the temperate and tropical family *Loranthaceae* (1300 species), growing on the branches of many trees. The Eurasian mistletoe (*Viscum album*) occurs mainly on apple trees, poplars, willows, and hawthorns. It has rootlike suckers, which penetrate into the host tissues, and woody branching stems, 24–35 in (60–90 cm) long, bearing oval leathery leaves and yellow male and female flowers borne on separate plants. The female flowers give rise to white berries, which are eaten by birds (which thereby disperse the seeds).

Mistletoe was once believed by the Druids to have magic powers and medicinal properties and is a traditional Christmas decoration.

mistral A cold dry northerly wind that is funneled down the Rhône Valley in S France to the Mediterranean Sea. Thick hedges and tree screens orientated E–W protect crops from its force.

Mistral, Frédéric (1830–1914) French poet. In 1854 he helped found the Félibrige, a movement dedicated to the regeneration of Provençal language and culture. His many works in the Provençal vernacular include the epic verse narratives *Mirèio* (1859) and *Lou Pouèmo dóu Rose* (1897). He won the Nobel Prize in 1905.

Mistral, Gabriela (Lucila Godoy Alcayaga; 1889–1957) Chilean poet, who worked as a teacher and cultural ambassador. Her volumes of poetry include *Desolación* (1922), published after the suicide of her fiancé, *Tala* (1938), and *Lagar* (1954). She was awarded the Nobel Prize in 1945.

Mitchell, George John (1933–   ) U.S. senator (1982–   ) and Senate majority leader (1989–   ). A Democrat from Maine, he gained recognition for his calming influence during the Iran–Contra hearings in 1987 and became known for his honesty and his willingness to accommodate. A lawyer, he was executive assistant to Sen. Edmund S. Muskie from 1962.

Mitchell, Margaret (1909–49) US novelist. Her single novel, the international best-seller *Gone with the Wind* (1936), is a historical romance set in Georgia during and after the Civil War. She was awarded a Pulitzer Prize in 1937. The film *Gone With the Wind* (1939) was one of the most popular ever made.

Mitchell, William ("Billy"; 1879–1936) US flier; born in France of American parents. During World War I he commanded US aviation forces and returned a war hero. Always an advocate of air power, he became assistant chief of the air service (1919) and was made a brigadier general (1920). Outspoken in his campaign for increased air power, he was relegated, as a colonel, to San Antonio (1925) where he continued his criticism. When the navy dirigible *Shenandoah* was lost in a storm (1925), he publicly criticized the inadequacies of the war and navy departments. His accusations resulted in a court-martial, a five-year suspension, and his resignation (1926). His predictions realized, he was awarded, posthumously, a special congressional medal (1948).

Mitchell, Mount 35 46N 82 16W A mountain in W central North Carolina, in the Black Mountains. It is the highest point (6684 ft; 2038 m) in the United States E of the Mississippi River.

mite A tiny *arachnid (up to 0.24 in [6 mm] long) comprising—with the *ticks—the worldwide order *Acarina* (or *Acari*; over 20,000 species). It has an unsegmented body and eight bristly legs. Mites occur in great abundance in a wide range of habitats, including soil, stored foods, fresh and salt water, plants, and decaying organic material; some are parasitic on animals. They can become serious pests and may also transmit diseases (including *typhus). *See also* harvest mite; itch mite; spider mite.

Mithra A Persian god of light, truth, and justice. He killed a cosmic bull, whose blood was the source of all animals and plants. The cult of *Mithraism flourished in the Roman Empire from the 2nd century AD, especially in the army, until the official adoption of Christianity in the 4th century.

Mithraism A mystery religion (*see* mysteries) that worshiped Mithra, the Persian god of the sun who represented justice and goodness. It spread through Asia Minor, finally reaching Rome in about 68 BC. Here Mithra was known as Mithras and was worshiped widely among Roman soldiers. He was regarded as the eternal enemy of evil, whose sacrifice of a bull symbolized the regeneration of life. Part of the cult's initiation ceremony was a bath in a sacrificed bull's blood. Mithraism rivaled Christianity until its decline in the 3rd century AD. Remains of a Roman temple to Mithras were discovered (1954) in London; parts of it can still be seen.

Mithridates VI Eupator (120–63 BC) King of Pontus and one of Rome's most persistent enemies. Mithridates extended his kingdom by invading Colchis and Lesser Armenia, antagonizing Rome by proceeding to Paphlagonia, Cappadocia, and Greece. Sulla, Lucullus, and Pompey in turn opposed him in three Mithridatic Wars (88–84, 83–81, 74–64) and he finally committed suicide.

mitochondria Granular rod-shaped structures that occur in the cytoplasm of nearly all □cells. They contain various enzymes that function in cellular *respiration and the metabolism of fat, glycogen, proteins, etc., to produce energy. Therefore in very active cells (i.e. those requiring more energy), such as heart muscle, mitochondria are large and numerous.

mitosis The process by which the nucleus of a somatic cell (i.e. any cell that is not a germ cell) duplicates itself exactly, producing two daughter nuclei with chromosomes that are identical to those of the parent nucleus. This nuclear division involves the separation of the two chromatids of each chromosome, which move apart to form two groups at opposite ends of the cell. In the final phase each group becomes enclosed in a new nuclear membrane. After this the cytoplasm usually divides to form two new cells. Mitosis occurs in most animals and plants during the normal growth and repair of tissues. *Compare* meiosis.

Mittelland Canal (*or* Ems-Weser-Elbe-Kanal) A canal in central Europe. Opened in 1938, it links the Dortmund-Ems Canal in W Germany with the Elbe River in E Germany. Length: 202 mi (325 km).

Mitterrand, François (Maurice) (1916–) French socialist politician; president (1981–). He held ministerial posts from 1947. He was president of a democratic-socialist union (1965–68) and in 1971 assumed leadership of the newly unified Socialist party. After two unsuccessful runs for the French presidency (1965, 1974) he defeated Giscard d'Estaing in 1981 to become the first socialist president in 35 years and then defeated Jacques Chirac in 1988.

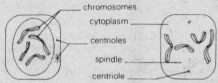

prophase *The genetic material becomes visible in the form of chromosomes and the nuclear membrane disappears.*

metaphase *The chromosomes become attached to the equator of a fibrous spindle.*

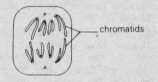

anaphase *The two chromatids of each chromosome move to opposite poles of the spindle.*

telophase *Nuclear membranes form around the two groups of chromatids, which become less distinct.*

MITOSIS *Division of the nucleus of an animal cell takes place in four phases, which grade into each other.*

mixed economy An economy in which there is neither complete capitalist control of resources, nor complete government control. Examples are the democracies of W Europe.

The aim in establishing mixed economies is to temper the "unacceptable face" of capitalism with its incentives and its efficient allocation of resources. Although some critics assert that mixed economies maintain the worst evils of capitalism, their undeniable capacity for economic growth has substantially improved the lot of the poorer sections of society. In mixed economies, governments seek to control the public services, the basic industries (e.g. coal and steel), and those enterprises that cannot raise adequate capital investment from private sources. This arrangement enables a measure of economic planning to be combined with a measure of free enterprise. In recent years some governments have intervened in the private sector to safeguard jobs in major industries (e.g. ship building, automobile manufacturing, etc.).

Mixtecs An American Indian people originating in W Oaxaca province (S Mexico). After the 10th century they gradually absorbed the neighboring *Zapotecs. The Mixtecs were excellent craftsmen, whose skill in gold working, mosaics, pottery, and painting spread over much of Mesoamerica, influencing both *Maya and *Aztec art styles.

Mizoguchi Kenji (1898–1956) Japanese film director. His films are characterized by a controlled visual style and by a persistent concern with the psychology of women. They include *The Life of O'Haru* (1952), *Ugetsu Monogatari* (1953), and *Street of Shame* (1956).

Mizoram A state of NE India, in tropical hills between Bangladesh and Myanmar. Its largely Christian tribes are subsistence farmers of rice, sugar, and potatoes. Mizoram was separated from Assam (1972), following the activities of secessionist factions. Area: 8195 sq mi (21,230 sq km). Population (1991): 686,217. Capital: Aijal.

m.k.s. system A system of *metric units based on the meter, kilogram, and second. It has now been replaced for scientific purposes by *SI units, which are derived from it. The main difference between the two systems is that in SI units, the m.k.s electrical units are rationalized (i.e. the factor 4π or 2π is introduced when it is demanded by the geometry).

Mnemosyne In Greek mythology, a daughter of the *Titans Uranus and Gaea. She is the personification of memory. After sleeping with Zeus for nine consecutive nights she gave birth to the *Muses.

moa An extinct flightless bird belonging to an order (*Dinornithiformes*; about 25 species) that occurred in New Zealand. Moas were 24–118 in (60–300 cm) tall and had a small head, a long neck, and long stout legs. They were fast runners but were hunted by early Polynesian settlers for food. Members of some smaller species may have survived until the 19th century.

Moabites A highly civilized Semitic tribe living E of the Dead Sea from the late 14th century BC. Closely associated ethnically with their neighbors and rivals, the Israelites, they successfully rebelled against Israelite occupation in the 9th century BC. In 582 BC, according to Josephus, they were conquered by the Babylonians. The Moabite Stone, found at Dibon near Amman (Jordan) in 1868 and dating to the 9th century BC, bears an inscription (in the Moabite alphabet) celebrating a Moabite victory against the Israelites.

Mobile 30 12N 88 00W A seaport in Alabama, on Mobile Bay at the mouth of the Mobile River. Founded in 1710, it was occupied by the French, British, and Spanish before being seized for the US in 1813 during the War of 1812. Industries include ship building, oil refining, textiles, and chemicals. Population (1990): 196,278.

Möbius strip In *topology, a one-sided surface with only one edge, made by taking a strip of paper, twisting it once and joining the ends. If cut in two lengthwise, it remains in one piece but with no twist. It was discovered by the German astronomer August Ferdinand Möbius (1780–1868).

Mobutu, Lake (former name: Lake Albert) A lake in Uganda and Zaïre. Discovered for Europeans by Baker in 1864, it is some 100 mi (160 km) long and is drained to the N by the Albert Nile River. Area: about 2064 sq mi (5346 sq km).

Mobutu, Sese Seko (Joseph Désiré M.; 1930–) Zaïrese statesman; president (1970–), having come to power in 1965 in a coup. In 1967 he founded the country's only political party—the Popular Movement of the Revolution—and the stability of his authoritarian government is fostered by his personal cult, Mobutuism.

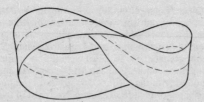

MÖBIUS STRIP *A surface with one side and one edge.*

moccasin (snake). *See* water moccasin.

Mocenigo A Venetian family from which came many of the *doges of the Venetian Republic. They included **Tommaso Mocenigo** (1343–1423), doge (1414–23); his nephew **Pietro Mocenigo** (1406–76), who was a distinguished admiral as well as doge (1474–76); Pietro's brother **Giovanni Mocenigo** (1408–85), doge (1478–85); and Giovanni's grandson **Andrea Mocenigo** (1473–1542), a historian.

Mocha (*or* Al Mukha) 13 20N 43 16E A town in W Yemen, on the Red Sea coast. It was famous for its export of high-quality coffee but declined following the rise of coffee growing in South America and Java in the early 18th century. Population: 5000.

mock epic A form of satiric verse that exposes the absurdity or worthlessness of a trivial subject or theme by treating it in the elevated style appropriate to a genuine *epic. The form originated in classical literature and was practiced by neoclassical writers in the late 17th and early 18th centuries. Examples include *Le Lutrin* (1674–83) by *Boileau and *The Rape of the Lock* (1712–14) and the *Dunciad* (1728–43) by *Pope.

mockingbird A songbird that belongs to an American family (*Mimidae*; 30 species) and is noted for its ability to mimic sounds. Mockingbirds live on or near the ground, feeding on insects and fruit. They were once prized as cage-birds. The common mockingbird (*Mimus polyglottus*), which ranges from S Canada to S Mexico, is about 10 in (25 cm) long with gray plumage and white wing bars.

mock orange A shrub, also called syringa, belonging to the genus *Philadelphus* (75 species), native to N temperate regions and commonly cultivated for ornament. They have simple leaves and fragrant white flowers resembling orange blossom. *P. coronarius* is the only native European species. Family: *Philadelphaceae*.

Modena (ancient name: Mutina) 44 39N 10 55E A city in N Italy, in Emilia-Romagna. Ruled by the Este family (1288–1860), it has an 11th-century romanesque cathedral, several palaces, and an ancient university (1175). The center of a rich agricultural area, its industries include agricultural engineering, textiles, and motor vehicles. Population (1991 est): 177,501.

modern art The art of the late 19th and 20th centuries, which has largely abandoned traditional subjects, aesthetic standards, and techniques of art. The development of modern art was stimulated by the decline of artistic patronage by church and state, giving the artist more freedom to experiment. These experiments have largely centered on the use of color and form as properties in their own right and not only as a means to mirror the real world (*see* photography). They can be traced back to *Manet and the impressionists. *Cézanne began the dissolution of one of the main foundations of Western painting since the Renaissance—the use of linear *perspective. It was completed by *cubism in the early 20th century. Variations of cubism were *futurism in Italy and *vorticism in England but in Russia it developed into a completely nonrepresentational geometric art in the form of *suprematism and *constructivism. Suprematism, constructivism, and neoplasticism (*see* Stijl, de) were highly influential in the 1920s at the German *Bauhaus school of design and geometric abstraction is still a leading artistic trend today in the form of *op art and *minimal art. Color used for its own sake was a major feature of French *fauvism in the early 1900s. Die *Brucke, the German counterpart of fauvism, was also part of another modern movement—*expressionism. However, these two trends were fused in the first abstract painting, which was produced by Kandinsky in about 1910. His heir in the 1940s, when the center of modern art shifted to New York City, was Jackson *Pollock, the inventor of *action painting. Other movements have explored modern concerns, such as the value of art (*see* dada), the world of dreams and the subconscious (*see* surrealism), and the role of the mass media in society (*see* pop art). *See also* abstract art; sculpture.

Modern Art, Museum of An art gallery in New York City devoted to late 19th- and 20th-century painting. Its extremely comprehensive collection contains major works from all significant movements in Europe and the US of the last century. It was opened in 1929.

modern dance A form of theatrical dance developed in central Europe and the US in the early 20th century in reaction to the technical virtuosity and fairy-tale subjects of *ballet. The early pioneers were the German dancers Kurt Joos and Mary Wigman and the US dancers Ruth St Denis and her husband, Ted Shawn, Isadora *Duncan, and Martha *Graham.

Modern dance has developed new kinds of movements to express feeling, particularly jerking, thrusting, and contracting movements. It is usually performed in simple clothing against austere scenery. Some of today's leading ballet choreographers, notably *Béjart, *Robbins, Merce Cunningham, Paul Tayler, Alvin Ailey, and Twyla Tharp have been influenced by modern dance.

Modernism A movement among Roman Catholic theologians that arose independently in several countries in the late 19th century. Its adherents sought to bring Roman Catholic thinking into harmony with modern philosophical and scientific trends and in particular with the new critical approach to the Bible. The historical accuracy of the Bible and the problems of dogmatic theology were held to be relatively unimportant. Pope Pius X condemned the movement officially in 1907 and many Modernist clergy were excommunicated.

modes Musical scales derived from ancient Greek music, on which European music was based up to the 16th century. Each mode consists of a different pattern of the five tones and two semitones of the octave; the patterns can be clearly demonstrated using the white notes of the piano keyboard. Some of the most common modes were the Ionian (C-C), the Dorian (D-D), the Lydian (F-F), and the Aeolian (A-A). The Ionian and Aeolian modes became the basis of the major and minor scales of the 17th century and after.

Modesto 37 39N 121 00W A city in central California, SE of Sacramento and E of San Francisco, on the Tuolumne River. Situated at the N end of the San Joaquin Valley, it serves as a processing center for the valley's farm goods and livestock. Wine is also produced. Population (1990): 164,730.

Modigliani, Amedeo (1884–1920) Italian painter and sculptor, born in Livorno of Jewish origin. His mature work, executed in Paris (1906–20), was influenced by *Cézanne and *Brancusi and, in its angular and elongated character, by Negro masks. From 1909 to 1915 he worked chiefly on sculptures; from

1915 until his death from tuberculosis, aggravated by drink and drug addiction, he painted many nudes and portraits.

Modigliani, Franco (1918–) US economist, winner of the Nobel Prize in economics (1985). Born in Rome, Italy, he came to the US during World War II and taught at various universities before becoming a professor at Massachusetts Institute of Technology. He was awarded the Nobel Prize for his work on the "life cycle theory," an analysis of people's savings.

Modoc North American Shapwailutan-speaking Indian tribe, similar to the Klamath Indians and found by the lakes of NE California and S Oregon. Known for their woven baskets, they fiercely defended their lands in the 1860s but were forced to live, side by side, on an Oregon reservation with their enemy, the Klamath. The Modoc Wars (or Lava Bed Wars; 1872–73), in which renegade Modocs attempted to leave the reservation, resulted in federal imprisonment. About 350 Modoc live on Quapaw Reservation in Oklahoma.

modulation A method of carrying information (the signal) on an electromagnetic wave or an oscillating electric current. In **amplitude modulation** (AM) the amplitude of a carrier wave is changed according to the magnitude of the signal. This is used in medium-wave sound broadcasting in which audio-frequencies (50–20,000 hertz) are carried on radio waves with a frequency of about one megahertz. In **frequency modulation** (FM) the frequency of the carrier wave is changed within a small bandwidth of the reference frequency. FM is used in VHF *radio (about 100 megahertz). Its main advantage over AM is its better signal-to-noise ratio.

In **pulse modulation** the carrier is a series of pulses. It is used in digital equipment, such as computers, and in telegraphy and telemetry. A continuous signal alters the height in pulse-amplitude modulation, the width in pulse-duration modulation, or the time between pulses in pulse-position modulation. Pulse-code modulation uses a coded pattern of pulses to carry the signal, e.g. in *Morse code.

Moers 51 27N 6 36E A city in NW Germany, in North Rhine-Westphalia in the *Ruhr. It grew rapidly in the 20th century as a coal mining center. Population (1988 est): 102,000.

Mogadishu (*or* Mogadiscio) 2 01N 45 25E The capital and main port of Somalia, on the Indian Ocean. It was founded as an Arab settlement in the 10th century and sold to Italy in 1905, becoming the capital of Italian Somaliland. It has a university (1969). It is the chief commercial center of the republic. During the civil war in the early 1990s, the city was heavily damaged. Population (1988): 1,000,000.

Mogilev 53 54N 30 20E A city in Belarus, on the Dnepr River. Founded in 1267, it passed to Lithuania and then to Poland before being annexed by Russia (1772). It produces metal goods, machinery, and chemicals. Population (1987): 359,000.

Mogul art and architecture A style that developed in N India under the patronage of the Mogul emperors. Originally much indebted to *Persian art, Mogul painting developed a more naturalistic style with small-scale scenes of court life and natural history as favored subjects. Book illustration was highly developed. Architecture reached its peak during the reign (1556–1605) of *Akbar, when attempts were made to fuse the opposing traditions of the indigenous Hindu architecture, characterized by solid rocklike masses and use of beams in building, with the Islamic tradition of mathematical clarity in design and use of true arches and internal spaces in construction (*see* Fatehpur Sikri). *See also* Indian art and architecture; Taj Mahal.

Moguls An Indian Muslim dynasty, descended from the Mongol leader
*Genghis Khan, that ruled from 1526 until 1858. Its founder was *Babur
(reigned 1526–30); he and the first 5 of his 18 successors, Humayun (1508–56;
reigned 1530–56), *Akbar (reigned 1556–1605), *Jahangir (1605–27), *Shah
Jahan (1627–58), and *Aurangzeb (1658–1707), are known as the Great
Moguls, and by the time of Aurangzeb the Empire spread from the far N to the
far S of India. During the late 17th and the 18th centuries Mogul power declined
in the face of opposition from Hindus to religious intolerance and of European
commercial expansion. The last emperor, Bahadur Shah II (1775–1862; reigned
1837–58), was deposed after the *Indian Mutiny and exiled to Burma.

MOGUL ART AND ARCHITECTURE *An example of late
Mogul painting, depicting dancers and musicians performing a nautch, a traditional Indian dance, inside a European
palace.*

Mohács, Battle of (August 29, 1526) The battle in which the Ottoman Turks
under *Suleiman the Magnificent defeated a vastly outnumbered Hungarian and
Bohemian army. The battle led to the submission of Hungary to Ottoman overrule.

mohair A wool-like fabric or yarn manufactured from the hair of *Angora
goats. Warm, light, and durable and frequently blended with wool, silk, or cotton, mohair is used for lightweight suiting, upholstery, and fluffy fashion
knitwear.

Mohammed (*or* Muhammad; c. 570–632 AD) According to Muslims, the last
of the prophets and preacher of *Islam to the Arabs. Mohammed is said to have
been born in Mecca, a member of the Quraysh clan, which dominated the town.
In 610, when he was about 40, he received revelations from God and called upon
his pagan fellow townsmen to prepare for the Last Day and to repent. The Meccans rejected him and threatened his life and in 622 he fled to Yathrib (*see* He-
gira), where he established the first Muslim community and began to spread
Islam. Yathrib now came to be called Medina, "City of the Prophet." By 629 the
Muslims in Medina were strong enough to defeat the still-pagan Meccans and
obtained control of Mecca. By the time of Mohammed's death, Islam had begun
to spread throughout Arabia. Mohammed's revelations were collected after his
death to form the *Koran. His tomb is venerated in the mosque at Medina.

Mohammed I Askia (d. 1538) Ruler of the West African empire of Songhai (1493–1528), which reached its greatest extent under his rule. He controlled the trade routes to North Africa and was an able administrator. An enthusiastic Muslim, he made the pilgrimage to Mecca in 1495–97.

Mohammed II (1430–81) Sultan of the Ottoman Empire (1451–81). Known as the Conqueror, his fame rests mainly on his conquest in 1453 of Constantinople, which as *Istanbul became the Ottoman capital. He also extended Ottoman territories in the Balkans and Asia Minor.

Mohammed Reza Pahlavi (1918–80) Shah of Iran (1941–79). He became shah when the Allies forced his father *Reza Shah Pahlavi, to abdicate in World War II. In 1979 civil war forced him into exile and an Islamic republic was established in Iran under the leadership of Ayatollah Khomeini.

Mohawk An Iroquoian-speaking American Indian tribe of New York state. They were one of the five tribes that formed the league of the *Iroquois, said to have been founded by the Mohawk chief *Hiawatha. Their culture was typical of that of the neighboring Iroquois tribes.

Mohegan North American Algonkian-speaking Indian tribe, found in E Connecticut, along the Thames River. United with the *Pequot under one chief, Sarcassus, they fought the English settlers in the *Pequot War (1637); under *Uncas, the Mohegan conquered other tribes and occupied most of S New England. A few remaining Mohegan live in Norwich, Conn.

Mohenjo-Daro The site in Sind (Pakistan) of a great city of the □Indus Valley civilization. First excavated in the 1920s, it has extensive brick-built remains. *See also* Harappa.

Mohican An Algonkian-speaking American Indian tribe of New England. Primarily cultivators, they lived in fortified communities of 20 to 30 houses or in enclosed villages, but were displaced by wars with the Mohawks. Each of their five tribal sections was governed by a chief (sachem) together with an elected council.

Mohole An unsuccessful research project embarked upon with US government funds but abandoned in 1966 because of its enormous cost. The aim was to obtain samples of the rocks of the earth's upper mantle by drilling down from the ocean floor through the crust to the *Mohorovičić discontinuity. Drilling was undertaken off W Mexico but the technological difficulties proved enormous.

Moholy-Nagy, László (1895–1946) Hungarian artist. His most influential work was produced while teaching at the *Bauhaus (1923–29), where his experimental abstract paintings and photographs culminated in his *Light-Space Modulators*, plastic mechanical constructions designed to show continuously changing effects of light. His last years were spent teaching in Chicago.

Mohorovičić discontinuity The boundary between the earth's crust and upper mantle, marked by a sudden increase in velocity in seismic waves as the denser mantle is reached. It lies at a depth of 20–22 mi (33–35 km) beneath the continents and 3–6 mi (5–10 km) beneath the oceans. It is named for the Croatian scientist Andrija Mohorovičić (1857–1936), who discovered it in 1909.

Mohs' scale A scale of hardness of minerals named for the mineralogist Friedrich Mohs (1773–1839). The 10 standard minerals in the scale, in ascending order of hardness, are: 1. talc, 2. gypsum, 3. calcite, 4. fluorite, 5. apatite, 6. orthoclase feldspar, 7. quartz, 8. topaz, 9. corundum, and 10. diamond. Each can be scratched by any mineral higher up the scale, and other minerals can be assigned numbers in the scale according to which materials will scratch them.

moiré pattern A wavy cloudy fabric design. Originally applied to mohair (hence its name), this watered effect is obtained by steam pressing the material, usually silk or rayon, between engraved rollers.

Mojave Desert (*or* Mohave Desert) A desert area in S California. It comprises part of the *Great Basin. Area: 15,000 sq mi (38,850 sq km).

Moji. *See* Kitakyushu.

mold Any fungus that forms a fine woolly mass growing on food, clothing, etc. Examples are the *bread mold and species of *Aspergillus* and *Penicillium*. *See also* slime mold.

Moldavia A former principality in SE Europe. It was occupied by the Mongols in the 13th century, becoming independent in the 14th century and encompassing Bukovina and Bessarabia. It became an Ottoman vassal state in the 16th century, losing Bukovina to Austria in the 18th century and Bessarabia to Russia in the 19th century. In 1859 Moldavia and Walachia formed Romania. Russian Moldavia became the *Moldavian Soviet Socialist Republic in 1940.

Moldova, Republic of A country in SE Europe, a constituent republic of the Soviet Union known as Moldavia until 1991. It was formed in 1940, mainly from areas of *Bessarabia (*see also* Moldavia). Its main industries are wine making, tobacco processing, and food canning, for it is very fertile, producing wheat, corn, fruit, and vegetables, as well as having many vineyards. It became independent in 1991 with the collapse of the Soviet Union. Moldova became a member of the Commonwealth of Independent States in 1991 and the UN in 1992. Area: 13,000 sq mi (33,670 sq km). Population (1987): 4,185,000. Capital: Kishinev.

mole (medicine) An area of darkly pigmented skin, known medically as a nevus. Many people have moles and the only reasons for doing anything about them are cosmetic unless they enlarge, bleed, or become painful, any of which may indicate malignant (cancerous) change.

mole (metrology; symbol mol) The *SI unit of amount of substance equal to the amount of substance that contains the same number of entities as there are atoms in 0.012 kg of carbon-12. One mol of any substance contains $6.022{,}52 \times 10^{23}$ entities (*see* Avogadro's number). The entities may be atoms, molecules, ions, electrons, etc.

mole (zoology) A burrowing mammal belonging to the family *Talpidae*, of Europe, Asia, and North America. The common Eurasian mole (*Talpa europaea*) is about 5.5 in (14 cm) long including its small bristly tail. It is thickset, with velvety-black fur, and has long-clawed digging forefeet. Moles make an extensive system of underground tunnels, feeding on earthworms and storing surplus worms in a "larder." Practically blind above ground, moles rapidly starve when prevented from digging. Order: *Insectivora*. *See also* desman.

mole cricket A large *cricket belonging to the family *Gryllotalpidae* (about 50 species); 1.3–2 in (35–50 mm) long, mole crickets are brown and have enlarged and toothed front legs, which are used for digging long shallow tunnels under damp ground. The female lays large numbers of eggs in an underground nest and the young (like the adults) feed on plant roots and insect larvae.

molecular biology The scientific discipline that deals with the molecular basis of living processes. Molecular biology involves both *biochemistry and *biophysics: its growth since the 1930s has been made possible by the development of such techniques as *chromatography, *electron microscopy, and *X-ray diffraction, which have revealed the structures of biologically important molecules, such as DNA, RNA, and enzymes. Heredity, and the development, organization, function, and malfunction of living cells, all depend on the physical and chemical properties of the molecules involved.

molecule The smallest portion of a compound that can exist independently and retain its properties. The atoms that make up a molecule are either bonded together covalently, e.g. CO_2, or electrovalently, e.g. NaCl. However, in crystalline substances the bonds extend throughout the whole crystal structure and the molecule has only a notional existence. In covalent gases and liquids, however, the molecule actually exists as a small group of atoms. **Molecular weight** (*or* relative molecular mass) is the ratio of the average mass per molecule to one-twelfth of the mass of an atom of carbon-12. It is thus the sum of the *atomic weights of the atoms comprising a molecule.

mole rat A burrowing *rodent superficially resembling a mole. Mole rats belong to three families found in Africa and Eurasia: *Bathyergidae* (16 species), *Spalacidae* (3 species), and *Rhizomyidae* (14 species). Mole rats of all three families are similar in appearance with small eyes and ears, a small tail, and powerful digging feet. They feed on roots and tubers.

Molière (Jean-Baptiste Poquelin; 1622–73) French dramatist, the father of modern French comedy. He left home in 1643 to establish a theatrical company and toured the provinces from 1645 to 1658. *Les Précieuses ridicules* (1659) was the first of a series of Paris productions for both court and public audiences that included *Tartuffe* (1664), *Dom Juan* (1665), *Le Misanthrope* (1666), *L'Avare* (1668), *Le Bourgeois Gentilhomme* (1670), and *Le Malade imaginaire* (1673). His ridicule of hypocrisy and his vigorous satire of contemporary manners and types brought him into constant conflict with the religious authorities. He frequently acted in the productions that he both wrote and directed, and he died after collapsing on stage.

Molina, Luis de (1535–1600) Spanish *Jesuit theologian. A professor at Évora in Portugal and later at Madrid, he is best known for his *Concordia liberi arbitrii cum gratiae donis* (1588), which founded the doctrine known as Molinism. This was an attempt to reconcile the concept of divine grace with man's free will. It precipitated a violent dispute between Molina's Jesuit supporters and the *Dominicans, which lasted for several centuries.

Molinos, Miguel de (c. 1640–97) Spanish mystic and priest, who was a leading advocate of *Quietism. From 1669 he lived chiefly in Rome, where he wrote his famous *Spiritual Guide* (1675). He was condemned to life imprisonment by the *Inquisition in 1687.

Molise A mountainous region in S central Italy. Formerly part of Abruzzi e Molise, it was established as a separate state in 1963. It is a poor underdeveloped agricultural region producing wheat, potatoes, maize, sheep, and goats. Area: 1713 sq mi (4438 sq km). Population (1991): 320,916. Capital: Campobasso.

mollusk An invertebrate animal belonging to the phylum *Mollusca* (about 100,000 species). Mollusks occupy marine, freshwater, and terrestrial habitats, being especially common on rocky coasts. They have a soft unsegmented body with a muscular foot, variously modified for crawling, burrowing, or swimming, and a thin dorsal mantle that secretes a shell of one, two, or eight parts. The shell is usually external, as in snails, but it may be internal, as in cuttlefish, or absent as in slugs. All except bivalves feed using a ribbon-shaped rasping tongue (radula). Most mollusks are herbivorous with some carnivorous and scavenging species. In the more primitive mollusks there are separate male and female sexes and eggs and sperm are released into the water, where fertilization takes place. Some of the more advanced gastropods and bivalves are hermaphrodite and in some gastropods and all cephalopods fertilization is internal. *See also* bivalve; cephalopod; chiton; gastropod.

molly An attractive tropical fish of the genus *Mollienesia*; 2–5 in (5–13 cm) long, several color varieties have been bred for use in aquaria, including the well-known sailfin mollies (*M. latipinna* and *M. velifera*), which have a bluish sheen and, in the male, a large sail-like dorsal fin. Family: *Poeciliidae*; order: *Atheriniformes*.

Molly Maguires (1862–76) US secret terrorist society in the Pennsylvania and West Virginia coalfields. Coal miners, dissatisfied with working and living conditions, banded together, took their name from an Irish antilandlord organization of the 1840s, and terrorized management and the police. James McParlan, a Pinkerton detective, spied on the group and in 1875–77 gave evidence that resulted in the hanging of 10 men.

Molnár, Ferenc (1878–1952) Hungarian dramatist and writer. He gained international success with his romantic and witty plays, notably *The Devil* (1907) and *The Red Mill* (1923). He also published novels and short stories. He emigrated to the US in 1940.

moloch A grotesque desert-dwelling Australian lizard, *Moloch horridus*, also called thorny devil. Its yellow-and-brown body is covered with thorny spines, which provide good camouflage. Ants are its chief food and a network of microscopic channels on its head collect dew, which drips into its mouth. Family: *Agamidae*.

Moloch A Semitic god whose worship was characterized by the sacrificial burning of children. There are several biblical references to his worship by the Israelites during the period of the Kings (c. 961–c. 562 BC) but his identity remains uncertain.

Molokai A mountainous US island in the N Pacific Ocean, in Hawaii. Father Damien worked in its leper colony. Pineapples and cattle are exported. Area: 261 sq mi (676 sq km). Chief settlement: Kaunakakai.

Molotov. *See* Perm.

Molotov, Vyacheslav Mikhailovich (V. M. Scriabin; 1890–1986) Soviet statesman, who assumed the name Molotov in 1906 to escape from the Imperial police. As prime minister (1930–41) and foreign minister (1939–49, 1953–56), Molotov signed the Soviet-German nonaggression treaty in 1939 and, after the German invasion in 1941, he negotiated alliances with the Allies. His subsequent attitude to the West (the frequency with which he said *niet*—no—in the UN was renowned) contributed to the prolongation of the Cold War. Disagreements with Khrushchev led to his demotion in 1956 and he was subsequently expelled from the Communist party. He was readmitted to the party in the 1980s.

The **Molotov cocktail**, named for him, is an incendiary hand-grenade.

Moltke, Helmuth, Graf von (1800–91) Prussian field marshal; chief of the general staff (1858–88). His reorganization of the Prussian army led to the Prussian victories in the wars against Denmark (1864) and Austria (1866) and in the Franco-Prussian War (1870–71). His nephew **Helmuth Johannes Ludwig von Moltke** (1848–1916) was chief of the German general staff (1906–14), directing at the outbreak of World War I the strategy devised by *Schlieffen. Held responsible for the defeat at the Marne, he was relieved of his command.

Moluccas (*or* Maluku) An Indonesian group of islands between Sulawesi and West Irian. It includes the islands of Ambon, Halmahera, and Ceram. Mountainous and volcanic, most are fertile and humid. The indigenous population fishes, hunts, and collects sago, while along the coasts the tropical rain forest is giving way to shifting cultivation; spices, fish, and copra are exported. *History*: before the Portuguese arrival (1512), the islands were ruled by Muslims and already famed for their cloves and nutmeg from which they gained the name of Spice Islands. After great European rivalry, Dutch control was established in the 19th century. With Indonesian independence (1949) the S Moluccas fought to secede but were subjugated by the new government (1950–56). Since 1966 S Moluccans in the Netherlands have drawn attention to their cause with violent protests. Area: about 28,766 sq mi (74,504 sq km). Population (1990): 1,856,000. Chief town: Ambon.

molybdenum (Mo) A very hard silvery-gray metal of high melting point, it was first prepared in 1782 by P. J. Hjelm (1746–1813). It occurs in nature as molybdenite (MoS_2) and as wulfenite (lead molybdenate; $PbMoO_4$). It is extracted by the reduction of molybdenum trioxide (MoO_3). Molybdenum is used in high-temperature filaments and as an alloying agent in the production of high-strength steels. Trace quantities of molybdenum are important for plant nutrition. At no 42; at wt 95.94; mp 4747°F (2617°C); bp 8342°F (4612°C).

Mombasa 4 04S 39 40E A port in Kenya, on an island in an inlet of the Indian Ocean. It was an important port for Arab traders and was taken in the 16th and 17th centuries by the Portuguese; the Arab influence remains strong. The modern deepwater port at Kinlindini handles most of Kenya's trade; industries include oil refining and a pipeline (opened 1977) supplies Nairobi. Population (1984 est): 425,600.

moment The product of a force and its perpendicular distance from the axis about which it acts. A moment produces a turning effect and is sometimes called a torque. The inertia of a body to a torque is called its **moment of inertia**. This quantity is equal to mr^2 for a single mass (m) rotating about an axis at a distance r from the axis. The moment of inertia of a system of masses is equal to the sum of these products.

momentum The linear momentum of a body is the product of its mass and its linear velocity. The angular momentum of a body is the product of its *moment of inertia and its angular velocity. Momentum is an important quantity in physics as during any process, for example a collision between two bodies, the total momentum of the system always remains constant (the law of conservation of momentum).

Mommsen, Theodor (1817–1903) German historian and politician. In his major historical work, *The History of Rome* (1854–85), Mommsen adopted a modern critical approach, effectively demythologizing Roman history. He also wrote on law and archeology.

Mon A people of lower Myanmar (Burma) and central Thailand. They speak an *Austro-Asiatic language, also known as Talaing. It is written in a script derived from *Pali, which the Burmese subsequently adopted. Between about 600 and 1000 AD Mon kingdoms dominated the area. After the fall of rival *Pagan, the Mons recovered independence (late 13th to mid-16th centuries) but were subjugated by the Burmese in the 18th century and now survive only as minority groups. They are village-dwelling rice farmers, whose Theravada Buddhism is tinged with earlier Pagan beliefs.

Monaco, Principality of A small country on the Mediterranean Sea, an enclave within French territory. It consists of three principal localities: the business district around the ports, Monte Carlo with its famous casino, and the capital Monaco. *Economy*: the main sources of revenue are tourism and the sale of postage stamps. *History*: ruled by the house of Grimaldi since 1297, it has been under French protection since 1641 (except for a period, 1815–61, of Sardinian protection). Executive power lies with the hereditary prince and the State Council, and legislative power with the prince and the National Council. In 1993,

Monaco joined the UN. Head of state: Prince Rainier III. Official language: French; Monégasque, a mixture of French and Italian, is also spoken. Official currency: French franc of 100 centimes. Area: 467 acres (189 hectares). Population (1989): 29,000.

Monadhliath Mountains (*or* Gray Hills) A mountain range in N Scotland, in the Highland Region. It lies between Loch Ness and the Spey River and reaches 3087 ft (941 m) at Carn Mairg.

Monaghan (Irish name: Contae Mhuineachain) A county in the NE Republic of Ireland, in Ulster bordering on Northern Ireland. It is generally low lying and undulating. Agricultural produce includes oats and potatoes; cattle rearing and dairy farming are also important. Area: 499 sq mi (1551 sq km). Population (1991): 51,262. County town: Monaghan.

mona monkey. *See* guenon.

monarch A widespread American *milkweed butterfly, *Danaus plexippus*. Light brown with black borders and white dots, the adults migrate southward to overwinter in semihibernation. In spring they move north, breeding on the way. Occasionally, individuals may reach Europe. The caterpillars are green with black and yellow bands.

monasticism A system under which men or women devote themselves to a religious life either in solitude or in special communities removed from society. St *Anthony of Egypt probably inaugurated Christian monasticism by organizing ascetic hermits under a rule (c. 305). They were, however, essentially solitaries; communal monastic life was introduced by Anthony's disciple, *Pachomius. Between 358 and 364 St *Basil drew up the rule that still governs the Orthodox Churches' religious communities. In the 6th century St *Benedict of Nursia introduced a monastic rule in Italy that remained the basic system in the West (*see* Benedictines). It underwent periodic reform, first at *Cluny in the 10th century. The rules of three orders founded in the 11th century—the Camaldolese (1012), *Carthusian (1084), and *Cistercian (1098)—were also stricter variants of the Benedictine rule. The mendicant friars (*see* Augustinians; Carmelites; Dominicans; Franciscans) also took vows and lived according to a rule, but not in seclusion: they continued to perform duties in the world. They had corresponding rules for women, however, who lived enclosed lives as nuns. Two military orders, the *Hospitallers and *Templars, followed monastic discipline. Both monks and nuns were required to take vows of poverty, chastity, and obedience and to devote their lives to prayer and work. Until the Renaissance revived secular learning, the monasteries were the main cultural centers, preserving and transmitting the learning of antiquity. Monasticism was also practiced by the ancient Jews (*see* Essenes), and there is a strong monastic tradition in Buddhism (*see* sangha; tri-ratna).

Monastir. *See* Bitola.

monazite A rare-earth mineral of composition $(Ce,La,Y,Th)PO_4$ and yellow to reddish-brown color, found as an accessory in acid igneous rocks and as placer deposits. Monazite is usually obtained as a by-product of titanium and zircon mining; it is the most common source of the rare earths.

Mönchengladbach (*or* München Gladbach) 51 12N 6 25E A city in NW Germany, in North Rhine-Westphalia. The site of a 13th-century cathedral, it is the center of the German textile industry and headquarters of the NATO forces in N central Europe. Population (1988): 255,000.

Monck, George, 1st Duke of Albemarle (1608–70) English general. Initially a Royalist in the Civil War, he was captured and imprisoned (1644–46).

Won over to the Parliamentary cause, he defeated the Scots at Dunbar (1650) and pacified Scotland. In the first *Dutch War he became a successful general at sea. In command of Scotland from 1654, he was largely responsible for the Restoration of Charles II.

Moncton 46 04N 64 50W A city and river port in E Canada, in New Brunswick. The railroad and transportation hub of the *Maritime Provinces, it also has light industry and the French-language University of Moncton (1864). Population (1986): 55,500.

Mond, Ludwig (1839–1909) German industrial chemist, who lived in Britain from 1862. He discovered nickel carbonyl and its application to the extraction of platinum from its ores, a method now known as the **Mond process**. He also made improvements to the *Solvay process.

Mondale, Walter F(rederick) ("Fritz"; 1928–) US vice president (1977–81). A lawyer, he worked with the Democratic Farmer-Labor party and was Minnesota's attorney general (1960–64). He succeeded Hubert *Humphrey in the US Senate (1965–77), where he was known as a liberal. Chosen to be Jimmy Carter's running mate in 1976, he was an active and effective vice president who worked closely with the president and was instrumental in the passage of labor and intelligence-control legislation. He and Carter were defeated (1980) in their bid for reelection. Mondale, chosen as the Democratic presidential nominee in the 1984 elections, named Geraldine *Ferraro as his running mate. Overwhelmingly defeated by incumbent Republican Ronald *Reagan, he returned to private law practice.

Mondrian, Piet (Pieter Cornelis Mondriaan; 1872–1944) Dutch painter, born in Amersfoot. His early still lifes and landscapes became increasingly architectural; however, while in Paris (1912–14) he came under the influence of *cubism. His first abstract compositions (1917) used only horizontal and vertical lines, primary colors, and black and white. During this period he helped to launch the art movement of de *Stijl. After 1919 his style, known as neoplasticism, influenced both the *Bauhaus school and the *international style in architecture. In New York after 1940 his style became more relaxed with such paintings as *Broadway Boogie Woogie*.

Monet, Claude (1840–1926) French impressionist painter, born in Paris (*see* impressionism). He spent his childhood in Le Havre, where his teacher *Boudin encouraged him to paint in the open air. After military service in Algeria (1860–62) he met *Sisley and *Renoir in Gleyre's studio. Initially influenced by the *Barbizon school, in the late 1860s he developed the impressionist technique in views of Paris and in the 1870s in boating scenes at Argenteuil. He excelled in his series of the same scenes painted at different times of day, e.g. *Gare St Lazare*, *Haystacks*, *Rouen Cathedral*, and the *Poplars*, the last of which anticipates *abstract art. His last works were his famous murals of water lilies (Orangerie, Paris).

monetarism A revision of old-established economic theories that rivals *Keynesianism. Monetarism's most celebrated proponent is the US economist Milton *Friedman. Monetarists believe that with the exception of *monetary policy government economic policy does not achieve its aims and is harmful. They regard responsible regulation of the money supply as essential to the wellbeing of the economy, advocating a gentle expansion of the money supply at roughly the rate of growth of the economy. Monetarists blame *inflation on overexpansion of the money supply. The essential difference between neo-Keynesians and monetarists is that the former believe in government regulation of the economy, whereas the latter do not.

monetary policy An economic policy in which the money supply is managed by the government, in order to influence the economy. Following the inflation of the 1970s and the impact of monetarist ideas (*see* monetarism), more attention is being paid to monetary policy.

money A medium of exchange. To be an efficient medium of exchange, money should be divisible (for small transactions), have a high value-to-weight ratio (to make it easy to carry about), be readily acceptable, and not easily counterfeited. Money also functions as means of credit and a store of wealth, for which purposes its value must remain stable. The depreciation in the value of money (*see* inflation) is an economic problem, at present besetting many countries. Money was reputedly invented by the Lydians in the 7th century BC. It originally took the form of something intrinsically valuable (such as a precious metal) but, so long as it is generally acceptable and retains confidence, this is not necessary. Indeed, most money is now in the form of paper, which is itself almost worthless. Individual countries have their own form of money (currency), which cannot be used in other countries; to be used in another country currencies have to be exchanged (*see* exchange rates). The total stock of money in the economy is known as the **money supply**.

money spider A tiny *spider of the family *Liniphiidae* (over 250 species). It has a reddish or black body and occurs in enormous numbers in fields, etc. Money spiders build sheetlike webs on vegetation to which they cling upside down, waiting to catch insects that drop onto the web. Immature spiders may be seen drifting considerable distances in the air, attached to silken gossamer threads.

moneywort A perennial herb, *Lysimachia nummularia*, also called creeping jenny, native to damp places in Europe. It has a creeping stem, up to 27 in (60 cm) long, shiny heart-shaped leaves, and yellow flowers borne individually on short stalks. Family: *Primulaceae*.

The Cornish moneywort (*Sibthorpia europaea*) is a small trailing perennial with minute pink flowers. Family: *Scrophulariaceae*.

Monge, Gaspard (1746–1818) French mathematician. He was one of the founders of descriptive geometry, the mathematics of projecting solid figures onto a plane, upon which modern engineering drawing is based. He became a close friend of Napoleon and was appointed minister for the navy (1792–93), but was stripped of all honors on the restoration of the Bourbons. He died in poverty.

Mongolian languages A group of languages that, together with *Turkic and *Manchu-Tungus, constitute the Altaic language family. Western Mongolian languages are spoken in parts of Russia, the Mongolian People's Republic, and Afghanistan; Eastern Mongolian is spoken in China and the Mongolian People's Republic. There are more than three million speakers of these languages, the majority of which remain unwritten.

Mongolian People's Republic A large sparsely populated country in NE central Asia, between Russia and China. It is mainly high plateau, rising to the Altai and Khangai Mountains in the W and extending into the Gobi Desert in the S. *Economy*: with its nomadic-pastoral tradition, it is still mainly dependent on livestock rearing, now organized in collectives and state farms. In recent years there have been attempts to increase crop growing. Copper mining is being introduced and other minerals include coal, oil, gold, tungsten, lead, and uranium. There is some light industry, mainly based in Ulan Bator. Exports, mainly to communist countries, include cattle and horses, wool, and hair. *History*: in the 13th century Genghis Khan ruled the Mongol empire from Karakoram in the N. As Outer Mongolia, the area was a province of China from 1691 to 1911, when it became an autonomous monarchy under Russian protection. Again under Chinese influence from 1919 to 1921, it then became independent and the Mongolian People's Republic was declared in 1924. Persecution of lama priests (*see* Tibetan Buddhism) precipitated the Lama Rebellion (1932), when several thousand Mongolians with several million head of livestock crossed the border into Inner Mongolia. After World War II its independence was guaranteed by the Soviet Union and China, but relations with the latter have deteriorated since the Sino-Soviet split in the early 1960s. Major political reform movements and US aid that began in the early 1990s paved the way for the transition to a more democratic state and economy. Head of State: Punsalmaagiyn Ochirbat. Official language: Khalkha Mongolian. Official currency: tugrik of 100 möngö. Area: 604,095 sq mi (1,565,000 sq km). Population (1990 est): 2,185,000. Capital: Ulan Bator.

Mongoloid The racial grouping comprising the populations of E Asia and the Arctic region of North America. They are characterized by medium skin pigmentation, the epicanthic fold of the upper eyelid, straight coarse black hair, a rather flat face with high cheekbones, slight facial and body hair, and a high percentage of B blood type. The American Indian peoples used to be classified as Mongoloid but now only the Eskimo peoples are included.

Mongols An Asiatic people united in the early 13th century by *Genghis Khan, who built up an empire that encompassed much of central Asia. Under his grandson *Kublai Khan the Mongols conquered China and ruled there as the *Yuan dynasty until 1368. They were subsequently confined to the area approximating to the present-day Mongolian People's Republic.

mongoose A carnivorous ☐mammal belonging to the family *Viverridae* (which also includes civets and genets), found in warm regions of the Mediterranean, Africa, and Asia. There are about 40 species, ranging in size from 20–40 in (50–100 cm) including the long tapering furry tail (10–20 in; 25–50 cm), with short legs, small ears, and long coarse gray-brown fur. Mongooses are renowned for catching snakes and rats and also eat eggs, small mammals, frogs, and birds. Chief genera: *Galidictis, Herpestes, Helogale*.

monism. *See* dualism.

Monitor and Merrimack Civil War naval battle at Hampton Roads, Va., in 1862; the first between ironclad ships. The *Monitor*, the Union ironclad, was engaged by the Confederate *Virginia* (formerly the *Merrimack*), a Northern-built steam frigate converted to an ironclad warship. After much shooting and attempts to ram each other, the *Virginia* returned to home base, each side confident of victory. Although the battle was indecisive, it showed the capabilities of ironclad vessels, raised the morale of both sides, and maintained the Union blockade. In 1978 the wreck of the victorious *Monitor* was identified in 230 ft (75 m) of water outside the harbor.

monitor lizard A lizard belonging to the Old World family *Varanidae* (30 species), occurring in tropical and subtropical regions; 6.5 in–10 ft (0.2–3 m) long, monitors have an elongated body and well-developed legs. They feed on mammals, snakes, lizards, eggs, and carrion. The rare Bornean earless monitor (*Lanthanotus borneensis*) lives in subterranean tunnels and is a good swimmer, feeding on fish and worms. *See also* Komodo dragon.

Moniz, Antonio Egas (1874–1955) Portuguese surgeon, who pioneered the use of brain surgery in the treatment of severe mental illness. In 1935 he performed the first operation of prefrontal lobotomy (*see* leukotomy) and shared the 1949 Nobel Prize with Walter Rudolf Hess (1881–1973).

MONITOR LIZARD *The Australian lace monitor, or goanna* (Varanus varius), *which reaches a length of 6 ft (1.8 m) or more and is mainly black and yellow.*

Monk, Thelonius (Sphere) (1920–82) US jazz pianist and composer, influential in the development of *bop. He developed a characteristic pianistic style and played alone or in small groups; his compositions include "Off Minor" and "Blue Monk."

monkey A tree-dwelling *primate. Monkeys are 8–43 in (20–110 cm) long and most have a long balancing tail of up to 100 cm used in climbing, although some are tailless. Agile and intelligent, they have fingernails and an opposable thumb enabling manual dexterity. Most monkeys are omnivorous but they prefer fruit, nuts, and other vegetation. *See also* New World monkey; Old World monkey.

monkey flower A fragrant annual or perennial herb or shrub of the mostly North American genus *Mimulus* (100 species), growing near streams and rivers. *M. guttatus* is a naturalized European species. Up to 24 in (60 cm) tall, it has simple toothed leaves and showy yellow tubular flowers with red spots, each with a two-lobed upper lip and a larger three-lobed lower lip. Family: *Scrophulariaceae. See also* musk.

monkey puzzle A coniferous tree, *Araucaria araucana*, also called Chile pine, native to Chile and Argentina and widely grown as an ornamental. Up to 100 ft (30 m) high (ornamental trees are much smaller), it has whorled horizontal branches covered with leathery prickly overlapping leaves, 1.2–1.6 in (3–4 cm) long. The globular spiny cones, 4–7 in (10–17 cm) long, ripen from green to brown and break up to release large seeds, which are edible when roasted. Family: *Araucariaceae.*

monkfish A *shark belonging to the family *Squatinidae*. It has a broad flattened head, an elongated tapering body, winglike pectoral fins, two dorsal fins, and no anal fin. Monkfish occur in tropical and temperate seas and feed on bottom-dwelling fish, mollusks, and crustaceans. A species of *anglerfish, *Lophius piscatorius*, is also called monkfish.

monkshood. *See* aconite.

Monmouth, James Scott, Duke of (1649–85) The illegitimate son of Charles II of England who led the Monmouth rebellion against his uncle James II. A Protestant, he became a focus of the opposition to the succession of the Roman Catholic James and was banished (1684). After James's accession (1685), Monmouth landed at Lyme Regis to raise a rebellion and was defeated, captured, and beheaded.

Monnet, Jean (1888–1979) French economist and public official, known for his contribution to European unity. He was deputy secretary general of the League of Nations (1919–23). In 1946 he inaugurated the Monnet Plan for the modernization of French industry and later drafted the *Schuman Plan to establish the European Coal and Steel Community, of which he was president (1952–55). His efforts culminated in the establishment of the EEC.

monocotyledons The smaller of the two main groups of flowering plants, which includes the palms, bananas, orchids, grasses, lilies, and many garden bulbs and corms—daffodils, irises, tulips, crocuses, etc. (*compare* dicotyledons). Monocots are characterized by having a single seed leaf (cotyledon) in the embryo. Typically the flower parts are in threes (or multiples of three) and the leaves have parallel veins. Very few monocots produce true wood. *See also* angiosperms.

Monod, Jacques-Lucien (1910–76) French biochemist, who proposed a mechanism for the regulation of gene activity. Monod and his colleague F. Jacob (1920–) postulated a regulatory gene that controlled the activity of a neighboring gene for protein synthesis. Their theory was later found to be largely true. Monod and Jacob shared the 1965 Nobel Prize with A. Lwoff (1902–).

monomer A simple molecule or group of atoms forming a repeated unit in a dimer (two molecules), trimer (three molecules), or polymer (*see* polymerization).

Monophysites (Greek *monos physis*: one nature) Supporters of the doctrine that the incarnate Christ had only a single divine nature. They opposed the orthodox teaching that he possessed two natures, human as well as divine. The doctrine was provoked by the dogmatic formulations of the Council of Chalcedon (451) and, despite attempts at reconciliation by the Byzantine emperors, the *Coptic and several other Eastern Churches were irrevocably schismatic by the mid-6th century.

monopoly An industry in which the market is supplied by one supplier. The monopolist can obtain a high profit by restricting supply and demanding a high price. Consumers are thus penalized and it is likely that with a secure market there will also be inefficiency in production. In the public sector of a mixed economy monopolies for the supply of public services (electricity, gas, transport, etc.) are commonplace. In the private sector they are usually restricted by legislation such as the *antitrust laws in the US.

monosaccharide (*or* simple sugar) A *carbohydrate consisting of a single sugar unit and possessing either a keto group ($C = O$) or an aldehyde group (CHO). Monosaccharides are classified according to the number of carbon atoms they possess—the most common being pentoses (with five) and hexoses (with six)—and they can exist as either straight-chain or ring-shaped structures. The most widely occurring monosaccharides are *glucose and *fructose.

monosodium glutamate The sodium salt of the amino acid glutamic acid, used widely in the food industry as a flavoring agent, especially in canned preserved foods.

monotheism Belief in only one God. The great monotheistic religions are Judaism, Christianity, and Islam. Earlier views that monotheism evolved out of *polytheism are now discredited, as Judaism and Islam in particular seem to have grown from conscious opposition to polytheistic systems.

Monothelites (Greek *monos, thelein*: one, (to) will) Supporters of the doctrine that the incarnate Christ possessed only one divine will. Monothelitism was conceived in 624 as a formula for reconciling the *Monophysite churches but failed in its purpose and was formally branded a heresy in 680.

monotreme A primitive *mammal belonging to the order *Monotremata*, found only in Australia (including Tasmania) and New Guinea. The name means "single hole," and monotremes have the reptilian characteristic of a single vent for passing urine, feces, and eggs or sperm. Monotremes lay eggs, suckling their young after these hatch. The only living monotremes are the *echidnas and *duck-billed platypus.

Monroe, James (1758–1831) US statesman; fifth president of the US (1817–25). After service in the Revolutionary War, Monroe studied law under Thomas *Jefferson and was a member of the Continental Congress (1783–86). Although he initially opposed the ratification of the US *Constitution, he served in the US Senate (1790–94) and was named US minister to France (1794–96). After a single term as governor of Virginia (1799–1802), Monroe was sent to France by President Jefferson and was instrumental in the negotiations leading to the *Louisiana Purchase (1803). He later served as a special US minister to Great Britain and Spain (1803–06). In 1811 he was again elected governor of Virginia but resigned that office to become secretary of state in the cabinet of Pres. James *Madison (1811–17) and briefly as secretary of war (1814–15). As the leader of the Jeffersonian Republicans, he was elected president in 1816. His two terms in office were marked by domestic prosperity and stable international relations. Most of the US border with Canada was finalized, and the former Spanish territory of Florida was acquired by the US in 1819. One of the most lasting achievements of the Monroe administration was the proclamation (1823) of the *Monroe Doctrine, which warned against European involvement in the western hemisphere.

Monroe, Marilyn (Norma Jean Baker *or* Mortenson; 1926–62) US film actress. Her childhood was spent in an orphanage and foster homes. Promoted as a sex symbol in such films as *Niagara* (1952) and *Gentlemen Prefer Blondes* (1953), she later developed a real acting talent and ability as a comedienne. Her third husband was Arthur *Miller, and her last film appearance was in *The Misfits* (1961), which he wrote. She died from an overdose of barbiturates.

Monroe Doctrine. *See* Monroe, James.

Monroe–Pinckney Treaty (1806) Agreement between the US and Britain regarding smuggling, blockading, and the illegal impressment of US sailors into the British Navy. Negotiated by US minister to Great Britain James *Monroe and William Pinckney with the British foreign secretary, it was not ratified by the US Senate.

Monrovia 6 20N 10 46W The capital and main port of Liberia, on the Atlantic Ocean. Founded in 1822 as a settlement for freed North American slaves, it was named for President Monroe of the US. The University of Liberia was founded in 1851. Population (1985): 500,000.

Mons (Flemish name: Bergen) 50 28N 3 58E A city in Belgium, situated between two important coal-mining regions. Notable buildings include the town hall (1443–67) and the Church of Ste Waudru (1450–1621). The battle of Mons took place here on Aug 23, 1914, at the beginning of World War I. Principally a commercial center, its industries include oil, cotton, porcelain, and tobacco. Population (1985): 90,500.

MARILYN MONROE *With Arthur Miller.*

Monsarrat, Nicholas (John Turney; 1910–79) British novelist. His best-known novel, *The Cruel Sea* (1951), was based on his naval experiences in World War II. Other novels include *The Tribe That Lost its Head* (1956) and *The Pillow Fight* (1965).

monsoon A seasonal large-scale reversal of winds in the tropics, resulting chiefly from the differential heating of the land and oceans. It is best developed in India, SE Asia, and China; N Australia and East and West Africa have similar wind reversals. The term is derived from the Arabic word *mawsim*, originally applied to the seasonal winds of the Arabian Sea. It is now commonly applied to the rainfall that accompanies the wind reversals, especially the period of heavy rainfall in S Asia extending from April to September, in which the winds are southwesterly.

Monstera A genus of large tropical American herbaceous plants (50 species) that climb by means of aerial roots. *M. deliciosa* is often grown as a house plant for its foliage and in the tropics for its edible green fruits. The leaves, up to 60 cm long, are perforated with slits or holes and the flowers resemble those of the *arum lily. Family: *Araceae*.

Montaigne, Michel de (1533–92) French essayist. Soon after the death of his father, a wealthy merchant, in 1568, he resigned his position as magistrate in Bordeaux and began composing his *Essais*. In 1580 he traveled extensively in Europe and was mayor of Bordeaux from 1581 to 1585. His *Essais*, which inaugurated a new literary genre, expressed his mature humanistic philosophy and constitute a moving self-portrait. They were published in two editions in 1580 and 1588, and a posthumous edition incorporated his final revisions. The *Essais* were translated into English by John Florio in 1603 and influenced the development of the English essay.

Montale, Eugenio (1896–1981) Italian poet. The stoic pessimism and symbolic imagery of his early poetry, especially in *Ossi di seppia* (1925), contrasts with the personal warmth of such later volumes as *Satura* (1971) and *Xenia* (1972). He was an opponent of fascism, and from 1947 literary editor of the newspaper *Corriere della Sera*. He published many translations and literary essays and won the Nobel Prize in 1975.

Montana The fourth largest US state. It is bounded by the Canadian provinces of Saskatchewan, Alberta, and British Columbia to the N; Idaho to the W and SW; Wyoming to the S; and South Dakota and North Dakota to the E. It is mountainous and forested in the W, rising to the Rocky Mountains, with the rolling grasslands of the Great Plains in the E. Its economy is predominantly agricultural, cattle ranching and wheat production being of greatest importance. Other crops include barley and sugar beet. It possesses important mineral resources, notably copper (at Butte) and coal. The extraction of the latter is possible through strip mining but this has caused environmental problems. There are several Indian reservations within the state, notably the Crow reservation. *History*: once the home of the buffalo and a large number of Indian tribes, including Blackfoot, Sioux, Shoshone, Arapaho, Cheyenne, and Flathead, Montana formed part of the Louisiana Purchase in 1803. The first explorations were probably undertaken by Lewis and Clark, but settlement began with the discovery of gold in the mid-19th century. The capital, Helena, originated as a mining camp called Last Chance Gulch. During the Indian wars the battle of *Little Bighorn (Custer's Last Stand) took place (1876). Range wars between sheep- and cattle-ranchers and struggles between copper companies for control of Montana's copper mines dominated the late 19th century. In 1909 open range areas were fenced in to allow farming of the land. All sectors suffered during the Depression, but World War II brought prosperity. Montana's energy industries flourished during the energy crisis of the 1970s. Area: 145,587 sq mi (377,070 sq km). Population (1990): 799,065. Capital: Helena.

Montanism An early Christian sect founded by a shadowy individual called Montanus in Asia Minor in the mid-2nd century. It spread to N Africa, where *Tertullian became an adherent. It was characterized by *millenarianism, prophesying, and insistence upon strict asceticism.

Mont Blanc (Italian name: Monte Bianco) 45 50N 6 52E The highest mountain in the Alps, on the French-Italian border. It was first climbed in 1786. A road tunnel (1958–62) beneath it, 7.5 mi (12 km) long, connects the two countries. Height: 15,771 ft (4807 m).

montbretia A perennial herb, *Crocosmia crocosmiflora* (a hybrid between *C. pottsii* and *C. aurea*), native to South Africa but naturalized in Europe and often grown as a garden ornamental. Up to 40 in (1 m) high, it has long stiff sword-shaped leaves and clusters of orange-red funnel-shaped flowers, up to 3 in (7.5 cm) across, with spreading petals. The name is also applied to the similar and related flowering herbs of the South African genus *Montbretia* (or *Tritonia*). Family: *Iridaceae*.

Montcalm, Louis Joseph de Montcalm-Grozon, Marquis de (1712–59) French general distinguished for his command (1756–59) against the British in Canada during the Seven Years' War. In 1756 he regained control of Ontario for the French, in 1757 he took Fort William Henry, and in 1758 repulsed the much larger British force from Ticonderoga. He died defending Quebec from assault by Gen. James *Wolfe, who, although victorious, was also mortally wounded.

Monte Bello Islands 20 30S 115 30E A group of uninhabited coral islands in the Indian Ocean, off the W coast of Western Australia. They were used for testing British nuclear weapons in 1952 and 1956.

Monte Carlo 43 44N 7 25E A resort in the principality of Monaco, on the Riviera. It is famous for its casino, automobile race, and other cultural and sporting events. Population (1982): 12,000.

Montefeltro An Italian noble family that ruled the city of Urbino between the 13th and 16th centuries. Originally rulers of the town of Mons Feretri from which they derived their name, the Montefeltri gave military support to the Holy Roman Emperor in his struggle against the pope (*see* Guelfs and Ghibellines). The best-known member of the family is the illegitimate **Federigo Montefeltro, Duke of Urbino** (1422–82), who distinguished himself as a military leader and as an art patron, especially of *Piero della Francesca. Urbino passed into the hands of the Rovere family in the 16th century because there were no Montefeltro heirs.

Montego Bay 18 27N 77 56W A port and tourist resort in NW Jamaica. Its chief exports are bananas and sugar. Population (1991): 83,446.

Montenegro (Serbo-Croat name: Crna Gora) A constituent republic of Yugoslavia, bordering on the Adriatic Sea. It is predominantly mountainous and forested. Stock raising is important, especially of sheep, goats, and pigs. *History*: it was declared a kingdom in 1910, becoming a province of the kingdom of the Serbs, Croats, and Slovenes (later Yugoslavia) in 1918. With Serbia it formed the new, smaller Yugoslavia in 1992. Area: 5387 sq mi (13,812 sq km). Population (1991): 616,327. Capital: Titograd.

Monterey 36 39N 121 45W A city in California, on Monterey Bay. One of California's oldest cities, it is a well-known retreat of artists and writers. It forms the background for several of John Steinbeck's novels. Population (1990): 31,954.

Monte Rosa 45 57N 7 53E A massif in S Europe, on the Swiss-Italian border in the Alps. The highest peak, the Dufourspitze, is, at 15,203 ft (4634 m), the highest in Switzerland.

Monterrey 25 40N 100 20W The third largest city in Mexico. Founded in 1579, it has many notable buildings including the 18th-century cathedral. Monterrey is a major industrial center specializing in metallurgy. Population (1986): 2,335,000.

Montespan, Françoise Athénaïs de Rochechouart, Marquise de (1641–1707) The mistress of Louis XIV of France from 1667 until replaced by the governess of their seven children—Mme de *Maintenon. Mme de Montespan remained at court until 1691, when she retired to a convent.

Montesquieu, Charles Louis de Secondat, Baron de (1689–1755) French historical philosopher and writer. Montesquieu's first work, the *Lettres persanes* (1721), was a brilliant satirical portrait of French institutions and society. It was a forerunner of the *Enlightenment. There followed the *Considérations sur les causes de la grandeur et de la décadence des romains* (1734) and the famous *Esprit des lois* (1748). This latter work, a comparative study of ideas on law and government, was perhaps the most important book of 18th-century France. It impressed even *Voltaire, who disliked Montesquieu intensely.

Montessori system A system of education for young children devised by the Italian doctor Maria Montessori (1870–1952). It places emphasis on development of the senses and envisages a limited role for the teacher as the child learns by itself through the use of didactic materials. Her first school opened in Rome in 1907 and her methods continue to be influential in nursery schools today.

Monteverdi, Claudio (1567–1643) Italian composer, a pupil of Marco Ingegneri (1545–92). From about 1590 to 1612 Monteverdi was court musician to the

Duke of Mantua. From 1613 until his death he was maestro di cappella at St Mark's Cathedral, Venice. Monteverdi was the first great composer of *opera; enlarging the orchestra, he employed a new range of instrumental effects and made use of an innovative harmonic style to achieve dramatic effects. He also influenced the development of the madrigal as an expressive form. His works include the operas *Orfeo* (1607) and *The Coronation of Poppea* (1642), a set of *Vespers* (1610), and many madrigals.

Montevideo 34 55S 56 10W The capital and main port of Uruguay, in the S on the Río de la Plata. Founded in 1726 by the Spanish as a defense against Portuguese attacks from Brazil, it suffered several occupations in the early 19th century before becoming capital of the newly independent Uruguay in 1828. In the 20th century it has developed rapidly, as both an industrial and a communications center, and it is now one of South America's largest cities. It is also a popular summer resort. The University of Uruguay was founded here in 1849. Population (1985): 1,251,647.

Montez, Lola (Marie Gilbert; 1818–61) Irish dancer and mistress of Louis I of Bavaria (1786–1868; reigned 1825–48). The hostility aroused by her influence led to the abdication of Louis in 1848 and her own expulsion. She later lived for several years in the US.

Montezuma II (1466–c. 1520) The last Aztec emperor of Mexico (1502–20). During his reign his empire was weakened by tribal warfare, which enabled the Spaniards, led by Hernán *Cortés, to establish themselves in Mexico. The emperor was captured by Cortés and was killed either by the Spaniards or by his own people during the Aztec attack on Cortés's force as it tried to leave Tenochtitlán.

Montfort, Simon de, Earl of Leicester (c. 1208–65) English statesman, born in Normandy; the son and namesake of the leader of the Crusade against the *Albigenses. After serving Henry III of England in Gascony, he joined the anti-Royalist faction that demanded greater control of the government, becoming the barons' leader in the subsequent *Barons' War. Initially successful, he became virtual ruler of England, summoning a parliament in 1265. In the same year, however, he was defeated and killed at Evesham.

Montgolfier, Jacques-Étienne (1745–99) French balloonist, who with his brother **Joseph-Michel Montgolfier** (1740–1810) invented the hot-air balloon. The hot-air balloon, so called because it derived its buoyancy from air heated by a fire, was publicly launched in 1782. A much larger balloon, which rose 6562 ft (2000 m), was demonstrated in June 1783 and in October a series of passenger-carrying ascents were made. Jacques-Étienne (who himself never made an ascent) then launched a free-flying balloon and in 1784 Joseph-Michel with five companions ascended in a steerable balloon. Their experiments aroused enormous interest in flying.

Montgomery 32 22N 86 20W The capital city of Alabama, on the Alabama River. Montgomery was the first capital (1861) of the Confederate states during the Civil War. In the mid-1950s it was the scene of a bus boycott by African Americans, which played an important part in the growth of the civil-rights movement and brought Martin Luther King to the nation's attention. Montgomery is an industrial city and agricultural trading center. Population (1990): 187,106.

Montgomery of Alamein, Bernard Law, 1st Viscount (1887–1976) British field marshal. In World War II he became commander of the Eighth Army (1942) and after the battle of Alamein drove *Rommel back to Tunis and surrender (1943), an achievement that brought him enormous popularity. Having played a major role in the invasion of Italy (1943), he became chief of land forces in the 1944 Normandy invasion. He helped plan the Arnhem disaster (September 1944), but restored his reputation by pushing back the subsequent German offensive, receiving Germany's surrender. After the war he was chief of the imperial general staff (1946–48) and deputy commander of NATO forces (1951–58).

month The time taken by the moon to complete one revolution around the earth. The complicated motion of the moon requires the starting and finishing points of the revolution to be specified. The length of the month depends on the choice of reference point. The **sidereal month**, of 27.32 days, is measured with reference to the background stars. The **synodic month**, of 29.53 days, is measured between two identical phases of the moon. The month is one of the basic time periods used in *calendars.

Montherlant, Henry de (1896–1972) French novelist and dramatist. He was born in Paris into an aristocratic family. His works celebrate the virtues of austerity and virility and concentrate on physical pursuits and relationships. They include *Les Célibataires* (1934), the tetralogy *Les Jeunes Filles* (1936–39), and *Le Chaos et la nuit* (1963), and his plays include *Malatesta* (1946) and *Port-Royal* (1954).

Montmartre. *See* Paris.

Montparnasse. *See* Paris.

Montpelier 44 16N 72 35W The capital city of Vermont, in N central Vermont, on the Winooski River. Settled in 1789, it became Vermont's capital in 1805. Besides state and federal business carried on in the city, there are also insurance companies headquartered there. Population (1990): 8,247.

Montpellier 43 36N 3 53E A city in S France, the capital of the Hérault department. A Huguenot stronghold, it was besieged and captured by Louis XIII in 1622. Notable buildings include the gothic cathedral, the university (founded 1289), and the Musée Fabre. Montpellier trades in wine and brandy and has numerous manufacturing industries. Population (1990): 210,866.

Montreal 45 30N 73 36W A city and port in E Canada, in Quebec on Montreal Island at the junction of the Ottawa and St Lawrence Rivers. Canada's largest city, it is also the greatest transportation, trade, and manufacturing center. Montreal employs cheap hydroelectricity for many industries, including oil refining, meat packing, brewing and distilling, food processing, textiles, and aircraft. It is the headquarters of banks, insurance companies, airlines, and railroads. Housing two English-speaking and two French-speaking universities, Montreal is a forum for politics, broadcasting, theater, film, and publishing. Two-thirds of the population is French speaking, making it the second largest French-speaking city in the world. Among its many beautiful buildings are Notre Dame Church, Christ Church Cathedral, and St James Cathedral. *History*: founded as Ville-Marie (1642), Montreal quickly became a commercial center. Captured by Britain (1760), it acquired an English-speaking merchant community that has dominated Quebec's economy ever since. Montreal was the venue of the world fair Expo '67 and the 1976 Olympics. Population (1991): 1,017,666.

Montreux 46 27N 6 55E A winter resort in W Switzerland, on Lake Geneva. Its 13th-century Château de Chillon is immortalized in Byron's poem the "Prisoner of Chillon." It holds an annual television festival awarding the Golden Rose of Montreux and a jazz festival. Tourism is an important source of income. Population (1980): 19,700.

Montrose, James Graham, 1st Marquess of (1612–50) Scottish general. In 1637 he signed the Covenant in support of Presbyterianism but became a rival of the anti-Royalist *Argyll. Montrose fought for Charles I in the English Civil War but after a series of victories (1644) his army was defeated (1645) and he fled to Europe. He returned in 1650 but was defeated, captured, and executed by the Parliamentarians.

Montserrat A British crown colony comprising one of the Leeward Islands, in the Caribbean Sea to the SE of Puerto Rico. It is largely mountainous with active volcanoes. *Economy*: chiefly agricultural, the main crops are cotton, coconuts, and fruit and vegetables, which with cattle are the main exports. Forestry is being developed. *History*: discovered by Columbus in 1493, it was colonized by the Irish in the 17th century. Formerly administratively joined to the Leeward Islands, it became a separate colony in 1960. It was part of the Federation of the West Indies (1958–62). Official language: English. Official currency: East Caribbean dollar of 100 cents. Area: 40 sq mi (106 sq km). Population (1980): 12,073. Capital and main port: Plymouth.

Montserrat 41 36N 1 48E An isolated mountain in NE Spain, NW of Barcelona. On its E slope is a Benedictine monastery housing a well-known carving, supposedly by St Luke, of the Virgin and Child. Height: 4054 ft (1235 m).

Mont St Michel 48 38N 1 30W A granite islet in NW France, in the Manche department in the Bay of St Michel. The islet is connected to the mainland by a causeway. It is about 256 ft (78 m) high and is crowned by a Benedictine monastery (founded 966 AD), which was used as a prison from the French Revolution until 1863.

Monza 45 35N 9 16E A city in Italy, in Lombardy. An important commercial city in the 13th century, it has a gothic cathedral. Umberto I was assassinated in Monza in 1900. Its manufactures include machinery and textiles. It is noted for its automobile-racing circuit. Population (1991 est): 123,188.

Moody, Dwight Lyman (1837–99) US evangelist. As a successful businessman in Chicago in the 1850s, he was an active lay worker in a Congregational Church. He first achieved fame as a preacher in England (1873–75), and together with his musical colleague Ira David Sankey (1840–1908) compiled a popular collection of hymns, the *Sankey and Moody Hymn Book* (1873). He founded the Moody Bible Institute (1899).

Moog synthesizer. *See* synthesizer.

moon The natural satellite of the earth. The moon orbits the earth every 27.32 days at a mean distance of 238,712 mi (384,400 km), keeping more or less the same face (the nearside) toward the earth. As it revolves, different *phases can be seen from earth, together with up to two or three lunar *eclipses per year. The moon is only 81 times less massive than the earth and has a diameter of 2148 mi (3476 km).

The major surface features are the light-colored highlands on the S nearside and most of the farside, and the much darker lava plains—the *maria. The maria and more especially the highlands are heavily cratered. These roughly circular walled depressions, ranging greatly in size, were produced by impacting bodies from space. The extremely tenuous atmosphere exposes the surface to considerable temperature extremes ($-292°F$ to $230°F$ [$-180°C$ to $+110°C$]). Much of our information about the moon has been derived from photographs and other measurements taken from orbiting US and Soviet satellites and later from moon-rock samples brought back (1969–72) by the Apollo astronauts and the unmanned Soviet Luna landers) and from experiments set up on the moon by the astronauts. The first landing on the moon was made by Neil *Armstrong and Buzz *Aldrin on July 20, 1969. *See* Apollo moon program.

moonfish A deep-bodied fish, also called opah, belonging to the genus *Lampris* and family *Lamprididae*, widely distributed in warm seas. Up to 7 ft (2 m) long, its body is colored blue above, rose-pink below, and is spotted with white; the fins are scarlet. It is uncommon and valued as food. Order: *Lampridiformes*.

moonflower. *See* morning glory.

Moonies. *See* Unification Church.

moon rat The largest living mammal of the order *Insectivora, Echinosorex gymnurus*, of Sumatra, Borneo, and S Asia. It is a *gymnure about 24 in (60 cm) long, black with a white head and long whiskery snout. A secretion of the anal glands gives it a characteristic smell.

moonstone A gem variety of feldspar, usually transparent or translucent orthoclase, albite, or labradorite. It shows a play of colors resembling that of opal.

Moore, Clement Clarke (1779–1863) US poet and teacher; author of *A Visit from St Nicholas* (1823). He taught Oriental and Greek literature at General Theological Seminary (1823–50) in New York City. His famous poem, written as a gift for his children, is better known by its opening words, " 'Twas the night before Christmas."

Moore, G(eorge) E(dward) (1873–1958) British philosopher. Moore's work centered on language and the analysis of its meaning. He maintained that the common usage of words is often profoundly different from their analytical meaning. Much of his published work is in the field of ethics and is concerned with the analysis of concepts of goodness. His books include *Principia Ethica* (1903) and *Ethics* (1912). He was professor of mental philosophy and logic at Cambridge (1925–39) and editor of the journal *Mind* (1921–47).

Moore, Henry (1898–1986) British sculptor. Moore studied at Leeds and the Royal College of Art (1921–24). His fascination with primitive African and Mexican art molded the development of his two characteristic themes: mother and child sculptures and reclining figures. The latter, a lifelong preoccupation, reached its apogee in the sculpture for UNESCO in Paris (1956–57). After devoting himself to abstract work in the 1930s, Moore reverted to the humanist tradition in the early 1940s with his celebrated drawings of sleeping figures in air-raid shelters. These, his *Madonna and Child* (1943–44), and family groups brought him international fame. His later output continued in this vein, together with more experimental abstract works, such as *Atom Piece* (1964–66).

Moore, Marianne (1887–1972) US poet. Her first volume, *Poems* (1921), contained poems contributed to the English imagist magazine *Egoist*. She edited the literary magazine *Dial* from 1925 to 1929. *Collected Poems* (1951) won the Pulitzer Prize. Her poetry is noted for its qualities of irony and sharply observed detail. She also published a verse translation of *The Fables of La Fontaine* (1954).

moorhen A gray-brown waterbird, *Gallinula chloropus*, also called common gallinule and waterhen, occurring worldwide except for Australia. It is 13 in (32 cm) long and has a red bill and forehead and a white patch beneath the tail. It breeds in thick vegetation near ponds and marshes and feeds on seeds, water plants, and aquatic invertebrates. Family: *Rallidae* (rails, etc.).

Moorish idol A deep-bodied tropical fish, *Zanclus canescens*, found in shallow Indo-Pacific waters. It has a black and yellow vertically striped body, about 7 in (18 cm) long, a beaklike mouth, and a greatly extended dorsal fin. It is the only member of its family (*Zanclidae*). Order: *Perciformes*.

Moors The conventional European name for the *Arab and *Berber inhabitants of NW Africa and, by extension, for the 8th-century Muslim conquerors of the Iberian Peninsula, whose armies consisted of both Arab and Berber troops. The word originates in the Roman name for that region of Africa—Mauretania. The Moors were the dominant power in Spain until the 11th century, after which they fell gradually under Christian rule (*see* Mudéjars). A highly civilized people, the Moors played a major role in transmitting classical science and philosophy to W Europe.

HENRY MOORE *The sculptor in the indoor studio at his home in England.*

moose. *See* elk.

Moose Jaw 50 23N 105 35W A city in W Canada, in S Saskatchewan. Founded in 1882, it is a railroad and farming center. Food processing, building materials, and oil refining are economically important. Population: 32,581.

moped. *See* motorcycles.

Moradabad 28 50N 78 45E A city in India, in Uttar Pradesh. Founded in 1625, it is an agricultural trading center and has metalworking, cotton-weaving, and printing industries. Population (1991): 416,836.

moraine The clay, stone, boulders, etc. (*see* till), carried along or deposited by glaciers. It may have been deposited by former glaciers as particular landforms or be actively transported on the ice surface, within the ice, or beneath the ice.

morality plays A form of vernacular religious drama popular in England and France from the late 14th to late 16th centuries. Similar in content and purpose to medieval sermons, morality plays were dramatized allegories of good and evil fighting for man's soul. They include *The Pride of Life*, *The Castle of Perseverance*, and *Everyman*, which is best known. They influenced Elizabethan drama and at the Reformation in England provided a vehicle for dramatizing the religious issues at stake. *See also* miracle plays.

moral philosophy. *See* ethics.

Moral Rearmament (MRA) An evangelical movement founded by a US evangelist and former Lutheran pastor, Frank Nathan Daniel Buchman (1878–1961), in the 1920s. It initially received most support at England's Oxford University and was called the Oxford Group until 1938. It seeks the regeneration of national and individual spirituality through conversion, God's personal guidance, and living in purity, unselfishness, honesty, and love.

Morandi, Giorgio (1890–1964) Italian still-life painter and etcher, born in Bologna. Although he also painted landscapes and flowerpieces, he is noted for his austere compositions of bottles and jars. He was associated with the school of *metaphysical painting.

Moravia (Czech name: Morava; German name: Mähren) An area and former province (1918–49) in the Czech Republic. Lying chiefly in the basin of the Morava River, it rises in the N to the Sudeten Mountains and in the E to the Carpathian Mountains. It contains important mineral deposits, including coal and iron ore. *History*: settled by Slavic tribes in the late 8th century AD, it formed the center of an important medieval kingdom (Great Moravia) until incorporated into the kingdom of *Bohemia in 1029; in 1849 it was made an Austrian crownland. It became part of the Republic of Czechoslovakia in 1918 and of the Czech Republic in 1993. Chief town: Brno.

Moravia, Alberto (Alberto Pincherle; 1907–90) Italian novelist. His early novels, beginning with *The Time of Indifference* (1929), criticized fascism and the corrupt middle-class society that allowed it to flourish. His later works, which include *The Woman of Rome* (1947), *Roman Tales* (1954), *Two Women* (1957), *The Lie* (1966), and *1934* (1983), concern themes of social alienation and the futility of sexual relationships. His literary and political essays are collected in *Man As an End* (1963).

Moravian Brethren A Protestant denomination that continues the ideals of the earlier Bohemian Brethren, a 15th-century group centered in Prague that practiced a simple unworldly form of Christianity. The Moravians date from the establishment of a community in 1722 by Count von *Zinzendorf on his estates in Saxony. In doctrine they are close to *Lutheranism but have a simplified Church hierarchy and liturgy. Hymn singing is important in their services. From the 1730s they were active missionaries; John *Wesley was among those whom they influenced. Many now live in North America.

moray eel A thick-bodied *eel of the family *Muraenidae* (over 80 species). Up to 5 ft (1.5 m) long, it is brightly colored and lacks pectoral fins. Moray eels live in rock crevices and reefs of warm and tropical seas and can be dangerous when disturbed.

MORAY EEL *The long jaws of a moray eel are armed with very sharp strong teeth, which are capable of inflicting a severe bite.*

Moray Firth An inlet of the North Sea in NE Scotland, extending SW from a line between Tarbat Ness in the Highland Region and Burghead in Grampian Region. Length: about 35 mi (56 km).

Mordvinian Autonomous Republic An administrative division in W central Russia. It is heavily forested. The majority of the population is Russian, 35% being Mordvinians, who speak a Finno-Ugric language. The area was annexed by Russia in the 16th century and became an autonomous republic in 1934. The region supports a wide range of industries, including timber, manufacturing of building materials, and textiles, but is predominantly agricultural: the main crops are cereals; sheep and dairy farming are also important. Area: 10,110 sq mi (26,200 sq km). Population (1986): 964,000. Capital: Saransk.

More, Henry (1614–87) English philosopher. One of the *Cambridge Platonists, More shared the group's interest in *Neoplatonism. *Descartes, whose work he helped publicize in England, was an early influence, but More later found his philosophy too materialistic. Although he was an opponent of religious fanaticism, More's own writings, such as *The Immortality of the Soul* (1659) and *Divine Dialogues* (1668), are more poetical and mystical than philosophical.

More, Sir Thomas (1477–1535) English lawyer, scholar, and saint, whose martyrdom horrified his contemporaries and has captured the imagination of succeeding generations. He joined Henry VIII's Privy Council in 1518 and succeeded Wolsey as chancellor in 1529. He resigned the chancellorship in 1532 in opposition to Henry's assumption of the supreme headship of the English Church. In 1534 More was imprisoned after refusing to swear to the new Act of Succession because it repudiated papal authority in England; he was brought to trial for treason in 1535. In spite of a brilliant self-defense, he was convicted on false evidence and beheaded. He was canonized by the Roman Catholic Church in 1935.

His best-known scholarly work is *Utopia* (1516), in which he discussed an ideal social and political system; he also wrote (c. 1513–c. 1518) an unfinished *History of King Richard III*.

Moreau, Gustave (1826–98) French symbolist painter, best known for his detailed and brilliantly colored biblical and mythological fantasies and as the enlightened teacher of *Matisse and *Rouault at the École des Beaux Arts. Most of his works are in the Musée Gustave Moreau, Paris.

Moreau, Jean Victor (1763–1813) French general. He fought in the Revolutionary Wars and, after Napoleon came to power (1799), became commander of the Rhine army, defeating the Austrians at Hohenlinden (1800). In 1804 he was arrested after becoming involved with anti-Bonapartists and was exiled. In 1813 he joined the coalition army formed to oppose Napoleon and died in the battle of *Dresden.

morel A fungus belonging to the genus *Morchella*. Morels are typically club-shaped with the surface of the cap pitted like a honeycomb. The edible common morel (*M. esculenta*) has a yellowish-brown cap, 1.6–3.1 in (4–8 cm) high, and a stout whitish stalk. It is found in clearings and hedgerows. Class: *Ascomycetes*.

Morelia (name until 1828: Valladolid) 19 40N 101 11W A city in Mexico, situated on the central plateau. It has a notable cathedral (17th–18th centuries) and is the center of a cattle-raising area. Population (1980): 297,554.

Morgagni, Giovanni Battista (1682–1771) Italian anatomist and founder of pathological anatomy. His great work, *On the Seats and Causes of Diseases as Investigated by Anatomy* (1761), was based on over 600 postmortem dissections. Morgagni was professor of anatomy at Padua University for nearly 60 years until his death.

Morgan An American all-purpose breed of horse descended from a stallion with some Thoroughbred and Arabian ancestry, born in about 1790 and named for its owner, Justin Morgan. The Morgan has a compact deep-chested body, powerful hindquarters, and a long crested neck and is usually bay. Height: 14–15 hands (1.42–1.52 m).

Morgan, Charles (1894–1958) British novelist and dramatist. With his novels, which include *The Fountain* (1932) and *The Voyage* (1940), he achieved a considerable reputation in Europe, becoming a member of the French Academy. In England he won greater success with his plays, especially *The River Line* (1949).

Morgan, Sir Henry (c. 1635–88) Welsh buccaneer. Said to have been kidnapped and taken to Barbados, he joined the buccaneers then raiding the Spanish in the Caribbean. In 1671 he led a band over the Isthmus of Panama and sacked the city (1671), thus opening the way to plunder in the S Pacific. He was knighted in 1674 and made lieutenant general of Jamaica.

Morgan, John Pierpont (1837–1913) US financier, who founded J. P. Morgan and Co, one of the most powerful US banking corporations. Son of a successful New York banker, Morgan amassed a fortune through gold speculation during the Civil War. In 1869 he gained control of the Albany & Susquehanna RR and continued to expand his railroad interests throughout the following decades. Morgan later supervised the organization of the United States Steel Corp (1901) and the International Harvester Corp (1902). As a prominent art collector, he was an important patron of the Metropolitan Museum in New York and founded the Pierpont Morgan Library. His son **John Pierpont Morgan, Jr.** (1867–1943) succeeded him as the chairman of J. P. Morgan and Co and helped to organize the credit requirements of the Allies in World War I.

Morgan, Thomas Hunt (1866–1945) US geneticist, who established that *chromosomes carried the units of inheritance proposed by Gregor *Mendel. Morgan was skeptical about Mendelian theory until he began his breeding experiments with the fruit fly *Drosophila*. He discovered that a number of genetic variations were inherited together and demonstrated that this was because their controlling genes occurred on the same chromosome (the phenomenon of linkage). Morgan was awarded a Nobel Prize (1933).

Morgan le Fay In *Arthurian legend, an evil sorceress who plotted the overthrow of her brother King Arthur. According to Malory's *Morte d'Arthur* (1485) she betrayed *Guinevere's adultery to Arthur. However, in the earlier *Vita Merlini* (c. 1150) by *Geoffrey of Monmouth she is a benevolent figure who lives in Avalon, where she once healed the wounded Arthur.

Morgenthau, Henry, Jr. (1891–1967) US statesman; secretary of the treasury (1934–45). An avid conservationist, he held several New York state conservation and agricultural positions (1928–32) during Franklin D. *Roosevelt's term as governor. After Roosevelt became president, Morgenthau was appointed secretary of the treasury, a post he held through the New Deal legislative programs and World War II. After his Morgenthau Plan for the postwar reconstruction of Germany met with Pres. Harry S. Truman's disapproval, he resigned and devoted the rest of his life to farming and philanthropic causes.

Mörike, Eduard Friedrich (1804–75) German poet and novelist. A rural clergyman, he found inspiration in country life, which supplied the subjects of his first distinguished collection of lyrics (*Gedichte*, 1838). The best of his prose works is the novella *Mozart auf der Reise nach Prag* (1856).

Moriscos Muslims forced to profess Christianity in Spain. Many Muslims continued to live in Spain after the formerly Muslim areas came under Christian rule and by the 15th century they were forced to become Christians or go into exile. Many chose to remain in Spain while privately remaining Muslims and eventually the government ordered their expulsion. Between 1609 and 1614 about 500,000 Moriscos were forced into exile, settling mainly in Africa.

Morisot, Berthe (1841–95) French painter, granddaughter of the artist *Fragonard. The first female impressionist and an outstanding painter of women and children, she was strongly encouraged by *Corot. *Manet, whose brother Eugène she married (1874), was influenced by her.

Morland, George (1763–1804) British painter, born in London. The son and pupil of the painter Henry Morland (c. 1730–97), he exhibited sketches at the Royal Academy when aged only 10. Popularized through engravings, his work, which included such picturesque rustic scenes as *The Inside of a Stable*, declined after 1794. His dissolute life finally resulted in imprisonment (1799–1802).

Morley, Edward Williams (1838–1923) US chemist, who investigated the relative atomic weights of hydrogen and oxygen. However, he is best known for his collaboration with Albert *Michelson in the *Michelson-Morley experiment.

Morley, Robert (1908–   ) British stage and film actor. His long career as a character actor dates from 1929, and his films include *Major Barbara* (1940), *Beat the Devil* (1953), and *Oscar Wilde* (1960). Other films are *The Trygon Factor* (1967), *Theater of Blood* (1973), and *The Blue Bird* (1976). Many of his later roles have been those of pompous eccentrics.

Morley, Thomas (1557–1603) English composer, music printer, organist of St Paul's Cathedral, and member of the Chapel Royal. A pupil of Byrd, he wrote madrigals, canzonets, songs, church music, and the textbook *A Plaine and Easie Introduction to Practicall Musicke* (1597).

Mormons Adherents of the Christian sect that is formally called the Church of Jesus Christ of Latter-Day Saints, founded in 1830 by Joseph Smith in New York state. A series of visions culminated in Smith's claim that he had discovered golden tablets that contained the Book of Mormon, a sacred book named for a primitive American prophet who had compiled it. After Smith's murder by a mob, the persecuted Mormons moved W under Brigham Young, establishing their headquarters at Salt Lake, Utah, in 1847. Attempting to revert to the simple sanctity of the early Christians, Mormons have no professional clergy, reject infant baptism, emphasize self-help to avoid want, abstain from alcohol and other stimulants, and run educational and missionary programs. Polygamy (*see* marriage), for which Mormons were once notorious, has been disallowed since 1890.

Mornay, Philippe de, Seigneur du Plessis-Marly (1549–1632) French Huguenot (Protestant) leader during the *Wars of Religion. Escaping the *St Bartholomew's Day Massacre (1572), he rose to a position of considerable influence as one of the chief confidants of Henry of Navarre, later Henry IV of France. When Henry was converted to Roman Catholicism, Mornay retained his Huguenot sympathies and lost the king's favor.

morning glory A trailing or twining plant of the genus *Ipomea*, native to tropical America and Australia and cultivated for its beautiful flowers. The leaves are often heart-shaped and the trumpet-shaped flowers, up to 5 in (12 cm) across, are deep blue, purple, pink, or white. Popular species are *I. purpurea* and *I. alba* (the moonflower). The seeds of certain varieties contain hallucinogens. Family: *Convolvulaceae*.

Moro, Aldo (1916–78) Italian statesman; Christian Democratic prime minister (1963–68, 1974–76) and foreign minister (1965–66, 1969–72, 1973–74). He included socialists in his first cabinet and in 1976 was instrumental in gaining communist support for the minority Christian Democratic government. In 1978 he was kidnapped and then murdered by the *Red Brigades.

Morocco, Kingdom of A country in NW Africa, bordering on the Atlantic Ocean and Mediterranean Sea. The Atlas Mountains crossing the center of the country rise to 13,665 ft (4165 m) at Mount Toubkal and separate the Atlantic coastal area from the Sahara. The population is mainly of Berber and Arabic origin. *Economy*: the chief occupations are agriculture and mining. Wheat, barley, maize, and citrus fruits are grown, mainly in the coastal areas N of the mountains; livestock, especially sheep and goats, is also important. Morocco is a leading exporter of phosphates, having about 40% of the world's known phosphate reserves. Other mineral resources are iron ore, coal, lead, zinc, cobalt, and manganese. Industries include food processing, textiles, and traditional handicraft industries; a major phosphoric acid plant has been developed. There is a thriving fishing industry, sardines and tuna being the chief catch. Morocco's hot sunny climate and Atlantic and Mediterranean beaches make it a popular tourist center. *History*: part of the Roman province of Mauretania, it fell to the Vandals in the 5th century AD. Conflict between Arabs and Berbers was virtually continuous; in the 15th and 16th centuries Morocco came under attack from Spain and Portugal and until the 19th century was a base for Barbary pirates. Its strategic importance was recognized by the European powers in the 19th century, French and Spanish interests conflicting with those of Germany. The Algeciras Conference was held (1906) to consider the Moroccan question. The French increased their control in the area and the appearance of a German warship at Agadir (1911) was interpreted by the French as a threat of war. Following the Agadir incident Morocco was partitioned into French and Spanish protectorates (1912) and the international zone of Tangier (1923). In 1956 the protectorates were relinquished and Morocco became a sultanate, later a kingdom (1957) under King Mohammed V; his son, Hassan II, acceded to the throne in 1961. In 1975 agreement was reached providing for the partition of Spanish Sahara (*see* Western Sahara) between Morocco and Mauretania; in 1979 Mauretania withdrew from Western Sahara and it came under Moroccan occupation but fighting continued between Moroccan troops and the Polisaro Front, a group that advocated Saharan nationalism. By a 1991 vote of the UN Security Council, plans were made for a referendum after a permanent cease-fire was in effect. Prime minister: Azzedine Laraki. Official religion: Islam. Official language: Arabic. Official currency: dirham of 100 centimes. Area: 144,078 sq mi (458,730 sq km). Population (1990): 26,249,000. Capital: Rabat.

Moroni 11 40S 43 16E The capital of the Comoro Islands, a port in the SW of Grande Comore island. Population (1977 est): 16,000.

Moroni, Giovanni Battista (c. 1525–78) Italian painter, born near Bergamo. He painted many altarpieces in Bergamo.

Morosini A noble Venetian family, prominent from the 10th century, that produced four *doges as well as distinguished generals, admirals, and churchmen. Best known is **Francesco Morosini** (1618–94), who was doge of Venice from 1688 until his death.

Morpheus In Greek mythology, a god of dreams, a son of Somnus, the god of sleep. He sent human forms into the dreams of sleeping men, while his brothers Phobetor and Phantasus sent animal and inanimate forms.

morphine A *narcotic analgesic drug obtained from *opium and used in medicine for the relief of severe pain. Its depressant effect on the brain accounts for the pain-killing properties; in high doses it also inhibits the breathing and cough centers. Other side effects include constipation, nausea, and vomiting. Morphine is an addictive drug and readily leads to severe physical dependence. Nalorphine is a specific antidote to morphine overdosage. *See also* drug dependence.

morphology (biology) The study of the form and structure of plants, animals, and microorganisms. *Anatomy is often used synonymously with morphology but in the former the emphasis is on the gross and microscopic structure of organs and parts.

morphology (language). *See* grammar.

Morphy, Paul Charles (1837–84) US chess player, who between 1858 and 1860 was regarded as the world's best player and whose games still fascinate chess enthusiasts. He traveled to Europe, defeating all opponents, but gave up chess to follow his legal career. This was unsuccessful and he became mentally unstable.

Morrill Land Grant Act (1862) US law that provided for the establishment and financial support of state institutions of higher learning, especially in the fields of agriculture and mechanical arts. Sponsored by US Representative Justin Smith Morrill of Vermont, it promoted education for the "industrial classes." *See also* Land-Grant College.

Morris, Desmond John (1928–) British zoologist, noted for his popularization of biology, especially in his books on human behavior. *The Naked Ape* (1967), *The Human Zoo* (1969), and *Manwatching* (1977) all set out to prove that human beings are still subject to the basic laws of animal behavior.

Morris, Gouverneur (1752–1816) US patriot, statesman, and diplomat. A member of the Continental Congress (1778–79), his financial expertise led to an appointment as assistant superintendent of finance (1781–85), during which time he devised the decimal coinage system, using dollars and cents, a term he invented. A delegate from Pennsylvania to the Constitutional Convention (1787), he played a major role in the final writing of the Constitution, although his idea of a strong central government was not incorporated. He was appointed US minister to France (1792–94), served as US senator (1800–03), and was made chairman of the Erie Canal Commission in 1810.

Morris, Robert (1734–1806) US patriot and businessman; born in England. He came to America in 1747 and by 1754 was a partner in a Philadelphia trading firm. A member of the Continental Congress (1775–78), he signed the Declaration of Independence and distinguished himself as a business and financial expert. He was recalled in 1781 to serve as superintendent of finance and was responsible for raising the funds for the Revolution. He reorganized government finances, established credit, founded the Bank of North America (1781), and established the US currency system. He was a US senator from Pennsylvania (1789–95).

Morris, William (1834–96) British designer, artist, and poet. Associated with the *Pre-Raphaelite Brotherhood, he later started a firm of decorators and designers (1861), who placed great importance on preindustrial crafts. He designed stained glass, carpets, and furniture, and his wallpaper designs are still used. His Kelmscott Press, founded in 1890, influenced book design and printing generally. The 19th-century *Arts and Crafts movement drew much of its inspiration from his work. He was also one of the founders of British socialism.

Morris dance A ritual English folk dance performed by groups of white-clad men wearing bells and often carrying sticks or handkerchiefs. A common theme is fertility through death and rebirth, symbolized by the carrying of green branches. Similar dances are found throughout Europe, India, and the Americas, often featuring animal characters or the black-faced Morisco (Moor), from which the name Morris is thought to derive.

Morris Jesup, Cape 83 40N 34 00W The N tip of Greenland, the world's most northerly land point, 440 mi (708 km) from the North Pole.

Morrison, Toni (Chloe Anthony Wofford; 1931–   ) US novelist. A graduate of Howard (1955) and Cornell (1957) universities, she worked in publishing from 1967. Her novels, dealing primarily with the lives of African Americans, include *The Bluest Eye* (1970), *Sula* (1973), *Song of Solomon* (1977), *Tar Baby* (1981), *Beloved* (1987), and *Jazz* (1992). In 1993 she was awarded the Nobel Prize in literature.

Morristown 40 48N 74 29W A city in N central New Jersey, NW of Newark. Settled about 1709–10, it was the site of Gen. George Washington's winter encampments of 1777 and 1779–80. The Morristown National Historical Park commemorates these and other significant Revolutionary War events. The telegraph was invented here by Samuel F. B. Morse and Alfred L. Vail. Industries include stone quarries, clothing, chemicals, and plastics. Population (1990): 16,189.

Morse, Samuel F(inley Breese) (1791–1872) US painter and inventor. He abandoned his first career as a successful portrait painter because he believed the US market was too limited. From the early 1830s, he worked for several years to perfect the electric telegraph before erecting the first telegraph line, between Washington and Baltimore (1844). Messages were sent by a system of dots and dashes that he had invented for the purpose (*see* Morse code). The first message sent, "What hath God wrought!" was particularly appropriate because the telegraph revolutionized communications.

Morse code The code invented by Samuel *Morse for transmitting telegraph messages. Each letter of the alphabet and number has a characteristic sequence of dots and dashes (short and long pulses), a dash being three times as long as a dot.

mortar (building material) A mixture of sand, hydrated lime, and Portland cement, used to bind together building bricks, etc. It is applied wet as a paste, which sets to a durable solid.

mortar (weapon) A short-barreled muzzle-loading artillery piece with a low-velocity high-angled trajectory. Although modern designs date from 1915, it originated before 1600. In World War II the largest Allied mortar had a caliber of 4.2 inches (107 mm), the German version being 8.3 inches (210 mm) with six barrels. Used against an enemy behind cover, mortars are principally used to fire high-explosive and smoke bombs.

mortgage Rights in property (usually land, buildings, etc.) given by a borrower (mortgagor) to a lender (mortgagee) as security for a loan. When all the money borrowed and the interest due under the mortgage have been repaid, it is redeemed.

Mortier, Édouard Adolphe Casimir Joseph, Duc de Trévise (1768–1835) French marshal, who fought in the Revolutionary and Napoleonic Wars. In 1803 he occupied Hanover but in 1805 was defeated at Dürnstein by the Russians. He subsequently served in the campaign against Prussia (1806–07) and in the *Peninsular War, winning at Ocaña (1809). He was Louis-Philippe's prime minister (1834–35) and died in an attempt on the king's life.

Mortimer, Roger de, 1st Earl of March (c. 1287–1330) English magnate. He led the baronial opposition to Edward II's favorites, (1320–22) and was im-

prisoned before fleeing to France. There he became the lover of Edward's queen
*Isabella with whom he secured Edward's deposition and murder in 1327. He
then ruled England in the name of Edward's son, Edward III, until the latter
caused him to be executed.

letters

A	·—	N	—·
B	—···	O	———
C	—·—·	P	·——·
D	—··	Q	——·—
E	·	R	·—·
F	··—·	S	···
G	——·	T	—
H	····	U	··—
I	··	V	···—
J	·———	W	·——
K	—·—	X	—··—
L	·—··	Y	—·——
M	——	Z	——··

numbers

1	·————
2	··———
3	···——
4	····—
5	·····
6	—····
7	——···
8	———··
9	————·
0	—————

punctuation marks

·	·—·—·—
,	——··——
:	———···
?	··——··
'	·————·
-	—····—
/	—··—·
(or)	—·—·——
"	·—··—·

MORSE CODE

Morton, James Douglas, 4th Earl of (c. 1516–81) Regent of Scotland
(1572–78) for James VI (later James I of England). Under Mary, Queen of
Scots, he was involved in the murder of Riccio (1566) and then of Darnley
(1567), for which he was eventually executed.

Morton, Jelly Roll (Ferdinand Joseph La Menthe; 1885–1941) US jazz pianist and composer, who began his career playing the piano in New Orleans'
Storyville brothels and made recordings in the 1920s with the group Morton's
Red Hot Peppers. Claiming that he "invented jazz in 1902," his reputation has
been the subject of controversy.

Morton, John (c. 1420–1500) English churchman. A supporter of the Lancastrian cause, under Henry VII he became archbishop of Canterbury (1486), chancellor (1487), and cardinal (1493). He is remembered for his argument—**Morton's Fork**—that both the rich and those who seemed to be less well off could
afford to contribute to royal requests for grants: those who lived in luxury obvi-
ously had the money to spare, while those who lived less extravagantly must
have saved money by their modest way of life.

mosaic A picture or ornamental design made from small colored cubes of
glass, stone, tile, etc. Mosaics were common in ancient Greece, where they were
principally used for floors and made from colored pebbles. During the Roman

Empire mosaics of opaque glass and glass covered with gold leaf became popular for wall and vault decoration, a development that reached its peak in the early Christian churches in Byzantium and Italy. The 6th-century decorations in S Vitale, in Ravenna, are among the most famous mosaics of the Middle Ages. During this period mosaics were no longer stylistically dependent on painting but, instead, led artistic trends with their use of two-dimensional forms, rich color, and lavish use of gold. During the Renaissance frescoes became the preferred form of church decoration but mosaics have been revived during the 20th century.

Mosaic law The collective name for the laws contained in the *Torah. They purport to have been revealed by God to Moses on Mount Sinai and in *Judaism they form the basis of *halakhah. In Christianity some of them are accepted, but most are rejected or interpreted allegorically.

mosasaur A member of an extinct family of huge marine lizards that lived during the Cretaceous period (135–65 million years ago). Up to 33 ft (10 m) long, mosasaurs had broad paddlelike limbs and a long flexible tail and were efficient swimmers, feeding on fish, cuttlefish, and squid.

moschatel A perennial herbaceous plant, *Adoxa moschatellina*, also called townhall clock, native to Eurasia and North America. Up to 4 in (10 cm) high, it has compound leaves with round-lobed leaflets and a squarish terminal cluster of greenish flowers. It has a musky smell and is the sole member of its family (*Adoxaceae*).

Moscow (Russian name: Moskva) 55 45N 37 42E The capital city of Russia, on the Moskva River. It is the economic and political center of Russia and an important transportation center. Industries include heavy engineering, cars, textiles, electronics, chemicals, publishing, and food processing. Moscow is at the center of the national railroad system and is an important river port. Its underground railroad (begun 1935) is of note. The city is based on a radial plan; the *Kremlin (citadel) and Red Square are at its heart. The Kremlin, triangular in shape, encloses a number of notable ecclesiastical buildings including the Cathedral of the Assumption (1475–79) and the Cathedral of the Annunciation (1484–89). Red Square is the traditional setting for military parades and demonstrations. Beyond its historical center Moscow is a modern city. It is a major cultural center; its many educational institutions include the University of Moscow (1755), the People's Friendship University (1960) for foreign students, and the Academy of Sciences. The Tretyakov Gallery of Russian Art (1856) is the most notable of its many museums. Other famous institutions include the Bolshoi Theater of Opera and Ballet (1780), the *Moscow Art Theater, and the Moscow State Circus. *History*: first documented in 1147, settlement actually dates back to prehistoric times. By the beginning of the 13th century it was the center of the Muscovy principality and became the seat of the Russian Church containing the Kremlin (1326). In 1712–13 the capital was transferred to St Petersburg (Leningrad) but Moscow remained significant. The city was invaded by Napoleon (1812) and the ensuing fire, started either by looting French soldiers or the Moscow people themselves, destroyed much of the city. The workers' movements in Moscow played an important role in the Revolution of 1905. In March 1918, it was chosen as the capital of the RSFSR and following the arrival of Lenin and other communist leaders (1922) was made the capital of the Soviet Union. Development programs were interrupted by World War II, during which the German invasion of the city was only halted by the severe weather and strong resistance. Since the war, programs of recovery and development have been followed and Moscow has developed an important tourist industry. It was chosen as the site of the 1980 Olympic Games. Moscow lost its status as capital of the USSR in the 1991 Soviet governmental collapse. Population (1991 est): 8,801,500.

Moscow Art Theater A Russian theater company founded in 1898 by Konstantin *Stanislavsky and Vladimir Nemirovich-Danchenko (1859–1948). Its first major success was a production of *The Seagull* by Chekhov, whose plays were ideally suited to the naturalistic acting style developed by Stanislavsky. Other dramatists whose plays received notable productions include Gorky, Tolstoy, and Maeterlinck. The company gained international acclaim on its first tour of Europe and the US in 1922 and has continued to maintain high standards of ensemble acting.

Moseley, Henry Gwyn Jeffries (1887–1915) British physicist, who, working under *Rutherford, discovered the connection between the frequency of the X-rays emitted by an atom of an element and its atomic number. This discovery provided a theoretical basis for the periodic classification of the elements. Moseley's career came to a tragic end when he was killed in World War I.

Moselle River (German name: Mosel R.) A river in W Europe, flowing N from NE France to join the Rhine River at Koblenz. It forms part of the border between W Germany and Luxembourg. Its valley is one of the main wine-growing areas of W Germany. Length: 340 mi (547 km).

Moses In the Old Testament, the lawgiver of Israel, who led the people from slavery in Egypt (Exodus) and, after wandering in the desert for 40 years, brought them to an area E of the Jordan River, the border of the Promised Land. He is the central figure in most of the Pentateuch (the first five Old Testament books). As a child in Egypt (according to the Old Testament), Moses was saved from the slaughter of all Hebrew male children ordered by Pharaoh by being hidden in bulrushes on the Nile; he was found and brought up by one of Pharaoh's daughters. On Mt Sinai he was given the Ten Commandments by Jehovah. He died at the age of 120, before the Israelites entered the Promised Land, which he was allowed to see from a distance (Mt Pisgah).

Moses, Grandma (Anna Mary Robertson M.; 1860–1961) US primitive painter, born in Greenwich, N.Y. (*see* primitivism). Entirely self-taught, she only turned seriously to painting at the age of 67 after a life as a farmer's wife. She specialized in naive and nostalgic scenes of farm life, popularized through prints and Christmas cards.

Mosley, Sir Oswald Ernald (1896–1980) British fascist. He was a member of Parliament as a Conservative (1918–22), an Independent (1922–24), and then a Labour representative (1924, 1926–31), serving as chancellor of the Duchy of Lancaster (1929–30). In 1932 he established the British Union of Fascists, which incited anti-Semitic violence, especially in London. In World War II he was interned (1940–43) and in 1948 founded the Union Movement.

mosque A Muslim place of worship. It evolved in various styles from a simple rectangular building, such as the first mosque built by Mohammed at Medina in 622 AD. Larger mosques are usually built around a courtyard, which is surrounded by arcades on all four sides. Prayers are said in a large covered area on the side facing Mecca, the direction being indicated by a niche (*mihrab*) in the wall. Mosques are often domed and have *minarets. Painting and sculpture of living beings are forbidden, but elaborate geometrical designs and Arabic calligraphy frequently adorn both exterior and interior walls. The mosque has traditionally been the center of Muslim life, intellectual and social as well as religious. The three most sacred mosques are those of Mecca, Medina, and Jerusalem.

Mosque of Islam. *See* Black Muslims.

mosquito A small fly belonging to a family (*Culicidae*; about 2500 species) of almost worldwide distribution, being especially abundant in the tropics. It has long legs, elongated mouthparts, and a long slender abdomen. In most species the males feed on plant juices, while the females bite and suck the blood of mammals, often transmitting serious human and animal diseases. The three important genera are *Anopheles*, *Aedes*, and *Culex* (including the common gnat, *C. pipiens*). The active larvae live in fresh water, feeding on algae, bacteria, and organic debris. Most breathe through a siphon at the rear end.

Mosquito Coast (*or* Miskito Coast) A coastal belt in Central America, bordering on the Caribbean Sea and extending from E Honduras into E Nicaragua. Its name derives from the former inhabitants of the area, the Mosquito (Miskito) Indians. The cultivation of bananas is the chief occupation. Average width: 40 mi (60 km).

moss A *bryophyte plant of the class *Musci* (or *Bryopsida*; about 15,000 species), growing worldwide (except in salt water) on moist soil, trees, rocks, etc. The moss plant is differentiated into stems and leaves and produces sex cells (gametes), which give rise to a spore capsule that grows from the plant on a long stalk. Mosses help control erosion by providing surface cover and retaining water. *Sphagnum*, responsible for peat formation, is the only economically important moss. The name is also applied to several unrelated plants, for example *Spanish moss.

Mössbauer effect The emission of a gamma ray (*see* gamma radiation) by an excited nucleus in a solid. Generally such an emission causes the nucleus to recoil, thus reducing the energy of the gamma ray. In the Mössbauer effect the recoil is distributed throughout the solid. The gamma ray therefore loses no energy and may then raise other nuclei into the same excited state. It was discovered by the German physicist Rudolph Mössbauer (1929–   ) and enables the structure of nuclei and molecules to be examined.

Mostaganem 36 04N 0 11E A port in NW Algeria, on the Mediterranean Sea. Founded in the 11th century, it has an 11th-century citadel. It trades in wine, fruit, and vegetables, and is at the head of a natural gas pipeline from Hasse R'Mel in the Sahara. Population (1987): 114,000.

Mostar 43 20N 17 50E A city in Bosnia and Hercegovina on the Neretva River. A center for Serbian culture with a university (1977), it is situated amid mountainous wine-growing country. Population (1981): 110,000.

most-favored-nation clause A clause in a trade agreement between two countries in which each country agrees that any more favorable agreement either may make with a third country shall also apply to the other country. The mechanism is at the heart of the *General Agreement on Tariffs and Trade (GATT), although GATT allows the clause to be waived in treaties with *developing countries and in certain cases involving the formation of a *customs union.

Mosul 36 21N 43 08E A city in N Iraq, close to the Turkish border. From 1534 to 1918 it was an important trading center in the Ottoman Empire, and Turkey continued to claim the town until 1926. Mosul's modern prosperity is derived from nearby oil fields. Its former Faculties of the University of Baghdad became Mosul University in 1967. Population (1985 est): 571,000.

motet A polyphonic composition (*see* polyphony) for voices, generally unaccompanied. In the medieval motet the fundamental tenor (holding) part was based on a slow-moving plainchant or popular song while the upper triplex (treble) and motetus (worded) parts had a different text and a quicker rhythm. The 16th-century motet with Latin text, used during church services but not a part of the liturgy, is found in its purest form in the works of Palestrina. In England a Latin motet was distinguished from an English *anthem. Since the 17th century the word has been used to describe a serious but not necessarily religious choral work.

mother-of-pearl. *See* pearl.

Motherwell, Robert (1915–91) US abstract painter. Largely self-taught, he turned to painting during World War II, under the influence of the European surrealists. He became a leading exponent of *action painting with his use of dripped and splattered paint, notably in his black and white series entitled *Elegy to the Spanish Republic*. His painting after this period became more structured, showing the influence of *Rothko.

moth orchid An epiphytic *orchid of the genus *Phalaenopsis* (about 40 species), native to SE Asia and E Australia. It has a very short stem bearing several broad leathery leaves and larger clusters of flowers. Moth orchids are popular hot-house ornamentals; hybrids produced usually have white or pink long-lasting flowers.

moths. *See* butterflies and moths.

motion pictures The art form and industry of films. The first motion picture exhibited to a public audience was made in 1895 by the French brothers Louis and Auguste *Lumière, whose equipment was developed from the inventions of Thomas *Edison, and the first commercial success was the American film *The Great Train Robbery* (1903). Influential pioneers of the silent film in the US were D. W. *Griffith, Mack *Sennett, and Charlie *Chaplin. In Europe, technological developments were creatively exploited by such directors as F. W. Murnau (1889–1931) in Germany and *Eisenstein in Russia. The end of the era of silent films was signaled by the success of Al *Jolson's *The Jazz Singer* (1927), which had a synchronized musical score; color film, introduced in the 1930s, added further popular appeal. The French directors René *Clair and Jean *Renoir made notable contributions to the early development of sound pictures. Between 1930 and 1945 the motion picture industry in the US became essentially an entertainment factory, controlled by giant Hollywood studios such as MGM and Paramount. The decline in audiences from the late 1940s because of the rival attraction of television caused the break-up of the Hollywood system. After World War II many of the most significant developments in motion pictures were initiated by directors in Europe, including Federico *Fellini and Michelangelo *Antonioni in Italy, Ingmar *Bergman in Sweden, Spain's Luis *Buñuel, and, later, François *Truffaut in France. Asian directors of note included Akira *Kurosawa in Japan and Satyajit Ray in India. British filmmakers included Carol Reed, David Lean, Tony Richardson, and Ken Russell. Directors such as Alfred *Hitchcock found their work acclaimed throughout the world. Many modern US directors, such as Stanley *Kubrick, Robert Altman, and Francis Ford Coppola, have often concentrated on films with a social message. Others, including George *Lucas and Steven Spielberg, have introduced a new era of futuristic films. Some actors, notably Woody *Allen, Clint Eastwood, Robert Redford, and Barbra Streisand, have also achieved success as directors.

motion sickness Nausea and sometimes vomiting caused by traveling in cars, buses, trains, planes, boats (sea sickness), or on any fast-moving machine. It arises when the constant movement disturbs the organs of balance in the inner ear, which causes nausea. Motion sickness is especially common in children and many of them grow out of it. It is treated with drugs to stop the nausea, particularly *antihistamines. As many of these cause sleepiness as well, a person driving should not take them.

motmot A bird of the tropical American family *Motmotidae* (8 species); 6–20 in (16–50 cm) long, motmots have short rounded wings, short legs, and long tails with elongated central feathers. The bill is broad and serrated and the plumage is green, blue, brown, and black. Motmots live in forests and prey on insects, spiders, worms, etc. Order: *Coraciiformes* (kingfishers, etc.).

motocross (*or* scrambling) A form of *motorcycle racing invented in Britain in 1927. It takes place on a circuit marked out across rough country. International events are for 250 cc and 500 cc machines.

motorcycle racing Racing single-seat motorcycles or sidecar combinations, in classes according to engine capacity. In **road racing**, run usually on special circuits, the main classes are 125, 250, 350, and 500 cc. The sport developed in Europe. World championships are awarded according to points won in Grand Prix and other races held in many countries. In the US the sport is regulated by the American Motorcyclist Association (AMA). **Motorcycle trials** are usually events in which a cross-country course has to be completed within a certain time, with points lost in observed sections of the course for stopping, touching the ground, etc. *See also* drag racing; motocross; rally; speedway.

motorcycles Two-wheeled engine-powered vehicles. The evolution of the motorcycle has been closely associated with the development of the *bicycle, *steam engine, and *car. The muscle-powered bicycle was in use by the mid-19th century but the concept of a steam-powered bicycle was first realized by S. H. Roper in the US in the 1860s. Similar machines were being built in Paris at about the same time by Pierre and Ernest Michaux. However, the true forerunner of the modern motorcycle was Gottlieb *Daimler's 1885 bicycle powered by an *Otto four-stroke engine. The first production model was Hildebrand and Wolfmüller's 1894 "Pétrolette." By 1900 there were some 11,000 motorcycles in France alone. During World War I, motorcycles (often in combination with sidecars) were extensively used. The interwar period—the great era of the motorcycle—saw the development of many classic designs: the Harley-Davidson in the US; the Brough Superior, Triumph Speed Twin, and Ariel Square Four in Britain; and the German DKW two-stroke and BMW four-stroke. All these were in military use in World War II. During and after the war some innovations were made, such as telescopic forks, sprung rear wheels, disc brakes, and starter motors, but the basic design remained unchanged. In the 1950s and 1960s interest in motorcycles in Europe and the US declined; their inherent danger and the status symbol of car ownership forced most European manufacturers out of business. The motor scooter, a low-powered Italian-originated version of the motorcycle, and the moped, an engine-assisted bicycle, acquired some popularity. In the 1970s, the Japanese, exploiting the closing of European factories, developed a whole new range of motorcycles, based on European designs. These machines now dominate world markets.

Mott, Lucretia Coffin (1793–1880) US reformer and pioneer in the woman's rights movement. As a Quaker lecturer, she preached against slavery, alcohol, and war. By 1833 she had formed the Philadelphia Anti-Slavery Society. With Elizabeth Cady *Stanton she initiated the 1848 Seneca Falls Convention, from which the woman's rights movement was born. She continued to work for suffrage and equal opportunities for all, especially women and African Americans.

Mo-tzu. *See* Mo-Zi.

mouflon A wild sheep, *Ovis musimon*, native to Corsica and Sardinia and introduced to other parts of Europe and to North America. Mouflons are about 25.5 in (65 cm) high at the shoulder and males have large curved horns, a distinctive rump patch, and a white saddle on the back.

Moulmein 16 30N 97 39E A port in Myanmar (formerly Burma), on the Salween River. The chief city of British Burma from 1826 until 1852, Moulmein has an important teak trade and exports rice. Population (1983 est): 220, 000.

MOTORCYCLES

1860s S.H. Roper Velocipede *One of the earliest steam-powered cycles, this machine survives in the Smithsonian Institution, Washington, DC.*

1894 Hildebrand and Wolfmüller "Pétrolette" *The first production motorcycle, it had direct rearwheel drive, pneumatic tires, and a 1488 cc engine. Production was 10 machines a day.*

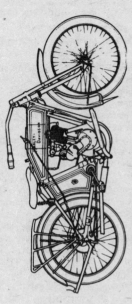

1885 Daimler *The forerunner of the modern motorcyle, it had a wooden frame, iron tires, and a 264 cc four-stroke engine.*

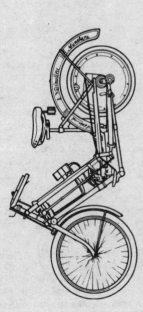

1917 Harley-Davidson *This 989 cc Vee-twin chaindrive machine had the first twist-grip throttle control.*

MOTORCYCLES

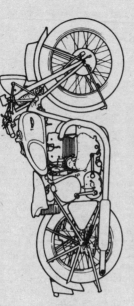

1938 Triumph 500 cc Speed Twin *Capable of over 100 mph, it was widely used by the police.*

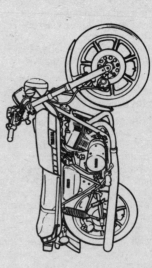

1979 Yamaha RD250 *A Japanese twin cylinder two-stroke with capacitor discharge ignition and disc brakes.*

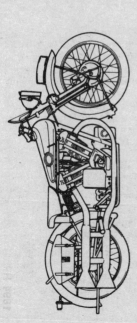

1930 Brough Superior *Built from 1919 to 1940 this Cadillac of motorcycles had a 980 cc Vee-twin JAP engine. Only 3000 were ever made.*

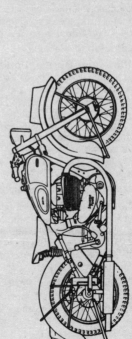

1949 Ariel Square Four *The compact arrangement of the four cylinders gave the machine its name. It had telescopic front forks and a sprung rear wheel.*

mountain. *See* orogeny.

mountain ash A tree, *Sorbus aucuparia*, also called rowan, native to temperate Eurasia and commonly cultivated as an ornamental. Up to 49 ft (15 m) high, it has long leaves with numerous paired leaflets and large clusters of small cream flowers, which give rise to bright-scarlet berries with a bitter acid taste, used to make wine and jelly. The similar and related American species is *S. americana*. Family: **Rosaceae*.

The Australian mountain ash (**Eucalyptus regnans*), up to 344 ft (105 m) high, is the world's tallest broad-leaved tree.

mountain beaver. *See* sewellel.

mountaineering A sport that developed in the mid-19th century. Interest in exploring mountains first grew in the 18th century; after Mont Blanc was climbed in 1786 by Michel Paccard and Jacques Balmat interest gradually extended to other areas of the Alps. The English Alpine Club, founded in 1857, was quickly followed by continental clubs. The Matterhorn was climbed in 1865 by Edward *Whymper's expedition, Mount Kilimanjaro in 1889 by Hans Meyer and Ludwig Purtscheller, and Mount Kenya in 1899. No peak over 25,646 ft (7817 m) was climbed until after World War II, when modern equipment and generous funding made high-altitude climbing possible. Annapurna I was climbed in 1950 by Maurice Herzog and Louis Lachenal and Mount Everest in 1953 by Sir Edmund *Hillary and *Tenzing Norgay. Now that the world's highest peaks have been conquered, mountaineering is largely a matter of finding new routes and new methods. Rock climbing and ice climbing, skills always intrinsic to mountaineering, have become independent sports; like mountaineering in general, they make use of such equipment as nylon ropes, down suits, and crampons and are organized through clubs.

mountain lion. *See* cougar.

Mountbatten of Burma, Louis, 1st Earl (1900–79) British admiral and colonial administrator; son of Prince Louis of Battenberg (1854–1921), who took the name Mountbatten and was created Marquess of Milford Haven in 1917, and of Princess Victoria of Hesse-Darmstadt, the granddaughter of Queen Victoria. He entered the Royal Navy in 1913 and in World War II was supreme Allied commander in SE Asia (1943–45), retaking Burma. As viceroy of India (1947) he presided over the transfer of power to India and Pakistan and was then governor general of India (1947–48). He was subsequently commander in chief of the Mediterranean fleet (1952–54) and first sea lord (1955–59), becoming an admiral in 1956. He died in Ireland, the victim of an IRA bomb.

Mounties. *See* Royal Canadian Mounted Police.

Mount of Olives The highest point in a small range of four summits situated just E of Jerusalem. It features in the Old and New Testaments. Its W slope was the site of the Garden of *Gethsemane. According to the Acts of the Apostles (1.2–12), Christ ascended to heaven from the Mount of Olives. Many churches and convents of various denominations have been built here since the 4th century AD or earlier.

Mount Rainier National Park A national park in S central Washington, SE of Seattle, in the Cascade Range, Mount Rainier, the focus of the park, which was established in 1899, is an extinct volcano that rises to 14,410 ft (4393 m) and has over 20 glaciers on it. The park is a popular winter sports area. Area: 378 sq mi (979 sq km).

Mount Rushmore National Memorial The gigantic sculpture of the heads of four US presidents—Washington, Jefferson, Lincoln, and Theodore

Roosevelt—carved (1927–41) to the design of the sculptor Gutzon *Borglum on the NE cliffs of Mount Rushmore, South Dakota. Each head is about 60 ft (18 m) high.

LORD MOUNTBATTEN *His outstanding contribution to public life was to oversee, as last viceroy of India, the establishment of Indian independence. Here he is greeted by Y. B. Chavan, India's defense minister (1962–66), at celebrations for Independence Day.*

Mount Saint Helens 46 12N 122 11W A volcano in SW Washington, in the S Cascade Range, NE of Vancouver, Canada. It is 9677 ft (2950 m) high, and, until 1980, had not erupted since 1857. In May 1980, a mammoth eruption blew the top off the mountain and caused widespread destruction in which more than 50 people died. The devastated area of about 172 sq mi (445 sq km) is included in Mount St Helens National Volcanic Monument, established in 1982. Minor eruptions since 1980 have caused minor damage.

Mount Vernon A national shrine in Virginia, S of Washington, DC, on the Potomac River. It was the home (1754–99) of George Washington, whose tomb lies in the grounds of the 18th-century Georgian mansion. The house, outbuildings, and gardens have been carefully restored and preserved.

Mount Wilson Observatory. *See* Hale Observatories.

Mourne Mountains A mountain range in Northern Ireland, in Co Down. It extends SW–NE between Carlingford Lough and Dundrum Bay, reaching 2798 ft (853 m) at Slieve Donard.

mourning dove A common North American *pigeon, *Zenaidura macroura*, that is adapted for survival in hot deserts; it can endure high body temperatures and dehydration and can fly long distances, enabling it to live far from water; 12 in (30 cm) long, it has a long pointed tail and gray-brown plumage with pink and violet patches on the neck.

mouse A *rodent belonging to the suborder *Myomorpha*. The house mouse (*Mus musculus*) is common in buildings worldwide and has long been associated with man. Grayish brown, it is 5.5–6 in (14–16 cm) long including its tail

(2.8–3.1 in; 7–8 cm) and feeds on a variety of foods, from sugar and grain to oil-based paints and putty.

Most mice—together with their larger relatives, the *rats—are grouped into the subfamilies *Murinae* of the Old World and *Cricetinae* of the New World (which also includes hamsters). There are separate subfamilies for African tree mice (*Dendromurinae*; 7 species), jumping mice (*Zapodinae*; 3 species), dormice, and other small groups.

mousebird. *See* coly.

mouse deer. *See* chevrotain.

Mousterian A stone-tool industry of the Middle *Paleolithic, associated with *Neanderthal man. Named for caves at Le Moustier in the Dordogne (SW France), the Mousterian occurs, with variants, throughout Eurasia from France to China and in N Africa. Spanning roughly the period of 70,000 to 35,000 BC, it is characterized by a wide variety of hand axes, scrapers, points, and blades, often made by the *Lavalloisian technique. Mousterian sites have provided the earliest evidence for formal burial of the dead.

mouthbrooder A fish belonging to one of several genera of *cichlid fishes. The eggs are carried in the mouth of the parent, usually the female, until they hatch. Chief genera: *Tilapia*; *Haplochromis*; *Pelmatochromis*. Other mouth-brooders include certain *fighting fish, *catfish, and cardinal fish.

mouth organ. *See* harmonica.

Mozambique, People's Republic of (Portuguese name: Moçambique) A country in S East Africa, bordering on the Indian Ocean. Extensive coastal plains, at their widest in the S, rise to plateaus inland with mountains reaching over 6500 ft (2000 m). The chief rivers, notably the Zambezi and Limpopo, flow E and provide both irrigation and hydroelectric power. Most of the population is African, mainly Bantu, with diminishing minorities of Europeans and others. *Economy*: chiefly agricultural, the staple food crops being rice and corn. The main cash crops of cashew nuts (of which Mozambique is the world's largest producer), cotton, and sugar are also the principal exports. Industry is, at present, based largely on food processing and textiles but there are plans to develop heavy industry. Mineral resources, including natural gas and high-grade iron ore, are largely unexploited except for coal and bauxite. The transit trade provides an important source of income and Mozambique was compensated for closing its routes to Rhodesia (now Zimbabwe) in 1976. *History*: the N coast was settled by Arabs from the 10th century and was explored by Vasco da *Gama in 1498, becoming a Portuguese colony in the early 16th century. In 1951 it became an overseas province of Portugal. From 1963 FRELIMO (Frente de Libertaçao de Moçambique) waged a guerrilla campaign that achieved the establishment (1975) of an independent socialist republic. Mozambique provided a base for *Mugabe's arm of the Zimbabwe guerrilla organization, the Patriotic Front, and its borders with Rhodesia (now Zimbabwe) were closed from 1976 until 1980. The South-African-backed Mozambique National Resistance (MNR) applied military pressure in Mozambique with raids on Maputo, the capital. South Africa claimed that the incursions were targeted at a guerrilla movement seeking to overthrow the South African government. In 1984 two US petroleum companies contracted with Mozambique to explore for oil. A nonaggression pact with South Africa was signed in 1984 and again in 1987, even though the South Africans continued to back the guerrillas. The civil war had a great impact on Mozambique's economy, killing hundreds of thousands and causing almost 250,000 to flee the country. In 1990, South Africa denounced the guerrillas and discontinued aid. Despite peace talks and reforms to democratize Mozambique, fighting continued. Official language: Portuguese; the main African language is Makua Lomwe. Official currency: Mozambique escudo of 100 centavos. Area: 303,070 sq mi (784,961 sq km). Population (1990): 14,718,000. Capital and main port: Maputo.

Mozarabs Christians living in Spain under Muslim rule. The Mozarabs (meaning "almost Arabs") were so called because in spite of their Christianity they adopted the Arabic culture of their Muslim rulers. They formed autonomous communities within the Muslim state.

Mozart, Wolfgang Amadeus (1756–91) Austrian composer, born in Salzburg, the son of the violinist and composer Leopold Mozart (1719–87). Mozart exhibited extraordinary musical talent at the age of four; in 1762 his father took him on a tour of Germany and to Paris and London, where he received adulation for his abilities. In 1770 in Rome Mozart was able to write out the entire score of a *Miserere* by Gregorio Allegri (1582–1652) after hearing the work twice; he earned the highest praise for his talents as performer, improviser, and composer. He continued to tour, composing piano sonatas, symphonies, and his early operas but failing to find a permanent position worthy of his exceptional talents. After a period of unhappy service with the archbishop of Salzburg (1779–81) he settled in Vienna as a freelance musician and teacher, composing such masterpieces as the operas *The Marriage of Figaro* (1786) and *Don Giovanni* (1787). The success of the latter obtained him belated recognition from the emperor but constant traveling, poverty, and frequent overwork contributed to his early death, possibly from typhus. Mozart achieved a fusion of the Germanic and Italianate styles of composition and his immense productivity enriched almost every musical genre. He composed 49 symphonies, over 40 concertos (of which those for piano [25], horn, violin, and clarinet are best known), 7 string quintets, 26 string quartets, numerous divertimenti, piano sonatas, violin sonatas, and much other music. Some of his finest works, such as the operas *Così fan tutte* (1790) and *The Magic Flute* (1791) and the *Jupiter* symphony (1788), were written in the last years of his life. His unfinished *Requiem* was completed after his death by Franz Süssmayr (1766–1803). *See also* Köchel, Ludwig von.

Mo-Zi (*or* Mo-tzu; ?470–391? BC) Chinese philosopher. Originally a follower of Confucius, Mo-Zi criticized him for stressing ritual rather than virtue. In his chief work, the *Mo-Zi*, he taught universal love, pacifism, and simplicity, principles that formed the basis of a short-lived religious movement, Moism. Although Moism as a religion had ceased to be practiced by the 2nd century BC, as a philosophy it is still highly regarded.

Mu'awiyah I (c. 602–80 AD) The first *caliph (661–80) of the Umayyad dynasty. He participated in the conquest of Syria, where he was made governor in 640. He fought against *Ali, after whose assassination he himself became caliph. Renowned for his tactful control of the Arabs, Mu'awiyah is blamed by Islam for turning the caliphate into a worldly kingship.

Mubarak, (Mohammad) Hosni (Said) (1928–   ) Egyptian statesman; president (1981–   ). A general, he commanded the Egyptian air force (1972–75) and was responsible for reorganization of the air units that fought successfully in the Yom Kippur War with Israel (1973). He became vice president to Anwar *Sadat in 1975 and succeeded him, upon his assassination, to the presidency in 1981. A cautious, conservative president, he held Egypt's inflationary economy in check and kept US-Egypt relations cordial, endorsing Egyptian support of US-led UN troops during the Persian Gulf War. He attempted, with some success, to end isolation from neighboring Arab countries and was very important in arranging the Middle East peace conference in November 1991.

mucous membrane A moist membrane that lines the digestive and respiratory tracts and the nasal sinuses. It is a type of *epithelium containing cells that
secrete **mucus**, a slimy substance that protects its surface and—in the digestive
tract—also lubricates the passage of food and feces. In the bronchi the mucus
traps particles that are inhaled with air.

Mozart *Lithograph by Jab from a painting by Hamman.
Many of Mozart's compositions for the piano were written
to display his abilities as an instrumentalist.*

Mudéjars (Arabic: vassal) The Muslims (*see* Moors) of Spain who had, by the
13th century, become subject to Christian rule during the reconquest of the Iberian peninsula. Many were of mixed *Berber and Spanish descent and continued
to preserve their Islamic religion and customs. They were the creators of an architectural style notable for its ornamental brickwork and use of ceramic tiling.
Many examples still survive in Castile and Aragon. *Compare* Mozarabs.

mudfish. *See* bowfin.

mudpuppy A salamander, *Necturus maculosis*, of North America. Gray-
brown, with four well-developed limbs, mudpuppies retain their dark-red gills
throughout their lives, even when mature at about five years old and 8 in (20 cm)
long. They are slow moving and generally hunt fish, snails, and other invertebrates at night. The female guards her eggs until they hatch. Family: *Proteidae*.
See also olm.

mudskipper A fish of the subfamily *Periophthalminae*, especially the genus *Periophthalmus*, found in swamps, estuaries, and mud flats of Africa, Polynesia, and Australia. Mudskippers have an elongated body, up to 12 in (30 cm) long, a blunt head, and dorsally protruding eyes. They are able to climb and walk over land using their limblike pectoral fins. Family: *Gobiidae* (*see* goby).

mufti A Muslim legal expert. They assist judges or private citizens by writing their opinions (*futwas* on legal matters. These only become precedents in cases of marriage, divorce, and inheritance. In the Ottoman Empire muftis were state officials, the grand mufti being the chief spiritual authority.

Mugabe, Robert (Gabriel) (1925–   ) Zimbabwe statesman; prime minister (1980–   ), and president (1987–   ). A teacher, he helped found the Zimbabwe African National Union (ZANU) in 1963 and, after ten years' (1964–74) detention in Rhodesia, formed the *Patriotic Front (PF) with Joshua Nkomo, leader of the Zimbabwe African People's Union (ZAPU). Based in Mozambique and Zambia respectively, they waged guerrilla warfare against the governments of Ian Smith and then Bishop Muzorewa until agreeing through talks (1979–80) to disarm (*see* Zimbabwe). His party's election victory (1980) brought Mugabe the leadership of newly independent Zimbabwe. Since that time he has consolidated his power and eliminated political opposition.

mugger A broad-snouted *crocodile, *Crocodylus palustris*, found in India, Sri Lanka, and Burma. It was formerly a sacred animal, kept in temples and tended by priests.

mugwort. *See* wormwood.

Mugwumps Group of US Republicans who supported Democrat Grover *Cleveland and would not vote for Republican James G. Blaine in 1884. Coined by New York newspaper editor Charles Dana, it means "big chief" in the Algonquian Indian language and is used to label any party member that does not support the party's candidate.

Muhammad. *See* Mohammed.

Muhammad Ahmad. *See* Mahdi, al-.

Muir, Edwin (1887–1959) Scottish poet. He moved to London in 1919, and during the 1930s he and his wife moved to Prague, where they translated the novels of Franz *Kafka and other major German writers. His reputation as a poet was established rather late in life with *The Voyage* (1946) and *The Labyrinth* (1949), in which he made distinctive use of traditional meters and diction. His *Autobiography* (1954) contains much of his best prose.

Muir, John (1838–1914) US naturalist and conservationist; born in Scotland. He settled in Wisconsin in 1849 and, after college (1859–63), traveled the country. He lived in Yosemite Valley for six years from 1868 and during a trip to Alaska (1879) discovered Glacier Bay. Due to his efforts and writings, the National Park bill (1890) established Yosemite and Sequoia national parks and paved the way for 13 national forests by 1897. The Muir Woods National Monument (1908) in California is named for him.

Mujibur Rahman, Sheik (1920–75) Bangladesh statesman; prime minister (1972–75). He was jailed in 1968 by *Ayub Khan's regime in Pakistan for campaigning for the independence of East Pakistan. Following the victory of his party, the Awami League, in the 1970 elections and victory in the subsequent civil war (1971), he became prime minister of the independent state of Bangladesh. He assumed dictatorial powers shortly before his assassination.

Mukden. *See* Shenyang.

mulberry A tree of the genus *Morus* (12 species), native to N temperate and subtropical regions. The black mulberry (*M. nigra*) is the species most commonly cultivated for its fruit. About 31 ft (12 m) high, it has toothed heart-shaped leaves and round green male and female flower clusters (catkins), borne usually on separate trees. The female flowers give rise to small berries that are grouped together to form a blackberry-like fruit, which has a pleasant slightly acid taste and is used in jellies, desserts, etc. The leaves of the white mulberry (*M. alba*) are the staple food of silkworms. Family: *Moraceae. See also* paper mulberry.

mule The sterile offspring of a female horse and a male ass. Mules are useful pack and draft animals, being hardy, sure-footed, and strong but smaller than a horse and requiring less food. *See also* hinny.

Mülheim an der Ruhr 51 25N 6 50E A city in NW Germany, in North Rhine-Westphalia on the Ruhr River. There is a 13th century castle. Its manufactures include power-station generators, pipes and tubes, and machinery. Population (1988): 170,000.

Mull An island off the W coast of Scotland, in the Inner Hebrides. It is chiefly mountainous and agriculture is restricted; sheep and cattle are raised. Other occupations include fishing, forestry, and tourism. Area: 351 sq mi (909 sq km). Chief town: Tobermory.

mullein A biennial or perennial herb of the genus *Verbascum* (about 300 species), native to N temperate Eurasia. The biennial common mullein (*V. thapsus*), also called Aaron's rod, occurs in dry limy regions. It has a single stem, 0.6–2 m tall, bearing large woolly leaves and a dense terminal spike of pale-yellow flowers. Some species, including the European dark mullein (*V. nigrum*), are grown as garden plants. Family: *Scrophulariaceae*.

Muller, Hermann Joseph (1890–1967) US geneticist, who discovered the ability of X-rays to induce changes (mutations) in genetic material. Although useful as an experimental tool, Muller recognized the danger of X-radiation to man. He was awarded a Nobel Prize (1946).

Müller, Paul Hermann (1899–1965) Swiss chemist, who discovered the insecticidal properties of *DDT (1939). Müller found it was relatively harmless to other forms of life and DDT became widely used to combat insect pests. Müller was awarded the 1948 Nobel Prize in medicine.

mullet A food fish, also called gray mullet, belonging to the genus *Mugil* (about 70 species), found in temperate and tropical coastal waters and estuaries. It has a slender silvery-green or gray large-scaled body, 12–35 in (30–90 cm) long, with two dorsal fins. It feeds in large schools on algae and small invertebrates. Family: *Mugilidae*; order: *Perciformes. See also* red mullet.

Mulliken, Robert Sanderson (1896–1986) US chemist and physicist, who developed *Schrödinger's theory of wave mechanics to provide a mathematical explanation of chemical bonding in terms of electron probabilities, orbitals, and energy levels. He received the 1966 Nobel Prize in chemistry for this work.

Mulroney, (Martin) Brian (1939–) Canadian statesman and lawyer; prime minister (1984–93). He practiced law in Montreal from 1962; in 1977 he was named to head the Iron Ore Company of Canada, where he proved himself adept at settling labor problems. Active in the Progressive Conservative party from law school days, he became the party's leader in 1983 and in September 1984 was elected prime minister, ousting Liberal party leader John *Turner. Mulroney pledged to strengthen Canada's economy, extend social services, and improve relations with the US; toward this end he held a two-day summit meeting with

President Reagan in 1986. His inability in 1990 to persuade all provinces to agree to the Meech Lake agreement of 1987, providing for Quebec's separateness, caused a decline in his popularity. He resigned in 1993.

Multan 30 10N 71 36E a city in central Pakistan. An ancient settlement on the key route to S India, it has often been besieged and occupied. Multan's textile manufacturing and cottage industries are noteworthy. Population (1981): 732,000.

multinational corporations Large business enterprises with headquarters (the parent company) in one country and operating divisions (subsidiaries) in one or more other countries. Strategic decision making usually takes place at the head office. Their command of large resources has led to demands for international legislation to control their activities.

multiple sclerosis A chronic and usually progressive disease of the nervous system in which the fatty sheaths that surround the nerves in the brain or spinal cord are destroyed, which affects the function of the nerves. The disease is also called disseminated sclerosis, as its effects are disseminated in different parts of the body. It usually begins in young adults, and the commonest initial symptoms are sudden severe blurring of the vision or weakness in one limb. The initial symptoms often resolve completely but later the disease returns and progresses slowly, causing permanent handicap.

multiple star A system of three or more stars that move in complex orbits under mutual gravitational attraction.

multiplexer In *telecommunications, a device that combines several signals so that they can be sent along a single transmission path, or channel, and reconstructed at the receiver. One method is to superimpose carrier waves of different frequencies (*see* modulation) on the signals. Multiplexers are used with radio transmissions, telephone lines, etc.

multiplier A number used in economic theory to indicate how many times a specific increase in income, demand, etc., will be multiplied to produce an increase in the overall income, demand, etc., in a nation's economy. For example, if an individual's income is increased by 10 as a result of a cut in direct taxation, half of this increase may be spent in such a way that it becomes income for others, who may in turn also spend half of their increased income. Thus the original 10 could be multiplied to produce a total of 20 of additional income, in which case the multiplier has a value of 2. Opinions differ as to the practical impact of the multiplier, depending on the prevailing view of what motivates consumption.

Mumford, Lewis (1895–1990) US social philosopher. Mumford's academic posts included research professorships at the Universities of Stanford (1942–44) and Berkeley (1961–62). He wrote widely on architecture and cities, arguing that technological society was repressive. His books include *Sticks and Stones* (1924), *Technics and Civilization* (1934), *Values for Survival* (1946), *In the Name of Sanity* (1954), and *The City in History* (1961).

mummers' play An English folk drama based on the legend of St George and the Seven Champions of Christendom; it was a dumb show (*mummer*, from Middle English *mum*, silent), traditionally enacted on Christmas Day by masked performers. Its plot largely consists of a duel between St George and an infidel knight, in which one of them is killed but is later brought back to life by a doctor. The play is still performed in a few villages in England and N Ireland.

mummy A human or animal body prepared and embalmed for burial according to ancient Egyptian religious practice. The internal organs were extracted and sealed in *Canopic jars and the body was desiccated by packing in dry natron, anointed, and encased in linen bandages.

mumps An acute virus infection that usually occurs in children. After an incubation period of 12 to 20 days the child develops headache and fever; later, the parotid salivary glands (situated under the ear) become tender and swollen. The disease is usually mild and resolves rapidly, but sometimes mild *meningitis develops. In adult male patients the infection may spread to the testicles, which may occasionally lead to sterility.

Munch, Charles (1892–1968) French conductor. He made his debut in Paris in 1932 and directed the Boston Symphony Orchestra from 1949 to 1962. In 1967 he founded the Orchestre de Paris but died on its first US tour.

Munch, Edvard (1863–1944) Norwegian painter and printmaker, who was a major influence on 20th-century German *expressionism. Largely self-taught, he developed his mature style in Berlin, following visits to Paris where he was influenced by *Gauguin and *Van Gogh. His symbolic paintings of love, death, and despair, including the famous *Cry* (1893; Nasjonalgalleriet, Oslo), reflect the pessimism caused by family tragedy. After 1910 he lived in Norway, where he painted murals for the festival hall of Oslo University (1913).

Münchhausen, Karl Friedrich, Freiherr von (1720–97) German soldier famous as a raconteur. His hyperbolic accounts of his feats passed into legend and were the subject of a series of adventure tales, *The Adventures of Baron Münchhausen* (1793), written by R. E. Raspe (1737–94).

Muncie 40 11N 85 22W A city in E Indiana, on the White River. It is the "typical American" town of the classic sociological study *Middletown* (1929) by Robert and Helen Lynd. An agricultural trading center, Muncie's varied manufactures include machine tools and glass. Population (1990): 71,035.

Munda Aboriginal tribes living mainly in the hills and forests of central and NE India. Munda languages form a subgroup of the *Austro-Asiatic language family. The northern branch of the Munda languages includes Santali, the most important. The Munda peoples are mainly slash-and-burn cultivators.

mung bean A *bean plant, *Phaseolus aureus*, also known as green gram, native to India and cultivated in tropical and subtropical regions chiefly as a vegetable crop. The slender pods contain up to 15 small edible seeds, which can be dried and stored or germinated in the dark to produce bean sprouts. Family: *Leguminosae*.

Munich (German name: München) 48 08N 11 35E A city in S Germany, the capital of Bavaria on the Isar River. It has a 15th-century cathedral and many baroque and rococo buildings, including Nymphenburg Palace (1664–1728). Its university was moved from Landshut in 1826. It is also noted for its technical university, opera, art galleries, and for its annual Oktoberfest (beer festival). A center of commerce, industry, and tourism, its manufactures include precision instruments, electrical goods, chemicals, and beer. *History*: Munich was from 1255 the residence and from 1506 the capital of the Dukes of Bavaria (from 1806 Kings). During the late 19th and early 20th centuries it flourished culturally, attracting such figures as the composer Wagner. The Nazi movement began here in the 1920s. Munich was severely bombed during World War II. Population (1991 est): 1,230,000.

Munich Agreement (1938) The settlement, resulting from the conference between Neville Chamberlain (UK), Daladier (France), Hitler (Germany), and Mussolini (Italy), that recognized Hitler's territorial claims to the *Sudetenland. Described by Chamberlain as achieving "peace in our time," it was followed in March 1939, by Hitler's invasion of Czechoslovakia and in September by World War II.

Munich Putsch (1923) The attempt by *Hitler to seize power in Germany. Hitler planned to form a national government after first seizing power in Bavaria. This attempt at revolution (German word: *Putsch*) failed and Hitler was imprisoned.

Munn v. Illinois (1877) US Supreme Court decision that upheld the right of states to control commerce within the state; one of the Granger cases. Grain elevator owners claimed that only the federal government had the right to regulate interstate trade. The court ruled that states could regulate private businesses that performed a public function, expecially if the business is carried on within the state.

Munro, Hector Hugh. *See* Saki.

Munsell color system A method of classifying *colors based on three parameters: hue (dominant color), luminosity (brightness), and saturation or chroma (strength, i.e. the degree to which it is a pure spectral color). The various colors are set out in a chart known as the color tree, in which the gradations of color are exhibited according to the three parameters. The Munsell color system is widely used in the paint industry. Named for Albert H. Munsell (1858–1918).

Münster 51 58N 7 37E A city and port in NW Germany, in North Rhine-Westphalia on the Dortmund-Ems Canal. It was an important member of the Hanseatic League and the capital of the former province of Westphalia. It has a 13th-century cathedral, restored after the damage of World War II, and a university (1773). Service industries provide employment for most of the workforce. Population (1991 est): 259,438.

Munster A province and ancient kingdom of the SW Republic of Ireland. It consists of the counties of Clare, Cork, Kerry, Limerick, Tipperary, and Waterford. Area: 9315 sq mi (24,125 sq km). Population (1991): 1,008,443.

Munthe, Axel (1857–1949) Swedish physician and author. Munthe practiced in Paris and Rome before retiring to Capri, where he built the Villa San Michele. *The Story of San Michele* (1929) described his early life and the building of the villa. It has been translated into 44 languages and remains a best-seller.

muntjac A small deer belonging to the subfamily *Muntiacinae* (6 species), occurring in forests of Asia, Sumatra, Java, and Borneo. The Indian muntjac (*Muntiacus muntjak*), also called barking deer or rib-faced deer, is 22 in (55 cm) high at the shoulder, chestnut above and paler beneath with short unbranched antlers and short sharp fangs. Muntjacs are mainly solitary and nocturnal, feeding on grass, leaves, and shoots.

Müntzer, Thomas (c. 1490–1525) German Protestant reformer and *Anabaptist leader. He began preaching reformed doctrines at Zwickau in 1520 but soon diverged from Luther's teachings. Claiming direct inspiration from the Holy Spirit, he called for radical social, political, and religious reform. He was driven out of several towns because of his subversive activities. A leader of the *Peasants' Revolt (1524–25), he was captured at the battle of Frankenhausen (1525) and executed.

Muntz metal A relatively hard strong type of *brass containing 60% copper and 40% zinc. It is not easily worked at room temperature and is usually shaped while hot or by casting. Named for G. F. Muntz (d. 1847).

muon A negatively charged unstable elementary particle (lifetime 2×10^{-6} second; mass 207 times that of the electron) that decays into an electron and two *neutrinos. It has a corresponding antiparticle. It was originally thought to be a meson (and was called the mu-meson) but is now classified as a lepton. *See* particle physics.

Muntjac *A male Indian muntjac showing the short antlers (about 5 in or 12 cm long), arising from hairy pedicles that extend down the face as bony ridges.*

mural painting The decoration of walls and ceilings by such varied techniques as *encaustic, *tempera, and *fresco painting. The design of murals is largely dependent on their architectural settings. *Renaissance painters often used perspective and architecture in their murals to create the illusion that the painted walls or ceilings were space extensions of the real architecture. Mural painting was revived during the 20th century, principally by the Mexican painters *Rivera, *Orozco, and *Siqueiros, who used it to reach a wider public with their social and political subject matter.

Murasaki Shikibu (?978–1026?) Japanese writer. She is most famous for her great saga, *The Tale of Genji*, which is probably the world's earliest novel. It deals chiefly with the love life of Prince Genji and is remarkable for its observations of nature and understanding of human emotions. It brought her such fame that she was invited to become lady-in-waiting to Shoshi, the consort of Emperor Ichijo.

Murat, Joachim (1767–1815) French marshal and king of Naples (1808–15). He served as a distinguished cavalry leader in Napoleon's campaigns in Italy (1796–97) and Egypt (1798–99) and fought at *Marengo (1800) and *Austerlitz (1805). In Naples, Murat introduced important administrative reforms. He treatied with the Austrians after Napoleon's defeat (1813) but subsequent attempts to regain his throne ended first in defeat at Tolentino and then in his capture and execution.

Murcia 38 59N 1 08W A city in SE Spain, in the province of Murcia. It was formerly the capital of the Moorish kingdom of Murcia and possesses a cathedral and university (founded 1915). Industries include silk and textiles. Population (1991): 318,838.

Murdoch, Iris (1919–) British novelist. Born in Dublin, she studied and taught philosophy at Oxford. Her first publication was a philosophical study, *Sartre* (1953). Her novels are elaborate and witty explorations of human relationships. They include *Under the Net* (1954), *The Bell* (1958), *A Severed Head* (1961), *The Black Prince* (1974), *The Sea, the Sea* (1978), *Nuns and Soldiers* (1981), *The Philosopher's Pupil* (1983), *The Good Apprentice* (1986), *The Book and the Brotherhood* (1988), and *The Message to the Planet* (1990).

Mureş River (Hungarian name: Maros) A river in E Europe, flowing W from the Carpathian Mountains in Romania across the Transylvanian Basin to join the Tisza River in Hungary. Length: 499 mi (803 km).

murex A *gastropod mollusk belonging to the family *Muricidae* (about 1000 species), mainly of tropical seas. Murex ⌐shells are elaborately ornamented with spines and frills; the snail feeds on other mollusks by drilling holes in their shells and extracting the flesh with its long proboscis. The Mediterranean *Murex trunculus* was the source of the dye Tyrian purple.

Murfreesboro 35 51N 86 23W A city in central Tennessee, SE of Nashville, on the W fork of the Stones River. Once the capital of Tennessee (1818–26), the city was the site of a strategic Civil War battle in December 1862–January 1863 and left the Union forces in control. The site is now part of the Stones River National Battlefield. Industries include textiles, clothing, electrical parts, luggage, furniture, and dairy products. Population (1990): 44,922.

Murillo, Bartolomé Esteban (1617–82) Spanish painter. He spent most of his life in Seville, working for the religious orders and helping to found the Spanish Academy (1660), of which he became first president. After abandoning his early realism, he painted urchins and religious scenes, particularly the Immaculate Conception, in an idealized style influenced by Rubens and the Venetians. Murillo was very popular until the 20th century, when there was a reaction against the sentimentality of such works as *The Two Trinities*.

Murmansk 68 59N 33 08E A port in Russia, on the Kola inlet of the Barents Sea. Its ice-free harbor was used by the Allied expedition against the Bolsheviks in 1918 and is an important fishing base. Population (1991 est): 472,900.

Murphy, Frank (1890–1949) US lawyer and statesman; associate justice of the US Supreme Court (1940–49). He was mayor of Detroit, Mich. (1930–33), governor-general and then US high commissioner of the Philippines (1933–36), and governor of Michigan (1937–39). Appointed US attorney general in 1939, he established a civil liberties division in the Department of Justice. His time on the Supreme Court, except for a brief military stint, found him defending the rights of Japanese-Americans (by his dissent in *Korematsu* v. *United States*; 1944), labor (by his vote in favor of *Thornhill* v. *Alabama*; 1940), and religion (by his dissent in *Wolf* v. *Colorado*; 1949).

Murray, Sir James (Augustus Henry) (1837–1915) British lexicographer. Largely self-educated, he became a teacher in 1870. After editing some early English texts, he was in 1878 appointed editor of the *New English Dictionary on Historical Principles* (later called the *Oxford English Dictionary*), to which he devoted the rest of his life, making a practical reality of this project and setting the standards of its scholarship.

Murray cod A carnivorous food and game fish, *Maccullochella macquariensis*, found in fresh waters of Australia. Up to 7 ft (2 m) long, it has a deep broad olive-green body with brown spots and a long dorsal fin.

Murray River The chief river in Australia. Rising near Mount Koscuisko, in New South Wales, it flows generally W and S forming the boundary between Victoria and New South Wales. It enters Encounter Bay on the Indian Ocean through Lake Alexandrina. The main tributaries are the Darling and Murrumbidgee Rivers; it also receives water from the Snowy Mountains hydroelectric scheme. Length: 1609 mi (2590 km).

Murrow, Edward R(oscoe) (1908–65) US radio and television journalist. He joined CBS in 1935 and became head of the European Bureau in 1937. After World War II he became a CBS vice president but continued to broadcast regularly and in the 1950s was a fearless critic of Sen. Joseph *McCarthy. He produced and hosted two influential television programs, *See It Now* (formerly *Hear It Now* on radio) and *Person to Person*. In 1961 he became director of the US Information Agency.

Murrumbidgee River A river in SE Australia, rising in the Eastern Highlands in New South Wales and flowing through the Australian Capital Territory before entering the Murray River. The Burrinjuck Dam provides water for irrigation. Length: 1050 mi (1690 km).

Murry, John Middleton (1889–1957) British literary critic. He married Katherine *Mansfield and was a friend of D. H. *Lawrence. He edited the literary magazines *Athenaeum* (1919–21) and *Adelphi* (1923–48). His many books include studies of Keats (1925, 1930, 1949) and Blake (1933) as well as an autobiography, *Between Two Worlds* (1935).

Muscat 23 37N 58 38E The capital of Oman, on the Gulf of Oman. Most port traffic is now handled at Matrah to the NW. There is an oil terminal to the W. Population (1982 est): 85,000.

Muscat and Oman. *See* Oman, Sultanate of.

muscle Tissue that is specialized to contract, producing movement or tension in the body. It contains long spindle-shaped cells (muscle fibers) that convert chemical energy (*see* ATP) into mechanical energy. Most of the body's musculature consists of voluntary muscle, which is consciously controlled via the central nervous system. It is also known as skeletal muscle (because it is attached to the bones) and striated (or striped) muscle (because of its banded appearance under the microscope). Individual muscles are made up of bundles of fibers enclosed in a strong fibrous sheath and attached to bones by tendons. Involuntary muscle occurs in the walls of hollow organs, such as blood vessels, intestines, and the bladder. It is responsible for movements not under conscious control and is regulated by the autonomic nervous system. Cardiac muscle is a special type of muscle found only in the heart: its rhythmic contractions produce the heartbeat.

muscovite. *See* micas.

Muscovy Company The first important English joint-stock company. Founded in 1553 to discover a northeast passage to the Orient, it was chartered in 1555 and granted a Russian trade monopoly, which it lost in 1698. It was dissolved in 1917.

Muscovy duck A large tropical American *perching duck, *Cairina moschata*. It has a glossy black plumage with white wing patches. The domesticated form is larger with a gray, white, or speckled plumage and a large scarlet caruncle on the bill.

muscular dystrophy A group of chronic and progressive disorders characterized by wasting and weakening of the muscle fibers. The disease is inherited and the commonest type, Duchenne muscular dystrophy, affects predominantly boys. The muscles affected and the rate of progress of the disease are both very variable. There is no specific treatment but physiotherapy and orthopedic measures can help those who suffer from the disease.

Muses In Greek mythology, the nine patrons of the arts and sciences, daughters of Zeus and *Mnemosyne. Calliope was the muse of epic poetry; Clio, history; Euterpe, flute playing and music; Erato, love poetry and hymns; Terpsichore, dancing; Melpomene, tragedy; Thalia, comedy; Polyhymnia, song and mime; and Urania, astronomy.

Musgrave Ranges A range of rocky granite hills in NW South Australia. It runs parallel to the Northern Territory border, reaching 4970 ft (1516 m) at Mount Woodruffe.

mushroom The umbrella-shaped spore-forming body produced by many fungi. (Sometimes the word toadstool is used for those species that are inedible or poisonous, mushroom being restricted to the edible species.) It consists of an erect stem (stipe) and a cap, which may be flat, conical, spherical, or cylindrical and has numerous radiating gills on its undersurface in which the spores are produced. The well-known edible mushrooms belong to the genus *Agaricus*; they have a smooth white or scaly brown cap with gills that are white, gray, or pink when immature and become deep brown at maturity. The field mushroom (*A. campestris*) has a white cap 1.6–3.1 in (4–8 cm) in diameter and deep-pink to brown gills.

music The art of organizing sounds, which usually consist of sequences of tones of definite *pitch, to produce melody, harmony, and rhythm. Musical cultures based on *scales evolved in such ancient civilizations as those of China, Persia, India, etc., as well as in Europe. Within each culture both *folk music and classical (*or* "art") music traditions exist. In Western music both traditions evolved from the Greek system of *modes established by Pythagoras and codified during the Middle Ages. In classical music modes became the basis for *plainchant and subsequently for *polyphony, which reached its peak in the 15th and 16th centuries. With the development of the major and minor scales in the early 17th century harmonic composition for instrumental ensembles and in *opera began to evolve. During the 17th and 18th centuries increasing attention was given to the development of musical form in classical music. By the beginning of the 19th century the dominant musical forms were the *sonata, *symphony, *concerto, and string quartet. Opera continued to flourish and *oratorio, invented during the 18th century, remained popular. The influence of romanticism in music gave rise to the tone poem (*see* symphonic poem) and an increasingly free attitude to traditional forms. *Chromaticism in the music of the late 19th and early 20th centuries led to *atonality and the adoption by some composers of *serialism. In the later 20th century composers have used unpitched sounds, electronic generators, tape recordings, synthesizers, and unconventional instrumental techniques to create music, as well as experimenting widely with musical forms. The 20th century has also seen the development of other important forms of popular music in the Western tradition, heavily influenced by African folk music. *See* jazz; rock; pop music.

musica ficta (Latin: false music) A modification of the pitch of certain notes, which, during the 11th to 16th centuries, was made in the course of musical performance. For instance, the harsh tritone F–B, known as *diabolus in musica* (Latin: the devil in music), was avoided by sharpening the F or flattening the B.

musical instruments Devices used to produce music. The chief characteristics of a musical instrument are its *timbre and range (i.e. the highest and lowest notes it can produce). In the *orchestra musical instruments are grouped into families. The *stringed instruments (*or* strings) include the violin, viola, cello, double bass, and harp (*see also* piano). The *wind instruments are divided into the woodwind (flute, clarinet, oboe, and bassoon) and brass (horn, trumpet, trombone, and tuba). The *percussion instruments include a whole range of instruments from the triangle and cymbals to the xylophone and timpani. Many instruments are used chiefly in jazz or pop (e.g. guitar, vibraphone, and maracas)

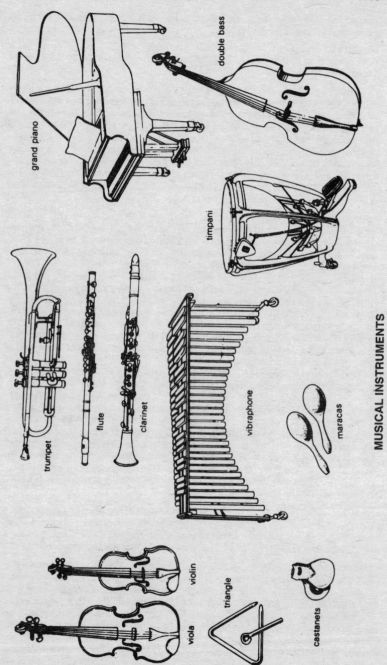

grand piano

double bass

timpani

trumpet

flute

clarinet

vibraphone

maracas

violin

viola

triangle

castanets

MUSICAL INSTRUMENTS

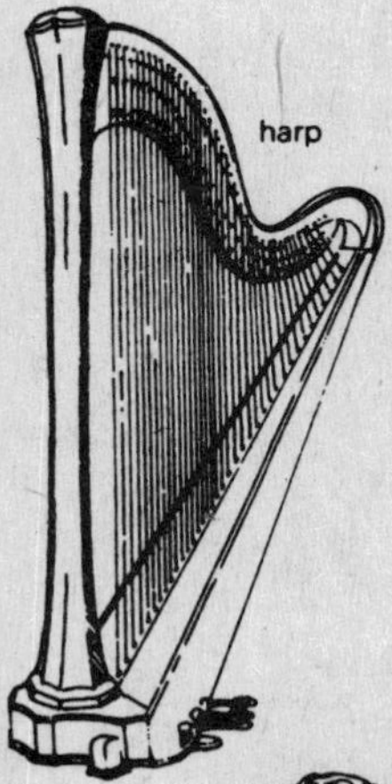

cymbals

koto

gong chimes

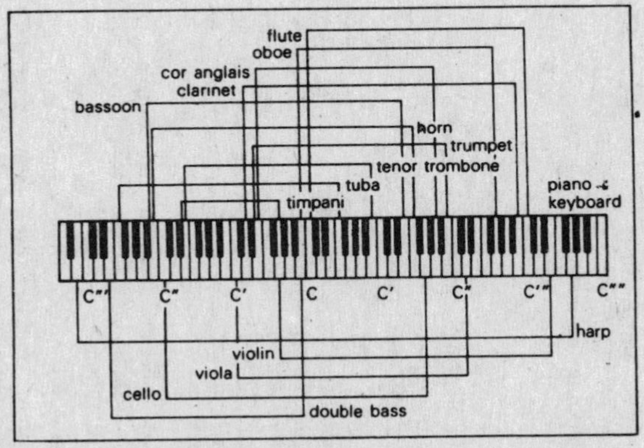

range of some musical instruments

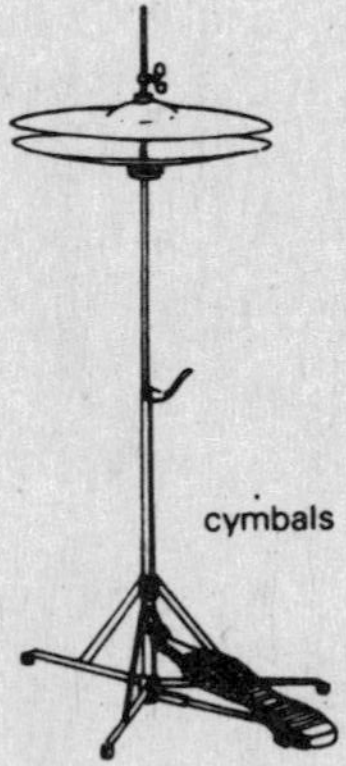

piano +
keyboard

flute
oboe
cor anglais
clarinet
bassoon

horn
trumpet
tenor trombone
tuba
timpani

harp

C'''
C''
C'
C
C'
C''
C'''

violin
viola
cello
double bass

harp

sitar

MUSICAL INSTRUMENTS

while others, such as the Indian sitar, the Japanese koto, and the Spanish castanets, feature predominantly in the music of particular countries.

musicals Light dramas combined with songs and dances. The genre evolved in the US in the late 19th century and was developed during the 1920s and 1930s by George *Gershwin, Cole *Porter, and Irving *Berlin. In *Oklahoma!* (1943) and other musicals of the 1940s, Richard *Rodgers and Oscar *Hammerstein attempted to integrate the dramatic and musical elements, a trend culminating in Leonard Bernstein's *West Side Story* (1957). Other notable creators of the musical include George M. Cohan, Jerome Kern, Kurt Weill, Lorenz Hart, Alan J. Lerner, Frederick Lowe, and Stephen Sondheim.

music drama. *See* opera.

music hall. *See* vaudeville.

Musil, Robert (1880–1942) Austrian novelist. He studied engineering and later philosophy and psychology and served as an officer in World War I. His fame was posthumous and due chiefly to his one major work, *The Man Without Qualities* (1930–43), a long novel describing life during the declining years of the Hapsburg empire. Of his other works, only the novel *Young Törless* (1906) is noteworthy.

musique concrète A type of musical composition invented by Pierre Schaeffer (1910–　) in 1948. Natural or man-made sounds are recorded on tape and arranged, often in an altered or distorted form, to form a composition made up of "concrete" or already existing sounds, as opposed to "abstract" musical tones.

musk (botany) A perennial plant, *Mimulus moschatus* (a species of *monkey flower), native to North America and grown as an ornamental for its musky fragrance; 8–24 in (20–60 cm) tall, it has oval leaves and tubular yellow flowers. The name is also applied to several other plants with a musky odor including the *moschatel, musk mallow (*Malva moschata*), musk rose (*Rosa moschata*), and musk stork's bill (*Erodium moschatum*).

musk (perfumery) An odorous substance obtained from the male *musk deer. It is included in perfumes because of the strength and persistence of its odor and it has been used as an aphrodisiac and stimulant.

musk deer A small solitary deer, *Moschus moschiferus*, found in mountain forests of central Asia. Musk deer are about 24 in (60 cm) high at the shoulder with long hind legs; males have no antlers but grow long fangs. They have been widely hunted for the secretion of their musk gland, which is used in the manufacture of perfumes.

musket A smoothbore firearm fired from the shoulder. The earliest form, known as a harquebus (*or* arquebus from German *Hackenbüsche*, hook gun), evolved in the 15th century as the first hand-held form of the *cannon—a development that depended on the matchlock as a means of igniting the charge. With a range of only 120 yd (110 m), the ball from the harquebus was unable to penetrate armor. In the second half of the 16th century a Spanish general invented a heavy shoulder weapon with a sufficiently large charge to penetrate even the finest armor—this musket still relied on the matchlock, essentially a fair-weather device. It was not until the mid-17th century that wheellocks (working on much the same principle as a flint lighter) and flintlocks were adopted for military use. The next landmark in the development of the musket was the *percussion cap at the beginning of the 19th century, which led to the breech-loading musket with cartridge and percussion-cap ammunition. Muskets were superseded by *rifles in the mid-19th century.

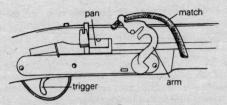

In the matchlock, a slow-burning match was forced into the powder pan by the arm when the trigger was pressed.

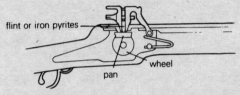

In the wheellock, the flint or iron pyrites was lowered onto a serrated wheel when the trigger was pressed. The sparks produced ignited the charge in the pan. The wheel, wound up by a key, also rotated when the trigger was pressed.

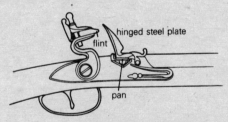

In the flintlock, pressing the trigger caused the flint to strike a hinged steel plate, forcing it back to expose the powder in the pan to the sparks.

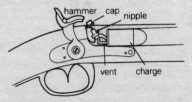

The percussion cap, containing mercury fulminate, was struck by the hammer when the trigger was pressed. The flame produced passed through the hollow nipple into the vent, where it fired the main charge.

MUSKET *The types of lock mechanism used in muzzle-loaders.*

musk ox A large hoofed ☐mammal, *Ovibos moschatus*, inhabiting the Arctic tundra of North America. About 59 in (150 cm) high at the shoulder, musk oxen have long dark shaggy hair and prominent horns, which curve down the sides of the skull and upward at the tip. They live in herds of 20–30 and feed on grass, etc. Bulls have a strong musky scent in the rutting season. Family: *Bovidae.

muskrat A large North American water.*vole, *Ondatra zibethica*, also called musquash. It grows up to 14 in (35 cm) long, excluding its black hairless tail, and its soft glossy coat is used in the fur trade. Muskrats inhabit marshland, living in earthmounds or burrowing in river banks. They feed on water plants, mussels, and crayfish. Family: *Cricetidae*. ☐mammal.

Muslim League An organization of Indian Muslims created to safeguard their rights in British India. Formed in 1906 as the All-India Muslim League, it generally supported British rule. In 1940, under the leadership of *Jinnah and with the prospect of Indian independence, the League began to press for a separate state for Indian Muslims. In 1947, after the founding of Pakistan, it became Pakistan's dominant political party. Supported mainly by the Westernized middle class, it split into three factions in the 1960s.

muslin A smooth delicately woven cotton fabric. Originally made in Mosul in Mesopotamia (hence its name), it is used for dresses and curtains. In the US coarser cotton fabrics used for shirts and sheeting are also called muslins.

musquash. *See* muskrat.

mussel A *bivalve mollusk belonging either to the family *Mytilidae* (marine mussels) or the superfamily *Unionacea* (freshwater mussels). Marine mussels have wedge-shaped shells measuring 2–6 in (5–15 cm), which are anchored to rocks by strands (byssus threads). Some species burrow into sand or wood. The edible mussel (*Mytilus edulis*) is an important seafood, being farmed commercially. Freshwater mussels inhabit ponds, lakes, and streams, embedded in mud or wedged between rocks.

Musset, Alfred de (1810–57) French poet and dramatist, one of the major figures of the romantic movement. He published his first volume of poetry, *Contes d'Espagne et d'Italie*, at the age of 20. He lived extravagantly, and his many volumes of poetry and drama include satires on the excesses of the romantic movement. His autobiographical *La Confession d'un enfant du siècle* (1836) includes an account of his love affair with George *Sand.

Mussolini, Benito (Amilcare Andrea) (1883–1945) Italian fascist dictator. Initially an ardent socialist, his support of Italian participation in World War I led to his expulsion from the Socialist party (1915). In 1919 he formed the Fasci di combattimento (*see* Blackshirts) in Milan and came to power following the *March on Rome (1922). He was prime minister until the murder of *Matteotti persuaded him to establish (1924–29) a dictatorship. As *duce* ("leader") his social policies, program of public works, maintenance of law and order, and conciliatory policies toward the Roman Catholic Church (*see* Lateran Treaty) initially impressed the Italian people. However, his expansionist foreign policy, especially his invasion of Ethiopia (1935), and his alliance with Hitler (the Rome-Berlin Axis, 1936) brought him increasing unpopularity. In 1939 he annexed Albania and after the outbreak of World War II he declared war on France and Britain (June 1940). The Italian war effort was disastrous, leading to defeats in E and N Africa and in Greece. Following the Allied invasion of Sicily, Mussolini was forced by the Fascist Grand Council to resign (July 1943). Rescued by the Germans to head a new fascist republic in N Italy, he was subsequently captured and shot by Italian partisans. His body was brought to Milan and hung up in a public square before burial.

MUSSOLINI

Mussorgski, Modest Petrovich (1839–81) Russian composer. At first an army officer and later a civil servant, he had little formal training beyond a few lessons with Balakirev. He developed a highly personal style, reproducing Russian speech rhythms in such works as the song cycles *The Nursery* (1868–72) and *Songs and Dances of Death* (1875–77). His masterpieces are the opera *Boris Godunov* (1868–72), the piano work *Pictures at an Exhibition* (1874), and the orchestral tone poem *A Night on Bald Mountain* (1860–66).

mustang The wild horse of North America. Mustangs are descended from the domesticated European stock of Spanish settlers and have become tough and small in the harsh conditions. Many were caught and tamed by cowboys and Indians, including the Mustang tribe, which was noted for its horse breeding. Wild herds were rapidly declining until protective legislation was passed in 1971.

mustard Any of various annual herbs of the genus *Brassica* and closely related genera, native to Europe and W Asia and cultivated chiefly for their seeds—source of the condiment mustard. They have branched stems, up to 0.6 in (1.5 cm) high, deeply lobed leaves, and terminal clusters of yellow flowers. The leaves may be used as fodder, fertilizer, vegetables, or herbs. The main species are the white or yellow mustard, *Sinapis alba* (or *B. hirta*), black or brown mustard (*B. nigra*), and Indian mustard (*B. juncea*).

Mustelidae A family of mammals of the order *Carnivora*. It includes the stoats, weasels, martens, badgers, skunks, and others. Mustelids typically have a long body and tail, short legs, and glands that secrete a musky fluid.

Mutanabbi, Abu At-Tayyib Ahmad Ibn Husayn al- (915–65 AD) Arab poet. From a poor but noble family, he learned his craft from the Bedouins and at Damascus, becoming a court poet in N Syria (948) and later in Egypt. He brought elaborate rhetorical innovations to the traditional odes (*qasidahs*) addressed to his patrons.

Mutare (former name: Umtali) 19 00S 32 40E A city in E Zimbabwe. Situated on the main railroad to Mozambique from Harare, it is an important market center for an area producing fruit and timber. Industries include paper milling, textiles, and food canning. Nearby national parks attract tourists. Population (1987): 75,358.

mutation A change in the hereditary material (*see* DNA) of an organism, which results in an altered physical characteristic. A mutation in a germ cell is inherited by subsequent generations of offspring; a change in any other cell (somatic cell) affects only those cells produced by division of the mutated cell. Gene mutations result from a change in the bases of the DNA molecule; chromosome mutations may be due to the addition or subtraction of bases and can usually be seen under a microscope. Both types of mutation affect the *genetic code and hence the corresponding function of the genes.

Very occasionally, mutations occur spontaneously and at random. They can also be induced by certain chemicals, ionizing radiation (such as X-rays), and by ultraviolet light. Most nonlethal mutations are of no benefit to the organism, but they do provide an important source of genetic variation in the population on which natural selection can act, which eventually results in the *evolution of new species.

Mutesa I (c. 1838–84) King of *Buganda in East Africa. An absolute ruler, Mutesa tried to play off the Arab intruders into his kingdom against the Europeans so that neither would become too powerful. He traded with both and encouraged Islam and Christianity.

mute swan An Old World *swan, *Cygnus olor*, found in marshy areas and estuaries and, as a semidomesticated ornamental bird, on rivers and lakes. It is 63 in (160 cm) long and has a long neck, white plumage, black legs, and an orange bill with a black base. Less vocal than other swans, it is also silent in flight.

Mutsuhito (1852–1912) Emperor of Japan (1867–1912), who presided over Japan's transformation into a modern state. The Meiji (Mutsuhito's title as emperor) restoration (1866–68) ended seven centuries of feudal rule and nominally returned full power to the throne, a change that culminated in the constitution promulgated by Mutsuhito in 1889.

muttonbird A bird whose chicks are collected for meat and oil. The name is used especially for the slender-billed shearwater (*Puffinus tenuirostris*) of Australia and the sooty shearwater (*Procellaria griseus*) of New Zealand. Both belong to the family *Procellariidae* (petrels).

mutualism. *See* symbiosis.

Muybridge, Eadweard (Edward James Muggeridge; 1830–1904) US photographer, born in Britain. He was a pioneer of action photography with his series of animals and humans photographed in consecutive stages of motion. He showed that a trotting horse momentarily raises all four legs simultaneously.

Muzorewa, Bishop Abel (Tendekai) (1925–   ) Zimbabwe statesman and bishop of the Methodist Church. One-time president of the African National Congress and the All-Africa Conference of Churches, Muzorewa negotiated a new constitution with Ian *Smith's government in 1978 and headed a nominally black government in *Zimbabwe until 1980, when Robert *Mugabe became prime minister.

Myanmar, Union of (former name: Socialist Republic of the Union of Burma) A country in SE Asia, on the Bay of Bengal and the Andaman Sea. The principal river system, that of the Irrawaddy and its main tributary, the Chindwin, forms a narrow plain running N-S, rising to the Arakan Mountains and the Chin Hills in the W and the Shan Plateau in the E. The Tenasserim Hills lie along the coast in the SE. The majority of the population, concentrated in the Irrawaddy delta, is Burmese, but there are several minorities, including the Shan, Karen, Chachin, and Chin peoples. *Economy*: priority has been given to the development of agriculture, the main crop being rice, and in 1976 plans were introduced by the government to set up cooperative farming, mainly on virgin land. Almost half the land (all of which is nationalized) is under forest and teak is a valuable export. There is some mining, especially of lead and zinc. Other industries are mainly based on food processing and all industry is now nationalized. Inland waterways provide an important means of communication. All foreign trade is carried out through government trading organizations and the main exports include rice and rice products, rubber, jute, and timber. *History*: by the 13th century the Burmese had developed a civilization based on Hinayana Buddhism. In the centuries following defeat by the Mongols in 1287, the area was under the rule of the Shans and the Mons. The rule of the Burmese Alaungpaya in the 18th century began a period of increased prosperity. After successive wars it came totally under British rule in 1885 as part of British India. In 1937 it attained a certain measure of self-government and was separated from India. In World War II it was occupied by Japanese forces, fighting first with the Japanese and later against them in support of the British. In 1948 it became a republic outside the Commonwealth. In 1962 its parliamentary democracy was overthrown in a military coup by Gen. U *Ne Win. Military rule ended in 1974 and a one-party socialist republic was formed. Following U Ne Win's resignation in 1981 Gen. San Yu was elected president. Myanmar avoided close ties with both East and West, maintaining a policy of strict neutrality. In 1983 a bomb explosion in Yangon, apparently aimed for visiting South Korean president Chin Doo Hunin, killed 21 people. The bombing was alleged by Myanmar to have been the work of North Korean terrorists, some of whom were captured. Myanmar, departing from its neutral stance, broke ties with North Korea. In 1988, Gen. Saw Maung took over the presidency and installed a military government, which refused to accept the results of 1990 elections in which the opposition party was victorious. Burma's name was officially changed to Myanmar in 1989. The 1991 Nobel Peace prize was awarded to Aung San Suu Kyi, the leader of the opposition party, for her efforts to democratize Myanmar. In 1992, the UN cited Saw Maung's government for human rights violations. Saw Maung retired in mid-1992 and was replaced by Gen. Than Shwe. Official language: Burmese. Official currency: kyat of 100 pyas. Area: 261,789 sq mi (678,000 sq km). Population (1990): 41,219,000. Capital and main port: Yangon (formerly Rangoon).

Mycenae An ancient citadel in the Peloponnese (S Greece). Famed in legend as the home of *Agamemnon, Mycenae attained its zenith between 1600 and 1200 BC. Massive fortifications, including the famous Lion Gate, attest Mycenae's military readiness and exquisite bronze daggers, gold masks, and silver drinking vessels from its royal graves indicate accompanying affluence.

Mycenaean civilization The civilization of Bronze Age Greece. It developed after about 1650 BC in mainland centers, such as *Mycenae and *Pylos, but after the collapse of the Minoan civilization (c. 1450 BC) its influence and political control extended to Crete. The Mycenaeans were a warrior aristocracy, identifiable with Homer's *Achaeans. They spoke a form of Greek, used *Linear B script, and lived in palaces decorated with frescoes and equipped with luxury stone and metal goods. About 1200 BC the palaces were destroyed, either by invaders or in internecine struggles, but recognizably Mycenaean culture survived in debased form until about 1100 BC.

mycology The branch of biology dealing with the study of fungi. Mycology was established as a separate discipline in the early 19th century, when the Swedish botanist Elias Fries (1794–1878) published the first scientifically based classification of the fungi (1821–32).

mycoplasma A minute organism that lacks a cell wall and belongs to the class *Mollicutes*, also called pleuropneumonia-like organisms (PPLOs). Regarded by some authorities as bacteria, mycoplasmas may be rounded, 150–300 nanometers in diameter, or filamentous, up to several micrometers long (*see* SI units). They are the cause of several plant and animal diseases; for example *Mycoplasma mycoides* causes pleuropneumonia in cattle.

MYCENAE *The entrance to the citadel of Mycenae is by the Lion Gate, set between massive walls of Cyclopean stonework.*

myelin A white fatty material that forms a sheath around the large nerve fibers of vertebrates and some invertebrates. Myelin acts as an insulator, thereby increasing the speed of conduction of impulses along the nerve fiber.

Mylae, Battle of (260 BC) A battle in the first *Punic War in which the Romans destroyed the Carthaginian fleet off Sicily. It was Rome's first naval victory.

My Lai A village in S Vietnam, where a massacre of about 347 civilians by US soldiers took place (Mar 16, 1968) during the Vietnam War. The incident was investigated only after it had been disclosed by an ex-serviceman (1969). The investigation resulted in the court-martial of several soldiers. Only one, Lt. William Calley, was convicted but his conviction was overturned. The incident provoked much criticism of the role of the US in Vietnam.

Mylodon A genus of extinct South American ground sloths dating from the Pleistocene epoch (one million years ago). About 118 in (300 cm) long, they had a specialized toe on the hind limb that was probably used for gripping branches or digging up tubers. *See also* Megatherium.

mynah A songbird belonging to a genus (*Acridotheres*) native to SE Asia. Mynahs usually have a dark plumage with bright wattles on the face. They feed chiefly on the ground and eat the insects found on cattle. The common mynah (*A. tristis*) lives in close proximity to man and has become a pest in some regions. The Chinese crested mynah (*A. cristatellus*) has been introduced to North America. Family: *Sturnidae* (starlings). *See also* hill mynah.

myocardial infarction Death of part of the heart muscle: the cause of what is popularly described as a heart attack. This is the most common cause of death in advanced societies and usually results from *atherosclerosis. The patient usually experiences sudden severe central chest pain, which may spread to the neck and arms and is usually accompanied by sweating and nausea. Most people who recover from heart attacks can eventually lead a full and active life: many have survived for as long as 40 years.

myopia. *See* nearsightedness.

Myrdal, Gunnar (1898–1987) Swedish sociologist and economist. Joint recipient of the 1974 Nobel Prize, Myrdal is best known for his study of the US racial problem, published as *An American Dilemma* (1944). His wife **Alva Myrdal** (1902–86) won the 1982 Nobel Peace Prize for her work for disarmament.

Myriapoda A group of terrestrial arthropods comprising the *centipedes, *millipedes, *pauropods, and *symphylids. They have elongated bodies and numerous walking legs.

Myrmidons A legendary Greek people from Thessaly. According to one legend, they originated on the island of Aegina when Zeus turned the ants (Greek *myrmex*, ant) into people. They are best known as the loyal warriors commanded by *Achilles in the Trojan War.

Myron (5th century BC) Athenian sculptor. His *Discus-Thrower* and *Marsyas*, described by ancient critics, are known through Roman copies. These freestanding figures show the new stances (made possible by the novel techniques of bronze working) that superseded the stylized poses derived from *kouros and *kore figures.

myrrh An aromatic yellow to red gum resin obtained from small tropical thorny trees of the genus *Commifera*, especially *C. myrrha*, *C. molmol*, and *C. abyssinica*, native to Africa and SW Asia. Myrrh exudes from the bark through slits and hardens on exposure to air. It is used in incense, perfumes, cosmetics, dentistry, and pharmaceuticals. Family: *Commiphoraceae*.

myrtle An evergreen shrub of the genus *Myrtus* (over 100 species). The common myrtle (*M. communis*), native to the Mediterranean area and W Asia, may grow to a height of 16 ft (5 m). It has aromatic dark-green shiny leaves, fragrant five-petaled white flowers, 2–3 cm across, with numerous stamens, and blue-black berries. An oil obtained from the leaves, flowers, and fruit is used in perfumery. Family: *Myrtaceae*. Other plants known as myrtle include the *sweet gale.

Mysore 12 18N 76 37E A city in India, in Karnataka. Industries include textiles, chemicals, and food processing and it has a university (1916). Population (1991): 480,006.

mysteries Secret religious cults in the ancient Mediterranean world that revealed their mystical rites only to initiates and promised them a life after death. Their initiation ceremonies, of which the details are often vague, involved purification, assimilation of occult knowledge, and acting out a sacred drama. The Egyptian cult of *Isis, the Greek *Eleusinian and *Orphic mysteries, and Roman *Mithraism are the most famous.

mystery plays. *See* miracle plays.

mysticism Belief in a type of religious experience in which the individual claims to achieve immediate knowledge of or temporary union with God. Mysticism is an element in most theistic traditions and the validity of the experience is often claimed to be established by the similarity of the accounts by mystics from totally different cultures of their visions, trances, and ecstasies. The usual preliminary is strict *asceticism. Christianity insists that a mystic should demonstrate his spiritual grace by practical works of charity. St *Francis of Assisi, St *Catherine of Siena, St *Teresa of Avila, St *John of the Cross, and *Julian of Norwich are among the many famous Christian mystics. Official Church attitudes have alternated between regarding mysticism as a special spiritual grace and suspecting it of verging on *Gnosticism, *pantheism, *Neoplatonism, or simply dangerous individualism. *See also* Sufism.

mythology Imaginative poetic stories, traditions, etc., concerning religious beliefs, gods, and supernatural and heroic human beings. Mythology often involves a cosmogony—an attempted explanation of the origin of the universe, of mankind, or of a particular race or culture. The term also refers to the formal study of such stories, traditions, etc. Myths have been interpreted in several ways. One ancient theory, first advanced by the Greek Euhemerus (300 BC) and called euhemerism, holds that there is an element of historical truth in myths and that mythical characters are only kings or other heroes given the honor of deification by the populace. *Plato also adopted a critical view of Greek mythology because of its immorality and sought to introduce worthier ideals by inventing more rational myths. Anthropology and psychoanalysis have thrown new light on the function of myths. Among primitive peoples they serve to provide an explanation or justification for social institutions. They also appear to embody universal values or patterns with regard to human psychology, as in Freud's interpretation of the child's relationship to its parents in terms of the *Oedipus myth. The mythologies of particular cultures have provided the material of most of the world's great literature and art, as in Egypt, Greece and Rome, and in Hinduism.

Mytilene (Modern Greek name: Mitilíni) 39 06N 26 34E The chief city of the Greek island of Lesbos, on the Aegean Sea. It is a port trading chiefly in olive oil, citrus fruits, and cereals.

myxoedema Underactivity of the *thyroid gland. Patients are slow, tired, dislike the cold, and have a slow pulse and reflexes. The skin may be thick and swollen. Myxoedema can be easily treated with thyroxine, the hormone produced by the thyroid gland.

myxomatosis An infectious disease of rabbits and hares that is caused by a virus. Symptoms include swollen eyes, nose, and muzzle, closed eyelids, and fever. The disease is usually fatal although some strains of rabbits show resistance. A vaccine is available to protect domestic rabbits. The disease was introduced to the UK and Australia during the 1950s as a pest-control measure.

Mzilikazi (c. 1790–1868) Zulu warrior, who in about 1840 founded the Matabele (*or* Ndebele) kingdom in S Rhodesia. A great military leader and an able administrator, Mzilikazi organized his new kingdom on military lines and withstood attacks from neighboring tribes and from the Afrikaners. Not long after his death his kingdom, under his son *Lobengula, was overwhelmed by the whites.

N

Nabis (Hebrew: prophets) A group of French artists formed in Paris in 1888. The leading members—Paul Sérusier (1863–1927), *Denis, *Bonnard, and *Vuillard—were united by their admiration for *Gauguin and Japanese prints. They applied their famous tenet that "a picture is . . . essentially a flat surface covered by colors in a certain order" to their activities as painters, poster and stained-glass designers, book illustrators, etc., thus influencing many branches of art. They disbanded in 1899.

Nablus 32 13N 35 16E A city on the *West Bank of the Jordan River. Nablus is the Shechem of the Old Testament: Jacob's Well is nearby. Population (1987 est): 106,944.

Nabokov, Vladimir (1899–1977) US novelist. Born into an aristocratic Russian family, he was educated at Britain's Cambridge University and lived in France and Germany before emigrating to the US in 1948. He achieved popular success with *Lolita* (1955), whose academic antihero lusts after young girls. His novels, noted for their elegant and witty word play, include *The Defense* (1930), one of several originally written in Russian, *Pale Fire* (1962), and *Ada* (1969). His other works include the autobiographical *Speak, Memory* (1967) and a translation of Pushkin's *Eugene Onegin* (4 vols, 1964).

nacre. *See* pearl.

Nadar (Gaspard Felix Tournachon; 1820–1910) French photographer, caricaturist, and writer, born in Paris. Although better known by his contemporaries as a novelist and essayist, his reputation now rests on his photographs of writers and artists, such as Baudelaire and Delacroix, and his pioneering aerial photographs taken from a balloon (1858).

Na-Dené languages An American Indian language group covering the N US, NW Canada, and Alaska. It includes the Athabascan, Tlingit, Haida, and Eyak subgroups. Athabascan is the largest group, consisting of more than 20 languages, and is also the most widespread, extending from the Yukon almost to the US border. Another subgroup of Athabascan origin, spoken on the N American Plains, includes *Navajo and several *Apache languages.

Nader, Ralph (1934–) US lawyer and consumer advocate. His book *Unsafe at Any Speed* (1965), which criticized the safety standards of the automobile industry, resulted in the passing of a car safety act in 1966. A champion of consumer rights, he founded the Center for the Study of Responsive Law in 1969. Among the many other consumer issues that he has investigated are fairness in advertising, nuclear power, and meat processing. Other works include *The Big Boys: Styles of Corporate Power* (1986).

Nader Shah (1688–1747) Shah of Persia (1736–47). Of Turkoman origin, he overthrew the Safavid dynasty to become shah. He had military successes but his internal policies led to many revolts. His attempt at introducing a new rite of Sunni Islam (*see* Sunnites) into Shiite Persia, and forcing his subjects to join it, failed. He was assassinated.

nadir. *See* zenith.

Naevius, Gnaeus (c. 270–c. 200 BC) Roman poet. He wrote a number of tragedies and comedies and an epic on the first Punic War, in which he related

the mythical origins of Rome (making Romulus a grandson of the Trojan Aeneas). Only fragments of his work are extant.

NAFTA. *See* North American Free Trade Agreement.

NAGA *A 10th-century sandstone panel from a temple in
central India depicting a naga encircled by a five-headed
cobra.*

naga In Hindu mythology, one of a race of minor serpent deities inhabiting an
underworld region called Patala, which is filled with gems. They are associated
with water and may be regarded as demons and a possible source of evil, but are
also worshiped as companions of the gods. Vishnu is often portrayed sleeping
on the naga Sesha, and there is a Buddhist legend of a naga raising the Buddha
on its coils above a flood sent to prevent his attaining enlightenment. Nagas are

variously depicted as half-snake and half-human, as many-headed cobras, or in human form posed beneath a canopy of cobras.

Nagaland A state in NE India, on the Burmese border. Mostly in the forested Naga Hills, it produces rice, other grains, pulses, sugar cane, and vegetables. Mahogany and other forest products are important. Local industries include weaving. *History:* after 1947 the Naga tribes resisted Indian rule as fiercely as they had Britain's, winning statehood in 1963. Further talks with the Naga underground movement led to the Shillong Peace Agreement in November 1975. Area: 6379 sq mi (16,527 sq km). Population (1991): 1,215,573. Capital: Kohima.

Nagarjuna (c. 150–c. 250 AD) Indian Buddhist monk and philosopher. Probably originally a brahmin from S India, he founded the Madhyamika (Middle Way) school of Mahayana Buddhism, noted for its highly intellectual approach to defining the nature of reality. Works attributed to him survive only in Tibetan and Chinese.

Nagasaki 32 45N 129 52E A port in Japan, in W Kyushu on the East China Sea. The first Japanese port to deal with European traders, it became a center of Christianity following its introduction by the Portuguese in the 16th century. On Aug 9, 1945, the second of the two atomic bombs used against Japan was dropped on Nagasaki, killing or wounding about 75,000 people, although the damage was not as extensive as at Hiroshima. Rapid rebuilding followed and the city is now an important center of the ship building industry. Its university was established in 1949. Population (1991): 443,823.

Nagorno-Karabakh A region (*oblast*) in Azerbaijan. It was formed in 1923 and its population comprises chiefly Azerbaijani and Armenians. It has metal and mineral deposits and supports many light industries but is chiefly agricultural: cotton, grapes, and wheat are grown. Area: 1700 sq mi (4400 sq km). Population (1987): 187,000. Capital: Stepanakert.

Nagoya 35 8N 136 53E A port in Japan, in SE Honshu on Ise Bay. The fourth largest city in the country, it was founded in 1610 and by World War II had developed into an important center for the manufacture of aircraft and ammunition. It was largely rebuilt following heavy bombing in 1945 and its industries now include steel and textiles. Its universities were established in 1939 and 1950. Population (1991): 2,158,784.

Nagpur 21 10N 79 12E A city in India, in Maharashtra. Founded in the early 18th century, it fell under British control in 1853. It grew with the arrival of the Peninsula Railroad (1867) and now has cotton, transport equipment, and metallurgical industries. Its university was established in 1923. Population (1991): 1,622,225.

Nagy, Imre (1896–1958) Hungarian statesman, who led the revolutionary government of 1956. As prime minister (1953–55) Nagy promised such reforms as an end to the forced development of heavy industry and agricultural collectivization, more consumer goods, occupational mobility, and the closure of labor camps. Opposed by Hungary's Stalinists, he was demoted and in 1956 expelled from the Communist party. In the subsequent *Hungarian Revolution Nagy again became prime minister but was abducted by Soviet troops and executed.

Naha 26 10N 127 40E A port in Japan, the main city of the *Ryukyu Islands and capital of Okinawa. It is the site of the University of the Ryukyus. Population (1991): 303,480.

Nahuatl The most widely used American Indian language of the Uto-Aztecan family, spoken in Mexico. It was the language of the *Aztecs and *Toltecs. A distinctive characteristic is the extensive use of the *tl* sound. The Nahua people are slash-and-burn cultivators, growing maize, beans, tomatoes, and chilies. Crafts, especially weaving, are well developed. The Nahua are nominally Roman Catholic, but pagan beliefs continue to flourish.

Nahum An Old Testament prophet who predicted the imminent destruction of the Assyrian capital of Nineveh by the Medes in 612 BC. **The Book of Nahum** describes this event in detail and interprets it as divine retribution.

naiads In Greek mythology, a class of *nymphs or female spirits of nature associated with rivers, lakes, and springs.

Naipaul, V(idiadhur) S(urajprasad) (1932–) West Indian novelist. He was educated at Oxford and now lives in England. A witty ironic tone characterizes his early comic novels, such as *A House for Mr Biswas* (1961), concerning the life of the poor in his native Trinidad. His later, more somber novels include *In a Free State* (1971), *Guerrillas* (1975), *A Bend in the River* (1979), *Among the Believers* (1981), and *Finding the Center* (1984). He has also published two travel books, a collection of essays (*The Return of Eva Perón*, 1980), and a history of Trinidad (*The Loss of El Dorado*, 1969).

Nairobi 1 17S 36 50E The capital of Kenya, situated on a plateau just S of the equator. Founded as a railroad center in the late 19th century, it is the administrative center of Kenya and trading center of a fertile agricultural region. Its varied manufactures include chemicals, textiles, glass, and furniture. The Nairobi National Park lies on the city's outskirts. The University of Nairobi was established in 1970. Population (1984): 1,505,000.

Naismith, James (1861–1939) US inventor of basketball; born in Canada. He was educated in Canada and then enrolled in the Springfield, Mass., Young Men's Christian Association (YMCA) Training School's physical education course. It was here, as a requirement of the course, that he invented basketball (1891), with two peach baskets and a soccer ball. He later taught physical education at the University of Kansas (1898–1937).

Najd (*or* Nejd) A region in Saudi Arabia, occupying the center of the country. It is largely desert and much of the population is nomadic. Formerly an independent kingdom, it became part of Saudi Arabia in 1932. Area: about 424,621 sq mi (1,100,000 sq km).

Nakasone, Yasuhiro (1918–) Japanese prime minister (1982–87). After graduation from law school (1941) and service in World War II, he served in the Japanese House of Representatives and also held several cabinet posts. Long a leader in the Liberal-Democratic party (LDP), he became prime minister in 1982. Elections called in 1983 saw a lessening of the LDP's power, but Nakasone remained in office. He broadened Japan's role internationally, especially in the development of Asia. In 1986, following the LDP's triumph in nationwide elections, he was selected as prime minister for a third term but resigned in 1987 and gradually stepped down (1989–90) as party leader in the aftermath of an influence-peddling scandal.

Nakhichevan Autonomous Republic An administrative division in the Azerbaidzhan Republic. It is populated mainly by Azerbaidzhani. The economy is predominantly agricultural, producing cereals, cotton, and tobacco. Industries include textiles and food processing. Area: 2120 sq mi (5500 sq km). Population (1991 est): 305,700. Capital: Nakhichevan.

Namaqualand (*or* Namaland; Afrikaans name: Namakwaland) An arid coastal area in SW Africa, extending S from near Windhoek (Namibia) into Cape Province (South Africa), divided by the Orange River into Little Namaqualand (S) and Great Namaqualand (N). It is occupied chiefly by Namas, consisting of Hottentot tribes, and has important diamond reserves.

Namib Desert A desert chiefly in W Namibia, extending some 994 mi (1600 km) along the Atlantic coast. It is arid and almost devoid of population.

Namibia (name until 1968: South West Africa) A territory in SW Africa, on the Atlantic Ocean. The narrow coastal plains of the Namib Desert rise to the central plateau, with the Kalahari Desert to the N. The Orange River forms its S boundary, and the Kunene and Okavango Rivers form part of its N boundary. The majority of the population is African, the largest group being the Ovambo. *Economy*: chiefly subsistence agriculture with emphasis on livestock, especially stock raising, and some dairy farming. Fishing is important, especially for pilchards. Rich mineral resources include diamonds (the main export), as well as copper, lead, zinc, tin, and vanadium; uranium has been found. Hydroelectricity is a valuable source of power. *History*: a German protectorate from 1884, during World War I it surrendered (1915) to South Africa, which administered South West Africa under a League of Nations mandate. In 1966 South Africa refused to acknowledge the declaration by the League's successor, the UN, that the mandate was at an end and was condemned by both the UN and the South West Africa People's Organization (SWAPO) as illegally occupying the territory. A constitutional solution put forward by South Africa in 1976 proved unacceptable to SWAPO and efforts to resolve the crisis continued. In 1988, South Africa agreed to independence for Namibia, linking it to Cuban troops leaving Angola. Elections under UN supervision for a 72-member assembly resulted in a SWAPO party majority. After a new constitution was passed by the assembly and a president was elected, Namibia formally achieved independence from South Africa in 1990. Talks between Namibia and South Africa in 1991 regarding Walvis Bay, an enclave of South Africa, were nonproductive. Official languages: Afrikaans and English. Official currency: South African rand of 100 cents. Area: 318,261 sq mi (824,269 sq km). Population (1992 est): 1,500,000. Capital: Windhoek. Main port: Walvis Bay (South Africa).

Namur (Flemish name: Namen) 50 28N 04 52E A city in S Belgium; strategically positioned at the confluence of the Sambre and Meuse Rivers. It was besieged and captured many times. Notable buildings include the 18th-century cathedral. Its chief manufactures are glass, paper, and leather and steel goods. Population (1991): 103,443.

Nanaimo 49 08N 123 58W A city and port in W Canada, in British Columbia on the E coast of Vancouver Island. With the main ferry links to the mainland, it is Vancouver Island's distribution center and the site of primary industries. Population (1991): 60,129.

Nanak (1469–1539) Indian founder of *Sikhism. Born near Lahore, a member of the mercantile Hindu class he traveled within and perhaps beyond India, visiting both Hindu and Muslim centers in search of spiritual truth. He settled finally in Kartarpur, where he attracted a large community of disciples. His teachings are contained in a number of hymns, many of which are extant.

Nana Sahib (Dandhu Panth; c. 1825–c. 1860) A leader of the *Indian Mutiny (1857). Adopted into a noble family, he led the revolt at Cawnpore, in which the British were massacred. When defeated in 1859 he was driven into the Himalayan foothills, where he probably died.

Nanchang 28 38N 115 56E A city in SE China, the capital of Jiangxi province and the site of its university. China's first commune was briefly established here in 1927. An ancient commercial center, it has varied manufactures. Population (1990): 1,086,124.

Nancy 48 42N 6 12E A city in NE France, the capital of the Meurthe-et-Moselle department on the Meurthe River. The former capital of the Dukes of

Lorraine, it passed to France in 1766. It has a fine collection of 18th-century buildings and is the site of a university (1572). Its varied industries include iron, salt, sodium, machinery, and textiles. Population (1990): 102,410.

Nanda Devi, Mount 30 21N 79 50E A mountain in NW India, close to the Tibetan border in the Himalayas. Height: 25,645 ft (7817 m).

Nanga Parbat, Mount 35 15N 74 36E A mountain in NE Pakistan, in the Himalayas. Height: 26,600 ft (8126 m).

Nanhai. *See* South China Sea.

Nanjing (Nan-ching *or* Nanking) 32 05N 118 55E A port in E China, the capital of Jiangsu province on the Yangtze River. An ancient cultural center, it was a Chinese capital (1368–1421, 1928–37) and the center of the Taiping Rebellion (1851–64). The university was established in 1902. It is a center of heavy industry. Population (1990): 2,090,204.

Nanking. *See* Nanjing.

Nanning 22 50N 108 19E A city in S China, the capital of Guangxi Zhuang AR. The commercial center of a rich agricultural area, it has many industries, including food processing and the manufacture of paper and agricultural machinery. Population (1990): 721,877.

Nansen, Fridtjof (1861–1930) Norwegian explorer, zoologist, and statesman. In 1888 he led an expedition across the Greenland icefield and in 1893, in the *Fram,* specially designed to resist icepacks, set sail across the Arctic. He allowed the vessel to drift attached to an icefloe. In 1895, with F. J. Johansen (1867–1923), he left the ship and reached 18 14N, the nearest point to the North Pole then attained. He subsequently contributed greatly to the League of Nations, becoming its high commissioner for refugees in 1920; he pioneered the **Nansen passport,** an identification card for displaced persons (1922). He won the Nobel Peace Prize (1923).

Nantes 47 14N 1 35W A major port in W France, the capital of the Loire-Atlantique department on the Loire estuary. Its commercial importance dates back to Roman times and it was here that the Edict of Nantes was signed in 1598. It has a 15th-century cathedral and a university (1961). Its port is accessible to oceangoing vessels and its industries include ship building, oil refining, and tanning. Population (1990): 251,133.

Nantes, Edict of (1598) A decree that guaranteed the French Protestants (*see* Huguenots) religious liberty. The edict, proclaimed by Henry IV, established the principle of religious toleration; by permitting the Huguenots freedom of worship and limited civil equality, Henry hoped to prevent further wars of religion in France. The Edict was revoked in 1685 by Louis XIV.

Nantucket An island off the coast of SE Massachusetts. A former whaling center, it is now chiefly a resort. Length: 15 mi (24 km). Width: 3 mi (5 km).

napalm An inexpensive jelly consisting of a mixture of the aluminum salts of *na*pathenic acid and *palm*itic acid used to thicken gasoline so that it can be used in incendiary bombs and flamethrowers. It was used in World War II, the Korean War, and in Vietnam. It ignites easily, burns at temperatures up to 1000°C, and is particularly effective against humans.

Naphtali, tribe of One of the 12 *tribes of Israel. It claimed descent from Naphtali, the son of Jacob by his concubine Bilhah. Its territory was NW of the Sea of Galilee.

naphthalene ($C_{10}H_8$) A white crystalline aromatic hydrocarbon that occurs in coal tar. It is used in the manufacture of dyes, synthetic resins, and mothballs.

Naphthol ($C_{10}H_7OH$) is the hydroxy derivative. It consists of two isomers; the most important, beta-naphthol, is used in antioxidants for rubbers and dyes and in drugs.

Napier 39 29S 176 58E A port in New Zealand, in E North Island on Hawke Bay. It is the most important center of New Zealand's wool trade. Population: 42,900.

Napier, John (1550–1617) Scottish mathematician, who invented *logarithms. In 1614 he published a table of logarithms to the base e, now known as Napierian logarithms. Logarithms to the base ten (common logarithms) were later adopted, following a suggestion by Henry *Briggs. Napier also produced an elementary calculating machine using a series of rods, known as **Napier's bones**.

Napier of Magdala, Robert Cornelis, 1st Baron (1810–90) British field marshal. He fought in the *Sikh Wars in India (1845–49) and during the Indian Mutiny helped to relieve Lucknow (1857). In 1868 he led the expedition to release British diplomats imprisoned in Ethiopia, capturing Magdala.

Naples (Italian name: Napoli; ancient name: Neapolis) 40 50N 14 15E A city in S Italy, the capital of Campania situated on volcanic slopes overlooking the Bay of Naples. It is an important port and a center of commerce and tourism. As well as traditional industries, such as textiles, food processing, and oil refining, newer industries (including the manufacture of cars and ball bearings) have grown up in recent years as a result of central government assistance. Its many historic buildings include medieval castles, a gothic cathedral (13th–14th centuries), the 17th-century Royal Palace, and the university (1224). The National Museum houses remains from Pompeii and Herculaneum. *History*: founded by Greek colonists about 600 BC, it fell to Rome in 326 but retained its Greek culture. It was under Byzantine rule (6th–8th centuries AD) and in 1139 it became part of the Norman kingdom of Sicily. It prospered under Charles I, the first Angevin king of Sicily, who made Naples his capital. Following the revolt known as the *Sicilian Vespers (1282), the island of Sicily passed to the House of Aragon and the Italian peninsula S of the Papal States became known as the kingdom of Naples (with Naples as its capital) until it fell to Garibaldi (1860) and was united with the rest of Italy (*see also* Sicily). From this time Naples lagged economically behind the N, resulting in considerable poverty. The city suffered further hardships during World War II, when it was badly damaged. Central government assistance during the postwar period has led to considerable improvements in the life of the city, based on a developed infrastructure (new roads, port installations, modernized transport and communications). Existing industries have been modernized and expanded and new industries have been established. Many thousands of its inhabitants, however, continue to live in slum conditions. Population (1991 est): 1,206,013.

Napoleon I (1769–1821) Emperor of the French (1804–15). Born Napoleon Bonaparte in Corsica, he became an artillery officer and rose to prominence in 1795, when he turned the guns of the Paris garrison—"a whiff of grapeshot"—on a mob threatening the government of the National Convention. Shortly afterward he married *Josephine de Beauharnais and in January 1796, was appointed to command the French army in Italy (*see* Revolutionary and Napoleonic Wars). His Italian campaign (1796–97) took the army from the brink of defeat by the Austrians to the conquest of Milan and Mantua. After Sardinia, Naples, and the papacy had sued for peace, Napoleon obtained the Directory's support for his plan to break British imperial power by conquering Egypt and India. In Egypt his great victory of the *Pyramids was undermined by Nelson's annihilation of a French fleet at *Aboukir Bay (1798) and in 1799 he returned unobtrusively to

France, where he joined a conspiracy against the tottering Directory. In the coup d'état of 18 Brumaire (Nov 9–10, 1799) he became first consul in a consulate formed on the Roman model; in 1802 he became consul for life and in 1804 had himself proclaimed emperor.

His outstanding domestic achievement was the legal codification, the *Code Napoléon*, that remains the basis of French law, but Napoleon achieved immortality with his exploits abroad. In 1802 he negotiated both the Treaty of Lunéville, which marked his defeat of the Austrians at Marengo, and the Treaty of Amiens with the British; however, his designs upon Italy, Germany, and Switzerland, led to a renewal of war in 1805. Despite the disaster at *Trafalgar (1805), which forced him to abandon his plan for the invasion of Britain, his land victories, especially at *Austerlitz (1805), *Jena (1806), and *Friedland (1806), drew almost every continental power within the French orbit.

Napoleon I *David's portrait (1821; Versailles) of the emperor crossing the Alps splendidly evokes the glory of the Napoleonic legend.*

Napoleon's supremacy was short-lived. The *Continental System failed to break the British by blockade and the protracted *Peninsular War (1808–14) drained French resources. In 1812 Napoleon invaded an increasingly recalcitrant Russia with half a million men, of whom nearly 400,000 died in the brutal Russian winter. In 1813 Europe rose against Napoleon, inflicting a massive defeat at Leipzig that forced his abdication and subsequent exile to Elba, of which he was given sovereignty. In 1815, however, he escaped, returned to a rapturous welcome in France, and attempted in the *Hundred Days to regain his former greatness. He suffered a decisive defeat at *Waterloo and spent the remainder of his life confined to the island of St. Helena. Napoleon's claim to the French crown was pursued after his death by the son of his marriage to Marie Louise of Austria (*see* Napoleon II), and then by his nephew, who became Emperor *Napoleon III. *See also* Bonaparte.

Napoleonic Code. *See* Code Napoléon.

Napoleonic Wars. *See* Revolutionary and Napoleonic Wars.

Napoleon II (1811–32) The title accorded by supporters of the Bonapartist claim to the French throne to the son of Napoleon I and Empress Marie Louise. At birth entitled king of Rome, he was brought up, after his father's fall (1814), in Austria, where he received the title duke of Reichstadt.

Napoleon III (1808–73) Emperor of the French (1852–70); son of Louis Bonaparte and Hortense de Beauharnais and nephew of Napoleon I. Pretender to the French throne during the reign of Louis Philippe (1830–48), Napoleon used the enormous prestige of his name to win the presidential election after the Revolution of 1848. By a coup d'état at the end of 1851, he dissolved the legislative assembly and, a year later, declared himself emperor. His domestic policies fostered industry and, with the planning work of Baron *Haussmann, transformed the face of Paris. Abroad, his diplomacy embroiled France in the Crimean War (1854–56), in war against the Austrians in Italy (1859), and in a desultory conflict in Mexico (1861–67). Finally, his aggressive stance toward Bismarck helped to cause the *Franco-Prussian War, in which the Second Empire was destroyed and Napoleon was driven into exile.

Nara 34 41N 135 49E A city in Japan, in S Honshu. Japan's first capital (710–84 AD), it contains many historic monuments, including a bronze Buddha 72 ft (16 m) high. Population (1990): 349,349.

Narayanganj 23 36N 90 28E A city in Bangladesh, the chief riverport of Dacca. It is a major trading center and together with Dacca forms the largest industrial region in the country. Population (1991): 268,952.

Narbonne 43 11N 3 00E A market city in SE France, in the Aude department. An important Roman settlement, it was formerly a port (silted up in the 14th century). Population (1975): 40,543.

Narcissus (botany) A genus of perennial herbaceous plants (about 40 species), native to Eurasia and N Africa and widely planted in gardens and parks. Growing from bulbs, they produce strap-shaped or rushlike leaves and erect flower stalks, usually up to 12 in (30 cm) high. The flowers are usually yellow, orange, or white, with a ring of petal-like segments surrounding a central crown. The *daffodils (*N. pseudonarcissus*) have large solitary yellow flowers with trumpet-shaped crowns; the sweet-scented jonquils (*N. jonquilla*) have clusters of smaller pale-yellow flowers with small cuplike crowns; and the poet's narcissus (*N. poeticus*) has solitary flowers with white petals surrounding a short fringed orange-tipped crown. Family: *Amaryllidaceae*.

Narcissus (Greek mythology) A beautiful youth who was punished for rejecting the love of the nymph Echo by being made to fall in love with his own reflection in a pool. He died and was transformed into a flower.

narcotics Drugs that cause stupor or sleep and relieve pain by depressing activity of the brain. The term is used particularly for *opium and its derivatives (opiates), including morphine and codeine. Synthetic narcotics include heroin, methadone, and pethidine. The main medical use of narcotics is for the relief of severe pain, but their use is strictly controlled by law in most countries because they carry the risk of *drug dependence. The term narcotics is also used more loosely for any addictive drug.

Narragansett North American Algonquian-speaking Indian tribe found in S New England. Chiefly in Rhode Island, they had an agricultural society. Partially wiped out from fighting the colonists in *King Philip's War (1675–76), they, along with other tribes in the area, relocated. Some descendants live in Rhode Island.

Narragansett Bay A bay in SE Rhode Island. It contains many islands including Rhode Island, Prudence Island, and Conanicut Island.

Narses (c. 480–574 AD) Byzantine general. Originally a slave in Emperor *Justinian I's household, Narses rose to become the emperor's confidant. In 551 he replaced *Belisarius as commander in Italy. He recaptured Rome and eventually subdued the Ostrogoths, governing Italy until 567.

Narva 59 22N 28 17E A port in Estonia on the Narva River near the Gulf of Finland. Peter the Great was defeated by the Swedes in a famous battle there in 1700. It is an important textile center and also possesses fish- and food-processing industries. Population (1991): 82,300.

Narvik 68 26N 17 25E An ice-free port in N Norway. Two naval battles between the British and Germans were fought here in 1940 and the port was occupied by the Allies from May 10 until June 9. It exports iron ore from the Kiruna-Gällivare mines in N Sweden. Population (1980): 20,000.

narwhal A gregarious Arctic toothed *whale, *Monodon monoceros*, up to 16 ft (5 m) long and feeding on fish and squid. Male narwhals have a long straight spirally twisted tusk that is derived from a tooth and grows to a length of 10 ft (3 m); its function is unknown. Family: *Monodontidae*.

NASA (National Aeronautics and Space Administration) The US civilian agency, formed in 1958, that is responsible for all nonmilitary aspects of the US space program. Its major projects have included the manned *Apollo moon program, *Skylab, and several highly successful *planetary probes. In addition it has launched many artificial *satellites belonging to the US and other nations. Space shuttles, designed to carry people and materials between earth and permanent space stations and to conduct scientific experiments in space, have made numerous flights since the first orbital mission in 1981. *See also* space shuttle.

Naseby, Battle of (June 14, 1645) The battle in the English *Civil War that decided Charles I's defeat. The *New Model Army under Fairfax and Oliver Cromwell routed Prince *Rupert's royalist forces at Naseby, near Market Harborough, Leicestershire, and in the following year Charles surrendered.

Nash, Ogden (1902–71) US humorous writer. He wrote witty comments on social and domestic life expressed in doggerel verse. He contributed to the *New Yorker* magazine, and his books include *Free Wheeling* (1931), *I'm a Stranger Here Myself* (1938), *You Can't Get There from Here* (1957), *Collected Verse* (1961), and *Marriage Lines* (1964). He collaborated with Kurt Weill and S. J. Perelman on the musical *One Touch of Venus* (1943).

Nash, Paul (1889–1946) British painter. After studying at the Slade School, he became known for his symbolic war landscapes during World Wars I and II, the finest example being *Totes Meer* (1940–41; Tate Gallery). Nash was also a leading member of Unit One (1933), a group of artists, including Barbara *Hepworth and Henry *Moore, dedicated to promoting modern art (particularly *abstract art) in the UK. His brother **John Nash** (1893–1977) produced fine watercolor landscapes and botanical illustrations.

Nash, Sir Walter (1882–1968) New Zealand statesman; Labor prime minister (1957–60). Born in Britain, he introduced successful anti-Depression policies while minister of finance (1934–49) and was also a member of the Pacific War Council (1942–44).

Nashe, Thomas (1567–c. 1601) British pamphleteer and dramatist. In *Pierce Penilesse* (1592) and other satiric pamphlets he attacked the Puritans and defended the theaters against them. Among other works are the comic masque *Summer's Last Will and Testament* (1592) and the pioneering picaresque novel *The Unfortunate Traveller* (1594). He collaborated with Ben Jonson and others on the satirical play *The Isle of Dogs* (1597).

Nashville 36 10N 86 50W The capital city of Tennessee, on the Cumberland River. Founded in 1779, it is the site of Vanderbilt University (1873) and is a major center for religious education. A center of the recording industry for country and western music, the Country and Western Music Hall of Fame and Museum are situated here. Since the 1930s, cheap electric power from the Tennessee Valley Authority has made it an important commercial and industrial city. Industries include railroad engineering, glass, printing and publishing, and clothing. Population (1990): 488,374.

Nasik 20 00N 73 52E A city in India, in Maharashtra on the Godavari River. It is a major Hindu pilgrimage center. Industries include printing and distilling. Population (1991): 646,896.

Nassau A former duchy, now in Hesse and Rheinland-Pfalz (Germany). In 1544 William the Silent, Count of Nassau, inherited the principality of *Orange, thus linking the two states. Nassau joined Napoleon's Confederation of the Rhine in 1806 and in 1866 came under Prussia.

Nassau 25 2N 77 25W The capital of the Bahamas, a port on New Providence Island. Built in 1729, it is an important tourist center. Population (1990): 172,196.

Nasser, Gamal Abdel (1918–70) Egyptian statesman; prime minister (1954–56) and president (1956–70). An army officer, he helped to found the nationalist Free Officers group, which overthrew the monarchy in 1952. He became prime minister and then president of the Republic of Egypt (United Arab Republic from 1958). His nationalization of the Suez Canal led to an unsuccessful Israeli and Anglo-French attack on Egypt (1956), after which he was established as a leader of the Arab world. His socialist and Arab nationalist policies brought him into frequent conflict with the West and the more conservative Arab states.

Nasser, Lake. *See* Aswan High Dam.

Nast, Thomas (1840–1902) US political cartoonist; born in Germany. He began drawing for *Harper's Weekly* in 1859 and then became a staff member (1862–86). His antislavery cartoons greatly helped the Union cause during the Civil War. He is best known for his cartoons attacking New York City's Boss Tweed (William Marcy *Tweed) and Tammany Hall, which were instrumental in the breakup of the Tweed Ring and the arrest of Tweed (1876). He created the symbols for the Republican and Democratic parties and popularized the US version of Santa Claus.

nasturtium An annual garden plant of the genus *Tropaeolum* (90 species), also called Indian cress, native to Central and South America. It has round parasol-like leaves with central stalks, and orange, yellow, pink, or red flowers, which are funnel-shaped with a long spur containing nectar. *T. majus* is the most popular ornamental species and its seeds may be used in salads. The canary creeper (*T. peregrinum*) has twining leafstalks. Family: *Tropaeolaceae*.

Natal 5 46S 35 15W A port in NE Brazil, the capital of Rio Grande do Norte state near the mouth of the Rio Potengi. The chief exports are sugar, cotton, and carnauba wax; industries include salt refining and the manufacture of textiles. It has a university (1958). Population (1980): 376,552.

Natal The smallest province in South Africa. The land rises sharply from the Indian Ocean in the E to the Drakensberg Mountains in the W. Economic growth has been rapid. Agriculture and forestry are important. Along the coast sugar cane is the major crop and inland pine, eucalyptus, and wattle plantations supply the timber and paper industries. Other products are tropical fruits, maize, and beef and dairy cattle. Industries include shipping, food processing, chemicals, and sugar and oil refining. Durban is the main industrial center and port. Coal is the chief mineral. *History*: the Boers attempted to establish a republic in Natal (1838) but this was annexed by Britain in 1843 and with additions became a province of the Union of South Africa (1910). Area: 33,578 sq mi (86,967 sq km). Population (1991): 2,074,134. Capital: Pietermaritzburg.

Nataraja In Hinduism, *Shiva in his aspect as lord of the cosmic dance, which symbolizes the constant activity of creation and dissolution. During the Middle Ages, in imitation of this divine dance, dancing became an important part of Hindu temple ritual.

Natchez A Muskogean-speaking North American Indian tribe of the Lower Mississippi. They were cultivators who, like the *Creeks, built mound temples and worshiped the sun. They were ruled by a despotic chief known as the Great Sun and had an elaborate system of social classes. The highest caste, the "suns," were obliged to marry members of the lowest caste, the commoners.

Natchez 31 34N 91 23W A city in SW Mississippi, on the E bank of the Mississippi River. Settled in 1716, it began its growth as a major cotton port in the early 19th century with the opening of the Mississippi River and the advent of the steamboat. It was also the end of the Natchez Trace (1801–08), a road from Nashville, Tenn., to Natchez. Natchez was the capital of Mississippi from 1817 to 1821. It is still an important shipping center for cotton and other agricultural products. The antebellum architecture and features of Natchez attract tourists. Population (1990): 19,460.

Natchez Trace A road that runs from Nashville, Tenn., to Natchez, Miss. Built over an old Indian trail by the US Army between 1801 and 1808, the road opened up Mississippi and enabled settlers to get to and from Nashville, the nearest major town. It became an important trade and postal route, but declined when the steamboat came into use on the river. Since 1938, it has been part of the Natchez Trace Parkway. Length: 500 mi (800 km).

Nathan, George Jean (1882–1958) US editor and drama critic. He was co-editor, with H. L. *Mencken, of *Smart Set* (1914–23), and with Mencken started *The American Mercury* in 1924, in which Nathan enhanced his reputation as a drama critic. He went on to cofound *American Spectator* in 1930 and continued to satirize American culture and to elevate theater standards in numerous magazines and newspapers. He published an annual, *Theatre Book of the Year* (1943–51), and many books of criticism.

Nation, Carrie (Amelia Moore; 1846–1911) US reformer. Her first husband, Dr. Charles Gloyd, whom she married in 1867, died from alcoholism. In 1877 she married David Nation, who divorced her in 1901. Living in Kansas, where prohibition was in effect but openly disobeyed, she took it upon herself to destroy, often using a hatchet, the illegal saloons. Through the 1890s and early

1900s, she continued her crusade in Kansas and cities on the east and west coasts, appearing in simulated religious dress, singing hymns, and quoting from the Bible—sometimes with followers. She also opposed short skirts and smoking and favored woman suffrage, but her fanaticism prevented endorsement from organized groups.

National Academy of Sciences (NAS) US organization, founded in 1863, that promotes the use of science for the general welfare. Composed of elected members from the science and engineering community who have distinguished themselves in research and development, the academy advises the government and informs the public through its publications.

National Aeronautics and Space Administration. *See* NASA.

National American Woman Suffrage Association (NAWSA) US organization, established in 1890, to promote voting rights for women. A result of the merger of the National Woman Suffrage Association (1869) and the National American Woman Suffrage Association (1869), it promoted woman suffrage on the national, state, and local level. Elizabeth Cady *Stanton served as one of its first presidents (1892–1900).

national anthem The official patriotic song of a country, sung or played on ceremonial occasions. The US anthem is "The *Star-Spangled Banner." Other well-known anthems are Britain's "God Save the King" and France's "La Marseillaise."

National Association for the Advancement of Colored People (NAACP) US civil rights organization, founded in 1909, that promotes equality for African Americans. Formed by the merging of W. E. B. *DuBois's black militant Niagara Movement and a group of interested whites, it sought to achieve equal rights for African Americans through education and legal and legislative means. Its Legal Defense and Education Fund was responsible for bringing about school desegregation in *Brown v. Board of Education of Topeka (1954). It is headquartered in New York City and membership comprises about 500,000 in almost 2000 local units.

National Country Party An Australian political party, formed in 1919 as the Country party, that represents the interests of farmers. It has held office only in coalition with the *Liberal party.

national forest US forest land, overseen by the Forest Service, a division of the Department of Agriculture, that is set aside for conservation and recreation. The Forest Service, established in 1905, protects water, forage, wildlife, recreation, and timber to be used in ways that "will best meet the needs of the American people," as reaffirmed in the Multiple Use and Sustained Yield Act (1960). About 200 million acres (81 million hectares) of forest areas in the US and its possessions are administered by the Forest Service.

National Gallery An art museum in London, containing the largest collection of paintings in Britain. Founded in 1824, it originally contained 38 paintings, bought from John Julius Angerstein (1735–1823). William Wilkins (1778–1839) built the present building (1832–38). The National Gallery has aimed to collect paintings of every leading school and period (except the modern) in Europe.

National Gallery of Art US museum, established in 1937, that houses the national art treasures. It is a branch of the Smithsonian Institution and, although privately funded at first, is maintained by the US government. Most gallery acquisitions are privately donated. Started off by Andrew W. *Mellon's collection of American portraits (he also funded the construction of the building), it houses European and American masterpieces.

National Greenback Party. *See* Greenback Party.

National Industrial Recovery Act (NIRA) US New Deal legislation, passed in 1933, to aid economic recovery during the Depression. It promoted fair competition, improved working conditions and labor standards, and increased consumer buying power. Industrial codes (about 550 in all) covered every facet of business from shortened working hours and child labor to pricing and production numbers and collective bargaining. To oversee implementation of the legislation, Pres. Franklin D. *Roosevelt established the National Recovery Administration (NRA). Although it was agreed that conditions had improved somewhat, the NIRA was ruled unconstitutional by the Supreme Court (*Schechter* v. *United States*; 1935).

nationalism A doctrine that claims to determine the unit of population entitled to have government of its own. In its revolutionary form it regards existing state boundaries as arbitrary. The doctrine developed in Europe around 1800. The Latin word *Natio* had simply meant a group, regardless of frontiers, as in *Montesquieu's reference to monks as the "pietistic nation." After the French Revolution, nationalists such as *Fichte and *Mazzini sought to make the boundaries of states coextensive with those of national habitation. Nations were supposed to be recognizable by certain distinguishing characteristics—for Fichte this was the use of a particular language. *Kant's doctrine of the autonomy of the will was used to provide philosophical backing for nationalism. While it was hoped that nationalism would make for peace, nationalistic aspirations in practice have often resulted in xenophobia, rivalry, and war.

National Labor Relations Board (NLRB) US federal agency, established in 1935, that governs labor relations. Its two main objectives are to correct unfair practices in business and labor unions and to insure the employee's freedom of choice, by secret ballot voting, to unionize. It administers the National Labor Relations Act (Wagner Act; 1935), which was amended by the Labor-Management Relations Act of 1947 (Taft-Hartley Act). There are five board members and a general counsel.

National Labor Relations Board v. Jones and Laughlin Steel Corp. (1937) US Supreme Court decision that dealt with the extent of federal regulatory power over interstate trade. The National Labor Relations Board (NLRB) directed Jones and Laughlin to rehire employees who had been fired for union activities. The steel company refused, and a federal court upheld their claim that the federal government could not rule on matters that affected interstate commerce only indirectly. The Supreme Court disagreed, ruled the direction of the NLRB constitutional, and ordered the workers rehired.

National Organization for Women (NOW) US organization, founded in 1966, that supports equal rights for women. Organized by feminist Betty Friedan and others, it advocates, through legislation, full equality for women, especially regarding the right to work and matters of marriage and divorce. It is a major force behind the campaign to ratify the Equal Rights Amendment.

National Park Service US government agency, established in 1916, a division of the Department of the Interior. It oversees the administration of all national historic, natural, cultural, and recreational areas, which include, among others, parks, monuments, rivers, parkways, seashores, reservoirs, and events. The oldest of the national parks is *Yellowstone National Park.

National Portrait Gallery An art museum in London founded in 1856 to house portraits that are authentic likenesses of famous personalities in British history. Its collection includes works by Holbein, Rubens, Reynolds, and Augustus John and an increasing number of photographs.

National Recovery Administration (NRA). *See* National Industrial Recovery Act.

National Republican party US political party, formed in 1828 by a faction of the Republican party that opposed Andrew *Jackson's reelection to the presidency in 1832. One of the party's leaders, Henry *Clay, ran against Jackson in the election, but lost. The party platform urged support of the second Bank of the United States. Short-lived, the party became part of the Whig Party by 1836.

National Security Acts (1947, 1949) US legislation that unified the military establishment, strengthened national security, and created the Department of Defense. In the 1947 law the Air Force became separate from the Army and equal to the Army and the Navy; the cabinet post of secretary of defense was created; and the National Security Council, *Central Intelligence Agency (CIA), National Security Resources Board (which no longer exists), and Joint Chiefs of Staff and several other boards were established. By the 1949 act the National Military Establishment was renamed the Department of Defense and raised to executive department level.

National Socialist German Workers' Party. *See* Nazi party.

Nation of Islam. *See* Black Muslims.

Native American Party. *See* Know-Nothing party.

NATO. *See* North Atlantic Treaty Organization.

Natron, Lake 2 20S 36 05E A lake in N Tanzania, in the *Great Rift Valley. It measures about 30 mi (56 km) by 15 mi (24 km) and contains salt and soda.

natterjack A short-legged European *toad, *Bufo calamita*. About 2.8 in (7 cm) long when fully grown, the natterjack has a yellow stripe down its back. It runs in a series of short spurts and if alarmed raises its inflated body on its hind legs to appear larger to the enemy.

Nat Turner Insurrection. *See* Turner, Nat.

natural gas A naturally occurring mixture of gaseous hydrocarbons consisting mainly of methane with smaller amounts of heavier hydrocarbons. It is obtained from underground reservoirs, often associated with *oil deposits. Like oil it originates in the bacterial decomposition of animal matter. It is a relatively cheap effective fuel, although in short supply (the present known reserves will be exhausted early next century). It also contains nonhydrocarbon impurities, the most important being helium, which is extracted commercially.

naturalism A literary and artistic movement of the late 19th century characterized by the use of realistic techniques to express the philosophical belief that all phenomena can be explained by natural or material causes. It was influenced by the biological theories of *Darwin, the philosophy of *Comte, and the deterministic theories of the historian *Taine. Its literary manifesto was *Le Roman expérimentale* (1880) by *Zola, whose sequence of 20 novels known as *Le Rougon-Macquart* (1871–93) was intended to demonstrate, by its concentration on the history of a single family, how human life is determined by heredity and environment. Writers influenced by naturalism include the dramatists *Hauptmann, *Ibsen, *Strindberg, and, in the 20th century, the US novelist Theodore *Dreiser. Its influence is also apparent in the work of such painters as *Courbet and *Van Gogh.

naturalization In law, the process by which an *alien, on taking an oath of allegiance, acquires the rights of a natural-born citizen of a country.

natural selection. *See* Darwinism.

Nauru, Republic of (*or* Naoero; former name: Pleasant Island) A small country in the central Pacific Ocean, NE of Australia comprising a coral island. The small population consists mainly of Naurians and other Pacific islanders. *Economy*: based entirely on the mining of phosphates, the only export. Deposits are expected to run out in the 1990s, but plans are underway to derive sufficient revenue by developing the island as a transport center and tax haven. *History*: discovered by the British in 1798, it was under British mandate from 1920 to 1947, when it came under the joint trusteeship of Australia, New Zealand, and the UK. In 1968 it became an independent republic and a special member of the British Commonwealth, with Hammer DeRoburt as its first president. He faced serious difficulties in 1983, which led to his resignation. Bringing a libel suit against a Guam newspaper for linking DeRoburt and the Nauru government with a loan to Marshall Island separatists, DeRoburt lost the case at great financial cost to the country. In addition, Nauru's proposal to ban the dumping of nuclear wastes in the Pacific was defeated by the superpowers. Four days after his resignation, DeRoburt was reelected. In 1989, Nauru accused Australia of exploiting and mismanaging Nauru's phosphate resources during the years before independence and sought compensation from them. In elections that year, President DeRoburt was defeated by Bernard Dowiyogo. Official language: English. Official currency: Australian dollar. Area: 8 sq mi (21 sq km). Population (1990 est): 8100. Capital and main port: Yaren.

Nausicaa In Greek legend, the daughter of Alcinous, king of Phaeacia. She gave help to the shipwrecked *Odysseus, and was offered by her father in marriage, but Odysseus, loyal to his wife, refused.

nautical mile. *See* mile.

nautilus One of several cephalopod mollusks with external shells. The pearly nautiluses (genus *Nautilus*; 3 species) live near the bottom of the Pacific and Indian Oceans. Up to 8 in (20 cm) across, they have 60–90 tentacles surrounding a horny beak and live in the outermost chamber of their flat coiled shells. The others serve as buoyancy chambers from which gases can be absorbed, thus enabling the animals to float at different depths.

The paper nautilus (*Argonauta argo*) is found in the Atlantic and Pacific Oceans. The female, 8 in (20 cm) long secretes from one of its tentacles a papery boat-shaped shell in which the eggs are laid and fertilized and develop. The male is much smaller (about 0.8 in [2 cm] long).

Navajo A North American Indian Athabascan-speaking people of New Mexico, Arizona, and Utah. Like their relatives, the *Apache, they migrated from the far north, probably during the 17th century. Unlike the Apache, they learned farming and adopted many traits from the *Pueblo Indians. Their social organization is based on the matrilineal principle and they live in small dispersed settlements, traditionally with little centralized political authority. They are farmers and herders and now the most numerous North American Indian tribe.

Navarino, Battle of (Oct 20, 1827) A naval battle arising from European intervention on behalf of Greece in the War of *Greek Independence from the Ottoman Empire. Ships of the French, Russian, and British navies destroyed the Ottoman-Egyptian fleet in the Bay of Navarinou in the Peloponnese. This was the last fleet action fought wholly under sail.

Navarre A former kingdom in N Spain, corresponding to the present-day Spanish province of Navarre and part of the French department of Basses-Pyrénées. Known as Pampalona until the late 12th century, it was ruled by Muslims until the late 9th century, when a Basque dynasty established control over the kingdom. In 1234 it passed to a French dynasty but in 1512 S Navarre was conquered by Ferdinand the Catholic of Aragon and united with Castile in 1515. French Navarre passed to the French crown in 1589.

navel A depression in the center of the abdomen that represents the site of attachment of the *umbilical cord of the fetus. Its medical name is the umbilicus. Occasionally babies are born with an umbilical hernia, in which the intestines protrude through the navel.

Navigation Acts A series of English acts originally to foster English shipping (1382, 1485, 1540) but subsequently to protect England's colonial trade, especially against its Dutch rivals. During the Commonwealth (1649–53) two ordinances (1650, 1651) respectively banned foreign trading in the colonies and restricted such trade to English or colonial ships, manned by predominantly English crews. These and similar Acts of 1660, 1672, and 1696 were repealed in 1849.

Navratilova, Martina (1956–) US tennis player; born in Czechoslovakia. She defected to the US in 1975 and won her first major title, the Wimbledon singles championship, which she won again in 1979 and 1982–87. The dominant women's player of the early 1980s, she took the US title in 1983–84 and 1986–87.

navy A nation's warships (*see* ships), together with their crews and supporting administration. Navies were built by the ancient Greek city states at first to protect their Mediterranean trade routes from pirates and later to undermine the sea power of their rivals and enemies. The first recorded sea battle took place between Corinth and Corcyra (*or* Corfu) in 664 BC and navies—typically comprising triremes—played an important part in both the Greek-Persian and Peloponnesian Wars. The first permanent naval administration was organized (311 BC) in ancient Rome, which was the supreme Mediterranean power by the early 2nd century BC (*see* Punic Wars). Rome's naval power passed after the collapse of the western Empire in the 5th century AD to the Byzantine (Eastern Roman) Empire. Meanwhile, the Vikings marauded northern waters, provoking Alfred the Great of England to create (9th century) the origins of the Royal Navy. The later Middle Ages saw the rise of Italian navies, outstandingly those of Venice and Genoa, and the decline of the Byzantine fleet, under the threat of the Ottoman Turks. By 1571, when, at Lepanto, the Turkish control of the Mediterranean was finally destroyed, Spain had emerged as the supreme naval power. England's defeat of the Spanish *Armada (1588) anticipated its subsequent emergence as a great naval power: by the late 17th century it had overtaken the Netherlands (*see* Dutch Wars) and by the early 19th century, France (*see* Revolutionary and Napoleonic Wars). British naval supremacy was threatened in the early 20th century by the German navy, which in spite of defeat in World War I again became a power to be reckoned with in the 1930s. By the end of World War II command of the seas had passed to the US navy. The navies of the US and Russia now dominate the seas and with their nuclear-powered missile-armed submarines also dominate most of the earth's surface.

Navy, Department of the US government military department within the Department of *Defense. Directed by the secretary of defense and the secretary of the navy, it comprises the US *Navy, the US *Marine Corps, and the US Coast Guard when it is operating as a service in the navy. Charged with the prosecution of war at sea when necessary and the maintenance of freedom on the seas, the department oversees the activities of its forces. Established in 1798, the department took over activities that had been the responsibility of the secretary of war.

Navy, United States Naval forces of the military. The navy's mission is to protect the United States by the effective prosecution of war at sea, including the seizure or defense of advanced naval bases (*Marine Corps); to support the forces of all military departments of the US; and to maintain freedom of the seas. Established in 1775, the navy is headed by the secretary of the navy and the chief of naval operations (CNO), the navy's highest ranking officer.

Naxalites An extremist communist movement centering on the town of Naxalbari in W Bengal (India). Dedicated to Maoist principles, it attempted a violent seizure of land for the landless in 1967.

Náxos A Greek island in the S Aegean Sea, the largest in the Cyclades. Náxos is traditionally the place where Theseus abandoned Ariadne. It was an ancient center of the worship of Dionysius. Area: 169 sq mi (438 sq km). Chief town: Náxos.

Nazareth 32 41N 35 16E A city in N Israel, between Haifa and the Sea of Galilee. The chief attractions of the city are the many churches, which commemorate its associations with the early life of Jesus Christ. Population: 33,000.

Nazi party (*N*ationalso*z*ialistische Deutsche Arbeiterpartei) The National Socalist German Workers' party, founded in 1919 as the German Workers' party and led from 1921 until his suicide in 1945 by Adolf *Hitler. *See also* fascism.

NAZI PARTY *Hitler's exploitation of the techniques of mass propaganda, notably at party rallies such as the one pictured here, helps explain his rise to power in prewar Germany.*

Nazirites (*or* Nazarites) In the Old Testament, a group of Israelites who consecrated themselves to God by taking special vows, originally perhaps for life but later for a certain period only. The vows were to abstain from wine, not to cut the hair, and to avoid contact with dead bodies. Samson and Samuel were Nazirites from birth.

N'djamena (name until 1973: Fort Lamy) The capital of Chad, a port in the SW on the Chari River. It was founded by the French in 1900. The University of Chad was established in 1971. Population (1992 est): 687,800.

Ndola 13 00S 28 39E A city in N Zambia, near the Zaïre border. It is an important commercial and distribution center for the *Copperbelt and has copper and cobalt refineries. Population (1988 est): 443,000.

Neagh, Lough A lake in Northern Ireland, divided between Co Antrim, Co Armagh, and Co Tyrone. It is the largest lake in the British Isles. Area: 150 sq mi (388 sq km).

Neanderthal man An extinct *hominid race that inhabited Europe and the adjacent areas of Africa and Asia between about 70,000 and 35,000 years ago. Characterized by heavy brow ridges, receding forehead, heavy protruding jaw, and robust bone structure, Neanderthal man nonetheless had a large cranial capacity and upright posture. They were cave-dwelling hunters who made tools and buried their dead in a manner implying some sort of cult and ritual (*see* Mousterian). Their status as a distinct species (*Homo neanderthalensis*) is now questioned and some paleontologists prefer to see them as a subspecies of *Homo sapiens* (*see* Homo).

neap tide A □tide of comparatively small range that occurs near the time of the moon's quarters. The range falls below the average range by 10 to 30% (high low tides and low high tides). *Compare* spring tide.

nearsightedness (*or* myopia) Inability to focus on distant objects. This is the commonest kind of visual defect and commonly runs in families; it is not due to excessive reading in bad light but to a slightly misshapen eyeball, in which the light rays are focused in front of the retina (light-sensitive layer). It is corrected by wearing glasses with concave lenses or contact lenses.

Nebraska A state in the midwestern US. It is bordered by Iowa and Missouri on the E with the Missouri River forming the boundary, by Kansas and Colorado on the S, by Wyoming on the W, and by South Dakota on the N. Part of the Central Lowlands cover the eastern third of the state, with the higher Great Plains in the W. Traditionally an agricultural state, it is still a leading producer of cattle, corn, and wheat. Most of the population is situated in the industrial E. Omaha, the largest city, and Lincoln are insurance centers. Food processing (especially meat) is a major industry; machinery, fabricated metal, transport equipment, chemicals, and printing and publishing are also important. *History*: originally inhabited by tribes of Pawnee, Cheyenne, Arapaho, and Sioux who hunted the vast herds of buffalo that roamed Nebraska's plains, the region was first explored by Francisco Vasquez de Coronado for Spain (1511). The French had developed the fur trade by the time the US acquired the area as part of the Louisiana Purchase in 1803. The Homestead Act (1862) and the arrival of the railroads (1867) encouraged settlement as hordes of pioneers traveled westward to claim the free land. Simultaneously with the arrival of the railroads, Nebraska achieved statehood (1867). The improved transportation spurred the development of cattle ranching. Nebraskan farmers were receptive to the Granger and Populist movements, and William Jennings Bryan, a native Nebraskan, became the national leader of both the Populists and the Democrats. Nebraska's well-being depended on its agricultural productivity, which was severely damaged by a devastating drought that came on the heels of the Depression of the 1930s. After World War II farm mechanization increased and new industries were developed; federal water projects helped the state, particularly with crop irrigation. During the economic recession of the early 1980s the economy remained generally strong with relatively low unemployment although the agricultural industry did suffer. Area: 77,227 sq mi (200,018 sq km). Population (1990): 1,578,385. Capital: Lincoln.

Nebuchadnezzar II (*or* Nebuchadrezzar; c. 630–562 BC) King of *Babylon (605–562). Nebuchadnezzar defeated the Egyptians at Carchemish (605 BC) and extended Babylonian power in Elam, N Syria, and S Asia Minor. He captured Jerusalem in 597 and again in 586, when he destroyed the city and forced the

Jews into exile (*see* Babylonian Exile). He restored Babylon to its former glory. Daniel's story of his madness is probably unhistorical.

nebula A cloud of interstellar gas and dust that becomes visible for one of three reasons. In an **emission nebula** the gas is ionized by ultraviolet radiation, generally from a hot star within the cloud; the ions interact with free electrons in the cloud, and light (predominantly red and green) is emitted. In a **reflection nebula** light from a nearby star is reflected in all directions by dust in the cloud, thus illuminating the cloud. The dust in a **dark nebula** reduces quite considerably the amount of light passing through it (by absorption and scattering) and a dark region is seen against a brighter background.

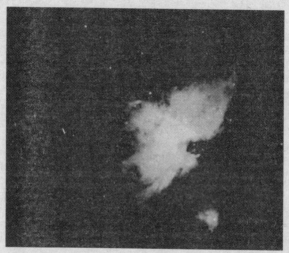

NEBULA *The Orion nebula, one of the brightest emission nebulae.*

Neckar River A river in SW Germany, flowing mainly N from the Black Forest past Stuttgart and Heidelberg to join the Rhine River at Mannheim. Length: 245 mi (394 km).

Necker, Jacques (1732–1804) French statesman. A successful banker, in 1768 he became a director of the French East India Company. In 1776 he was appointed director of the treasury and in 1777, director general of finance. In retirement from 1781 to 1788, he was recalled to his former post on the eve of the French Revolution in the hope that he would deal with the economic crisis. He persuaded Louis XVI to summon the States General and suggested reforms that aroused the enmity of the aristocrats, who secured his dismissal. Reappointed after the storming of the Bastille, he resigned in 1790. His daughter was Mme de Staël.

nectar A sugary solution produced by glandular structures (nectaries) in animal-pollinated flowers. Nectar attracts insects, birds, or bats to the flower and encourages pollination as the animal collects nectar from different sources.

nectarine. *See* peach.

needlefish A carnivorous fish, also called garfish, belonging to the family *Belonidae* (about 60 species), that occurs in tropical and warm-temperate seas. It has a slender silvery-blue or green body, up to 4 ft (1.2 m) long, with elongated jaws and numerous sharp teeth. Species include the European garfish (*Belone belone*). Order: *Atheriniformes*.

Neer, Aert van der (c. 1603–77) Dutch landscape painter, famous for his moonlight, sunset, and firelight scenes. He also painted ice-bound canals and other winter landscapes.

Nefertiti (died c. 1346 BC) The cousin and chief wife of *Akhenaton of Egypt. She is depicted with her six daughters and the king in many scenes of personal and domestic life, a unique exception to the priestly conventions of Egyptian royal portraiture. Her portrait bust is perhaps the best-known work of Egyptian art.

Negev A desert in S Israel. In recent years large areas have been irrigated by pipeline from the Jordan River and many farming communities established, including over a hundred *kibbutzim*. Area: about 4632 sq mi (12,000 sq km).

Negrín, Juan (1889–1956) Spanish politician. A moderate socialist, Negrín became prime minister of the Republic in 1937 during the *Spanish Civil War. He centralized the military forces of the Republic but Negrín's dependence on the Communist party brought opposition that forced his resignation.

Negri Sembilan A state in W Peninsular Malaysia, on the Strait of Malacca. It is hilly, producing mainly rubber, rice, coconuts, and tin. Area: 2550 sq mi (6605 sw km). Population (1980): 563,955. Capital: Seremban.

Negro, Río 1. (Portuguese name: Rio Negro) A river in NE South America. Rising in E Colombia as the Guainía, it flows generally E into Brazil, joining the Amazon River about 10 mi (16 km) below Manaus. Length: about 1400 mi (2250 km). **2.** A river in S Argentina, rising in the Andes and flowing generally SE across Patagonia to the Atlantic Ocean. Length: 630 mi (1014 km).

Negroid The racial grouping comprising populations of sub-Saharan Africa. They are characterized by heavy skin pigmentation, curly to kinky dark hair, broad nose and lips, slight body hair, and high frequency of blood type Ro in the Rh system. Two subtypes exist: the taller darker Congoloid race and the shorter and lighter pygmies, Bushmen, and Hottentots, collectively known as Capoids.

Negros A volcanic island in the central Philippines, in the Visayan Islands. The chief industry is sugar production. Area: 5278 sq mi (13,670 sq km). Chief town: Bacolod.

Nehemiah In the Old Testament, a Jewish leader of the 5th century BC. He was cupbearer to the Persian king but was granted permission to return to Jerusalem in 444 BC, where, despite opposition, he planned and supervised the restoration of the city walls. In 432 he visited Jerusalem a second time and initiated a number of religious and social reforms. **The Book of Nehemiah**, recording his activities, is by the author of *Chronicles and *Ezra.

Nehru, Jawaharlal (1889–1964) Indian statesman; the first prime minister of independent India (1947–64). Educated in England, he returned to India in 1912 to practice law but soon left his profession to follow Mahatma *Gandhi; in 1929 he was elected president of the *Indian National Congress in succession to his father Motilal Nehru (1861–1931). Between 1921 and 1945 he served nine prison sentences for participating in the movement of noncooperation against the British. After World War II he was a central figure in the negotiations for the creation of an independent India. Throughout his long premiership he was held in high esteem both in his own country and abroad. He carried through many social reforms and maintained a policy of nonalignment with foreign powers, although he was finally forced to enlist US support against Chinese border attacks in 1962. Vijaya *Pandit was his sister and Indira *Gandhi his daughter.

JAWAHARLAL NEHRU *Two members of a political dynasty view exhibits at the Summer Palace in Peking. With Nehru is his daughter, Indira Gandhi, who later became prime minister.*

Neill, A(lexander) S(utherland) (1883–1973) Scottish educationalist, child psychologist, and writer. The best-known British exponent of child-centered education, Neill founded Summerhill (1921), a coeducational boarding school, famous for its informal atmosphere and liberal educational techniques. His books include *Hearts, Not Heads* (1945) and *Talking of Summerhill* (1967).

Neisse River 1. (*or* Glatzer Neisse; Polish name: Nysa) A river in SW Poland, flowing NE to join the Oder River near Brzeg. Length: 159 mi (244 km). **2.** (*or* Lusatian Neisse) A river rising in NW Czechoslovakia and flowing mainly N to the Oder River near Gubin in Poland. It forms part of the border between Germany and Poland. Length: 140 mi (225 km).

Nejd. *See* Najd.

Nekrasov, Nikolai Alekseevich (1821–78) Russian poet. After rejecting the military career proposed by his father, he became a successful editor and manager of various literary periodicals. The main theme of his poetry is the oppression and character of the Russian peasants. He frequently drew on traditional folk songs, especially in his poems for children.

nekton An ecological division of aquatic animals that includes all those swimming actively, i.e. by their own efforts, in the open waters of a sea or lake (*compare* plankton). The nekton includes fishes, squids, turtles, seals, and whales.

Nelson, Horatio, Viscount (1758–1805) British admiral. At the outbreak of the French Revolutionary Wars he was given a command in the Mediterranean. In 1794, at Calvi, he lost the sight in his right eye but went on to play an important part in the victory off Cape St Vincent (1797), for which he was knighted. Shortly afterward he lost his right arm in action but in 1798 he destroyed France's naval power in the Mediterranean by his great victory in the battle of the *Nile. Nelson spent the following year in Naples, where he fell in love with Emma, Lady *Hamilton. Returning to England in 1800, Nelson, now Baron Nelson of the Nile, received a hero's welcome but his affair with Emma Hamilton caused scandal. Given command in the Baltic, he was responsible for the victory at Copenhagen (1801). In 1803 he became commander in the Mediterranean. He blockaded Toulon but in 1805 the French escaped, with Nelson hot in pursuit, and the ensuing chase culminated in the battle of *Trafalgar (1805). Nelson directed this British triumph from aboard the *Victory* (□ships) but was himself mortally wounded.

HORATIO NELSON *Portrait (1798–1800) by Guy Head.*

Nelson, Willie (1933–) US singer and composer, who earned the nickname "King of Country Music" for such creations as "Crazy" and "Night Life." A country music "outlaw," he wore baggy clothing, had a scruffy beard, braided his long hair, and wore his trademark red bandanna. Nelson worked toward a purer sound in country music that appealed to all audiences. His later country hits, such as "On the Road Again" and "Always on My Mind," often crossed over to become hits on the popular music charts. He also acted in films, including *The Electric Horseman, Honeysuckle Rose,* and *Songwriter.*

Neman River (*or* Nyeman R.) A river rising in Belarus, it flows mainly NW through Lithuania to enter the Baltic Sea. Length: 582 mi (937 km).

nematode A spindle-shaped colorless worm, also called roundworm, belonging to the phylum *Nematoda* (over 10,000 species). Most nematodes are less than 0.12 in (3 mm) long and have a mouth at one end, sometimes containing teeth or stylets, and usually a short muscular pharynx leading to the intestine. The sexes are generally separate. Nematodes live almost everywhere in soil, fresh water, and the sea. Some are parasites of plants or animals; others feed on dead organic matter. Many damage crops or parasitize domestic animals and man. *See also* Ascaris; eelworm; filaria; guinea worm; hookworm; pinworm; vinegar eel.

Nemertina. *See* ribbonworm.

Nemery, Jaafar Mohammed al (1930–) Sudanese statesman; president (1971–85). An army officer, Nemery came to power in a coup in 1969 and was chairman of a revolutionary council before becoming president. In 1972 he negotiated an end to the 17-year revolt of the non-Muslims in the S, but N–S tensions remained. In the early 1980s, he was threatened by opposition from Libya and was ousted in a coup in 1985.

Nemesia A genus of annual herbs native to South Africa. They are up to 12 in (30 cm) tall, with narrow leaves and showy white, yellow, red, pink, or purple two-lipped flowers, sometimes spurred, with spotted centers. Many species are popular ornamentals, especially *N. strumosa*, *N. floribunda*, and *N. versicolor*. Family: *Scrophulariaceae*.

Nemesis In Greek mythology, a goddess personifying the gods' anger at and punishment of human arrogance or *hubris. According to Hesiod, she is the daughter of night. She is associated with just vengeance and especially the punishment that befalls the impious.

Nennius (9th century AD) Welsh antiquary. He is traditionally held to be the author of *Historia Britonum*, a summary of Roman, Saxon, and Celtic legends concerning the early history of Britain. It contains the earliest reference to King *Arthur and mentions the poets *Aneirin and *Taliesin.

neoclassicism 1. In art and architecture, a style dominant in Europe from the late 18th to mid-19th centuries. Originating in Rome in about 1750, it later spread throughout Europe and to the US. Although essentially a revival of classical art and architecture, it was distinguished from similar revivals by its new scientific approach to the recreation of the past. This was largely stimulated by archeological discoveries at *Pompeii, *Herculaneum, and elsewhere. Key figures in the early development of neoclassicism were the art historian *Winckelmann, who promoted enthusiasm for Greek art, and *Piranesi, who did the same for Roman art. Early neoclassical painters included *Mengs and Benjamin *West but the best known were Jacques Louis *David and *Ingres, who worked in France. Here neoclassicism developed under the stimulus of the *Enlightenment as a reaction to the frivolity of the *rococo style. The neoclassical penchant for themes of self-sacrifice in painting made it popular during the French Revolution. Other leading neoclassicists were the sculptors *Canova and *Thorvalsden and the architects Robert Adam, Soufflot, Claude-Nicholas Ledoux, and Friedrich Gilly. *See also* Empire style. **2.** A style of composition originating in the 1920s. It was characterized by the use of counterpoint, small instrumental forces, and the use of such 18th-century forms as the concerto grosso. The leading practitioners of musical neoclassicism were *Stravinsky and *Hindemith.

neodymium (Nd) A *lanthanide element, occurring in the mineral monazite. It is used with lanthanum in *misch metal in lighter flints and, as the oxide

(Nd_2O_3), together with praseodymium, to produce special dark glasses used in welding goggles. At no 60; at wt 144.24; mp 1872°F (1021°C); bp 5560°F (3068°C).

neoimpressionism. *See* pointillism.

Neolithic The final division of the *Stone Age. It is characterized by the development of the earliest settled agricultural communities and increasing domestication of animals, apparently occurring first in the Middle East during the 9th millennium BC (*see* Çatalhüyük; Jericho). Although man still used only stone tools and weapons, he evolved improved techniques of grinding (as opposed to flaking) stone and the invention of pottery facilitated food storage and preparation.

Neo-Melanesian The form of *pidgin English widely used in Melanesia and New Guinea as a trade and mission language, which has become the native language of some communities. It has a more restricted vocabulary than that of English, on which it is based, a simplified grammar, and a modified sound system.

neon (Ne) A noble gas present in very small amounts in the earth's atmosphere, discovered in 1898 by Ramsay and M. W. Travers (1872–1961) by fractional distillation of liquid air. In an electrical discharge tube, neon glows orange-red and it is commonly used in advertising signs and voltage indicator lamps. Although some ion-pairs have been reported (for example NeH^+), no stable compounds similar to those of krypton and xenon are yet known. At no 10; at wt 20.179; mp −415°F (−248.67°C); bp −410.9°F (−246.05°C).

neoplasticism. *See* Stijl, de.

Neoplatonism The philosophy, formulated principally by *Plotinus, that emphasizes an eternal world of order, goodness, and beauty, of which material existence is a weak and unsatisfactory copy. The chief influences were Plato's concept of the Good, the analysis of love in the *Symposium*, and the speculations about the soul and immortality in the *Phaedo*; Plotinus had little interest in Plato's political and other systems. Neoplatonism helped to shape both medieval Christian theology and Islamic philosophy. *See also* Platonism.

Neoptolemus In Greek legend, king of Epirus, the son of *Achilles. He took part in the *Trojan War after his father's death and killed *Priam at the altar of Zeus.

neorealism An Italian literary movement that originated during the early years of the fascist regime in the 1920s and flourished openly after its fall in 1943. Notable writers included the novelists Cesare *Pavese, Alberto *Moravia, and Ignazio *Silone, all of whom suffered political persecution for their accurate portrayal of social conditions. The term neorealism has also been applied to certain Italian films made after World War II. Often using nonprofessional actors and shot on real locations, neorealist films include *De Sica's *The Bicycle Thief* (1948).

neoteny The condition in which larval characteristics persist in an animal when it reaches sexual maturity. The *axolotl is a neotenous salamander that rarely assumes the typical adult form under natural conditions, although metamorphosis can be triggered by injection of thyroid hormone. Neotony is also known in certain tunicates (primitive marine chordates).

Nepal, Kingdom of A landlocked country in the Himalayas, between China (Tibet) and India. Most of the country consists of a series of mountain ranges and high fertile valleys, with some of the world's highest peaks, including Mount Everest, along its N border and a region of plain and swamp in the S. Its predominantly Hindu population is of Mongoloid stock, the Gurkhas having been the dominant group since 1769. *Economy*: chiefly agricultural, the main crops are rice, maize, millet, and wheat. Forestry is also important. Mineral resources are sparse, although some mica is being mined. Hydroelectricity is being developed on a large scale and some industry is being encouraged, including jute and sugar. Tourism is an important source of revenue. Exports, mainly to India, include grains, jute, and timber, as well as medicinal herbs from the mountains. *History*: the independent principalities that comprised the region in the Middle Ages were conquered by the Gurkhas in the 18th century and Nepal was subsequently ruled by the Shah family and then by the Rana, who continue to reign. In 1959 a new constitution provided for an elected parliament, but in 1960 the king dismissed the new government and in 1962 abolished the constitution. There is now a pyramidal structure of government by local and national councils (*panchayat*). Until 1990, executive power lay with the king. In 1990, he relinquished many of his powers and lifted the ban on political parties. Elections in 1991 produced a multiparty coalition government. In international relations Nepal tries to keep a balance between the two neighboring great powers. Head of state: King Birendra Bir Bikram Shah Dev. Prime Minister: Girja Prasad Koirala. Official language: Nepali. Official currency: Nepalese rupee of 100 paisa. Area: 54,600 sq mi (141,400 sk km). Population (1990 est): 19,158,000. Capital: Kathmandu.

nephritis (*or* Bright's disease) Inflammation of the kidneys. It may result from infection, as in *pyelitis, or from a disorder of the body's system that affects the kidneys (called glomerulonephritis), which causes protein, cells, and blood to appear in the urine and swelling of the body tissues (*see* edema). This sometimes occurs in children after a streptococcal infection of the throat and often resolves, but other types of glomerulonephritis, occurring more often in adults, may become chronic and result eventually in kidney failure or *uremia.

Neptune (astronomy) The most distant giant planet, orbiting the sun every 165 years at a mean distance of 2793 million mi (4497 million km). It is somewhat smaller (30,750 mi [49,500 km] in diameter) and more massive (17.3 earth masses) than *Uranus, exhibits a similar featureless greenish disk in a telescope, and is thought to be almost identical to Uranus in atmospheric and internal structure. It has two *satellites. Neptune's existence was predicted by John Couch Adams and Urbain Leverrier. It was discovered in 1846 by J. G. Galle, using Leverrier's predicted position.

Neptune (mythology) An early Italian god associated with water. When seapower became important to Rome, he became the principal Roman sea god and was identified with the Greek *Poseidon. He is usually portrayed holding a trident and riding a dolphin.

neptunium (Np) The first synthetic transuranic element, produced in 1940 at Berkeley, Calif., by bombarding uranium with neutrons. Trace quantities are produced in natural uranium ores by the same reaction. It is available in small quantities in nuclear reactors and forms halides (for example NpF_3, $NpCl_4$) and oxides (for example NpO_2). At no 93; at wt 237.0482; mp 1185°F (640°C); bp 7063°F (3902°C).

nereids In Greek mythology, a class of *nymphs or female spirits of nature associated with the sea. They were the daughters of the sea god Nereus and Doris, daughter of Oceanus. The best-known Nereids were *Amphitrite, wife of Poseidon, and *Thetis, mother of Achilles.

Nereus A primitive Greek sea god, father of the *Nereids. He had prophetic powers and was capable of changing his form.

Nergal A Mesopotamian god of hunger and devastation and ruler of the under-world . He is also described as a protective god capable of restoring the dead to life and features in the *Epic of Gilgamesh*.

Neri, St Philip (1515–95)   Italian mystic, who founded the Congregation of the Oratory (*see* Oratorians). Settling in Rome (c. 1533), he organized a body of laymen dedicated to charitable works. He was ordained in 1551, becoming a priest at the Church of San Girolamo. Over its nave he built an oratory to hold religious meetings and concerts of sacred music, from which both the name of Neri's order and the word *oratorio* derive. He later ordained his followers, finally installing them in Sta Maria at Vallicella in 1575. Feast day: May 26.

Nernst, Walther Hermann (1864–1941) German physical chemist, who first stated the third law of *thermodynamics. He also explained the ionization of certain substances when dissolved in water and showed that hydrogen and chlorine combine, when exposed to light, as a result of a chain reaction involving free radicals. He won the 1920 Nobel Prize for Chemistry.

Nero (Claudius Caesar) (37–68 AD) Roman emperor (54–68), notorious for his cruelty. His early reign was dominated by his mother *Agrippina the Younger, *Seneca, and Sextus Afranius Burrus but by 62 Nero had thrown off these influences: Agrippina was murdered (59), Burrus died, perhaps by poison (62), and Seneca retired (62). Also in 62, he murdered his wife Octavia in order to marry Poppaea, who herself died in 65 after being kicked by her husband. Nero ruled with a vanity and irresponsibility that antagonized most sectors of society. A conspiracy to assassinate him, after which Seneca was forced to kill himself, failed in 65. In 68, however, revolts in Gaul, Spain, and Africa and the mutiny of his palace guard forced him to flee Rome and precipitated his suicide.

Neruda, Pablo (Neftalí Ricardo Reyes; 1904–73)   Chilean poet. He served in the diplomatic service from 1927 to 1943, was elected a Communist senator in 1943, and was appointed ambassador to France by Salvador *Allende in 1970. The nihilism of his early poetry, such as *Residencia en la tierra* (1925–31), was later replaced by social commitment in *Canto general* (1950) and other works. He won the Nobel Prize in 1971.

Nerva, Marcus Cocceius (c. 30–98 AD) Roman emperor (96–98), chosen by the Senate to succeed Domitian. Nerva's brief rule was enlightened: land was allotted to poorer citizens, treason charges were abolished, and administration was improved.

Nerval, Gérard de (Gérard Labrunie; 1805–55)   French poet. His childhood interest in the occult was furthered by travels in the Near East, described in *Voyage en Orient* (1851). His best-known works, which anticipate the techniques of symbolism (*see* symbolists) and *surrealism, include the story *Sylvie* (1854), the sonnets *Les Chimères* (1854), and the collection of prose and poetry, *Le Rêve et la vie* (1855). His writing was affected by his thwarted love for an actress and by his mental breakdowns, which recurred from 1841 until his suicide in 1855.

nerve. *See* neuron.

nerve gases War gases that inhibit the action of the enzyme acetylcholinesterase, which is essential for the transmission of impulses from nerve to nerve or muscle. Death results from paralysis of the diaphragm leading to asphyxiation. Most nerve gases are derivatives of phosphoric acid and they are toxic in minute quantities (1 mg can be lethal). *See* chemical warfare.

Nervi, Pier Luigi (1891–1978) Italian engineer and architect, famous for his inventive use of reinforced concrete. His first major building, a stadium in Florence (1930–32), features a concrete cantilevered spiral staircase and curved roof. It was followed between 1935 and 1941 by a series of aircraft hangars (now destroyed) with vaults of lattice-patterned beams. In 1949 he designed the great exhibition hall in Turin and in 1953 was one of the architects of the UNESCO building in Paris. Among his later works were two sports stadiums for the 1960 Rome Olympics and San Francisco Cathedral (1970). He was a professor at Rome University from 1947 to 1961.

nervous system The network of nervous tissue in the body. This comprises the central nervous system (CNS), i.e. the *brain and *spinal cord, and the peripheral nervous system. The latter includes the cranial and spinal nerves with their *ganglia and the autonomic nervous system (ANS). The ANS controls unconscious body functions, such as digestion and heartbeat, and is coordinated by the *hypothalamus. The nervous system is chiefly responsible for communication both within the body and between the body and its surroundings. Incoming information passes along sensory *neurons to the brain, where it is analyzed and compared with *memory; nerve impulses then leave the central nervous system along motor nerves, carrying signals to all parts of the body and enabling it to respond continuously. Man's success as a species is largely due to the complexity of his nervous system.

Ness, Loch A deep lake in N Scotland, in the Highland Region in the Great Glen. The sight of a monster (the **Loch Ness monster**) has frequently been reported. Length: 22 mi (36 km). Depth: 754 ft (229 m).

Nesselrode, Karl Robert, Count (1780–1862) Russian statesman. He represented Russia at the Congress of Vienna (1814–15) and became foreign minister in 1822, dominating the formation of Russian foreign policy until his death. Nesselrode's intransigent policy in the Balkans contributed largely to the outbreak of the *Crimean War in 1853.

Nessus In Greek legend, a centaur who attempted to rape Deianira, the wife of *Heracles, who killed him with an arrow tipped with the *Hyrda's poisonous blood. Before he died, Nessus deceitfully told Deianira that she should save some of his own infected blood as a potion to win back Heracles' love. She smeared the centaur's blood on Heracles' shirt and thus caused his death.

nest A structure built or taken over by animals to house their eggs, their young, or themselves. The greatest variety is found among birds, whose nests are typically bowl-shaped and constructed of twigs, leaves, moss, fur, etc., woven or glued together. The nests of certain swifts are made entirely of saliva and form the major ingredient of bird's nest soup. Some birds nest on the ground, without using any nesting material; others use holes, either naturally occurring or excavated in trees. Nest building in birds is a complex behavior, triggered by hormones, in which some components are instinctive and others learned. Nests are also built by ants, termites, bees, and wasps, which construct elaborate tunnel systems, and by fish, amphibians, reptiles, and small mammals.

Nestor In Greek legend, a king of Pylos. His 11 brothers were killed by *Heracles. As a commander in the *Trojan War during his old age, he acted as a wise counselor to the quarrelling Greek leaders.

Nestorians The adherents of the Christological doctrines of the Syrian bishop Nestorius (died c. 451). Appointed Patriarch of Constantinople (428), he maintained, probably in overreaction to *Monophysite theories, that there were two persons, not merely two natures, in the incarnate Christ, and that the Virgin Mary could not therefore properly be called the Mother of God. He was accused of heresy and deposed (431). His supporters in his E Syrian homeland formed their own church, centered on Edessa. Expelled from Edessa (489), they established themselves in Persia until virtually annihilated by the 14th-century Mongol invasions.

Netherlandic A subgroup of the Western *Germanic languages. It first appears in documents in the 12th century. It is now spoken in Holland and Belgium, where it is called Dutch and Flemish respectively, although the two are in fact the same language. It is the parent language of Afrikaans and is also spoken in parts of Indonesia as a result of Dutch colonization.

Netherlands, Kingdom of the A country in NW Europe, on the North Sea. It is almost entirely flat except for some low hills in the SE, and considerable areas of land have been reclaimed from the sea. Rivers, including the Scheldt, Maas, and Rhine, together with the many canals form an efficient system of inland waterways. *Economy*: although popularly considered to be an agricultural nation, industry and commerce are the principal sources of income. Highly developed industries include oil and gas, chemicals, electronics, printing, metals, and food processing. The production of coal, once important, ceased in 1975, when all mines were closed. Agriculture is highly mechanized and market gardening is important. There is also considerable livestock farming, dairy produce being one of the principal exports together with flower bulbs, fuels, chemicals, textiles, and machinery. There is a thriving fishing industry and oysters are a valuable product. Tourism is an important source of revenue as is the Europort at *Rotterdam. *History*: until 1581 the Netherlands formed with present-day Belgium and Luxembourg the region often referred to as the Low Countries. It was under Roman occupation from the 1st century BC to the 4th century AD. It was then overrun by German tribes, of which the Franks had established dominance over the area by the mid-5th century. After the partition of the Frankish empire in 843 the region formed (855) part of Lothair's inheritance and was called Lotharingia. The following centuries saw the rise of powerful principalities, notably the bishopric of Utrecht and the counties of Holland and Guelders, which were fiefs of the German kings before coming under the influence of Burgundy from the 14th century and the Hapsburg Emperor Charles V in the early 16th century. Commercial prosperity and the persecution of Protestants fostered a growing movement for independence from the rule of Charles's son Philip II of Spain. In 1581, during the *Revolt of the Netherlands, the seven N provinces—Holland, Zeeland, Utrecht, Overijssel, Gröningen, Drenthe, and Friesland—proclaimed their independence as the United Provinces of the Netherlands under the leadership of William the Silent. War with Spain continued intermittently until, at the conclusion of the Thirty Year's War, Spain recognized the independence of the Dutch Republic in the Peace of Westphalia (1648). In the 17th century, under the rule of the House of Orange-Nassau, from which the stadtholder (chief magistrate) was elected until 1795, the Netherlands reached a peak of prosperity (based on trade and fishing) and international prestige, forming a considerable overseas empire. In the 18th century, however, after the death of William III of Orange, who in 1688 had become king of England, the Netherlands declined. In 1795 it fell to Revolutionary France and in 1806 Napoleon made his brother Louis Bonaparte king of Holland. Following Napoleon's defeat the former Dutch Republic was reunited with the S provinces (the Spanish Netherlands until 1713 and then the Austrian Netherlands), which had remained loyal to the Hapsburgs in the 16th century, to form the Kingdom of the Netherlands (1814). In 1830 the S revolted against the union, forming Belgium (1831), and in 1867 Luxembourg became an independent state. The Netherlands, which flourished economically in the second half of the 19th century, remained neutral in World War I but in World War II was occupied by Germany (1940–45) in spite of fierce Dutch resistance. In 1948 the Netherlands joined with Belgium and Luxembourg to form the *Benelux economic union; it was a founder member of the EEC. The immediate postwar period was dominated by the Dutch colony of Indonesia's fight for independence, achieved in 1950 after bitter and bloody conflict. The peaceful assimilation of nonwhite immigrants from the former colonies was marred in the 1970s following terrorist activities by the South Moluccans, who were protesting against the Indonesian occupation of their country. In 1980 Queen Juliana abdicated and was succeeded as head of state by her daughter Princess Beatrix. As part of a 1979 NATO agreement the Netherlands agreed to allow the deployment of medium-range missiles on its soil. The final decision on deployment was postponed, however, in response to widespread antinuclear sentiments in the country. In the early 1990s, with the Cold War at an end, the Netherlands turned to the European Community (EC), supporting closer EC ties and ratifying the *Maastricht Treaty. Many expressed concern that the national language, Dutch, would limit communication in a unified Europe. Official language: Dutch. Official currency: guilder of 100 cents. Area: 15,892 sq mi (41,160 sq km). Population (1990 est): 14,864,000. Capitals: Amsterdam (legal and administrative); The Hague (seat of government). Main port: Rotterdam.

Netherlands Antilles (Dutch name: Nederlandse Antillen) Two groups of West Indian islands in the Lesser Antilles, in the Caribbean Sea some 497 mi (800 km) apart. The S group lies off the N coast of Venezuela and consists of *Curaçao, *Aruba, and Bonaire; the N group (geographically part of the Leeward Islands) consists of St Eustatius, Saba, and the S part of *St Martin. Under Dutch control since the 17th century, the islands became self-governing in 1954. The economy is based chiefly on oil refining, centered on Curaçao and Aruba. Area: 390 sq mi (996 sq km). Population (1992 est): 192,000. Capital: Willemstad.

net national product. *See* gross national product.

Neto, Agostinho (1922–79) Angolan statesman; president (1975–79). A physician, he led the MPLA (Popular Movement for the Liberation of Angola) in the struggle against Portuguese rule (1962–74) and on independence became Angola's first president.

nettle An annual or perennial herb of the genus *Urtica* (about 30 species), found in temperate regions worldwide. Up to 5 ft (1.5 m) in height, it has simple leaves with toothed margins and bears clusters of small green unisexual flowers. Stems and leaves may have stinging hairs. Family: *Urticaceae*.

Dead nettles are annual or perennial herbs of the genus *Lamium* (about 40 species), occurring in Europe, temperate Asia, and N Africa. They bear clusters of tubular two-lipped flowers. Family: *Labiatae*.

nettle rash. *See* urticaria.

Neuchâtel (German name: Neuenburg) 47.00N 6 56E A city in W Switzerland, on Lake Neuchâtel. It possesses a university (1909) and the Swiss Laboratory of Horological Research. Industries include watchmaking and chocolate production; wine trading is important. Population (1986): 32,700.

Neue Kunstlervereinigung (New Artists' Association) An organization of artists founded in Munich in 1909 by *Kandinsky and *Jawlensky, among others. Its aim to provide more favorable exhibiting conditions for modern art in Munich was largely fulfilled in its large exhibition of international contemporary art in 1910. Disagreements among the members resulted in the defection in 1911 of Kandinsky and Marc, who then founded The *Blue Rider.

Neumann, (Johann) Balthasar (1687–1753) German architect, born in Bohemia. One of the greatest rococo architects, Neumann was a military engineer before being appointed court architect to the bishop of Würzburg (1719), for whom he built his most famous palace. He also designed churches, of which the church of Vierzehnheiligen (1743–72), with its complex plan and lavish ornamentation, was his masterpiece.

Neumann, John von (1903–57) US mathematician, born in Hungary. He invented *game theory, the branch of mathematics that analyzes stragegy and is now widely employed for military purposes. He also set quantum theory upon a rigorous mathematical basis.

neuralgia Sharp or burning pain arising from nerves. Causalgia, one form of neuralgia, is pain arising from a single nerve and is usually caused by an injury to that nerve. The commonest form is trigeminal neuralgia, in which paroxysms of pain affect one side of the face, particularly the cheek, along the course of the trigeminal nerve.

neuritis Inflammation of the nerves. This can be caused by leprosy and multiple sclerosis. However, most diseases of peripheral nerves are caused not by inflammation but by degeneration of the nerve, and the word **neuropathy** is used to describe this. Neuropathies can be caused by a variety of conditions, including diabetes, alcoholism, lead poisoning, and vitamin deficiencies, such as beriberi and pellagra.

neurohormone A chemical (*see* hormone) that is secreted by nerve cells and modifies the function of other organs in the body. The *hypothalamus, for example, releases several hormones that cause the *pituitary gland to secrete its own hormones, the kidney to retain water in the body, and the breast to produce milk.

neurology The study of the structure (neuroanatomy), function (neurophysiology), and diseases (neuropathology) of the *nervous system. A neurologist is a physician who specializes in the diagnosis and treatment of nervous diseases.

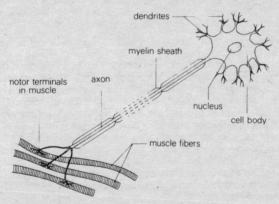

NEURONE *When a nerve impulse transmitted down the axon of a neurone reaches the motor terminals in muscle fibers the muscle is stimulated to contract.*

neurone (*or* nerve cell) The functioning unit of the *nervous system. A neurone consists of a cell body, containing the nucleus; small irregular branching processes called dendrites; and a single long nerve fiber, or axon, which may be ensheathed by layers of fatty material (myelin) and either makes contact with other neurons at *synapses or ends at muscle fibers or gland cells. When a neuron is stimulated from outside or by another neuron, a nerve impulse is transmitted electrochemically down the axon (*see* action potential). The frequency of these impulses is the basis for the control of behavior. Bundles of nerve fibers are bound together to form **nerves**, which transmit impulses from sense organs to the brain or spinal cord (sensory nerves) or outward from the central nervous system to a muscle or gland (motor nerves).

Neuroptera An order of slender carnivorous insects (4500 species) with long antennae and two similar pairs of net-veined wings. The order includes the *alderflies, *snakeflies, and *dobsonflies (suborder *Megaloptera*) and the *lacewings and *antlions (suborder *Plannipennia*).

neurosis A mental illness in which insight is retained but there is a disordered way of behaving or thinking that causes suffering to the patient (*compare* psychosis). Th symptoms of neurosis vary considerably: they include a pathologically severe emotional state, as in *anxiety or *depression; distressing behavior and thoughts, as in *phobias or *obsessions; and physical complaints, as in *hysteria. A neurosis with psychological symptoms is known as a **psychoneurosis**. Neurotic symptoms usually arise through a complex interaction between *stress and a vulnerable personality. Treatment for neurosis can include *tranquilizers, *psychotherapy, and *behavior therapy.

Neusiedl, Lake (German name: Neusiedlersee) A lake in Austria and Hungary. Having no natural outlet, its area varies with the rainfall. Many species of bird are to be found on its reedy shore. Area: about 135 sq mi (350 sq km).

Neuss 51 12N 06 42E A city in NW Germany, in North Rhine-Westphalia near the Rhine River. Known for its annual rifle-shooting contest, it is a canal port and industrial center. Population (1991 est): 147,019.

Neustria The W Frankish kingdom created by the partition in 511 of the possessions of *Clovis I. Approximately the size of N France, it was the rival to *Austrasia (the E kingdom) until 687, when *Pepin of Herstal, mayor of the palace (viceroy) of Austrasia, defeated the Neustrians at Tertry.

neutrality The legal status of a country that remains impartial in relation to other countries that are at war (belligerents). In *international law the rights and obligations of a neutral state are mainly contained in the Hague Conventions V and XIII (1907; *see* Hague Peace Conferences) on neutrality in land war and on the sea, respectively. A neutral state must treat belligerents in the same way in matters not relating to war and must not assist either side in furthering its war aims. In particular it must prohibit the use of its territory for the purpose of equipping for war or recruiting men, and it may use force if necessary to prevent any violation of its neutrality. The most important right conferred by neutrality is inviolability of territory: belligerents may not carry on warfare in a neutral state's territory, which includes its water and air space. The term "nonbelligerence" is used when a state that is theoretically neutral is, in fact, sympathetic to one belligerent, for example the relationship between the US and the UK between 1939 and 1941.

neutrinos A group of three elementary particles and their antiparticles. They are classified as leptons, have no charge, and are probably massless. One type of neutrino is associated with the *electron, one with the *muon, and one with the *tau particle.

neutron An elementary particle that is a constituent of all atomic nuclei except hydrogen − 1. It has no electric charge and its mass is slightly greater than that of the *proton. Inside the nucleus the neutron is stable but when free it decays by the *weak interaction to a proton, an electron, and an antineutrino (*see* beta decay). Its mean life is about 12 minutes. The neutron was discovered by *Chadwick in 1932. *See also* particle physics.

neutron bomb. *See* nuclear weapons.

neutron star A star that has undergone *gravitational collapse to the extent that most of the protons and electrons making up its constituent atoms have coalesced into neutrons. The density is extremely high (about 10^{17} kg m^{-3}) and the pressure exerted by the densely packed neutrons can support the star against further contraction. Neutron stars are thought to form when the mass of the stellar core remaining after a *supernova exceeds about 1.4 times the sun's mass. *See also* pulsar.

Neva, Battle of the (July 15, 1240) The battle in which Sweden was defeated by the forces of Prince Aleksandr Yaroslavich of Novgorod (who thus received the name Nevsky; *see* Alexander Nevsky). His victory ended the expansionist ambitions of Sweden into NW Russia.

Nevada One of the mountain states in the W US. It is bounded by Utah and Arizona on the E, California on the SW and W, and Oregon and Idaho on the N. Lying almost wholly within the Great Basin, most of the state consists of a vast plateau with several high mountain ranges rising to well over 5250 ft (1600 m). The only major river is the Colorado, in the SE. The Hoover, or Boulder, Dam, one of the world's major dams, impounds Lake Mead along the Colorado. Nevada is the most arid US state. Many water projects throughout the state supply drinking water and irrigation. Over 85% of Nevada is federally controlled in the form of water projects and military installations. Most of the population and manufacturing industries are located in the two main cities of Las Vegas and Reno. Copper smelting is a major industry; others include stone, clay, and glass products, cement, food processing, and more recently space, electronics, and the atomic industries. A mineral-rich state, it produces metallic ores and other minerals. Tourism (largely because of the state's legalized gambling) is by far the most important industry. Las Vegas, which is also famous for its nightlife, and Lake Tahoe are two of the chief tourist attractions. The land and climate are unfavorable for agriculture but some dairying and livestock raising, especially cattle and sheep, are carried on. *History*: first explored by Americans, the state was ceded to the US by Mexico in 1848 as part of the *Mexican War settlement. The Mormons founded the first permanent settlement in 1858. It became a state in 1864 following the discovery of the Comstock Lode, the richest known US silver deposit (now depleted). During the 1970s Nevadans began suit against the federal government for repossession of its land resources. The movement became known as the Sagebrush Rebellion. The growth of high-technology industries contributed to Nevada's expansion, and in the 1980s it had become one of the fastest-growing states. Area: 110,540 sq mi (286,297 sq km). Population (1990): 1,201,833. Capital: Carson City.

Nevelson, Louise (Louise Berliawsky; 1900–88) US sculptor and painter, born in Russia. She used scraps of everyday objects—wood, metals, and plastics—to create her futuristic sculptures. Her "black boxes" of the 1950s, filled with odd pieces of wood and wheels, were wall structures painted black. In the 1960s and 1970s she constructed metal and Plexiglass sculptures, usually painted white or gold. Her works include *Sky Cathedral* (1958), *Daun's Wedding Feast* (1959), *Homage to the World* (1966), *Transparent Sculpture VI* (1967–68), *Night Presence IV* (1972), and the White Chapel of the Good Shepherd at St Peter's Lutheran Church in New York City (1977–78).

Nevers 47 00N 3 09N A city in central France, the capital of the Nièvre department on the Loire River. It has a 13th-century cathedral and a palace (15th–16th centuries) and its industries include light engineering and pottery. Population (1982): 45,000.

Nevis. *See* St Kitts-Nevis.

nevus. *See* birthmark.

Newark 40 44N 74 11W A city in New Jersey, on Newark Bay, part of the Greater New York Metropolitan Area. Founded in 1666, it attracted several inventors, whose developments included patent leather (1818), malleable cast iron (1826), the first photographic film (1888), and electrical measuring instruments (1888). The state's largest city, it is the focus of air, road, and rail routes. Industries include cutlery, jewelry, and chemicals. Population (1990): 275,233.

New Bedford 41 38N 70 56W A city in SE Massachusetts, on Buzzard's Bay at the mouth of the Acushnet River, SE of Fall River. Its history is steeped in the whaling business; during the 18th and 19th centuries it was a major shipping and whaling port, and fishing is still important. Industries include food processing, textiles and clothing, and rubber and metal products. Population (1990): 99,922.

New Britain A volcanic island in the SW Pacific Ocean, in Papua New Guinea, the largest of the Bismarck Archipelago. Copra and some minerals are exported. Area: 14,100 sq mi (36,520 sq km). Chief town: Rabaul.

New Brunswick A province of E Canada, on the Gulf of St Lawrence. Heavily forested, it consists of rugged uplands with fertile river valleys; the population is concentrated in the *St John River Basin. There is some mixed farming and fishing is important along the Bay of Fundy. Lead, zinc, and some copper are mined at Bathurst. Forestry was a major activity during the last century but overcutting and the loss of protected British markets led to a decline in the industry. Today lumbering and the manufacture of pulp and paper serve mainly local needs. In an attempt to encourage industrial development the federal government has spent considerable sums of money on improving the infrastructure (factories, roads, etc.). *History*: slow settlement by French peasants, beginning in the 17th century, ended shortly after Britain's control of the coastal areas was confirmed in 1731. Colonization from Britain and New England followed, and New Brunswick became a separate colony (1784). It prospered and was a founding member of the Dominion of Canada. Area: 627,835 sq mi (72,092 sq km). Population (1991): 723,900; approximately 30% are French speaking. Capital: Fredericton.

New Brunswick 40 29N 74 27W A city in NE New Jersey, on the S bank of the Raritan River, W of Perth Amboy. Rutgers University (1766) is here. Settled in 1681, its chief manufactures are drugs and medical supplies. Population (1990): 41,711.

New Caledonia (French name: Nouvelle Calédonie) A French island in the SW Pacific Ocean. Together with its dependencies (the Isle of Pines, the Loyalty Islands, and others) it forms a French overseas territory. The main industries are nickel mining and processing and meat preserving. Nickel, copra, and coffee are exported. Area: 7374 sq mi (19,103 sq km), including dependencies. Population (1992): 174,000. Capital: Nouméa.

Newcastle 32 55S 151 46E A city in Australia, in New South Wales on the mouth of the Hunter River. Iron and steel industries are important, using coal from the Newcastle-Cessnock field. Population (1991 est): 432,600.

Newcastle, Thomas Pelham-Holles, 1st Duke of (1693–1768) British statesman; Whig prime minister (1754–56, 1757–62). He resigned as prime minister in 1756 because of early reverses in the *Seven Years' War but returned in 1757 with foreign affairs in the hands of Pitt the Elder. His brother **Henry Pelham** (1696–1754) was prime minister (1743–54) in the Broad-Bottom administration, which included members of opposing political factions.

Newcastle, William Cavendish, Duke of (1592–1676) British soldier, author, and patron of the arts. He fought for the Royalists in the Civil War and after their defeat at *Marston Moor (1644) he went into exile. Returning at the Restoration, he became a patron of writers, including Jonson and Dryden.

Newcastle disease. *See* fowl pest.

Newcastle-under-Lyme 53 00N 2 14W A city in the Midlands of England, in Staffordshire. There are traces of a 12th-century castle built by John of Gaunt. The principal industries are coal mining, bricks and tiles, clothing, paper, and machinery. Nearby is Keele University (1962). Population (1981): 72,853.

Newcastle upon Tyne 54 59N 1 35W A city in NE England, on the N bank of the Tyne River opposite Gateshead, with which it is linked by a tunnel and five bridges. It is the principal port and commercial and cultural center of NE England, with a 14th-century cathedral and a university (1852). The principal industries include shipbuilding, marine and electrical engineering, chemicals, flour milling, soap, and paints. *History*: on the site of a Roman settlement, Newcastle derives its name from the castle (1080) built as a defense against the Scots. Newcastle's well-known trade in coal developed in the 13th century. Population (1981): 192,454.

Newchang. *See* Yingkou.

Newcombe, John (1944–   ) Australian tennis player, who was Wimbledon singles champion in 1967, 1970, and 1971 and US singles champion in 1967 and 1973. Also an outstanding doubles player, he won three successive titles at Wimbledon (1968–70).

New Comedy The final period of Greek comic drama, lasting from c. 320 BC to the mid-3rd century BC and characterized by well-constructed plays on domestic themes. The role of the chorus diminished as the plots became more complicated. The leading writers of this period were *Menander and *Philemon, whose plays influenced the development of comedy in Rome and later in W Europe. *See also* Middle Comedy: Old Comedy.

Newcomen, Thomas (1663–1729) English blacksmith, who in 1712 constructed an early steam engine. It was based on Thomas *Savery's engine and was widely used for pumping water out of mines. It was extremely inefficient, however, and it was not until *Watt invented the separate condenser that steam engines became suitable for use in transportation.

New Deal (1933–41) The sweeping legislative program proposed by Pres. Franklin D. *Roosevelt to help the nation recover from the effects of the *Depression and to initiate social and economic reforms. Promising to offer the Americn people a "new deal," Roosevelt embarked on an ambitious program of emergency legislation during the first hundred days of his administration in 1933. In order to deal with the country's severe economic crisis, the president ordered a four-day bank holiday during which the *Federal Reserve System was completely reorganized; credit, currency, and foreign exchange were regulated; the gold standard was abandoned; and the dollar was devalued. These measures enabled the nation's banks to reopen on a sound basis and averted impending economic catastrophe. The next stage in the New Deal program was the establishment of federal agencies to provide work, relief, and public works programs for the millions of Americans who had lost their jobs. These programs included the *Civilian Conservation Corps, the *Agricultural Adjustment Act, the *National Industrial Recovery Act, and the Tennessee Valley Authority, which was ostensibly set up as a flood control program, but which improved the social and economic status of the undeveloped region by promoting farming and industry. The early New Deal programs achieved notable successes, and they were supplemented in 1935 by the establishment of the *Works Progress Administration (WPA), the *National Labor Relations Board, and the *Social Security Act, which provided retirement and disability payments for all American workers. Although the Roosevelt administration faced opposition from conservative members of Congress and from several adverse rulings of the Supreme Court, the New Deal effectively brought the country out of the Depression and established the social and economic policies carried on by succeeding administrations.

New Economic Policy (NEP) An economic policy adopted by the Soviet Union between 1921 and 1929. Introduced by Lenin, the NEP replaced War Communism, a period during the civil war of forced labor and brutal requisitioning of food supplies. The NEP, by contrast, gave concessions to private enterprise in agriculture, trade, and industry and aimed at the political neutralization of the peasants. Although the NEP met with considerable success, it was followed under Stalin by more radical policies and the *five-year plans.

New England An area in the extreme NE US, bordering on the Atlantic Ocean. It consists of the states of Maine, New Hampshire, Vermont, Massachusetts, Rhode Island, and Connecticut. Explored and named by Capt. John Smith (1614), it was first settled by the Puritans (1620). Poor agriculturally, it developed industry early, especially fishing and textiles. Despite the decline of its textile industry the area is now of major economic importance with a flourishing tourist industry. Area: about 63,300 sq mi (164,000 sq km).

New England A district of Australia, in New South Wales. Predominantly agricultural, it occupies the N Tableland between the Moonbi Range and the Queensland border. A separatist movement has existed since the early 20th century but so far has been unsuccessful in making the district a separate state.

New England Confederation A union in 1643 of four colonies—Massachusetts, Plymouth, Connecticut, and New Haven—for purposes of safety, defense, and mutual cooperation. Factors prompting confederation were Indian wars, threat of foreign invasion, desire for a state religion, and the need for mutual cooperation in intercolony matters. Maine and Rhode Island were excluded because of religious differences. It disbanded in 1684.

Newfoundland A province of E Canada, consisting of the sparsely populated Coast of *Labrador on the Atlantic Ocean and the triangular island of Newfoundland, lying between the Ocean and the Gulf of St Lawrence. The island consists of a low forested plateau rolling gently to the NE. Its interior is fairly infertile and most of the population lives along the irregular coast, especially in the SE. Pulp and paper has replaced the declining fisheries as the major industry. Iron, lead, zinc, and copper are mined. *History*: discovered by John Cabot (1497), Newfoundland became an English fishing station where settlement was actively discouraged until the 19th century. The island won representative government (1832) and developed steadily until World War I, when it became a dominion. In 1927 it won possession of Labrador's interior and in 1949 became the newest Canadian province. In the last 50 years Newfoundland has not been very prosperous. The island still has a rich tradition of folk song and storytelling. Area: 143,044 sq mi (370,485 sq km). Population (1981 est): 567,681. Capital: St John's.

Newfoundland dog A breed of working dog originating in Newfoundland. Massively built and strong swimmers, Newfoundlands have been used for lifesaving at sea. The heavy dense black, brown, or black-and-white coat enables them to withstand icy water. Height: 28 in (71 cm) (dogs); 26 in (66 cm) (bitches).

New France The French colonies in E Canada. From about 1600 French trading posts extended along the St Lawrence River to the Great Lakes. France lost these colonies to Britain in the *Seven Years' War (1756–63).

New Frontier Pres. John F. *Kennedy's name for the theme of his administration's (1962–63) legislative program. First used in his nomination acceptance speech (1960), he referred to "new frontiers" at home, abroad, and in space that would be challenging, even perilous at times, but would be met and conquered.

New Granada A Spanish colony in South America, which in 1717 became a viceroyalty comprising modern Colombia, Ecuador, Panama, and Venezuela (which was later detached). It was liberated by Simón *Bolívar in 1819. From 1830 to 1858 Colombia and Panama formed the Republic of New Granada.

New Guinea An island in the SW Pacific Ocean, the second largest island in the world, separated from Australia by the Torres Strait. It consists of the Indonesian province of *Irian Jaya in the W and *Papua New Guinea in the E. Mountainous and forested, it is largely undeveloped and is famed for its unique species of butterflies and birds. Its linguistically diverse tribal population consists of Melanesian, Negrito, and Papuan ethnic groups. *History*: known to Europeans from 1511, the island was colonized by the Dutch in the 18th century. In 1828 the Dutch controlled the W part; this became part of Indonesia in 1963. The SE was colonized by Britain and the NE by Germany in the late 19th century. Area: 299,310 sq mi (775,213 sq km).

New Hampshire A NE state in New England. It is generally hilly, with many lakes; a low-lying area adjoins the Atlantic Ocean in the SE. Manufacturing is the principal source of employment, centered mainly in the S. Electrical and other machinery together with paper and wood are the principal products. Tourism is the other major industry. The state's farmers produce livestock, dairy and poultry products, and vegetables. Mining is of minor importance and the large deposits of granite are no longer quarried to any great extent. *History*: one of the 13 original colonies, it was first settled by English colonists about 1627, becoming a royal province in 1679. One of the first states to declare its independence, it became a state in 1788. Area: 9304 sq mi (24,097 sq km). Population (1990): 1,109,252. Capital: Concord.

New Harmony 38 08N 87 56W A town in SE Indiana, on the E bank of the Wabash River at the Illinois border, NW of Evansville. George Rapp named it Harmonie when he settled here in 1815. Rapp's utopian colony disbanded in failure in 1824. Robert Owen's experimental utopian society, New Harmony, (1825–28) also failed, but the name remained. The chief economic activity is agriculture. Population (1990): 846.

New Haven 41 18N 72 55W A city and seaport in Connecticut, on Long Island Sound. It is best known as the site of Yale University (1701). It was here that Charles Goodyear invented vulcanized rubber. Industries include hardware, watches, and firearms. Population (1990): 130,474.

New Haven Colony Colony in S Connecticut and SE New York on the N shore of Long Island, established in 1638 as Quinnipiac by Puritans John Davenport (1597–1670) and Theophilus Eaton (1590–1658) and their followers. A theocracy, rule was based on interpretation of the Bible and voting and office-holding eligibility required church membership. Renamed New Haven in 1640, it became part of the New England Confederation in 1643 and eventually included settlements at Guilford, Milford, Stamford, and Branford, Conn., and at Southold, Long Island. The smallest of the Puritan colonies, it was absorbed into Connecticut Colony in 1664.

New Hebrides (French name: Nouvelles-Hébrides). *See* Vanuatu.

Ne Win (1911–) Burmese statesman; prime minister (1958–60, 1962-74); president (1974–81). From 1943 he fought for the independence of Burma (now Myanmar) and, when this was achieved in 1948, became defense minister. In 1958 he became prime minister after forcing U *Nu's resignation and, after leaving office in 1960, again seized power in 1962. In 1972 the 1947 constitution was abolished and replaced (in 1974) by one introducing a single-party assembly and the presidency of Ne Win. Although he stepped down in 1985, he continued to be influential in government affairs.

New Ireland A volcanic island in the SW Pacific Ocean, in Papua New Guinea in the Bismarck Archipélago. Copra is exported. Area: 3340 sq mi (8650 sq km). Chief town: Kavieng.

New Jersey A state in the NE US, on the mid-Atlantic coast. It is bounded by the Atlantic Ocean on the E, by Delaware (across the Delaware Bay) on the S, by Pennsylvania (across the Delaware River) on the W, and by New York on the N. The Kittatinny Mountains extend across the NW corner of the state, SE of which lies a belt of lowland containing most of New Jersey's major cities. The remaining area to the S consists of coastal plains, which cover more than half the state. One of the most highly urbanized and densely populated states, it is a major industrial center. The most important economic activity is manufacturing, with chemicals, textiles, electrical machinery, and processed foods the major products. Although mining is relatively unimportant, New Jersey is a center for copper smelting and refining as well as a major producer of titanium concentrate. Agriculture is also well developed and a variety of crops are grown, including asparagus, tomatoes, peppers, sweet corn, potatoes, and peaches. Its beaches, forests, and mountain regions form the basis of a thriving tourist industry. *History*: originally inhabited by the Delaware Indians, the region was first explored by Henry Hudson on a voyage for the Dutch East India Company. Other Europeans conducted explorations in the early 17th century. Eventually Dutch trading posts sprang up, but the area was taken over in 1664 by the British, who held it until Delaware declared its independence as one of the 13 original colonies. Many important battles of the American Revolution took place in New Jersey, including those at Trenton, Princeton, and Monmouth. New Jersey became a state in 1787. The 19th century was a period of tremendous economic growth, accompanied by political corruption. The corruption was targeted by Gov. Woodrow *Wilson's reform movement (1910–12), which served as a springboard for his nomination for president. The state's highly industrial economy also saw great expansion during and after World War II. In the 1970s casino gambling in Atlantic City was legalized, which served as a boost to the seaside resort and the state's tourist industry. The huge Meadowlands Sports Complex, completed in 1981 in East Rutherford, has also encouraged tourism. Political corruption surfaced once again and New Jersey figured prominently in the Abscam investigations of 1980–81. Area: 7836 sq mi (20,295 sq km). Population (1990): 7,730,188. Capital: Trenton.

New Jersey Plan (1787) Plan for national government put forth at the Constitutional Convention of 1787 by William *Paterson of New Jersey. The plan aimed at accommodating the smaller states and called for equal representation of states in a federal legislature, as opposed to representation by population as formulated in the *Virginia Plan. Eventually parts of both plans were incorporated in the *Connecticut Compromise, which called for a federal bicameral legislature.

New London 41 21N 72 06W A city and seaport in Connecticut, at the mouth of the Thames River on Long Island Sound. The US Coast Guard Academy and a US naval submarine base (1916) are located here. The annual Harvard-Yale boat race is held here on the Thames River. Industries include ship building and textiles. Population (1990): 28,540.

Newman, John Henry, Cardinal (1801–90) British churchman and a leader of the *Oxford Movement, until his conversion to Roman Catholicism (1845). He was educated at Oxford, later becoming a fellow and tutor there. While vicar of St Mary's, Oxford (1827–43), he published *Parochial and Plain Sermons* (1834–42) and began the series entitled *Tracts for the Times* in 1833. He wrote many of these, including the most controversial one, *Tract 90*, which argued that the Thirty-Nine Articles were not incompatible with Roman Catholicism. Of his later works the most famous are *Idea of a University* (1852), his poem, *Dream of Gerontius* (1866), and a theological work, *Grammar of Assent* (1870). His spiritual autobiography, *Apologia pro vita sua* (1864), was a reply to Charles Kingsley's criticisms of Roman Catholicism. He was made a cardinal in 1879.

Newman, Paul (1925–   ) US film actor. He has frequently played cynical and witty heroes, notably in *Hud* (1963), *Butch Cassidy and the Sundance Kid* (1969), and *The Sting* (1973); among his other films are *Buffalo Bill and the Indians* (1976), *Slap Shot* (1977), *Absence of Malice* (1981), *The Verdict* (1982), *The Color of Money* (1986, for which he won an Academy Award), and *Mr. and Mrs. Bridge* (1991). From 1968 he also directed and produced films. A political activist, he supports nuclear disarmament. He is married to the US actress Joanne Woodward.

new math The new methods of teaching mathematics and presenting mathematical relationships that incorporate some of the concepts of formal logic. *Set theory and *vectors, for example, formerly considered advanced and abstract, are now taught at an early stage in school mathematics and form part of the logical basis of further learning. New applications of mathematics are being developed to deal with computers, automation, and the accompanying changes in social organization, for example operational research.

New Mexico One of the mountain states in the SW US. It is bordered by Texas on the E, by Texas and Mexico on the S, by Arizona on the W, by Colorado on the N, and by Oklahoma on the NE. There are three main physical regions: a flat tableland in the E, a central mountainous region cut N–S by the Valley of the Rio Grande, and a region of mountains and plains in the W. A generally arid state, its irrigation problems have been mitigated by the presence of two important rivers, the Rio Grande and the Pecos. The relatively sparse population is mainly concentrated in the urban centers, especially in Albuquerque. Its rich mineral wealth forms the basis of the economy. Its oil and natural gas deposits are especially important, and it is a leading producer of uranium ore, manganese ore, and potash. There are also large commercial forests. Livestock is the main agricultural product, and crops include hay, cotton, wheat, and sorghum grains. There is limited manufacturing. Tourism is an important source of revenue. *History*: inhabited by Indians for some 20,000 years, the region was dominated by the Pueblos when the first Europeans arrived. In the 16th century the Spanish explored the territory. Their efforts to establish missions and form ranching communities were met with tremendous resistance from the Indians. When Mexico achieved independence from Spain (1821), the area became a Mexican province, passing to the US after the Mexican War (1846–48). Settlement continued via the Santa Fe Trail. With the defeat of the Apache chief Geronimo (1886), Indian resistance was finally broken. A boom in ranching, accelerated by the arrival of the railroads (1879), encouraged development, and New Mexico became a state in 1912. In 1943, Los Alamos Laboratories was built by the US government as a center for atomic research. Intense scientific labor at Los Alamos came to fruition in the world's first atomic bomb, exploded

near Alamagordo in July 1945. The growth of military installations greatly enhanced the state's economic and population growth. Still a relatively poor state
with high unemployment, New Mexico's economic difficulties of the early
1980s increased tensions among the Anglo, Indian, and Spanish communities.
Area: 121,666 sq mi (315,113 sq km). Population (1990): 1,515,069. Capital:
Santa Fe.

New Model Army The parliamentary army formed in 1645 during the English *Civil War. It was organized by Sir Thomas *Fairfax and united the various local armies. Led by Oliver *Cromwell, it wielded increasing political
power, emerging the victor from its power struggle with the *Long Parliament.
In 1650 Cromwell became its commander in chief.

New Netherland A Dutch colony in North America. Established in 1613, the
colony was centered on New Amsterdam, which after its conquest by the English (1664) was renamed New York.

New Orleans 30 00N 90 03W A city and major port in Louisiana. Known as
the Crescent City because of its location on a bend in the Mississippi River, it is
one of the leading commercial and industrial centers of the South with food processing, oil, chemical, ship building, and ship-repairing industries. The Vieux
Carré (French Quarter) has many historic buildings, including St Louis Cathedral (1794) and the Cabildo (1795). An educational center, New Orleans is the
site of several universities. The famous Mardi Gras festival is held annually. *History*: founded in 1718, New Orleans became the capital of the French colonial
region of Louisiana before passing to Spain in 1763. It returned briefly to France
in 1803 but passed to the US in the same year. Jazz had its origins among the
African-American musicians of New Orleans during the late 19th century. Population (1990): 496,938.

New Orleans, Battle of (1815) US victory and final battle of the *War of
1812. Although it is considered a decisive, morale-boosting battle of the war, it
was fought, due to slow communication, two weeks after the peace treaty at
Ghent was signed. Aided by the Creoles and the pirate band of Jean *Lafitte,
Andrew *Jackson's forces held off the British invasion from ships in the Gulf of
Mexico. British casualties were high—almost 300 were killed.

New Orleans style The original style of jazz, which developed in the Storyville district of New Orleans. The New Orleans style began around 1890 with
the band of Buddy Bolden (1868–1941) and continued until the 1920s when
*swing bands gained popularity. In New Orleans jazz, the melody of a song was
treated as a basis for improvisation by the cornet, clarinet, or trombone, supported by double bass, drums, guitar, and piano. Important New Orleans jazz
musicians include Louis Armstrong and Jelly Roll Morton. *Compare* Dixieland.

Newport 41 13N 71 18W A city in SE Rhode Island, on the S end of Aquid-
neck Island in Narragansett Bay. Settled in 1639, it grew as a shipbuilding center, port, and cultural center. In the mid-19th century it became popular with the
wealthy, who began to build luxurious summer homes. The naval base, established in the late 19th century and expanded after World War I, also helped the
economy. Today, tourism is very important. Many of the summer mansions are
open to the public and events such as the America's Cup Yacht races and Tennis
Week are traditional. Population (1990): 28,227.

Newport (Welsh name: Casnewydd ar Wysg) 51 35N 3 00W A port in South
Wales, the administrative center of Gwent near the mouth of the Usk River. Iron
and steel, engineering, chemicals, and fertilizers are important industries. Its
parish church became the cathedral for the Monmouth diocese in 1921. Population (1983): 130,200.

Newport News 36 59N 76 26W A city and seaport in SE Virginia, on the James River estuary. A major shipbuilding and ship-repair center, its manufactures include metal products and building materials. Population (1990): 170,045.

New Siberian Islands (Russian name: Novosibirskiye Ostrova) A Russian archipelago off the N coast, between the Laptev Sea and the East Siberian Sea. Kotelny, Faddeyevskii, and New Siberia are the largest islands and the Lyakhov Islands to the S are sometimes considered part of the group. There is no permanent population. Total area: 13,549 sq mi (35,100 sq km), including the Lyakhov Islands.

New South Wales A state of SE Australia, bordering on the Pacific Ocean. It consists of extensive plains in the W, separated from the narrow coastal belt by the *Great Dividing Range with the *Snowy Mountains and part of the Australian Alps in the SE. The chief rivers are the Murray, Darling, and Murrumbidgee. It is the most populous and economically important state of Australia. Agricultural products include beef cattle, cereals (of which wheat is the most important), fruit and vegetables (especially in the S *Riverina district), wool, and dairy products, which includes large quantities of butter and milk products processed at cooperative factories along the coast. Fishing, including oyster farming, and forestry are also important. Minerals extracted include coal, silver, lead, zinc, and copper. Over half the population live in Sydney, where most of the industries are located; these include the manufacture of iron and steel, textiles, electrical goods, and chemicals. Separatist movements, resenting the domination of the state, exist in the districts of *New England and Riverina. Area: 309,433 sq mi (801,428 sq km). Population (1992 est): 5,984,500.

New Spain, Viceroyalty of (1535–1821) A Spanish colony in the New World comprising modern Mexico, the SW US, and parts of Central America. It was established under Antonio de *Mendoza.

newspaper A publication issued at regular intervals and containing information and opinion about current affairs. The earliest newspaper may have been the ancient Roman *Acta Diurna* (59 BC) but newspapers in their modern form originated in Europe in the 17th century. The political influence of newspapers was quickly appreciated by governments, which introduced such legislation as the Stamp Act (1712), imposing a duty of a halfpenny on each half-sheet and a penny on each whole sheet. The most notable victory in the campaign for press freedom was made in the 18th century in England by John *Wilkes, who obtained the right to publish parliamentary reports, but not until 1855 was the Stamp Act repealed. The rapid expansion of newspapers during the 19th century was influenced by improvements in printing technology, the establishment of international news agencies, and the increase in literacy. Popular *journalism was pioneered in the US by such newspapers as the *San Francisco Examiner* (1880) and the *Morning Journal* (1895), both founded by William Randolph *Hearst. Technological improvements continued in the 20th century, including color printing, computer-aided typesetting, and satellite transmission of data.

New Sweden (1638–55) Swedish colony in N Delaware on the W bank of the Delaware River; sponsored by the New Sweden Company, a group of Swedish and Dutch under the leadership of Peter Minuit, former governor of the New Netherland (New York) colony. The Swedes remained, settled Fort Christina (now Wilmington) and the surrounding area, and persevered until 1655 when the colony was captured by New Amsterdam's Peter *Stuyvesant.

newt A salamander belonging to a family (*Salamandridae*) occurring in Europe, Asia, and North America. The European smooth newt (*Triturus vulgaris*) is greenish brown with dark-brown spots and has a black-spotted orange belly. It grows to a length of 4 in (10 cm) (including a 2 in [5 cm] tail). Newts live mainly on land, hibernating under stones in winter and returning to water to breed in spring. The European fire salamander (*Salamandra salamandra*) bears live young and produces a poisonous skin secretion when harmed.

NEWT *The European palmate newt* (Triturus helveticus), *like other newts, become totally aquatic during the breeding season. After an elaborate courtship display the male deposits sperm masses (spermatophores), which are taken into the cloaca of the female and fertilize the eggs internally.*

New Testament The 27 books that constitute the second major division of the Christian *Bible. The title is intended to convey the belief that the books contain the fulfillment of prophecies made in the *Old Testament. Written in Greek, the New Testament has four divisions: the four Gospels (Matthew, Mark, Luke, and John); the *Acts of the Apostles; the *Epistles, mainly written by St Paul; and the Book of *Revelation. It covers a period from the birth of *Jesus to the spread of Christianity throughout the Roman Empire and was written between about 50 and 100 AD.

newton (N) The *SI unit of force defined as the force required to give a mass of one kilogram an acceleration of one meter per second per second. Named for Sir Isaac *Newton.

Newton, Sir Isaac (1642–1727) British physicist and mathematician, who was a professor at Cambridge University (1669–1701). One of the greatest scientists of all time, Newton did much of his original work in his parents' home immediately after his graduation, while Cambridge was closed (1665–67) during the Great Plague. His first discovery was the law of gravitation, apocryphally inspired by the realization that an apple falling from a tree is attracted by the same force that holds the moon in orbit. Gravitation required a precise definition of force, which Newton also supplied in his laws of motion (*see* Newtonian mechanics). Newton's second major work in this period was the invention of the calculus; *Leibniz and Newton bickered for some years as to who had the idea first. Probably they both invented the method independently. His third contribution was in optics: he recognized that white light is a mixture of colored lights, which can be separated by refraction. His incorrect belief that this effect could not be corrected, when it occurs as the chromatic aberration of a lens, inspired him to invent the reflecting telescope. Newton's principle publications were

Philosophiae naturalis principia mathematica (1686–87) and *Optics* (1704), which held that light is a corpuscular phenomenon.

He was president of the Royal Society from 1703 until his death and was knighted in 1705. A considerable amount of Newton's later life was spent delving into alchemy, astrology, and theological speculation. From biblical chronology he calculated the day of the earth's creation to be about 3500 BC. Einstein said of him, "In one person, he combined the experimenter, the theorist, the mechanic and, not least, the artist in exposition."

Newtonian mechanics The branch of *mechanics concerned with systems in which the results of *quantum theory and the theory of *relativity can be ignored. Also known as classical mechanics, it is based on *Newton's three laws of motion. The first law states that a body remains at rest or moves with constant velocity in a straight line unless acted upon by a *force. This law thus defines the concept of force. The second law, which defines mass, states that the *acceleration (*a*) of a body is proportional to the force (*f*) causing it. The constant of proportionality is the mass (*m*) of the body: $f = ma$. The third law states that the action of a force always produces a reaction in the body. The reaction is of equal magnitude but opposite in direction to the action.

Newton's rings A series of light and dark rings formed in a plano-convex lens if monochromatic light is shone onto the lens when it rests on a plane mirror. First observed by *Newton, they are caused by *interference between light reflected by the mirror and light reflected at the curved surface of the lens.

New Wave (*or* Nouvelle Vague) A group of French film directors in the late 1950s whose films were characterized by their informal and highly original individual styles. The directors, most of whom were associated with the magazine *Cahiers du Cinéma* and the *auteur theory of film criticism, included *Truffaut, *Chabrol, *Resnais, and *Godard.

New Westminster 49 10N 122 58W A city and port in W Canada, in British Columbia on the Fraser River. Bordering on E Vancouver, it manufactures wood products, foods, and oil. Population: 38,393.

New World A name for the American continent, used especially by early emigrants from Europe and in describing the geographical distribution of plants and animals. *Compare* Old World.

New World monkey A *monkey native to the Americas. There are two families: the *Cebidae* (37 species) including *uakaris, *sakis, *titis, *howlers, *capuchins, *squirrel monkeys, *spider monkeys, *woolly monkeys, and the *douroucouli; and the *Callithricidae* (33 species) containing *marmosets and *tamarins. New World monkeys are restricted to Central and South America and are largely arboreal and vegetarian.

New York A state in the NE US. It is bordered by Canada and Lake Ontario on the N, by Vermont, Massachusetts, and Connecticut on the E, by Pennsylvania, New Jersey, and the Atlantic Ocean on the S, and by Pennsylvania, Lake Erie, and Canada on the W. It is basically an upland region, dissected by the valleys of the Mohawk and Hudson Rivers. Traffic flowing from the Great Lakes to the major port of New York City has provided many opportunities for industrial development and today New York is the chief manufacturing state in the US. Its varied products include clothing, electrical machinery, and processed foods; printing and publishing are among the most notable industries. The presence of New York City also makes it the commercial, financial, and cultural center of the nation. The most important agricultural activity is dairying; other leading products include apples, grains, and potatoes. *History*: first explored by Giovanni da Verrazano (1524) and Henry Hudson (1609), the region was the home of Iroquois, Algonquin, Mohegan, and other Indian tribes. The area was originally a Dutch colony (1624) known as New Netherland with New Amsterdam as the capital. In the Second Dutch War (1664–67) Peter Stuyvesant was forced to surrender the colony to the British, who renamed it in honor of the Duke of York and held it until it declared its independence (1776) as one of the 13 original colonies. New York figured prominently in the American Revolution, with close to one-third of the war's battles being fought on its soil. The important Battle of Saratoga (1777), a decisive victory for the colonists, took place there. New York became a state in 1788. In the 19th century the growth of commerce was facilitated by the opening of the Erie Canal (1825). Rapid industrial growth followed, particularly in textiles. Formerly a predominantly agricultural region, the growth of industry marked a new direction for New York's economy. During the 1880s the reform movements that flourished throughout the Northeast, including abolitionism and women's suffrage, found a favorable climate in New York. The waves of immigration that had begun in the mid-1800s continued into the early 20th century. Industrial expansion brought New York to the forefront in manufacturing, and it became the leading manufacturing state as well as the state with the largest population. Although the population declined after World War II, it is still the second-largest after California. New York City remains the country's largest metropolis. Many prominent political leaders were native sons, including five presidents (Martin Van Buren, Millard Fillmore, Chester A. Arthur, Theodore Roosevelt, and Franklin Delano Roosevelt) and three distinguished governors (Alfred E. Smith, Thomas E. Dewey, and Nelson A. Rockefeller). Following World War II the demographics of New York began to change significantly, with a shift from the urban areas into the suburbs, a trend also marked by the movement of many urban businesses to outlying areas. Area: 49,576 sq mi (128,402 sq km). Population (1990): 17,990,445. Capital: Albany.

New York 40 45N 74 00W The largest US city, situated in New York state on New York Bay at the mouth of the Hudson River. Divided into five boroughs—*Manhattan, *Brooklyn, the *Bronx, *Queens, and Richmond (coextensive with *Staten Island), it is the nation's leading seaport and one of the most important business, manufacturing, communications, and cultural centers in the country. As one of the world's financial centers (*see* Wall Street), it is the site of many large corporations and the New York and American Stock Exchanges. The principal manufactures include furs, jewelry, chemicals, metal products, and processed foods. New York is also the main center of US television and radio and book publishing. Its most notable features include Central Park, the fashionable shops of Fifth Avenue, the *Statue of Liberty, Times Square, *Greenwich Village, the Brooklyn Bridge (1883), Rockefeller Center, St Patrick's Cathedral (1858–79), and a large number of extremely tall buildings (skyscrapers), such as the Empire State Building (1931), the UN Headquarters (1951), and the World Trade Center (1973), which give Manhattan its characteristic skyline. Its cultural life is exceptional. As well as the famous Broadway theater district and the Lincoln Center for the Performing Arts, which houses two opera companies, a symphony orchestra, and a ballet company, there are numerous museums, art galleries, and libraries. The most notable educational institutions include Columbia University (founded as King's College in 1754), the City University of New York (1847), and New York University (1831). *History*: on Sept 3, 1609, Henry Hudson sailed into New York Bay and his glowing reports attracted its founding Dutch colonists, who arrived in 1620. In 1625 New Amsterdam, situated at the S tip of Manhattan, became the capital of the newly established colony of New Netherland and the following year the whole island of Manhattan was bought from the Indians for the equivalent of $24. In 1664 the city was captured by the English for the duke of York and promptly renamed. In the 17th century it became a base for prosperous merchants and such pirates as Captain Kidd. From 1789 until 1790 it was the first capital of the US. The opening of the Erie Canal in 1825 ensured its preeminence as a commercial city and seaport. Following the Civil War, it began to merge with neighboring towns, such as Brooklyn, and the metropolis began to form. Early in the 20th century the arrival of millions of European immigrants supplied New York with limitless cheap labor. In recent years many of its middle-class inhabitants have moved to the suburbs of the metropolis and the city subsequently lost a considerable amount of tax revenue. During the mid-1970s New York's financial crisis worsened and the city was narrowly saved from bankruptcy by emergency loans. Population (1990): 7,322,564.

New York Times Company v. Sullivan (1964) US Supreme Court decision that upheld the First Amendment's freedom of the press clause. The suit was brought against *The New York Times*, which had published an advertisement in which police action in Montgomery, Ala., was criticized, by the Montgomery police commissioner. The Supreme Court reversed a state court libel decision that had been in the commissioner's favor. The court stated that, unless malice could be proven, public officials cannot seek libel damages for criticism of their official functions.

New Zealand, Dominion of A country in the Pacific Ocean, to the SE of Australia. It consists of two main islands, *North Island and *South Island, together with several smaller ones, including *Stewart Island to the S. *Ross Dependency and the *Tokelau Islands are dependencies, and the *Cook and Niue Islands are self-governing. Most of the population is of British descent with a large Maori minority. *Economy*: the main basis of the economy is livestock rearing, especially sheep farming. Farms are highly mechanized and there is considerable research into agricultural science and technology. Meat, wool, and dairy products are the main exports, which were adversely affected when the UK joined the EEC in 1973. However the effects were less than had been feared and New Zealand has opened up markets in other parts of the world. Mineral resources include coal, gold, limestone, and silica sand, and oil and natural gas have been found. New Zealand's swift-flowing rivers make hydroelectricity a valuable source of power. Timber production has increased in recent years and there is a growing pulp and paper industry. Other industries, such as food processing and textiles, have also been expanding and tourism is of growing importance. *History*: from about the 14th century the islands were inhabited by the Maoris, a Polynesian people. The first European to discover New Zealand was *Tasman in 1642, who called it Staten Land, later changed to Nieuw Zealand; in 1769 the coast was explored by *Cook. During the early part of the 19th century it was used as a whaling and trading base. By the Treaty of *Waitangi in 1840 the Maori chiefs ceded sovereignty to Britain and a colony was established. British settlement increased rapidly and sheep farming developed on a large scale. After two wars with the Maoris over land rights, peace was reached in 1871. New Zealand was made a dominion in 1907 and became fully independent by the Statute of Westminster in 1931. By the early part of the 20th century its social administration policy was one of the most advanced in the world. Free compulsory primary education was introduced in 1877 and in 1893 New Zealand became the first country in the world to give women the vote. It played an important part in both world wars. Since World War II New Zealand has played an increasing role in international affairs, especially in the Far East. In 1985, New Zealand banned all nuclear warships from its ports. The country's economy suffered severe recession in the late 1980s, and although efforts to curb inflation, including a price and wage policy, were ultimately successful, the slow economic recovery resulted in record-low popularity for the ruling National party by the end of 1992. Prime Minister: James Bolger. Offical language: English. Official currency: New Zealand dollar of 100 cents. Area: 103,719 sq mi (268,704 sq km). Population (1992 est): 3,400,000. Capital: Wellington. Main port: Auckland.

Nexø, Martin Andersen (1869–1954) Danish novelist. His upbringing in the slums of Copenhagen led him to become a socialist and subsequently a communist. He achieved worldwide fame with his novels *Pelle erobreren* (*Pelle the Conqueror*; 1906–10) and *Ditte menneskebarn* (*Ditte: Daughter of Man*; 1917–21), depicting the struggles of the working class. In 1949 he left Denmark and settled in East Germany.

Ney, Michel, Prince of Moscow (1769–1815) French marshal, whom Napoleon described as "the bravest of the brave." He served throughout the Revolutionary Wars and, under Napoleon, won the great victory at Elchingen (1805) and fought at *Jena (1806) and *Friedland (1807). His extraordinary courage in the French retreat from Moscow (1812–13) prompted Napoleon's accolade. When Napoleon returned from Elba, Ney rallied to the former emperor's cause and after his defeat at Waterloo was shot as a traitor.

Nez Percé A North American Indian people of the plateau region of Idaho. Their culture, typical of this area, was based on salmon fishing. After acquiring horses in the 18th century, they frequently left their riverside villages to hunt buffalo on the Plains and thus acquired many Plains Indian traits. They became expert horse breeders possessing large herds. Their language belongs to the Sahaptin division of the *Penutian family.

Ngo Dinh Diem (1901–63) Vietnamese statesman; president of South Vietnam (1955–63). Unsympathetic to Ho Chi Minh's *Viet Minh, he went into exile, returned just before the partition of Vietnam, was appointed prime minister (1954), and in 1955 abolished the monarchy and became president. He was assassinated, together with his brother Ngo Dinh Nhu, in a military coup in 1963 (*see* Vietnam War).

Nha Trang 12 15N 109 10E An ancient port in S Vietnam, at the mouth of the Cai River. Nearby are four shrines dating from the 7th to 12th centuries. The chief industry is fishing. Population (1989): 213,700.

Niagara Falls Two waterfalls on the US-Canadian border, on the Niagara River between Lakes Erie and Ontario. The American Falls, 167 ft (51 m) high and 1000 ft (300 m) wide, are straight while the Horseshoe Falls (Canada), 162 ft (49 m) high and 2600 ft (790 m) wide, are curved. Much of their flow is diverted to generate electricity but they remain spectacular tourist attractions. Shipping between the two lakes is diverted past the Falls by way of the Welland Ship Canal.

Niagara Falls 43 06N 79 04W A city in SE Ontario, Canada, on the Niagara River, oppposite Niagara Falls, NY, to which it is connected by a bridge. The chief economic activity is tourism, which centers on Horseshoe Falls, the Canadian side of Niagara Falls. Other industries include fertilizer, chemicals, cereals, and silverware. Population (1986): 72,100.

Niagara Falls 43 06N 79 02W A city in W New York, NW of Buffalo on the Niagara River, opposite Niagara Falls, Canada. Tourism is the main economic activity; American Falls, the US side of Niagara Falls and surrounding exhibits of the history of the falls and of the area attract many visitors. Manufactures include chemicals, metals, petroleum, wood and paper products, and foodstuffs. Population (1990): 61,840.

Niamey 13 32N 2 05E The capital of Niger, on the Niger River. It has grown rapidly as the country's administrative and commercial center. Its university was founded in 1973. Population (1988): 392,170.

Nibelungenlied (German: *Song of the Nibelungs*) A Middle High German epic poem composed in the 13th century but drawing on much earlier material. Its main theme is the disastrous rivalries following *Siegfried's killing of the Burgundian princes called Nibelungs and his seizure of their treasure. A variant of the story also occurs in the Old Norse *Volsungasaga* (*see* sagas), in which Siegfried is called Sigurd. *Wagner's operatic cycle, *The Ring of the Nibelung*, makes use of elements from both the Germanic and Old Norse versions.

Nicaea, Councils of Two ecumenical councils of the Christian Church held at Nicaea, now Iznik (Turkey). **1.** (325) The council that was summoned by the Byzantine emperor Constantine to establish Church unity and suppress *Arianism. The number of participating bishops was, according to later reports, 318. The *Nicene Creed was the major doctrinal formulation. **2.** (787) The council that was summoned by the Byzantine empress Irene to condemn *iconoclasm. Its initial assembly at Constantinople (786) was disrupted by iconoclasts, but the following year it met at Nicaea and approved a formula for restoring the veneration of icons.

Nicaragua, Republic of A country in Central America between the Caribbean Sea and the Pacific Ocean. Swamp and dense tropical forest on the Caribbean coast, and a broader plain with lakes on the W rise to a central mountain range. Lake Nicaragua in the SW is the largest in Central America. The population is mainly of mixed Indian and Spanish descent, with minorities of African and other descent. *Economy*: chiefly agricultural, the main crops are maize, rice, cotton, coffee, and sugar. Development plans include large irrigation schemes. Production of bananas, formerly the main crop in the E, has been reduced in recent years. There is considerable livestock rearing, and meat packing is an important industry. Minerals include gold, silver, and copper, and large quantities of natural gas were found in 1974. Oil deposits are being explored. Industries, on a small scale, include food processing, textiles, and oil refining. The main exports are cotton, coffee, sugar, beef, and timber. *History*: sighted by Columbus in 1502, it was colonized by Spain from 1522, becoming part of the captaincy general of Guatemala. It broke away from Spain in 1821 and formed part of the Central American Federation until 1838, when Nicaragua became a republic. A treaty with the US in 1916 gave the latter an option on a canal route through Nicaragua as well as naval-base facilities. From 1933 the government was dominated by the Somoza family, opposition to which culminated in a civil war that forced (1979) the resignation and exile of the president, Gen. Anastasio Somoza (1925–80). The victorious Sandinista National Liberation Front (FSLN) established a government that instituted socialist policies. Accusing the Sandinistas of supplying arms to the El Salvador rebels, the US supported an army of "Contras" that fought the government. US aid to the Contras was a major obstacle to normal Nicaraguan-US relations in the late 1980s. Declining US support for the Contras in the wake of the *Iran-Contra Affair, a regional peace plan spearheaded by Oscar *Arias Sanchez, and a more conciliatory attitude by the government and the Contras led to a lessening of tensions during late 1987 and early 1988. A temporary truce was agreed upon in 1988. Violeta Barrios de Chamorro, of the National Opposition Union (UNO), was elected president in 1990 and worked to demobilize both Contra and federal troops and to reduce inflation. Economic difficulties and civil strife hampered government reform efforts in 1992–93. Head of state: Pres. Violeta Barrios de Chamorro. Official language: Spanish. Official currency: cordoba of 100 centavos. Area:

57,143 sq mi (148,000 sq km). Population (1990): 3,606,000. Capital: Managua. Main ports: Corinto (on the Pacific coast) and Bluefields (on the Caribbean).

Nice 43 42N 7 16E A city in SE France, the capital of the Alpes-Maritimes department, one of the leading resorts of the French Riviera. Notable landmarks include the Promenade des Anglais. It has a large trade in fruit and flowers. Population (1990): 345,625.

Nicene Creed The statement of Christian belief accepted as orthodox by the first Council of *Nicaea (325). The Nicene Creed used in the *Eucharist service of Orthodox, Roman Catholic, and Protestant Churches is a version of this creed, considerably expanded in the sections on Christ (*see* Filioque) and the Holy Spirit.

Nichiren Buddhism A popular Japanese Buddhist school named for its founder, a 13th-century monk and prophet. He militantly opposed other Buddhist sects and held that *The Lotus Sutra* contained the true teaching and that the historical Buddha was identical with eternal Buddha-nature, in which all men participate. The sincere invocation of the mantra of homage to *The Lotus Sutra* is sufficient to gain enlightenment.

Nicholas I, St (d. 867) Pope (858–67 AD). In the West Nicholas successfully defended and expanded papal authority against both secular rulers, such as *Lothair, and local bishops, notably *Hincmar of Reims. In the East Nicholas strongly opposed the appointment of *Photius as patriarch of Constantinople and declared him deposed. Photius then declared Nicholas (867) deposed, but Photius's overthrow prevented further hostilities. Feast day: Nov 13.

Nicholas I (1796–1855) Emperor of Russia (1825–55), notorious as an autocrat. Nicholas's accession was followed by the *Dekabrist revolt, which though unsuccessful hardened his conservatism. His ambitions in the Balkans precipitated the *Crimean War.

Nicholas II (1868–1918) The last Emperor of Russia (1894–1917). Nicholas's ambition in Asia led to the unpopular *Russo-Japanese War, which in turn precipitated the *Revolution of 1905. Forced to accept the establishment of a representative assembly (*see* Duma), Nicholas nevertheless continued attempts to rule autocratically. In 1915 he took supreme command of Russian forces in World War I, leaving Russia to the mismanagement of the Empress *Alexandra and *Rasputin. After the outbreak of the Russian Revolution in 1917, Nicholas was forced to abdicate (March). He and his family were imprisoned by the Bolsheviks and executed at Ekaterinburg (now Sverdlovsk).

Nicholas, St (4th century AD) The patron saint of Russia, sailors, and children. He is thought to have been Bishop of Myra in Asia Minor and his alleged relics are in the Basilica of S Nicola, Bari. Legends telling of his gifts of gold to three poor girls for their dowries gave rise to the practice of exchanging gifts on his feast day, Dec 6. This custom has been transferred to Dec 25 in most countries.

Nicholas of Cusa (1401–64) German prelate and scholar. He was made a cardinal in 1448, appointed bishop of Brixen (present-day Bressanone) in 1450, and became a papal legate. He is known for the breadth of his learning. He wrote important works on mysticism, mathematics, biology, and astronomy.

Nicholson, Ben (1894–1982) British artist. His first one-man exhibition (1922) reflected the influence of *cubism and de *Stijl. Some of his best abstract works were produced in the 1930s, while a member of the British art group Unit One (*see* Nash, Paul). These include white-painted plaster reliefs of rectangles combined with circles. He was the son of **Sir William Nicholson** (1872–1949), an artist renowned for his posters.

Nicholson, Jack (1937–   ) US film actor. Following his success as a supporting actor in *Easy Rider* (1969), he became one of the film industry's most respected stars. His films include *Chinatown* (1974), *The Passenger* (1974), *Batman* (1989), and *A Few Good Men* (1992), as well as *One Flew Over the Cuckoo's Nest* (1975) and *Terms of Endearment* (1983), for each of which he won an Academy Award.

JACK NICKLAUS

Nicholson, William (1753–1815) British chemist, who in 1800 discovered *electrolysis by passing a current from a voltaic pile through water and noting the bubbles of gas being given off.

Nicias (c. 470–413 BC) Athenian general and politician. An aristocratic opponent of the demagogue *Cleon, Nicias negotiated a temporary peace with Sparta in the Peloponnesian War (peace of Nicias, 421). He opposed Alcibiades' imperialist designs and only reluctantly commanded the ill-fated Athenian campaign to Sicily, during which he and nearly his entire force perished.

nickel (Ni) A hard silvery metal similar to iron, discovered in 1751 by A. F. Cronstedt (1722–65). It occurs in nature chiefly as pentlandite, NiS, and pyrrhotite, (Fe,Ni)S, which are found in Canada and Australia. Iron meteorites typically contain from 5 to 20% nickel. It is chemically similar to cobalt and copper, and forms a green oxide (NiO), the chloride ($NiCl_2$), the sulfate ($NiSO_4$), and other compounds. It is used widely in alloys, such as stainless steel, Invar, Monel, armor plating, and in coinage. Finely divided nickel is also used as a catalyst for hydrogenation reactions in organic chemistry. At no 28; at wt 58.71; mp 2650°F (1453°C); bp 4954°F (2732°C).

Nicklaus, Jack (William) (1940–   ) US golfer, who has won more major championships than any other. Between 1959 and 1986, he won two US amateur championships, four US and three British Open championships, five US Professional Golfers Association championships, and six Masters championships. In 1988, he was voted "Golfer of the Century." From 1990, he also played on the Senior Tour.

Nicobar Islands. *See* Andaman and Nicobar Islands.

Nicolai, Otto Ehrenfried (1810–49) German conductor and composer of operas. He held posts in Rome and Vienna and is remembered for *The Merry Wives of Windsor* (1849).

Nicolson, Sir Harold (George) (1886–1968) British diplomat and literary critic. Born in Iran and educated at Oxford, he worked in the diplomatic service until 1929 and was later a member of Parliament (1935–45). In 1913 he married the novelist Victoria Sackville-West (1892–1962). He published political studies, critical appreciations of Verlaine, Byron, Tennyson, and others, and several volumes of his *Diaries*.

Nicopolis, Battle of (Sept 25, 1396) The battle in which a coalition of Crusaders under Emperor *Sigismund, at the request of the Byzantine emperor, Manuel II Palaeologus (1350–1425; reigned 1391–1425), were decisively defeated by the Turks under Sultan Bayezid I (1347–1403; reigned 1389–1403). It contributed greatly to further Turkish advances and the ultimate fall of the Eastern Roman (Byzantine) Empire.

Nicosia (Greek name: Leukosía; Turkish name: Lefkosa) The capital of Cyprus, on the Pedieas River. Originally known as Ledra it has been successively under Byzantine, Venetian, Turkish, and British control. It possesses many old buildings, including the Cathedral of St Sophia (completed 1325), now the main mosque in Nicosia. Its industries include textiles, food processing, and cigarettes. Population (1990 est): 168,800.

nicotine ($C_{10}H_{14}N_2$) A toxic colorless oily liquid alkaloid that rapidly turns brown on exposure to air. It is obtained from the dried leaves of the tobacco plant and is present in small quantities in cigarettes.

nicotinic acid. *See* vitamin B complex.

Niebuhr, Barthold Georg (1776–1831) German historian. Niebuhr served as Prussian ambassador in Rome from 1816 to 1823, when he joined the staff of Bonn University. His *History of Rome* (1811–32) was significantly different from previous works on the ancient world, as he adopted a more critical approach and stressed the importance of external factors in the development of Rome. His ideas and methods influenced many scholars, including Theodor *Mommsen.

Niebuhr, Reinhold (1892–1971) US minister, philosopher, and theologian. He was pastor of Detroit's Bethel Evangelical Church (1915–28) where he saw labor injustices in the automobile industry. He taught at Union Theological Seminary (1928–60) and through the 1930s was a pacifist, political activist, and socialist. During the 1940s, however, he favored the war to stop Hitler and totalitarianism and after 1945 cofounded Americans for Democratic Action and was an adviser to the State Department. His early writings—*Moral Man and Immoral Society* (1932) and *Christianity and Power Politics* (1940)—reflected his socialist years. His later works—*A Nation So Conceived* (1963) and *Man's Nature and His Communities* (1965)—dealt with his theory of political realism.

Nielsen, Carl (August) (1865–1931) Danish composer and conductor. He began his musical career as a violinist. Nielsen developed the principle of progressive tonality (beginning in one *tonality and ending in another) in his six symphonies, of which the fourth, entitled *The Inextinguishable* (1914–16), and the fifth (1922) are the best known. He also composed concertos for the violin, flute and clarinet, the operas *Saul and David* (1900–02) and *Maskarade* (1904–06), chamber music, and choral music.

Niemeyer, Oscar (1907–   ) Brazilian architect. A disciple of Le Corbusier with whom he collaborated on the Ministry of Education (1937–43) in Rio de

Janeiro, Niemeyer has made a major contribution to the development of modern architecture in Brazil. His first independent buildings included a casino, club, and church at Pampulha in Bel Horizonte. He has achieved international fame for his designs for □Brasília, notably the president's palace (1959) and the cathedral (1964).

Nietzsche, Friedrich (1844–1900) German philosopher. A friend of Wagner, Nietzsche was influenced by the writings of *Schopenhauer and *Goethe. His first book, *The Birth of Tragedy* (1872), argued that Wagnerian opera was the successor to Greek drama. Nietzsche rejected Christianity and its morality and attempted a "transvaluation of all values." He argued that the "will to power" (the title of his posthumously edited notebooks) was the crucial human characteristic. In *Thus Spake Zarathustra* (1883–92), he eulogizes the man who is free, titanic, and powerful, an ideal adopted by the Nazis for the Aryan superman. His often obscure writings have been variously interpreted by 20th-century psychologists and existentialists. After 1889 he was permanently insane.

Niger, Republic of A large landlocked country in West Africa. Lying mainly in the Sahara, it consists of desert in the N merging to semidesert in the S and rising to the central Aïr mountains. In the extreme SW it is drained by the Niger River, bordered by fertile flood plains. Approximately half the population are Hausa, with large proportions of Zerma, Songhai, and Fulani. *Economy*: agriculture, particularly livestock raising, is important but it suffered badly from the droughts of the late 1960s and early 1970s in the Sahel. Crops include groundnuts, millet, beans, and cassava, with cotton and rice being grown in the wetter river districts. Mineral resources include salt, natron, and tin; important uranium deposits in the N are being exploited. *History*: occupied by France (1883–99), it became a territory of French West Africa in 1904. It was made an autonomous republic within the French Community in 1958 prior to gaining full independence in 1960 with Hamani Diori as president. Diori was overthrown in a military coup led by Maj. Gen. Seyni Kountché, who subsequently became president. Kountché died in 1987, and under a new constitution adopted in 1989, Niger once again had a civilian government; however, the country still operated under a single-party system. A more democratic constitution was approved in 1992, but the government faced a disintegrating economy and internal rebellions. Official language: French. Official currency: CFA (Communauté financière africaine) franc of 100 centimes. Area: 458,075 sq mi (1,186,408 sq km). Population (1990 est): 7,691,000. Capital: Niamey.

Niger River The third longest river in Africa. Rising in the S highlands of Guinea, near the Sierra Leone border, it flows NE and then SE through Mali, Niger, and Nigeria to enter the Gulf of Guinea. It has one of the largest hydroelectric-power plants in Africa. Length: 2600 mi (4183 km).

Niger-Congo languages An African language family spoken in central and S Africa. It is subdivided into six groups: the *West Atlantic languages; the Mande languages spoken in Guinea, Mali, and Sierra Leone; the Voltaic languages spoken in Upper Volta, Ghana, and the Ivory Coast; the *Kwa languages of West Africa, such as Yoruba and Igbo; the Benue-Congo group, which includes the *Bantu languages; and the Adamawa-Eastern group spoken in Nigeria. The whole family is sometimes included in the larger Niger-Kordofanian classification, which relates it to the Kordofanian languages of the Sudan.

Nigeria, Federation of A large country in West Africa, on the Gulf of Guinea. Mangrove swamps along the coast give way to tropical rain forests inland rising to open savanna-covered plateaus, with mountains in the E reaching heights of over 5000 ft (2000 m). The N is semidesert and the Niger River flows through the W. The inhabitants are mainly Hausa and Fulani in the N,

Yoruba in the W, and Ibo in the E. *Economy*: since the discovery of oil in the 1960s and 1970s there has been a dramatic expansion in the economy and a shift away from agriculture to industry. Oil production accounts for about 90% of exports although production has declined in recent years; Nigeria is a member of OPEC and the world's eighth largest producer. There are also important reserves of natural gas and other minerals, including tin, coal, iron ore, and columbite (of which Nigeria is the world's main supplier). Manufacturing industries have undergone rapid expansion, including brewing, aluminum, motor vehicles, textiles, and cement. Hydroelectricity is a valuable source of power, particularly since the opening of the Kainji Dam on the Niger River (1969). Agriculture is still important and diverse although output has declined in recent years and it suffered severely through the prolonged drought in the Sahel. The main cash crops are groundnuts and cotton in the N and palms, coconut, and rubber in the S. Livestock, fishing, and forestry for timber are also important. *History*: in the Middle Ages there were highly developed kingdoms in the area, such as those of the Hausa in the N and the Yoruba (e.g. Oyo, Benin) in the SW; the Ibo occupied the SE. The coast was explored in the 15th century by the Portuguese, who developed the slave trade, in which the Dutch and English also participated. In 1861 Lagos was annexed by Britain and in 1886 the Royal Niger Company was incorporated to further British interests. By 1906, the British were in control of Nigeria, which was divided into the protectorate of Northern Nigeria and the colony (of Lagos) and protectorate of Southern Nigeria. These were united in 1914. Nigeria became a federation in 1954, gained independence in 1960, and became a republic within the Commonwealth in 1963. The government was overthrown in a violent military coup in 1966 and, after a further coup, a new government was formed under Lt. Col. Gowon. In 1967 the Eastern Region, which contained the homeland of the Ibo, withdrew to form the Republic of *Biafra under Lt. Col. Odumegwn Ojukwu's leadership. Civil war followed, lasting until Biafra's surrender in 1970. Gowon was overthrown in a coup in 1975. In 1979 Alhaji Shehu Shagari became president. He was reelected in 1983. On the last day of 1983 the Shagari government was overturned, and a military regime under Maj. Gen. Mohammed Buhari was installed. Buhari's inability to solve the country's political and particularly its economic problems led to his overthrow in 1985. He was succeeded by Maj. Gen. Ibrahim Babangida, who began the gradual process of a return to civilian rule. By 1991, local elections had been held, and a commission had been formed to establish voting registration centers. In 1992 and 1993, election results were canceled, and Babangida resigned in Aug 1993. Military leaders took control of the government in Nov 1993. Official language: English; the main African languages are Yoruba, Hausa, and Ibo. Official currency: naira of 100 kobo. Area: 356,669 sq mi (923,773 sq km). Population (1990 est): 118,865,000. Capital and main port: Lagos.

nightblindness Inability to see in dim light. This is the earliest sign of vitamin A deficiency and is seen most commonly in young children in poor countries. Vitamin A is found in fruit, vegetables, and fish-liver oil. Preparations of vitamin A and cod-liver oil are used in treatment.

night heron A nocturnal *heron belonging to a subfamily (*Nycticoracini*; 9 species) occurring worldwide. Night herons are comparatively short-legged and squat, with a short neck and a broad bill. Birds of the main genus (*Nycticorax*) are mostly black-headed with long white ornamental head plumes.

nightingale A plump woodland bird, *Luscinia megarhynchos*, that winters in tropical Africa and breeds in S Europe and Asia Minor during the summer. It is about 6 in (16 cm) long with reddish-brown plumage and pale underparts and feeds on ground insects and spiders. Nightingales are noted for their beautiful song and were popular as cagebirds. The thrush nightingale (*L. luscinia*) is a closely related similar species. Family: *Turdidae* (thrushes).

Nightingale, Florence (1820–1910) British hospital reformer and founder of the nursing profession. With strong religious convictions, Nightingale trained as a nurse and was appointed a nursing superintendent in London in 1853. On the outbreak of the Crimean War, in 1854, she volunteered to lead a party of nurses to work in the military hospitals. She set about transforming the appalling conditions, earning herself the title Lady with the Lamp from her patients. After the war she was instrumental in obtaining improved living conditions in the army and, in 1860 she established a school for nurses, the first of its kind.

FLORENCE NIGHTINGALE *The legendary Lady with the Lamp tending patients in the hospital at Scutari, during the Crimean War.*

nightjar A nocturnal bird belonging to a subfamily (*Caprimulginae*; 60–70 species) occurring in most temperate and tropical regions, also called goatsucker. About 12 in (30 cm) long, nightjars have a soft mottled gray, brown, and reddish plumage with spotted and barred underparts and a long tail. Its short bill has a wide gape surrounded by long sensitive bristles enabling it to catch insects in flight. Family: *Caprimulgidae*; order: *Caprimulgiformes* (frogmouths, nightjars, etc.).

nightmares Frightening *dreams, from which the sufferer often wakes with a feeling of suffocation. They are distinguished from **night terrors**, in which a child wakes suddenly in panic but later cannot remember the incident. Nightmares are more common during states of anxiety and depression and in people taking certain sleeping tablets. *See also* sleep.

nightshade One of several plants of the family *Solanaceae. The most notorious is *deadly nightshade (or belladonna). The **woody nightshade**, or bittersweet (*Solanum dulcamara*), is a scrambling shrubby perennial, up to 7 ft (2 m) tall, of Eurasia and N Africa. It has oval leaves, the lower ones much divided, and loose clusters of flowers with five spreading purple lobes and conspicuous yellow stamens. The red berries are poisonous. The **black nightshade** (*S. nigrum*) is an annual, up to 20 in (50 cm) high, widely distributed as a weed. It has oval pointed leaves, small yellowish flowers, and poisonous black berries.

The unrelated **enchanter's nightshade** (*Circaea lutetiana*), of Eurasia, is a herbaceous perennial of shady places. Up to 24 in (60 cm) tall, it has large heartshaped leaves and a terminal spike of tiny white flowers. Family: *Onagraceae*.

nihilism A view that rejects all traditional values and institutions. *Turgenev invented the label in *Fathers and Sons* (1861) for the philosophy of the character of Basarov, which was based on that of Dmitrii Pisarev (1840–68). The political expression of nihilism is anarchy; its 19th-century Russian proponents held that progress is impossible without the destruction of all existing organizations. Nihilism also undermines accepted standards in *ethics and *aesthetics.

Niigata 37 58N 139 2E A city in Japan, in NW Honshu. The main port for the Sea of Japan, its industries include chemicals and oil refining. Its university was established in 1949. Population (1991): 487,856.

Nijinsky, Vaslav (1890–1950) Russian ballet dancer. In 1909 he joined Diaghilev's company in Paris, and quickly achieved an international reputation for his daring and sensitive dancing. Michel *Fokine created *Petrushka, Scheherazade*, and other ballets for him, and from 1913 he also began to choreograph. He retired in 1919 suffering from schizophrenia and was cared for by his wife until his death.

Nijmegen (German name: Nimwegen) 51 50N 5 52E A city in the E Netherlands, in Gelderland province. The Treaties of *Nijmegen (1678–79) were signed here. Its university was founded in 1923. It is an important industrial center with chemicals and engineering. Population (1991 est): 145,782.

Nijmegen, Treaties of (1678–79) The peace treaties between France and, respectively, the Netherlands (1678), Spain (1678), and the Holy Roman Empire (1679) that ended the third *Dutch War. Terms were least favorable to Spain, Louis XIV securing Franche-Comté and a naturally defensible frontier with the Spanish Netherlands.

Nike The Greek personification of victory, often portrayed as an aspect of *Athena. Among larger representations is the famous statue discovered in Samothrace in 1836 and now in the Louvre, Paris.

Nikisch, Arthur (1855–1922) Hungarian conductor. A brilliant student at the Vienna conservatory, he directed the Leipzig Opera (1879–87), the Boston Symphony Orchestra (1889–93), and then the Leipzig Gewandhaus and Berlin Philharmonic Orchestras concurrently (1895–1922).

Nikolaev 46 57N 32 00E A port in S Ukraine, at the confluence of the Bug and Ingul Rivers about 40 mi (64 km) from the Black Sea. Long a naval base, it has important ship building and flour-milling industries. Population (1991 est): 512,000.

Nikopol 47 34 N 34 25E A city in Ukraine, on the Dnepr River. It is important as the center of a region having the world's largest manganese reserves. Population (1991 est): 159,000.

Nile, Battle of the (Aug 1, 1798) A naval battle in which the British, under *Nelson, defeated the French during *Napoleon's invasion of Egypt (*see* Revolutionary and Napoleonic Wars). This engagement severed communications between France and Napoleon's army in Egypt and gave Britain control of the Mediterranean.

Nile River A river in N Africa, the longest river in the world. The longest of its three main tributaries, the White Nile, rises in Burundi as the Luvironza River before joining the Kagera River to enter Lake Victoria, the chief reservoir of the Nile. It emerges as the Victoria Nile at Jinja to flow northward—through Lake Mobutu—becoming the White Nile at its confluence with the Bahr el Ghazal. At Khartoum it is joined by the Blue Nile (which rises in the Ethiopian highlands) and later by the Atbara River before flowing through a broad delta into the Mediterranean Sea. The Nile's annual floodwaters have supported cultivation on its floodplains since ancient times. To provide the increasing amounts of water required for irrigation, vast dams have been constructed, including the Aswan Dam and *Aswan High Dam. Length: 4187 mi (6741 km).

nilgai A large antelope, *Bosephalus tragocamelus*, inhabiting Indian forests and plains. Up to 55 in (140 cm) high at the shoulder, male nilgais have a slate-gray coat with white underparts and develop short horns and a throat tuft. Females are smaller and tawny brown. They live in small herds, browsing on shrubs and fruit.

Nilo-Saharan languages A family of African languages that covers the smallest geographical area of all the African language groups. It is also the least clearly defined group, there being very great variety within its constituent languages. It includes the Nilotic languages of the Chari-Nile group, such as Dinka and Nuer.

nimbostratus A form of *cloud common in temperate latitudes. Dark gray and solid in appearance it has a low base but may show extensive vertical development. Precipitation of snow or rain is often prolonged although not usually heavy.

Nîmes 43 50N 4 21E A city in S France, the capital of the Gard department. An important Roman settlement, it was a Protestant stronghold (16th–17th centuries). It has several notable Roman remains, including an amphitheater and the temple of Diana; the Pont du Gard lies to the NE. A trading center for wine and brandy, its manufactures include textiles, footwear, and agricultural machinery. Population (1990): 133,607.

Nimitz, Chester W(illiam) (1885–1966) US admiral. In World War II, as commander of the Pacific Fleet after Pearl Harbor (1941), he complemented Gen. Douglas *MacArthur's command of the SW Pacific. His victories along the island chains from Japan to New Guinea, which destroyed the Japanese fleet, were made possible by his use of aircraft carriers as support bases.

Nimrod A legendary biblical figure described in Genesis as a mighty hunter. He founded a Mesopotamian kingdom that included the cities of Babel, Erech, and Akkad and is credited with building the cities of Nineveh and Kalhu (modern Nimrud).

Nimrud An Assyrian capital (ancient Kalhu) near Mosul (Iraq). Founded about 1250 BC it was destroyed by the Medes in 612 BC. *Layard's excavations (1845–51) of the 9th-century city yielded gigantic sculptures of winged bulls and a library of *cuneiform tablets. *See also* Nineveh.

Nin, Anaïs (1903–77) US writer; born in France. She spent part of her childhood in the US and most of her young adult years in France. Influenced by the surrealist writers in Paris and her personal experience with psychoanalysis, she developed her own style of writing, concentrating on themes of women and women's problems. Her works include the novels *The House of Incest* (1937), *Winter of Artifice* (1939), *The Four-Chambered Heart* (1950), *A Spy in the House of Love* (1954), and *The Novel of the Future* (1970); short stories *Under a Glass Bell* (1944) and *Ladders to Fire* (1946); and her diaries, which appeared in six volumes.

ninety-five theses. *See* Luther, Martin.

Nineveh An Assyrian capital (modern Kuyunjik) near Mosul (Iraq). Nineveh was made co-capital with □Nimrud by *Sennacherib (c. 700 BC). The Medes sacked it in 612 BC. Sculptures, reliefs, and inscriptions illuminate Assyrian life at

NIMRUD *British archeologists directed the excavation and removal of the statue of the winged bull, now in the British Museum, London. It was at first believed to have been the site of Nineveh.*

this period, but *Layard's great find was the library of *Ashurbanipal, which preserved masterpieces of *cuneiform literature, including the epic of *Gilgamesh.

Ningbo (*or* Ning-po) 29 54N 121 33E A river port in E China, in Zhejiang province near the East China Sea. Important for overseas trade (5th–9th centuries), it was also a religious center and has many temples. Its industries include textiles and food processing. Population (1990): 552,540.

Ningxia Hui Autonomous Region (*or* Ningsia Hui AR) An administrative division in N China. It occupies a plateau and is largely desert, with nomadic herdsmen in the N and some cultivation in the S. Area: 25,896 sq mi (66,400 sq km). Population (1990): 4,655,451. Capital: Yinchuan.

Niobe In Greek mythology, the daughter of Tantalus and wife of the king of Thebes. She took great pride in her many children and arrogantly urged the Thebans to worship her instead of Leto, the mother of only two children, Apollo and Artemis. When the Thebans consented to this, Apollo and Artemis avenged their mother's honor and killed Niobe's children. Overcome by grief, Niobe wandered to Mount Sipylus in Lydia, where Zeus changed her into a stone column or statue, the face of which was said to shed tears continually.

niobium (Nb) A soft ductile white metal, discovered in 1801. It was formerly known as columbium in the US. Niobium is used in specialist alloys in spacecraft, and at low temperatures it has superconducting properties. Its compounds include the white oxide (Nb_2O_5), which has interesting structural properties, and the volatile fluoride and chloride (NbF_5, $NbCl_5$). At no 41; at wt 92.9064; mp 4479°F (2468°C); bp 8576°F (4742°C).

nipa A small *palm tree, *Nipa fruticans*, of brackish waters and estuaries of SE Asia. It has a creeping trunk and large feathery foliage, which is used for thatching and basket making. The fruits are sometimes eaten and the flowers are used commercially as a source of sugar.

Nippur A city of ancient *Sumer (modern Niffer in central Iraq). From about 2600 BC it was Sumer's chief religious center with a *ziggurat dedicated to Enlil (built c. 2000 BC) and temples to *Ishtar (Inanna). Quantities of tablets bearing religious, literary, and other texts have been discovered.

Nirenberg, Marshall Warren (1927–   ) US biochemist, who developed a technique for breaking the genetic code. Nirenberg used synthetic RNA of known base sequence and determined for which amino acid it coded. He shared a Nobel Prize (1968) with *Khorana and Robert W. Holley (1922–   ) for this work.

nirvana The supreme goal of Buddhism, in which liberation from the limitations of existence and rebirth are attained through the extinction of desire. Whereas the *Theravada school sees nirvana as the negation of the mundane, the *Mahayana regards it as the ultimate achievement of man's essential Buddhanature. In Hinduism nirvana also means spiritual release in the sense of freedom from reincarnation or of union with God or the Absolute.

Niš 43 20N 21 54E A city in E Yugoslavia, in Serbia on the Nišava River. For five centuries to 1877 it was a center for Serbian resistance to Turkish control. Its products include locomotives and textiles, and it has a university (1965). Population (1991): 247,898.

Nishinomiya 34 44N 135 22E A city in Japan, in S Honshu on Osaka Bay. A heavy industrial center, it is traditionally known for its *sake* (a Japanese rice wine). Population (1991): 426,711.

Niterói 22 54S 43 06W A city in SE Brazil, in Rio de Janeiro state on Guanabara Bay opposite the city of Rio de Janeiro. Although largely residential, it has ship building and textile industries and is a popular resort. Population (1980): 386,185.

nitric acid (HNO_3) A fuming corrosive liquid made by the oxidation of ammonia by air in the presence of a platinum catalyst or the action of sulfuric acid on sodium or potassium nitrate. It is widely used in the manufacture of fertilizers and explosives and in other chemical processes.

nitrocellulose. *See* cellulose nitrate.

nitrogen (N) A colorless odorless gas, discovered by D. Rutherford (1749–1819) in 1772. It makes up 78% of the earth's atmosphere by volume. The element exists as diatomic molecules (N_2) bonded very strongly together. This bond must be broken before nitrogen can react, which accounts for its chemical inertness. It forms a range of chemical compounds including ammonia (NH_3), the oxides (N_2O, NO, N_2O_3, NO_2, N_2O_5), nitric acid (HNO_3), and many nitrates (for example $NaNO_3$). Liquid nitrogen has a wide range of cryogenic applications. Ammonia (NH_3) and nitrates are of great importance as fertilizers. Nitrates are also used in explosives as a source of oxygen, which they liberate when heated. Sodium and potassium nitrates occur naturally in some desert areas. Nitrogen gas is used to provide an inert gas blanket in some welding applications. At no 7; at wt 14.0067; mp $-345.75°F$ ($-209.86°C$); bp $-320.4°F$ ($-195.8°C$).

nitrogen cycle The sequence of processes by which nitrogen and its compounds are utilized in nature. Nitrogen gas in the air is converted (fixed) to ammonia by lightning, cosmic radiation, certain soil bacteria, and fertilizer manufacturers (*see* nitrogen fixation). Nitrifying bacteria in the roots of leguminous

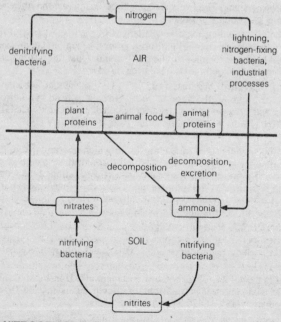

NITROGEN CYCLE

plants convert ammonia to nitrites and then to nitrates. Some nitrates are reduced by denitrifying bacteria to nitrogen, but most are used by plants to manufacture amino acids and proteins. When animals eat plants some of this nitrogenous plant material is incorporated into animal tissues. Nitrogenous excretory products and dead organic matter decompose to produce ammonia, so completing the cycle.

nitrogen fixation The conversion of atmospheric nitrogen gas into nitrogen compounds. The process occurs naturally by the action of bacteria in the roots of leguminous plants (see nitrogen cycle). Industrial methods of fixing nitrogen are of immense importance in the manufacture of nitrogen fertilizers. One method is the reaction of nitrogen with oxygen to give nitric oxide in an electric arc. The process is only economical in regions in which cheap hydroelectric power is available. The major method of fixing nitrogen is the *Haber-Bosch process for making ammonia.

nitroglycerin ($C_3H_5(NO_3)_3$) A yellow oily highly *explosive liquid. It is used as an explosive either alone or as *dynamite or *gelignite.

Niue 19 02S 169 55W A fertile coral island in the S Pacific Ocean, belonging to New Zealand. Copra and bananas are exported. Area: 100 sq mi (260 sq km). Population (1980 est): 3288. Chief town: Alofi.

Niven, David (1909–83) British film actor. His early films include *The Prisoner of Zenda* (1937) and *Wuthering Heights* (1939), and he later appeared in many stylish comedies and action films, including *Separate Tables* (1958), *The Guns of Navarone* (1961), and *Candleshoe* (1977). He published two highly successful volumes of autobiography, *The Moon's a Balloon* (1972) and *Bring on the Empty Horses* (1975).

Nixon, Richard Milhous (1913–94) US statesman; Republican president (1969–74). A Californian-born lawyer, he was elected in 1946 to the US House of Representatives, where he was a member of the Un-American Activities Committee. In 1950 he was elected to the Senate as a staunch anticommunist. He achieved early political power partly by discrediting Democratic opponents as communist sympathizers. He was Eisenhower's vice president from 1953 until 1960, when he became the Republican presidential candidate. He was defeated by John F. *Kennedy and, when in 1962 he failed to win the governorship of California, his political career seemed over. However, Nixon returned to national politics in the mid-1960s and in 1968 narrowly defeated Hubert Humphrey for the presidency. As president he reduced US troop commitments abroad and in 1973 ended US military involvement in Vietnam. In 1972 he visited the People's Republic of China, a move that was to lead to the establishment of diplomatic relations with China. Participation in illegal efforts to ensure re-election in 1972 and the subsequent cover-up attempt led to the *Watergate scandal. Under threat of impeachment he became the first president to resign office. President *Ford granted him a free pardon after succeeding him as president. In private life he wrote *RN: The Memoirs of Richard Nixon* (1978), *The Real War* (1980), and *In the Arena* (1990).

Nizam al-Mulk (c. 1018–92) Persian statesman, who was vizier (minister; 1063–92) to the *Seljuq sultans *Alp-Arslan and Malik-Shah. Nizam al-Mulk, who wielded almost absolute power, governed the Seljuq empire at its zenith. He was the author of *The Book of Government*, in which he expressed his political and orthodox religious views. Shortly before Malik-Shah's death, Nizam al-Mulk was assassinated, probably by a rival at court.

Nizhnii Tagil 58 00N 59 58E A city in Russia, on the Tagil River and on the E slopes of the Ural Mountains. Its metallurgical industries arise from the surrounding iron-mining region. Population (1991 est): 439,200.

Nizhny Novgorodo (*or* Nishnii Novgorodo; name 1932–91: Gorkii, Gorki, *or* Gorky) 56 20N 44 00E A city in central Russia, on the Oka and Volga Rivers. It is one of the country's most important industrial cities, whose manufactures include machinery, chemicals, and textiles. Its trade fair was the most important in Russia until it was discontinued in 1917. The city was renamed in 1932 in honor of the writer Maksim Gorki. Population (1991 est): 1,445,000.

RICHARD M. NIXON *President (1969–74) who, as a result of the Watergate scandal, became the first to resign the presidency.*

Nkomo, Joshua (1917–) Zimbabwean politician. Secretary general of the Rhodesian African Railway Union in Rhodesia (1945–50), Nkomo became president of the Zimbabwe African People's Union (ZAPU) in 1961. With headquarters in Zambia, it allied with Robert Mugabe's Zimbabwe African National Union (ZANU) in 1976 to form the *Patriotic Front (PF) against the government of Ian Smith in Rhodesia (*see also* Zimbabwe). Nkomo became a minister in Mugabe's government in 1980 but was dismissed (1982) when arms caches were found on his farms.

Nkrumah, Kwame (1909–72) Ghanaian statesman; prime minister (1957–60) and then president (1960–66). A student in the US and the UK, after returning home he formed (1949) the Convention People's party, which with a policy of noncooperation with the British took the Gold Coast to independence as Ghana in 1957. Nkrumah was deposed by a military coup while visiting China in 1966. He sought exile in Guinea, where Sékou Touré made him co-head of state. An advocate of African unity, he wrote *Toward Colonial Freedom* (1947) and *Handbook of Revolutionary Warfare* (1968).

No A form of Japanese theater, the early development of which is associated with the work of the actor and dramatist *Zeami Motokiyo (1363–1443). Originating in religious ritual and folk dances and strongly influenced by Zen Buddhism, it is performed with a minimum of scenery and properties and is characterized by the use of dance, mime, and masks. The acting is highly stylized. A traditional No program lasts several hours and consists of five plays separated by three comic interludes known as *Kyogen*. It has remained an aristocratic form, contrasting with the more realistic *Kabuki* drama.

Noah An Old Testament figure. After God had determined to destroy the human race because of its wickedness (Genesis 6–8), he made a covenant with Noah as the only man worthy of being saved from the coming flood. Noah was instructed to build an ark for his family and representatives of each animal species, and they would be preserved after the flood subsided. Noah and his sons Ham, Shem, and Japheth and their wives became the ancestors of the present human race. Several other cultures have similar legends about a catastrophic primeval flood.

Nobel, Alfred Bernhard (1833–96) Swedish chemist and businessman. From his invention of dynamite (1867) and a smokeless gunpowder (1889) and his exploitation of the Baku oil fields he amassed a considerable fortune, leaving much of it as a foundation for the **Nobel Prizes**. Five of the annual awards—(for physics, chemistry, physiology or medicine, literature, and peace) are made by various Swedish academies, except for the Peace Prize, which is awarded by a committee elected by the Norwegian parliament. A sixth prize, for economics, instituted in memory of Alfred Nobel, has been financed by the Swedish National Bank since 1969.

nobelium (No) A synthetic transuranic element discovered in 1957 by bombarding curium with carbon ions in an accelerator. Five isotopes with short half-lives have been discovered. Named for Alfred Nobel. At no 102; at wt (255).

Nobile, Umberto (1885–1978) Italian aeronautical engineer and aviator. He designed the airships *Norge* and *Italia*, piloting the *Norge* in *Amundsen's flight over the North Pole (1926). In 1928 he flew the *Italia* across the Pole but crashed on the return journey, being rescued after 40 days.

Noble, Sir Andrew (1831–1915) British physicist, who founded the science of ballistics. In conjunction with Sir Frederick *Abel he improved the quality of gunpowder and made many innovations in artillery design.

noble gases (*or* inert gases) The elements forming group O of the *periodic table: helium, neon, argon, krypton, xenon, and radon. All are colorless odorless tasteless gases, which are slightly soluble in water. They are virtually inert chemically owing to their filled outer electron shells, although complexes of xenon and krypton have recently been isolated (e.g. XeF_4). Helium is commercially obtained from natural gas, the others (apart from radon) from the distillation of air. Their inertness suits them for such applications as arc welding and filling incandescent lamps.

noble metals Metals, such as gold, silver, and platinum, that do not rust or tarnish in air or water and are not easily attacked by acids.

	1983	1984	1985	1986
Physics	S. Chandrasekhar W. Fowler	Carlo Rubbia Simon van der Meer	Klaus von Klitzing	Gerd Biner Heinrich Rohrer Ernst Ruska
Chemistry	H. Taube	Robert B. Merrifield	Herbert A. Hauptman Jerome Karle	Dudley Herschbach Yuan T. Lee John C. Polanyi
Medicine	B. McClintock	Niels K. Jerne Georges J. F. Koehler Cesar Milstein	Michael S. Brown Joseph L. Goodstein	Stanley Cohen Rita Levi-Montalcini
Literature	William Golding	Jaroslav Seifert	Claude Simon	Wole Soyinka
Peace	L. Walesa	Desmond Tutu	International Physicians for the Prevention of Nuclear War	Elie Wiesel
Economics	G. Debreu	Richard Stone	Franco Modigliani	James McGill Buchanan

NOBEL *prize winners.*

Nobunaga Oda (1534–82) Japanese general, hero of many legends. *See* Oda Nobunaga.

Noctiluca A genus of minute single-celled animals (☐Protozoa) found in coastal waters throughout the world. They are pinkish, about the size of a pin-head, have a single flagellum that wafts food particles toward the mouth, and are luminescent. Class: **Flagellata.*

noctuid moth A moth belonging to the family *Noctuidae* (about 20,000 species), also called owlet moth, widespread in Eurasia and North America. The adults are usually dull brown or gray and fly at night. The caterpillars, which are also known as **army worms and **cutworms, are active at night, eating plant roots and stems.

noctule An insect-eating **bat, *Nyctalus noctula*, of Eurasia. About 5 in (12 cm) long, it has bright-chestnut fur and long narrow wings. Noctules hibernate only from December to January Family: *Vespertilionidae.*

noddy. *See* tern.

Noel-Baker, Philip John (1889–1982) British campaigner for disarmament and Labour politician. He worked at the League of Nations (1919–22) and helped to draft the UN Charter; he was an MP (1929–31, 1936–50). The author of *The Arms Race: A Programme for World Disarmament* (1958), in 1959 he was awarded the Nobel Peace Prize.

Noguchi, Hideyo (1876–1928) Japanese bacteriologist, who discovered that paralysis in syphilitic patients was caused by spirochete organisms in the central nervous system. Noguchi also investigated snake venoms, poliomyelitis, and trachoma. He died of yellow fever while he was undertaking research into the disease in Africa.

Nolan, Sidney (1917–92) Australian painter, born in Melbourne. Largely self-taught, he first painted abstract works, influenced by **Klee and **Moholy-Nagy but is internationally known for his paintings of Australian historical figures, and landscapes of the outback.

Nolde, Emil (E. Hansen; 1867–1956) German expressionist painter and print-maker. Although briefly associated (1906–07) with Die **Brucke, he developed an independent style characterized by his distorted forms and clashing colors. Deeply religious, he painted many biblical scenes, bleak landscapes of the Baltic coast, and still lifes of flowers.

Nollekens, Joseph (1737–1823) British neoclassical sculptor (*see* neoclassicism). After executing several portrait busts in Rome (1760–70), he became highly successful with his portrait sculptures in England. His sitters included King George III, the painter Benjamin West, and the political leaders William Pitt the Younger and Charles James Fox. He was also a sculptor of tombs and mythological subjects.

nomads Peoples who live in no fixed place but wander periodically according to the seasonal availability of food, pasture, or trade and employment. Hunters and gatherers (e.g. Australian Aborigines) usually live in small bands that spend anything from a few days to a few weeks in a vicinity, moving within a loosely defined and often extensive territory. Pastoralists (e.g. many central Asian tribes) often move between summer and winter pastures (*see* transhumance). Traders, tinkers, entertainers, and those who provide certain crafts and services, such as the **gypsies, often travel widely seeking employment and customers for services.

SIDNEY NOLAN Dead Duck Mine.

Nome 64 30N 165 30W A port in W Alaska, on the S shore of the Seward Peninsula. Founded as Anvil City during the gold rush of 1868, it has fishing and handicraft industries. Population (1990): 3500.

nominalism The medieval philosophical theory that general terms (called universals) have no real existence, that is, there is no abstract entity corresponding to a universal. Thus, there exists no such thing as blueness, but only individual blue things (called particulars). Nominalism, therefore, contrasts with *realism. *William of Ockham, *Hobbes, and certain modern analytic philosophers have all made varying statements of nominalist theory.

nomograph (*or* nomogram) A *graph showing the relationship between three variable quantities, enabling the value of one variable to be read off if the other two are known. It can take the form of a series of curves on a graph of two quantities, corresponding to constant values of a third. Or it can consist of three straight lines calibrated with the values of the variables. A fourth line is drawn between two known points on two of the straight lines: the point at which this fourth line cuts the third straight line gives the value of the unknown quantity.

Nonconformists In its original early-17th-century sense, the term referred to members of the Church of England who did not conform with its rituals. After the Act of Uniformity (1662), the term's scope widened to include members of dissenting Protestant sects, such as the Quakers and Methodists.

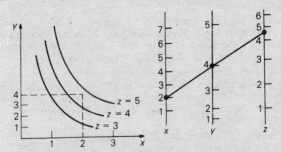

NOMOGRAPH *If x = 2 and y = 4, a value of approximately 4.5 for z is obtained from the two forms of nomograph shown.*

non-Euclidean geometry A form of *geometry in which *Euclid's postulates are not satisfied. In *Euclidean geometry if two lines are both at right angles to a third they never meet (i.e. they remain parallel). In, for example, hyperbolic (or elliptic) geometry they eventually diverge (or converge). Non-Euclidean geometry was developed independently by *Lobachevski (published 1831) and *Bolyai (published 1836). *See also* Riemannian geometry.

Non-Intercourse Act (1809) US law that allowed trade with nations except Britain and France until they stopped the blockade of neutral nations. It superseded the *Embargo Act of 1807.

Nono, Luigi (1924–90) Italian composer. A pupil of Francesco Malipiero (1882–1973), he married Schoenberg's daughter Nuria. Nono's compositions frequently employ serialism; many of them consist of settings of texts by Marxist writers. They include *La fabbrica illuminata* (for mezzo-soprano and tape; 1964) and *Non consumiamo Marx* (for voices and tape; 1969).

Nonproliferation of Nuclear Weapons, Treaty on the. *See* disarmament.

nonsense verse A genre of comic verse that is structured according to a kind of surreal logic that defies rational interpretation. It is characterized by strict rhyme schemes and the use of meaningless neologisms. The genre, predominantly English, is usually dated from the publication of *The Book of Nonsense* by Edward *Lear in 1846. Other outstanding writers of nonsense are Lewis *Carroll and Hilaire *Belloc. *See also* limerick.

Nootka A North American Indian people of the NW Pacific coast region who speak a *Wakashan language. They were traditionally hunters, fishers, and expert whale catchers, using large canoes and harpoons. They practiced the *potlatch as did their neighbors, the *Kwakiutl.

noradrenaline (*or* norepinephrine) A hormone that is secreted by the central core (medulla) of the adrenal glands. It is a *catecholamine, structurally similar to *adrenaline but producing different effects in certain target organs, especially the heart, the rate of which it decreases. Noradrenaline is taken up and stored by cells of the sympathetic nervous system and subsequently released by nerve endings to excite adjacent nerves in the transmission of impulses. In the hypothalamus it is thought to inhibit transmission of impulses.

Nordenskjöld, Nils Adolf Erik, Baron (1832–1901) Swedish navigator. After exploration in Spitsbergen he became the first, in the *Vega*, to navigate the *Northeast Passage (1878–79).

Norfolk 36 54N 76 18W A seaport in Virginia, on Hampton Roads. Founded in 1682, it suffered considerable damage in the American Revolution and the US Civil War. It is the headquarters of the US Atlantic Fleet. Norfolk's industries include textiles, cars, and ship building. Population (1990): 261,229.

Norfolk A county of E England, bordering on the North Sea. It is mainly agricultural with arable farming and intensive turkey rearing. Fishing is centered on Great Yarmouth. Tourism is important, especially in Great Yarmouth and on the Norfolk Broads. Area: 1067 sq mi (5355 sq km). Population (1987): 736,000. Administrative center: Norwich.

Norfolk, Thomas Howard, 3rd Duke of (1473–1554) English statesman; the uncle of two of Henry VIII's wives. He became president of the privy council in 1529 and in 1536 suppressed the *Pilgrimage of Grace. He lost power after 1542 and was imprisoned under Edward VI for involvement in treason (1546). His son **Thomas Howard, 4th Duke of Norfolk** (1538–72) was imprisoned (1559–60) by Elizabeth I for planning to marry Mary, Queen of Scots. He subsequently participated in *Ridolfi's plot against Elizabeth and was executed.

Norfolk Island 29 05S 167 59E A mountainous Australian island in the SW Pacific Ocean. Formerly a British penal colony, some of the descendants of the *Bounty* mutineers were resettled here from *Pitcairn Island (1856). Area: 14 sq mi (36 sq km). Population (1986): 2367. Chief town: Kingston.

Norman 35 13N 97 26W A city in central Oklahoma, on the Canadian River, SW of Oklahoma City. Founded in 1889, it became the home of the University of Oklahoma in 1892. Oil wells and petroleum production are important to the economy. Population (1990): 80,071.

Norman art and architecture The styles that flourished in Normandy and the lands that the Normans had conquered in the 11th and 12th centuries, notably the *romanesque architectural style. First appearing in England before the Norman conquest in Westminster Abbey (consecrated 1065), Norman architecture later developed into a distinctive native style. Characteristic Norman features include massive walls, rounded arches, two-tower church façades and abstract geometrical ornamentation on columns, etc. In S Italy the Norman style was fused with the native Saracen and Byzantine traditions. In the other arts the most notable Norman achievement was the *Bayeux tapestry.

Norman conquest (1066–72) The conquest of England by William, duke of Normandy (*see* William the Conqueror). After defeating Harold II at the battle of Hastings (1066), William captured London and was crowned. Local uprisings were suppressed by 1070 and with the defeat of the Scots in 1072 the conquest was complete. The Norman influence on Anglo-Saxon England was fundamental. Although structures of government continued virtually unaltered, the English aristocracy was replaced by Normans and other continentals and *feudalism was introduced. Latin became the language of government and Norman French, the literary language; the Norman influence was also felt in church organization and architecture.

Normandy (French name: Normandie) A former province in N France, on the English Channel. It now comprises the planning regions of **Basse-Normandie**, with an area of 6787 sq mi (17,583 sq km) and a population (1975 est) of 1,303,600, and **Haute-Normandie**, with an area of 4732 sq mi (12,258 sq km) and a population (1975 est) of 1,595,400. A fertile agricultural area with sheep and dairy farming, it also produces flax, hemp, and apples. *History*: during the medieval period Normandy flourished as a major state. William II, duke of Normandy, conquered England (1066) to become William I of England. Disputed between England and France during the following centuries, it finally reverted to France in 1449. During World War II it suffered severe damage, the Normandy invasion taking place in 1944.

Norman French The dialect spoken in Normandy during the early Middle Ages and by the Norman invaders of England. Their speech influenced English and introduced new words to the language.

Normans Viking settlers in N France (later Normandy) whose rule, under their leader Rollo, was formally recognized (911) by Charles the Simple (879–929; reigned 898–923). Further expansion in Normandy followed and by the end of the 11th century they had also conquered England (*see* Norman conquest) and much of S Italy and Sicily and had established crusading states in the E, besides gaining a foothold in Wales and Scotland. Noted for their military dynamism and inventiveness (they introduced the castle into England) they adopted and adapted existing administrative practices in countries they conquered with great success, normally possessing a stable government working in close harmony with the Church.

Norns In Norse mythology, the fates, three females who shape the life of man. They are Urth (the past), Verthandi (the present), and Skuld (the future).

Norris, Frank (Benjamin Franklin N.; 1870–1902) US naturalist writer. He was a correspondent for several newspapers and a magazine from 1895–1902. He wrote *McTeague* (1899) and the first two parts—*The Octopus* (1901) and *The Pit* (1903)—of a trilogy, *Epic of the Wheat*. The third part, *The Wolf*, was never finished.

Norrköping 58 35N 16 10E A port in SE Sweden, on an inlet of the Baltic Sea. Its industries include ship building, engineering, and textiles. Population (1992 est): 120,756.

Norsemen. *See* Vikings.

North, Frederick, Lord (1732–92) British statesman; prime minister (1770–82). He was a Lord of the Treasury (1759–65) and chancellor of the exchequer (1767–70) before becoming prime minister, as which his policies were largely dictated by George III. He was severely criticized for precipitating the *American Revolution (1775–83), and for British defeats in the conflict, and eventually resigned.

North America The third largest continent in the world, in the N of the W hemisphere bordering on the Arctic Ocean, the N Pacific Ocean, the N Atlantic Ocean, the Gulf of Mexico, and the Caribbean Sea. The Isthmus of Panama links it with South America. It is generally accepted as consisting of *Canada, the *United States of America, *Mexico, *Central America, *Greenland, and the *West Indies. The mountains of the Western Cordillera extend down its entire W coast descending E to the Great Plains before rising to the Appalachian Mountains further E, which are separated from the Canadian Shield by the Great Lakes. Area: over 9,500,000 sq mi (24,000,000 sq km). Population (1990 est): 400,000,000.

North American Free Trade Agreement (NAFTA) Pact among the United States, Canada, and Mexico to reduce and eliminate trade and other economic barriers among the three countries. Signed in December 1993, it went into effect on Jan 1, 1994, and was designed to be fully implemented over 15 years, forming a free-trade zone with a population of more than 370,000,000. Economic areas covered in the agreement included agriculture, manufacturing, and services. President Clinton made NAFTA's passage a centerpiece of his economic program but needed massive Republican support to push the bill through Congress.

North American Indian languages A geographical classification of the languages of the indigenous peoples of North America. It is estimated that these languages originally numbered about 300; at least a third of these are dead or dying out, but the number of speakers of a few, such as *Navaho, is increasing. Highly diverse, these languages have been classified in various ways and about 57 families have been identified. *Sapir arranged these into six phyla (1929): *Eskimo-*Aleut; *Algonkian-*Wakashan; *Na-Dené; *Penutian; *Hokan-*Siouan; and *Aztec-Tanoan.

Northampton 52 14N 0 54W A city in central England, the administrative center of Northamptonshire on the Nene River. A manufacturing center, Northampton has undergone considerable expansion since its designation as a new town in 1968. Population (1984): 163,000.

Northampton 39 59N 83 56W A city in W central Massachusetts, on the W bank of the Connecticut River, north of Springfield. Smith College (1871) is there. Products manufactured include cutting utensils, wiring, and optical instruments. Population (1990): 29,289.

North Atlantic Drift One of the major ocean currents of the world, flowing NE across the Atlantic from the *Gulf Stream.

North Atlantic Treaty Organization (NATO) An alliance formed in 1949 by Belgium, Canada, Denmark, France, Iceland, Italy, Luxembourg, the Netherlands, Norway, Portugal, the UK, and the US; Greece and Turkey joined in 1952, West Germany in 1955, and Spain in 1982. It was formed during the *Cold War to protect the Western world against possible Soviet aggression. All member states are bound to protect any member against attack. NATO began to reexamine its role in the early 1990s as the nations of eastern Europe turned away from communism, as the Soviet Union collapsed, and as weapons treaties diminished the threat of global war. NATO seeks to encourage economic and social cooperation among its member states. Its secretariat headquarters is in Brussels and its military headquarters near Mons.

North Borneo. *See* Sabah.

North Brabant (Dutch name: Noord-Brabant) A province in the S Netherlands, bordering on Belgium. Its fertile coastal lowlands, which produce wheat and sugar beet, were badly flooded in 1953. Area: 1896 sq mi (4911 sq km). Population (1988): 2,156,000. Capital: 's Hertogenbosch.

North Cape (Norwegian name: Nordkapp) 71 11N 25 40E A promontory in Norway, on the island of Magerøy. It is the most N point in Europe.

North Carolina A state in SE US. It is bounded on the N by Virginia, on the E by the Atlantic Ocean, on the S by South Carolina and Georgia, and on the W by Tennessee. The extensive coastal plain stretches westward—from the indented coastline to the Piedmont Plateau and the Appalachian Mountains in the E. It is heavily populated and the leading industrial state in the South, producing textiles, furniture, and processed foods. It is the nation's major producer of tobacco and tobacco products. *History*: first visited by Giovanni da Verrazano (1524), the region was inhabited by Tuscarora, Catawba, and Cherokee Indians. Sir Walter Raleigh tried and failed to establish the first British New World settlement there in the 1580s. With the colonization of the eastern seaboard, small farms gradually grew up, but settlement was hampered by political conflict with North Carolina's colonial proprietors from Virginia. Indian resistance also discouraged settlement. One of the 13 original colonies, it shares its early history with South Carolina. In 1713, North Carolina became a separate colony, and in 1729 it became a royal colony. At the time of the American Revolution it was the first colony to direct its delegates to vote for independence. Following the war, because of strong sentiments against a powerful central government, North Carolina did not ratify the US Constitution or become a state until 1789. The forced removal of the Cherokees (beginning in 1835) spurred expansion into the region. Although antislavery sentiments ran high, it supported the Confederate cause in the Civil War. Reconstruction marked the beginnings of the modern era; industry saw enormous growth and the traditional plantation system was replaced by farm tenancy. Expanded educational opportunities contributed to development, and following World War II industrial diversification and the arrival of hydroelectric power brought prosperity. North Carolina is a bellwether state, a forerunner in the area of social legislation and a major industrial force in the South. Area: 52,586 sq mi (136,197 sq km). Population (1990): 6,628,637. Capital: Raleigh.

North Dakota A state in the N central US. Minnesota lies to the E, South Dakota to the S, Montana to the W, and Canada to the N. It comprises three main physical regions: the Red River Valley along the E border, the Central Lowlands just W of this strip, and the Great Plains in the SW. The population is sparse, particularly in the W. Agriculture and mining are the two principal economic activities; its coal and oil reserves are among the country's largest and it is a major producer of wheat. The small manufacturing sector is growing, especially food processing. *History*: explored by Pierre de la Verendryé (1738) and the Lewis and Clark Expedition (1804–05), the area (except for a portion) formed part of the Louisiana Purchase (1803); the remainder was obtained from the British in 1818. Early attempts to settle were made by Scottish and Irish families at Pembina in 1812, but settlement was slow until the Indians were forcibly subdued in the 1860s. With the arrival of the railroads and the defeat of the Sioux chief Sitting Bull, the area was ripe for settlement. It formed part of the territory of Dakota from 1860 until 1889 when it was made a separate state. Large numbers of Europeans immigrated to the area in the late 1800s. Agrarian dissatisfaction and the emergence of the Populist party laid the groundwork for numerous reforms. Subsequently drought, dust storms, and the Depression of the 1930s brought severe hardship, but North Dakota experienced recovery with World War II. The construction of air bases and missile sites in the 1960s boosted the local economy. Oil was discovered in 1951 and with the energy shortage of the 1970s, the state undertook efforts to develop further its own energy supplies. Area: 70,665 sq mi (183,022 sq km). Population (1990): 638,800. Capital: Bismarck.

Northeast Caucasian languages A group of about 25 languages of the NE region of the Caucasus, also called the Nakho-Dagestanian family. Chechen, the most important, is part of the Nakh subdivision. The Dagestanian subdivision may be further divided into the Avar-Ando-Dido languages, of which Avar is the most important and the only one that is written; the Lakk-Dargwa languages; and the Lezgian languages.

Northeast Passage (Russian name: Severny Morskoy Put) The sea route along the N Eurasian coast, kept open in summer by Russian icebreakers. It was first traversed by the Swedish explorer Niels Nordenskjöld (1878–79). *See also* Northwest Passage.

Northern Areas The northernmost districts administered by, although technically not part of, Pakistan, principally Baltistan, Hunza, and Gilgit.

Northern Ireland. *See* Ireland.

Northern Marianas. *See* Mariana Islands.

Northern Rhodesia. *See* Zambia.

Northern Territory An administrative division of N central Australia, bordering on the Timor and Arafura Seas. It consists chiefly of a plateau with Arnhem Land in the N (containing Australia's largest Aborigine reservation) and the Macdonnell Ranges in the S. SW of Alice Springs and close to the geographical center of the continent stands *Ayers Rock. The main agricultural activity is the rearing of beef cattle; these are transported in trains of trailers (road trains) along the highways, the chief means of transport. Minerals are important, especially iron ore, manganese, copper, gold, and bauxite. There are also large deposits of uranium, as yet unexploited, but possibly containing a quarter of all the world's known resources of high-grade ore. In 1978 the Northern Territory became an independent state, although the federal government retained control over uranium. Area: 519,770 sq mi (1,346,200 sq km). Population (1992 est): 168,000. Capital: Darwin.

NORTHERN TERRITORY *A waterhole on the Finke River at Glen Helen Gorge 100 mi (160 km) W of Alice Springs.*

Northern War, Great (1700–21) The war fought between Russia, Denmark, and Poland, on one side, and Sweden, on the other. *Charles XII of Sweden, whose Baltic supremacy was opposed by his neighbors, defeated Denmark, then Russia at Narva (1700), and Poland (1706). He was subsequently overcome by the Russians under Peter the Great (Poltava, 1709) and fled to the Turks, who defeated the Russians at Pruth River (1711). After returning to Sweden Charles suffered a series of setbacks and was forced to initiate peace negotiations. At the same time he continued hostilities, in the course of which he died (1718). The war between Denmark, Poland, and Sweden was ended by the Treaties of Stockholm (1719–20). The Treaty of *Nystad (1721) between Russia and Sweden marked Russia's emergence as the major Baltic power.

North German Confederation (1867–71) An alliance of German states under Prussian leadership formed by Bismarck following victory in the Austro-Prussian War (1866). It formed the basis of the German Empire, proclaimed in 1871.

North Holland (Dutch name: Noord-Holland) A province in the W Nether-lands, between the North Sea and the IJsselmeer. Much of it lies below sea level. The province contains major urban centers, including Amsterdam, and its indus-trial activities include ship building, textiles, and motor vehicles. Its farms produce mainly dairy and livestock products. Area: 1124 sq mi (2912 sq km). Population (1988): 2,353,000. Capital: Haarlem.

North Island The most northerly of the two principal islands of New Zealand, separated from South Island by Cook Strait. It consists chiefly of a central vol-canic plateau with fertile coastal and valley lowlands. Area: 44,281 sq mi (114,729 sq km). Population (1991): 2,549,707.

North Ossetian Autonomous Republic An administrative division in Russia. The Ossetians are a Caucasian people, known for their wood and silver carving. The region has metal and oil deposits and industries include textiles and food processing. The main crops are grain, cotton, and grapes. Area: 3088 sq mi (8000 sq km). Population (1991 est): 642,500. Capital: Ordzhonikidze.

North Platte A river that rises in N central Colorado and flows N and then E through Wyoming into Nebraska where it meets the South Pla1980

tte River at North Platte to become the Platte River. Numerous dam/reservoir systems along the river provide irrigation and flood control for the surrounding valleys. Length: 680 mi (1095 km).

North Rhine-Westphalia (German name: Nordrhein-Westfalen) A *Land* in W Germany, bordering on the Netherlands and Belgium. It was formed in 1946. Rich in minerals, including coal, it contains the vast Ruhr industrial region and is one of the world's most densely populated areas. Its many industries include steel, textiles, and chemicals. Area: 13,147 sq mi (34,057 sq km). Population (1991 est): 17,349,700. Capital: Düsseldorf.

Northrop, John Howard (1891–1987) US biochemist, who isolated and pu-rified various digestive enzymes and showed that they were all proteins. He re-ceived the 1946 Nobel Prize.

North Sea A section of the Atlantic Ocean in NW Europe, between the British Isles and the continent N of the Strait of Dover. The entire floor is part of the continental shelf, with an average depth of about 914 ft (300 m). It is fished for over 5% of the world's catch, consisting especially of cod, herring, and mack-erel; recent exploitation of *North Sea oil and natural-gas finds have further in-creased its economic importance. Freak high tides have flooded large areas of coastal lowlands, especially in the Netherlands and E England.

North Sea oil The *oil deposits that were discovered under the North Sea in the 1960s. Exploration and development has been carried out by multinational companies from the US and Europe. The area is divided into UK, German, Nor-wegian, Danish, and Dutch sectors. The UK has the largest of these. Discovered reserves in the North Sea contain an estimated 2.5 billion tons but exploration is still continuing and new oil fields are being developed.

North Star. *See* Polaris.

North Uist. *See* Uist.

Northumberland The northernmost county of England, bordering on Scot-land and the North Sea. The main river, the Tyne, flows SE. There are outstand-ing Roman remains, notably Hadrian's Wall. The main agricultural activity is sheep farming. Area: 1944 sq mi (5033 sq km). Population (1981): 299,905. Ad-ministrative center: Newcastle-upon-Tyne.

Northumberland, John Dudley, Duke of (1502–53) English statesman, who was virtual ruler of England (1549–53) under Edward VI, a minor. In 1553 he married his son Guildford Dudley to Lady Jane *Grey, whom he persuaded the king to name as his heir. On Edward's death Jane was proclaimed queen but lack of support forced a surrender to Mary (I). Northumberland was executed.

Northumbria A kingdom of Anglo-Saxon England north of the Humber, formed in the 7th century by the union of the kingdoms of Deira and Bernicia. Northumbria became politically preeminent in England in the 7th century under *Edwin, Saint *Oswald, and *Oswin. Northumbrian scholarship was also unrivaled, boasting such great names as *Bede and *Alcuin. By 829, however, Northumbria had recognized the overlordship of Wessex and in the late 9th century its unity was destroyed by the Danes.

Northwest Caucasian languages A group of languages of the NW region of the Caucasus, also called the Abkhazo-Adyghian family. It includes Abkhaz, Abaza, Adyghian, Kabardian (Circassian), and Ubykh. All but Ubykh are written. A distinctive feature is the small number of vowel sounds and great number of consonants.

Northwest Company A Canadian fur-trading company, founded in 1783, that became a bitter rival of the *Hudson's Bay Company. Conflict between them ended in their forced merger in 1821.

North-West Frontier Province A province in NW Pakistan, SE of Afghanistan in the Himalayas and lower mountains. Its Pathan inhabitants mostly herd livestock or cultivate grains, fruit, sugarcane, and tobacco. There is little industry, but the province controls the strategic Khyber Pass to Afghanistan. Over the centuries each great power in the region has sought to control the province, but it has usually remained semiautonomous because of its rugged terrain and fierce inhabitants. Area: 28,773 sq mi (74,522 sq km). Population (1983 est): 11,658,000. Capital: Peshawar.

Northwest Ordinance (1787) US congressional ordinance that outlined government for territories carved out of the newly created Northwest Territory and any future territories. Each territory would have a congressionally appointed governor, secretary, and three judges. When a population of 5,000 males, eligible to vote, had been reached, the territory could elect a legislature and send one nonvoting representative to the US House of Representatives. Statehood could be attained with a population of at least 60,000. A minimum of three and maximum of five states could be carved from the Northwest Territory and all rights, including freedom from slavery, would be accorded citizens of the territory.

Northwest Passage The sea route along the coast of North America, between the Atlantic and Pacific Oceans. It was first traversed by Roald Amundsen (1903–06) and since 1969 has been used for transporting Alaskan oil. *See also* Northeast Passage.

Northwest Territories A territory of N Canada, stretching from 60°N to the North Pole. It consists of the districts of *Franklin, *Keewatin, and *Mackenzie. The territory has never undergone much development, largely because of its harsh climate. One of the most sparsely populated areas in the world, two-thirds of the people are Indians and Eskimos, who traditionally live nomadically by hunting, trapping, and fishing. The Eskimos are increasingly settling in larger communities around cooperatives and government institutions. Rich in mineral resources, the economy is dominated by the mining industry; pitchblende, silver zinc, lead, tungsten and gold are all extracted. The area also has vast oil reserves. In 1982 a plan to divide the Northwest Territories into two regions was approved by voters. An agreement was drawn up and signed in 1991, and a 1992 referendum authorized splitting up the territory. The eastern part, called Nunavut, meaning "Our Land," is to be administered by the Inuit (Eskimos). A seven-year transition period is planned. Area: 1,253,432 sq mi (3,246,389 sq km). Population (1991): 57,649. Capital: Yellowknife.

Northwest Territory Area established by Congress in 1787 and defined as W of Pennsylvania, N of the Ohio River to the Great Lakes, and E of the Mississippi River. The Northwest Ordinances (1785; 1787) determined the method of land sale and government. Eventually, the states of Ohio (1803), Indiana (1816), Illinois (1848), Michigan (1837), Wisconsin (1848), and a small part of Minnesota (1858) evolved from the territory.

Norway, Kingdom of (Norwegian name: Norge) A country in N Europe occupying the W part of the Scandinavian Peninsula. It borders on the Arctic Ocean (N), the Norwegian Sea (W), and the Skagerrak (S). It is largely mountainous, reaching heights of almost 8000 ft (2500 m), with a heavily indented coastline. There are numerous glaciers, and forests cover approximately one-quarter of the country. The archipelago of Svalbard and Jan Meyen Island are also part of Norway together with the dependencies of Bouvet Island, Peter I Island, and Queen Maud Land. Norway is one of the most sparsely populated countries on the continent. *Economy*: abundant hydroelectric power has enabled Norway to develop as an industrial nation. Chemicals, engineering, ship building, and food processing are all important while forestry is a major source of wealth, especially for the pulp and paper industry. Norway is one of the world's great fishing nations and fish is one of the principal exports. It also has one of the world's largest merchant fleets. Revenues from tourism are important. Minerals include iron ore, limestone, coal, copper, zinc, and lead. Heavy borrowing to finance the development of offshore oil and gas deposits (discovered 1968), which have proved to be considerably less than was first thought, led to a balance-of-payments deficit; however, Norway has become Europe's largest exporter of oil and natural gas. Its inhabitants enjoy one of the world's highest standards of living. *History*: its early history was dominated by the Vikings. The many local chieftains were not subjected to a single ruler until the reign of Harold I Haarfager (died c. 930). Christianity was introduced in the 10th century and became established under Olaf II Haraldsson (reigned 1015–28). During the reign (1204–63) of Haakon IV Haakonsson, Norway acquired Iceland and Greenland and in the 14th century, under Margaret, was united with Sweden and Denmark. Sweden broke free in 1523 but Norway remained under Danish domination until 1814, when it was united with Sweden under the Swedish crown, while maintaining internal self-government. Only in 1907 was full independence achieved. Norway declared its neutrality in both world wars but from 1940 to 1944 was occupied by the Germans, who established a government under Quisling. Abandoning isolationism after World War II, Norway joined the UN (of which the Norwegian Trygve Lie was first secretary general) and NATO. In 1972 Norwegians rejected membership of the EEC in a referendum. In common with other Scandinavian countries Norway has a highly developed social-welfare system. Head of state: Harald V. Prime Minister: Gro Harlem Brundtland. Official language: Norwegian. Official religion: Evangelical Lutheran. Official currency: Krone of 100 ore. Area: 125,053 sq mi (323,886 sq km). Population (1990 est): 4,214,000. Capital and main port: Oslo.

Norwegian A North Germanic language of the West Scandinavian division, spoken in Norway. There are two distinct forms known as Dano-Norwegian (Bokmål or Riksmål) and New Norwegian (Nynorsk or Landsmål). Bokmål derives from written Danish, the language used during the union with Denmark (1397–1814). Nynorsk was created by the scholar Ivar Aasen (1813–96) to revive the tradition of Old Norwegian, which was closely related to *Old Norse speech. Bokmål is more widely used.

Norwegian Antarctic Territory The area in Antarctica claimed by Norway, lying S of latitude 60°S and between longitudes 20°W and 45°E. It consists of the end of Coats Land, Queen Maud Land, and islands. There have been many research stations from various nations along the mountainous coast.

Norwich 52 38N 1 18E A city in E England, on the Wensum River. In the late 16th century it became a major textile center. It has a Norman cathedral (1096) and keep, many medieval churches, and is the site of the University of East Anglia (1963). Industries include shoe manufacturing, electrical and other machinery, food and drink, chemicals, printing, and bookbinding. Population (1991): 121,000.

nose The organ of smell, which is also an entrance to the respiratory tract. The external nose, which projects from the face, has a framework of bone and cartilage and is divided into two nostrils by the nasal septum. It leads to the nasal cavity, which is lined by *mucous membrane, extends back to the pharynx and windpipe, and is connected to the air *sinuses of the skull. Hairs in the nostrils filter particles from inhaled air, which is further cleaned, warmed, and moistened in the nasal cavity. The membrane at the top of the nasal cavity contains olfactory cells, which are sensitive to different smells and are connected to the brain via the olfactory nerve.

Nostradamus (Michel de Notredame; 1503–66) French physician and astrologer, who became famous with his publication of *Centuries* (1555–58), in which he made a number of prophecies in the form of rhyming quatrains. Some of his prophecies, which are obscure and open to various interpretations, appeared to come true and Charles IX appointed him his physician on his accession (1560).

notebook computer A small lightweight portable computer. Typically, a notebook computer weighs less than 6 lb (2.7 kg); it takes its name from the fact that it is about the size of a notebook. It can fit easily into a briefcase.

nothosaur A primitive marine reptile of the Jurassic period (200–135 million years ago); 0.98 in–20 ft (0.3–6 m) long, nothosaurs had a long neck and tail and long limbs partly modified into paddles. They fed on fish, which were gripped tightly with long sharp teeth.

notochord A flexible skeletal rod that runs along the length of the body in the embryos of all animals of the phylum Chordata (including vertebrates). In primitive chordates, such as the lancelets and lampreys, the notochord persists throughout life as the main axial support, but in vertebrates it is incorporated into the backbone as the embryo develops.

Notoungulata An extinct order of mammals whose remains have been found mainly in South America. Notoungulates ranged from small rabbitlike forms to the massive *Toxodon*, which stood over 7 ft (2 m) high at the shoulder. They had three-toed feet, with either claws or hooves, and lived from the Paleocene epoch to the Pleistocene epoch (about 70 million to 2.5 million years ago).

Notre-Dame de Paris The gothic cathedral built (1163–1345) on the Île de la Cité, Paris, to replace two earlier churches. The nave, choir, and west front were completed by 1204; the innovative flying buttresses and the great rose windows, which still retain their 13th-century stained glass, are notable features. Damaged during the French Revolution, Notre-Dame was saved from demolition and redecorated for Napoleon's coronation (1804) and was subsequently fully restored (1845–64) by *Viollet-le-Duc.

Nottingham 52 58N 1 10W A city in N central England, the administrative center of Nottinghamshire on the River Trent. Charles I raised his standard there in 1642 at the outbreak of the Civil War. Notable buildings include the castle (built by William the Conqueror and restored in 1878). Nottingham's chief industries are hosiery, bicycles, cigarettes, pharmaceuticals, engineering, brewing, and printing. The university dates from 1948. Population (1981): 271,080.

Nottinghamshire A county in the East Midlands of England. It consists mainly of lowlands, crossed by the Trent River, with the Pennine uplands in the W and the remnants of Sherwood Forest (famous for its associations with the Robin Hood legend) in the SW. Agriculture is important with arable and dairy farming, orchards, and market gardening. It contains important coalfields. Gypsum, limestone, and gravel are also extracted. The main industrial town is Nottingham. Area: 2164 sq km (835 sq mi). Population (1981): 982,631. Administrative center: Nottingham.

Nouakchott 18 09N 15 58W The capital of Mauritania, in the W near the Atlantic coast. A small village until the 1950s, it was developed as the capital after independence in 1960. Its modern port is situated 4 mi (6.4 km) from the city. Population (1988): 393,325.

Nouméa 22 16S 166 26E The capital of New Caledonia. A port, it exports nickel, chrome, manganese, and iron. Population (1989): 65,110.

nouveau roman An experimental type of novel pioneered by French writers in the 1950s. The leading exponents include Nathalie *Sarraute, Alain *Robbe-Grillet, and Michel *Butor. Reacting against traditional realistic concepts of character and narrative, their works are characterized by a distrust of psychological motives, detailed descriptions of external reality, and the avoidance of any kind of value judgment.

Nouvelle Vague. *See* New Wave.

nova A star that suddenly increases in brightness by perhaps 10,000 times or more and then fades over months or years, usually to its original brightness. Novae all appear to occur in binary systems in which there is (usually) a *white dwarf with a large close companion star. Gaseous material flowing from the large star is thought to accumulate on the white dwarf and trigger the immense nova eruption. Novae are considered *variable stars.

Novalis (Friedrich Leopold, Freiherr von Hardenberg; 1772–1801) German romantic poet and writer. After studying law, he became an auditor. The death of his fiancée (1797) inspired his celebration of death and love in the *Hymnen an die Nacht* (1800); he himself died prematurely of tuberculosis. His unfinished novel *Heinrich von Ofterdingen* (1802) typifies the romantic belief in the transforming power of art.

Nova Lisboa. *See* Huambo.

Novara 45 27N 08 37E A city in NW Italy, in Piedmont. It has several notable buildings, including a 13th-century town hall. As well as a rice-milling industry, there are textile and chemical plants. Population (1991 est): 103,349.

Nova Scotia A province of E Canada. It consists of a peninsula protruding into the Atlantic Ocean, and *Cape Breton Island. Mostly rolling hills and valleys, Nova Scotia was originally covered by mixed forest but has been largely replanted with conifers. Economic growth is restricted by limited resources and the distance from important markets. Coal output is down significantly, but Nova Scotia also mines gypsum, salt, and copper. Agriculture includes dairying, mixed farming, livestock, and fruit. Iron and steel, pulp and paper, fishing, and tourism are also economically important. *History*: from the first colonization (1605), Britain and France contested the area, Britain eventually gaining possession (confirmed by the Treaty of Paris in 1763). Largely settled by Scots, Nova

Scotia prospered in the 19th-century age of sail. But since joining Canada (1867), its economy has lagged. Area: 20,402 sq mi (52,841 sq km). Population (1991): 899,942. Capital: Halifax.

Novaya Zemlya A Russian archipelago off the N coast, between the Barents and the Kara Seas. It is a continuation of the Ural Mountains and consists almost entirely of two islands separated by a narrow strait. There is no permanent population, and the N island is always icebound. Total area: about 32,040 sq mi (83,000 sq km).

novel An extended work of prose fiction dealing with the interaction of characters in a real or imagined setting. The term derives from Italian *novella*, meaning a short tale or anecdote. Latin forerunners of the novel are the picaresque *Satyricon* of Petronius (1st century AD) and *The Golden Ass* by Apuleius (2nd century AD). Cervantes's *Don Quixote* (1605) is considered the most important early novel. In England, a particular combination of social, economic, and literary conditions led to the development of the novel in the 18th century. The first notable English novelists included *Richardson, *Fielding, and *Defoe. The novels of the great 19th-century writers, notably *Melville and *Twain in the US, *Dickens in England, *Tolstoy and *Dostoievsky in Russia, and *Balzac and *Flaubert in France, together constitute one of the great achievements of world literature. In the 20th century the novel has been strongly influenced by developments in psychology and philosophy, and the various proliferating categories of novel—such as *science fiction, the *detective story, and the *nouveau roman—appeal to all levels of readership. *See also* picaresque novel.

November Eleventh month of the year. Derived from *novem*, which means nine in Latin, it was the ninth month in the ancient Roman calendar. It has 30 days. The zodiac signs for November are Scorpio and Sagittarius; the flower is the chrysanthemum, and the birthstone is the topaz. In the US, Veterans Day is Nov 11, and Thanksgiving is celebrated on the fourth Thursday of the month.

Novgorod 58 30N 31 20E A city in Russia, on the Volkhov River. It has varied manufacturing industries and is a famous tourist center, although many of its magnificent buildings, including the St Sofia Cathedral (1045–50), were badly damaged during World War II. *History*: it is one of Russia's oldest towns, dating at least to the 9th century, and was a notable trading center in the Middle Ages. Self-governing from 1019, it was forced to acknowledge Tatar overrule in the 13th century and that of Moscow in the 15th century. It was held by the Swedes from 1611 to 1619 and subsequently declined. Population (1991 est): 233,800.

Novi Sad 45 15N 19 15E A port in N central Yugoslavia, in Serbia on the Danube River. It is an important center of Serbian culture with a university (1960). Population (1991): 264,533.

Novokuznetsk 53 45N 87 12E A city in W central Russia. Kuznetsk, a village on the right bank of the Tom River, was founded in 1617 and the industrial town of Stalinsk was developed on the opposite bank in the 1930s. The conurbation was named Novokuznetsk in 1961. It has two large iron plants and is the center of a coal-mining region. Population (1991 est): 601,900.

Novosibirsk 55 04N 83 05E A city in W central Russia, on the Ob River and the Trans-Siberian Railroad. The most important economic center in Siberia, it has machine-building, textile, chemical, and metallurgical industries. Nearby is the Academic Community (Akademgorodk), a complex of science research institutes. Population (1991 est): 1,446,000.

Novotný, Antonín (1904–75) Czechoslovak statesman. One of the founding members of the Czechoslovak Communist party (1921), he was first secretary of the party (1953–68) and president of Czechoslovakia (1957–68). He was forced to resign in the face of the reform movement led by *Dubček, after whose fall Novotný was reinstated as a party member.

Noyes, Alfred (1880–1958) British poet. He wrote patriotic verse about the sea and several epic narrative poems including *Drake* (1906–08) and *The Torchbearers* (1922–30). His traditional views on literature and politics were expressed in his literary criticism and his autobiography, *Two Worlds for Memory* (1953).

Nu, U (*or* Thakin Nu; 1907–) Burmese statesman; prime minister (1948–56, 1957–58, 1960–62). A leading nationalist from the 1930s, he became prime minister on the achievement of independence. He sought to establish parliamentary democracy but when his Anti-Fascist People's Freedom League split in 1958 he was forced by *Ne Win to resign. He was restored, together with parliamentary government, in 1960 but was again deposed in 1962 and in 1966 withdrew into exile. He returned to Burma in 1980 and, in 1984, helped to found the National League for Democracy.

Nubia A region of NE Africa, in the Nile valley, approximately between Aswan (Egypt) and Khartoum (Sudan). Much of Nubia is now drowned by Lake Nasser. From about 2000 BC the Egyptians gradually occupied Nubia, which they called Cush. Trade, especially in gold, flourished. By the 15th century BC Nubia had an Egyptian viceroy. As Egyptian power waned, Nubian kings, based at Napata and *Meroë, became influential, even dominating Egypt itself (c. 730–670). Their independent nation, culture, and language lasted until the 4th century AD.

Nubian Desert A desert in the NE Sudan, between the Nile River and the Red Sea. It consists of a sandstone plateau with peaks of up to 7411 ft (2259 m) near the coast. Area: about 154,408 sq mi (400,000 sq km).

nuclear energy The energy evolved by nuclear fission or nuclear fusion. The energy is liberated in fission when a heavy atomic nucleus, such as uranium, splits into two or more parts, the total mass of the parts being less than the mass of the original nucleus. This difference in mass is equivalent to the *binding energy of the nucleus and most of it is converted into kinetic energy (i.e. the increased velocity with which the parts move) according to Einstein's law, $E = mc^2$. In a fusion reaction, two light nuclei, such as hydrogen or deuterium, combine to form a stable nucleus, such as helium; as the nucleus formed is lighter than the sum of the component nuclei, again energy is released in accordance with Einstein's law.

In the case of fission, when a nucleus of uranium 235 atom is struck by a neutron, a U-236 nucleus is formed, which immediately splits into two roughly equal parts, two or three neutrons being liberated at the same time. As these neutrons can then cause further fissions, a chain reaction builds up and a lump of U-235 will disintegrate almost instantaneously with enormous explosive power, provided that it is in excess of the critical mass (*see* nuclear weapons).

In nuclear power stations the fission reaction is harnessed to produce heat at a controlled rate (to raise steam to drive a turbine) in one of two ways. Both use natural uranium, which contains only 0.7% of the fissionable U-235 isotope, nearly all of the rest being the isotope U-238. The U-238 isotope absorbs the fast-moving neutrons emitted by the fission of U-235 and prevents a chain reaction from occurring in natural uranium. There are, however, two ways of producing a chain reaction. One is to use a moderator to slow down the fast neutrons so that they are not absorbed by U-238 nuclei (*see* thermal reactor). The other is to enrich the natural uranium with extra quantities of U-235 (or plutonium-239) so that there are sufficient neutrons to sustain the chain reaction in spite of absorption by U-238 (*see* fast reactor). All present commercial reactors are thermal, although the fast reactor is under development.

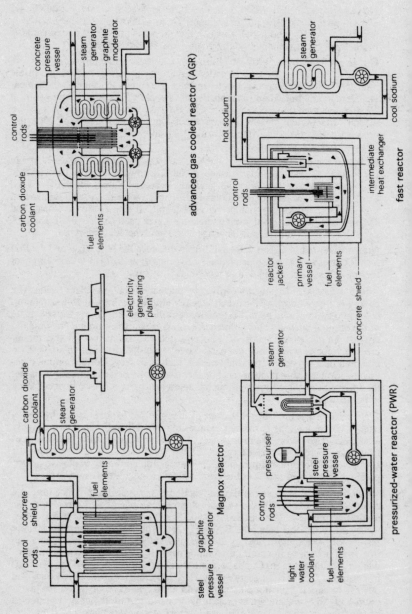

NUCLEAR ENERGY

Magnox reactor

control rods
concrete shield
steel pressure vessel
graphite moderator
fuel elements
carbon dioxide coolant
steam generator
electricity generating plant

advanced gas cooled reactor (AGR)

control rods
carbon dioxide coolant
fuel elements
concrete pressure vessel
steam generator
graphite moderator

pressurized-water reactor (PWR)

control rods
light water coolant
fuel elements
pressuriser
steel pressure vessel
steam generator
concrete shield

fast reactor

control rods
hot sodium
cool sodium
steam generator
reactor jacket
primary vessel
fuel elements
intermediate heat exchanger
concrete shield

1857

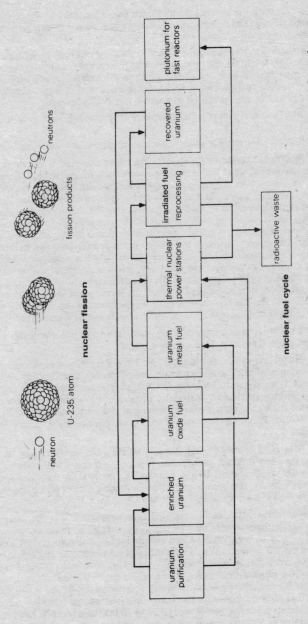

NUCLEAR ENERGY

U-235 atom   fission products

neutron   neutrons

nuclear fission

uranium purification → enriched uranium → uranium oxide fuel → uranium metal fuel → thermal nuclear power stations → irradiated fuel reprocessing → recovered uranium → plutonium for fast reactors

radioactive waste

nuclear fuel cycle

NUCLEAR ENERGY *Natural uranium metal fuel clad in Magnox (magnesium alloy) is used in Magnox thermal reactors. Enriched uranium dioxide pellets clad in steel are used in AGR and PWR fuel elements. Plutonium for fast reactors and recycled enriched uranium is obtained by reprocessing spent fuel from thermal reactors. The electricity generating plant is similar with all reactor types.*

The fusion process is the basis of the hydrogen bomb (*see* nuclear weapons) and the □thermonuclear reactor, which is unlikely to be a source of energy until the 21st century.

The importance of nuclear energy is that it will almost certainly be increasingly needed to supply world energy requirements as reserves of fossil fuels diminish. It is also important as a source of energy to power submarines, a very small quantity of nuclear fuel providing a very large amount of energy—about 7×10^{13} joules per kilogram, compared to about 4×10^7 J/kg for coal.

nuclear fission. *See* fast reactor; nuclear energy; nuclear weapons; thermal reactor.

nuclear fusion. *See* nuclear energy; nuclear weapons; thermonuclear reactor.

nuclear magnetic resonance (NMR) An effect observed when an atomic nucleus is exposed to radio waves in the presence of a magnetic field. A strong magnetic field causes the magnetic moment of the nucleus to precess around the direction of the field, only certain orientations being allowed by quantum theory. A transition from one orientation to another involves the absorption or emission of a photon, the frequency of which is equal to the precessional frequency. With magnetic field strengths customarily used the radiation is in the radio-frequency band. If radio-frequency radiation is supplied to the sample from one coil and is detected by another coil, while the magnetic field strength is slowly changed, radiation is absorbed at certain field values, which correspond to the frequency difference between orientations. An NMR spectrum consists of a graph of field strength against detector response. This provides information about the structure of molecules and the positions of electrons within them, as the orbital electrons shield the nucleus and cause them to resonate at different field strengths.

nuclear reactor A device for producing *nuclear energy in a usable form. *See* fast reactor; thermal reactor; thermonuclear reactor.

Nuclear Regulatory Commission (NCR) US agency that licenses and regulates the uses of nuclear energy to protect public health and safety and the environment. It regulates the building and operating of nuclear reactors and the ownership and use of nuclear materials. Inspections after licensing are routinely carried out by the commission to ensure adherence to safety rules. Established in 1974, it took over functions formerly assigned to the Atomic Energy Commission.

Nuclear Test-Ban Treaty (1963) A treaty banning nuclear testing by its signatories on the ground, in the atmosphere, in space, and under water. The signatories were the US, the Soviet Union, and the UK; many other countries agreed to adhere to the treaty. It made no attempt to limit nuclear stockpiling and therefore was rejected as ineffectual by France and China. *See also* disarmament.

nuclear weapons Missiles, bombs, shells, or land mines that use fission or fusion of nuclear material (*see* nuclear energy) yielding enormous quantities of heat, light, blast, and radiation. The first **atomic bomb** (*or* fission bomb), manufactured by the US in World War II, was dropped on Hiroshima in 1945. It consisted of two small masses of uranium 235 forced together by a chemical explosion to form a supercritical mass, in which an uncontrolled chain reaction occurred. Below the critical mass (estimated at between 35–44 lb [16–20 kg]) a chain reaction does not occur, as too many neutrons escape from the surface. The bomb had an explosive power equivalent to 20,000 tons of TNT. Later models used plutonium 239 to even greater effect.

The **hydrogen bomb** (fusion bomb *or* thermonuclear bomb) consists of an atom bomb surrounded by a layer of hydrogenous material, such as lithium deuteride.

The atom bomb creates the necessary temperature (about 180,000,000°F [100,000,000°C]) needed to ignite the fusion reaction (*see* thermonuclear reactor). Hydrogen bombs have an explosive power measured in tens of megatons (millions of tons) of TNT. The first hydrogen bomb was exploded by US scientists on Eniwetok Atoll in 1952 and although it has never been used in war, hydrogen bombs have been tested by the Soviet Union, Britain, France, and China. Further testing was prohibited by the *Nuclear Test-Ban Treaty of 1963. The **neutron bomb** (*or* enhanced radiation bomb) is a nuclear weapon designed to maximize neutron radiation. It is lethal to all forms of life but, having reduced blast, leaves buildings, etc., relatively undamaged.

nucleic acids Organic compounds, found in the cells of all living organisms, that consist of a mixture of nitrogenous bases (purines and pyrimidines), phosphoric acid, and a pentose sugar. The sugar is ribose in the ribonucleic acids (*see* RNA) and deoxyribose in the deoxyribonucleic acids (*see* DNA). Nucleic acids store genetic information in living organisms and interpret that information in protein synthesis. *See also* nucleoprotein.

nucleolus A small dense body, one or more of which can be seen within the *nucleus of a nondividing cell. It contains RNA and protein and is involved in the synthesis of *ribosomes.

nucleon A collective name for a proton or neutron. *See also* mass number.

nucleoprotein A compound consisting of a *nucleic acid associated with one or more proteins. The nucleoprotein of cell nuclei—the chromosomes—consists of DNA and proteins, mainly histones; cytoplasmic nucleoproteins—the *ribosomes—are ribonucleoproteins comprising some 60% protein and 40% RNA. *Viruses also consist of nucleoprotein.

nucleus (biology) A large granular component of nearly all □cells. It is usually spherical or ovoid in shape and is surrounded by a nuclear membrane, which is perforated with pores to allow exchange of materials between the nucleus and cytoplasm. The nucleus contains the *chromosomes, made up of the hereditary material (DNA), and is therefore essential for the control and regulation of cellular activities, such as growth and metabolism. During cell division the chromosomes are involved in the transfer of hereditary information (*see* meiosis; mitosis).

nucleus (physics) The central core of the atom (*see* atomic theory) discovered by Rutherford in 1911. All nuclei consist of protons and neutrons (jointly called nucleons), except for hydrogen, which consists of a single proton. The constituent nucleons are held together by the *strong interaction, which at the minute distances within the nucleus (of the order 10^{-15} m) is some one hundred times stronger than the electromagnetic interaction between protons. The number of protons in the nucleus determines its charge and atomic number; the number of neutrons (in addition to the number of protons) determines the mass number and the isotope. **Nuclear physics** is the study of the structure and reactions of the nucleus. *See also* particle physics.

Nuevo Laredo 27 30N 99 30W A city in N Mexico, on the Rio Grande. It is an important point of entry from Mexico into the US. Population (1980): 203,300.

Nu Jiang. *See* Salween River.

Nuku'alofa 21 09S 175 14W The capital of Tonga in the S Pacific, in N Tongatabu. It is the site of the Royal Palace (1865–67) and Royal Tombs. Copra and bananas are exported. Population (1986): 28,900.

Nukus 42 28N 59 07E A city in Uzbekistan, the capital of the Kara-Kalpak associated republic, on the Amu Darya River. Its industries include food processing. Population (1991 est): 179,600.

Nullarbor Plain A plain of SW South Australia and SW Western Australia, bordering on the Great Australian Bight. It consists of a treeless arid plateau with extensive limestone areas and is crossed by the Trans-Australian Railway. Area: 100,000 sq mi (260,000 sq km).

numbat A rat-sized *marsupial, *Myrmecobius fasciatus*, of open eucalyptus woods in SW Australia, also called marsupial (*or* banded) anteater. It is slender and rust-colored, with white stripes across the back and a long tail, and it feeds on ants and termites with its long sticky tongue. Numbats have no pouch. Family: *Dasyuridae*.

NUMBAT *This marsupial is well adapted for feeding on ants and termites, having a long sticky tongue, many small teeth, and powerful claws for digging up nests.*

numbers Mathematical symbols used to denote quantity. The natural numbers, 1, 2, 3, 4, 5 . . . , etc., were developed first by the Hindus and Arabs for simple counting. Subtraction led to negative numbers and to zero, which together with natural numbers make up the set of integers . . . $-3, -2, -1, 0, 1, ...$ Division of whole numbers results in fractions or rational numbers. Some numbers, such as $\sqrt{2}$, cannot be expressed as the ratio of two integers. These are called irrational numbers and they occur as the solutions to simple algebraic equations. They can be calculated to any required accuracy but cannot be written as exact values. Other numbers, called transcendental numbers, do not come from algebraic relationships. Some of these occur as basic properties of space, for example π, the ratio of a circumference of a circle to its diameter. Real numbers include all rational and irrational numbers. The equation $x^2 = -1$ can have no real solution for x, since the square of any number is positive.

The imaginary number, $i = \sqrt{-1}$, was introduced to overcome this problem. *See* complex numbers; number theory.

Numbers The fourth book of the Old Testament, attributed to Moses. It derives its name from the two records of a census that it mentions. The narrative covers the Israelites' journey from Mt Sinai to the borders of Canaan and gives the reasons for their failure to enter Canaan. It recounts the subsequent 40 years wandering in the wilderness and includes miscellaneous laws relevant to the eventual occupation of the Promised Land.

number theory The study of the properties of *numbers. It includes various theorems about *prime numbers, many of which are unproved but apparently true, and the study of Diophantine equations (named for *Diophantus of Alexandria), i.e. equations that have only integer solutions. *Fermat's last theorem deals with the solution of one of these equations and is a famous unproved theorem. Although number theory has existed for thousands of years, its development has been continuous and it now includes analytic number theory, originated by *Euler in 1742; geometric number theory, which uses such geometrical methods of analysis as Cartesian coordinates (*see* coordinate systems), *vectors, and *matrices; and probabilistic number theory, based on *probability theory.

Numidia An ancient kingdom of N Africa, W of *Carthage. Its *Berber population was nomadic until Masinissa (c. 240–149 BC), Rome's ally during the second and third *Punic Wars, promoted agriculture and urbanization. After supporting Pompey against Julius Caesar (46 BC), Numidia lost its monarchy and became part of the Roman province of Africa.

numismatics (*or* coin collecting) Collecting and studying coins, medals, or banknotes as a hobby or as a form of historical research. Collecting Greek and Roman coins became popular among aristocrats in Renaissance Italy, although collections then often included copies. During the 19th century numismatics became popular among a wider public; catalogues were produced and societies formed. Museums are now the greatest collectors, while private collectors usually specialize in one field. Coins in good condition are a form of investment, the best being "proof" coins, struck especially for sale to collectors.

Nummulites A genus of protozoan animals, sometimes called money fossils, that was abundant during the Eocene epoch (about 54–38 million years ago) although only one species has survived. Some limestones are almost entirely composed of their shells, which were disk-shaped and biconvex. Order: *Foraminifera*.

nunatak A rock peak protruding above the surface of an ice sheet. Nunataks occur in Greenland, the word originating from the Eskimo language.

Nuneaton 52 32N 1 28W A city in central England, in Warwickshire. Besides its coal-mining industry, Nuneaton manufactures textiles, cardboard boxes, and bricks. Its name refers to the 12th-century Benedictine nunnery, now in ruins. Population (1984): 72,000.

Nuremberg (German name: Nürnberg) 49 27N 11 05E A city in Germany, in Bavaria on the Pegnitz River. It was severely bombed during World War II because of its engine industry and is now a major center of the metalworking and electrical industries. It shares a university with Erlangen. *History*: a medieval trading center, it became the center of the German Renaissance, when the mastersingers' contests were held there. It was the site of the Nazi party congresses (1933–38) and the war-crime trials following World War II. It is the birthplace of Albrecht Dürer and Hans Sachs. Population (1991 est): 494,000.

Nuremberg Trials (1945–46) The trials of *Nazi criminals after World War II. An international military court was set up by the Allied Powers in Nuremberg to try Nazi individuals or groups who had violated the rules of war or committed crimes against humanity, such as the mass murders of Jews in *concentration camps. Twelve men were sentenced to hang (including Göring, who committed suicide before the sentence could be carried out, Ribbentrop, Frank, Streicher, and Jodl) and six others were imprisoned for various terms (including Hess, who remained in Spandau until his death). The trials of the war criminals created precedents, chiefly that war crimes are the responsibility not merely of the state but also of the individual.

Nureyev, Rudolf (1938–93) Russian ballet dancer. He danced with the Leningrad Kirov Ballet from 1958 until 1961, when he defected from Russia. In 1962 he joined the Royal Ballet, where he frequently partnered Margot *Fonteyn in such ballets as *Giselle* and *Swan Lake*. In 1977 he starred in the film *Valentino*. He became an Austrian citizen in 1982.

Nurhachi (1559–1626) Manchu chieftain, who founded the Qing dynasty of China. He unified the Juchen tribes of Manchuria to found the Manchu state. He organized all his subjects under the *Banner System, creating a powerful base from which his successors conquered all China.

Nurmi, Paavo Johannes (1897–1973) Finnish middle-distance and long-distance runner. He broke over 20 world records and won 12 Olympic medals, 9 gold and 3 silver. He was Olympic 10,000 meters champion in 1920 and 1928 and in 1924 won both the 1500 meters and the 5000 meters. He was in the habit of running carrying a stopwatch.

nursery rhymes Traditional verses said or sung to small children. They are usually for amusement only, although some, such as counting rhymes, are also instructional. They vary greatly in age and origin: some probably originate in ancient folklore, while others were first composed as popular ballads in the 19th century. The earliest known collection, *Tommy Thumb's Song Book* (1744), includes such perennial favorites as "Sing a Song of Sixpence" and "Who Killed Cock Robin?"

nurse shark A *shark, *Ginglymostoma cirratum*, that occurs in warm shallow waters of the Atlantic Ocean. Yellow-brown or gray-brown and up to 14 ft (4.2 m) long, it is considered dangerous to man only when provoked. Live young are born. Family: *Orectolobidae*.

nursing The medical specialty concerned with the care of the sick. Nursing originated in the religious orders, becoming increasingly secularized in Protestant countries after the Reformation; the standards of professional nursing were established by Florence *Nightingale after her work in the Crimea. Nurses are responsible for the day-to-day welfare of patients and for carrying out routine medical and surgical procedures under the supervision of a doctor. Apart from nursing in hospitals, the profession includes the work of nurse-midwives, home and school nurses, public health nurses, nurse practitioners, and physicians' assistants.

Nusa Tenggara (former name: Lesser *Sunda Islands) A volcanic Indonesian island group E of Java, the chief islands being Bali, Lombok, Sumbawa, Sumba, Flores, and Timor. Area: 28,241 sq mi (73,144 sq km).

nut Loosely, any edible nonsucculent fruit, including the groundnut (peanut) and Brazil nut. Botanically, a nut is a large dry fruit containing a single seed that is not released from the fruit at maturity. An example is the chestnut.

nutcracker A songbird of the genus *Nucifraga* found in coniferous forests of E Europe and Asia. The nutcracker (*caryocatactes*) is dark brown speckled with white, about 13 in (32 cm) long, and cracks open pine cones with its sharp bill to extract the seeds. Clark's nutcracker (*N. columbianus*) is gray with a black tail and wings patched with white. Family: *Corvidae* (crows, jays, magpies).

nuthatch A small stocky bird belonging to a family (*Sittidae*: 30 species) occurring everywhere except South America and New Zealand. Nuthatches have long straight bills, for hammering open nuts, and long-clawed toes, for running up and down tree trunks in search of insects. The European nuthatch (*Sitta europaea*), about 5.5 in (14 cm) long, has a blue-gray upper plumage with paler underparts and a black eyestripe.

nutmeg A fragrant tropical evergreen tree, *Myristica fragrans*, native to Indonesia but widely cultivated in SE Asia and the West Indies. Growing to 65 ft (20 m) high, it has oval pointed leaves and tiny male and female flowers borne on separate trees. The yellow fleshy fruit, about 1.2 in (3 cm) across, splits when ripe to expose the seed, which has a red fleshy covering (aril). The dried aril (mace) and whole or ground seeds (nutmeg) are used as spices. Family: *Myristicaceae*.

nutria. *See* coypu.

nux vomica A poisonous evergreen tree, *Strychnos nux-vomica*, also called the koochla tree, native to lowlands of Myanmar and India. It has simple leaves and clusters of tubular flowers, each with five spreading lobes. The seeds of the orangelike fruits contain the highly poisonous substances strychnine and curare. Family: *Strychnaceae*.

Nuzi An ancient *Hurrian city SW of Kirkuk (N Iraq). Nuzi flourished in the 15th century BC before being absorbed into the Assyrian Empire. Excavations here in the 1920s revealed a prosperous trading center with archives detailing legal, commercial, and military activities.

nyala An antelope, *Tragelaphus angasi*, of SW Africa. About 40 in (100 cm) high at the shoulder, nyalas are shy and nocturnal, inhabiting dense undergrowth, and have spiral-shaped horns and a grayish-brown coat with vertical white stripes on the flanks. The mountain nyala (*T. buxtoni*) lives in mountainous regions of S Ethiopia.

Nyasa, Lake. *See* Malawi, Lake.

Nyeman River. *See* Neman River.

Nyerere, Julius (Kambarage) (1922–　　) Tanzanian statesman; president (1962–85). Educated at Makerere College (Uganda) and Edinburgh University, in 1954 Nyerere formed the Tanganyika African National Union, which led the fight for independence (achieved in 1960). He became chief minister (1960), prime minister (1961), and then president of Tanganyika, which was renamed Tanzania in 1964 after union with Zanzibar. Nyerere defended the one-party state as being more appropriate for a developing country and was a prominent advocate of African unity. Under his leadership Tanzania raised its literacy rate dramatically and was instrumental in the overthrow of Amin in Uganda in 1979. He retired as president in 1985 while retaining party leadership.

Nyköping 58 45N 17 03E A seaport in E Sweden, on the Baltic coast. A center of commerce and industry, its manufactures include machinery and textiles. Population (1978 est): 64,099.

nylon A synthetic material with a translucent creamy white appearance, widely used both in fiber form and in solid blocks because of its lightness, toughness, and elasticity. It is made by *polymerization of diamine with *fatty acid or by polymerizing a single monomer, in both cases to form a polyamide. Nylon is used to make small engineering components, such as bearings and gears, because it is hard wearing and easy to machine. It is also spun and woven into fabrics for clothing, etc., and can be colored with pigments. Introduced commercially in 1938, nylon was the first truly synthetic fiber.

nymph A stage in the life cycle of insects that show incomplete *metamorphosis, including dragonflies, grasshoppers, and bugs. The egg hatches into a nymph, which undergoes a series of molts to form a line of nymphs that show increasing similarity to the adult.

nymphalid butterfly A butterfly belonging to the widely distributed family *Nymphalidae*, also called brush-footed butterfly. Nymphalids are characterized by small hairy forelegs, useless for walking. Many, including the migratory *red admiral and *painted lady, are strong fast fliers. The adults are generally orange or brown with black markings and the caterpillars are commonly brown or black and covered with branched spines.

Nymphenburg porcelain Porcelain produced at a factory established (1753) near Munich. It is famed for rococo figures designed by F. A. Bustelli (1723–64). They include Italian comedy, chinoiserie, and mythological models. After Bustelli died, tablewares, particularly tea services, were made, often based on Meissen. The factory still copies its early models.

nymphs In Greek mythology, female spirits of nature, often portrayed as youthful and amorous dancers or musicians. They were long-lived, though not immortal, and usually benevolent. The several classes of nymphs associated with particular natural phenomena include the *dryads, the *naiads, and the *nereids.

Nyoro A Bantu-speaking people of the W lakes region of Uganda. They were traditionally divided into three distinct groups: the Bito clan from whom the hereditary paramount chief (Mukama) always came, the aristocratic Huma pastoralists, and the subordinate Iru cultivators. The Bito and Huma are thought to have originally come from the N as conquering invaders. They are a patrilineal people who live in small scattered settlements.

Nysa River. *See* Neisse River.

Nystad, Treaty of (1721) The peace treaty between Russia and Sweden that concluded the Great *Northern War. Sweden was obliged to cede large tracts of territory, including Livonia, and Russia gained its long-coveted access to the Baltic Sea, thus becoming a European power.

Nyx (Latin name: Nox) A Greek goddess, the personification of night. She was the daughter of Chaos and her offspring included Thanatos (Death), Hypnos (Sleep), the *Fates, and *Nemesis. She lived in Tartarus, from which she emerged as Hemera, the goddess of day.

O

Oahu An island in Hawaii, the most populous and the administrative center. The Japanese attack on *Pearl Harbor (1941) was decisive in bringing the US into World War II. Area: 608 sq mi (1584 sq km). Chief city: Honolulu.

oak A deciduous or evergreen □tree or shrub of the genus *Quercus* (over 800 species), found in N temperate and subtropical regions. The simple leaves usually have lobed or toothed margins and the yellow male catkins and tiny green female flowers are borne on the same tree. The fruit—an acorn—is a hard oval nut partly enclosed by a round cup. Often 98–131 ft (30–40 m) high, many species are important timber trees, especially the common or pedunculate oak (*Q. robur*) and the *durmast oak (both Eurasian) and the North American white oak (*Q. alba*) and live oaks. Several are planted for ornament, including the Eurasian Turkey oak (*Q. cerris*), the North American red oak (*Q. rubra*), which has a red autumn foliage, and the Mediterranean *holm oak. The cork oak (*Q. suber*) is the main commercial source of *cork. Family: *Fagaceae*.

Oakland 37 50N 122 15W A port in California, on San Francisco Bay and connected with San Francisco by the San Francisco–Oakland Bay Bridge (1936). Oakland's industries include chemicals and shipbuilding. Population (1990): 372,242.

Oakley, Annie (Phoebe Anne Oakley Mozee; 1860–1926) US sharpshooter. From 1885 she and her husband, Frank Butler, performed daring acts of marksmanship in Buffalo Bill's Wild West Show. A musical, *Annie Get Your Gun* (1948) with music by Irving Berlin, was based on her life.

oak moss An edible *lichen, *Evernia prunastri*, found in mountainous regions of the N hemisphere. It has a pale greenish-gray body, 1.2–3.1 in (3–8 cm) long, with numerous pointed branches. Its heavy fragrance makes it of value in perfumery and it is used in the preparation of drugs for treating wounds and infections.

Oak Ridge 36 02N 84 12W A city in Tennessee. It contains the Oak Ridge National Laboratory (1943) for nuclear research. Population (1990): 27,310.

oarfish A *ribbonfish of the genus *Regalecus*, especially *R. glesne*, found in all seas. It has a long silvery ribbonlike body, up to 30 ft (9 m) long, a long red dorsal fin that extends forward to form a crest, long red oarlike pelvic fins situated near the pectoral fins, and no anal or tail fins. □oceans.

OAS. *See* Organisation de l'Armée secrète; Organization of American States.

oasis An area within a desert where water is available for vegetation and human use. It may consist of a single small spring around which palms grow or be an extensive area where the water table is at or near the ground surface.

Oates, Joyce Carol (1938–) US writer. She writes about violence and of mental and economic poverty. Her collections of short stories include *By the North Gate* (1963), *Wheel of Love* (1970), *Last Days* (1984), *The Assignation* (1988), and *Heat and Other Stories* (1991). Among her novels are *Expensive People* (1968), *Them* (1969), *Wonderland* (1971), *The Assassins* (1975), *Childworld* (1976), *Bellefleur* (1980), *A Bloodsmoor Romance* (1982), *The Profane Art* (1983), *Marya: A Life* (1986), *You Must Remember This* (1987), *American Appetites* (1989), and *Because It Is Bitter, and Because It Is My Heart* (1990).

Oates, Lawrence Edward Grace (1880–1912) British explorer. He participated in R. F. *Scott's expedition to the Antarctic (1910–12). They reached the Pole but on the return journey Oates, fearing that his lameness (resulting from frostbite) might hinder the expedition, walked out into the blizzard to die. His gallant act failed to save his companions.

Oates, Titus. *See* Popish Plot.

oat grass A perennial *grass of either of the genera *Arrhenatherum* (about 6 species), native to temperate Eurasia, and *Danthonia* (over 100 species), native to S temperate regions. Tall oat grass (*A. elatius*) has been introduced as a pasture grass to many countries; *Danthonia* species are important forage grasses.

oats Annual *grasses belonging to the genus *Avena* (10 species), native to temperate regions. The common oat (*A. sativa*) was first cultivated in Europe and is grown widely in cool temperate regions. Up to 40 in (1 m) high, it has a branching cluster of stalked flowers; the grain is used as a livestock feed, especially for horses, and for oatmeal, breakfast cereals, etc. The straw is used for livestock fodder and bedding. Wild oats, especially *A. fatua*, can be a serious weed in cereal crops.

OAU. *See* Organization of African Unity.

Oaxaca (*or* Oaxaca de Juárez) 17 05N 96 41W A city in S Mexico, in the Atoyac Valley. Founded in 1486 by the Aztecs, it has flour-milling, cotton, textile, and handicraft industries. Its university was established in 1827. Population (1980): 157,000.

Ob River A river in N central Russia, flowing N from the Altai Mountains to the **Gulf of Ob** on the Kara Sea. One of the world's largest rivers, its drainage basin covers an area of about 1,131,000 sq mi (2,930,000 sq km). Length: 2287 mi (3682 km).

Obadiah An Old Testament prophet who predicted the downfall of Edom, the traditional enemy of Israel. **The Book of Obadiah** records his prophecy and is the shortest book of the Old Testament.

Obelia A genus of marine invertebrate animals belonging to a suborder (*Leptomedusae*) of *coelenterates. Their life cycle alternates between a sedentary asexual phase (*see* polyp) and a free-swimming sexual phase (*see* medusa). The polyps occur in small whitish or brownish colonies attached to the sea bottom, rocks, shells, etc., of shallow coastal waters. Order: *Hydroida*; class: *Hydrozoa*.

obelisk A stone monument generally shaped as a tall tapering rectangular column of stone, ending in a pyramid-like form. First used by the Egyptians, they have also been employed in the modern age. They were normally made of a single piece of stone and erected for religious or commemorative purposes. Perhaps the most famous are those known as *Cleopatra's Needles.

Oberammergau 47 35N 11 07E A town in S Germany, in the Bavarian Alps. It is noted for its passion play, performed every 10 years following a vow made by the villagers (1633) when they were saved from the plague. Population (1980): 5,000.

Oberhausen 51 27N 6 50E A city in NW Germany, in North Rhine-Westphalia on the Rhine-Herne Canal in the *Ruhr. It is a port and industrial center. Population (1991 est): 224,000.

oboe A woodwind instrument with a double reed, made in three jointed sections and having a conical bore and small belled end. It derives from the ancient shawm. It has a range of about three octaves above the B-flat below middle C and because of its constant pitch usually gives the A to which other orchestral instruments tune.

Obote, (Apollo) Milton (1925–   ) Ugandan statesman; prime minister (1962–66) and president (1966–71, 1980–85). He formed (1958) the Uganda People's Congress, which opposed the existence of the kingdom of *Buganda within Uganda. On independence he became prime minister and in 1966 deposed Mutesa II of Buganda (1924–69). He was overthrown by *Amin in 1971, reelected in 1980, and ousted again in 1985.

Obrenović A Serbian ruling dynasty that came to power in 1815, when *Karageorge was assassinated, probably by *Miloš Obrenović. This led to a feud between the Karadordević and Obrenović families, which lasted until *Alexander, the last Obrenović monarch, was assassinated in 1903.

O'Brien, Edna (1936–   ) Irish author. Her novels include *The Country Girls* (1960), *The Lonely Girls* (1962; filmed as *The Girl With Green Eyes*, 1965), *Casualties of Peace* (1966), *Night* (1972), and *The Dazzle* (1981). She has also written plays, film scripts, and short stories.

O'Brien, Flann (Brian O'Nolan; 1911–66) Irish novelist and journalist. His best-known novel is *At Swim-Two-Birds* (1939), an exuberant comic mixture of folklore, farce, and lyricism that was praised by James Joyce and Dylan Thomas. Other novels include *The Dalkey Archive* (1964) and *The Third Policeman* (1967). He wrote a satirical column for the *Irish Times* under the name Myles na Gopaleen.

O'Brien, William (1852–1928) Irish nationalist politician and journalist. He made a great impression as a fiery member of Parliament (from 1883) in the *Home Rule party. He later became more moderate, forming (1910) a short-lived political party that attempted to reconcile different opinions in Ireland.

O'Brien, William Smith (1803–64) Irish politician. A member of Parliament (1828–48), he was at first a moderate constitutionalist but in the 1840s became a prominent member of the *Young Ireland group and led the abortive 1848 rebellion. O'Brien was transported to Australia but subsequently pardoned.

obscenity. *See* censorship.

obsidian A black glassy volcanic rock with a conchoidal fracture. It is of rhyolitic composition (*see* rhyolite) and contains less water and less crystalline material than pitchstone, a similar volcanic glass. Obsidian is formed by the rapid cooling of acid lava.

obstetrics. *See* gynecology.

O'Casey, Sean (1880–1964) Irish dramatist. Born into a poor Protestant family in Dublin, he was largely self-educated and became involved in the Irish nationalist movement. His early realistic tragicomedies, such as *The Shadow of a Gunman* (1923) and *Juno and the Paycock* (1924), were produced at the Abbey Theatre and dealt with Ireland in the time of the "Troubles." In 1926 he went to live in England. His later work includes the antiwar play *The Silver Tassie* (1929), *Red Roses for Me* (1943), *The Bishop's Bonfire* (1955), and *The Drums of Father Ned* (1958). He published six volumes of autobiography (1939–54).

Occam. *See* Ockham.

occultation The temporary disappearance of one astronomical body behind another, as when the moon passes in front of and obscures a star. *See also* eclipse.

occultism Theories and practices based on a belief in hidden supernatural forces that are presumed to account for phenomena for which no rational or scientific explanation can be provided. Occultists set great store by ancient texts, secret rituals, esoteric traditions, and the powers of the human mind as keys to the understanding of the universe. *Theosophy, *satanism, *alchemy, *astrology, the *Kabbalah, *gnosticism, and various methods of divination, such as the *I Ching, are all manifestations of occultism.

occupational therapy The ancillary medical specialty concerned with restoring the physical and mental health of the sick and disabled. The occupational therapist plays an important role in keeping long-term hospital patients interested and usefully occupied, in helping them gain confidence to return to work, and—if necessary—in training disabled persons for new employment. Occupational therapy is of great importance in *geriatrics.

oceanarium A large display tank in which species of marine animals and plants are maintained in the conditions of their natural environments. The first public oceanarium was founded in 1938 at Marineland, Fla.

Oceania The islands of the Pacific Ocean, usually taken to exclude Japan, Indonesia, Taiwan, the Philippines, and the Aleutian Islands, but often including Australasia.

Ocean Island (*or* Banaba) 00 52S 169 35E An island in the SW Pacific Ocean, in Kiribati. Rich in phosphate, it was mined by the UK from 1900 to 1979, when supplies were exhausted. After a long legal battle the Banabans accepted compensation for the loss of their island. Resettled on Rabi Island in Fiji during World War II, they have demanded independence from the government of Kiribati. Area: about 2 sq mi (5 sq km).

oceanography The study of the oceans, particularly their origin, structure, and form, the relief and sediments of the sea floor, and the flora and fauna they contain. The physical and chemical properties of sea water, waves, currents, and tides are also involved. The structural geology of the oceans is a major element in the theory of *plate tectonics.

oceans The large areas of water (excluding lakes and seas) covering about 70% of the earth's surface. The whole water mass is known as the hydrosphere. The oceans are the Pacific (covering about one-third of the world), Atlantic, Indian, and Arctic; the Southern Ocean (waters south of 40°S) is sometimes distinguished. Major structural features of the oceans are the continental margins (continental shelf and slope), mid-ocean ridges, ocean basins, and trenches (the deepest parts of the oceans). Research vessels, such as *Glomar Challenger*, drill into the ocean floor at many locations, and provide much data that assists in the understanding of geology.

Oceanus In Greek mythology, a river issuing from the underworld and encircling the earth. It was personified as a *Titan, a son of Uranus and Gaea and father of the gods and nymphs of the seas and rivers.

ocelot A *cat, *Felis* (*Panthera*) *pardalis*, also called painted leopard, of Central and South American forests; 40–59 in (100–150 cm) long including the tail (12–20 in; 30–50 cm), it has a black-spotted buff coat with stripes on the legs—an attractive target for hunters. It frequently hunts by night to avoid capture, searching for small mammals and reptiles.

ocher A natural pigment, either red or yellow, consisting of hydrated ferric oxide with various impurities. It is therefore a type of *limonite deposit. It has been used as a pigment since prehistoric times and was important in medieval fresco painting.

Ochoa, Severo (1905–93) US biochemist, who won a Nobel Prize in physiology or medicine (1959). Born in Spain, he studied medicine at Madrid University. He was one of the first to demonstrate the role of adenosine triphosphate (ATP) in the storage of the body's energy. This led to the discovery of the

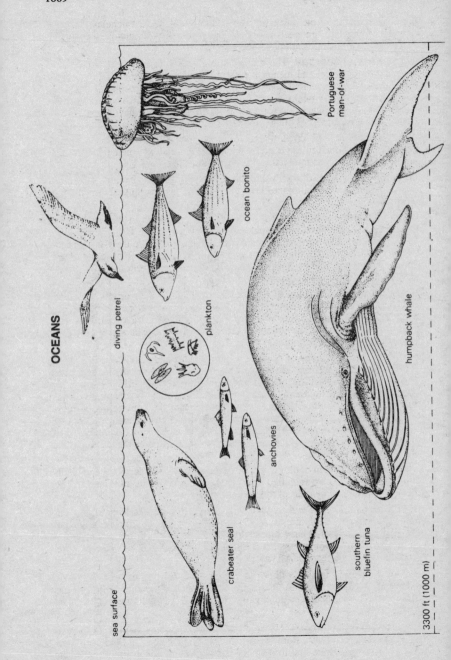

OCEANS

sea surface

diving petrel

Portuguese man-of-war

ocean bonito

plankton

anchovies

crabeater seal

humpback whale

southern bluefin tuna

3300 ft (1000 m)

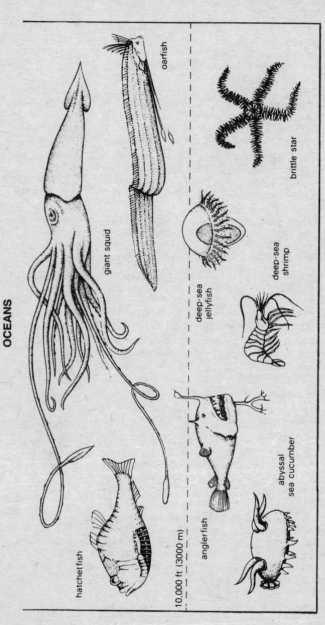

OCEANS

oarfish

giant squid

deep-sea jellyfish

brittle star

deep-sea shrimp

hatchetfish

anglerfish

abyssal sea cucumber

10,000 ft (3000 m)

OCEANS *A selection of animals and plants found at different depths of the ocean.*

enzyme polynucleotide phosphorylase, which was later used to synthesize ribonucleic acid (RNA).

Ockham's Razor The metaphysical principle, associated with the English medieval philosopher *William of Ockham, that "Entities should not be multiplied unnecessarily." In analyzing a problem one should always choose the hypothesis that makes the least number of assumptions; only indispensible concepts are real.

O'Connell, Daniel (1775–1847) Irish politician, who aroused popular support in the 1820s for the right of Roman Catholics to sit in the British Parliament. Himself a Catholic, his election to Parliament in 1828 forced the government to concede *Catholic emancipation. Thereafter, O'Connell was dubbed the Liberator. He subsequently worked for the repeal of union with Britain.

O'Connor, Feargus (1794–1855) Irish politician. From 1832 to 1835 he was a radical member of Parliament. He then became a leading Chartist (*see* Chartism), editing the radical newspaper *Northern Star*. He was elected again to Parliament in 1847 and presented the 1848 Chartist petition. In 1852 he was pronounced insane.

O'Connor, Frank (Michael O'Donovan; 1903–66) Irish short-story writer. During the 1930s he was director of the Abbey Theatre and a friend of W. B. *Yeats. He published many collections of stories, from *Guests of the Nation* (1931) to *My Oedipus Complex* (1964), and several translations from Gaelic.

O'Connor, Sandra Day (1930–) US jurist; the first woman appointed to the Supreme Court (1981–). She practiced law in Arizona and became that state's assistant attorney general (1965–68), was Republican majority leader of the state senate (1972–74), and sat on Arizona's Court of Appeals (1979–81). A conservative, she was appointed to the Supreme Court by Pres. Ronald Reagan.

octane number A measure of the extent to which a fuel causes *knocking in a gasoline engine. It is the percentage by volume of *iso*-octane (C_8H_{18}) in a mixture of *iso*-octane and *n*-heptane (C_7H_{16}), which has the same knocking characteristics as the fuel under specified conditions.

Octavia (d. 11 BC) The sister of Emperor Augustus, who married her to Mark Antony (40) to seal their reconciliation. Antony divorced her in 32, when he returned to Egypt and Cleopatra.

Octavian. *See* Augustus.

October Tenth month of the year. Derived from *octo*, which means eight in Latin, it was the eighth month in the ancient Roman calendar. It has 31 days. The zodiac signs for October are Libra and Scorpio; the flowers are cosmos and calendula, and the birthstones are opal, tourmaline, and beryl. In the US, Columbus Day falls on Oct 12, and Halloween is observed on the 31st.

octopus An eight-armed *cephalopod mollusk belonging to the genus *Octopus*, found in most oceans. Octopuses are 2–213 in (5–540 cm) long and a large species may have an armspan of 354 in (900 cm). The common octopus (*O. vulgaris*), weighing up to 4.4 lb (2 kg), has a pair of well-developed eyes, a ring of tentacles around its horny beak, and a saclike body. Octopuses feed mainly on crabs and lobsters and may eject a cloud of ink when alarmed. Family: *Octopodidae*; order: *Octopoda*.

Oda Nobunaga (1534–82) Japanese feudal lord, who began the reunification of feudal Japan. By careful administration, skillful diplomacy, the selection of able generals, and the adoption of novel military tactics based on formations of infantry armed with the newly introduced arquebus, Nobunaga achieved domination between 1560 and 1582 over Kyoto and central Japan. He was treacherously assassinated.

Odense 55 24N 10 25E A seaport in S Denmark, on the island of Fyn. Its gothic cathedral was founded by *Canute II and contains his tomb and shrine. Odense University was established in 1964. It is the birthplace of Hans Christian Andersen. Its varied industries include ship building, sugar refining, textiles, and iron founding. Dairy produce is the main export. Population (1988 est): 175,000.

Oder River (Polish and Czech name: Odra) A river in E Europe. Rising in the Oder Mountains of the Czech Republic, it flows N and W through Poland and enters the Baltic Sea at Szczecin. Linked by canals to both E and W Europe, it is of great commercial importance. Length: 551 mi (886 km).

Oder-Neisse Line The boundary between Germany and Poland confirmed by the Allies at the *Potsdam Conference (1945) at the end of World War II. The line ran S from Swinoujście on the Baltic Sea to the Czechoslovak border, following the Oder and Neisse Rivers. It was recognized by East Germany and Poland in 1950 but not by West Germany until 1970.

Odessa 46 30N 30 46E A port in S Ukraine, on the Black Sea. Fishing and whaling as well as ship repairing are important activities and industries include engineering, chemicals, and oil refining. *History*: founded in the 14th century as a Tatar fortress, it passed to Russia in 1791 and became a naval base. It was the scene in the Revolution of 1905 of the mutiny on the *Potemkin*, the subject of a remarkable film by Eisenstein. Population (1987): 1,141,000.

Odets, Clifford (1906–63) US dramatist. He joined the Communist party in 1934 and was a founding member of the Group Theater, which produced his first successful play, *Waiting for Lefty* (1935). He later became a Hollywood scriptwriter. His other plays include *Awake and Sing* (1935), *Golden Boy* (1937), *The Big Knife* (1949), and *The Country Girl* (1950).

Odin The principal god of the Teutonic peoples, the husband of *Frigga and, according to some legends, the father of *Thor. Also known as Woden and Wotan, he was the god of war, learning, and poetry and possessed great magical powers. He was the protector of slain heroes, who were brought to *Valhalla by his servants, the *Valkyries. His desire for learning was so great that he gave up his right eye to drink from Mimir's well of knowledge. The Old English form of his name, *Woden*, is preserved in *Wednesday*. □Ragnarök.

Odoacer (c. 433–93 AD) King of Italy (476–93). A German chieftain, he served with various Roman commanders before rebelling and deposing the last Western Roman emperor, *Romulus Augustulus. After acknowledging the overlordship of the Eastern Roman emperor, Zeno (reigned 474–91), he ruled Italy competently until overthrown and killed by the Ostrogothic king, *Theodoric the Great.

Odontoglossum A genus of epiphytic *orchids (about 250 species) native to mountainous areas of tropical America. Each large swollen stem base bears one or more leaves, and the flowers, which are borne on a spike, vary greatly in color and size. Many *Odontoglossum* species have been crossed both within the genus and with other orchid genera to produce hundreds of beautiful hybrids, prized by orchid growers.

Odo of Bayeux (c. 1036–97) Bishop of Bayeux (1049–97). The half-brother of William the Conqueror, he took part in the Norman conquest of England and helped rule the country during William's absences but subsequently rebelled against William II. He died on the First Crusade.

Odysseus (*or* Ulysses) A legendary Greek king of Ithaca and hero of Homer's *Odyssey*, notable for his cunning. His many adventures during his voyage home from the *Trojan War included encounters with the Cyclops *Polyphemus, the cannibalistic Laestrygones, the enchantress *Circe, and the goddess Calypso, with whom he lived for eight years. Having reached Ithaca, he was reunited with his faithful wife *Penelope after killing her suitors with the help of his son Telemachus.

OECD. *See* Organization for Economic Cooperation and Development.

Oedipus In Greek legend, a king of Thebes who unwittingly fulfilled the prophecy of the oracle at Delphi that he would kill his father and marry his mother. He was brought up by Polybus, king of Corinth. He killed his true father, Laius, in a roadside quarrel, and after winning the throne of Thebes by solving the riddle of the *sphinx he married his mother, the widowed Jocasta. When they discovered the truth, Jocasta committed suicide and Oedipus blinded himself and went into exile. The story is the subject of Sophocles' best-known tragedy.

Oedipus complex The unconscious sexual feelings of a boy for his mother, which are accompanied by aggressive feelings for his father. According to psychoanalysis this is a normal desire, made unconscious by *repression. The female equivalent (in which a girl desires her father) is called the **Electra complex**.

Oehlenschläger, Adam (Gottlob) (1779–1850) Danish poet and playwright. He was the founder of Danish romanticism and Denmark's greatest poet. His works include the blank-verse tragedies *Hakon Jarl* and *Baldur hin Gode* (*Balder the Good*), based on Norse legend and published in *Nordiske Digte* (1807). He also wrote lyric poetry and a ballad cycle based on the poetic Edda, *Nordens Guder* (*The Gods of the North*; 1819).

Oersted, Hans Christian (1777–1851) Danish physicist; professor at Copenhagen University. He discovered the magnetic effect of an electric current and thus established the relationship between electricity and magnetism. He did not, however, take an active part in the elucidation of this discovery. The c.g.s. unit of magnetic field strength is named for him.

Offa (d. 796) King of Mercia (757–96) and overlord of all England S of the Humber. He engaged in trade with Charlemagne, although Charlemagne had refused to marry his daughter to Offa's son. He accepted greater papal control of the Church, introduced a new currency, and devised a code of laws. **Offa's Dyke**, an earthwork dividing England from Wales, built c. 784–c. 796, marks the frontier established by his wars with the Welsh.

Offaly (Irish name: Uabh Failghe) A county in the central Republic of Ireland, in Leinster bordered in the W by the River Shannon. It is chiefly low lying, containing part of the Bog of Allen in the N. Agricultural produce includes oats, barley, and wheat; cattle are reared. Area: 770 sq mi (2000 sq km). Population (1991): 58,448. County town: Tullamore.

Off-Broadway theaters Small-scale professional theaters in New York City that specialize in noncommercial and experimental productions. They were responsible for the most lively drama in the US in the 1950s and 1960s.

Offenbach (am Main) 50 06N 8 46E A city in S central Germany, in Hessen on the Main River. It is noted for its leather industry. Population (1991 est): 115,000.

Offenbach, Jacques (J. Eberst; 1819–80) German composer of French adoption and Jewish descent. He adopted the name of the town in which his father lived. A professional cellist, at the age of 30 he began writing a series of popular operettas, including *Orpheus in the Underworld* (1858), *La Belle Hélène* (1864), and *La Vie Parisienne* (1866). He also composed one grand opera, *The Tales of Hoffman* (produced posthumously; 1881).

Office of Strategic Services (OSS) (1942–45) US World War II information-gathering agency. Created to gain access to enemy war information, to demoralize the enemy, and to act as liaison with the underground resistance forces within enemy countries, it was administered by Maj. Gen. William Donovan (1883–1959). The *Central Intelligence Agency later assumed many of its activities.

O'Flaherty, Liam (1897–1984) Irish novelist. Born in the Aran Islands, he worked his way around the world before starting his literary career in London in 1922. His novels, chiefly concerned with themes of violence and terrorism, include *The Informer* (1925) and *The Assassin* (1928). *The Pedlar's Revenge and Other Stories* was published in 1976. After 1935 he lived mostly in the US.

Ogaden, the A semidesert area in E Ethiopia, enclosed by Somalia except to the W. The nomadic inhabitants are chiefly Muslim Somalis. In the 1960s a claim to the area by Somalia provoked border clashes. Somalia invaded the Ogaden in 1977 but withdrew (1978) in the face of counteroffensives launched by Ethiopia with Cuban and Soviet aid. Guerrilla fighting continued until the end of the 1980s. *See also* Ethiopia.

Ogam (*or* Ogham) A script found in about 400 Celtic inscriptions in Ireland and W Britain, dating from the 5th to the 7th centuries AD. It is alphabetic and consists of 20 letters, each made from a number of oblique or straight strokes on either side of a central dividing line.

Ogbomosho 8 05N 4 11E The third largest city in Nigeria, on the Yorubaland plateau. Agricultural trade is important and there are local craft industries, including textiles and woodworking. There are also shoe and tobacco factories. Population (1990 est): 628,000.

Ogden, C(harles) K(ay) (1889–1957) British writer and scholar. With I. A. *Richards he wrote *The Meaning of Meaning* (1923). From 1925 he developed *Basic English, with a restricted vocabulary of 850 words, intended as a practical medium of international communication.

Oglethorpe, James Edward (1696–1785) English general and colonizer. While serving in Parliament, he promoted the establishment of a colony in North America for indigent debtors and persecuted Protestants. In 1733 he led the first group of settlers to the colony that was to become Georgia. He repulsed a Spanish attack against it (1742).

Ogooué River (*or* Ogowe R.) A river in W central Africa. Rising in the SW Congo, it flows mainly NW and W through Gabon to enter the Atlantic Ocean. Length: 683 mi (970 km).

O'Hara, John (Henry) (1905–70) US novelist. After working as a journalist he began publishing ironic stories about middle-class life in the 1930s. His best-known novels are *Appointment in Samarra* (1934), *Butterfield 8* (1935), *Pal Joey* (1940), *Ten North Frederick* (1955), and *From the Terrace* (1958).

O'Higgins, Bernardo (?1778–1842) Chilean national hero. The son of an Irish-born soldier who became Spanish colonial governor, he fought with José de *San Martin against Spain and liberated Chile. He was made dictator of the country in 1817 but his wide-ranging reforms created much resentment and he was deposed after a revolt in the provinces.

Ohio A midwestern state in the US. It is bounded on the E by Pennsylvania and West Virginia, on the S by West Virginia and Kentucky, on the W by Indiana, and on the N by Michigan and Lake Erie. The flat or rolling land of W Ohio gives way in the E to the hill and valley region of the Appalachian Plateau. A major industrial state, it lies at the center of the most industrialized area of the US and is strategically located near many rich markets. The leading industrial products are transportation equipment, raw and fabricated metals, nonelectrical machinery, and rubber. It also exploits its abundant natural resources, including clay and stone, lime, coal, natural gas, and oil. Agriculture is important, especially livestock. *History*: Miami, Shawnee, Erie, and Ottawa Indians were the indigenous inhabitants when European explorers arrived. Robert Cavalier, sieur de La Salle (1669) claimed the area for France in 1669. Subsequent Anglo-French rivalry over control of the territory culminated in the French and Indian War, in which England won the region (1763). After the American Revolution the area became part of the Northwest Territory (1787). Ohio became a separate territory in 1799 and a state in 1802. Rapid industrial development, facilitated by the earlier building of railroads and canals, took place after the Civil War. Cleveland became the site of a growing petroleum industry. Flooding, a long-standing problem in Ohio, took a devastating toll in 1913 and prompted the establishment of many state and national water-control projects. The Depression caused severe hardship for factory workers and farmers, but World War II brought economic prosperity. The national energy crisis of the late 1970s resulted in a boom for Ohio's coal industry, and prosperity continued until the 1980s when the entire nation experienced a slowdown. Area: 41,222 sq mi (106,764 sq km). Population (1990): 10,847,115. Capital: Columbus.

Ohio River A river flowing mainly SW from Pittsburgh in W Pennsylvania to join the Mississippi (in Illinois) as its main E tributory. Length: 980 mi (1577 km).

ohm (Ω) The *SI unit of electrical resistance equal to the resistance between two points on a conductor when a potential difference of one volt between the points produces a current of one ampere. This definition replaced the former definition, which was based on the resistance of a specified column of mercury. Named for Georg *Ohm.

Ohm, Georg Simon (1787–1854) German physicist, who discovered in 1827 that the current flowing through a wire is proportional to the potential difference between its ends (*see* Ohm's law). Ohm also found that the electrical resistance of a wire is proportional to its length and inversely proportional to its cross-sectional area. The unit of electrical resistance is named for him.

Ohm's law The basic law of electric current, named for its discoverer, Georg *Ohm. The current, I, flowing through an element in a circuit is directly proportional to the voltage drop, V, across it. It is written as $V = IR$, where R is the resistance of the circuit element.

oil There are three types of oil: lipids (*see* fats and oils), *essential oils, and mineral oil.

Petroleum (*or* rock oil) is the thick greenish mineral oil that occurs in permeable underground rock and consists mainly of *hydrocarbons, with some other elements (sulfur, oxygen, nitrogen, etc.). It is believed to have derived from the remains of living organisms deposited many millions of years ago with rock-forming sediments. Under the effects of heat and pressure this organic material passed through a number of chemical and physical changes ending up as droplets of petroleum, which migrated through porous rocks and fissures to become trapped in large underground reservoirs, often floating on a layer of water and held under pressure beneath a layer of natural gas (mostly methane).

Mineral oil was used in the 4th millennium BC by the Sumerians to reinforce bricks, and the Burmese were burning it in oil lamps in the 13th century AD. However, the modern oil industry began when oil was discovered in Pennsylvania in 1859 and has grown with the development of the internal-combustion engine, which is entirely dependent on it as a fuel.

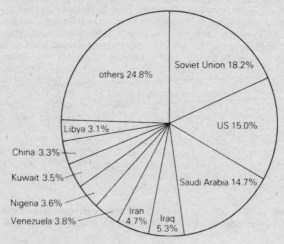

OIL *World crude petroleum production.*

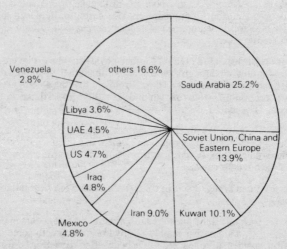

OIL *World crude petroleum reserves.*

The presence of oil in underground reservoirs is detected by geologists, who seek evidence of the type of structures in which oil is known to occur and measure the gravitational force in likely areas to identify variations of rock density; depth is determined by such measures as the behavior of sound waves produced by small surface explosions. Exploratory narrow-bore drillings are then made to determine the extent of a reservoir. The actual oil well is made by drilling through the rock with a rotating bit supported in a wider shaft; a specially prepared mud is pumped through the hollow bit to collect the debris, which is forced back up the shaft around the drilling bit. When the oil is reached, the pressure of the mud is used to control the pressure of the oil so that none is wasted by "gushers"; when the mud has been removed from the shaft the flow is controlled by valves. This method of sinking wells enables oil over 3 mi (5 km) below the surface to be mined. Drilling for oil below the sea is achieved in a similar manner, except that the drilling rig has to be supported on a base, which has legs sunk into the seabed.

Petroleum has no uses in its crude form and has to be refined by fractional distillation (i.e. separating the components according to their boiling points) before it is of commercial value. Natural gas is widely used as a substitute for coal gas and as a source of power in the refinery. Products made by blending the distillation fractions include aviation fuel, gasoline, kerosene, diesel oil, lubricating oil, paraffin wax, and petroleum jelly. In addition to fractional distillation, other processes, such as catalytic cracking, are used to split the larger molecules into smaller ones to increase the yield of gasoline and to reduce the viscosity of heavier oils. Catalytic reforming is used to make a number of valuable chemicals (petrochemicals), which are required to manufacture detergents, plastics, fibers, fertilizers, drugs, etc.

As one of the world's primary energy sources, the price, conservation, and political significance of oil are extremely controversial issues. In 1961 the *Organization of Petroleum Exporting Countries (OPEC) was set up to protect producing countries from exploitation. Its advent ended the era of cheap energy and prices for petroleum products rose sharply during the ensuing decade. In 1974 the International Energy Agency (IEA) was established to protect consumers. Since then various factors, including the flow of North Sea oil, have helped to stabilize prices, although the Iranian revolution of 1979 temporarily led to world shortages and further price increases.

World oil reserves are as difficult to estimate as future world consumption. Reserves depend on the estimates for undiscovered sources, while consumption depends on the projected growth of usage, the price of oil in relation to its competitors, and the extent to which nuclear energy will be utilized.

oil beetle A heavy-bodied flightless beetle belonging to the family *Meloidae* (about 2000 species). If disturbed, it discharges evil-smelling oily blood—an example of reflex bleeding—as a defense mechanism. It has a similar lifestyle to the *blister beetle.

oilbird A South American cave-dwelling bird, *Steatornis caripensis*, also called guacharo. It is 12 in (30 cm) long and has a fan-shaped tail, a white-spotted black-barred brown plumage, and a hook-tipped bill surrounded by long bristles. It lives in colonies, uses echolocation inside caves, and feeds on fruit. It is the only member of its family (*Steatornithidae*); order: *Caprimulgiformes* (frogmouths, nightjars, etc.).

oil-immersion lens A lens system used in some *microscopes in which the gap between the objective lens and the specimen is filled with oil (usually cedarwood oil). It increases the amount of light entering the system.

oil palm A *palm tree, *Elaeis guineensis*, native to tropical West Africa and cultivated in Africa, Indonesia, Malaysia, and tropical America as the source of palm oil. Growing to a height of 49 ft (15 m), the palms produce fleshy fruits, 1.2 in (3 cm) long, containing a white kernel within a hard black shell. Palm oil is extracted from the pulp and kernel and is used in making soaps, margarine, lubricants, etc. The residual meal from the kernels is a valuable livestock feed.

oilseeds Oil-bearing seeds of plants from which the edible oil is extracted for making margarine, soaps, etc. Examples include rapeseed, cottonseed, groundnuts, and soybeans. The oil is obtained from the seeds by expelling it under pressure or by extracting it using a solvent (with a solvent recovery cycle); the **oilcake** remaining after most of the oil has been removed is called expellers or extractions, respectively. Both forms of oilcake are widely used as animal feeds.

Oise River A river in N France, flowing mainly SW from the Belgian Ardennes to join the Seine River at Conflans. Length: 188 mi (302 km).

Oistrakh, David (1908–75) Russian violinist. He made his debut in Moscow in 1933 and won the International Violin Competition in Brussels in 1937. He played frequently in the West, and was well known for his performances of the Brahms, Tchaikovsky, and Prokofiev violin concertos. His son and pupil, the violinist **Igor Oistrakh** (1931–   ), often gave joint recitals with him and has also conducted.

Oita 33 15N 131 36E A port in Japan, on the NE coast of Kyushu. An important town in the 16th century, it is now an expanding industrial center with an oil refinery and iron and steel industries. Population (1991 est): 412,860.

Ojibwa A North American Indian people of the Great Lakes region, who speak a language of the Algonkian family. They are also known as Chippewa; those who now live near Lake Winnipeg in Canada are called Saulteaux. They were traditionally hunters, fishers, and gatherers, who wandered in small bands and sheltered in simply made dome-shaped wigwams. Shamans exercised considerable influence.

Ojos del Salado 27 05S 68 05W A mountain peak on the border between Argentina and Chile, the second highest peak in the Andes. Height: 22,550 ft (6873 m).

okapi A hoofed mammal, *Okapia johnstoni*, of central African rain forests. Okapis are about 60 in (150 cm) high at the shoulder and have a dark-brown coat with horizontal black and white stripes on the legs and rump, which provide camouflage. The smaller male has short bony backward-pointing horns. They were unknown to science until 1901. Family: *Giraffidae* (giraffes).

Okavango Swamp A marshy area in NE Botswana, into which the Okavango River drains. It supports a rich and varied wildlife.

Okayama 34 40N 133 54E A city in Japan, in SW Honshu. A commercial and industrial center, it has a 16th-century castle and a traditional Japanese garden (1786). Its university was established in 1949. Population (1991 est): 597,238.

Okeechobee, Lake A large freshwater lake in S Florida. It drains into the Atlantic Ocean through the *Everglades. Area: 700 sq mi (1813 sq km).

Okefenokee Swamp A swamp area extending through SE Georgia and NE Florida. In 1937 a large proportion of it was designated the Okefenokee National Wildlife Refuge; the wildlife includes alligators, snakes, and birds.

O'Keeffe, Georgia (1887–1986) US painter. Her first one-person show was presented in 1917 by the photographer Alfred *Stieglitz, whom she married in 1924. She specialized in semiabstract paintings of flowers, bones, architecture, and landscapes inspired by the countryside of New Mexico.

Okeghem, Jean d' (c. 1425–c. 1495) Flemish composer, noted for his innovative counterpoint. He was composer to Charles VII, Louis XI, and Charles

VIII of France and his pupils included Josquin des Prez. He wrote much church music, including 16 masses and 9 motets.

OKAPI *The closest living relative of the giraffe, this nocturnal animal becomes very docile and breeds readily in captivity.*

Okhotsk, Sea of A section of the N Pacific Ocean off the E coast of Russia, separated from the main ocean by Kamchatka and the Kuril Islands.

Okinawa A mountainous Japanese island, the main one of the *Ryukyu group. During World War II it was captured by US forces in a major amphibious operation and was only returned to Japan in 1972, the US retaining military bases there. Chief products are fish, rice, sugar cane, and sweet potatoes. Area: 454 sq mi (1176 sq km). Population (1991): 1,229,000. Capital: *Naha.

Oklahoma A state in the S central US. It is bounded on the E by Missouri and Arkansas, on the S by Texas, on the W by Texas and New Mexico, and on the N by Colorado and Kansas. It has a diverse landscape, with uplands in the W, the lowlands of the Arkansas River Valley and coastal plain in the center and S, and wooded hills in the E. An oil-rich state, agriculture (especially cattle) remains a major source of revenue. Most industry is located around Oklahoma City and Tulsa (one of the world's leading oil centers). The most important manufacturing industries are food processing, nonelectrical machinery, fabricated metal products, and electrical and transport equipment. *History*: occupied by Plains Indians including Apache, Comanche, Kiowa, and Osage, Oklahoma was acquired by the US as part of the Louisiana Purchase (1803). In 1834 the land was designated Indian Territory by the federal government, a repository for Indians evicted from their homelands. The opening of the cattle routes, such as the Chisholm Trail (1860s), which traversed the territory, brought pressure on the government to allow settlement. Homesteading runs and "land lotteries" subsequently brought settlers when a strip of land was released for settlement. In 1906 white settlers were allowed access to the remainder of the Indian Territory. In the 1890s and early 1900s Oklahoma became a major oil producer. It became a state in 1907. Oklahoma was severely affected by the great drought of the 1930s (during the Depression), and thousands saw their farms turn to dust, forcing them to become migrant laborers. During World War II the economy expanded and diversified, allowing for gradual but solid growth after the war. During the postwar period and into the present, energy-related industries have contributed to Oklahoma's position as a rapidly growing state. Area: 69,919 sq mi (181,089 sq km). Population (1990): 3,145,585. Capital: Oklahoma City.

Oklahoma City 35 28N 97 33W The capital city of Oklahoma, on the North Canadian River. Founded in 1889, it expanded rapidly following the discovery of oil (1920s). Today it is a commercial, industrial, and distribution center for an oil-producing and agricultural area. Oklahoma City University was established in 1904. Population (1990): 444,719.

okra An annual African herb, *Hibiscus esculentus*, also called lady's fingers or gumbo, widely cultivated in the tropics and subtropics. It grows 40–80 in (1–2 m) high and has heart-shaped leaves and five-petaled yellow flowers with a crimson center. The pods are picked before they are ripe and eaten fresh, canned, dried, or pickled. They may be used to thicken stews and soups. The seeds are a coffee substitute. Family: *Malvaceae*.

Olaf I Tryggvason (c. 964–c. 1000) King of Norway (995–c. 1000). He took part in the Viking attacks on England (991–94) but the English king, Ethelred the Unready, became his godfather when Olaf was confirmed as a Christian at Andover (994). Olaf subsequently imposed Christianity on Norway. A hero of Scandinavian literature, he died at the hands of the Danes in the battle of Svolder.

Olaf II Haraldsson, Saint (c. 995–1030) King (1015–28) and patron saint of Norway. Baptized in 1013, he attempted to complete the conversion of Norway to Christianity. He was overthrown by Canute II of England and Denmark and died, attempting to regain his kingdom, at the battle of Stikelstad.

Olaf V (1903–91) King of Norway (1957–91). A talented sportsman, he took part as a yachtsman in the 1928 Olympic Games. In 1929 he married Princess Märtha of Sweden. His son Harald succeeded as Harald V.

Öland A long narrow island in Sweden, in the Baltic Sea separated from the mainland by the Kalmar Sound. Area: 520 sq mi (1347 sq km). Chief town: Borgholm.

Olbers, Heinrich Wilhelm Matthäus (1758–1840) German astronomer, who was the first to point out the paradoxical nature of the night sky (*see* Olbers' paradox). He was also one of the first astronomers to detect and study the asteroids, discovering Pallas in 1802 and Vesta in 1804.

Olbers' paradox Why is the sky dark at night? Heinrich *Olbers argued, in 1826, that if the universe were infinite, uniform, and unchanging, with innumerable stars, then the night sky would be covered in stars and appear as bright as the average star, i.e. the sun. The paradox is resolved by the facts that the universe does not extend infinitely in space and time and is expanding rather than remaining static and unchanging; as the galaxies recede, their radiation suffers a *red-shift (i.e. is diminished in energy), which increases with distance.

Old Believers A schismatic sect of the Russian Orthodox Church that rejected the liturgical reforms of the Patriarch of Moscow (1667). Its members were mainly peasants, who suffered much persecution. The majority, who evolved their own Church hierarchy, was eventually recognized by the state (1881), but the remainder split up into small and often eccentric sects.

Oldcastle, Sir John (c. 1378–1417) English soldier and leader of the *Lollards. An ardent supporter of *Wycliffe, whose works he distributed, he was arrested for heresy and imprisoned in the Tower of London (1413). He escaped but was recaptured four years later and hanged. Shakespeare's character Falstaff is partly based on him.

Old Catholics Christian Churches from several European countries that separated from the Roman Catholic Church at various times and in 1932 entered into communion with the Church of England. They comprise the Church of Utrecht, which supported *Jansenism against Roman Catholic orthodoxy (1724), the Old Catholic Churches of Germany, Switzerland, and Austria, which rejected papal infallibility (1870), the National Polish Church (established 1897), and the Yugoslav Old Catholic Church (1924).

Old Comedy The first period of Greek comic drama, lasting up to the end of the 5th century BC. The episodic choral plays of this period contained elements of song, dance, topical satire, and political criticism and ranged in style from bawdy slapstick to lyrical grace. All the surviving examples are by *Aristophanes. *See also* Middle Comedy; New Comedy.

Oldenburg 53 08N 8 13E A city in NW Germany, in Lower Saxony on the Hunte River. The capital of the former duchy of Oldenburg, it has a 17th-century palace. It is an agricultural and industrial center. Population (1991): 143,131.

Oldenburg, Claes (Thure) (1929–) US sculptor, born in Sweden. He became a leading exponent of *pop art in the 1960s, first with his re-creation of ordinary environments, notably *The Store* (1960–61), and later with his "soft sculptures," in which vinyl and stuffed canvas are shaped into everyday objects, such as bathtubs, typewriters, etc.

Old English sheepdog A breed of working □dog originating in England. It has a compact body, a characteristic ambling gait, and a long dense shaggy coat that may be gray or blue-gray with white markings. These dogs are also known as bobtails because their tails are docked at birth. Height: 22–26 in (55–66 cm).

Oldham 53 33N 2 07W A city in N England, in Greater Manchester. Traditionally a cotton-spinning town, Oldham now also has electronics, textile machinery, plastics, and clothing industries. The town hall is a copy of Ceres' Temple in Athens. Population (1981): 107,800.

old man cactus A succulent desert *cactus of the genus *Cephalocereus* (50 species), especially *C. senilis*, native to tropical and subtropical America. Its sturdy stems are coated with long strands of white hair at maturity and may reach of height of 39 ft (12 m).

old man's beard. *See* Clematis.

Old Norse A North Germanic language formerly spoken in Iceland and Norway (c. 1150–c. 1350). It is the language of the Norse *sagas and was closely related to the contemporary speech of Denmark and Sweden. From this group the modern Scandinavian languages are derived.

Old Testament The collection of 39 books constituting the sacred scriptures of *Judaism. Together with the *New Testament they also form the first of the two major divisions of the Christian *Bible. The title derives from the Latin word for *covenant and refers to the pact between God and Israel, a concept that underlies the authors' view of history and is the major theme throughout. The books claim to cover the period from the creation of the universe and man (Adam) to about 400 BC. They are traditionally divided into three parts: the Law or *Torah, the first five books, traditionally ascribed to Moses and often called the Pentateuch by scholars; the Prophets, which are most of the books bearing the names of individual prophets and containing much historical information; and the Writings or Hagiographa (Hebrew: *Kethubim*), the latest books admitted to the canon of the Hebrew Old Testament (c. 100 AD), i.e. Psalms, Proverbs, Job, Ruth, Lamentations, the Song of Solomon, Ecclesiastes, Esther, Daniel, Chronicles, Ezra, and Nehemiah.

Olduvai Gorge A site in N Tanzania yielding an important sequence of Lower *Paleolithic fossils and tools. Here L. S. B. *Leakey found remains of the *Australopithecus* he called *Zinjanthropus* (c. 1,750,000 years old) and the *hominid *Homo habilis* (c. 2,000,000 years old), one or both of which manufactured crude pebble choppers.

Old World A name for Europe, Africa, and Asia, used especially by early emigrants from Europe. *Compare* New World.

Old World monkey A *monkey belonging to the family *Cercopithecidae* (58 species), native to Africa or Asia. There are both terrestrial and arboreal species, active mainly by day and either omnivorous or vegetarian. They inhabit forest, savannah, swamps, and rocks. *See also* baboon; colobus; guenon; langur; macaque.

oleander A poisonous evergreen shrub, *Nerium oleander*, also called rosebay, native to the Mediterranean region and widely cultivated in warm regions for its attractive flowers. Up to 23 ft (7 m) high, it has long narrow leaves, clusters of white, pink, or purplish five-petaled flowers (up to 3 in [7.5 cm] across), and dangling pods. Family: *Apocynaceae*.

oleaster A shrub or tree, *Elaeagnus angustifolia*, also called Russian olive, found throughout S Europe and sometimes cultivated for its ornamental silvery foliage. It grows 6.5–40 ft (2–12 m) high and bears small fragrant yellowish flowers. The olive-shaped yellowish fruits have a silvery scaly coat and are dried and used in cakes as Trebizond dates. Family: *Elaeagnaceae*.

olefines. *See* alkenes.

Oligocene epoch. *See* Tertiary period.

oligopoly An economic market structure in which there is imperfect competition between a few suppliers. Oligopoly is common in Western economies today. Economic theory is not as successful at predicting the market trends in an oligopoly as it is under the extremes of *monopoly and *perfect competition, because the action of each firm in an oligopoly affects the policies of the others.

olingo A mammal belonging to the genus *Bassaricyon* (3 species), found in tropical forests of South America. Olingos are 30–37 in (75–95 cm) long including the tail (16–19 in; 40–48 cm), with buff-colored or golden fur. They apparently nest in hollow trees and feed chiefly on fruit. Family: *Procyonidae* (raccoons, kinkajous, etc.); order: *Carnivora*.

Oliphant, Sir Mark Laurence Elwin (1901–) Australian physicist, who in 1934 discovered *tritium while bombarding deuterium with deuterons. His work contributed to the development of the hydrogen bomb. He also designed the first proton synchrotron accelerator.

Olivares, Gaspar de Guzmán, Conde-Duque de (1587–1645) Spanish statesman. The chief minister of Philip IV (1621–43), he combined reform, especially economic, with a grand imperial vision and attempted to make all the

Spanish kingdoms provide him with men and money. Dissatisfaction exploded under the strain of Spain's participation in the *Thirty Years' War into revolt in Portugal and Catalonia and led to his downfall. Olivares supported the painters Rubens and Velázquez and the writer Lope de Vega.

olive An evergreen tree, *Olea europaea*, native to W Asia but cultivated throughout Mediterranean and subtropical regions for its fruits. Up to 40 ft (12 m) high, it has a gnarled gray trunk and lance-shaped leathery gray-green leaves. Small greenish-white flowers produce fleshy oval berries containing a hard stone. Unripe green olives and ripe black olives are usually pickled for use in hors d'oeuvres and other dishes. **Olive oil**, pressed from the fruit, is one of the finest edible oils and can be consumed without refining or processing. It is also used in making soaps, cosmetics, and textiles. Olive wood resists decay and is used for furniture and ornaments. Family: *Oleaceae*.

Olives, Mount of (*or* Olivet) 31 47N 35 15E A hill to the E of the old city of Jerusalem. Near its foot is the Garden of Gethsemane, the scene of the betrayal of Christ (Mark 14.26–50) and it is the traditional site of Christ's Ascension (Acts 1.2–12). Height: 2686 ft (817 m).

olive shell A *gastropod mollusk of the family *Olividae* (300 species) of warm shallow seas. The shiny □shell, 0.4–5 in (1–12 cm) long, is roughly cylindrical with a short spire and is covered by the mantle. The animals prey on smaller mollusks on sandy seabeds.

Olivier, Laurence (Kerr), Baron (1907–89) British actor. He played many Shakespearean and a number of outstanding modern roles while with the Old Vic Theatre Company from 1937 to 1949. His films include the Shakespeare adaptations *Henry V* (1944), *Hamlet* (1948), and *Richard III* (1956). He was director of Britain's National Theatre Company from 1961 to 1973, during which time he played many leading roles, including Shakespeare's Othello (filmed 1965) and in plays by Chekhov, O'Neill, and Ionesco. He was knighted in 1947 and created a life peer in 1970.

olivine A group of rock-forming silicate minerals, varying in composition between the end-members forsterite (Mg_2SiO_4) and fayalite (Fe_2SiO_4). Olivines are green, brownish green, or yellowish green, with a conchoidal fracture. Those rich in magnesium occur in basic and ultrabasic igneous rocks, while fayalite occurs in acid igneous rocks. Peridot is a pale green gem variety. Olivine is believed to be a major constituent of the earth's upper mantle.

olm A cave-dwelling salamander, *Proteus anguineus*, found in the Carpathian Mountains. Growing to about 12 in (30 cm), it is white and has bright-red gills throughout its life. The eyes are covered with skin but are clearly visible in young larvae. Although sightless, olms prey on small worms and can survive for long periods without feeding. Family: *Proteidae*. *See also* mudpuppy.

Olmecs An ancient American Indian people of the Gulf Coast of Mexico. Between about 1200 and 400 BC they evolved the first important Mesoamerican culture, with great ceremonial centers at La Venta and San Lorenzo. They invented a hieroglyphic script and a calendar. Outstanding stone carvers, they produced both monumental basalt heads and small jade figures.

Olomouc (German name: Olmütz) 49 48N 17 15E An industrial city in the Czech Republic, in N Moravia. Its notable historic buildings include the gothic cathedral and the town hall with its 15th-century astronomical clock. The university was founded in 1576. Population (1991): 105,690.

Olsztyn (German name: Allenstein) 53 48N 20 29E A market city in NE Poland. It was founded in 1334 by the Teutonic Knights. Industries include the manufacture of leather. Population (1992 est): 164,000.

LAURENCE OLIVIER *Preparing for a scene in his third Shakespearean film,* Richard III.

Olympia A sanctuary of *Zeus, established about 1000 BC in the NW *Peloponnese, in W Greece. From 776 BC until at least 261 AD it was the venue of the *Olympic Games. Extensive excavations from 1881 have revealed no important buildings before the 6th century BC, when the temple of Hera and the stadium were built. In 457 BC the temple of Zeus in the Altis (sacred grove), which later held *Phidias's famous statue, was completed. Public buildings and monuments, a gymnasium, wrestling area, baths, and guest houses for officials and competitors were built later. The sanctuary was finally closed by the Christian Emperor Theodosius (390 AD).

Olympia 47 03N 122 53W A seaport and the capital of Washington, on Puget Sound. Founded in 1850, it possesses a fine capitol building (1893). Industries include timber, fishing, and mining. Population (1990): 33,729.

Olympic Games A quadrennial international sports contest. The modern games derive from the ancient Greek athletic festival held at *Olympia, first recorded reliably in 776 BC; however, the games probably date back to the 14th century BC and originated in a religious ceremony. Corrupted in Roman times, they were banned by *Theodosius the Great (393 AD). They were revived at Athens in 1896, largely through the efforts of Baron Pierre de Coubertin (1863–1937), a French educator, who wished to improve national and international understanding through sport. The Winter Olympics were first held in 1924. The Games are governed by the International Olympic Committee, a self-elected international body. Although officially a contest between individuals, hosted by a particular city, the Games are often seen as a competition between countries.

Olympic National Park A national park in NW Washington, mainly in the Olympic Mountains but including a narrow strip along the Pacific Ocean. Established in 1938, the park preserves the glaciered Olympic Mountains, as well as rain forests along the coast. Mount Olympus, the highest point, rises to 7954 ft (2425 m). Area: 1401 sq mi (3629 sq km).

Olympus, Mount (Modern Greek name: Óros Ólimbos) 40 05N 22 21E A small group of mountains in NE central Greece, held in ancient times to be the home of the gods. Highest point: 9570 ft (2917 m).

Om In Indian religions, the greatest of the mantras or mystical sounds embodying and representing spiritual power. In Sanskrit *Om* comprises three sounds *A, U, M* (the vowels being equivalent to *O*), which represent the three Vedic scriptures, the three worlds (earth, atmosphere, heaven), the *Trimurti or some other triple, and ultimately the essence of the universe.

Omaha 41 15N 96 00W A city in Nebraska, on the Missouri River. The state's main commercial center, industries include meat processing and agricultural machinery. Omaha is a center for medical research. Population (1980): 311,681.

Oman, Sultanate of (name until 1970: Muscat and Oman) A country in the Middle East, in E *Arabia. It is mainly flat but rises to 10,194 ft (3107 m) near the coast in the N. The majority of the population is Arab, Ibadhi Muslim by religion, nomadic, and illiterate. *Economy*: oil, which has been extracted since 1967, accounts for about 90% of the country's revenue. There is also beef production, fishing for sardines, tuna, and sharks, and the growing of such produce as cereals, tobacco, and dates; dates, limes, and pomegranates are the chief export crops. *History*: Oman was settled by the Portuguese, Dutch, and English in the 16th century. Since the 19th century Britain has been influential in Oman. It supported the present sultan's overthrow of his father in 1970 and has helped fight the guerrillas in *Dhofar. Head of State: Sultan Qaboos ibn Sa'id. Official language: Arabic. Official currency: Rial Omani of 1000 baiza. Area: 120,000 sq mi (300,000 sq km). Population (1990 est): 1,530,000. Capital: Muscat.

Omar (*or* Umar) (d. 644 AD) The second *caliph (634–44), who is regarded by Islam as the founder of the Muslim state. Omar continued the Muslim conquests and in 638 visited Jerusalem after its capture. He was murdered in Medina by a discontented slave.

Omar Khayyam (?1048–1122?) Persian poet, who was famous as a mathematician and made astronomical observations for the reform of the calendar. His poems, characterized by an agnostic and hedonistic philosophy, were written in the form of *ruba'is* (quatrains). The free translation of 75 of them by Edward *Fitzgerald in 1859 became widely popular; more recent translations have been made by the British poets Robert Graves and John Heath Stubbs (1918–   ).

Omayyads. *See* Umayyads.

ombres chinoises (French: Chinese shadows) A form of shadow puppet drama introduced into 18th-century Europe by travelers returning from the Far East. It was popularized in France by the opening of a shadow theater at Versailles in 1774. The technique involved the representation of brief amusing episodes by black silhouettes cast from solid puppets.

ombudsman A person appointed to investigate grievances against central-government administration. The post originated in Sweden in 1809 and exists in most Scandinavian countries.

Omdurman 15 37N 32 29E A city in the Sudan, on the Nile River. The Mahdi made it his capital in 1885 but his successor, the Khalifa, was defeated by Anglo-Egyptian forces under Lord Kitchener in the battle of Omdurman (1898). The Islamic University of Omdurman was founded in 1961. Commerce includes hides, textiles, agricultural produce, and handicrafts. Population (1983): 526,300.

Omsk 55 00N 73 22E A port in central Russia at the confluence of the Irtysh and Om rivers. Also on the Trans-Siberian Railway, it is a significant transportation center and has important engineering industries and oil refineries. Population (1991 est): 1,166,800.

onager A small wild *ass, *Equus hemionus onager*, of Iran. Onagers have a yellow-brown summer coat, which becomes darker in winter, and roam dry grassland in small herds.

Onassis, Aristotle Socrates (1906–75) Greek businessman, who owned one of the largest independent shipping lines in the world. He started his business in 1932 and during the 1950s became one of the first to construct supertankers. In 1968 he married Jacqueline *Kennedy, his second wife, after a long relationship with Maria *Callas.

Oñate, Juan de (d. 1630) Spanish conquistador. In about 1595 he settled the territory NW of Central America, New Mexico, and in 1601 sought the mythical kingdom of Quivira. Later, seeking a strait to the Pacific, he reached the Colorado River and Gulf of California.

Ondes Martenot (English: Martenot waves) An electronic musical instrument invented in 1928 by Maurice Martenot. It consists of oscillators that produce signals, which are then mixed, amplified, and emitted through a loudspeaker. The frequency of the notes is determined by a keyboard and a special metal ribbon, by means of which glissandi can be produced. The keys can also be moved laterally to produce microtonal variations in pitch. The instrument plays an important part in Messiaen's symphony *Turangalîla* (1948).

Onega, Lake A lake in NW Russia, the second largest in Europe. It forms part of the water route from the Gulf of Finland to the White Sea. Area: 3817 sq mi (9887 sq km).

Oneida 43 04N 75 40W A city in New York state. A religious society, the Oneida Community, was established nearby in 1848. Its members, who made silverware and steel traps, held all property in common, but social experiments ceased when it became a joint stock company in 1881. Population (1990): 10,850.

Oneida North American Iroquoian-speaking Indian tribe, part of the *Iroquois League, found in central New York. Descendants of the Oneida now live in New York, Wisconsin, and Canada.

O'Neill, Eugene (1888–1953) US dramatist. The son of actors, he was brought up in the theater and worked for six years as a sailor. He began writing one-act plays while recovering from tuberculosis in a sanatorium. He won critical recognition with *Beyond the Horizon* (1920), *Emperor Jones* (1920), *Anna Christie* (1921), and *Desire Under the Elms* (1924). *Mourning Becomes Electra* (1931) transplants Aeschylus's trilogy to Civil War New England. His finest plays, including *The Iceman Cometh* (1946) and *Long Day's Journey into Night* (1956; written 1940–41), were written while he was suffering from Parkinson's disease and alcoholism. He won the Nobel Prize in 1936.

O'Neill, Thomas P(hilip), Jr. ("Tip"; 1912–94) US politician; speaker of the House of Representatives (1977–87). A Democrat from Massachusetts, he

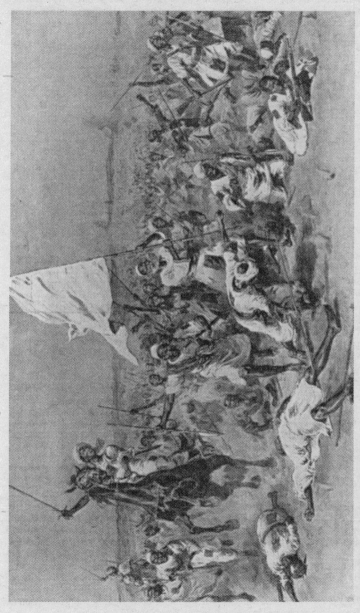

OMDURMAN *A painting of the Battle of Omdurman (1898) showing the first charge of the Dervishes.*

served in the House of Representatives (1952–87). As Speaker he effectively worked behind the scenes to bring opposing factions together in compromise. He wrote *Man of the House* (1987).

EUGENE O'NEILL *Playwright whose dramas earned him the Nobel Prize in literature and four Pulitzer Prizes.*

onion A hardy herbaceous perennial plant, **Allium cepa*, probably native to central or W Asia but now cultivated worldwide, mainly in temperate regions, for its edible bulb. The mature plant has a leafless stalk, about 40 in (1 m) high, which bears a round head of small white flowers, and six long slender leaves growing directly from the bulb. Onions are grown either from seed or from tiny bulbs called sets, produced in the flower head. Immature bulbs, together with their leaves, are eaten raw in salads, etc.: these are spring, or green, onions (*see* scallion). Family: *Liliaceae*.

Onitsha 6 10N 6 47E A port in S Nigeria, on the Niger River. It suffered damage during the civil war (1967–71). It is an important trading center. Agricultural products are the main exports and manufacturing is being developed, including textiles, printing, and tire retreading. Population (1992 est): 337,000.

Onsager, Lars (1903–76) US chemist, born in Norway. His study of the thermodynamics of irreversible processes helped to solve the problems of separating uranium 235 from uranium 238 by gaseous diffusion, which was essential to the production of nuclear fuel. For this work Onsager was awarded the Nobel Prize in 1968.

Ontario The second largest province in Canada, stretching from the Great Lakes N to Hudson Bay. It lies mainly on the mineral-rich Canadian Shield, a rocky forested plateau with many lakes and rivers. Most of the population live in the gentle fertile lowlands near the S Great Lakes, dominated by the highly industrialized belt stretching from Toronto to Windsor. Manufacturing is very important, especially the production of motor vehicles, steel, pulp and paper, textiles, machinery, petrochemicals, and food products. Ontario is Canada's leading mining province, producing half the world's nickel as well as copper, iron, zinc, gold, and uranium. The province's farmers produce tobacco, fruit, vegetables, and dairy products. Ontario is the wealthiest and most populous Canadian province, the country's political and economic heartland, and the cultural and educational center of English-speaking Canada. *History*: penetrated by French explorers and fur traders in the 17th century, Ontario became British (1763) and was settled by *Loyalists after the American Revolution. The province benefited greatly from the formation of Canada (1867), which provided it with a vast hinterland and a larger domestic market. Area: 344,090 sq mi (891,194 sq km). Population (1991): 10,084,855. Capital: Toronto.

Ontario, Lake A lake in E North America, the smallest and easternmost of the Great Lakes. It is fed by the Niagara River and empties into the St Lawrence River. Area: 7313 sq mi (18,941 sq km).

ontogeny. *See* phylogeny.

ontology The branch of philosophy that deals with the theory of being and considers questions about what is and what is not. Ontological theories may assert that only minds exist (extreme *idealism), or that only physical objects do (*see* materialism). The term was introduced by *Wolff to cover one of the chief concerns of *metaphysics.

o'nyong-nyong An acute viral infection occurring in East Africa. The disease, transmitted by mosquitoes, is characterized by a rash, aching joints, headache, and fever. Patients usually recover with rest and drugs to relieve the pain and fever.

onyx A semiprecious stone consisting of a variety of *chalcedony characterized by straight parallel bands, often distinctly colored. Onyx occurs in the lower part of steam cavities in igneous rocks. **Sardonyx** (birthstone for August) is a variety with reddish bands.

oolite A variety of *limestone consisting mainly of beds of ooliths, approximately spherical concretions of calcite accumulated in concentric layers around a nucleus (for example a grain of sand or fragment of a shell). Ooliths of greater diameter than 0.08 in (2 mm) are called pisoliths and the resultant rocks pisolites. Although most oolites are calcareous, oolitic ironstones also occur.

Oort cloud A cloud of 10 million or more comets, thought to move around the sun in near-circular orbits that lie in a zone far beyond Pluto's orbit. A comet can be perturbed out of the cloud by, say, a passing star and sent toward the sun, taking many thousands of years to complete its orbit. The cloud is named for the Dutch astronomer Jan Hendrik Oort (1900–   ).

opah. *See* moonfish.

opal A semiprecious stone consisting of a hydrous amorphous variety of silica. Common opal is a dull-white or milky-blue color, with yellow, brown, or red tinges due to impurities. The precious variety, used as a gem, shows a characteristic internal play of colors (opalescence) resulting from internal reflection and refraction of light passing through adjacent thin layers of different water content. It occurs in cavities in many rocks, deposited by percolating silica-bearing water; geyserite is a variety deposited from hot springs. The variety diatomite, made up of diatom skeletons, is used industrially as an insulator, abrasive, and filtering agent. The main sources of opal gems are Australia and Mexico. Birthstone for October.

Op art A form of abstract art, developed in the 1950s and 1960s, that exploits optical techniques to produce dramatic effects, such as the illusion of movement. Violent color contrasts and subtly distorted patterns are commonly used. Notable exponents include Victor *Vasarely in the US and Bridget *Riley in the UK.

OPEC. *See* Organization of Petroleum Exporting Countries.

Open Door A policy promulgated by the US in 1899 to ensure equal trading rights in China for all countries. Its own trade with China threatened by the growing influence there of the other major powers, the US sought and received the guarantee by Britain, France, Germany, Italy, and Japan of the maintenance of Chinese integrity.

open-hearth process A technique for making *steel from *pig iron, scrap steel, and iron ore. It was developed in the 1850s and is still used, although *electric-arc furnaces are being used increasingly, especially for high-grade steel. The process uses gaseous fuel, which is preheated by the exhaust gases from the furnace. The molten metal lies in a shallow pool at the bottom or hearth of the furnace.

opera A staged dramatic work in which all or most of the text is set to music. Opera originated in Florence in the early 17th century as the result of attempts to revive Greek tragedy and to reproduce its musical elements. These became the aria, recitative, and chorus of operatic convention. Opera began in the court but quickly became a popular public entertainment. The earliest opera still in the modern repertory is Monteverdi's *Orfeo* (1607). In *opera seria, the Italian style of opera developed by such composers as Scarlatti, Lully, and Handel, vocal ability became the dominant feature until Gluck reaffirmed the importance of the dramatic element in the mid-18th century. *Opera buffa developed in the early 18th century and was originally performed between the acts of opera seria. At the end of the 18th century Mozart perfected opera buffa, giving it greater depth and expression. In the early 19th century the influence of romanticism gave rise to the works of Weber and Meyerbeer, while the Italian *bel canto tradition was maintained by Bellini, Rossini, and Donizetti. In the mid-19th century Wagner evolved the theory of music drama, in which the musical and dramatic elements of opera were integrated. He applied it to his opera cycle *Der ring des Nibelungen* (1869–1876) and his subsequent operas, which embodied his theory of the *gesamtkunstwerk* (German: complete work of art). Verdi extended the emotional and dramatic range of Italian opera and in his late works assimilated the Wagnerian technique of continuous music in each act in place of the traditional division into separate numbers. The realism of Bizet's *Carmen* (1875) influenced Leoncavallo, Mascagni, and Puccini. In the 20th century a wide variety of operatic styles have flourished, including the dramatic realism of Janáček and the neoclassicism of Stravinsky. Richard Strauss's operas were greatly influenced by Wagner, as was Debussy's opera *Pelléas et Mélisande* (1902). Schoenberg and Berg applied atonal and serial techniques to opera. Other important operatic composers of the 20th century include Prokofiev, Britten, Henze, and Tippett. *See also* opéra comique; comic opera; operetta.

opera buffa A form of comic *opera containing some spoken dialogue. It evolved in Italy in the 18th century, an early example being *Pergolesi's *La* *serva padrona* (1733). The French genre, *opéra bouffe*, evolved from it in the 19th century and is typified by *Offenbach's operettas.

opéra comique 1. A type of French comic opera of the 18th century with spoken dialogue. 2. In the 19th century, any French opera with spoken dialogue, a category including Bizet's *Carmen* and Gounod's *Faust*.

opera seria A type of *opera common in the 18th century, characterized by a mythological or heroic plot, an Italian libretto, and a formal musical scheme of recitatives and arias.

Operation Desert Storm (Jan–Feb 1991) The response by a coalition of UN countries led by the US to Iraq's invasion and annexation of Kuwait in Aug 1990. After coalition forces built up forces in Saudi Arabia and after attempts to settle the issue peacefully failed, the war to free Kuwait began on Jan 17, 1991, with sustained air attacks on Iraq and Kuwait. Iraq's leader, Saddam *Hussein, then ordered missile attacks on coalition troops in Saudi Arabia and on Israel. A ground assault on Kuwait and Iraq began on Feb 23, 1991, and within 100 hours the coalition forces under Gen. Norman *Schwartzkopf had regained Kuwait. Coalition losses were extremely light; Iraq's were heavy.

ophthalmology The medical specialty concerned with the study, diagnosis, and treatment of diseases of the eye. Ophthalmologists are doctors specializing in this. **Optometry** is the assessment and correction of visual defects, and opticians are not doctors: ophthalmic opticians both test eyesight and prescribe suitable lenses; dispensing opticians make and fit glasses.

Ophüls, Max (M. Oppenheimer, 1902–57) German film director. He worked mostly in France, Italy, and the US. His stylish and elaborate romantic films include *Letter From An Unknown Woman* (1948), *La Ronde* (1950), and *Lola Montes* (1955).

Opitz (von Boberfeld), Martin (1597–1639) German poet and man of letters. Educated at Heidelberg, he served in the courts of various German nobles until he was appointed historiographer to Ladislaus IV of Poland. His own verse, for example *Teutsche Poemata* (1624), lacks originality but was, with his translations and critical works, especially *Buch von der teutschen Poeterey* (1624), extremely influential in providing a model for German verse and in introducing the work of the *Pléiade, Sidney's *Arcadia*, and other foreign writers.

opium The dried juice obtained from the seed capsule of the *opium poppy. A narcotic drug, opium has been used for centuries in medicine for the relief of pain. Although still sometimes given in the form of laudanum (tincture of opium), its main legitimate uses today include the extraction of its active ingredients—*morphine (first isolated in 1803), codeine, papaverine, etc.—and preparation of their derivatives (e.g. heroin). Because opium causes *drug dependence and overdosage can be fatal, its preparation and use are strictly controlled (in spite of this, illegal trading in opium continues). India and Turkey are the main opium-producing countries.

opium poppy An annual *poppy, *Papaver somniferum*, cultivated since ancient times in N temperate and subtropical regions as the source of *opium; 12–24 in (30–60 cm) tall, it has large white to purple flowers with dark centers and the fruit is a round capsule. Opium is extracted from the latex of the plant, which exudes from notches made in the half-ripened capsule and hardens on exposure to air.

Opium Wars 1. (1839–42) The war between Britain and China precipitated by the confiscation by the Chinese government of British opium stores in Canton and the murder of a Chinese by British sailors. The British victory was confirmed by the Treaty of Nanking in which five *treaty ports were opened to British trade and residence. **2.** (1856–60) The war between Britain and France, on one side, and China. Its immediate cause was the boarding of a British ship by Chinese officials. The allied victory opened further ports to Western trade (Treaty of Tientsin, 1858, to which the Chinese agreed in the Peking Convention, 1860) and led to the legalization of opium.

Opole (German name: Oppeln) 50 40N 17 56E A city in SW Poland, on the Oder River. It was the capital (1919–45) of the German province of Upper Silesia. Industries include the manufacture of machinery, chemicals, cement, and textiles. Population (1992 est): 128,900.

Oporto (Portuguese name: Pôrto) 41 09N 8 37W The second largest city in Portugal, on the Douro River near the Atlantic coast. Built on terraces, it has many tall granite houses and a modernized 13th-century cathedral; its university was founded in 1911. It is famous for the export (chiefly to Britain) of its port wine; other exports include fruit, olive oil, and cork. Population (1991): 350,000.

opossum A New World *marsupial belonging to the family *Didelphidae* (65 species). Opossums are the only marsupials outside Australasia. The common, or Virginian, opossum (*Didelphys marsupialis*) is cat-sized, with a large pouch containing up to 16 teats; it produces at least two litters of young every year. After about three months the young ride on their mother's back, leaving the pouch free for another litter. Opossums live in crevices and abandoned burrows, feeding on both animal and vegetable matter. □mammal.

OPOSSUM *Young common opossums cling to their mother's fur after emerging from the pouch and remain close to her for about three months before leading an independent existence.*

Oppeln. *See* Opole.

Oppenheimer, J. Robert (1904–67) US physicist, who contributed to quantum mechanics and particle physics. In 1943 he was put in charge of the development of the atom bomb at Los Alamos, NM. After the war he was appointed chairman of the advisory committee to the Atomic Energy Commission but as a result of his opposition to the development of the hydrogen bomb, he lost his post in 1953 and was labeled a security risk by Sen. Joseph *McCarthy's committee. He also served as director (1947–66) of Princeton's Institute for Advanced Study.

opposition An alignment of two celestial bodies in the solar system, usually the sun and a planet, that occurs when they lie directly opposite each other in the sky. The angle planet-earth-sun is then 180°. Venus and Mercury cannot come to opposition with the sun. For the other planets, opposition is the most favorable time for observation.

Ops A Roman fertility goddess, wife of Saturn, identified with the Greek *Rhea. She was usually worshiped together with a primitive rustic god, Consus.

optical activity The rotation of the plane of polarization of plane *polarized light as it passes through certain solutions and crystals. The angle through which the plane is rotated is directly proportional to the path length of the light in the substance and, in the case of a solution, to its concentration. If the plane is rotated clockwise (looking at the oncoming light) the substance is said to be dextrorotatory and is indicated by the prefix *d*–. Levorotatory substances, indicated by *l*–, rotate the plane counterclockwise.

optics The branch of physics concerned with *light and vision. Optics is divided into two major branches: geometrical optics and physical optics. Geometrical optics studies the geometry of light rays as they pass through an optical system. Physical optics is the study of the properties of light including *diffraction, *interference, and polarization (*see* polarized light) and the interaction between light and matter as in *refraction, *scattering, and absorption.

option The right to buy or sell something at an agreed price by a specified date. Usually the option costs a sum of money (the option money), which is not returned if the option is not taken up. Options are sought for such diverse assets as the right to buy a house, the film rights of a book, or a line of stocks or shares. On stock and commodity exchanges options to buy shares or commodities (a call option) or to sell them (a put option) are regular features of trading.

Opuntia. *See* prickly pear.

Opus Dei (Latin: God's work) **1.** In Benedictine monasticism, the monk's primary duty of prayer. It specifically refers to the recitation of prescribed prayers (the Divine Office) at set times known as the canonical hours, namely matins, lauds, prime, terce, sext (noon), nones, vespers, and compline. **2.** An international Roman Catholic organization originating in Spain (1928). It was founded to spread Christian ideals, particularly in university and government circles, and its members include priests and laymen.

orache An annual branching herb or small shrub of the genus *Atriplex* (about 100 species), occurring worldwide on sea shores and waste land and growing 40 in–5 ft (1–1.5 m) high. The leaves are narrow or triangular and, in some species, may be used as a vegetable. Tiny green flowers are borne in a branching cluster and the fruit is surrounded by a winglike membrane. Family: *Chenopodiaceae*.

oracle A response given by a deity, usually through the medium of a priest or priestess, to an individual's inquiry; also, the sacred place at which such responses were sought. Although occurring in Egyptian and other ancient civilizations, the best-known oracles were those of classical Greece. The oldest was that of Zeus at Dodona, where the oracle was interpreted from the rustling of the leaves of oak trees. At the oracle of Apollo at Delphi, which attained great political influence during the 6th and 7th centuries BC, the oracular pronouncements made by the Pythian priestess in a state of frenzy were interpreted in verse by the priests.

Oracle. *See* teletext.

Oradea 47 03N 21 55E A city in NW Romania, on the Crişul Repede River. It is situated in a wine-producing area where many Neolithic, Roman, and other artifacts have been found. Its varied industries include the manufacture of machine tools, chemicals, and food products. Population (1992): 220,848.

oral contraceptive A hormonal drug—usually a mixture of an *estrogen and a synthetic *progesterone—taken in the form of tablets ("the Pill") by women to prevent conception. Oral contraceptives act by preventing the monthly release of an egg cell from the ovary. They are taken every day from the 5th to the 26th day of the menstrual cycle (menstruation occurs during the week in which they are not taken). The Pill may cause fluid retention, depression, high blood pressure, weight gain, and in rare cases thrombosis.

Oran (Arabic name: Wahran; French name: Ouahran) 35 45N 0 38W A port in Algeria, on the Mediterranean Sea. Under intermittent Spanish occupation from the 16th to the 18th centuries, it was occupied by France from 1831 until Algerian independence (1962). It has a university (1965). Exports include cereals, wine, wool, and esparto grass. Population (1987): 628,558.

orange One of several small evergreen □trees or shrubs of the genus *Citrus*, native to SE Asia but cultivated throughout the tropics and subtropics. The thick oval shiny leaves have winged stalks and the fragrant white five-petaled flowers are borne in clusters. The globular fruit has a dimpled orange or yellow rind and a juicy pulp, rich in sugars, acids, and vitamin C. Fruit of the sweet orange (*C. sinensis*) is eaten fresh while that of the Seville orange (*C. aurantium*) is used to make marmalade. Oranges are also used in soft drinks and confectionery. Family: *Rutaceae. See also* tangerine.

Orange The ruling dynasty of the Netherlands since 1815. In the 16th century the prince of Orange, in S France, married into the House of *Nassau, a member of which, *William the Silent, became prince of Orange-Nassau (1544) and led the Revolt of the Netherlands against Spain. He and his descendants (one of whom became William III of England) were *stadtholders (chief magistrates) of the United Provinces of the Netherlands until its collapse in 1795. In 1815 the family were restored as monarchs of the newly established kingdom of the Netherlands. The principality of Orange was seized by Louis XIV in 1660.

Orange 44 08N 4 48E A city in SE France, in the Vaucluse department. It was the capital of the principality of Orange in the Middle Ages, the descendants of which formed the House of Orange. There are several notable Roman remains. Population (1975): 26,468.

Orange Free State (Afrikaans name: Oranje Urystaat) An inland province in South Africa. Much of the province consists of the undulating plain of the Highveld. It is predominantly rural, with agriculture as the leading economic activity. Wheat, maize, and stock rearing are important. Mining has developed recently; diamonds, gold, uranium, and coal are produced. Chemicals, fertilizers, and oil from coal are manufactured. The province has a strong Afrikaner culture. *History*: first settled by Voortrekkers in the early 19th century, it was under British rule as the Orange River Sovereignty from 1848 until an independent Orange Free State was recognized in 1854. It joined the Union of South Africa in 1910. Area: 49,886 sq mi (129,152 sq km). Population (1991): 1,929,392. Capital: Bloemfontein.

Orange Order An Irish sectarian society, named for William III of England (previously William of Orange), pledged to maintain the Protestant succession. Formed in 1795, following William's defeat of the Roman Catholic former king James II, it provided the backbone of Ulster resistance to the *Home Rule movement. The embodiment of Protestant Unionism, its parades have contributed to the political unrest of Northern Irish politics.

Orange River A river in SW Africa. Rising in NE Lesotho, it flows mainly W across the South African plateau to the Atlantic Ocean. The largest river in South Africa, it forms part of the border between South Africa and Namibia. In 1963 the **Orange River Project** was begun to provide, through a series of dams, irrigation and hydroelectric power. Length: 1300 mi (2093 km).

orangutan A long-armed great *ape, *Pongo pygmaeus*, of Borneo and Sumatra. Orangutans grow up to 47 in (120 cm) tall, with arms spanning more than 79 in (200 cm), and have long coarse reddish-brown hair. Mainly vegetarian, they are especially fond of durian fruit. They are the only great apes outside Africa and there are fewer than 5000 individuals in the wild.

Oratorians Communities of Roman Catholic priests who live together without taking vows and who devote themselves to teaching, preaching, prayer, and administration of the sacraments. There are two orders: the Italian Oratory of St Philip Neri (founded 1564) and the French Oratoire de Jésus-Christ (1611). The former has oratories in England founded by Cardinal Newman. The latter runs seminaries for the training of priests.

oratorio A musical composition, usually on a religious subject, for soloists, chorus, and orchestra. The name derives from the Oratory of St Philip Neri in 16th-century Rome (*see* Oratorians), where semidramatized versions of biblical stories were performed with musical accompaniment. Among notable oratorios are the *St Matthew* and *St John Passions* of J. S. Bach, Handel's *Messiah*, Haydn's *The Creation.*, Mendelssohn's *Elijah*, Berlioz's *Childhood of Christ*, Elgar's *Dream of Gerontius*, and Tippett's *A Child of Our Time*.

orbital An atomic orbital is the region around the nucleus in which there is an appreciable probability that an electron will be found. In *wave mechanics an electron does not have a fixed orbit as it does in the *Bohr atom; it has instead an orbital in which there is a probability distribution, given by a wave function, that it will be found in a particular region. Each orbital has a fixed energy and a shape determined by three *quantum numbers, one (n) indicating the most probable distance of the electron from the nucleus, one (l) giving its angular momentum, and one (m) giving the orientation of the orbital if it is not spherical. In the formation of a covalent bond between two atoms, a molecular orbital containing two electrons is formed.

orb weaver A *spider belonging to a widely distributed family (*Argiopidae*; over 2500 species), noted for its geometrically designed web. For example, the web of the orange-garden spider (*Miranda aurantia*), common in grass and bushes, has a zigzag band and reaches 24 in (60 cm) across.

Orcagna, Andrea (Andrea di Cione; c. 1308–c. 1368) Florentine artist. His only certain surviving painting is the altarpiece in the Strozzi Chapel of Sta Maria Novella, Florence; as a sculptor he is known for his marble tabernacle in Orsanmichele. He became architect to Orsanmichele (1355) and to the Duomo in Florence (1357 and 1364–67) and in Orvieto (1358).

orchestra A body of instrumentalists playing music written or arranged for a specific combination of instruments. The modern **symphony orchestra** evolved from the small and variously constituted orchestras of the 18th century; its original instrumentation (first and second violins, violas, cellos, double basses, bassoons, oboes, flutes, horns, and timpani) being that of the typical symphony. Such orchestras were directed from a continuo keyboard instrument or by the leader of the first violin section. In the 19th century the orchestra was enlarged and the range of instruments widened by the addition of clarinets, trumpets, trombones, and percussion instruments; later the harp, cor anglais, piccolo, bass clarinet, contra bassoon, and tuba were added. In the late 19th century the number of woodwind and brass was increased, and such instruments as the saxophone, saxhorn, Wagner tuba, glockenspiel, and xylophone were occasionally used. The role of the conductor became increasingly important from the early 19th century onward. In the 20th century the piano, guitar, mandolin, marimba, vibraphone, as well as various electric and electronic instruments have all had orchestral parts written for them. The modern symphony orchestra comprises at least a hundred players. The **chamber orchestra** corresponds in size to the smaller orchestras of the 18th century.

orchid A herbaceous perennial plant of the family *Orchidaceae* (about 20,000 species), found worldwide, especially in damp tropical regions. Most temperate orchids grow normally in the soil (i.e. they are terrestrial), while tropical orchids tend to grow nonparasitically on trees (i.e. as epiphytes) and form pseudobulbs (storage organs) at the base of the stem. Orchid flowers vary greatly in shape, color, and size and occur usually in clusters. Each flower consists of three petal-like sepals and three petals—the lowest (labellum) being very distinctive. The one or two stamens and stigma are fused to form a central column that bears pollen grains grouped into masses (pollinia), which are transferred to other flowers by insects. The flowers of many species are adapted to receive only a particular species of insects in order to restrict natural hybridization; examples are the bee, fly, and spider orchids (genus *Ophrys*). The fruit is a capsule containing enormous numbers of tiny seeds, which are dispersed by wind. Many orchids are cultivated for ornament, both commercially for the florist trade and by amateur growers (*see* Cattleya; Cymbidium; Odontoglossum; slipper orchid); one genus—*Vanilla*—is of commercial importance as the source of vanilla flavoring.

orchil (*or* archil) One of several *lichens (*Umbilicaria, Roccella, Evernia, Lecanova*, and *Ochrolechia*) from which a violet dye can be extracted by fermentation. The name is also applied to the dye itself.

Orczy, Baroness Emmusca (1865–1947) British novelist. Born in Hungary, she went to London to study art. Her best-known novel is *The Scarlet Pimpernel* (1905), concerning the adventures of an English nobleman who smuggles aristocrats out of Revolutionary France.

Order of the British Empire, The Most Excellent A British order of knighthood, instituted in 1917 and having five classes: Knights or Dames Grand Cross (GBE); Knights or Dames Commanders (KBE or DBE); Commanders (CBE); Officers (OBE); and Members (MBE). Its motto is *For God and Empire*.

orders of architecture The fundamental elements of classical □architecture, comprising five main types of supportive column—Doric, Tuscan, Ionic, Corinthian, and Composite. The column was first employed by the Egyptians but it was developed by the Greeks and Romans to such an extent that the proportions between the column's constituent parts determined the proportions of the entire building.

Each order usually consists of four main parts, the base, shaft, *capital, and entablature, these having individual shapes and types of decoration. The first order to be developed, the Doric, takes two forms: the Greek Doric, which has no base, and the Roman Doric, more slender in proportion and with a base. Roman Doric's unadorned and unfluted counterpart is the Tuscan order. The Ionic first appeared in Asia Minor in about the 6th century BC and was adopted by the Greeks in the 5th century BC. It has slender proportions and a capital adorned with four spiral scrolls (volutes), two at the front and two at the back.

The most decorative order, the Corinthian, was developed by the Romans, although it was occasionally used in ancient Greece. The Romans also combined the Corinthian capital of *acanthus leaves with the volutes of the Ionic capital to form the Composite order.

A **pilaster** is a rectangular column attached to the wall. It conforms to the system of orders but, unlike the cylindrical column, is usually only decorative in function.

Ordovician period A geological period of the Lower Paleozoic era, between the Cambrian and Silurian periods. It lasted from about 515 to 445 million years ago. It is divided into the Upper and Lower Ordovician, based on the graptolite fossils that are abundant in the deepwater deposits.

ore A rock body or mineral deposit from which one or more useful materials, usually metals, can be economically extracted. The metal content of the various ores differs; iron ore contains about 20–30% iron, whereas copper ores may contain only 0.5% copper. The gangue is the waste material left when the desired mineral has been extracted.

Örebro 59 17N 15 13E A city in S Sweden. An ancient city, it was largely rebuilt following a fire in 1854. It has a university (1967) and its manufactures include footwear, machinery, and chemicals. Population (1992 est): 122,042.

oregano An aromatic perennial herb, *Origanum vulgare*, native to the Mediterranean and W Asia. The dried leaves and flowers are used as a culinary flavoring and the plant is a source of essential oils. Family: *Labiatae*.

Oregon A state on the NW Pacific coast; bordered by California and Nevada to the S, the Pacific Ocean to the W, Washington to the N, and Idaho to the E. Its topography is diverse, the Cascade Range extends N–S dividing the state between the valleys of the W and the dry plateau areas of the E. The Willamette Valley contains the major settlements. The economy is based predominantly on agriculture and forestry. Oregon is the nation's leading timber state and approximately half its area is forested; the Douglas fir is especially important. Much of the timber is used to produce plywood, pulp, and paper. Agriculture includes cattle ranching in the drier areas, dairy farming in the valleys, and wheat growing in the NE; specialized crops, such as cherries, are also grown. Hydroelectric-power resources have led to the development of metal-processing industries. *History*: originally occupied by several Indian tribes, the first extensive US exploration was by the *Lewis and Clark Expedition (1805). Fur traders became active shortly thereafter. There was considerable migration of settlers from the Midwest along the famous *Oregon Trail during the mid-19th century. It became a territory in 1848 and a state in 1859, after being separated from Washington (1853). Industrial development and the state's relatively unspoiled environment spurred growth in the 20th century. Area: 96,981 sq mi (251,180 sq km). Population (1990): 2,842,321. Capital: Salem.

Oregon Trail An overland route from the Missouri to the Columbia River, first followed by explorers and fur traders, and later by settlers. Traversing more than 2000 mi (3200 km) of frontier territory, the Oregon Trail began at Independence, Mo., crossed the Rockies at the South Pass, then followed the course of the Colorado and Snake rivers, and ended at Astoria, a fur trading center at the outlet of the Columbia River. During the Great Migration of 1842–43, thousands of settlers from the American Midwest followed the route of the Oregon Trail in wagon trains to establish new homes and towns in the Oregon territory.

Oregon Treaty (1846) US-British agreement that settled the N boundary line of the US west of the Rocky Mountains. A compromise, the treaty set the boundary at the 49th parallel except for the island of Vancouver. The British, through the *Hudson's Bay Company, retained free navigation rights on the *Columbia River.

Orel (*or* Oryol) 52 58N 36 04E A city in W Russia. Founded in 1564, it was severely damaged in World War II. Industries include engineering. The writer Turgenev was born there, and his house is now a museum. Population (1991 est): 345,000.

Orenburg (name from 1938 until 1957: Chkalov) 51 50N 55 00E A city in W Russia, on the Ural River. It was founded in 1735 by the Cossacks on the site of present-day Orsk, subsequently being moved downstream. Industries include engineering and consumer-goods manufacture. Population (1991 est): 556,500.

Orense 42 20N 7 52W A city in NW Spain, in Galicia on the Miño River. It possesses a cathedral and a remarkable bridge built in 1230. Industries include iron founding and flour milling. Population (1991): 101,623.

Oresme, Nicole d' (c. 1320–82) French philosopher and churchman. He became master of the College of Navarre at Paris in 1355 and later Bishop of Lisieux (1377). His writings deal with politics, natural science, geometry, and economics. He was also an early advocate of the theory that the earth revolves around other bodies.

Orestes In Greek legend, the son of *Agamemnon, king of Mycenae, and *Clytemnestra. Encouraged by his sister *Electra, he avenged his father's murder by killing his mother and her lover Aegisthus. In the dramatic trilogy of *Aeschylus he is pursued by the *Erinyes until he is acquitted at the Areopagus in Athens by the deciding vote of Athena.

Øresund (*or* Öresund). *See* Sound, the.

orfe A carnivorous food and game fish, *Idus idus*, also called ide, found in rivers and lakes of Europe and NW Asia. Its stout elongated body, 12–20 in (30–50 cm) long, is blue-gray or blackish with a silvery belly. The golden orfe is a reddish-gold variety. Family: *Cyprinidae*; order: *Cypriniformes*.

Orff, Carl (1895–1982) German composer, teacher, conductor, and editor. He developed a monodic style of composition characterized by lively rhythms; his best-known work is the scenic oratorio *Carmina Burana* (1935–36), based on 13th-century Latin and German poems found in a Benedictine monastery in Bavaria. Orff also developed educational percussion instruments, such as the stone chimes.

organ A musical wind instrument of early origin, which developed from the reed pipes and the *hydraulis. The modern organ consists of a large number of graduated pipes, some of which contain reeds, fitted over a wind chest and blown by manual or electric bellows. The pipes are made to sound by depressing keys or pedals. Each pipe sounds one note, but groups of duplicate pipes, called stops, can be made to sound together or successively. Different stops have different tone colors, many of which resemble orchestral instruments. An organ console may have as many as five or more keyboards, known as the great, swell, choir, solo, and echo, as well as pedals. Each keyboard has a separate range of stops and different characteristics; the swell, for example, has shutters over the pipe holes that allow crescendos and decrescendos.

Coupler mechanisms allow one keyboard to become automatically linked to another. These allow, for example the pedals, which normally play the deepest notes, to play notes many octaves higher.

The action linking keys and pipes consists of a series of rods called a tracker action or wires conveying electrical impulses. The modern **electronic organ** consists of a series of electronic oscillators to produce notes, which are then amplified.

organic chemistry. *See* chemistry.

Organisation de l'Armée secrète (OAS) An organization of French settlers in Algeria opposed to Algerian independence from France. The OAS was established in 1961 and led by General Raoul Salan. Its campaign of terrorism in Algeria and France included the attempted assassination in September 1961, of the French president, de Gaulle, who by March 1962, had reached agreement with the Algerian nationalists (*see* Front de Libération nationale). Salan was captured in April (and imprisoned 1962–68) and the OAS collapsed.

Organization for Economic Cooperation and Development (OECD) An international organization founded in 1961 to further economic growth among its members, expand world trade, and coordinate aid to developing countries. It succeeded the Organization for European Economic Cooperation, which had been set up in 1948 to coordinate the *Marshall Plan for European economic recovery after World War II. The headquarters of the OECD are in Paris.

Organization of African Unity (OAU) An intergovernmental organization of independent African countries. It was founded in 1963 to provide a forum for discussion of political and economic problems affecting African states and to formulate policies toward such problems. The OAU meets annually but maintains a standing committee in Addis Ababa (Ethiopia).

Organization of American States (OAS) A body founded in 1948 to foster mutual understanding and cooperation between American republics and collective security. It is based on the principle of the *Monroe Doctrine. In 1962 Cuba was expelled from the OAS because of its acceptance of nuclear missiles from the Soviet Union.

Organization of Central American States An international organization founded in 1951. Its members include Costa Rica, El Salvador, Guatemala, Honduras, and Nicaragua, and its headquarters are in Guatemala City. Its aim is to promote social, cultural, and economic development through joint action.

Organization of Petroleum Exporting Countries (OPEC) An organization founded in 1960 to represent the interests of the 13 chief oil-exporting nations (Algeria, Ecuador, Gabon, Indonesia, Iran, Iraq, Kuwait, Libya, Nigeria, Qatar, Saudi Arabia, United Arab Emirates, and Venezuela) in dealings with the major oil companies. OPEC was long the only really successful primary-product *cartel, deciding in 1973 to double its share in the receipts from oil exported; later attempts to control the price of oil were not as successful.

organ-pipe cactus A branching columnar *cactus, of the genus *Lemacrocereus* or *Cereus*, especially *L. thurberi*, which resembles a candelabrum and is found in deserts of the S US and Mexico. Up to 33 ft (10 m) high, the fruit is edible.

organ-pipe coral A *coral, *Tubipora musica*, occurring in shallow waters of the Indian and Pacific Oceans. It is composed of a colony of long upright stalked *polyps supported by bright-red skeletal tubes of fused spicules. Order: *Stolonifera*.

organum (Latin: organ, instrument) A type of medieval polyphonic vocal composition in which a plainchant melody was accompanied by voices at the fixed intervals of the octave and fourth or fifth. *See also* ars antiqua.

oribi A rare antelope, *Ourebia ourebi*, of African grasslands. About 35 in (90 cm) high at the shoulder, oribis have slender legs, large ears, a fawn coat, and a short bristly tail; males have short straight horns. Hiding among long grass during the day, they graze in small herds at dawn and dusk.

orienteering A navigational sport, held over rugged country, that originated in Sweden in 1918 and is designed to test both intellectual and athletic ability. Using a map and compass, competitors run around a series of control points that must be visited in the prescribed sequence. Distances range from 2–8 mi (3–13 km).

origami The oriental art of paper folding, which developed into a traditional Japanese craft. It is used in the formal ceremonial wrapping of gifts and to construct models of birds, animals, sailing boats, etc., which can often be made to move, e.g. birds that flap their wings. It now enjoys a wide popularity outside Japan.

Origen (c. 185–c. 254 AD) Egyptian theologian and Father of the Church, born at Alexandria, son of a Christian martyr. As head of Alexandria's catechetical school he gained fame as a teacher. He was ordained in Palestine (c. 230), but the bishop of Alexandria immediately unfrocked him, maintaining that he was unfit for priesthood because he had castrated himself. He then settled in Caesarea, where he founded a school. During the persecution of Emperor Decius (c. 250) he was imprisoned and tortured at Tyre. The most famous of his many influential works are his critical edition of the Bible, the *Hexapla*, and his theological treatise, *De principiis*.

original sin In Christian doctrine, the inherent wickedness of mankind occasioned by Adam's fall (Genesis 3). After much debate by the Church Fathers, St *Augustine of Hippo's diagnosis, that it is inescapably transmitted to us by our parents and that only the divine initiative of *grace can redeem us, was accepted as orthodox (*see also* Pelagius). St Thomas *Aquinas accorded greater scope to the human will, and after the Reformation the concept of original sin became unfashionable among many theologians. Many modern thinkers reject it or interpret it symbolically.

Orinoco River (Spanish name: Río Orinoco) The third largest river system in South America. Rising in S Venezuela, it flows in an arc forming part of the Venezuela-Colombia border before entering the Atlantic Ocean via an extensive delta region. It provides an important communications system; oceangoing vessels can penetrate upstream for about 226 mi (364 km). Drainage basin area: 365,000 sq mi (940,000 sq km). Length: about 2575 km (1600 mi).

oriole A songbird belonging to an Old World family (*Oriolidae*; 28 species) occurring mainly in tropical forests. Orioles generally have a black-and-yellow plumage, measure 7–12 in (18–30 cm), and feed on fruit and insects. The golden oriole (*Oriolus oriolus*) is the only species reaching Europe, visiting Britain in the summer.

American orioles belong to the family *Icteridae* (87 species); 6–21 in (16–54 cm) long, they usually have a black plumage with red, yellow, or brown markings.

Orion A very conspicuous constellation that lies on the celestial equator and can therefore be seen from most parts of the world. The brightest stars, *Rigel and the slightly fainter *Betelgeuse, lie at opposite corners of a quadrilateral of stars with Bellatrix and Saiph, both 2nd magnitude, at the other corners. Inside the quadrilateral three 2nd-magnitude stars form **Orion's Belt**, S of which lies the **Orion nebula**, one of the brightest emission □nebulae.

Orissa A state in E India, on the Bay of Bengal. Its coastal plain extends through the Eastern *Ghats via broad valleys into interior highlands. Orissa is grossly overcrowded and its inhabitants farm rice, turmeric, and sugar cane.

Fishing, forestry, and the mining of iron ore, manganese, chromite, and coal are economically important. There is also some heavy industry. *History*: known from ancient times, Orissa ruled a maritime empire during the 1st millennium AD. Partitioned by Muslim conquerors (17th century), it gradually fell under British domination (18th–19th centuries). Area: 60,132 sq mi (155,782 sq km). Population (1991): 31,512,070. Capital: Bhubaneswar.

Orizaba 18 51N 97 08W A city and resort in E central Mexico. It is the chief center of the textile industry. Population (1980): 114,850.

Orkney Islands (*or* Orkneys) A group of about 70 islands off the N coast of Scotland, separated from the mainland by the Pentland Firth. About 20 of the islands are inhabited; the chief ones are Mainland (Pomona), South Ronaldsay, Westray, Sanday, and Hoy. The population is of Scandinavian descent, reflecting the Islands' long connections with Norway and Denmark. Agriculture is of major importance within the Islands' economy, producing chiefly beef cattle and poultry. It serves as a base for the exploitation of North Sea oil. Area: 376 sq mi (974 sq km). Administrative center: Kirkwall.

Orlando 28 33N 81 21W A city in central Florida. A tourist resort, it is the commercial center for citrus growing. Walt Disney World is situated nearby. Population (1990): 164,693.

Orlando, Vittorio Emanuele (1860–1952) Italian statesman; prime minister (1917–19). Representing Italy at the Paris Peace Conference (1919) after World War I, his failure to secure sufficiently favorable terms for Italy led to his resignation. He supported Mussolini and *Matteotti's murder in 1924, retiring from politics until after World War II. He was elected to the Senate in 1948.

Orléans 47 54N 1 54E A city in N France, the capital of the Loiret department on the Loire River. In 1429, during the Hundred Years' War, the city was delivered from the English by Joan of Arc. Its cathedral, which was destroyed by the Huguenots in 1568, was rebuilt in the 17th century. The focal point of road and rail routes, Orléans has an extensive trade in wine, brandy, and agricultural produce. Its manufactures include machinery, electrical goods, and textiles. Population (1990): 107,965.

Orléans, Charles, Duc d' (1394–1465) French poet. He was captured by the English at the battle of Agincourt (1415) and spent the next 25 years in prison in England, where he wrote a collection of poems in English. His son became Louis XII of France.

Orléans, Louis Philippe Joseph, Duc d' (1747–93) French revolutionary. A cousin of Louis XVI of France, he nevertheless supported the dissident Third Estate at the beginning of the *French Revolution. He joined the radical Jacobins in 1791 and voted for the execution of the king. He was himself executed after his son (later King Louis Philippe) had joined the Austrian coalition against France.

Orléans, Siege of (October 1428–May 1429) English siege of the strategically important city of Orléans during the *Hundred Years' War, undertaken with little success on either side until the arrival of *Joan of Arc to relieve the city. Her achievement of this aim was a notable factor in French military resurgence and signaled the beginning of the end of English occupation.

Orlov, Grigori Grigorievich, Count (1734–83) Russian soldier, who was the lover of *Catherine the Great. Orlov and his brother **Aleksei Grigorievich Orlov** (1737–1807) led the coup d'état that placed Catherine on the throne in 1862. Grigori Orlov had a favorable position at court but exerted little influence over Catherine.

Ormandy, Eugene (E. Blau; 1899–1985) Hungarian-born US conductor. His early career was as a violinist, but he turned to conducting soon after settling in the US in 1921. He was conductor of the Philadelphia Orchestra, in succession to Stokowski, from 1938 to 1980.

ormolu (French: *d'or moulu*, powdered gold) Ornamental gilded bronze usually used as embellishment on furniture. The 17th- and early 18th-century technique applied the gold coating by means of a mercuric process, which released poisonous fumes. This was abandoned in favor of applying gold dust in a varnish. Ormolu mounts were frequent in French 18th- and 19th-century furniture.

Ormonde, James Butler, 1st Duke of (1610–88) Anglo-Irish general, who in the *Civil War commanded the Royalist army in Ireland (1641–50). After the Restoration of the monarchy, he was Lord Lieutenant of Ireland (1661–69, 1677–84).

Ornithischia An order of herbivorous *dinosaurs that lived in the Jurassic and Cretaceous periods (200–65 million years ago). They had hip bones arranged like those of birds (the name means "bird hips") and a horny beak at the front of the jaw (teeth were present only at the rear). Some were bipedal while others evolved to become quadrupedal and heavily armored. There were both amphibious and terrestrial forms. *See* Iguanodon; Stegosaurus; Triceratops.

Ornitholestes A dinosaur that lived in North America during the Jurassic and Cretaceous periods (200–65 million years ago). About 7 ft (2 m) long, it was lightly built and moved on its long slender hind limbs balanced by a long stiff tail. Its fore limbs were short with long slender clawed fingers and it probably lived in forest undergrowth, catching birds, lizards, and mammals.

ornithology The study of *birds. Ornithology is a popular pastime as well as a branch of zoology; the records of bird spottings made by amateur ornithologists can be valuable to professional scientists in helping to determine the ecology and behavior of bird populations. Recovery of rings used in bird-ringing experiments provides information regarding the dispersion and migration of birds. Many species are protected by legislation, and such bodies as the Audubon Society exist to promote the establishment of bird sanctuaries and general interest in birds.

orogeny A period of mountain building. Several major orogenies have occurred in the earth's geological history, the main ones since the Precambrian being the Caledonian (in the Lower Paleozoic), Variscan (including the Armorican and Hercynian phases, in the Upper Paleozoic), and the Alpine (in the Tertiary). **Orogenesis** is the process of mountain building, including folding, faulting, and thrusting, resulting from the collision of two continents, which compresses the sediment between them into mountain chains (*see* plate tectonics).

Orontes River A river in SW Asia. Rising in Lebanon, it flows mainly N through Syria and then SW past Antioch (Turkey) to enter the Mediterranean Sea. Length: 230 mi (370 km).

Orozco, José (1883–1949) Mexican mural painter. His early watercolors of prostitutes were so bitterly attacked that he sought refuge in the US (1917–20). In 1922, however, the Mexican Government commissioned him, *Rivera, *Siqueiros, and others to paint murals in the National Preparatory School, Mexico City. Renewed criticism of his social and political subject matter led to his second visit to the US (1927–34), where he made his name with murals for several educational institutions.

Orpheus A legendary Greek poet and musician, the son of the muse Calliope by either Apollo or Oeagrus, king of Thrace. After sailing with the *Argonauts he married *Eurydice. After her death, he descended to Hades to recover her. *Persephone, charmed by his playing on the lyre, released Eurydice but Orpheus lost her when he disobeyed the gods' command not to look back at her. He met his death at the hands of the Maenads, followers of *Dionysus, who dismembered him. He was believed to be the founder of the *Orphic mysteries, a cult dating from the 7th century BC, which was concerned with the liberation of the soul from the body.

Orphic mysteries An esoteric religious cult (*see* mysteries) in ancient Greece and S Italy. It was based on poems, probably datable to the 7th century BC, which its adherents believed were written by *Orpheus. According to these, the material world was made from the ashes of the Titans, whom Zeus destroyed for devouring his son Dionysus. Vegetarianism, participation in the mystical rites, and high ethical standards were demanded of initiates.

orphism An abstract form of *cubism, which developed in France about 1912. Albert Gleizes (1881–1953), Jean Metzinger (1883–1956), and Gino *Severini all contributed to this brightly colored flat patterned style but the chief exponent, *Delaunay, preferred to call his version *simultaneisme*. His work became purely abstract by 1914, greatly influencing *Klee and *Kandinsky.

Orr, Bobby (Robert Gordon O.; 1948–   ) Canadian hockey player. He played for the Boston Bruins (1967–76). The holder of many scoring records for defensemen, he was named the National Hockey League's top defenseman eight times (1968–75).

orrisroot The fragrant rhizome (underground stem) of several European plants of the genus *Iris*, chiefly *I. florentina, I. pallida* and *I. germanica*. It is dried and ground for use in perfumes and medicines.

Orsini A Roman family, originating in the 10th century, that led the propapal (Guelf) faction in Rome during the 13th century. Several members became high-ranking clerics, including two popes, Celestine III (reigned 1191–98) and Nicholas III (reigned 1277–80). They remained a dominant force in the politics of Rome and the papacy during the early modern period, attaining princely status in 1629.

Orsk 51 13N 58 35E A city in W Russia, at the confluence of the Ural and Or rivers. It has an oil refinery and also manufactures heavy machinery. Population (1991 est): 275,600.

Ortega y Gasset, José (1883–1955) Spanish philosopher and writer. He became professor of metaphysics at Madrid University in 1910. His philosophy was chiefly concerned with what he called "the metaphysics of vital reason." In his best-known book, *La rebelión de las masas* (1930), he attacked mass rule, which, he argued, would lead to chaos.

Ortelius, Abraham (1527–98) Flemish cartographer. Ortelius traveled widely, buying and selling antiquities and maps. His *Theatrum orbis terrarum* (1570), a collection of maps charting the whole world, became the definitive contemporary cartographical system. Ortelius became geographer to Philip II of Spain in 1575.

orthicon A television camera tube in which a low-energy electron beam scans a target screen, consisting of a thin dielectric plate with a mosaic of photosensitive squares on one side and a thin metallic coating on the other. Each square and its metallic electrode form a tiny capacitor; when light falls on a photosensitive element the capacitor becomes charged. The scanning beam discharges these capacitors and thus becomes modulated by the pattern of light falling on the screen.

ORTELIUS *The* Theatrum orbis terrarum *was enlarged and reissued until 1612 and this miniature map of Palestine was first published in 1601. It shows the route taken by Moses and the Israelites on the flight from Egypt.*

orthoclase An alkali potassium *feldspar, $KAlSi_3O_8$. It is formed at intermediate to low temperatures and crystallizes in the monoclinic crystal system, often with twinned crystals. Orthoclase is found in acid igneous rocks and in many metamorphic rocks. It is white, pink, or greenish gray, and is softer than quartz, with a duller luster. Commercially, orthoclase is frequently obtained from pegmatites; it is used in the manufacture of glass, ceramic glazes, and enamels.

orthodontics. *See* dentistry.

Orthodox Church The federation of self-governing Churches historically associated with the eastern part of the Roman Empire and separated from the Latin Church since 1054 (*see* Filioque); also called the Eastern Orthodox Church. The four ancient *patriarchs of Orthodoxy are of Constantinople (which has primacy of honor), Alexandria, Antioch, and Jerusalem; in addition there are patriarchs of Moscow, Georgia, Serbia, Bulgaria, and Romania. Independent or autocephalous Orthodox Churches exist in Greece, Cyprus, Albania, Czech Republic, Slovakia, and Poland. There are congregations in other countries, many established by Russian immigrants after the Revolution. Government is by bishops, who must be unmarried, priests, who may marry but only before ordination, and deacons, who play an important liturgical role. The Orthodox Church claims the authority of *Apostolic Succession and regards itself as the one true Church, accepting as doctrine only the *Nicene Creed. Its worship is sacramental and centered on the Eucharist and the ancient liturgies of St John Chrysostom and St Basil, which are always solemnly celebrated and sung without accompaniment. Communion is given in both kinds. The veneration of *icons is a distinctive feature of Orthodox worship; statues and other three-dimensional images are forbidden. Easter is the main feast of the Church year, which follows the Julian calendar and therefore varies considerably from Western custom in dating major Christian festivals. *See also* Greek Orthodox Church; Russian Orthodox Church.

orthopedics The medical specialty concerned with treating deformities caused by disease of and injury to the bones and joints. This includes the use of surgery, manipulation, traction, etc., in correcting deformities and fractures, together with rehabilitation to enable patients to lead an independent life. The availability of artificial hip joints has greatly extended the scope of orthopedics in the treatment of severe arthritis of the hip.

Orthoptera A mainly tropical order of generally large stout-bodied insects (15,000 species), including the *grasshoppers and *crickets. The hind legs are enlarged and specialized for jumping and the large blunt head has biting jaws for feeding on vegetation. Typically there are two pairs of wings—the front pair thicker—but few species are good fliers. Many species produce sounds by rubbing one part of the body against another (stridulation).

ortolan A Eurasian *bunting, *Emberiza hortulana*, about 6 in (16 cm) long, having a brown-streaked plumage with a yellow throat and pinkish belly. Prior to its autumn migration to N Africa and the Middle East it stores large amounts of fat and for this reason it is trapped in large numbers as a table delicacy.

Oruro 17 59S 67 08W A city in central Bolivia, 12,160 ft (3705 m) above sea level. It is the center of an important tin-mining area; other minerals worked include silver, copper, and wolfram. It has a technical university (1892). Population (1989 est): 176,700.

Orvieto 42 43N 12 06E A city in central Italy, in Umbria. It is reputed to be the site of the Etruscan city Volsinii, which was destroyed by the Romans in 280 BC. Notable buildings include the gothic cathedral and several palaces. A popular tourist center, it is also famous for its white wine. Population: 23,220.

Orwell, George (Eric Blair; 1903–50) British novelist. Born in India, he was educated at Eton and served in the Burmese Imperial Police from 1922 to 1927. In *Down and Out in Paris and London* (1933) and *The Road to Wigan Pier* (1937) he described his experience of poverty. He criticized official communist policies and practices in *Homage to Catalonia* (1936), an autobiographical account of the Spanish Civil War, and expressed his anti-Stalinist convictions in the political allegory *Animal Farm* (1945). *Nineteen Eighty Four* (1949) is a deeply pessimistic view of a totalitarian future.

Oryol. *See* Orel.

oryx A desert antelope, *Oryx gazella*, which comprises two races, beisa and gemsbok, of S and E Africa. Up to 47 in (120 cm) high at the shoulder, oryxes have long slender straight horns and are grayish brown with black markings on the face and legs. The herds feed at night on desert plants. The white Arabian oryx (*O. leukoryx*) and the grayish-white N African scimitar-horned oryx (*O. tao*) are both endangered species.

Osaka 34 40N 135 30E A port in Japan, in SW Honshu on the Yodo delta. The third largest city in Japan, it was a leading commercial center by the 17th century. Imperial palaces were built here from the 4th century AD and an ancient Buddhist temple (593 AD) still remains. It is overlooked by the 16th-century castle (reconstructed). A cultural center, it possesses several universities and has a famous puppet theater. Together with Kobe, Kyoto, and several small cities it now forms the **Osaka-Kobe** industrial area, second in importance only to the Tokyo-Yokohama area, and in common with Tokyo suffers from serious atmospheric pollution as well as traffic congestion. Major industries are textiles, steel, electrical equipment, and chemicals. Population (1990): 2,613,199.

Osborne, John (1929–) British dramatist. One of the original *Angry Young Men, he gave expression to the rage and frustration of a whole generation in the character of Jimmy Porter, the disillusioned antihero of *Look Back in Anger* (1956). His criticism of contemporary Britain continued in such plays as *The Entertainer* (1957), *West of Suez* (1971), and *Watch it Come Down* (1976).

Oscar. *See* Academy of Motion Picture Arts and Sciences.

Oscar II (1829–1907) King of Sweden (1872–1907) and of Norway from 1872 until its final separation from Sweden in 1905. He was also a writer, especially of poetry.

Osceola (?1800–38) Seminole Indian leader. Rebelling at attempts to relocate his people from Georgia to west of the Mississippi River, he settled in Florida with a band of followers. In 1835 he was responsible for killing a US Indian agent, precipitating the Second Seminole War (1835–42). Entrenched in the Everglades, he fought guerrilla style until he was captured (1837) while under a flag of truce. He died while in prison.

oscilloscope. *See* cathode-ray oscilloscope.

Oshawa 43 53N 78 51W A city and port in central Canada, in S Ontario on Lake Ontario. A prosperous agricultural center, it houses a major motor-vehicle factory. Other industries include metal goods, furniture, glass, and plastics. Population (1991): 129,344.

Oshogbo 7 50N 4 35E A city in SW Nigeria. It developed as a commercial center after the arrival of the railroad (1906). Its main exports are cocoa and palm oil; there are also local tobacco-processing, cotton-weaving, and dyeing industries. Population (1992 est): 442,000.

osier A small *willow tree, *Salix viminalis*, 10–33 ft (3–10 m) high, with flexible hairy branches used in basket making. The long narrow dark-green leaves are smooth above and white and silky beneath, with inrolled margins. Osiers are found in marshy areas throughout central and S Eurasia and often cultivated.

Osijek 45 33N 18 42E A city in Croatia, on the Drava River. An agricultural trading center, it manufactures agricultural machinery and footwear. Population (1991): 165,000.

Osipenko. *See* Berdyansk.

Osiris The Egyptian god of the dead, the brother and husband of *Isis; as the father of *Horus (the sun), he was also the god of renewal and rebirth. He was killed by his evil brother *Set. After Isis had magically reconstructed his body, he became ruler of the underworld. The pharaohs, and later all men who passed the judgment of good and evil, became identified with Osiris after death. He is usually portrayed holding the royal flail and crook. He was identified by the Greeks with *Dionysus.

Osler, Sir William (1849–1919) Canadian physician, who pioneered modern clinical teaching methods. In 1872 Osler identified the particles in blood known as *platelets. He was appointed professor of medicine at the new Johns Hopkins University, Baltimore, in 1888. Osler introduced new attitudes and ideas to teaching medicine, encouraging examination of patients in the wards and the use of laboratories by students. In 1905 he became Regius Professor of Medicine at Oxford University. A classics scholar, he bequeathed his library to McGill University, Montreal.

Oslo (former name [1877–1925]: Kristiania) 59 56N 10 54E The capital and main port of Norway, situated in the SE at the head of Oslo Fjord. It is the financial and industrial center of Norway. The principal industries include the manufacture of consumer goods and ship building. A cultural center, Oslo is the site of a university (1811), the National Theater, and several notable museums. Fine

buildings include the 17th-century cathedral and the 19th-century royal palace.
History: founded in the 11th century as a defensive post against the Danes, it became capital in 1299. It developed into an important trading post under the influence of the Hanseatic League and was rebuilt after a fire in the 17th century. It was occupied by the Germans in World War II. Population (1992 est): 467,000.

OSIRIS *The third innermost coffin of Tutankhamen, made of gold, portrays the pharaoh as Osiris.*

Osman I (c. 1258–c. 1326) Emir of the small Turkish state in Asia Minor that later developed into the *Ottoman Empire. He was the eponymous ancestor of the Ottoman sultans. Under Osman the state expanded mainly at the expense of the Byzantines and shortly before he died Bursa was captured.

osmiridium A naturally occurring alloy of osmium and iridium, with minor quantities of platinum, rhodium, and ruthenium. It is used for fountain pen nibs because it is hard and resistant.

osmium (Os) An extremely hard bluish-silver metal of the platinum group. It is one of the densest elements known (relative density 22.6). Its major use is in the production of hard alloys with other noble metals, for pen nibs and electrical contacts. The tetroxide (OsO$_4$) is volatile (bp 266°F; 130°C) and very toxic. At no 76; at wt 190.2; mp 5513°F (3045°C); bp 9081°F (5027°C).

osmosis The passage of a solvent from a less concentrated into a more concentrated solution through a semipermeable membrane (one allowing the passage of solvent, but not solute, molecules). Osmosis stops if the pressure of the more concentrated solution exceeds that of the less concentrated solution by an amount known as the **osmotic pressure** between them. In living organisms the solvent is water and osmosis plays an important role in effecting the distribution of water in plants and animals: the passage of water into and out of cells is determined by the osmotic pressures of the extracellular and intracellular solutions. Osmosis can be used in the *desalination of water.

Osmunda A genus of stout leathery *ferns (about 12 species), found in wet tropical and temperate regions. Their short thick branching rhizomes give rise to branching fronds, 20–71 in (50–180 cm) high, made up of light-green tapering leaflets with expanded bases. The upper leaflets of the larger central fertile fronds are reduced to veins covered with clusters of brown pear-shaped spore capsules, which resemble flower clusters in the royal fern (*O. regalis*). The root and rhizome fibers are used as a culture medium for orchids. Family: *Osmundaceae*.

Osnabrück 52 17N 8 03E A city in NW Germany, in Lower Saxony on the Hase River. The 13th-century romanesque cathedral and episcopal palace (1667–90) survived the bombing of World War II. It has iron, steel, and car industries. Population (1991 est): 163,000.

osprey A large *hawk, *Pandion haliaetus*, also called fish hawk, occurring worldwide (except in South America) around coasts and inland waters. It is 25.5 in (65 cm) long and its plumage is brown above and white below. It feeds mostly on pike and trout, caught in its talons, which are covered with rough spikes to help grasp prey. The recent decline in numbers has been due mainly to pesticide poisoning.

Ossa, Mount 41 52S 146 04E A mountain in Australia, the highest peak of Tasmania in the Duana Range. Height: 5305 ft (1617 m).

Ossetia. *See* North Ossetian Autonomous Republic; South Ossetian autonomous region.

Ossetic A language belonging to the *Iranian family and spoken in the N Caucasus by the Ossetes. The Ossetes are descended from the ancient Alani, a Scythian tribe. The language is written in the Cyrillic alphabet and has absorbed many influences from Russian and the other Caucasian languages.

Ossian (3rd century AD) A legendary poet and warrior who, as Oisin, features in the *Fenian cycle. The Scots poet James Macpherson (1736–96) claimed to have discovered remains of Ossian's poetry in the Highlands and published his "translations" from the Gaelic between 1760 and 1763. These included the epic poem *Fingal* (1762). Macpherson's work was in fact his own, largely based on a few well-known Gaelic fragments. Although denounced as forgeries by Dr Johnson, the poems were enthusiastically received throughout Europe and had a great influence on European romanticism.

Ossietsky, Carl von (1888–1938) German pacifist and journalist. He founded a pacifist organization in 1920 and became editor of a liberal newspaper in 1927. Following his arrest in 1933 he spent the rest of his life in a concentration camp and in hospitals. He won the Nobel Peace Prize in 1935.

Ossining 41 10N 73 52W A city in New York state. Known as Sing Sing until 1901, it is the site of the Sing Sing state prison, once notorious for its severe discipline. Population (1990): 22,852.

Ostade, Adrian van (1610–85) Dutch painter and etcher, born in Haarlem. Influenced by *Brouwer, he specialized in scenes of peasant life.

Ostend (Flemish name: Oostende; French name: Ostende) 51 13N 2 55E A seaport in NW Belgium, on the North Sea. Ostend is a pleasure resort, with a casino, a promenade, and a royal chalet. It is the headquarters of the country's fishing fleet and maintains a cross-Channel ferry service to Dover, Eng. Industries include ship building and fish processing. Population (1981 est): 69,678.

Ostend Manifesto (1854) US communication that stated the intention of the US to seize Cuba if Spain would not sell it to the US. When Spain refused US minister Pierre Soulé's offer to buy Cuba, he, under direction from the US secretary of state, met with James Y. Mason and James Buchanan, US ministers to France and Britain respectively, at Ostend, Belgium, where they signed the manifesto. Condemned in the US, the manifesto was never issued.

osteoarthritis A disease of the joints in which their internal surfaces are rubbed away and they become swollen and painful. This becomes increasingly common as people age: almost all very old people have some osteoarthritis, but it may affect younger people as well. The joints that bear most weight are most commonly affected: back, hips, and knees. Drugs can reduce the pain of the joints but cannot reverse the disease. Artificial hips and knees can be surgically installed to relieve the pain and allow greater movement. *See also* arthritis.

osteology. *See* bone.

osteomalacia Softening of the bones due to shortage of vitamin D: adult *rickets. It is seen most commonly in pregnant women and in old people whose diet is deficient in vitamin D or who do not have access to much sunshine (which activates vitamin D). Fractures occur very easily in osteomalacia. Treatment is with vitamin D preparations.

osteomyelitis Infection of bone. This occurs most commonly in poor communities. Children, particularly boys, are more often affected; symptoms are a high fever and acute pain in the bone affected, which is classically around the knee. Before antibiotics were available death or physical handicap often resulted, but these are now rare and the infection is readily cured with antibiotics.

osteopathy A system of healing by manipulation and massage, based on the theory that nearly all diseases are due to the displacement of bones, especially the bones of the spine. Osteopathy is undoubtedly of use in treating dislocations, fractures, and disorders of the joint, but the theory behind it is unacceptable to the medical profession and osteopathy is not legally recognized as a branch of orthodox medicine. Many doctors of medicine are vehemently opposed to osteopathy.

osteoporosis Weakening of the bone. This occurs most commonly in old people, particularly women, but it also affects bones that are immobilized for long periods. The immobilized bone of a young person will usually regain its strength after mobilization, but an elderly patient's osteoporotic bones are more difficult to treat.

Ostia A town of ancient Rome, at the mouth of the Tiber River. It was probably founded about 350 BC, although it is dated by tradition to the 7th century BC. A major naval base under the Republic, its prosperity was greatest in the 2nd century AD, when it was an important commercial center. It was abandoned in the 9th century. Impressive Roman ruins have been excavated.

ostracism The method in 5th-century BC Athens of banishing unpopular citizens. Each citizen inscribed on a potsherd (*ostrakon*) the name of his candidate for banishment. The man receiving most votes was exiled for 10 years. Instituted to curb tyranny, ostracism was in practice uncommon. Prominent ostracized Athenians included Aristides and Themistocles.

Ostracoda A subclass of small *crustaceans (2000 species), 0.04–0.16 in (1–4 mm) long, also called mussel or seed shrimps, found in fresh and salt water. Ostracods have a bean-shaped two-sided carapace, from which protrude two pairs of large hairy antennae and two pair of legs for swimming or walking. Most ostracods live on or near the bottom and eat anything, but particularly decaying vegetation or small animals. The females lay eggs on stems and leaves of water plants.

Ostrava 49 50N 18 15E An industrial city in the Czech Republic, in N Moravia on both sides of the Ostravice River. It is a major coal-mining center; other industries include iron and steel processing, engineering, and chemicals. Population (1991): 327,553.

ostrich A flightless African bird, *Struthio camelus*, occurring in open grassland and semidesert regions. Males reach 8 ft (2.5 m) tall and are black with white wing and tail plumes; females are smaller and mainly brown. Ostriches have a long almost naked neck, a small head, and a ducklike bill used to feed on plant material. They can reach speeds of up to 40 mph (65 km per hour). Domesticated birds are farmed commercially for leather and ornamental feathers. It is the largest living bird and the only member of its family (*Struthionidae*). Order: *Struthioniformes*.

Ostrogoths A branch of the *Goths, originally based in the Ukraine, but forced W of the Dniester River by the *Huns (375 AD). In the 6th century they frequently invaded N Italy and captured much of the Balkans. Between 493 and 526 *Theodoric, their leader, ruled Italy. On his death the Roman Empire, after a long struggle, destroyed the Ostrogoths (562).

Ostrovskii, Aleksandr Nikolaevich (1823–86) Russian dramatist. He established his reputation with realistic comedies about the merchant class, making use of the knowledge of corruption that he had gained as a civil servant. His best-known plays include *Easy Money* (1856) and the tragedy *The Storm* (1859), which became the basis of *Janacek's opera *Katya Kabanova*.

Ostwald, (Friedrich) Wilhelm (1853–1932) German chemist, born in Riga, who was a pioneer in the field of physical chemistry. His greatest work was in developing the theory of catalysis for which he was awarded the Nobel Prize in 1909. He also contributed to the philosophy of science and was an ardent positivist.

Oswald, Lee Harvey (1939–63) The presumed assassin of Pres. John F. *Kennedy. Renouncing his citizenship in 1959 to live in the USSR, he returned in 1962. He shot Kennedy in Dallas, Tex., on Nov 22, 1963. Two days later he was killed by Jack Ruby, a nightclub owner, in the Dallas police headquarters. Following an investigation into the assassination, the Warren Commission ruled in 1964 that Oswald had acted alone.

Oswald, Saint (c. 605–41) King of Northumbria (634–41) after defeating and killing the Welsh king, Cadwallader. Converted to Christianity while in exile on Iona, he restored Christianity in Northumbria with the help of St. *Aidan. Oswald was killed in battle by Penda. Feast day: Aug 5.

Oswald of York, St (d. 992 AD) English churchman. Bishop of Worcester and later Archbishop of York, he founded many new monasteries and was a leading initiator of Anglo-Saxon monastic reform. Feast day: Feb 28.

Oświęcim (German name: Auschwitz) 50 02N 19 11E A town in S Poland. It was the site of a notorious Nazi concentration camp during World War II. Population: 41,000.

Oswiu (*or* Oswy; d. 670) King of Northumbria (655–70) and overlord (655–57) of all England S of the Humber, after his forces had killed Penda of Mercia in battle. He summoned the Synod of *Whitby (664) to resolve the differences between the Roman and Celtic Churches.

Otis, Elisha Graves (1811–61) US inventor, who in 1852 designed the first safety elevator, that is one that would not fall to the ground if the cable broke. In 1854 Otis publicly demonstrated the elevator's safety by arranging for the cable of an elevator in which he was riding to be cut.

Otranto 40 08N 18 30E A small port in SE Italy, in Apulia on the Strait of Otranto. Dating from Greek times, it became an important Roman port, later destroyed by Turks (1480). Its ruined castle provided the setting for Horace Walpole's gothic novel *The Castle of Otranto*. Population: 4151.

Ottawa 45 25N 75 43W The capital of Canada, in SE Ontario on the Ottawa River. It is two-thirds English speaking and one-third French speaking. Ottawa University was founded in 1848 and the Carleton University in 1942. *History*: founded (as Bytown) in the early 19th century as a lumbering center, it became capital of the United Provinces of Canada in 1858, and national capital in 1867. Population (1991): 313,987.

Ottawa North American Algonkian-speaking Indian tribe, found in Ontario, Canada; Michigan, and Wisconsin. Traders, they allied with the French during the *French and Indian War and, under Chief *Pontiac, fought British expansion. Today the Ottawa live in Oklahoma, Michigan, Wisconsin, and Manitoulin Island, Ontario.

Ottawa Agreements (1932) Preferential tariff rates negotiated between the UK and its dominions at the Imperial Economic Conference held at Ottawa (Canada).

Ottawa River A river in central Canada, rising in W Quebec and flowing W, then SE down the Ontario-Quebec border to join the St Lawrence River, as its chief tributary, at Montreal. The numerous rapids along its lower and middle courses are used to generate electricity. It is linked with Lake Ontario by the Rideau Canal. Length: 696 mi (1120 km).

otter A semi-aquatic carnivorous □mammal belonging to the subfamily *Lutrinae* (18 species), distributed worldwide except in Polar regions, Australasia, and Madagascar. Otters have a cylindrical body with waterproof fur, short legs, partially webbed feet, and a thick tapering tail.

The Eurasian otter (*Lutra lutra*), grows to a length of about 4 ft (1.2 m) and a weight of about 22 lb (10 kg). Otters inhabit waterways, lakes, and coasts, feeding on frogs, fish, and invertebrates. Chief genera: *Lutra, Paraonyx*; family: *Mustelidae. See also* sea otter.

otterhound A breed of dog of uncertain ancestry, used to hunt otters. It is a strongly built powerful swimmer with large webbed feet and a large head with long drooping ears. Otterhounds have a dense water-resistant undercoat and a long shaggy outer coat, which can be any color. Height: 24–27 in (61–69 cm).

otter shrew A semiaquatic carnivorous mammal belonging to the family *Potamogalidae* (3 species), of West and central Africa. Up to 24 in (60 cm) long, they have long slender brown and white bodies with a shrewlike snout and a flattened tail for swimming. They forage for aquatic invertebrate prey. Order: *Insectivora*.

OTTAWA *The center block of the neo-Gothic Parliament buildings (1859–65) on Parliament Hill. The Peace Tower at the center separates the Commons wing (on the left) from the Senate wing (on the right).*

Otto (I) the Great (912–73 AD) Holy Roman Emperor (936–73; crowned 962). He subdued his rebellious vassals, defeated a Hungarian invasion at the great victory of Lechfeld (955), and extended his influence into Italy. He deposed Pope John XII, replacing him with Leo VIII, and established bishoprics as a means of controlling his domains.

Otto IV (c. 1175–1218) Holy Roman Emperor (1198–1215; crowned 1209). He was elected emperor in opposition to the candidate of the Hohenstaufen family but was crowned by Pope Innocent III in return for promising to keep out of Italian territorial disputes. In 1210, however, he invaded S Italy and, after being decisively defeated by France, a Hohenstaufen ally, at *Bouvines (1214), was formally deposed.

Otto, Nikolaus August (1832–91) German engineer, who in 1876 devised the four-stroke cycle, known as the Otto cycle, for the *internal-combustion engine. His engine made the development of the automobile possible.

Ottoman Empire A Turkish Muslim empire ruling large parts of the Middle East as well as territories in Europe from the 14th to the 20th centuries. Its capital was *Istanbul (formerly Constantinople) and its rulers descendants of its founder *Osman I. Originating around 1300 as a small Turkish state in Asia Minor, in 1453 the Ottomans captured Constantinople and destroyed the Eastern Roman (Byzantine) Empire. Ottoman power culminated in the 16th century with the conquest of Egypt and Syria (1517) and, under *Suleiman the Magnificent, Hungary (1529) and territories in the Middle East and N Africa. From the 17th century the Empire declined. Attempts at modernization were only partly successful and in the 1908 *Young Turks revolution a group of army officers seized power. In World War I the Ottomans supported Germany and defeat brought the loss of territories outside Asia Minor. This humiliation led to the nationalist revolution of Kemal *Atatürk, which replaced the Ottoman Empire with the state of Turkey (1922).

Otway, Thomas (1652–85) British dramatist. His best-known plays are the sentimental tragedies *The Orphan* (1680) and *Venice Preserved* (1682), written for the actress Elizabeth Barry (1658–1713), whom he loved. He also wrote Restoration comedies and adapted plays by Racine and Molière.

Ouagadougou 12 25N 1 30W The capital of Burkina Faso. Founded in the 11th century as the center of a Mossi empire, it was captured by the French in 1896. Its university was founded in 1974. It is an important communications center. Population (1985): 441,514.

Oudenaarde, Battle of (July 11, 1708) A battle in the War of the *Spanish Succession in which the British, Dutch, and Austrians defeated the French. The allied commanders, Marlborough and Prince Eugene of Savoy, unexpectedly joined armies and forced the French to fight a surprise battle.

Oudry, Jean-Baptiste (1686–1755) French *rococo painter and tapestry designer. A pupil of the portraitist Nicholas de Largillière (1656–1746), he was a portrait and still-life painter before specializing (from about 1720) in animal and hunting scenes. As head of the *Beauvais (1734) and *Gobelin (1736) tapestry works, and as favorite painter of Louis XV, he achieved a wide reputation. His illustrations to La Fontaine's *Fables* are particularly well known.

Ouessant. *See* Ushant.

Oujda 34 41N 1 45W A city in E Morocco, near the Algerian border. It is a meeting point of the Moroccan and Algerian railroads. Population (1982): 260,082.

Oulu (Swedish name: Uleåborg) 65 00N 25 26E A seaport in NW Finland, on the Gulf of Bothnia. It has a university (1959) and its industries include ship building and saw milling. Population (1992 est): 102,032.

ounce. *See* snow leopard.

Ouse River The name of several rivers in England, including: **1.** A river in NE England, flowing mainly NE through Yorkshire to join the Trent River forming the Humber estuary. Length: 57 mi (92 km). **2.** A river in S England, flowing E and S across the South Downs to the English Channel at Newhaven. Length: 30 mi (48 km). *See also* Great Ouse River.

Ouspensky, Peter (1878–1947) Russian-born occultist. He trained as a scientist but as *Gurdjieff's close associate (1915–24) he became interested in methods of developing man's consciousness. He taught in London (1924–40) and New York (1940–47) and his writings include *Tertium Organum* (1912) and *A New Model of the Universe* (1914).

Outer Mongolia. *See* Mongolian People's Republic.

ouzel. *See* ring ouzel.

ouzo A Greek liquor flavored with aniseed, similar to *absinthe. It is drunk cold with water, in which it becomes cloudy.

ovary 1. The organ of female animals in which the *egg cells (ova) are produced. In mammals (including women) there are two ovaries close to the openings of the Fallopian tubes, which lead to the uterus (womb). They produce both eggs and steroid hormones (*see* estrogen; progesterone) in a regular cycle (*see* menstruation). The ovaries contain numerous follicles, some of which—the Graafian follicles—mature to release egg cells at ovulation, after which they form yellowish hormone-producing bodies (*see* corpus luteum). **2.** The part of a flower that contains the *ovules. It is situated at the base of the carpel(s) and becomes the fruit wall after fertilization.

ovenbird A small brown passerine bird belonging to a diverse family (*Furnariidae*; 221 species) occurring in tropical America and ranging in size from 5–11 in (12–28 cm). Ovenbirds usually build elaborate nests in tunnels and crevices but the family name is derived from the nests of the genus *Furnarius*, which build large ovenlike globes from wet clay.

Overijssel A province in the NE Netherlands bordering on Germany. Reclamation in the W has made it an inland province. Dairy farming and the production of fodder crops are especially important. Recently developed industries produce textiles, machinery, and salt. Area: 1516 sq mi (3927 sq km). Population (1981 est): 1,027,836. Capital: Zwolle.

overture An orchestral composition serving to introduce an opera, oratorio, or play or a one-movement work with a programmatic title played in the concert hall (**concert overture**). In the 18th century the two principal forms of opera overture were the **Italian overture**, consisting of a slow movement between two quick ones, from which the symphony evolved, and the **French overture**, consisting of a slow introduction, a quick fugal section, and often a slow final section or separate dance movement.

Ovid (Publius Ovidius Naso; 43 BC–17 AD) Roman poet. After his education he traveled extensively in Greek territories. His poems include the *Amores* and the *Ars amatoria*, both demonstrating his clear and polished style and his characteristic theme of love; the *Heroides*, love letters addressed by legendary heroines to their lovers; and the *Fasti*, a poetic treatment of festivals and rites in the Roman calendar, which he never completed. His greatest work, the *Metamorphoses*, is a poem in 15 books including mythological and historical tales linked by the theme of transformation. In 8 AD he was exiled by the emperor Augustus to Tomi, a remote township on the Black Sea, possibly because of some association with Augustus's licentious daughter, Julia. Despite appeals for mercy in his poems *Tristia* and *Epistulae ex Ponto*, he remained there until his death.

Oviedo 43 21N 5 50W A city in N Spain, in Asturias. It possesses a 14th-century cathedral and a university (founded 1608). Industries include mining and food processing. Population (1991): 194,919.

ovule The structure within the *ovary of a flower that contains an egg cell and nutritive tissue. After fertilization it develops into the *seed containing the embryo.

ovum. *See* egg.

Owen, Robert (1771–1858) British philanthropist and manufacturer. Born in Wales, in 1800 he became manager of the mills at New Lanark, Scotland, where he established a model community. He introduced better working conditions and housing and established the first infant school in Britain (1816). His advocacy from 1817 of "villages of unity and cooperation" for the unemployed anticipated *cooperative societies and he established such communities at New Harmony, Indiana (1825), Orbiston, Scotland (1826), Ralahine, Ireland (1831), and Queenswood, England (1839). Owen was also active in the trade-union movement.

ROBERT OWEN *This contemporary engraving shows his model community at New Lanark: the school and kitchens (left), the cotton factories (right), and the village band (lower right-hand corner).*

Owen, Wilfred (1893–1918) British poet. His poetry written during World War I was motivated by horror at the brutality of war, pity for its victims, and anger at civilian complacency. His most famous poems include "Strange Meeting" and "Anthem for Doomed Youth." While in a hospital near Edinburgh in 1917 he met Siegfried *Sassoon, who edited his *Poems* (1920). He was killed in action.

Owen Falls 0 29N 33 11E A cataract in Uganda, on the Victoria Nile River just below Lake Victoria. The **Owen Falls Dam** (completed 1954) provides hydroelectric power for much of Uganda and Kenya and is used to control the flood waters.

Owens, Jesse (John Cleveland O.; 1913–80) US sprinter, long jumper, and hurdler. In 1935 he set six world records in 45 minutes (in the long jump, 100 yards, 220 yards, 220 meters, 220 yards hurdles, and 220 meters hurdles). At the Berlin Olympics (1936) he won four gold medals; this success of a black athlete was inconsistent with the racist theories of Hitler, who refused to congratulate him. He was awarded the Presidential Medal of Freedom in 1976.

owl A nocturnal bird of prey belonging to an order (*Strigiformes*) of worldwide distribution. There are two families: *Strigidae* (typical owls) and *Tytonidae* (barn and bay owls). Owls have a large head with large forward-facing eyes surrounded by a facial disk of radiating feathers, soft plumage, usually brown and patterned, and a short sharp hooked bill. With acute vision and hearing and silent flight, owls hunt mammals, birds, and insects, disgorging the remains in hard pellets. They range in size from the *pygmy owls to the large *eagle owls; most are arboreal but some live in swamps, cactus deserts, or on the ground. *See* barn owl; burrowing owl; fish owl; little owl; snowy owl; tawny owl.

owlet frogmouth A solitary arboreal bird belonging to a family (*Aegothelidae*; 7 or 8 species) occurring in Australian forests. They have a gaping mouth surrounded by long sensitive bristles and feed at night on insects. The little owlet frogmouth (*Aegotheles cristatus*) is 9 in (22 cm) long and has a gray-brown plumage with brown underparts. Order: *Caprimulgiformes* (nightjars and nighthawks).

owlet moth. *See* noctuid moth.

ox. *See* cattle.

oxalic acid (*or* ethanedioic acid; $(COOH)_2$) A colorless poisonous soluble crystalline solid. Potassium and sodium salts are found in plants. Industrially it is prepared from sawdust treated with sodium and potassium hydroxides. Oxalic acid is used as a metal cleaner and for bleaching textiles and leather.

oxbow lake. *See* lake.

Oxenstierna, Axel, Count (1583–1654) Swedish statesman; chancellor (1612–54). He gained great power during the reign of Gustavus II Adolphus, being the effective controller of national finance and commerce. After Gustavus's death in 1632, he directed Sweden in the Thirty Years' War and gained favorable terms at the Peace of *Westphalia. During the minority (1632–44) of Queen *Christina he dominated the regency council, and continued to influence government until his death.

oxeye daisy A perennial herb, *Chrysanthemum leucanthemum*, also called moon daisy or marguerite, found in grassland and wasteland throughout Europe; 8–27.5 in (20–70 cm) high, it has large solitary flower heads, 0.98–2 in (2.5–5 cm) in diameter, with long white rays surrounding a yellow central disk. Family: *Compositae*.

Oxford 51 46N 1 15W A city in S central England, on the Rivers Thames and Cherwell. Important from Saxon times and heavily fortified, Oxford's fame as a center of learning dates from the 13th century, when the first university colleges were founded (*see* Oxford, University of). In the Civil War, Oxford was the Royalist headquarters. The college buildings dominate the center of the city but there is considerable industrial development. It has one of the world's greatest libraries (the *Bodleian Library, 1602). Population (1981): 98,521.

Oxford, Provisions of (1258) The scheme of constitutional reform imposed upon Henry III by his barons at Oxford following their opposition to excessive taxation. Royal authority was to be contained by an advisory council of 15 barons, which was to reform government. The pope absolved Henry from his promise to observe the Provisions (1261), which led to the *Barons' War.

Oxford, 1st Earl of. *See* Harley, Robert, 1st Earl of Oxford.

Oxford, University of One of the oldest universities in Europe, whose fame dates from the 13th century. It is organized as a federation of colleges, which are governed by their own teaching staff ("Fellows"), admit students, maintain their own property (which includes residential accommodation, libraries, playing fields, etc.), and provide members of the University's administrative and legislative bodies, its many faculties, departments, and committees. The University is responsible for organizing a lecture program, maintaining the large libraries (such as the *Bodleian Library), providing all laboratories, and conducting examinations. The University includes University College, (founded in 1249), All Souls (1438), Christ Church (1546), and Lady Margaret Hall (1878), which was the first women's college, and Green College (1979).

Oxford Group. *See* Moral Rearmament.

Oxford Movement A movement within the Church of England in the 19th century aimed at emphasizing the Catholic principles on which it rested. Led by *Newman, *Keble, *Pusey, and *Froude of Oxford University, it was initiated in 1833 by Keble's sermon "On the National Apostasy." Aided by their *Tracts for the Times*, the Tractarians, as they came to be called, unleashed a spiritual force that did much to invigorate Anglicanism.

oxidation and reduction Oxidation is the chemical combination of a substance with oxygen. An example is the combustion of carbon to carbon dioxide: $C + O_2 \rightarrow CO_2$. The converse process, removal of oxygen, is known as reduction; an example is the reduction of iron oxide to iron: $Fe_2O_3 + 3C \rightarrow 2Fe + 3CO$. The terms oxidation and reduction have been extended in chemistry. Thus, reduction also refers to reaction with hydrogen and oxidation to removal of hydrogen. More generally, an oxidation reaction is one involving loss of electrons and a reduction reaction is one in which electrons are gained. Thus, the conversion of ferrous ions to ferric ions is an oxidation: $Fe^{2+} - e \rightarrow Fe^{3+}$. A compound that supplies oxygen or removes electrons is an **oxidizing agent**, whereas one that removes oxygen or supplies electrons is a **reducing agent**. Usually oxidation and reduction reactions occur together. Thus, in the reaction of ferric ions (Fe^{3+}) with stannous ions (Sn^{2+}), the ferric ions are reduced to ferrous ions (Fe^{2+}) and the stannous ions oxidized to stannic ions (Sn^{4+}): $2Fe^{3+} + Sn^{2+} \rightarrow 2Fe^{2+} + Sn^{4+}$. Reactions of this type are called **redox reactions**.

oxidation number (*or* oxidation state) The number of electrons that would have to be added to an atom to neutralize it. Thus Na^+, Cl^-, and He have oxidation numbers of 1, −1, and 0, respectively. Rules have been developed for assigning oxidation numbers to covalently bound atoms depending on the electric charge that the atom would have if the molecule ionized.

oxlip A perennial herb, *Primula elatior*, found throughout Europe and W Asia. It is similar to the *cowslip but has larger more flattened pale-yellow flowers with a darker yellow throat. The name is also given to hybrids between the primrose and cowslip. Family: *Primulaceae*.

Oxnard 34 12N 119 11W A city in SW California, W of Los Angeles, near the E end of the Santa Barbara Channel. Sugar beet refining and citrus fruit processing are the principal industries. Population (1990): 142,216.

oxpecker An African songbird of the genus *Buphagus*, also called tickbird, that feeds on ticks and maggots pecked from the hides of cattle and game animals. The yellow-billed oxpecker (*B. africanus*) is about 8 in (20 cm) long with sharp claws for clinging to the backs of its hosts and a stiff tail used for support in climbing over them. Oxpeckers remove parasites from their hosts but also feed on the blood from the sores. Family: *Sturnidae* (starlings).

Oxus River. *See* Amu Darya River.

oxygen (O) A colorless odorless gas discovered by J. *Priestley. The element exists in two forms—the diatomic molecule (O_2), which constitutes 21% of the earth's atmosphere, and trace amounts of the highly reactive triatomic allotrope, ozone (O_3), which is formed in the upper atmosphere by the interaction of ultraviolet radiation with oxygen and by lightning discharges. The ozone layer is important in absorbing harmful ultraviolet rays from the sun. Oxygen is very reactive and forms oxides with most elements (for example Na_2O, MgO, Fe_2O_3, Cl_2O_7, XeO_3). In addition to its vital importance for plants and animals, its major use is in the production of steel in blast furnaces. It is obtained by the distillation of liquid air. At no 8; at wt 15.9994; mp −361.1°F (−218.4°C); bp −297.35°F (−182.96°C).

oxygen cycle The process by which oxygen—present in the atmosphere or dissolved in water—is taken in by plants and animals for use in *respiration (intercellular combustion of food materials to provide energy) and released into the environment as a waste product, mostly in the form of free oxygen (by plants in *photosynthesis). Oxygen is often combined in organic and inorganic compounds, which may also be considered as part of the cycle. *See also* carbon cycle; nitrogen cycle.

Oyo Empire A kingdom in SW Nigeria and the most powerful state in West Africa from the mid-17th until the mid-18th centuries. Oyo then began to decline relative to Dahomey and during the next century was broken up by *Fulani invasions, European intrusions, and civil war. Oyo is now a province in Western State, SW Nigeria.

oyster A sedentary *bivalve mollusk belonging to the family *Ostreidae* (true oysters), of temperate and warm seas. The lower plate (valve) of the shell is larger and flatter than the upper valve; they are held together by an elastic ligament and powerful muscles. Edible oysters are cultivated for their white flesh; pearl oysters (family *Aviculidae*) are cultivated for their pearls, which they make by coating a grain of sand lodged inside their shell with calcareous material.

oystercatcher A black or black-and-white wading bird belonging to a family (*Haematopodidae*; 4 species) occurring in temperate and tropical coastal regions; 16–20 in (40–50 cm) long, oystercatchers have long pointed wings, a long wedge-shaped tail, pink legs, and a long or flattened orange-red bill specialized for opening bivalve mollusks and probing in mud for worms and crustaceans. Order: *Charadriiformes*.

Ozark Plateau (*or* Ozark Mountains) An eroded plateau in S Missouri and N Arkansas, reaching over 2000 ft (600 m) in the Boston Mountains. Forestry and mining are important; minerals include lead and zinc.

ozone (O_3) A pale blue gaseous form of *oxygen, formed by passing an electrical discharge through oxygen (O_2). Ozone is a poisonous unstable gas. It is used as an oxidizing agent, for example in water purification. It is present in small amounts in the atmosphere, mostly in the *ozone layer.

ozone layer (*or* ozonosphere) The zone in the upper atmosphere in which the gas ozone (triatomic oxygen; O_3) forms in its greatest concentrations. This is generally between about 6–30 mi (10–50 km) above the earth's surface. Ozone forms as a result of the dissociation by solar ultraviolet radiation of molecular oxygen into single atoms, some of which then combine with undissociated oxygen molecules. It absorbs in the 230–320 nm waveband, protecting the earth from dangerous excessive ultraviolet radiation.

P

Pabst, G(eorge) W(ilhelm) (1885–1967) Austrian film director. His films are distinguished by their innovative realistic techniques and their social criticism of decadence and nationalism in Germany. They include *Pandora's Box* (1929), the antiwar *Westfront 1918* (1930), *Die Dreigroschenoper* (1931), and *Kameradschaft* (1931).

paca A large nocturnal *rodent, *Cuniculus paca*, of Central and South America. Up to 34 in (60 cm) long, with a tiny tail and spotted coat, it is found in damp places near rivers and swamps, feeding on leaves and fruit and living in burrows. Part of the skull is specialized as a resonating chamber. It is hunted by all kinds of predators, including man. Family: *Dasyproctidae*.

Pacaraima Mountains A mountain range in NE South America. Comprising part of the Guiana Highlands, it extends W–E along part of the Brazil-Venezuela and Brazil-Guyana borders reaching 9219 ft (2810 m) at Mount Roraima.

pacemaker A small section of specialized heart muscle that initiates heartbeat. It is situated in the right atrium and contracts spontaneously: the impulse to contract is transmitted from the pacemaker to both atria and then to the ventricles. If the pacemaker ceases to function (heart block) it may be replaced by an artificial battery-operated device that stimulates the heart to contract. If required permanently it is surgically implanted under the skin.

Pachomius, St (c. 290–346 AD) Egyptian hermit, who founded the first monastery in 318 at Tabenna, on the Nile River, and the first Christian rule involving a uniform communal existence. Until then *monasticism had been practiced only by solitaries in the desert. Feast day: May 14.

pachyderm A thick-skinned *mammal, such as the elephant, rhinoceros, or hippopotamus. Early naturalists classified these animals, together with pigs and walruses, in a group called *Pachydermata*. The classification is now abandoned but the term is still used.

Pachymeres, Georgius (1242–c. 1310) Byzantine historian and writer. Pachymere's most important work was a history of the period 1261 to 1308, under the emperors *Michael VIII Palaeologus and Andronicus II Palaeologus (1260–1332; reigned 1282–1328). Other works include an outline of Aristotelian philosophy and a treatise on the Holy Spirit. The latter work is significant in that it accepts the controversial Roman *Filioque clause of the formula of St *John of Damascus.

Pacific, War of the (1879–84) The war between Chile and the allies Bolivia and Peru. Also called the Nitrate War, it was provoked by a dispute over Chile's exploitation of nitrate deposits in Bolivia. Within two years Bolivia was defeated, and Peru's capital of Lima captured. According to the peace terms, finally agreed in 1884, Peru and Bolivia ceded territories to Chile, Bolivia losing all access to the sea.

Pacific Islands, Trust Territory of the A UN trust territory administered by the US. It comprises the *Marshall Islands, the Federated States of *Micronesia, and Belau; the Mariana Islands were included until 1978. Taken by Japan from Germany (1914), the islands were captured by the US in World War II (1944) and the trusteeship established in 1947.

Pacific Ocean The world's largest and deepest ocean, covering a third of its surface. It extends between Asia, Australia, Antarctica, and America. It contains a multitude of volcanic and coral islands in the tropical SW and reaches its maximum depth in the *Marianas Trench. The S and E are marked by a uniform climate with steady winds, but the W is known for its typhoons, which often cause coastal flooding. The Pacific has some diurnal and mixed tides, while Tahitian tides follow the sun and not the moon. Its vast mineral resources are unexploited.

pacifism The group of doctrines, religious, moral, or political, that urge nonparticipation either in any war whatsoever or in particular wars that are held to be unjustified. In ancient societies it was assumed that membership of the society involved fighting for it when necessary. This view was not held by early Christians, although not all Christians have been unanimously pacifist; in fact Christian pacifism was relatively unimportant from Constantine's period to the Reformation, when first *Anabaptists, and then *Quakers, adopted total pacifism. In modern times conscientious objectors have been recognized in both World Wars and have often served with distinction in noncombatant (medical) units. Moreover, nonviolent methods of attaining political ends were shown to be effective by *Gandhi in the 1920s, although his achievement was to some extent diminished by the slaughter between Hindus and Muslims that followed his years of pacifism. Martin Luther *King, Jr., adapted Gandhi's methods to the US civil-rights movement.

Pacino, Al(fred) (1940–) US film actor, whose strong portrayal of a blind retired military officer in *Scent of a Woman* (1992) won the Best Actor Academy Award for 1992. Noted for his meticulous research of his character's world, he was nominated consistently for Academy Awards. *The Godfather* (1972), *Dick Tracy* (1990), and *Glengarry Glen Ross* (1992) earned him consideration for Best Supporting Actor, and other Best Actor nominations came for *Serpico* (1973), *The Godfather, Part II* (1974), *Dog Day Afternoon* (1975), and *And Justice for All* (1979).

pack rat A North American *rodent belonging to the genus *Neotoma* (20 species), also called wood rat. With body length of 6–9 in (15–23 cm), it has a hairy tail and inhabits rocky and wooded country, nesting in a pile of twigs and feeding on seeds and vegetation. Family: *Cricetidae*.

Padang 1 00S 100 21E A port in Indonesia, in W Sumatra. An early Dutch settlement, it flourished when railroads were built in the 19th century. It exports coal, cement, coffee, copra, and rubber. Its university was established in 1956. Population (1980): 480,922.

paddlefish One of two species of freshwater *bony fish, *Polyodon spathula* of North America or *Psephurus gladius* of China, also called duckbill cat. Paddlefishes have a smooth body, with an enormous paddle-shaped snout, and feed by straining planktonic organisms from the water. Family: *Polyodontidae*; order: *Acipenseriformes*.

Paderewski, Ignacy (Jan) (1860–1941) Polish pianist, composer, and statesman. Having studied at Warsaw, Berlin, and Vienna, he achieved an international reputation as a performer and composed a piano concerto and many solo pieces. He was the first prime minister (1919) of newly independent Poland but resigned after 10 months to return to his musical career.

Padua (Italian name: Padova) 45 24N 11 53E A city in NE Italy, near Venice. An important city in Roman and Renaissance times, it has several notable buildings, including a 13th-century cathedral and the Basilica of St Anthony, in front of which stands one of Donatello's most famous works, the equestrian statue of

Gattamelata. Galileo taught at its university (founded in 1222). Machinery and textiles are produced. Population (1991 est): 218,000.

Paestum The Roman name for Posidonia, a colony of *Sybaris founded about 600 BC on the SW coast of Italy. Paestum is famed for the three great Doric temples the remains of which still stand there. Named for the Greek sea god *Poseidon, it was conquered by Rome in 273 BC and became celebrated in Latin poetry for its twice-flowering roses.

Páez, José Antonio (1790–1873) Venezuelan revolutionary. The leader of a band of cowboys (*llaneros*), he allied himself with *Bolívar against Spain. After the liberation he took Venezuela out of the confederation of Gran Colombia and became its first president (1831).

Pagalu. *See* Equatorial Guinea, Republic of.

Pagan The former capital of Burma on the Irrawaddy River SE of Mandalay. Founded in about 849 AD, Pagan was refounded after the decree adopting Buddhism as the state religion (1056). Hundreds of brick-built temples, monasteries, and pagodas survived Pagan's sack by the Mongols (1287) and some, such as the Ananda temple (1090) and Shwezigon pagoda (12th century), are still in use.

Paganini, Niccolò (1782–1840) Italian virtuoso violinist. After an adventurous youth he toured Europe, astonishing audiences with his techniques, such as left-hand pizzicato, multiple stopping, and artificial harmonics. His skill inspired Liszt and Schumann to compose piano music of transcendent difficulty. He composed six violin concertos, various showpieces for violin, including a set of variations on the G string, and 24 caprices, one of which became the basis for compositions by Rachmaninov, Brahms, and others.

PAGODA *The exuberantly curving roofs of the typical multistoried Chinese pagoda contrast with the more restrained Japanese form.*

pagoda A Buddhist shrine in the form of a tower for housing relics of the Buddha. Pagodas originated in India, where their standardized form of a basic unit repeated vertically in diminishing sizes was evolved. From India the pagoda spread to Sri Lanka (where it is called a dagoba), SE Asia, China, and Japan. Japanese pagodas are usually five-storied wooden structures built around a central timber post to provide stability against earthquakes. *See also* stupa.

Pago Pago 14 16S 170 43W The capital of American Samoa, in SE Tutuila on the S Pacific Ocean. A US naval base (1872–1951), it is a port exporting canned tuna. Population (1990): 3519.

Pahang A large state in SE Peninsular Malaysia, on the South China Sea. Lying mainly in the Pahang River basin it rises to the Cameron Mountains in the W. Rubber, rice, coconuts, gold, and tin are produced. Area: 13,873 sq mi (35,931 sq km). Population (1980): 770,644. Capital: Kuantan.

Pahang River The longest river in Peninsular Malaysia, rising in the NW and flowing generally S then E through the state of Penang to enter the South China Sea. Length: 200 mi (322 km).

Paige, Satchel (Leroy Robert P.; 1906–82) US baseball player. Long a pitcher in African-American baseball leagues, he became a member of the Cleveland Indians in 1948 when African Americans began to be allowed in the major leagues. He also pitched for the St Louis Browns (1951–53) and other teams and was elected to the Baseball Hall of Fame in 1971.

Paine, Thomas (1737–1809) British writer and political theorist. His pamphlet *Common Sense* (1776) initiated the American movement toward independence. In 1791–92 his *Rights of Man* was published, in support of the French Revolution and in opposition to *Burke's *Reflections*. Indicted for treason, Paine fled to France, where he was elected to the French Convention. While imprisoned by Robespierre, he wrote the second part of his *Age of Reason* (1796), a deist manifesto that held that "all religions are in their nature mild and benign."

paint A finely powdered insoluble pigment suspended in a binding medium; on application to a surface the volatile components of the binding medium evaporate, the drying oils oxidize, and the resins polymerize, leaving a decorative or protective skin. The pigments impart color and opacity to the skin and extenders (such as barium sulfate, calcium carbonate, or asbestos) are mixed with the pigments to strengthen the skin and reduce raw-material costs. The binding medium consists of a drying oil (e.g. linseed oil or tung oil), a resin (rosin or a synthetic alkyd), a thinner (turpentine, benzene, etc.), and a drier to accelerate film formation. Water-based emulsion paints consist of emulsions of a synthetic resin (e.g. polyvinyl acetate, polystyrene, acrylic resins) in water.

Painted Desert An area in N central Arizona, bounded by the Little Colorado River on the E and S and on the N by the Colorado River. It is about 15–20 mi (24–32 km) wide. At an average altitude of 5000 ft (1525 m), it was named by Joseph C. Ives and John Strong Newberry in 1858 because of the wide range of colors in aged rocks exposed by erosion. Area: 7500 sq mi (19,425 sq km).

painted lady An orange, black, and white butterfly, *Vanessa cardui*, of worldwide distribution. It cannot survive cold winters but migrates from warmer regions each year. The caterpillars feed mainly on thistles and nettles. The American painted lady (*V. virginiensis*) is similar but less widespread.

painting In art, the creation of an aesthetic entity by the skilled covering of a surface with paint. Suitable painting surfaces include paper, canvas, walls, and ivory, and among the many techniques of painting are oil, *watercolor, *tempera, *encaustic, *fresco, and, the most modern method, *acrylic painting. The main subjects of painting were religious until the Renaissance period, when portraits, landscapes, *genre, and *still life began to assume an independent existence.

The principal painting styles in the history of art have been classical (ancient Greek and Roman), Byzantine, romanesque, gothic, Renaissance, mannerist, baroque, rococo, neoclassical, impressionist, and abstract.

Paisley, Ian (1926–) Northern Irish politician; an uncompromising defender of Protestant unionism. A minister of the Free Presbyterian Church of Ulster from 1946, he was a Protestant Unionist member of Parliament in the Northern Irish Parliament (1970–72) before becoming (1974) a Democratic Unionist member of Britain's House of Commons.

Paiute North American Shoshonean-speaking Indian tribe, found in Utah, Arizona, Nevada, and California (Southern Paiute) and in parts of Oregon, California, Nevada, and Idaho (Northern Paiute). Basically farmers, weavers, and hunters, they were relocated after 1850 to reservations within the boundaries of their original lands.

Pakistan, Islamic Republic of A country in S Asia, bordering on Iran, Afghanistan, China, and India. The W is mountainous and the E has areas of desert, while the Indus River rises in the Himalayas in the N and flows S across plateau and the Indus Plain to the Arabian Sea. The country is arid with great extremes of temperature but the plain is very fertile, except in areas that have become saline or waterlogged. The population, which is increasing rapidly, is a mixture of many Asian and Middle Eastern racial groups. Of the languages spoken Punjabi is the most commonly used, although Urdu is the language of the educated. 97% of the population is Muslim. *Economy*: mainly agricultural, producing chiefly rice, wheat, sugar cane, and cotton. Productivity has improved during the 1960s and 1970s with increased mechanization, the use of chemical fertilizers, improved strains of crops, and the reclamation of saline land. Irrigation, on which agriculture is dependent, has also been extensively developed since the Indus Waters Treaty was concluded with India (1960). Industry has developed successfully since 1947, at which time the area had very little. Although industry employs only 14% of the workforce and is still largely dependent on imported machinery, petroleum, chemicals, and metals, Pakistan has become a major exporter of cotton and cotton yarn and cloth. Chemical fertilizers, cement, sugar, and handicrafts are also produced, and a steel industry is being developed. Fishing is increasingly important. Resources include coal (mainly low-grade), iron ore, copper, limestone, oil, and large quantities of natural gas. Hydroelectric power is also produced. *History*: the history of Pakistan is that of *India until 1947, when it was created to satisfy the *Muslim League's demand for a separate state for the Muslim minority. It consisted then of two separate areas; West Pakistan comprised Baluchistan, the Northwest Frontier, West Punjab (now Punjab province), and Sind, while East Pakistan was formed from East Bengal. The question of control over Kashmir is still unsettled. The most serious problem has been the unification of Pakistan's diverse population groups, divided by geography, race, and extremes of wealth and poverty. The unifying force of the common religion has not been able to contain demands for regional autonomy and increased democracy. Thus each of Pakistan's three constitutions (1956, 1962, 1973) has been replaced by martial law. Regional unrest was especially serious in East Pakistan, which had a larger population but less political and military power than West Pakistan. The electoral victory in East Pakistan of the Awami League (1970), which demanded regional autonomy, led to its secession as *Bangladesh (1971). This was affected after a two-week civil war in which Indian forces intervened and defeated the Pakistani army, which consisted of troops from West Pakistan. Regionalism later led to guerrilla fighting in Baluchistan and the Northwest Frontier province (1973 onward). On Jan 30, 1972, Pakistan withdrew from the Commonwealth of Nations. Allegations of ballot rigging following the 1977 elections triggered off more violent unrest, which led finally to a military coup led by Gen. Zia ul-Haq. Demonstrations and riots followed when the former prime minister, Zulfikar Ali Bhutto, was executed for conspiracy to murder (1979). Gen. Zia became president in 1978 and held parliamentary elections in 1985. He was killed (1988) in a plane crash and was succeeded by the opposition party leader, Benazir Bhutto, the daughter of Zulfikar Ali Bhutto. She became the first female president in the nation's history. She was dismissed in 1990 amid charges of corruption and of lack of control and direction, but remained influential in politics and regained the prime ministry in Oct 1993. Official language: Urdu. Official currency: Pakistan rupee of 100 paise. Area (excluding Jammu and Kashmir): 310,322 sq mi (803,943 sq km). Population (1990 est): 113,163,000. Capital: Islamabad.

Palaeologus The ruling dynasty of the Eastern Roman Empire from 1261 to 1453. Originating in the 11th century, the first Palaeologus emperor was *Michael VIII Palaeologus and they ruled until the fall of Constantinople to the Turks in 1453. During this period Byzantine culture underwent a major revival.

palate The roof of the mouth, which is divided into two parts. The soft palate at the back of the mouth is composed of mucous membrane and prevents food passing into the nose during swallowing. From its center hangs down a flap of tissue, the uvula. The hard palate, further forward, is composed of two fused halves made up of the palatine bone and part of the maxillary (upper jaw) bones. During development the two halves of the palate may fail to fuse, leading to a *cleft palate.

Palatinate Two historic regions of Germany: the Lower (*or* Rhenish) Palatinate is now in Rheinland-Pfalz, Baden-Württemberg, and Hessen and the Upper Palatinate is now in Bavaria. In 1156 the title of count palatine (originally a judicial officer) was bestowed by Emperor Frederick I on his half-brother Conrad, whose territories included what later became the Rhenish Palatinate. When, in 1214, it passed to the *Wittelsbach family, their lands in Bavaria became the Upper Palatinate. From 1356 the counts palatine were *electors of Holy Roman Emperors. During the Reformation the Palatinate became a center of Protestantism and the claim by the Protestant, Elector Frederick, the Winter King, to the Bohemian throne precipitated the *Thirty Years' War. The two Palatinates were separated from 1648 until 1777 but in the early 19th century the Lower Palatinate was divided between France and various German states and the Upper Palatinate passed to Bavaria.

Palau. *See* Belau.

Palawan A mountainous island in the W Philippines, between the South China and Sulu Seas. Sparsely populated, its chief products are timber, mercury, and chromite; fishing is important. Area: 4550 sq mi (11,785 sq km). Chief town: Puerto Princesa.

Palembang 2 59S 104 45E A port in Indonesia, in S Sumatra on the Musi River. It was the capital of a Hindu Sumatran kingdom (8th century AD) and Dutch trade began here in 1617. Its university was established in 1960. The export center of local oil fields, it has Indonesia's largest refinery and many oil-based industries. Population (1980): 787,187.

Palencia 41 01N 4 32W A city in N central Spain, in León. It possessed Spain's first university, founded in 1208 and moved to Salamanca in 1239. The gothic cathedral contains paintings by El Greco, including *St Sebastian*. Manufactures include iron and porcelain. Population (1982): 67,250.

Paleocene epoch. *See* Tertiary period.

paleography The study of ancient handwriting. Paleography originated as an adjunct to textual criticism of Greek and Latin manuscripts but is now applied to all kinds of scripts. Paleographers assess the cultural and historical implications of the development of writing styles and the output of individual scriptoria (scribal centers) and scribes. Recent technical aids include computerized surveys of large numbers of manuscripts and ultraviolet photography to render faint writing legible.

Paleolithic The earliest division of the *Stone Age. It extends roughly from the emergence of man, or at least of some hominid capable of making simple pebble tools, to the end of the last ice age. The Paleolithic is conventionally divided into three phases: Lower, beginning as much as 3,500,000 years ago and characterized by pebble-tool and hand-axe manufacture; Middle, beginning about 70,000 years ago and associated with *Neanderthal man and *Mousterian industries; and Upper, beginning about 40,000 years ago and associated in Europe with *Cro-Magnon man and cave art.

paleomagnetism The history of the earth's magnetic field (*see* geomagnetic field) as determined from the remanent magnetism of rocks. The study assumes that the principal component of igneous and sedimentary rocks' magnetism was determined at or near to the time at which the rocks were formed. Paleomagnetism provides evidence for continental drift (*see* plate tectonics) and the movement of the magnetic poles.

paleontology The study of ancient organisms from their *fossil remains in the rocks. Their taxonomy, anatomy, ecology, and evolution are studied. Fossils are used to correlate bodies of rock and establish their stratigraphic relationships with each other; this field is called biostratigraphy. Modern methods of *dating rocks by radiometric means give their absolute dates rather than their order in the stratigraphic column. The study of ancient microscopic organisms is called **micropaleontology** and the fossils are known as microfossils.

Paleo-Siberian languages A diverse group of languages of Siberia comprising four unrelated groups: Yeniseian; Luorawetlan, which includes Chuckchi, Koryak, and Aliutor; Yukaghir, which includes Yukaghir and also Omok and Chuvan, both now extinct; and Gilyak, the only one of its group.

Paleozoic era The era of geological time between the Precambrian and the Mesozoic, lasting from about 590 to 240 million years ago. It is divided into the Upper Paleozoic, which contains the Cambrian, Ordovician, and Silurian periods, and the Lower Paleozoic, containing the Devonian, Carboniferous, and Permian. It is the first era of *Phanerozoic time. The Caledonian and Variscan orogenies both occurred in this era.

Palermo 38 08N 13 23E A port in Italy, the capital of Sicily. Founded by the Phoenicians in the 8th century BC, it first established itself as chief town of the island under the Arabs (9th–11th centuries). Its many notable buildings include the gothic cathedral and the Norman palace (now the regional parliament). It has ship building and textile industries. Population (1991 est): 734,238.

Palestine (*or* Holy Land) A historic area in the Middle East, consisting of the area between the Mediterranean Sea and the Jordan River. It now comprises *Israel and territories belonging to Jordan and Egypt. Sacred to Jews, Christians, and Muslims alike, and caught as it has been between a succession of surrounding empires, the area has been much fought over. It has been inhabited since prehistoric times. Toward the end of the 2nd millennium BC it was settled by the Hebrew people, who in the Old Testament were led out of Egypt by Moses, and in about 1000 BC a Hebrew kingdom was founded by Saul. Following the reign of Solomon it was split into Israel, later conquered by the Assyrians, and Judah (*see* Judea), later conquered by the Babylonians (*see* Babylonian exile), who destroyed the *Temple of Jerusalem (rebuilt in 516 BC under the Persians). The Romans conquered the Jewish state that existed briefly in 142–63 BC and also destroyed the Temple (70 AD) while violently suppressing a Jewish revolt. From the late 4th century AD many Jews left Palestine, which became a center first for Christian and later for Muslim pilgrimage (following Arab conquest in 636 AD). Christianity was reinstated in the area by the conquest of the Crusaders (1099 until the 13th century). After a period of Egyptian rule it fell to the Ottoman Turks (1516), who ruled it until World War I. During the 1830s Palestine, inhabited chiefly by Arab peasants, was opened up to European influence and from the mid-19th century Jews returned from the *Diaspora to settle in Palestine. The late 19th century saw the beginning of *Zionism and in 1909 Tel Aviv, the first new Jewish city, was founded. By 1914 there were 100,000 Jews in Palestine, although their numbers were reduced by almost half during World War I, in which they were sympathetic to the Allies. In 1918 Palestine was captured by the British; British administration, effective from 1920, was confirmed by a League of Nations mandate (1922). By the *Balfour Declaration (1917) the British supported the Jewish demand for a Jewish nation in Palestine. This provoked unrest and terrorism among the Arab population, who felt increasingly threatened by Jewish immigration. In 1947 the problem was referred to the UN, which decided to divide Palestine into two separate states, Jewish and Arab. As this was accepted by the Jews but not the Arabs, Britain renounced its mandate in 1948. The state of Israel was then proclaimed and immediately attacked by the surrounding Arab countries. They were repulsed but the rest of Palestine was divided between Jordan and Egypt. *See also* West Bank.

Palestine Liberation Organization (PLO) An organization of various Palestinian groups opposed to the existence of the state of Israel. Formed in 1964 and led by Yasser Arafat since 1968, the PLO has not been able to maintain unity among all the Palestinian groups; in particular, the Popular Front for the Liberation of Palestine (PFLP), led by Dr. George Habash, has remained independent. The PLO has nonetheless managed to gain support from the *Arab League, which recognized it as the sole legitimate representative of the Palestinian people in 1974. Terrorism was long the PLO's chief means of confrontation with Israel. In 1993 substantial progress was made in peace negotiations between the PLO and Israel.

Palestrina, Giovanni Pierluigi da (?1525–94) Italian composer. He spent most of his life in Rome, as chorister, choirmaster, or maestro at churches including St Peter's. One of the greatest masters of *polyphony, he composed 93 masses, 179 motets, and many other pieces, mainly for church use. He was twice offered posts elsewhere (Venice and Mantua) but each time he asked too high a salary.

Palgrave, Francis Turner (1824–97) British poet and anthologist. A friend of Tennyson, he published several volumes of verse and became professor of poetry at Oxford. He is best remembered for his influential anthology of English verse, *The Golden Treasury* (1861).

Pali An *Indo-Aryan language originating in N India. It is the language of the Theravada Buddhist canon and is used throughout the Theravada countries of SE Asia but disappeared from India itself during the 14th century.

Palio A horse race run in July and August in the main piazza of Siena. It is named for the painted silk banner that the winner receives. The Palio first took place in 1482 and is accompanied by considerable pageantry.

Palissy, Bernard (1510–89) French potter, famous for his rustic ware, a richly colored lead-glazed earthenware. His dishes are ornamental in relief with mythological subjects or reptiles, plants, etc. He enjoyed court patronage in the 1560s but was persecuted as a Huguenot and died in prison. He is also known for his writings on religion, science, and philosophy.

Palladianism An architectural style developed in 16th-century Venetia by *Palladio. It was based on classical Roman public architecture and the theories of *Vitruvius and it placed great importance on symmetrical room planning and a harmonious system of proportions. Largely disseminated by Palladio's books, *I quattro libri dell' architettura* (1570), it was first introduced into England in the early 17th century by Inigo *Jones and it was revived early in the 18th century. The style was widely used in England for public buildings and country houses, and imitated in Europe, Russia and North America, where it influenced southern plantation homes. It was eventually replaced by *neoclassicism in the mid-18th century.

PALLADIANISM *Chiswick House (begun 1725), which was designed by England's Lord Burlington for his own use.*

Palladio, Andrea (1508–80) Italian architect, born in Padua. One of the most sophisticated and widely imitated of classical architects, Palladio is famous for developing the architectural style now known as *Palladianism. Trained as a stonemason, Palladio designed most of his buildings in and around Vicenza. His first job was the remodeling of the basilica in Vicenza (begun 1549) and from that emerged a hugely successful career. He produced villas, for example the Villa Rotonda (near Vicenza) and Villa Barbaro (Maser); palaces, for example the Palazzo Chericati (1550s); churches, the most famous being S Giorgio Maggiore in Venice (begun 1566).

palladium (Pd) A silvery-white noble metal of the platinum group, discovered by W. H. Wollaston (1766–1828) in 1803, and named for the asteroid Pallas, which was discovered at about the same time. Palladium readily absorbs hydrogen and is used as a catalyst for hydrogenation reactions; it is alloyed with gold to form white gold. At no 46; at wt 106.4; mp 2828°F (1552°C); bp 5689°F (3140°C).

Palladium In Greek and Roman religion, an ancient image of Athena, originally the wooden image kept in the citadel of Troy and believed to have been sent from heaven by Zeus. The safety of the city depended on it. It was stolen by Odysseus and Diomedes, who thus made possible the capture of Troy. It was believed to have been taken to Athens or Sparta, or to Rome (by *Aeneas).

Pallas The second largest (377 m [608 km] in diameter) *minor planet, the orbit of which lies between those of Mars and Jupiter.

Pallas's cat A small wild *cat, *Felis* (or *Otocolobus*) *manul*, of Tibet, Mongolia, and Siberia. About 20 in (50 cm) long, with a very thick tail and long yellow-gray fur, it has a small face with low-set ears—an adaptation for stalking small mammals from the cover of rocks and boulders.

palm A monocotyledonous plant of the family *Palmae* (or *Arecaceae*; about 2500 species), occurring in tropical and subtropical regions. Ranging from 40–196 ft (1–60 m) in height, palms typically have an unbranched trunk crowned with a cluster of leaves, which are pleated and fan-shaped or featherlike and often very large (up to 49 ft [15 m] long). The flowers are usually grouped into large clusters and give rise to berries or drupes (stone fruits). Palms are commercially important as a source of food (*see* coconut; date; sago), oil (*see* oil palm), wax (*see* carnauba), and various fibers and building materials.

Palma (*or* Palma de Mallorca) 39 35N 2 39E The capital of the Spanish Balearic Islands, in Majorca on the Mediterranean Sea. Its historic buildings include the gothic cathedral (1230–1601) and the 14th-century Bellver Castle. Noted as a tourist resort, it is also a port and commercial center; industries include textiles, footwear, and such crafts as pottery. Population (1986): 321,100.

Palm Beach 26 41N 80 02W A town and fashionable winter resort in SE Florida, on Lake Worth (a lagoon). It is an extension of the much larger West Palm Beach. Population (1990): 9814.

palm civet A mammal of the family *Viverridae* that is smaller than the true civets and more omnivorous than the *genets. Most palm civets are Asian—the two-spotted palm civet (*Nandinia binotata*) is the only African species. The masked palm civit (*Paguma larvata*) of SE Asia is up to 55 in (140 cm) long including the tail (20–25.5 in; 50–65 cm) and is mainly arboreal, feeding on fruit, insects, and some vertebrates.

Palmer, Arnold (1929–   ) US professional golfer, who did much to make golf a spectator sport. US amateur champion in 1954, he won the US Open championship (1960), Masters championship (1958, 1960, 1962, 1964), British Open championship (1961, 1962), and many other events. From the mid-1980s he competed in golf's senior events.

Palmer, Samuel (1805–81) British landscape painter and etcher, born in London. He first exhibited at the Royal Academy at the age of 14 but his best landscapes, often moonlit and either in sepia or watercolor, were painted during his association (1826–35) with a group of painters in Shoreham, who shared Palmer's admiration for William *Blake. His imaginative and mystical approach to art declined into conventionality in the late 1830s.

Palmerston, Henry John Temple, 3rd viscount (1784–1865) British statesman; Liberal prime minister (1855–58, 1859–65). He entered Parliament in 1807 as a Tory, but by 1830 he had joined the Whigs (later Liberals). His markedly nationalistic foreign policy sought to defend constitutional states and prevent a Franco-Russian combination. As prime minister Palmerston supported the Confederacy in the Civil War but was dissuaded by his colleagues from actively involving Britain.

Palmerston North 40 21S 175 37E A city in New Zealand, in S North Island. It is a center for the agricultural area of the Manawatu Plain and is the site of Massey University (a branch of Victoria University, Wellington). Population (1989 est): 67,500.

palmistry The study of the lines and ridges on the palm of the hand in order to interpret character and divine the owner's future. Although without scientific basis, palmistry (or chiromancy as it is also called) provides common-sense evidence of a person's way of life and habits and from these something may be deduced of his character and interests.

Palm Springs 33 49N 116 34W A city in California. Long known for its hot springs, it is a popular resort with golf courses and an aerial tramway. Population (1990): 40,181.

Palm Sunday The Sunday before Easter, commemorating Christ's last triumphal ride into Jerusalem (Mark 11). In many Churches crosses or branches of palm leaves are distributed on this day.

palmyra A *palm tree, *Borassus flabellier*, cultivated in India and Sri Lanka. The timber is used for construction and the leaves are used for thatch and made into a type of paper. The sugary sap from the flower heads is fermented to give palm wine and the kernels of the fruits are eaten.

Palmyra (*or* Tadmor) 34 36N 38 15E An ancient Syrian desert city on the route of the E–W caravan trade in the 2nd and 3rd centuries AD. Palmyra came under Roman control in the 1st century AD but under *Zenobia regained its independence from 270 until 272, when it was reconquered and then destroyed; subsequently rebuilt, it was taken by the Muslims in 634. The ruins of the ancient city include the remains of the Temple of Bel (Palmyra's chief deity). Inscriptions in the Palmyric alphabet (developed from the *Aramaic) provide important information on Palmyra's trade.

Palo Alto 32 27N 122 09W A city in W central California, SE of San Francisco, at the S tip of San Francisco Bay. Stanford University (1885) is here. Population (1990): 55,900.

Palo Alto, Battle of (1846) First US-Mexican clash of the *Mexican War. US Gen. Zachary *Taylor, returning to Fort Texas on the Rio Grande near Brownsville, Tex., was blocked by the Mexicans under Gen. Mariano Arista. The American force, although smaller, was victorious, forcing the Mexicans back across the border.

palolo worm (*or* paolo worm) A large marine *annelid worm, *Eunice viridis*, of the S Pacific. Palolo worms hunt for small prey among coral reefs and their reproduction is synchronized by the phases of the moon. The rear portion of the worm, containing eggs or sperm, separates and swims to the surface, discharging its gametes in the sea. Swarming worms are a local delicacy. Class: *Polychaeta*.

Palomar, Mount A mountain in California. It is the site of the Mount Palomar Observatory operated by the Carnegie Institute of Washington and the California Institute of Technology. Its 200 in (508 cm) reflecting telescope is among the largest in the world. Height: 6140 ft (1870 m). *See also* Hale Observatories.

palomino A horse that has a yellow or golden coat and a white or silver mane and tail. Palominos are often Arabs or American quarter horses but may be of any light saddle-horse breed. They are recognized as a color breed in the US but do not breed true.

palynology (*or* pollen analysis) The study of pollen grains and their distribution in sedimentary rocks in order to provide information about life and environmental conditions of past geological ages. Pollen is extremely resistant to decay and therefore well preserved in rocks. The different genera and species are also very distinctive; therefore the presence of a certain type of pollen indicates the dominant flora—and therefore the climate and other conditions—of the period studied.

Pamirs (*or* Pamir) A mountainous area of central Asia, situated mainly in Tajikistan and extending into China and Afghanistan. It consists of a complex of high ranges rising over 20,000 ft (6000 m), with the Tian Shan in the N, the

Kunlun and Karakoram in the E, and the Hindu Kush in the W. Its highest point is Mount Communism, at 24,590 ft (7495 m).

Pampas The flat treeless plains of Argentina. These extend W from the Atlantic Ocean to the Andes and are bordered by the Gran Chaco in the N and Patagonia in the S. They are of major agricultural importance in the E, producing wheat, corn, and beef in particular.

pampas cat A small wild *cat, *Felis colocolo*, of South America. About the size of a domestic cat, with a long tail and grayish coat, it once hunted in grassland and swamps but is now very rare.

pampas grass A perennial *grass of the genus *Cortaderia*, native to South America and widely cultivated as an ornamental. *C. argentea* grows in dense clumps, with leaves up to 7 ft (2 m) long and flowering stems exceeding 10 ft (3 m) in length. The flowers usually form silvery-white plumes, although various color varieties are possible.

Pamplona 42 49N 1 39W A city in NE Spain, in the Basque Provinces. It has a cathedral and holds a renowned fiesta (during which bulls are driven through the streets to the bullring), described by the novelist Ernest Hemingway in *The Sun Also Rises* (1926). It is an agricultural center and its industries include traditional crafts and chemicals. Population (1991): 179,251.

Pan The Greek god of shepherds and their flocks, the son of Hermes. He is usually portrayed with the legs, ears, and horns of a goat. He lived in the mountains and was associated especially with Arcadia, where he sported with the nymphs and played his pipes, known as the syrinx (*see* panpipes). He was believed to be the source of a sudden inexplicable fear, or panic, which sometimes overcame travelers in wild and remote places.

Panama, Isthmus of A narrow strip of land linking North and South America, between the Caribbean Sea and the Pacific Ocean. Length: 420 mi (676 km). Minimum width: 31 mi (50 km).

Panama, Republic of A country in Central America occupying the Isthmus of Panama, which connects Central and South America. The *Panama Canal crosses the isthmus, bisecting the country and providing passage between the Atlantic (via the Caribbean Sea) and Pacific Oceans. Narrow coastal plains rise to volcanic mountains. The population is largely of mixed Indian, European, and African descent. *Economy*: considerable revenue comes from receipts from the Panama Canal and from international capital. The main agricultural products are bananas, rice, sugar, and corn; fishing (especially for shrimps) is growing in importance. Industries include oil refining, cement production, and paper and food processing. Tourism is an increasing source of revenue. The main exports include refined oil, bananas, shrimps, and sugar. *History*: discoverd by Columbus in 1502 and soon colonized by the Spanish; in 1513 Balboa made his famous journey across the isthmus. Panama later became part of the viceroyalty of Peru and then of New Granada. In 1821 it became part of newly independent Colombia, from which it broke free in 1903 after a revolution supported by the US. Its political history has been turbulent. A military coup in 1968 brought Gen. Omar Torrijos to power and in 1972 a new constitution gave him full executive powers for six years, while also initiating a presidency. In 1978 Torrijos accordingly retired as head of state but retained his command of the National Guard and effectively remained in control until his death in 1981. Panama helped to form the so-called Contadora group, an alliance of Latin American countries. In 1988, the US accused Gen. Manuel Noriega, effective leader of Panama, of drug smuggling. In a 1989 invasion, the US ousted Noriega, who fled and sought asylum for a time in the Vatican embassy. Brought to the US for trial, he was convicted of drug charges in 1992. Official language: Spanish. Official currency: balboa of 100 centésimos. Area: 29,201 sq mi (75,650 sq km). Population (1992): 2,515,000. Capital and main port: Panama City.

Panama Canal A canal across the Isthmus of Panama connecting the Atlantic and Pacific Oceans. Some 51 mi (82 km) long, it was begun by the French Panama Canal Company under Ferdinand de *Lesseps but construction was halted in 1889 by bankruptcy. In 1903 the US acquired the construction rights from newly independent Panama and the canal was opened in 1914. By the 1903 treaty the US acquired sovereignty in perpetuity over the **Panama Canal Zone**, a region extending 3 mi (5 km) on either side of the canal. In return Panama received $10 million and an annuity. In 1978 two treaties provided for Panamanian sovereignty over the canal and the Zone by 2000 and for their neutrality and in 1979 Panama assumed territorial jurisdiction over the former Canal Zone. Area: 647 sq mi (1676 sq km).

Panama City 5 58N 79 31W The capital of Panama, situated in the center of the country near the Pacific end of the Panama Canal. Founded by the Spanish in 1519 on the site of an Indian fishing village, it was destroyed by Henry Morgan and his pirates in 1671 and rebuilt two years later 5 mi (8 km) to the SW. It became capital of the newly independent Panama in 1904 and has expanded considerably since the opening of the Canal in 1914. The University of Panama was founded in 1935 and that of Santa Maria de la Antigua in 1965. Population (1990): 411,549.

Pan-American Highway A system of highways connecting North and South America. When completed it will consist of about 16,150 mi (26,000 km) of roadway. First proposed as a single route, it is now a whole network of roads. Between Texas and Panama it is called the Inter-American Highway. The sections through the Central American states were built with US aid, while Mexico financed and built its own section. It will eventually connect with roads leading to Santiago, Buenos Aires, Montevideo, and Rio de Janeiro.

Panay An island in the central Philippines, in the Visayan Islands. Mountainous in the W, its central fertile plain produces rice, maize, and sugar. It also has timber, fishing, and copper and coal-mining industries. Area: 4744 sq mi (12,287 sq km). Chief town: Iloilo.

Panchen Lama In *Tibetan Buddhism, the title of the chief abbot of Tashilhunpo monastery at Zhikatse, ranking second to the *Dalai Lama. He is said to be a reincarnation of Amitabha, the Buddha of Infinite Light. The present Panchen Lama was enthroned in 1952 at Tashilhunpo, where he apparently still resides despite the Chinese occupation of Tibet and the exile of the Dalai Lama.

pancreas A gland, about 6 in (15 cm) long, situated in the abdomen behind the stomach. When food passes into the intestine the pancreas secretes several digestive enzymes that drain into the intestine through the pancreatic duct. In addition, small clusters of cells (called islets of Langerhans) scattered throughout the pancreas secrete the hormones *insulin and *glucagon, which control blood-sugar levels.

panda A bearlike mammal belonging to the family *Procyonidae* (raccoons, kinkajous, etc.). The giant panda (*Ailuropoda melanoleuca*) is very rare; it lives in the cold bamboo forests of central China, feeding on young bamboo shoots. Giant pandas are up to 5 ft (1.6 m) long, weigh 165–220 lb (75–100 kg), and have bold black-and white-markings.

The red panda (*Ailurus fulgens*), also called the lesser panda, lives in the forests of the Himalayas and W China; 31–43 in (80–110 cm) long including the bushy tail (12–20 in; 30–50 cm), it is red-brown with black markings on its white face.

Red pandas live in trees and feed on the ground at twilight on roots, nuts, lichens, and bamboo shoots.

PANDA *The elongated wrist bone of the giant panda acts like a thumb, enabling it to manipulate the bamboo shoots on which it feeds.*

Pandanus. *See* screw pine.

Pandarus In Greek legend, a Trojan archer who wounded the Greek commander Menelaus and was killed by Diomedes. In the medieval story concerning Troilus and Cressida he is the lovers' go-between.

Pandit, Vijaya Lakshmi (1900–   ) Indian diplomat; sister of Jawaharlal *Nehru. She was imprisoned as a member of *Gandhi's movement of noncooperation with the British. Following independence she was ambassador to the Soviet Union (1947–49) and to the US (1949–51); she then became president of the UN General Assembly (1953–54) and high commissioner to the UK (1955–61).

Pandora In Greek mythology, the first woman, fashioned by *Hephaestus and invented by Zeus as his revenge on *Prometheus, who had stolen fire from heaven. She married Epimethus, brother of Prometheus. Her dowry was a box, which when opened, released all the varieties of evil and retained only hope.

pangolin An armored mammal belonging to the genus *Manis* and order *Pholidota* (7 species), of Africa and S Asia, also called scaly anteater; 12–31 in (30–80 cm) long with long prehensile tails, pangolins are covered on their backs with overlapping horny scales. Toothless, with a long sticky tongue and strong claws, they sleep in deep burrows, emerging at night to feed on ants and termites. They can walk on their hind legs, climb trees, and curl up into a tight ball if attacked.

Pan Gu (*or* P'an Ku) In Chinese Taoist mythology, the first man. His knowledge of *yin and yang enabled him to shape the world.

Pan Gu (*or* P'an Ku; 32–92 AD) Chinese historian. He expanded the work of *Si-ma Qian to cover the history of the Han dynasty until his own time. His great work *The History of the Former Han* started the Chinese tradition of compiling dynastic histories.

panic grass An annual or perennial *grass of the genus *Panicum* (500 species), mostly of the tropics and subtropics. The flowering stems, up to 31 in (80 cm) high, have many branches, each bearing several slender-stalked spikelets (flower clusters). Some species are cultivated for their grain (*see* millet).

Panini (6th or 5th century BC) Indian grammarian. Panini's analysis of Sanskrit, the *Ashtadhyayi*, is one of the earliest studies of a language and the most comprehensive grammatical work to appear before the 19th century. Although intended to regulate the use of Sanskrit rather than to teach it, the *Ashtadhyayi* is still used in some Brahman schools.

Pankhurst, Emmeline (1858–1928) British suffragette, who founded, the Women's Social and Political Union (1903). She was imprisoned several times for destroying property, undergoing hunger strikes and forcible feeding. During World War I, she abandoned her militancy and encouraged the industrial recruitment of women. *See* women's movement.

P'an Ku. *See* Pan Gu.

panorama A narrative scene or landscape painted on a large canvas, which was either hung up around the walls of a circular room or slowly unrolled before an audience. The first panorama was produced by the Scottish painter Robert Barker (1739–1806) in 1788. An antecedent of films, panoramas provided a popular form of entertainment as well as fulfilling an educational function in the 19th century.

panpipes (*or* syrinx) An ancient musical instrument consisting of a row of small graduated pipes bound together. It is played by blowing across the holes. According to Greek legend it was invented by the deity Pan, who pursued the nymph Syrinx. When she was changed into a reed by Apollo, Pan made the instrument from the reed stem.

pansy A popular annual or perennial garden plant that is a hybrid of the wild pansy (*Viola tricolor*), developed in the early 19th century. There are now many varieties, up to 8 in (20 cm) high, with leafy stems and (usually) yellow, orange, purple, brown, or white flowers, up to 2 in (5 cm) across. The wild pansy, or heartsease, found throughout Eurasia, has small flowers colored purple, yellow, and white. Family: *Violaceae*. *See also* violet.

Pantelleria Island (ancient name: Cossyra) A volcanic island in Italy, in the Mediterranean Sea. Produce includes wine and raisins. Area: 32 sq mi (83 sq km). Chief town: Pantelleria.

pantheism Any belief or doctrine presenting the natural world, including man, as part of the divine. Pantheism is a predominant tendency in Hinduism but is frowned on by orthodox Christianity. *Spinoza's phrase equating God and Nature (*Deus sive natura*) was an influential formulation of the idea, which enjoyed some currency among 19th-century philosophers. The romantic poets, particularly *Wordsworth, were also attracted to pantheism.

Pantheon 1. A temple dedicated to the worship of many gods. The most famous is that in Rome begun in 27 BC but rebuilt about 118 AD under Emperor Hadrian. It is a daring circular design built in concrete and topped by a huge concrete dome 142 ft (43 m) wide. In 609 AD it became the Church of Sta Maria Rotonda. 2. A building honoring the famous. The best known is that in Paris designed by *Soufflot in 1759.

panther A color variety of leopard that has a great deal of black pigmentation, which sometimes extends to the tongue and gums. Panthers can occur among a litter of normally spotted leopards.

panzer A mechanized division of the German army. The term panzer, meaning a coat of armor, has become widely used to denote armored forces, tanks, self-propelled artillery, and armored troop carriers.

papacy The office of the pope as temporal head of the Roman Catholic Church. Popes claim to be elected in direct line from St *Peter, to whom Christ deputed his authority on earth (Matthew 16.18–19) and who became the first bishop of Rome. The keys symbolizing this authority are still a papal emblem. The bishop of Rome, however, was not immediately recognized as preeminent and the title Pope was only formally reserved for him in 1073. In W Europe the papacy's political influence spread rapidly after 600 and Pope Leo III's coronation of *Charlemagne (800) marked the beginning of a relationship between the papacy and Holy Roman Empire that dominated Europe until the Reformation. In the East the papacy's attempt to assert its authority by excommunicating the Patriarch of Constantinople brought about the schism between the Roman Catholic and Orthodox Churches (1054; *see also* Filioque). Lesser and temporary schisms were caused by the election of antipopes, notably during the 14th century, when, after the popes had been in exile in Avignon (1309–77; *see* Avignon papacy), there was a period called the *Great Schism (1378–1417) during which there were rival popes in France and Rome. The Reformation seriously weakened the papacy's spiritual and temporal power, although papal territories in Italy remained under the pope's sovereignty. During the unification of Italy, these *papal states were appropriated (1870) and the pope's authority over the Vatican City was only formally acknowledged by the Italian state in the Lateran Treaty (1929). In 1870 the promulgation of the doctrine of papal infallibility caused further schism (*see* Old Catholics). In the 20th century the papacy has resolutely opposed communism and has participated tentatively in the ecumenical movement to heal earlier schisms.

Papadopoulos, George (1919–   ) Greek colonel, who led the military regime that seized power in Greece in 1967. He ruled by decree with the official title of prime minister, and then president, until overthrown by a military revolt in 1973.

papain A protein-digesting enzyme found in the fruit of the *papaw tree (*Carica papaya*). It is used in biochemical research and as a meat tenderizer.

papal states The central Italian states under papal sovereignty between 756, when *Pepin the Short presented Ravenna to Pope Stephen II (reigned 752–57), and 1870. They included parts of Emilia-Romagna, Marche, Umbria, and Lazio. They were a major obstacle to the 19th-century movement for Italian unification (*see* Risorgimento) but, despite papal opposition, were finally annexed in 1870. The popes refused to recognize their loss of temporal power until the *Lateran Treaty (1929) established the Vatican City as an independent papal state.

papaw (*or* papaya) A small tropical American tree, *Carica papaya*, cultivated throughout the tropics. About 25 ft (7.5 m) tall, it has lobed toothed leaves crowded at the tips of the branches and fragrant creamy-white flowers. The yellowish fruit resembles an elongated melon: its succulent pinkish or orange flesh encloses a mass of seeds. The fruits are eaten fresh, boiled, and in preserves or pickles and are a commercial source of the enzyme papain. Family: *Caricaceae*.

Papeete 17 32S 149 34W The capital of French Polynesia, in NW Tahiti. A tourist center, it is a stop on many Pacific routes. Population (1988): 23,555.

Papen, Franz von (1879–1969) German statesman and diplomat; chancellor (1932). A Catholic Center party politician with extreme right-wing views, he resigned the chancellorship after six months because of lack of cabinet support for his policies and then persuaded Hindenburg to appoint Hitler as chancellor (1933). Papen was ambassador to Austria (1934–38) and then to Turkey (1939–44). He was found not guilty at the Nuremberg war trials and only served three years of an eight-year prison sentence imposed by a German court.

paper A substance in sheet form made from the pulped cellulose fibers of wood, grass, cotton, etc., and used for writing and printing on, wrapping, cleaning, etc. The Chinese invented paper (c. 2nd century BC) and the Arabs learned the secret in 768 AD from Chinese prisoners of war at Samarkand. From Arab manufacture in the Middle East and Spain, paper spread to Byzantium (mid-11th century) and thence all over Europe. Foreign competition meant a slow start to British paper making, the first successful mill being set up about 1589. All early paper was handmade: shallow wooden frames (molds) with wire mesh bases (*see also* watermark) were dipped into vats of pulp and shaken until the pulp fibers felted together. The resulting sheets were dried, pressed, and, if necessary, sized (dipped in a gelantinous solution to render the surface less permeable). A machine for making paper in a continuous role (or web) was not invented until 1798, in France. Brought to England in 1803 by Henry Fourdrinier (1766–1854), this machine, of which variants are still in use, picked up the pulp (about 99% water) on a traveling wire mesh and shook it until the fibers were interlaced and the water drained off, before passing it through pressing and drying rollers.

The **pulp** for papermaking is obtained chiefly from wood, but also from esparto grass, rags, and increasingly from recycled wastepaper. Wood pulp may be produced by direct grinding of whole logs, as in making newsprint. For whiter, higher quality paper, the wood undergoes a more complex chemical treatment. Esparto grass and rags are used for strong durable high-quality paper, such as bank notes and legal documents. Recycled wastepaper often requires careful sorting and de-inking and is usually mixed with fresh wood pulp.

paper mulberry A shrub or small tree, *Broussonetia papyrifera*, native to E Asia and Polynesia but planted elsewhere as an ornamental, especially in the US. Up to 50 ft (15 m) tall, it has oval pointed leaves, flowers in catkins, and round rough fruits, 1 in (2.5 cm) across. Its bark is used in paper making and to produce tapa cloth in Polynesia. The bast fibers form the basis of coarse fabrics. Family: *Moraceae*.

papilionid butterfly A butterfly belonging to the widely distributed mainly tropical family *Papilionidae* (about 800 species). Papilionids comprise the *swallowtail butterflies, with tail-like projections on the hindwings, and the parnassians, which are mainly alpine.

papilloma A harmless tumor that grows from the surface of the skin or from the lining of a hollow organ, for example the bladder, womb, or lungs. *Warts and *polyps are types of papilloma. If they bleed or undergo any other change they are best treated by removal.

papillon A breed of toy dog, possibly of Spanish origin, associated with such illustrious owners as Mme de Pompadour and Marie Antoinette. Its name is derived from its large forward-facing ears, which resemble the wings of a butterfly (French word: *papillon*). The tail is held over the back and the long fine coat is white with colored patches. Height: 8–11 in (20–28 cm).

Papineau, Louis Joseph (1786–1871) French-Canadian politician. He served in Lower Canada's legislature from 1808 and was Speaker (1815–37). He

PAPER

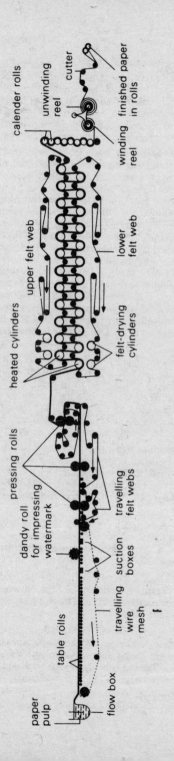

PAPER *The Fourdrinier paper-making machine is one of the longest machines in use.*

was against British rule in Canada and fought for French-Canadian rights. Opposed to the joining of Upper and Lower Canada, he put forth the "92 Resolutions" (1834), a list of French-Canadian grievances and demands. Although the resolutions were passed in the assembly, they were not enforced and he fled to the US (1837) and eventually to Paris (1839–44). He came back to a united Canada and served in the legislature (1848–54).

Pappus of Alexandria (3rd century BC) Greek mathematician, who wrote an encyclopedia consisting of eight volumes, much of which survives. It summarized Greek mathematics, of which virtually all our knowledge is due to Pappus.

paprika. *See* Capsicum.

Papua New Guinea, State of A country in the Pacific Ocean, E of Indonesia. It consists of the E part of *New Guinea and several islands, including the Bismarck Archipelago (including New Britain and New Ireland), the N part of the Solomon Islands (including Bougainville), and the Admiralty Islands. Most of the population are Melanesians. *Economy*: subsistence agriculture and the growing of cash crops, such as coconuts, cocoa, coffee, and rubber, are the chief occupations. Livestock rearing is being developed and the country's dense rain forest provides timber. The chief mineral resource and export is copper, the main source being on the island of Bougainville. Other exports include gold, coffee, cocoa, timber, and copra. *History*: the SE part of the island of New Guinea was annexed by Queensland in 1883, becoming a British colony in 1888, known as the Territory of Papua. The NE part was formerly a German territory and came under Australian rule in 1914 as the Trust Territory of New Guinea. In 1921 the two territories including their islands were merged, later becoming a UN Trusteeship under Australia. It was renamed Papua New Guinea in 1971, achieved self-government in 1973, and became fully independent in 1975. Civil war in 1990 involved a separatist movement by Bougainville islanders due to the closing of one of the world's largest copper mines. Peace talks brought about meetings to discuss the mine's—and the island's—future. Prime minister: Rabbie Namaliu. Official language: English; Pidgin is widely spoken. Official currency: kina of 100 toca. Area: 178,656 sq mi (462,840 sq km). Population (1990 est): 2,423,000. Capital and main port: Port Moresby.

papyrus An aquatic reedlike plant, *Cyperus papyrus*, up to 10 ft (3 m) tall, originally cultivated in the Nile delta of Egypt and now growing wild in parts of Africa and in Syria. It was used by the ancient Egyptians to make paper: the thick triangular stems were split into thin strips, which were pressed together while still wet. It was also used for rope, mats, sails, and shoes, and the pith was a common food. Family: *Cyperaceae*.

parabola The curve formed by a *conic section, in which the distance from a fixed point (focus) and a fixed line (directrix) are equal. In *Cartesian coordinates a standard form of its equation is $y^2 = 4ax$, for a parabola that is symmetrical about the x-axis and cuts it at the origin (vertex).

Paracel Islands An archipelago of coral islands and reefs in the South China Sea, SE of Hainan Island. They lie above oil deposits and were seized by China from Vietnam in 1974.

Paracelsus (Theophrastus Bombastus von Hohenheim; 1493–1541) Swiss physician, whose radical ideas influenced the development of medicine during the Renaissance. Paracelsus established a reputation for arrogance and aroused controversy by publicly burning the works of *Avicenna and *Galen, denouncing quack remedies, and clashing with the medical establishment. He stressed the importance of chemical compounds in treating disease, refuted the notion that mental illness was caused by demons, and linked goiter with minerals in drinking water.

parachuting The use of a parachute (a fabric canopy) to float down to the ground, usually from an aircraft, either if the aircraft is about to crash, as a way of landing troops in an area, or as a form of sport. Parachutes were used for entertainment long before they were used for safety; the first successful jump was made in 1797 and the first contest held in 1926. In accuracy competitions a contestant uses vents in his parachute to steer himself onto a target area, a red or orange cross with arms 16 ft (5 m) long and 3 ft (1m) wide. In the middle is a red disk, 4 in (10 cm) in diameter. The best parachutists land exactly on the disk. *See also* skydiving.

paraffin wax A wax obtained during the refining of crude *oil. Fully refined, it is a white tasteless solid (mp 5060°C) consisting of higher *alkanes; it is extensively used in the manufacture of waxed papers, candles, and polishes (especially microcrystalline wax polishes).

Paraguay, Republic of A landlocked country in the center of South America. It is divided by the Paraguay River into two zones: an area of fertile plains and hills to the E and the semidesert of the Gran Chaco to the W. The great majority of the population is of mixed Spanish and Guaraní Indian descent. *Economy*: chiefly agricultural, livestock rearing is of particular importance. Meat packing is one of the main industries, and meat was one of the principal exports, especially to Europe, although this has been reduced since the EEC ban on meat imports. Others include cotton, oilseed, and timber. The main crops are cotton, soybeans, cassava, and sugarcane and there are extensive forests, some of them unexploited. Mineral resources are on the whole sparse, but some limestone, salt, and kaolin is produced. Hydroelectricity is being developed, especially for the export of power to neighboring countries. *History*: explored by the Spanish in the early 16th century, it became a Spanish colony, forming part of the viceroyalty of Peru and later (1776) of the new viceroyalty of Río de la Plata. It became independent of Spain in 1811, and in 1814 José Gaspar Rodríguez de Francia (1766–1840) was elected dictator, becoming dictator for life in 1817. From 1844 to 1870 Paraguay was ruled by the López family. The population suffered great losses in the War of the *Triple Alliance (1865–70) against Brazil, Argentina, and Uruguay and again in the *Chaco War (1932–35) with Bolivia. A period of political unrest was ended in 1954, when Gen. Alfredo Stroessner (1912–   ) seized power and became president. He was ousted in 1989 and replaced by Gen. Andrés Rodriguez, who instituted political reforms. The country's first municipal elections were held in 1991, and a new constitution was adopted in 1992. Juan Carlos Wasmosy was elected president in 1993 in the nation's first multiparty free elections. Paraguay is a member of the OAS and LAFTA. Official language: Spanish; the majority speak Guaraní. Official currency: guaraní of 100 céntimos. Area: 157,042 sq mi (406,752 sq km). Population (1989 est): 3,613,000.

Paraguay River (Portuguese name: Rio Paraguai) A river in South America. Rising in Brazil in Mato Grosso state, it flows generally S to join the Paraná River in SW Paraguay. It is an important means of transport and communications, especially in Paraguay. Length: about 1500 mi (2400 km).

Paraguayan War. *See* Triple Alliance, War of the.

parakeet A small seed-eating *parrot characterized by a long tapering tail and a predominantly green plumage and found especially in SE Asia and Australia. Large flocks may damage crops; brightly colored species are popular as cage birds. *See also* budgerigar; rosella.

paralysis Failure of a muscle or a group of muscles to work. This is most commonly caused by damage to the nerve (and its connections) supplying the muscle, as resulting from injury or infection (*see* poliomyelitis), but it may also be due to failure of the nerve impulse to be transmitted to the muscle (as in myasthenia gravis) or by wasting of the muscle (as in *muscular dystrophy). Paralysis is seen most commonly in Western countries following a *stroke: this causes damage to the part of the brain that controls movement and commonly results in **hemiplegia**, i.e. one half of the body and face becomes paralyzed. *Multiple sclerosis also causes paralysis. **Paraplegia** (paralyzed legs) results from injury to the spinal cord. **Quadriplegia** (paralyzed legs and arms) results when the spinal cord is damaged close to the brain.

paramagnetism A form of *magnetism occurring in materials that when placed in a *magnetic field have an internal field stronger than that outside. This is caused by the presence in atoms or molecules of electrons with unpaired spins. The atom or molecule therefore acts like a tiny magnet (*see* ferromagnetism). In the presence of an external magnetic field these microscopic magnets tend to align with the field, reinforcing it. The effect is destroyed by random thermal motion and, except at low temperatures and high field strengths, the *permeability (a measure of the extent of alignment) is inversely proportional to the temperature.

Paramaribo 5 52N 55 14W The capital and main port of Suriname, near the N coast on the Suriname River. Founded by the French in 1540, it was later under English and then Dutch rule. It has developed considerably since World War II. The University of Suriname was founded in 1968. Population (1985 est): 77,500.

Paramecium A genus of microscopic single-celled animals (☐Protozoa), called slipper animalcules, found in fresh water. They are slipper-shaped, 0.004–0.011 in (0.1–0.3 mm) long, and covered with cilia, which are used for swimming and to waft bacteria and small protozoa's into the gullet. They reproduce asexually by binary *fission and sexually by *conjugation. Class: **Ciliata*.

Paraná 31 45S 60 30W A city in E Argentina, on the Paraná River. It is an outlet for agricultural produce (especially cattle, sheep, and grain). Notable buildings include the Cathedral of Paraná (1883). Population (1991 est): 277,000.

Paraná River (Spanish name: Río Paraná) A river in South America. Formed by the confluence of the Rio Grande and Rio Paranaíba in SE central Brazil, it flows generally S for 1800 mi (2900 km) to join the Uruguay River and form the Río de al Plata. The Itaipu Dam, the world's largest dam, which is sited at Foz do Iguaçu near the Paraguayan border, was opened in 1982; the hydroelectric power station is expected to be in full operation by 1989, with a capacity of 12.6 million kW. The cost is being shared by Brazil and Paraguay.

paranoia A mental disorder in which the patient is governed by a rigid system of irrational beliefs (delusions). The sufferer may believe that he is being persecuted by others, or betrayed, or that he is overwhelmingly important. The condition, which can result from *schizophrenia, *alcoholism, or *manic-depressive psychosis, is treated according to the cause. *See also* personality disorder.

paraplegia. *See* paralysis.

parapsychology Scientific investigation into paranormal phenomena. Proper subjects for research include *ghost and *poltergeist hauntings, *extrasensory perception, and *spiritualism. The London Society for Psychical Research (founded in 1882) was the first of numerous kindred organizations throughout the world, but mainstream science is still skeptical about their methodology and conclusions.

Paraquat $(C_9H_{20}N_2(SO_4)_2)$ The trade name for a yellow water-soluble solid that is used as a weedkiller. It is highly toxic and some deaths have resulted from swallowing quantities in excess of one gram. It concentrates in the lungs and also causes kidney damage. Treatment for Paraquat poisoning, by *activated charcoal or some other absorbing material, is only effective if carried out immediately.

parasite An organism living in or on another organisms of a different species (called the host), from which it obtains food and protection: the relationship may or may not be harmful to the host. A facultative parasite is one that becomes parasitic only under certain conditions, while an obligate parasite must always live parasitically. Many parasites have complex life cycles, with one or more intermediate hosts (of different species) supporting the parasite in the immature stages of its development. The study of parasites—**parasitology**—is of great importance in medicine since many parasites either cause or transmit disease. Disease-causing parasites include bacteria and other microorganisms (*see* infection) and tapeworms; mites, ticks, and fleas are examples of external parasites that transmit disease. Many plants are either partly or completely parasitic, usually on other plants. Mistletoe is a partial parasite.

parasol mushroom An edible mushroom, *Lepiota procera*, found in clearings and around the edges of deciduous woods. Its cap, 4–8 in (10–20 cm) in diameter, is grayish brown with darker scales. The scales form rings on the stem, which has a double collar just below the cap.

parathyroid glands Two pairs of small endocrine glands lying immediately behind the thyroid gland. These glands secrete **parathyroid hormone** in response to a reduction in the level of calcium in the blood. This hormone causes the release of calcium from the bones and its transfer to the blood. Deficiency of parathyroid hormone (and therefore lack of calcium in the blood) results in muscle spasms and cramps (tetany).

paratyphoid fever Infection of the digestive tract caused by the bacterium *Salmonella paratyphi*. It is a mild form of *typhoid fever and can be treated by antibiotic drugs.

parchment Animal skin, usually of the goat, sheep, or calf, treated for writing on but untanned. It derives its name from Pergamum, where in the 2nd century BC the development of improved methods of cleaning, stretching, and scraping skins enabled them to have writing on both sides. It was used for manuscripts and early bound books. More delicate skin from young animals is called vellum. Parchment now often describes high-grade paper manufactured from wood pulp and rag, treated with a special finish. *See also* leather.

parchment worm An *annelid worm, belonging to the genus *Chaetopterus*, that lives in a U-shaped tube made of parchmentlike material on muddy shores of the Atlantic and Pacific Oceans. Up to 10 in (25 cm) long, the worm draws in a current of water by beating its paddle-shaped appendages, trapping food particles in a bag of mucus. Parchment worms are strongly luminescent. Class: *Polychaeta*.

Pardubice (German name: Pardubitz) 50 03N 15 45E A city in the Czech Republic, in E Bohemia on the Elbe River. It has an architecturally distinguished square containing a 16th-century gothic castle and the Green Gate (1507). Population (1980 est): 93,000.

Paré, Ambroise (1510–90) French surgeon and one of the fathers of modern surgery. As barber-surgeon to the army, Paré discarded the practice of treating wounds with boiling oil and hot irons in favor of cleansing, the use of ointments, and surgery to tie off major arteries.

parenchyma The general packing tissue of plants, consisting of simple undifferentiated cells. In young stems, parenchyma encloses the vascular (conducting) tissue and provides support for the plant.

Pareto, Vilfredo (1848–1932) Italian economist and sociologist. Pareto's early work in economics culminated in Pareto's Law, which held that the distribution of incomes could be defined by a mathematical formula. His later sociological work *The Mind and Society* (1916) attacked political liberalism while supporting the free market economy. He is also known for his theory on the rise and fall of governing elites.

Paris 48 52N 2 18E The capital of France and a department of the Paris Region, situated in the N of the country on the Seine River. One of Europe's greatest cities, Paris dominates France as the administrative, commercial, and cultural center. It is also an important industrial base, and many international organizations, including UNESCO, have their headquarters here. The city is in turn dominated by its river, which contributes to the division of Paris into several distinct districts, each with its own characteristics. At the heart of the city, the Île de la Cité contains the cathedral of *Notre-Dame, the Palais de Justice, and the 13th-century Sainte Chapelle. On the Left Bank lie Montparnasse and the Latin Quarter, which is known for its associations with writers and artists and still contains some faculties of the university of the Sorbonne (founded in the 12th century) although much of it has now been moved to other sites. On the Right Bank stands the Palais du Louvre, one of the world's most important museums. Further W is a series of radiating boulevards meeting at the Place Charles de Gaulle (formerly Place de l'Étiole), which were laid out by Baron *Haussmann in the 19th century. The Champs Élysées runs from the *Arc de Triomphe at the center of the Place Charles de Gaulle to the Place de la Concorde. Further N lies Montmartre (the artists' colony of Paris until the migration to Montparnasse in the 1920s), dominated by the Basilica of the Sacré Coeur (1919). The tunnels beneath Montmartre, created by quarrying, are now a major problem, causing subsidence and structural damage to buildings. To the S of the Seine, the *Eiffel Tower, built for an exhibition in 1898, is another reminder of the 19th century. *History*: the earliest known settlement was on the Île de la Cité in Roman times. According to legend, St Denis became the first bishop in the 3rd century AD and Ste Geneviève saved the city from sacking by German tribes in the 5th century. In the 6th century Clovis made it the capital of his Frankish kingdom but it later suffered attacks from Vikings. It regained importance as the capital under the *Capetians and from the 13th century its independence as a city increased. Since the storming of the Bastille (1789), heralding the beginning of the French Revolution, it has been the scene of many revolts, such as the *July Revolution and the *Revolution of 1848; the most recent disturbance was in May 1968. Occupied by the Germans in World War II, it was liberated by the Allies in 1944. Population (1990): 2,175,110.

Paris In Greek legend, a son of *Priam and Hecuba. He was brought up as a shepherd on Mount Ida. His abduction of *Helen with the help of Aphrodite caused the *Trojan War, during which he killed Achilles and was himself killed by Philoctetes. *See also* Eris.

Paris, Matthew. *See* Matthew Paris.

Paris, Treaties of 1. (1763) The treaty that ended the *Seven Years' War. France ceded its North American territories E of the Mississippi River to Britain and Louisiana to Spain, from which Britain acquired Florida. Britain also gained

Minorca, Senegal, Grenada, St Vincent, Dominica, and Tobago. **2.** (1783) The treaty that ended the *American Revolution. US independence was recognized and Britain ceded Florida to Spain. **3.** (1814) The peace between France and the victorious allies (Prussia, Russia, Austria, Britain, Sweden, and Portugal) that confirmed Napoleon's abdication and limited France to its 1792 boundaries. **4.** (1815) The peace following Napoleon's final defeat at Waterloo that reduced France to its 1789 boundaries. **5.** (1856) The peace that ended the *Crimean War. Russia guaranteed the neutrality of the Black Sea and ceded S Bessarabia to Moldavia.

PARIS *The Eiffel Tower, probably the city's most famous landmark, seen behind the Alexander III Bridge over the River Seine.*

Paris Peace Conference (1919–20) A conference of representatives of the Allied and Associated Powers held after World War I. Proceedings were dominated by the US (Woodrow Wilson), France (Clemenceau), the UK (Lloyd George), and Italy (Orlando). Five treaties arose from the conference: *Versailles with Germany (1919); Saint-Germain with Austria (1920); Neuilly with Bulgaria (1919); Trianon with Hungary (1920); and Sèvres with Turkey (1920). In addition the conference ratified the Covenant of the *League of Nations.

parity The concept of left- and right-handedness. According to the law of conservation of parity, no fundamental distinction exists between left and right and the laws of physics apply equally to left- and right-handed systems. In 1957 this principle was shown to be violated in *weak interactions between certain elementary particles (*see* particle physics). For example, when a neutron decays the electron produced is always left-polarized (i.e. spins in a direction opposite to that of its motion), whereas if parity was conserved there would be equal numbers of left- and right-polarized electrons. This lack of parity provides a fundamental distinction between left and right. The parity of elementary particles is expressed as a *quantum number.

Park, Mungo (1771–c. 1806) Scottish explorer. A surgeon, he made two explorations of the Niger River. In 1795–96 he ascended the Niger from the mouth of the Gambia River, crossed the Sénégal Basin, and was imprisoned by Arabs. Escaping, he eventually returned to The Gambia. His *Travels in the Interior Districts of Africa* (1797) related his adventures. In 1805, under government patronage and with 40 companions, he resumed his exploration. The expedition was attacked by natives and Park died.

Park Chung Hee (1917–79) South Korean statesman and general; president from 1963 until his murder in 1979. He served in the Japanese army in World War II and then in the South Korean army. He led the coup that established a military regime in 1961, becoming president two years later. In 1972 he declared martial law and assumed quasi-dictatorial powers.

Parker, Charlie (Christopher) (1920–55) US jazz saxophonist and composer, known as "Bird" or "Yardbird." With Dizzy *Gillespie he originated the *bop style of jazz and appeared with a number of bands. In the 1950s he made recordings with a band containing strings and wind and was regarded as one of the greatest jazz musicians.

Parker, Dorothy Rothschild (1893–1967) US humorous writer. Famous as a wit, she established her reputation while working as drama critic for *Vanity Fair* and the *New Yorker* (1927–33). She is best known for her short stories and sketches, collected in *Here Lies* (1939), but she also wrote poems, collected in *Not So Deep As a Well* (1936), plays, and filmscripts.

Parkes, Sir Henry (1815–96) Australian statesman; prime minister of New South Wales (1872–75, 1877, 1878–83, 1887–89, 1889–91). Born in England, he emigrated to Australia in 1839. He campaigned (1849–52) against the British transportation of convicts to Australia and as prime minister worked for the federation of the Australian states and for compulsory free education.

Parkinson, (Cyril) Northcote (1909–93) British author, historian, and journalist. He wrote the well-known *Parkinson's Law* (1958), a study of business administration containing the aphorisms that work expands to fill the time allotted to it and that subordinates multiply at a fixed rate regardless of the amount of work produced. His other books include *Britain in the Far East* (1955), *The Law and the Profits* (1960), and *Big Business* (1974).

parkinsonism (*or* Parkinson's disease) A chronic disease affecting the part of the brain controlling voluntary movement, first described in 1817 by a British physician, James Parkinson (1755–1824). Sometimes the disease may result from infection, side effects of drugs, or injury, but usually no cause is apparent. The symptoms are tremor of the hands and mouth, stiffness, and difficulty in initiating movements. It occurs most commonly in older people and can often be treated effectively with drugs, including *L-dopa, or surgery.

Parkman, Francis (1823–93) US historian. *The Oregon Trail* (1849) is an account of an adventurous expedition undertaken to gain knowledge of the American Indians. Thenceforth he suffered from illness and blindness but completed a monumental colonial history of *France and England in North America* (9 vols,

1851–92). Other works, which often dealt with events in Canadian history, include *History of the Conspiracy of Pontiac* (1851) and *The Old Regime in Canada* (1874).

Parks, Gordon, Sr (1912–   ) US photographer and motion picture director. He worked for *Life* magazine (1948–68) during which time he often photographed African-American ghetto life. He wrote *The Learning Tree* (1963) and directed the movies *Shaft* (1971) and *Leadbelly* (1976).

parlement The supreme court of France until the French Revolution. The parlement of Paris developed in the 12th century out of the king's court. Membership was at first elective but by the 14th century seats could be bought and in 1614 became hereditable with the introduction of the *paullete* (annual right), which secured a seat by payment of an annual fee. From its duty, and right of refusal, to register royal edicts the parlement derived considerable political power and by the 17th century had become a bastion of reaction. It impeded government attempts to put its own house in order and in 1792, in the wake of the French Revolution, the parlement of Paris, together with its less influential provincial counterparts, was abolished.

Parliament The legislative assembly of the UK; it consists of the sovereign, the House of Lords, and the House of Commons; its seat is the *Palace of Westminster. Parliament developed in the 13th century from the *Curia Regis (King's Court), in which the monarch consulted with his barons. In 1213, 1254, and 1258 representatives of the shires were also summoned to attend Parliament and in 1265 the Parliament summoned by Simon de *Montfort included borough representatives—the origins of the House of Commons. By the reign of Edward III (1327–77) Lords and Commons, meeting separately, were recognized constituents of government. Increasingly assertive under Elizabeth I (1559–1603), its conflict with James I and Charles I over the extent to which the crown was answerable to Parliament led to the Civil War (1642–51) and the establishment of republican government under Oliver Cromwell. Following the Restoration of the monarchy in 1660, the attempts of James II to rule arbitrarily led to the Glorious Revolution (1688), which achieved the beginning of parliamentary ascendancy over the crown. The 18th century saw the emergence of party politics (*see* Whigs; Tories) and of a *prime minister and the development of *cabinet government. In the 19th century the *Reform Acts greatly reduced the influence of the House of Lords, which lost its veto power by the Parliament Act (1911).

Parma 44 48N 10 19E A city in N Italy, in Emilia-Romagna. Dating from Roman times, it became an important cultural center in the Middle Ages. Its university was established in 1222 and it has a romanesque cathedral and a 16th-century palace, damaged in 1944 during World War II. The center of an agricultural district, Parma's industries include the manufacture of Parmesan cheese, perfume, fertilizers, and glass. Population (1980 est): 175,932.

Parmenides (c. 510–c. 450 BC) Greek philosopher, born at Elea (S Italy). According to Parmenides, things either are or are not. Only "being" is real; "not-being" is illusory. For change to occur "being" must become "not-being," which is absurd. Therefore change does not occur. But our senses indicate that change does occur: therefore our senses are misleading, and "being," as apprehended by reason, is the only reality. Parmenides described "being" as finite, spherical, timeless, undifferentiated, and indivisible. His doctrines strongly influenced *Plato. *See also* Heraclitus; Zeno of Elea.

Parmigianino (Girolamo Francesco Maria mazzola; 1503–40) Italian mannerist painter and etcher, whose nickname derives from his birthplace, Parma.

After painting frescoes in S Giovanni Evangelista, Parma, he moved to Rome (1524) but was forced to flee to Bologna during the sack of Rome (1527). Characteristic of his elongated figure style is the *Madonna with the Long Neck* (Palazzo Pitti, Florence). His portraits include *Self-Portrait in a Convex Mirror* (Kunsthistorisches Museum, Vienna). □mannerism.

Parnassians A group of French poets in the mid-19th century who reacted against the subjectivism of the romantics and whose poetry was characterized by objective restraint and verbal and technical precision. They were led by *Leconte de Lisle, whose disciples included Theodore de *Banville, *Sully-Prudhomme, and J.M. de Hérédia (1842–1905).

Parnassus, Mount (Modern Greek name: Parnassós) 38 32N 22 41E A mountain in S central Greece, held in ancient times as sacred to the god Apollo and the Muses. Height: 8061 ft (2457 m).

Parnell, Charles Stewart (1846–91) Irish politician, who in 1880 became the leader of the *Home Rule party in the British House of Commons. Parnell, a member of Parliament from 1875, reconciled constitutional and radical forces and enjoyed widespread popular support in Ireland. He allied his party with the Liberals in 1886, when Gladstone introduced the Home Rule bill. Parnell remained a dominant political figure until 1890, when he was named in a divorce suit brought against Katherine O'Shea, whom he then married.

Páros A Greek island in the S Aegean Sea, in the Cyclades. Marble has been quarried here for sculpture since ancient times. Area: 75 sq mi (195 sq km).

parquetry The inlaying of geometrically shaped pieces of wood into the plane surfaces of furniture, floors, staircases, etc. The word is often now used to describe geometric *marquetry, particularly as used on 17th- and 18th-century furniture.

Parr, Catherine (1512–48) The sixth wife (1543–47) of Henry VIII of England. She was noted for her kindness to her three stepchildren. After Henry's death, she married (1547) Thomas, Baron Seymour of Sudeley (d. 1549).

Parrish, Maxfield (Frederick) (1870–1966) US illustrator and artist. He illustrated books and magazine covers and painted posters and murals, the most well-known of which is on a wall in the St. Regis Hotel in New York City. A painter of intricate, decorative designs, he illustrated Washington *Irving's *Knickerbocker's History of New York* (written in 1809), and Kenneth *Grahame's *The Golden Age* (1895) and *Dream Days* (1898).

parrot A bird belonging to the family (*Psittacidae*; 300 species) occurring worldwide in warm regions; 4–40 in (10–100 cm) long, parrots have a compact body, a short neck, and strong rounded wings suited for fast flight over short distances. The plumage is typically brightly colored and the short stout hooked bill is used to open nuts and to feed on fruits and seeds. Most are arboreal and excellent climbers, having clawed feet and rough scaly toes. They are gregarious and have a harsh screaming voice. Order: *Psittaciformes. See also* cockatoo; kakapo; kea; lory; lovebird; macaw; parakeet.

parrot fish A fish, also called parrot wrasse, belonging to the family *Scaridae* found among tropical reefs. Up to 48 in (1.2 m) long, it has a deep often brilliantly colored body and the teeth are fused to form a hard beak, which is used to feed on coral, mollusks, and seaweed. Order: *Perciformes*.

parsec A unit of distance, used in astronomy, corresponding to a parallax of one second of arc; 1 parsec = 3.26 light-years or 3.084×10^{16} meters.

Parseeism The religion of the descendants of Persians who fled their country in the 8th century AD to avoid persecution following the Arab conquest. Mostly located in Bombay, Madras, Calcutta, and Karachi, they continue to practice *Zoroastrianism in two sectarian forms.

parsley A fragrant biennial herb, *Petroselinum crispum*, native to the Mediterranean region but widely cultivated. The compound leaves are curled or frilled and have an aromatic flavor. They are used fresh or dried in fish and meat dishes, soups, garnishes, and bouquets garnis. The flowering stems, up to 40 in (1 m) high, bear clusters of small yellowish flowers. Family: *Umbelliferae*.

parsnip A hairy strong-smelling biennial plant, *Pastinaca sativa*, native to grassland and wasteland of temperate Eurasia and widely cultivated throughout temperate regions for its large starchy white taproot, which is eaten as a vegetable or used as cattle feed. The leaves consist of paired lobed toothed leaflets on a long furrowed stalk and the clusters of tiny yellow flowers are borne on stems up to 5 ft (150 cm) high. Family: *Umbelliferae*.

Parsons, Talcott (1902–78) US sociologist. His early theories, first expounded in *The Structure of Social Action* (1937), underwent extensive change in *The Social System* (1951), becoming a functionalist (*see* functionalism) systems approach and later incorporating evolutionism and cybernetics. The consequences for adopting such an approach are represented in his analysis of social stratification, in which he emphasized its integrative supportive role. His work has been criticized for obscurity and failure to deal with conflict, power, and deviance.

parthenogenesis A method of reproduction in which the egg develops without *fertilization to produce an individual usually identical to the parent. It occurs commonly among lower plants and animals, particularly aphids, ants, bees, and wasps, principally to accelerate the production of individuals at certain times of the year. In many species, for example aphids, sexual reproduction does take place from time to time to provide genetic variation.

Parthenon A temple on the hill of the Acropolis in □Athens dedicated to the goddess Athena. Built between 447 and 432 BC by *Ictinus and *Callicrates at the instigation of *Pericles, it represents the summit of classical Greek architecture. Its rectangular colonnaded exterior of Doric columns originally contained a walled chamber with *Phidias's gold and ivory statue of Athena. In the 5th century AD it became a Christian church and in the 15th century a mosque. It was blown up by the Turks in 1687. Much that remained of its adorning sculpture was removed by Lord Elgin in the 19th century (*see* Elgin Marbles).

Parthia The region S of the Caspian Sea approximating to present-day Khorasan (NE Iran). Inhabited by seminomadic tribes, Parthia, once a feudal confederacy of vassal kingdoms under the Achaemenians and then the Seleucids, controlled a great empire from about 250 BC to 224 AD with its capital at *Ctesiphon. Parthia's famous cavalry and mounted archers harassed Rome's eastern frontiers, overwhelming Crassus's army in a humiliating defeat at *Carrhae in 53 BC. In 224 AD the Parthian empire was conquered by the *Sasanians of Persia.

particle physics The study of elementary particles and their interactions. Until the discovery of the *electron (J. J. Thomson; 1898), the atom had been thought of as a minute indivisible "billiard ball." The existence of the electron and the discovery of the *proton (Rutherford; 1914) made it clear that the atom had an internal structure. When the *neutron was discovered (Chadwick; 1932), it appeared that the whole universe was constructed of just these three particles. The outstanding problem was the nature of the force that held neutrons and protons together in the atomic nucleus. The only two fundamental forces known at that time were the gravitational force and the electromagnetic (em) force; the gravitational force was too weak to account for the great stability of the nucleus and the em force had no effect on the electrically uncharged neutron.

In 1935 *Yukawa suggested that there might be in nature a short-lived particle (later called the meson) that jumped between protons and neutrons and held them together in much the same way as two tennis players are held together by the ball passing between them. This concept of exchange forces and the subsequent discovery of short-lived particles led to intensive research into particle physics throughout the world (*see* accelerators). By the 1960s some 200 "elementary" particles had been identified and it became clear that there were four basic types of force; in addition to gravitational and em forces there were *strong interactions (100 times more powerful than em forces) and *weak interactions (10^{10} weaker than em forces). It also became evident that some elementary particles were more elementary than others. In general, there are now believed to be two classes: leptons (the electron, muon, tau particle, and *neutrinos), which interact by the em or the weak forces and have no apparent internal structure; and hadrons (including the proton, neutron, ion, etc.), which interact by the strong interaction and do appear to have an internal structure.

During the past 20 years the main preoccupation of particle physicists has been the elucidation of hadron structure. The current model is based on Murray Gell-Mann's concept of the quark, introduced in 1963. In this model, hadrons themselves are divided into two classes: baryons, which decay into protons; and mesons, which decay into leptons and *photons or into proton pairs. Baryons consist of three quarks and mesons consist of a quark-antiquark pair. Thus all the matter in the universe is now seen as being made of leptons and quarks.

Although the quark concept was introduced as a theoretical construct and a single quark has never been identified experimentally, there is now a considerable amount of evidence that they actually exist. Quark theory is fairly elaborate; quarks have fractional electronic charges ($+\frac{2}{3}$ or $-\frac{1}{3}$ of the electronic charge) and come in five "flavors" called up (u; $+\frac{2}{3}$), down (d; $-\frac{1}{3}$), charmed (c; $+\frac{2}{3}$), strange (s; $-\frac{1}{3}$), and bottom (b; $-\frac{1}{3}$). For each flavor there is an equivalent antiquark ($\bar{u}, \bar{d}$, etc.). The proton consists of uud ($\frac{2}{3}+\frac{2}{3}-\frac{1}{3}=1$) and the neutron consists of udd ($\frac{2}{3}-\frac{1}{3}-\frac{1}{3}=0$).

In this limited form quark theory conflicted with the *Pauli exclusion principle and it therefore became necessary to introduce the concept of "color." Thus each flavor of quark can have one of the three colors red, yellow, or blue, with antiquarks having the corresponding anticolors. "Color" in this sense has no connection with visual color but the analogy is useful. All hadrons are regarded as white and baryons must consist of a red, a blue, and a yellow (since these visual colors produce white); mesons consist of a quark of any color and its corresponding anticolor. *See also* antimatter; charm; quantum number; strangeness.

Parton, Dolly (Rebecca) (1946–) US singer and actress, whose country charm brought her fame in the worlds of music and film. Already a country music star, she captivated 1970s audiences with her unusual, almost childlike voice and her flashy appearance. Her films, which she began making in the 1980s, include *9 to 5* (for which she wrote the award-winning title song), *The Best Little Whorehouse in Texas*, *Rhinestone*, and *Steel Magnolias*.

partridge A small gamebird native to the Old World but widely introduced elsewhere. Partridges are 10–16 in (25–40 cm) long and have rounded bodies with short rounded wings and a low gliding flight. The European partridge (*Perdix perdix*) is a common farmland bird and has a grayish plumage with a red face and tail and a dark U-shaped marking on its belly. Family: *Phasianidae* (pheasants, quail, partridges). *See also* francolin.

Partridge, Eric (Honeywood) (1894–1979) British lexicographer, born in New Zealand. After World War I he settled in England, where he produced many witty, idiosyncratic, and learned works, including *A Dictionary of Slang and Unconventional English* and an etymological dictionary called *Origins*, both of which have had numerous editions.

Pasadena 34 10N 118 09W A city in California. It is a winter health resort and well-known residence for Los Angeles film stars. The Tournament of Roses and the Rose Bowl football game are held annually. The California Institute of Technology was established in 1891. Population (1990): 131,591.

Pasadena 29 42N 95 13W A city in SE Texas, just SE of Houston. Sam Houston defeated Mexico's Gen. Santa Anna here in 1836, and Texas independence was established. Oil is refined and petroleum, metal, plastic, paper, and rubber products are manufactured. Population (1990): 119,363.

pascal (Pa) The *SI unit of pressure equal to one newton per square meter. Named for Blaise *Pascal.

Pascal, Blaise (1623–62) French mathematician, physicist, and theologian. He made a study of conic sections when still in his teens; later he studied the mathematics of *probability, in collaboration with Pierre de Fermat, and invented Pascal's triangle for calculating the coefficients of a binomial expansion. He also made discoveries in *fluid mechanics, notably that the pressure in a fluid is everywhere equal (**Pascal's principle**). In 1641 he invented the first calculating machine. At the age of 31 he had a mystical experience and from then on devoted his life to religion. In the same year he became a Jansenist and his *Lettres provinciales* (1656–57) defended *Jansenism against the *Jesuits. His greatest work was *Pensées sur la religion* (1669), a poetical and metaphysical treatise on human nature.

pasha An honorary title applied in the Ottoman Empire to military, naval, and civil commanders. It was abolished in Turkey in 1934 but lasted until 1952 in Egypt.

Pashto The language of the Pathan people of N Pakistan and Afghanistan, which belongs to the *Iranian family. Pashto is the official language of Afghanistan. There are two main dialects, Pashto in Afghanistan and Pakhto in Pakistan. Both are written in a modified Arabic script.

Pašić Nicola (1845–1926) Serbian statesman. Pašić was prime minister of Serbia (1891–92, 1904–05, 1906–08, 1909–11, 1912–18). After World War I he was a representative of the newly formed Yugoslavia at the Paris Peace Conference. In 1921 he became prime minister of Yugoslavia, serving until 1924 and again from 1924 to 1926. He believed in a centralized Yugoslavia and Serbian supremacy within it.

Pasionaria, La. *See* Ibarruri, Dolores.

Pasolini, Pier Paolo (1922–75) Italian film director. His films include original treatments of Greek legends, such as *Oedipus Rex* (1967) and *Medea* (1969), a highly acclaimed biblical film, *The Gospel According to St Matthew* (1964), Marxist allegories, such as *Theorem* (1968) and *Pigsty* (1969), and anthologies of bawdy entertainment, such as *The Decameron* (1970).

passage rites Rituals and ceremonies performed on a person's transition from one social status to another. The most common are those at birth, puberty, marriage, death, and succession to office. Practices vary greatly but a pattern consisting of three stages is common to many such rites. First, there is a rite of separation, removing the subject from his previous status; next, a transitional stage in which the person is suspended between statuses; and finally, a rite of aggregation, in which the new status is conferred. In many primitive societies such rites are thought to be essential to ensure success in the new role. *See also* initiation rites.

Passchendaele. *See* World War I.

passenger pigeon A slender long-winged *pigeon, *Ectopistes migratorius*, once common in deciduous woodlands of North America but extinct by the end of the 19th century. It was 12.5 in (32 cm) long and had a pointed tail and a slate-gray plumage with a deep pink breast. It fed on beech nuts, acorns, and fruits and was highly migratory, able to fly long distances for food, and formed flocks numbering millions of birds. Harvesting of eggs, chicks, and adults and rapid deforestation led to its extinction.

passerine bird A bird belonging to the order *Passeriformes*, which includes over half (about 5100) of all bird species. Passerines—the perching birds—are characterized by their feet, which are specialized for gripping branches and stems. They are the most highly evolved birds and occur in large numbers in almost every habitat, although few live or feed in water. Most species are between 5–8 in (12–20 cm) in length, although some are as small as 3 in (7.5 cm), with others reaching 46 in (117 cm). There are both migratory and sedentary species. Passerines are often of economic importance—as a source of food, for their ornamental plumage, or as cage birds. Some species, such as the *quelea and *Java sparrow are serious crop pests. The order is divided into four major groups (suborders): *Eurylaimi* (broadbills); *Tyranni* (includes manakins, ovenbirds, pittas, and tyrant flycatchers); *Menurae* (lyrebirds and scrubbirds); and— the largest and most advanced group—*Oscines* (*see* songbird).

passionflower A climbing plant of the genus *Passiflora* (500 species), native chiefly to tropical and subtropical America and cultivated for ornament. The leaves may be simple or deeply lobed; some are modified as tendrils. The distinctive flowers each consist of a cup-shaped base with five colored sepals and petals at its upper edge surmounted by a colored fringe. From the center of this protrudes a stalk bearing the stamens and ovary. The fruit is a berry or capsule, which in some species (e.g. *P. quadrangularis*) is edible (passionfruits *or* granadillas). Family: *Passifloraceae*.

Passion plays Religious dramas concerning the Crucifixion and Resurrection of Christ and often including other related religious episodes. They were performed on Good Friday throughout medieval Europe and survived after the Reformation in Switzerland, Austria, and Germany. The Passion play at *Oberammergau in Germany, the best-known modern example, has been performed every 10 years since 1634 in fulfillment of a vow made by the villagers during an epidemic of the plague.

Passover (Hebrew word: *Pesah*) One of the three biblical pilgrimage festivals (the others are Weeks and Tabernacles). It commemorates the Exodus from Egypt and also incorporates a spring harvest festival. In Judaism, it is celebrated for seven or eight days, beginning on the eve of the first day with a formal meal (*see* haggadah). Unleavened bread (*matzah*) is eaten, all leaven being removed from the house. In Christianity it has been replaced by *Easter.

Passy, Frédéric (1822–1912) French economist and politician, whose efforts for peace were rewarded with the first Nobel Peace Prize (1901), which he won jointly with *Dunant. He established a peace arbitration society (Ligue international de la Paix, 1867) and helped found the International Parliamentary Union (1889), as well as arbitrating in international disputes.

pasta An originally Italian dough made from semolina obtained from durum wheat and water, sometimes with the addition of eggs. Among the many varieties of pasta are spaghetti (long thin rods), macaroni (short hollow thicker tubes), lasagne (flat rectangular pieces), ravioli (little squares of pasta stuffed with meat), and tagliatelle (long flat ribbons). Pasta is usually served with well-flavored sauces.

Pasternak, Boris (1890–1960) Russian poet and novelist. He was born into a cultured Jewish family and studied music and philosophy. He published several volumes of symbolist poetry between 1917 and 1923 and many translations during the 1930s. His epic novel *Dr Zhivago* was banned in Russia but became internationally successful after its publication in Italy in 1957. Under severe political pressure, he declined the Nobel Prize in 1958.

Pasteur, Louis (1822–95) French chemist and microbiologist, who made great advances in the prevention and treatment of diseases caused by microorganisms. A tanner's son, Pasteur became a science teacher and pursued his interest in chemistry; in 1848 he discovered two different optically active forms of tartaric acid that had differing biological properties. In 1854 Pasteur was appointed dean of the faculty of sciences at Lille University. He found that fermentation was caused by microorganisms and that, by excluding these, souring or decay could be prevented (*see* pasteurization). Although partially paralyzed in 1868, Pasteur's interest in germs and disease directed his attention to anthrax (the life cycle of the causative bacillus in cattle had been studied by *Koch). By 1881 Pasteur had devised a means of safely inducing immunity to the disease by injecting a vaccine of heat-treated (attenuated) live anthrax bacilli. Pasteur also produced a vaccine for chicken cholera and—in 1885, his most spectacular achievement—an effective rabies vaccine. The Pasteur Institute was founded in 1888 to treat rabies and has since developed into a world center for biological research.

pasteurization Heat treatment used to destroy the microorganisms in milk. The method involves heating milk for 30 minutes at 140°F (60°C), which kills the tuberculosis bacteria without damaging the milk protein. This process is named for Louis *Pasteur, who demonstrated that heat could prevent the spoilage of wine and beer caused by fermentation of yeasts and other microorganisms.

Pasto 1 12N 77 17W A city in SW Colombia, on a slope of the Pasto volcano. It is the commercial center of an agricultural and cattle-rearing area. The University of Nariño was founded in 1827. Population (1985): 197,407.

Patagonia A geographic area of S South America in Argentina and Chile, extending S of the River Colorado to the Strait of Magellan. It consists chiefly of an arid plateau rising to the Andes. Sheep raising is the principal economic activity. It contains the major oil field of Comodoro Rivadavia, Argentina's chief source of oil, and the Río Turbio coal field. Area: about 300,000 sq mi (777,000 sq km).

patas monkey An *Old World monkey, *Erythrocebus patas*, of African grasslands. Patas monkeys are 43–46 in (110–160 cm) long including the tail (20–30 in; 50–75 cm) and are mainly terrestrial and omnivorous. They live in well-ordered troops (hence, their alternative name—military monkeys). A white-nosed eastern race is called the nisnas monkey.

patchouli An aromatic herb, *Pogostemon patchouli*, native to Malaysia. It contains a fragrant essential oil used in perfumery in SE Asia. The dried leaves are used as an insect repellent. Family: *Labiatae*.

Paterson, William (1745–1806) US jurist and politician; born in Ireland. He held various state positions in New Jersey and went to the Continental Congress (1780–81) and Constitutional Convention (1787), where he proposed the *New

Jersey Plan, parts of which were adopted. He served as US senator (1789–90), governor of New Jersey (1791–93), and associate justice of the Supreme Court (1793–1806).

PATAS MONKEY *These monkeys have long tails and are well adapted for climbing trees and rocks, although they usually remain on the ground.*

Paterson 40 55N 74 10W A city in New Jersey, part of the Greater New York Metropolitan Area. Founded in 1791, it became known as the Silk City in the 19th century, because of its large silk industry. Its varied manufactures today include cotton, paper, and chemicals. Population (1990): 140,891.

Pathans A large group of tribes of N Pakistan and SE Afghanistan who speak the *Pashto language. They are also known as Pashtuns. Each tribe is subdivided into a number of patrilineal clans, said to be descended from a common ancestor. Genealogical lines of many generations are remembered and determine land rights, succession, and inheritance. Devout Muslims, the Pathans are farmers and warriors, many entering into military service.

pathology The branch of medicine concerned with the study of disease and disease processes in order to understand their causes and nature. The specialty originated in the mid-19th century, when *Virchow demonstrated that changes in the structure of cells and tissues were related to specific diseases. Cellular pathology advanced further with the work of Pasteur and Koch on the bacterial cause of disease, but it was not until the beginning of the 20th century that the knowledge gained in the laboratory was applied to the treatment and prevention of disease in patients. Examples of early work in the science of clinical pathology include Schick's test for diphtheria and Wassermann's test for syphilis. Chemical pathology developed from the observation of changes in the composition and structure of blood in disease, notably with the work of Banting and Best on the importance of insulin in diabetes and contributions from such hematologists as Landsteiner in the discovery of the blood groups. Today pathology includes studies of the chemistry of blood, urine, feces, and diseased tissue, obtained by biopsy or at autopsy, together with the use of X-rays and many other investigative techniques.

Patinir, Joachim (*or* Patenier; c. 1485–1524) Flemish painter, noted for his panoramic landscape views, which dwarf the religious themes that were his ostensible subjects. His paintings include *St Christopher* and *St Jerome* (both Prado).

Pátmos A Greek island in the E Aegean Sea, in the Dodecanese. St John the Divine is believed to have written the Book of Revelation there. Area: 13 sq mi (34 sq km).

Patna 25 37N 85 12E A city in India, the capital of Bihar on the Ganges River. It was founded in 1541 on the former site of Pataliputra, ancient capital of the Maurya and Gupta empires. Population (1991): 916,980.

pato A four-a-side equestrian sport related to *polo and *basketball, played in Argentina. The mounted players try to throw a ball, to which are attached six leather handles, into a goal (a net attached to a post).

Paton, Alan (1903–88) South African novelist. His best-known novel, *Cry, the Beloved Country* (1948), is a passionate indictment of injustice in South African society. His other works include *Too Late the Phalarope* (1953), also dealing with South African social problems, *The Land and the People of South Africa* (1955), *Ah, But Your Land Is Beautiful* (1982), and a collection of short stories, *Debbie Go Home* (1961). He was national president of the Liberal party from 1953 to 1960.

Patras (*or* Pátrai) 38 14N 21 44E A port in W Greece, in the N Peloponnese on the Gulf of Patras. The War of Greek Independence began there in 1821. Exports include currants, raisins, tobacco, and olive oil. Its university was established in 1966. Population (1991): 155,180.

patriarch 1. In the Old Testament, *Adam and the other ancestors of the human race before the Flood, as well as the later forebears of the Hebrew nation: Abraham, Isaac, Jacob, and Jacob's 12 sons who gave their names to the 12 tribes of Israel. **2.** In the Orthodox Church, the title of a bishop with jurisdiction over other bishops. At the Council of Chalcedon (451) five such sees were recognized: Alexandria, Antioch, Constantinople, Jerusalem, and Rome. The patriarch of Constantinople took the title Ecumenical Patriarch, despite Rome's objections (*see* papacy).

patricians The hereditary aristocracy of ancient Rome. Originally the sole holders of political and religious offices, the patricians were gradually forced during Republican times to admit *plebeians to political offices and their privileged position was eroded.

Patrick, St (c. 390–c. 460 AD) The patron saint of Ireland. Legend tells of his abduction from Britain by Irish marauders at the age of 16. A local chief's slave in Antrim, he later escaped to Gaul, finally returning to Ireland as a missionary. He established an archiepiscopal see at Armagh and by the time of his death had firmly established Christianity in Ireland. His only certain works are a spiritual autobiography, the *Confession*, and the *Epistle to Coroticus*. Feast day: Mar 17. Emblems: snakes and shamrock.

Patriotic Front (PF) A black nationalist organization, founded in 1976, to oppose the government of Ian Smith in Rhodesia (now *Zimbabwe). Its two wings—the Zimbabwe African National Union (ZANU), led by Robert *Mugabe, and the Zimbabwe African People's Union (ZAPU), led by Joshua *Nkomo—were based in Mozambique and Zambia respectively. In the elections

(1980) that followed the Lancaster House agreements, Mugabe became prime minister of Zimbabwe.

Patroclus In Homer's *Iliad*, the companion of Achilles. During the Trojan War he was killed by Hector while wearing the armor of Achilles.

Patti, Adelina (Adela Juana Maria; 1843–1919) Italian-born US operatic soprano. She specialized in the Italian coloratura repertoire, singing both in the US and Europe.

Patton, George S(mith) (1885–1945) US general. Gaining experience in the strategy of armored warfare during his service in World War I, Patton was successively placed in command of the US tank corps in North Africa (1941), the Seventh Army in Sicily (1943), and the Third Army in France (1944) during World War II. Following the *D-Day invasion of Normandy, he led a spectacular advance to the Moselle. In the Ardennes he cleared the W bank of the Rhine and encircled the Ruhr, an operation that was decisive in the final military defeat of Nazi Germany. Patton distinguished himself as an uncompromising commander who demanded total discipline and dedication from his subordinate officers and troops.

Pau 43 18N 0 22W A city in SW France, the capital of the Pyrénées-Atlantique department. It was the former capital of Béarn and residence of the French Kings of Navarre. Pau is a tourist resort and trades in horses, wine, and leather. Population (1982): 86,000.

Paul I (1754–1801) Tsar of Russia (1796–1801). Paul reversed many of the enlightened policies of his mother, Catherine the Great, and pursued an inconsistent foreign policy that isolated Russia. His incompetence and despotism led to his assassination.

Paul I (1901–64) King of the Hellenes (1947–64). The third son of Constantine I, he lived mostly in exile from 1917 to 1935, and again during World War II, succeeding his brother George II (1890–1947; reigned 1922–23, 1935–47). In 1938 Paul married Frederika (1917–   ) of Brunswick.

Paul III (Alessandro Farnese; 1468–1549) Pope (1534–49). First of the *Counter-Reformation popes, Paul restored the *Inquisition, summoned the Council of *Trent, and actively supported the new orders, especially the *Jesuits. However, he was also noted for his nepotism and worldliness. He was a considerable patron of learning and the arts.

Paul VI (Giovanni Battista Montini; 1897–1978) Pope (1963–78). Succeeding *John XXIII, Paul continued his predecessor's policies of reform, reconvening the second *Vatican Council after his election. While working for ecumenicism and administrative reform he maintained papal authority and traditional doctrines, notably in the encyclical *Humanae Vitae* (*Of Human Life*; 1968), which reiterated the Church's position on birth control.

Paul, St (c. 3–c. 64 AD) Christian Apostle, born Saul of Tarsus, who spread Christianity among the Gentiles; the 13 Epistles attributed to him form a major part of the New Testament. The son of a Pharisee and a Roman citizen, he was educated at Jerusalem and was initially anti-Christian, having participated in the martyrdom of St *Stephen. While traveling to Damascus, he had a vision that led to his conversion to Christianity. He began his activity as an Apostle in Damascus, later joining the other Apostles in Jerusalem. His important missionary work consisted of three journeys in which he traveled to Cyprus, Asia Minor, Macedonia, Greece, Ephesus, and elsewhere, establishing churches or bringing support to previously established Christian communities. After his third journey, he returned to Jerusalem and was arrested by Roman soldiers in order to protect him from the hostility of the mob, who attacked him for teaching transgression of the Mosaic Law. He eventually appealed to Caesar and, as a Roman citizen, was taken to Rome for trial. He was imprisoned for two years; here the New Testament account (in Acts) ends. It appears that he may have been released, before being arrested a final time and beheaded under Nero. Paul's influence was decisive in extending Christianity beyond the Jewish context of the Church at Jerusalem, and the Pauline Epistles formed the basis of all subsequent Christian theology. Feast day: June 29.

Pauli, Wolfgang (1900–58) US physicist, born in Austria, who in 1925 formulated the *Pauli exclusion principle for which he received the 1945 Nobel Prize. In 1931 he postulated that some of the energy of a *beta decay was carried away by massless particles, which *Fermi named neutrinos.

Pauli exclusion principle The principle that no two *fermions may exist in the same state. It is most commonly applied to atomic electrons, which cannot have the same set of *quantum numbers. Named for Wolfgang *Pauli.

Pauling, Linus Carl (1901–) US chemist, who originated and developed important concepts concerning the structure of molecules. Successfully using new analytical techniques, Pauling elucidated the nature of chemical bonding in both simple and complex molecules, publishing his highly influential book *The Nature of the Chemical Bond*, in 1939. He received the Nobel Prize for chemistry (1954) for his research and the Nobel Peace Prize (1962) for his pacifist stance against the use of nuclear weapons.

Paulinus of Nola, St (c. 353–431 AD) Christian Latin poet, born at Bordeaux. After a political career as a senator, consul, and governor of Campania, he became a Christian and was ordained in 394. Bishop of Nola from 409 until his death, he is famous for his poetic epistles. Feast day: June 22.

Paulus, Friedrich (1890–1957) German field marshal in World War II. In command of the Sixth Army on the Eastern Front, he captured Stalingrad (1943) but his army was forced to surrender, thus ending the German offensive in the Soviet Union. *See* Stalingrad, Battle of.

Pausanias (2nd century AD) Greek traveler, whose *Description of Greece* is an invaluable source for places and buildings now destroyed. His accuracy and judgment are attested by his description of those that survive.

Pau-t'ou. *See* Baotou.

Pavarotti, Luciano (1935–) Italian operatic tenor. He made his debut at La Scala, Milan, in 1966 and at the Metropolitan Opera in New York in 1968. He has become known for his performances of the works of Bellini, Verdi, and Puccini.

Pavese, Cesare (1908–50) Italian novelist and poet. He was imprisoned for his antifascist journalism in 1935 and later joined the resistance movement. His best-known novels, which concern human isolation, include *Il compagno* (1947) and *La luna e i falò* (1950). He also published poetry and numerous translations of works by US and English writers. Lonely throughout his life, he committed suicide at a time when he was receiving most public recognition. His diaries were published posthumously as *Il mestiere di vivere* (1952).

Pavia (ancient name: Ticinum) 45 12N 9 09E A city in Italy, in Lombardy on the Ticino River. Dating from Roman times, it has a 12th-century church, in which St Augustine is buried, a 15th-century cathedral, a monastery, several palaces and a university (1361). Pavia is the center of an agricultural region and produces sewing machines, metal goods, textiles, and furniture. Population (1990 est): 80,700.

Pavia, Battle of (Feb 24, 1525) A major engagement in the Italian wars between *Francis I of France and the Hapsburg emperor *Charles V. It marked the beginning of Hapsburg ascendancy in Italy. Some 23,000 Hapsburg troops relieved the besieged city of Pavia, captured Francis, and virtually destroyed the French army of 28,000.

Pavlodar 52 21N 76 59E A port city in NE Kazakhstan, on the Irtysh River. It was founded in 1720 but remained small until the mid-20th century, when it became an important industrial center: food processing is the principal activity. Population (1991 est): 342,500.

Pavlov, Ivan Petrovich (1849–1936) Russian physiologist noted for his studies of digestion and his demonstration of the *conditioned reflex. Pavlov showed how heartbeat is regulated by the vagus nerve and how eating stimulates secretion of digestive juices by the stomach. Pavlov extended his theories of reflex behavior to cover aspects of human behavior, such as learning.

Pavlov was a persistent critic of the communist regime although it continued to provide him with facilities for research. He was awarded the 1907 Nobel Prize.

Pavlova, Anna (1885–1931) Russian ballet dancer. She joined Diaghilev's company in Paris in 1909, and from 1914 she devoted her career to international tours with her own company. She created the chief role in *Les Sylphides* and was especially associated with *Le Cygne*, choreographed for her by *Fokine in 1907.

pawnbroking The lending of money on the security of an item of personal property. An article pawned is pledged to the pawnbroker but can be redeemed within a specified time by the repayment of the loan plus *interest.

Pawnee A confederation of Caddoan-speaking North American Indian tribes of the Platte River area, Nebraska. They were typical of the Eastern Plains Indian semiagricultural and buffalo-hunting culture. Their villages consisted of large circular earth-covered lodges. Shamans were important. The Pawnees worshiped the sun, had a star cult, and observed the morning-star ceremony in which a captured maiden was sacrificed by cutting out her heart.

Pawtucket 41 53N 71 23W A city in NE Rhode Island, on the Blackstone River. The site of the first US cotton mill (1790), its industries include textiles, silks, machinery, and paper. Population (1990): 72,644.

Paxinou, Katina (1900–72) Greek actress. As well as acting in classical Greek tragedies she translated and produced British and US plays for the Greek National Theater. Her films include *For Whom the Bell Tolls* (1943) and *Mourning Becomes Electra* (1947).

Payne-Aldrich Tariff Act (1909) US law that attempted reform of tariffs. Originally two separate proposals—by Sereno E. Payne in the House and Nelson Wilmarth Aldrich in the Senate—the merged compromise bill did not greatly change tariff rates and did not include an originally proposed inheritance tax.

Paysandú 32 21S 58 05W A port in W Uruguay, on the Uruguay River. Accessible to oceangoing vessels, its chief exports are cereals, flax, and livestock. It is a meat-processing center and has tanning and sugar-refining industries. Population (1985): 75,000.

Paz, Octavio (1914–) Mexican poet, critic, and diplomat, whose early poetry was influenced by Marxism and surrealism. His mature poetry is philosophical and deals with the problem of solitude; the collection *La estación violenta* (1958) contains his best-known poem, "Piedra del sol." He was awarded the Nobel Prize in literature in 1990.

Pazzi conspiracy (1478) A plot to assassinate Lorenzo and Giuliano de' *Medici in Florence Cathedral. It was led by their political and business rivals, the Pazzi, and was supported by the papacy. Giuliano died but the Medici maintained control of the government and many of the conspirators were captured and killed. A war with the papacy followed but Lorenzo's dominance over Florence had been demonstrated.

pea An annual herb of the genus *Pisum* (about 6 species), native to the Mediterranean area and W Asia, especially the widely cultivated *P. sativum*. The leaves consist of paired oval leaflets and have curling tendrils used for climbing. The white flowers have a large rear petal and two smaller wing petals enclosing a cuplike keel petal. The edible round seeds are contained in an elongated pod and are an important source of protein for man and livestock. Family: *Leguminosae*.

Peace Corps A US government agency and volunteer program established in 1961 by Pres. John F. *Kennedy to provide the underdeveloped countries of the world with skilled technical advisers, teachers, and agricultural experts. Since the inception of the program, thousands of Peace Corps volunteers, all of whom must be US citizens and over 18 years of age, have served in various capacities throughout the Third World, contributing their expertise to the improvement of economic and social conditions and promoting friendship between their host countries and the US.

Peace River A river in W Canada, whose headstreams (Finlay and Parsnip Rivers) rise in the British Columbia Rockies. Flowing generally NE across the N Alberta plains, it empties into the Slave River. It is mostly navigable and is also tapped for hydroelectricity. Its valley is fertile farmland, with important oil and timber reserves. Length: 1195 mi (1923 km), including Finlay River.

peach A small tree, *Prunus persica*, probably native to China but widely cultivated in Mediterranean and warm temperate regions. Up to 20 ft (6 m) high, it has toothed glossy green leaves and pink flowers, borne singly or in groups in the leaf axils. The round fleshy fruit (a *drupe) has a distinct cleft and thin velvety skin, yellowish with a crimson tinge. The sweet white or yellow flesh encloses a wrinkled stone. Peaches are eaten fresh, canned, or in preserves. Nectarines (*P. persica* var. *nectarina*) are varieties with smooth-skinned fruits. Family: *Rosaceae*.

peacock. *See* peafowl.

Peacock, Thomas Love (1785–1866) British satirical novelist. He worked for the East India Company from 1819 to 1856 and was a close friend of Shelley. His seven novels, which include *Nightmare Abbey* (1818) and *Gryll Grange* (1860), satirize contemporary fashions and ideas.

peacock butterfly A common Eurasian *nymphalid butterfly, *Inachis io*. The adults are brownish purple with a bright eyespot on each wing. They fly from early spring well into summer. The black spiny caterpillars are gregarious and feed on stinging nettles.

pea crab A small pea-shaped *crab belonging to the genus *Pinnotheres*. The female lives within the shell of certain bivalve *mollusks, such as oysters and mussels, obtaining food and shelter but not harming its host (*see* commensalism). The larvae and usually the males are free-swimming. Tribe: *Brachyura*.

peafowl An Old World gamebird belonging to a genus (*Pavo*; 2 species) native to lowland forests of India and SE Asia. Peafowl are 30 in (75 cm) long and the female (peahen) has a green-brown plumage; males (peacocks) have elaborate lacy tails 60 in (150 cm) long, the feathers of which are tipped by blue-and-bronze markings and raised over the body during display. The blue (Indian) peacock (*P. cristatus*) is a metallic blue color and has been domesticated as an ornamental bird. Family: *Phasianidae* (pheasants, partridges, etc.); order: *Galliformes* (pheasants, turkeys, etc.).

Peale, Charles Wilson (1741–1827) US artist, who painted portraits of the famous, including George *Washington. His son **Rembrandt** (1778–1860) carried on the tradition of portrait painting and was also known for his historical paintings, including *The Court of Death* (1820). Other members of the family, including sons **Raphaelle** (1774–1825), **Rubens** (1784–1865), **Titian** (1799–1885), and **Franklin** (1795–1870), and brother **James** (1749–1831) and his children, worked on miniature, still life, animal, natural history, and portrait paintings.

peanut The fruit of *Arachis hypogea*, also called groundnut or earthnut, native to tropical South America but widely cultivated in the tropics. The plant is an erect or creeping annual, 11–18 in (30–45 cm) high, with compound leaves and yellow flowers. After fertilization the flower stalk elongates, pushing the developing pod below the soil to ripen underground. The pod has a thin spongy wall and contains one to three seeds (the nuts), which are highly nutritious. They are used in cooking, canned, and made into peanut butter and peanut oil (used in margarine). Family: *Leguminosae*.

pear A tree of the genus *Pyrus* (about 20 species), native to temperate Eurasia. The numerous cultivated varieties of orchard and garden pears are derived from *P. communis*. Up to 43 ft (13 m) high, it has oval leaves and bears clusters of five-petaled white flowers. The fruit, which narrows toward the stalk, has freckled brownish-yellow or russet skin surrounding sweet gritty flesh and a core of pips; it is eaten fresh or canned and used to make an alcoholic drink, perry. The wood is used for furniture making. Family: *Rosaceae*.

pearl A natural calcareous concretion formed in certain bivalve mollusks popularly known as pearl oysters or pearl mussels. Used for jewelry since earliest times, pearls are usually white or bluish gray and of globular, oval, pear-shaped, or irregular form. A pearl is formed around a foreign body, such as a worm larva, either against the inner side of the shell (a blister pearl) or within the mollusk sealed off as a cyst. It consists of concentric films of nacre, consisting of aragonite, which also forms the smooth lustrous lining (mother-of-pearl) in the shells of pearl-bearing mollusks. Cultured pearls are beads of mother-of-pearl artificially inserted into the mollusk, where they are left for three to five years. Artificial pearls are usually glass beads with a coating prepared from fish scales. Birthstone for June.

pearlfish An eel-like parasitic fish, also called fierasfer or cucumber fish, belonging to the family *Carapidae* (about 27 species), found in shallow tropical marine waters. About 6 in (15 cm) long, it lives in the bodies of echinoderms and mollusks (including pearl oysters), feeding on their reproductive and respiratory organs. The larvae are components of *plankton. Order: *Perciformes*.

Pearl Harbor An inlet of the Pacific Ocean, in Hawaii on Oahu Island. Following the US annexation of Hawaii in 1900, it became a US naval base. On Dec 7, 1941, the Japanese launched an air attack on US military installations in Hawaii. Four battleships were lost in Pearl Harbor and 3300 service personnel killed. This action precipitated US involvement in World War II. It is now a naval shipyard, supply center, and submarine base.

pearlite A constituent of *steel. It has a regular structure of alternate layers of ferrite (pure iron) and amentite. The name comes from its iridescent appearance under a microscope.

Pearl River. *See* Zhu Jiang.

pearlwort A small tufted or matted annual or perennial herb of the genus *Sagina* (about 20 species), native chiefly to N temperate regions. It has small narrow stalkless leaves and tiny four-petaled white flowers. The evergreen *S. subulata* is cultivated as a rock-garden or border plant. Family: *Caryophyllaceae.*

Pears, Sir Peter (1910–86) British tenor. He was well known for his performances of Bach and Schubert and was closely associated with the music of his friend *Britten, who wrote many works and operatic roles for him, such as the role of Aschenbach in the opera *Death in Venice* (1973).

Pearse, Patrick Henry (1879–1916) Irish nationalist, Gaelic enthusiast, and teacher. Pearse became a leader of the Irish Republican Brotherhood (*see* Fenians) and in the *Easter Rising of 1916 proclaimed an independent Irish republic with himself as president. The insurgents were defeated and Pearse and 14 others were executed. Pearse realized the military futility of the rising but believed a blood sacrifice was required for Irish nationalism.

Pearson, Lester B(owles) (1897–1972) Canadian statesman and diplomat; Liberal prime minister (1963–68). Ambassador to the US (1945–46), chairman of NATO (1951), and delegate to the UN, Pearson played a key role in settling the Suez crisis (1956), which earned him the Nobel Peace Prize in 1957.

Peary, Robert Edwin (1856–1920) US explorer in the Arctic. A draftsman and surveyor, he explored areas of Greenland (1886–92). In 1893 he began his efforts to reach the North Pole. In 1909, in the last of six expeditions, he became the first to reach the North Pole. Although his claim was disputed by Frederick Cook, Peary's feat was recognized by Congress in 1911. He achieved the rank of rear admiral.

Peary Land An area in N Greenland, between Victoria Fjord and the Greenland Sea. It is the most northerly land area in the world and was named for the Arctic explorer Robert E. Peary, who first explored it in 1892.

Peasants' Revolt (1381) The only major popular revolt in England during the Middle Ages. It was occasioned by heavy *poll taxes and reflected a general discontent with government policies. The rising was led by Wat *Tyler and John *Ball. The peasants marched on London, where they were joined by disaffected craftsmen, artisans, and lesser clergy. They achieved initial success, taking the Tower of London, but the revolt soon collapsed and its supporters were ruthlessly suppressed.

Peasants' War (1524–25) A peasant uprising in S Germany, precipitated by economic hardship. The revolt was condemned by Luther and crushed by the Swabian League. Some 100,000 peasants died.

peat Partially decomposed dark-brown or black plant debris laid down in waterlogged conditions in temperate or cold climates. The remains of *Sphagnum* (peat or bog moss) are important constituents. Peat is the starting point for the formation of coal and is itself used as a fuel. The more alkaline fen peat is used for horticultural purposes.

pecan. *See* hickory.

peccary A small gregarious hoofed mammal belonging to the genus *Tayassu* (2 species) of South and Central American forests. Resembling a pig, the collared peccary (*T. tajacu*) is dark gray with a light stripe from chest to shoulder and grows to a length of 35 in (90 cm). It has two pairs of short tusks. The white-lipped peccary (*T. albirostris*) is darker and larger and has a white patch on the snout. Both are omnivorous. Family: *Tayassuidae.*

Pechora River A river in NW Russia. Rising in the Ural Mountains, it flows generally N to enter the Barents Sea and is navigable for much of its length. Length: 1127 mi (1814 km).

Peckinpah, Sam (1926–84) US film director. His Westerns, which include *Guns in the Afternoon* (1962) and *The Wild Bunch* (1969), show the western myth in conflict with historical progress and include powerful scenes of violence. His other films include *Straw Dogs* (1971) and *The Getaway* (1973).

pecking order (*or* dominance hierarchy) A pattern of social structure found in certain animal groups that denotes the order of precedence of individuals, particularly in relation to feeding. It was first described—and is particularly well developed—in birds, in which the aggressive behavior shown by members of the hierarchy to all those inferior to them takes the form of pecking. It can occur between different species competing for the same food or among a single-species population, especially under captive conditions.

Pecos River A river rising in N New Mexico and flowing SSE through Texas, to join the Rio Grande. It is an important source of irrigation. Length: 1180 km (735 mi).

Pécs (German name: Fünfkirchen) 46 04N 18 15E An industrial city in SW Hungary. An old trading center, it became an important humanist center (14th–15th centuries) and has the earliest established university in the country (1367; reopened 1922). Its rapid growth in the 19th and 20th centuries was based on nearby coalfields. Population (1991 est): 170,023.

pectin A carbohydrate found combined with cellulose in the cell walls of plants. Ripening fruits change any other pectic compounds present into jelly-like pectin—an essential ingredient for the jelling of jam.

pediatrics The medical specialty concerned with the problems and illnesses of infants and children from birth (or premature birth) to adolescence. Pediatricians must have a detailed knowledge of obstetrics, genetics (to deal with inherited diseases), and psychology. Their work includes the management of handicaps at home and in school as well as the treatment and prevention of childhood diseases.

Pedro I (1798–1834) Emperor of Brazil (1822–31). The son of John VI of Portugal, Pedro became regent in Brazil in 1821 and declared its independence in 1822. On John's death (1826) he refused the Portuguese crown, which was granted to Pedro's daughter. Forced to abdicate in 1831, Pedro returned to Portugal.

Pedro II (1825–91) Emperor of Brazil (1831–89), following the abdication of his father Pedro I. His reign saw an era of prosperity, in spite of wars against Argentina and Paraguay. His gradual abolition of slavery alienated the landowners, who joined the army in deposing him and declaring a republic in 1889.

Pedro the Cruel (1334–69) King of Castile and León (1350–69). He ruled with great cruelty and his brother, Henry of Trastamara (1333–79; reigned, as Henry II, 1369–79), attempted, with French help, to depose him in 1367. England was drawn into the conflict on Pedro's side and Spain thus became a battlefield of the *Hundred Years' War between France and England. Pedro was killed by Henry after defeat at the battle of Montiel.

Peel, Sir Robert (1788–1850) British statesman; Conservative prime minister (1834–35, 1841–46). Elected to Parliament in 1809, he was twice home secretary (1822–27, 1828–30). In the Tamworth manifesto (1834), a speech to his constituents, he stated a program of reform that clearly identified the *Conservative party. His second ministry reintroduced the income tax (1841) and reduced duties on food and raw materials. He is best remembered for the repeal of the

*Corn Laws (1846), which caused his followers, the Peelites, to defect from the Conservative party; they subsequently joined the Liberals.

Peele, George (1556–96) English dramatist. In 1581 he moved from Oxford to the active literary society of London. A prolific writer, his works include the pastoral *The Arraignment of Paris* (1584), the chronicle play *Edward I* (1593), and the satirical play *The Old Wives' Tale* (1595), as well as poems and pamphlets.

Peenemünde 54 09N 13 46E A fishing village in Germany, on the Baltic coast. The Rocket Test Center was opened in Peenemünde in 1937 and it was here that flying bombs (V1) and German rockets (V2) were developed under Wernher von *Braun during World War II.

peepul. *See* bo tree.

peerage In the UK and Ireland, the temporal hereditary nobility, a body originating in the council of the Norman kings of England, and the life peers, appointed primarily in recognition of public service. The five ranks of the hereditary peerage are, in descending order, duke, marquess, earl, viscount, and baron. A life peer has the rank of baron. All peers are permitted to sit in the House of Lords.

peewit. *See* lapwing.

Pegasus (astronomy) A large constellation in the N sky that contains the **Square of Pegasus**, formed from three of the brightest 2nd- and 3rd-magnitude stars in the constellation together with the 2nd-magnitude star Alpheratz in Andromeda.

Pegasus (Greek mythology) A winged horse that sprang from the blood of *Medusa when she was beheaded by Perseus. It carried the legendary hero Bellerophon in his battles but unseated him when he attempted to ride to heaven. It became a constellation and the bearer of thunderbolts for Zeus.

pegmatite A very coarse-grained igneous rock, usually occurring in veins or dikes within or around bodies of granite. Crystals over 35 ft (10 m) across have been found in pegmatites. Most consist largely of alkali feldspar and quartz but many also contain accessory minerals that are otherwise rare, and these may be of economic importance.

Pegu 17 18N 96 31E A city in S Myanmar (formerly Burma). The former capital of the Mon kingdoms, which dominated Burma at intervals from the 6th century AD until the 17th century, it has an enormous reclining statue of Buddha, 181 ft (55 m) long. Population (1983): 255,000.

Péguy, Charles (1873–1914) French poet and essayist. From his socialist bookshop he published the journal *Cahiers de la quinzaine* (1900–14), which expressed the literary ideals of his generation. He was killed in action in World War I.

Pei, I(eoh) M(ing) (1917–) US architect, born in China. He started his own architecture firm in 1955 and was responsible for designing Mile High Stadium in Denver (1956). Through the 1960s he designed many urban complexes as well as the East-West Center at the University of Hawaii and the Everson Museum of Art in Syracuse, NY (1968). He planned the John Hancock Building (1973) and a wing of the Museum of Fine Arts (1981) in Boston, the East Building of the National Gallery of Art (1978), the US embassy in Peking (1979), and renovations to the Louvre Museum (Paris) in the 1980s.

Peipus, Lake (Russian name: Ozero Chudskoye) A lake in Estonia and Russia. It is drained by the Narva River N into the Gulf of Finland. Area: 1356 sq mi (3512 sq km).

Peirce, Charles Sanders (1839–1914) US philosopher and logician. He spent much of his career in government service, rather than academic life, and his influential *Collected Papers* were only published posthumously (1931–58). Peirce believed that an idea could best be defined by examination of the consequences to which it led. This concept became known as *pragmatism, a name that he later changed to pragmaticism. His work on formal logic was immensely significant.

Peking. *See* Beijing.

Pekingese An ancient breed of toy □dog originating in China and brought to the West by British forces who sacked the Imperial Palace, Peking, in 1860. The Pekingese has a long straight coat forming a luxuriant mane on the shoulders and it may be of any color. The short-muzzled face is always black. Height: 6–9 in (15–23 cm).

Peking man A type of fossil *hominid belonging to the species *Homo erectus* and represented by skeletal remains found at Chou-K'ou-Tien (*or* Zhou kou tian) cave near Peking (now called Beijing). Formerly known as *Sinanthropus*, Peking man lived during the middle Pleistocene period (c. 500,000 years ago), used flint and bone tools, hunted, and could make fire.

Pelagius (c. 360–c. 420 AD) The originator of the heretical Christian doctrine known as Pelagianism. Born in Britain, he settled in Rome (c. 380) and later preached in Africa and Palestine. He rejected the doctrines of original sin and predestination, believing in man's free will and inherent capacity for good. These beliefs were hotly disputed by St *Augustine and a series of synods. Pope Innocent I finally condemned them in 417 and excommunicated Pelagius.

Pelargonium. *See* geranium.

Pelasgians (*or* Pelasgi) The inhabitants of Greece before the 12th century BC. They spoke a non-Greek language and lived mainly in the N Aegean. They were scattered during Bronze Age infiltrations of Greek-speaking peoples from the N.

Pelé (Edson Arantes do Nascimento; 1940–   ) Brazilian soccer player, who played for Santos (1955–74), the New York Cosmos (1975–77), and Brazil. The greatest inside forward of his time, he became a world star at 17 when Brazil first won the World Cup (1958). He scored over 1300 goals.

Pelée, Mount (French name: Montagne Pelée) 14 18N 61 10W An active volcano on the West Indian island of Martinique. In 1902 an eruption engulfed the town of St Pierre. Height: 4800 ft (1463 m).

Peleus In Greek legend, a king of Phthia in Thessaly. He was married to *Thetis and was the father of Achilles.

Pelham, Henry. *See* Newcastle, Thomas Pelham-Holles, 1st duke of.

pelican A large waterbird belonging to a family (*Pelecanidae*; 7 species) occurring on lakes, rivers, and coasts of temperate and tropical regions, 49–71 in (125–180 cm) long, pelicans are typically white with dark wingtips and have short legs, strong feet, a short tail, and very large wings. Their long straight pointed bills have a distensible pouch underneath, in which fish are held before being swallowed. Order: *Pelecaniformes* (gannets, pelicans, etc.).

Pella The capital, about 24 mi (39 km) NW of Thessaloniki (N Greece), of Macedon (*see* Macedonia) from about 400 to 167 BC. Archelaus I (reigned 413–399) established his court here and it is the birthplace of Alexander the Great.

pellagra A disease caused by deficiency of nicotinic acid (*see* vitamin B complex). It occurs mainly in poor countries in people whose diet consists predominantly of maize. The disease causes dermatitis, diarrhea, and delirium or depression. Health can be rapidly restored by giving nicotinic acid, nicotinamide or a diet rich in milk, yeast, beans, or peas.

PELÉ *In Brazil he is often nicknamed* La Perola Negra, *the Black Pearl.*

Pelletier, Pierre Joseph (1788–1842) French chemist, who in 1817 isolated *chlorophyll. He also isolated a number of naturally occurring *alkaloids, including *quinine and *strychnine, which were later introduced into medical preparations by François *Magendie.

Peloponnesus (Modern Greek name: Pelopónnesos) The S peninsula of Greece, joined to central Greece by the Isthmus of Corinth. It includes the towns of Corinth, Patrás (the chief port), and *Sparta. Area: 8354 sq mi (21,637 sq km). Population (1991): 605,663.

Peloponnesian War (431–404 BC) The conflict between Athens and Sparta and their allies, in which Sparta was finally victorious. According to the Athenian historian Thucydides, the war was caused by Spartan fear of Athenian imperialism. Sparta's superior infantry invaded Athens in 431 while Athens, under Pericles, relying for security on walls connecting it to its seaport, attacked at sea. Lacking conclusive victories, both sides agreed to the peace of *Nicias (421). In 415, however, Athens led by *Alcibiades set out to conquer Sicily, which retaliated with Spartan help and destroyed the Athenian fleet (413). The war continued until Sparta under *Lysander captured the partially rebuilt Athenian fleet (405) and besieged Athens, which then surrendered (404).

Pelops The legendary Greek founder of the Pelopid dynasty of Mycenae, a son of *Tantalus. He won his bride Hippodamia by winning a chariot race with the help of his driver Myrtilus. When Myrtilus demanded his reward, Pelops refused and instead drowned him. The curse pronounced by the dying Myrtilus was passed on to his son *Atreus and all his descendants until it was exorcised by the purification of *Orestes.

pelota A generic name for a variety of court games played with a ball using the hand or a racket or bat. They derive from *real tennis and are widely played in the Basque provinces.

Pelotas 31 45S 52 20W A seaport in S Brazil, in Rio Grande do Sul state on the São Gonçalo Canal. The chief exports are meat, wool, and hides. Population (1980): 197,092.

Peltier effect. *See* thermoelectric effects.

pelvis A basin-like structure composed of the hip bones and lower part of the spine. It protects the soft organs of the lower abdomen and provides attachment for the bones and muscles of the legs. The pelvis is larger in women since it must allow the passage of a baby during childbirth.

Pemba 5 10S 39 45E An island in Tanzania, off the NE coast of the mainland. Its major industry is the growing of cloves, of which it is the world's largest producer. Area: 380 sq mi (984 sq km).

PEN The acronym of the International Association of Poets, Playwrights, Editors, Essayists, and Novelists, an organization founded in 1921 to promote international fellowship between professional writers. Its presidents have included H. G. *Wells and Heinrich *Böll.

penal law State and federal statutes that determine the acts and circumstances that amount to a crime (a wrong against society prohibited by law) and the punishment for crimes. Most crimes entail both an act (*actus reus*) and a mental element (*mens rea*). However, there is a growing number of crimes in which no mental element is necessary, such as most driving offenses; insanity, infancy (children under the age of ten), or duress (an act committed under threat of death or serious personal injury) may excuse a crime, but ignorance of the law does not if, in cases involving a mental element, the offender intends the result of his acts.

Penang A state in NW Peninsular Malaysia, on the Strait of Malacca, consisting of Penang island and Province Wellesley on the mainland. Ceded to the East India Company in 1786, the island was the first British settlement in Malaya and rapidly became a commercial center. The main products are rice, rubber, and tin. Area: 398 sq mi (1031 sq km). Population (1990): 1,142,200. Capital: Georgetown.

Penates. *See* Lares and Penates.

pencil cedar A *juniper tree, *Juniperus virginiana*, native to E and central North America and quite widely cultivated for ornament. It has scalelike leaves and blue berrylike fruits, up to 0.24 in (6 mm) long. Its aromatic wood has been used to line clothing chests and cupboards (it repels moths) and for making lead pencils. The tree usually grows to a height of 49 ft (15 m).

Penda (d. 655) King of Mercia (c. 634–55), who made Mercia one of the most powerful English kingdoms. He remained heathen but permitted the conversion of his people to Christianity. He was killed in battle by Oswiu, king of Northumbria.

Penderecki, Krzystof (1933–) Polish composer. He studied in Kraków. His music, for which he has devised a special system of notation, is characterized by note clusters, special tone colors, and unusual sound effects. His compositions include *Threnody for the Victims of Hiroshima* (for strings; 1961), *De Natura Sonoris I* (for orchestra; 1966), the choral work *Utrenja* (1969–71), and a symphony (1973). He also composed *Polish Requiem* (1980–83).

Pendleton Act (1883) US law that reformed the civil-service system. Sponsored by Sen. George H. Pendleton (1825–89), the bill established the Civil Service Commission to set rules and oversee the granting of government jobs based on competitive examination rather than the spoils system.

pendulum A device in which a mass (the bob) swings freely about a fixed point with a constant period. In the ideal simple pendulum the bob is connected to the fixed point by a length (l) of weightless string, wire, etc. Its period is $2\pi(l/g)^{1/2}$, where g is the *acceleration of free fall, and is independent of the mass of the bob. A compound pendulum consists of a bob attached to the fixed point via two rigid rods. Pendulums are used to regulate a clock mechanism and in instruments that determine the value of g.

Penelope In Homer's *Odyssey*, the wife of *Odysseus. During her husband's absence she put off her many suitors by saying that she must first make a shroud for her father-in-law Laertes. Each night she unraveled what she had woven by day. After 20 years Odysseus returned and killed the suitors.

Penghu Islands (English name: Pescadores) A Taiwanese archipelago of about 64 small islands in Taiwan Strait. Area: 49 sq mi (127 sq km). Population (1978 est): 112,000. Main island: Penghu.

penguin A flightless black-and-white seabird belonging to a family (*Spheniscidae*; 14–18 species) occurring on cold coasts of the S hemisphere. Penguins are adapted for aquatic life, having wings reduced to narrow flippers giving fast propulsion when chasing fish and squid and escaping predators; 16–47 in (40–120 cm) long, they have dense plumage enabling them to tolerate extreme cold. Penguins are highly gregarious and often migrate long distances inland to nest in "rookeries." Order: *Sphenisciformes. See also* emperor penguin; fairy penguin.

penicillins A group of *antibiotics. The first penicillin was isolated from the mold *Penicillium notatum*, in 1929, by Sir Alexander *Fleming but was not used to treat infections in man until 1941. Some penicillins must be injected (e.g. benzylpenicillin); others can be taken by mouth (e.g. phenoxymethylpenicillin). Semisynthetic penicillins (e.g. flucloxacillin, methicillin) are effective against infections resistant to naturally occurring penicillins. Ampicillin is a broad-spectrum penicillin, i.e. it kills many species of bacteria. Penicillins can cause severe allergic reactions in susceptible patients.

Penicillium A genus of fungi (about 250 species) that are common molds in soil and on organic matter. The observation of the antibacterial action of *P. notatum* by Sir Alexander *Fleming led to the discovery of penicillin and other antibiotics. *P. camemberti* and *P. roqueforti* are important in cheese making. Family: *Eurotiaceae*; class: *Ascomycetes*.

Peninsular Campaign (1862) US Civil War offensive by the Union Army to take Richmond, Va. Conceived by Union Gen. George B. *McClellan, the Union strategy was to leave Washington protected by 40,000–50,000 troops to proceed, with the rest of the Union Army, from the peninsula between the York and James Rivers to Richmond. McClellan's troops forced Confederate retreats at Yorktown and Norfolk, thus opening up both rivers for the Union fleet, but the Army was stopped near Richmond by Confederate forces under Gen. Joseph *Johnston and later Gen. Robert E. *Lee. The stalemated Battle of Seven Pines and the Seven Days' battles assured the safety of the Confederate capital. Casualties throughout the campaign were high on both sides.

Peninsular War (1808–14) That part of the Napoleonic Wars fought in Spain and Portugal. The French took Portugal in 1807 and in 1808 Napoleon's brother, Joseph *Bonaparte, replaced Ferdinand VII as king of Spain. Popular revolts broke out and turned into a vicious *guerrilla war. The Spanish rebels managed an initial victory at Bailén but against crack French troops could do no more than resist the sieges of Gerona and Zaragoza. British troops under the command of the duke of *Wellington eventually liberated the Peninsula. After their victory at Vitoria (1813) they invaded France, helping to force Napoleon's abdication (1814).

penis The male copulatory organ of mammals, some reptiles, and a few birds. In man (and other mammals) it contains a tube (urethra) through which both semen and urine can be discharged. The urethra is surrounded by specialized erectile tissue (making up the bulk of the penis): this becomes engorged with blood during sexual excitement, enabling the penis to be inserted into the vagina. The corresponding part in women is the **clitoris**, a small erectile mass of tissue situated in front of the urinary opening.

Pen-ki. *See* Benxi.

Penn, William (1644–1718) English Quaker and founder of Pennsylvania, son of Admiral Sir William Penn (1621–70). Expelled from Oxford (1661) because of his refusal to conform to the restored Anglican Church, he joined the Quakers in 1664. In 1668 he was imprisoned in the Tower for his writings. Here he wrote *No Cross, No Crown* (1669), a classic of Quaker practice. From 1682 he was involved in the establishment of Quaker settlements in America, including Pennsylvania, for which he drew up a constitution, The Frame of Government, allowing freedom of worship. He accomplished peaceful relations with the Indians and designed the city of Philadelphia during his two visits to the colonies (1682–84; 1699–1701). His Charter of Privileges (1701) established a legislature. He was imprisoned for treason and later for debts.

Pennines (*or* Pennine Chain) An upland range in N England. It extends from the Cheviot Hills in the N to the valley of the Trent River in the S. Sometimes known as the "backbone of England" it is the watershed of the chief rivers in N England. It rises to 2930 ft (893 m) at Cross Fell. The **Pennine Way**, a footpath 250 mi (400 km) long, extends between Edale in Derbyshire and Kirk Yetholm in the Borders Region of Scotland.

Pennsylvania A middle Atlantic state. It is bordered on the E by New York and New Jersey, on the S by Delaware, Maryland, and West Virginia, on the W by West Virginia and Ohio, and on the N by Lake Erie and New York. The state is dominated by the uplands of the Appalachian Plateau. Much of the land is under forest or farmed, although it is generally considered to be an urbanized industrial state, dominated by Philadelphia in the E and Pittsburgh in the W. It is a leading iron and steel producer and provides nearly all the country's hard coal. Oil has long been important and the world's first oil well was drilled near Titusville in 1859. Dairy farming predominates in the NE, while the fertile lands of the SE yield cereals, fruit, and vegetables. This latter area is associated with the Pennsylvania Dutch, whose highly decorated barns can be seen throughout the area. *History*: originally the home of the Delaware, Susquehanna, Shawnee, and other Indian tribes, Pennsylvania was first settled by Swedes in 1643. Control passed to the Dutch and then to the British, who granted the region to Quaker William Penn in 1681. Under Penn the colony became a refuge for persecuted religious groups (the Pennsylvania Dutch still live there in large numbers) and a peaceful and successful community, enjoying good relations with the Indians, grew up. The French and Indian Wars (1754–63) interrupted this peace as did the American Revolution two decades later. Benjamin Franklin and other

Pennsylvanians became strong voices in the colonial independence movement, and it was at Philadelphia that the signing of the Declaration of Independence took place. Pennsylvania, the nation's capital from 1790 to 1800, achieved statehood in 1787. The late 1700s saw the beginning of iron smelting, and the building of canals (1820s) and railroads facilitated continuing economic expansion. Pennsylvania fought with the Union in the Civil War and was the site of the great Gettysburg campaign (1863). From the close of the Civil War until the end of World War II, Pennsylvania experienced rapid economic and industrial growth with coal mining, oil drilling, and steel production dominating. The state's economy suffered after World War II, but its strong and diversified economic foundation sustained its position as a wealthy and powerful state. Heavy industry was hard hit by the recession of the early 1980s but increasing US energy needs resulted in growing markets for Pennsylvania's coal. Area: 45,333 sq mi (117,412 sq km). Population (1990): 11,881,643. Capital: Harrisburg.

Pennsylvanian period. *See* Carboniferous period.

pennyroyal A perennial herb, *Mentha pulegium*, native to wet places throughout Eurasia and naturalized in North America; 4–20 in (10–50 cm) tall, it has small strongly scented hairy oval leaves and widely spaced whorls of tubular pink or lilac flowers. It is used as a flavoring and to scent soap. Family: *Labiatae*.

Penobscot North American Algonkian-speaking Indian tribe, found in SE Maine in the Penobscot Bay area. Farmers and fishermen, they were members of the Abnaki Confederacy until 1749, when they made their own peace with the British. Today, descendants of the Penobscot live in Old Town, Me, and have limited representation in the state legislature.

Pensacola 30 25N 87 13W A resort city in W Florida, on the W coast of Pensacola Bay, SE of Mobile, Ala. Settled by the Spanish in 1698, it came under US administration in 1821 as part of Florida Territory. A major US naval flight training base is there. Besides tourism, fish processing and shipping are the major industries. Population (1990): 58,165.

Pentagon The headquarters of the Defense Department, a massive five-sided building in Virginia built (1941–43) during World War II. It houses all three services, the army, navy, and air force, and extends over 34 acres (14 hectares).

Pentagon Papers (1967–69) Confidential US government papers on the US military situation in Indochina, especially Vietnam. In 1971 several newspapers, including *The New York Times*, started referring to and publishing parts of the study, which revealed that information about Vietnam had been withheld from the US public. The Justice Department, basing its argument on violation of national security, ordered *The Times* to stop publication and prosecuted Daniel Ellsberg, accused of stealing the papers he helped to write, for espionage; both charges were dismissed.

Pentateuch (Greek: five books) The title used by biblical scholars for the first five books of the *Old Testament, traditionally ascribed to Moses. *See also* Torah.

pentathlon An athletic competition comprising five events, the winner being the competitor with the highest total. It originated in an Olympic contest of sprinting, long jumping, javelin throwing, discus throwing, and wrestling (instituted in 708 BC). The women's version, an Olympic event from 1964, consisted of the 100 m hurdles, shot put, high jump, long jump, and 800 m run before it was expanded to six events (heptathlon). The men's pentathlon has been replaced in major competitions by the *decathlon. It has not been an Olympic event since 1924. It comprises the long jump, javelin throw, 200 m sprint, discus throw, and 1500 m run. The **modern pentathlon** is a sporting competition comprising five events: a 5000 m cross-country ride (on horseback), fencing, pistol shooting, a 3000 m swim, and a 4000 m cross-country run. It was first included in the Olympic Games in 1912.

Pentecostal Churches A Christian movement originating in revivalist meetings in the US in 1906. In Pentecostal assemblies people seek spiritual renewal through baptism by the Holy Spirit, as took place on the first Pentecost (Acts 2.1–4). Glossolalia (speaking in tongues, or making utterances in an unknown language under the influence of intense religious experience) is an accompanying phenomenon in many cases as is the ability to perform faith healing. Certain charismatic preachers, generally laymen, evoked an enormous response, especially in the US, where the largest number of Pentecostal Churches are found.

pentlandite The principal ore mineral of nickel, (Ni,Fe)S, founded in association with pyrrhotite and chalcopyrite in basic and ultrabasic igneous rocks. It is mined in Canada, Australia, and Russia.

Penutian languages A major family of North American Indian languages spoken along the NW Pacific coast, on the Columbia River plateau, and in California. There are four main divisions: *Chinook and Tsimshian; Coos, Takelma, and Kalapooia; the Sahaptin group, which includes *Nez Percé; and the Californian group.

Penza 53 11N 45 00E Capital city of Russia's Penza region. Founded in 1666, it suffered repeated Tartar attacks. Long an agricultural center, food processing remains important. Other industries include machine manufacturing and paper making. Population (1991 est): 551,500.

peony A large perennial herb or shrub of the genus *Paeonia* (33 species) of N temperate regions, often cultivated for its showy flowers. The large glossy deeply cut leaves arise from underground stems or woody aerial shoots and the solitary white, pink, crimson, or yellow flowers are about 4 in (10 cm) across, with in-curving petals and a fleshy central disk supporting the stigma and numerous stamens. The fruit is a large leathery pod containing black seeds. Family: *Paeoniaceae*.

Peoria 40 43N 89 38W A city in Illinois, on the Illinois River. The state's second largest city, it is the grain and livestock center for an extensive agricultural area. Population (1990): 113,504.

Pepin (II) of Herstal (d. 714 AD) Ruler of the Franks (687–714). He became mayor of the palace (viceroy) of *Austrasia in 679 and virtual ruler of all the Franks after defeating *Neustria at Tertry (687). The Merovingian kings remained nominal rulers until the overthrow of the dynasty by his grandson *Pepin the Short.

Pepin the Short (d. 768 AD) King of the Franks (751–68) after overthrowing the *Merovingians. The son of *Charles Martel, Pepin founded the *Carolingian dynasty and was crowned king by St Boniface. He checked Lombard expansion and in 756 presented Pope Stephen II with the territories around Ravenna—the nucleus of the *papal states. His son *Charlemagne inherited the Frankish kingdom in 771.

pepper A condiment derived from a perennial climbing vine, *Piper nigrum*, native to India. Up to 33 ft (10 m) high, it bears chains of up to 50 inconspicuous flowers that form berrylike fruits (or peppercorns), about 0.20 in (5 mm) in diameter. Whole peppercorns yield black pepper while white pepper is obtained from peppercorns with the outer part of the fruit wall removed. Family: *Piperaceae*.

The fleshy red and green peppers are the fruits of *Capsicum* species.

pepperbox A 19th-century firearm, usually a pistol, with a cluster of barrels, each fired separately. Most bizarre was the *Mariette* design (1837) with 18 barrels, firing in groups of three.

peppered moth A European *geometrid moth, *Biston betularia*, the typical form of which has a similar coloration to the lichen-encrusted tree bark on which it rests. During the past century a dark form, var. *carbonaria*, has become common in sooty industrial areas, where it is better camouflaged—and thus better protected from predators—than the typical form.

peppermint A perennial herb, *Mentha* × *piperata*: a hybrid between water mint (*M. aquatica*) and *spearmint. It has smooth dark-green leaves and oblong clusters of reddish-lilac flowers and is the source of oil of peppermint, used as a flavoring.

pepsin A protein-digesting enzyme found in gastric juice. The inactive form, pepsinogen, is secreted by glands in the stomach wall and converted to pepsin by the hydrochloric acid in the stomach. Pepsin is a powerful coagulant of milk.

peptic ulcer An inflamed eroded area in the wall of the stomach (**gastric ulcer**) or, more commonly, the duodenum (**duodenal ulcer**). Ulcers are very common but it is not known exactly why they occur; they are more common in people who secrete excessive amounts of stomach acid. They may cause abdominal pain, nausea, and vomiting. Serious complications occur when the ulcer bleeds or perforates (bursts). In some patients ulcers disappear as quickly as they come; others require drugs, a special diet, or even surgery (especially if an ulcer perforates).

peptide A chemical compound comprising a chain of two or more *amino acids linked by peptide bonds (–NH–CO–) formed between the carboxyl and amino groups of adjacent amino acids. Polypeptides, containing between three and several hundred amino acids, are the constituents of *proteins. Some peptides are important as hormones (e.g. *ACTH) and as antibiotics (e.g. bacitracin, gradmicidin).

Pepys, Samuel (1633–1703) English diarist. His long career in naval administration culminated in his appointment as secretary to the Admiralty (1669–88). He was also a member of Parliament and president of the Royal Society. His *Diary*, which extends from 1660 to 1669 and includes descriptions of the Restoration, the Plague, and the Fire of London, is the intimate record of a man for whom every detail of life held interest. It was written in code and deciphered in the early 19th century.

Pequot North American Algonquian-speaking Indian tribe, related to the *Mohegan, found in Connecticut, Rhode Island, and E Long Island, New York. The *Pequot War (1637) forced the few surviving Pequot to seek refuge with neighboring tribes; they were eventually placed by the English in villages near New London, Conn., sold into slavery, or sent to the West Indies.

Pequot War (1637) US colonial war with the *Pequot Indians in Connecticut. Colonists, in retaliation for the murders of colonial traders, attacked the Pequots at Mystic and burned their fort and village. Those who escaped were pursued to swamps near present-day Westport in S Connecticut where the rest of the tribe, with the exception of some women and children, was annihilated.

Perak A populous state in NW Peninsular Malaysia, on the Strait of Malacca. In the Kinta Valley are important tin mines, and rubber, coconuts, and rice are produced. Area: 7980 sq mi (20,668 sq km). Population (1990): 2,222,200. Capital: Ipoh.

Perceval A hero of *Arthurian legend, who played a leading part in the quest of the *Holy Grail. In *Chrétien de Troyes' romance, *Conte du Graal*, and in *Wolfram von Eschenbach's *Parzival*, he succeeds in the quest, but in later romances *Galahad is the only Arthurian knight to succeed in the quest.

Perceval, Spencer (1762–1812) British politician; prime minister (1809–12) remembered for his assassination by a mad and bankrupt broker, John Bellingham.

perch One of two species of freshwater food and game fish belonging to the genus *Perca*. The common perch (*P. fluviatilis*) of Eurasia has a deep elongated body, usually about 10 in (25 cm) long, and is greenish in color, with dark vertical bars on its sides, reddish or orange lower fins, and a spiny first dorsal fin. The yellow perch (*P. flavescens*) is North American. Perch usually live in shoals, feeding on fish and invertebrates. Family: *Percidae*; order: *Perciformes*. *See also* climbing perch; sea bass.

Percheron A breed of heavy draft □horse originating in the Perche district of France. It has a deep muscular body, powerful neck and shoulders, and a characteristically small refined head. Percherons are commonly black or gray. Height: 5–6 ft (1.63–1.73 m) (16–17 hands).

perching duck A *duck belonging to a tribe (*Cairinini*) found chiefly in tropical woodlands. Perching ducks nest in treeholes and have long-clawed toes for gripping branches. Drakes are larger and have brighter colors than females. *See* Mandarin duck; Muscovy duck.

percussion cap A device, which came into use in the early 19th century, for igniting the charge in firearms, enabling breech-loading *muskets and *rifles to be developed. Percussion muskets with cartridge ammunition were soon widely adopted in place of flintlocks.

percussion instruments Musical instruments that are struck by the hand or by a stick to produce sounds. The family includes the triangle, gong, rattle, block, cymbals and whip, as well as the pitched xylophone, glockenspiel, bells, celesta, and vibraphone. *Compare* drums; stringed instruments; wind instruments.

Percy, Sir Henry (1364–1403) English rebel, called Hotspur. Together with his father, Henry, 1st earl of Northumberland (1342–1408), he led the most serious revolt against Henry IV, whom they had helped to the throne in 1399. Headstrong and fearless (hence his nickname) Percy was defeated and killed at Shrewsbury. He appears in Shakespeare's *Henry IV*, Part I.

Père David's deer A rare Chinese deer, *Elaphurus davidianus*, now found only in parks and zoos. About 48 in (120 cm) high at the shoulder, it has a long tail, splayed hooves, and a reddish-gray coat with a white ring around the eye. The male has long branching antlers. A French missionary, Père Armand David (1826–1900), described specimens in the Chinese emperor's hunting park in 1865.

peregrine falcon A large powerful *falcon, *Falco peregrinus*, occurring in rocky coastal regions worldwide. It is 13–19 in (33–48 cm) long and has long pointed wings and a long tail. The male is blue-gray with black-barred white underparts; females are browner. It feeds mainly on ducks, shorebirds, and mammals, soaring high and diving at great speed.

Pereira 4 47N 75 46W A city in W Colombia. Notable buildings include the cathedral (1890) and the university (1961). An agricultural trading center, it has coffee-processing, brewing, and clothing industries. Population (1985): 233,271.

PÈRE DAVID'S DEER *This species would probably now be extinct if a breeding herd had not been established in England at about 1900. All specimens living today are believed to be descended from this herd.*

Perelman, S(idney) J(oseph) (1904–79) US humorous writer. After publishing his first book in 1929, he worked for a time as a Hollywood scriptwriter, notably on some Marx Brothers films. In the 1930s he began contributing to the *New Yorker*, in which he published most of his short stories and sketches. One of the leading American humorists, he published numerous collections of his pieces, including *Strictly From Hunger* (1937), *Crazy Like a Fox* (1944), *The Most of S. J. Perelman* (1958), *Baby, It's Cold Inside* (1970), and *Eastward, Ha!* (1977).

perennials Plants that can live for many years. In herbaceous perennials, such as the iris and daffodil, aerial parts die down each winter and the plants survive in the form of underground organs (rhizomes, bulbs, corms, etc.). Woody perennials—trees and shrubs—have woody stems, which overwinter above ground. Woody perennials may or may not shed their leaves in winter.

Pérez de Cuéllar, Javier (1920–) Peruvian diplomat; UN secretary-general (1982–91). He served as Peruvian ambassador to Switzerland (1964–66), USSR (1969–71), the UN (1971–75), and Venezuela (1978). From 1975 until 1979 he was under-secretary of the UN in Cyprus. He succeeded Kurt *Waldheim as secretary-general in 1982 and was elected to a second term in

1986. He urged negotiations during the Lebanon crises and the *Falkland Islands War, mediated a successful end to the Iran–Iraq War in 1988, and worked to gain Namibia's independence in 1989. His attempts in 1990–91 to prevent war in the Persian Gulf were not successful.

Pérez Galdós, Benito (1843–1920) Spanish novelist. He wrote a series of 46 historical novels about 19th-century Spain, *Episodios nacionales* (1873–1912), and a second series of novels about contemporary society, of which the best known are *Fortunata y Jacinta* (1886–87) and the *Torquemada* sequence (1889–95). He also wrote several successful plays.

perfect competition A theoretical market structure in economic theory in which no producer supplies a sufficiently large portion of the market to be able to influence prices or to make an exorbitant profit. Perfect competition ensures that resources in the economy are allocated in the most efficient way but is rarely found in practice. *Compare* monopoly; monopsony; oligopoly.

perfect number An integer that is equal to the sum of all its factors (except itself); for example $28 = 1 + 2 + 4 + 7 + 14$. If the sum of all the factors of n is greater or less than n, then n is called excessive or defective respectively. *See also* numbers.

Perga (modern name: Ihsaniye) 36 59N 30 46E An ancient city in SW Turkey, near Antalya. It was the starting point of St Paul's first missionary journey (Acts 13.13) and remains include a theater, an agora, and basilicas.

Pergamum An ancient city of W Asia Minor. After about 230 BC it became capital of a powerful Hellenistic kingdom, allied with Egypt and Rome against the *Seleucids. Pergamum became rich largely from *parchment and luxury textiles mass-produced by slave labor. Pergamene sculptors led artistic fashion, its library rivaled that of *Alexandria, and the architecture of the upper city was magnificent. The last king bequeathed his realm to Rome (133 BC).

Pergolesi, Giovanni (Battista) (1710–36) Italian composer. He spent most of his short life in or near Naples. His comic intermezzo *La serva padrona* (1733) was influential in the development of *opera buffa. His last work was a *Stabat Mater* (for soprano, alto, and orchestra; 1736).

Perkins, Frances (1882–1965) US stateswoman and reformer. She headed the Consumers' League of New York (1910–12) and served on various New York state industrial commissions. An advocate of better working conditions and unemployment insurance, she was secretary of labor during Pres. Franklin D. *Roosevelt's administrations (1933–45), the first woman appointed to a cabinet position. She was responsible for overseeing and implementing *New Deal legislation. She later served on the Civil Service Commission (1946–53).

Pericles (c. 495–429 BC) Athenian statesman, who presided over Athens' golden age. According to *Plutarch, Pericles became leader of the democratic party in 461 and secured power shortly afterward, following the ostracism of his rival *Cimon. He dominated Athens until 430 by virtue of his outstanding oratory and leadership and his reputation for honesty. Under Pericles, Athens asserted its leadership of the *Delian League and revolts among its members were suppressed: following the Thirty Years' Peace with Sparta, Pericles was able to reduce Euboea (445) and then Samos (439). By 431, rivalry between Athens and Sparta had led to the outbreak of the *Peloponnesian War. The effectiveness of Pericles' strategy, which emphasized Athenian naval power, was undermined by the plague of 430 and Pericles briefly lost office. He died shortly after his reinstatement.

In 447 Pericles initiated the great program of public works on the *Acropolis. He also fostered the work of many eminent men, including the playwright Sophocles, the philosopher Anaxagoras, and the sculptor Phidias.

peridotite An ultrabasic igneous rock consisting mainly of olivine; some varieties contain other ferromagnesian minerals, but none contain feldspar. The earth's mantle, believed to be mainly olivine, is sometimes called the peridotite shell. Peridotites are coarse-grained and occur beneath many mountain chains and island arcs.

perigee The point in the orbit of the moon or of an artificial satellite around the earth at which the body is nearest the earth. *Compare* apogee.

Perigordian A culture of the Upper *Paleolithic. Perigordian is the preferred French designation for the pre-*Solutrean industries in W Europe, excluding the typologically different *Aurignacian. Upper Perigordian is approximately equatable with *Gravettian.

Périgueux 45 12N 0 44E A city in SW France, the capital of the Dordogne department. It has Roman remains and a 12th-century cathedral and is renowned for its *pâté de foie gras*, truffles, and wine. Manufactures include hardware and chemicals. Population (1975): 37,670.

perihelion The point in the orbit of a body around the sun at which the body is nearest the sun. The earth is at perihelion on about Jan 3. *Compare* aphelion.

Perilla A genus of herbs (4–6 species), native to India and SE Asia, with simple purplish-green leaves and spikes of tubular lilac flowers. They are cultivated as a source of a fast-drying oil, derived from the seeds and used in printing inks, paints, and varnishes. The leaves are used as a condiment. Family: *Labiatae.*

Perim Island 12 40N 43 24E A South Yemeni island in the Bab (strait) el-Mandeb, off the SW tip of the Arabian Peninsula. It belonged to Aden from 1857 to 1967. Area: 5 sq mi (13 sq km).

period (geology.) *See* geological time scale.

period (physics) The interval of time between successive identical configurations of a vibrating system. It is the reciprocal of the frequency of the system.

periodic motion Any motion that repeats itself at constant intervals. The interval of time between successive identical positions is known as the *period of the motion and the maximum displacement of the system from its stationary position is called the amplitude. Examples of periodic motion include a swinging *pendulum, a bouncing ball, and a vibrating string. An important class of periodic motion is *simple harmonic motion.

periodic table A tabular arrangement of the chemical *elements in order of increasing atomic number, such that physical and chemical similarities are displayed. The earliest version of the periodic table was devised in 1871 by D. *Mendeleyev, who successfully predicted the existence of several elements from gaps in the table. The rows across the table are known as periods and the columns as groups. The elements in a group all have a similar configuration of outer electrons in their atoms and therefore show similar chemical behavior. The *halogens, for example, form a group in column 7A. Across each period, atoms are electropositive (form positive ions) to the left and electronegative to the right. For example, in the first period fluorine (F) is the most electronegative element and lithium (Li) the most electropositive. *Atomic theory explains this behavior using the concept of electron shells, corresponding to different energy levels of the atomic electrons. Atoms combine in order to form complete outer shells. The shells are built up by filling the lower energy states (inner shells)

PERIODIC TABLE

1A	2A	3B	4B	5B	6B	7B	8	8	8	1B	2B	3A	4A	5A	6A	7A	0
1 H																	2 He
3 Li	4 Be											5 B	6 C	7 N	8 O	9 F	10 Ne
11 Na	12 Mg			← TRANSITION ELEMENTS →								13 Al	14 Si	15 P	16 S	17 Cl	18 Ar
19 K	20 Ca	21 Sc	22 Ti	23 V	24 Cr	25 Mn	26 Fe	27 Co	28 Ni	29 Cu	30 Zn	31 Ga	32 Ge	33 As	34 Se	35 Br	36 Kr
37 Rb	38 Sr	39 Y	40 Zr	41 Nb	42 Mo	43 Tc	44 Ru	45 Rh	46 Pd	47 Ag	48 Cd	49 In	50 Sn	51 Sb	52 Te	53 I	54 Xe
55 Cs	56 Ba	57† La	72 Hf	73 Ta	74 W	75 Re	76 Os	77 Ir	78 Pt	79 Au	80 Hg	81 Tl	82 Pb	83 Bi	84 Po	85 At	86 Rn
87 Fr	88 Ra	89‡ Ac															

† Lanthanides

57 La	58 Ce	59 Pr	60 Nd	61 Pm	62 Sm	63 Eu	64 Gd	65 Tb	66 Dy	67 Ho	68 Er	69 Tm	70 Yb	71 Lu

‡ Actinides

89 Ac	90 Th	91 Pa	92 U	93 Np	94 Pu	95 Am	96 Cm	97 Bk	98 Cf	99 Es	100 Fm	101 Md	102 No	103 Lr

first. The first shell takes two electrons, the second, eight, and so on. In larger atoms the inner electrons screen the outer electrons from the nucleus, resulting in a more complex shell-filling sequence. This explains the partly filled shells of the *transition elements, which form the middle block of the table, in what are known as the long periods. The short periods are from lithium (Li) to neon (Ne) and from sodium (Na) to argon (Ar). The *noble gases in column 0 have complete outer shells and are generally chemically inactive.

periodontal disease Disease of the gums and other structures surrounding the teeth, formerly known as pyorrhea. Caused by the action of bacteria on food debris that forms a hard deposit (tartar) in the spaces between the gums and teeth, it results in swelling and bleeding of the gums: eventually—if untreated—the teeth become loose and fall out. Periodontal disease is the major cause of tooth loss in adults: it may be prevented (and the early stages treated) by regular brushing, scaling, and polishing, to remove the tartar. Advanced cases require surgery.

Peripatus A common genus of wormlike *arthropods belonging to the mainly tropical subphylum *Onychophora* (about 90 species). The soft unsegmented body, about 2 in (50 mm) long, bears 14–44 short stumpy legs. The animals live in moist dark places, in rock crevices, or under stones or rotting logs and feed on insects. The young develop within the body of the mother and at birth resemble the adults.

periscope An optical device consisting, typically, of a tube in which mirrors or prisms are arranged so that light passing through an aperture at right angles to the tube is reflected through the length of the tube to emerge at an aperture at the other end also at right angles to the tube. Periscopes in their simplest form, with cardboard or plastic tubes, are used to see over the heads of a crowd; in their more sophisticated form, they are designed to be extendible and are used by submerged submarines to see above the surface of the water. In this form they may contain aiming devices for weapons, infrared screens, etc.

Perissodactyla An order of hoofed mammals (16 species) that includes *horses, *tapirs, and *rhinoceroses. The name—meaning odd-toed—reflects the fact that the weight of the body is carried mainly by the central (third) digit of the foot. They are herbivorous, grazing or browsing on leaves, but have evolved separately from other hoofed mammals and have only a single stomach, which is less efficient than the digestive system of *ruminants. *Compare* Artiodactyla.

peritonitis Inflammation of the peritoneum—the membrane that lines the abdominal cavity. This is a serious condition that results from the bursting of an abdominal organ (such as the appendix, gall bladder, or spleen) or of a peptic ulcer. Alternatively it may result from bacterial infection. The patient will be very ill, possibly in shock, with a painful and rigid belly. An operation is essential to repair the perforated organ and cleanse the abdomen; antibiotics are also given.

periwinkle (botany) An evergreen creeping shrub or perennial herb of the genus *Vinca* (5 species), native to Europe and W Asia. The attractive solitary blue or white flowers are tubular with five lobes and the fruit is usually a long capsule. They thrive in shade and are cultivated as ornamentals: *V. major* is an important species. Family: *Apocynaceae*.

periwinkle (zoology) A *gastropod mollusk belonging to the family *Littorinidae*, also called winkle. The common edible winkle (*Littorina littorea*) of European seashores is about 0.8 in (2 cm) high and has a dark-green rounded shell with a pointed spire and grazes on algae. The flat-sided periwinkle (*L. littoralis*) lacks the spire and occurs in many colors.

Perm (name from 1940 until 1957: Molotov) 58 01N 56 10E A port in W Russia, on the Kama River. Its varied industries include engineering, chemical manufacturing, and oil refining. The *Permian period was first identified here. Population (1991 est): 1,100,400.

permafrost The permanent freezing of the ground, sometimes to great depths, in areas bordering on ice sheets. During the summer season the top layer of soil may thaw and become marshy, while the frozen ground below remains an impermeable barrier. Problems arise with the construction of roads and buildings in permafrost areas due to the freeze-thaw processes. Permafrost posed problems in the building of the Alaskan pipeline, completed in 1977.

Permalloy An *alloy of one part iron to four parts nickel, often with other metals added. It has a high magnetic permeability, which makes it useful for parts of electrical machinery that are subjected to alternating magnetic fields.

permeability, magnetic A measure of the response of a material to a *magnetic field. Magnetic permeability, μ, is the ratio of the magnetic *flux induced in the material to the applied magnetic field strength. The relative permeability, μ_r, is the ratio of μ in the medium to that in a vacuum, μ_o (*see* magnetic constant). Paramagnetic materials have a μ_r greater than unity because they reinforce the magnetic field. Ferromagnetic materials can have a μ_r as high as 100,000. Diamagnetic materials have a μ_r of less than one.

Permian period The last geological period of the Paleozoic era, between the Carboniferous and Triassic periods, lasting from about 280 to 240 million years ago. Widespread continental conditions prevailed, which continued into the Triassic, and the two periods are often linked together as the Permo-Triassic, during which the New Red Sandstone was laid down.

permittivity The absolute permittivity of a medium is the ratio of the electric displacement to the electric field at the same point. The absolute permittivity of free space is called the *electric constant. The relative permittivity (*or* dielectric constant) of a capacitor is the ratio of its capacitance with a specified dielectric between the plates to its capacitance with free space between the plates.

Pernik 42 36N 23 03E A city in W Bulgaria, situated on the Struma River near Sofia. It has engineering and iron and steel industries with coal mining nearby. Population (1987 est): 97,250.

Perón, Juan (Domingo) (1895–1974) Argentine statesman; president (1946–55, 1973–74). Elected in 1946 after winning popular support as head of the labor secretariat, his position was strengthened by the popularity of his second wife, **Evita Perón** (Maria Eva Duarte de P.; 1919–52), who was idolized by the poor for her charitable work. After her death, support for Perón waned and he was deposed. He went into exile but remained an influential political force in Argentina, returning in 1973, when he was reelected president. He died in office and was succeeded by his third wife **Isabel Perón** (María Estella P.; 1930–), who was deposed by the army in 1976.

Perot, H(enry) Ross (1930–) US business and political leader. After graduating from the Naval Academy and completing his naval service (1953–57), he became a sales executive for International Business Machines (IBM). Frustrated with IBM's policies, he left to found (1962) Electronic Data Systems (EDS). In 1984 he became a billionaire by selling EDS to General Motors. Noted for his patriotic stances, Perot made himself available for the 1992 presidential election, portraying himself as a reformer outside the usual political channels. His criticisms of government operations unexpectedly drew wide support from voters and enlivened the 1992 campaign.

JUAN PERÓN *He is seen here with his beautiful and popular second wife Evita, a former actress, who was responsible for many reforms (including female suffrage) during his first presidency.*

Perpendicular The style of ☐gothic architecture predominant in England between 1370 and the mid-16th century. The name derives from the panel-like effect of the window design, with its pronounced vertical mullions broken regularly by horizontal divisions. Gloucester Cathedral choir (c. 1357) is an early example. The Henry VII chapel, Westminster Abbey (1503–19), is a masterpiece of the Perpendicular style.

perpetual-motion machine A hypothetical machine that produces continuous and unending motion without drawing energy from an outside source. Although such a machine would contravene the laws of *thermodynamics and therefore cannot be made, there have always been, and indeed still are, hopeful inventors who believe that it is possible to find loopholes in the laws of nature. A perpetual-motion machine would need to be frictionless (in contravention of the second law of thermodynamics) or would need to be able to create energy to overcome the friction (in contravention of the first law). Using the heat of the ocean to drive a ship (perpetual motion of the second kind) is also impossible, because it would contravene the second law.

Perpignan 42 42N 2 54E A city in S France, the capital of the Pyrénées-Orientales department situated near the Spanish border. The capital of the former province of Roussillon in the 17th century, it has a gothic cathedral and a 13th-century castle (the former residence of the kings of Majorca). Perpignan is a tourist and commercial center, trading in wine, fruit, and vegetables. Population (1990): 108,049.

Perrault, Charles (1628–1703) French poet and fairytale writer. As a member of the Académie Française he opposed *Boileau by championing the modern writers against the ancients. He is best known for his collection of fairytales, *Contes de ma mère l'Oye* (1697), translated into English in 1729 and best known by the English title, *Tales of Mother Goose.*

Perrin, Jean-Baptiste (1870–1942) French physicist, who discovered that cathode rays carry a negative charge and therefore consist of particles and not waves, as many physicists then thought. He also used Einstein's equations for the Brownian movement to determine the approximate size of molecules.

Perry, Oliver Hazard (1785–1819) US naval officer, who fought in the war in Tripoli (1801–05) and in the *War of 1812, in which he commanded the US fleet on Lake Erie and was victorious over the British fleet. After the war he served with the navy in the Mediterranean and in South America. *See also* Lake Erie, Battle of. His brother **Matthew Calbraigh Perry** (1794–1858) was also a naval officer. After service in the *War of 1812, Perry established an educational program for US naval officers (1833) and was later given command of the USS *Fulton*, the first steam-powered vessel in the US Navy (1837). Placed in command of the navy's African Squadron (1843), he helped to suppress the slave trade, and during the *Mexican War, he participated in the naval operations at Vera Cruz. In 1852 he was selected by Pres. Millard *Fillmore to undertake a naval expedition to Japan in order to secure US trading rights there. Anchoring at Yedo Bay at the head of the impressive American Eastern Squadron, he persuaded the Japanese to open diplomatic and economic relations with the US, thus ending Japan's traditional isolation.

Perse, Saint-John (Alexis Saint-Léger; 1887–1975) French poet. He was born in the West Indies, served as a diplomat in the Far East, and became secretary general of the Foreign Ministry in 1933. From 1940 to 1958 he lived in the US. His volumes of poetry, written in long free-verse lines, give prominence to landscapes and the sea and include the long poem *Anabase* (1922), translated by T. S. Eliot in 1930, and *Chronique* (1960). He won the Nobel Prize in 1960.

Persephone (Roman name: Proserpine) Greek goddess of the underworld, daughter of Zeus and *Demeter. She was abducted by *Hades, who made her queen of the underworld. Zeus, moved by Demeter's sorrow for her daughter, allowed her to spend part of each year on earth. Her return to the earth symbolized the regeneration of natural life in the spring.

Persepolis An ancient Persian city in Fars province, Iran. *Darius I (reigned 522–486 BC) planned Persepolis as the ceremonial capital of his empire and its wealth and splendor were legendary. Among the buildings on the vast central terrace were the apadana (royal audience hall), which was approached by monumental stairways flanked by reliefs of tribute bearers, and *Xerxes' throne hall. The Achaemenian royal tombs are nearby. *Alexander the Great destroyed Persepolis in 330 BC.

Perseus (astronomy) A constellation in the N sky near Cassiopeia, lying in the Milky Way. The brightest stars are the 2nd-magnitude Mirfak and the eclipsing binary *Algol.

Perseus (Greek mythology) The son of Zeus and Danae. One of the greatest Greek heroes, he beheaded the *Medusa with the help of Athena, who gave him a mirror so that he could avoid looking at the Gorgon and so escape being turned to stone. He rescued Andromeda, daughter of the Ethiopian king, and married her. She had been chained to a rock as a sacrifice to a sea monster, which Perseus turned to stone by showing it the Medusa's head.

Pershing, John J(oseph) (1860–1948) US general. A graduate of West Point, Pershing served in the Indian Wars in the Southwest and in the *Spanish-American War. After leading the army in an unsuccessful pursuit of the Mexican revolutionary and outlaw Pancho *Villa (1916), he was appointed commander of the *American Expeditionary Force (AEF) to France during World War I. A sound administrator as well as a strong military leader, he strengthened the AEF, insisting on its independence from the other Allied forces. After the war, he served as army chief of staff from 1921 until his retirement from active duty in 1924.

Persia. *See* Iran.

Persian A language belonging to the *Iranian language family. It is the official language of Iran and is written in a modified Arabic script.

Persian art and architecture The styles associated with the three principal phases of the Persian empire: *Achaemenian (550–331 BC), *Sasanian (224–651 AD), and Islamic. The splendors of Achaemenian and Sasanian architecture are represented respectively by *Persepolis and *Ctesiphon. Sasanian kings commissioned monumental relief sculptures to commemorate victories and coronations. The Persian tradition of fine craftsmanship in metalwork, glassware, and ceramics dates from this period. After 651, Persian styles became an aspect of international trends in *Islamic art. Calligraphy and book illustration became important, the latter evolving into the renowned 15th-, 16th-, and 17th-century Persian miniature painting. The love of subtly brilliant colors is epitomized in the famous Persian carpets and in the architectural use of turquoise colored tiles.

Persian cat A domesticated cat, also called a Longhair, having a long flowing coat with a ruff or frill around the neck. The 20 or so recognized breeds are characterized by their short bodies, deep flanks, short legs, and short bushy tails. The head has a snub nose, large round eyes, and small wide-set ears and the coat may be of any color, although the Blue Persian is most popular.

Persian Empire. *See* Achaemenians.

Persian Gulf An arm of the Arabian Sea, extending some 590 mi (950 km) NW beyond the Gulf of Oman. The large offshore oil deposits are exploited by the surrounding *Gulf States. Area: 89,942 sq mi (233,000 sq km).

Persian Wars. *See* Greek–Persian Wars.

persimmon A tree of the genus *Diospyros* that produces edible fruits. These are the Japanese persimmon (*D. kaki*), the American persimmon (*D. virginiana*), and the Asian date plum (*D. lotus*). Up to 100 ft (30 m) high, they have dark-green oval leaves and produce round orange, yellow, or red fruits, 2–3.1 in (5–8 cm) across. Persimmons are eaten fresh, cooked, or candied. Family: *Ebenaceae*.

perspective Any means of rendering objects or space in a picture to give an illusion of their depth. Perspective in a single object is known as foreshortening and can be seen in even primitive works as a result of accurate observation. The laws of true perspective of an entire scene, known as linear perspective, were formulated by *Brunelleschi in the 15th century and became one of the *Renaissance artists' most important scientific investigations. The earliest known scientific perspective (1436) was constructed by *Alberti in his treatise on painting. Guide lines converge on one, two, or three points on the horizon line, known as vanishing points, according to whether the orientation of a scene is central, angular, or oblique.

perspiration. *See* sweat.

Perth 31 58S 115 49E The capital of Western Australia on the Swan River. Founded in 1829, it expanded following the discovery of gold (1893) at Kalgoolie. It is the commercial and cultural center of the state; the University of Western Australia was founded in 1913 and there are two cathedrals. Its port, *Fremantle, and Kwinana, both to the S, are growing industrial centers. Population (1990): 1,193,100.

Perth 56 24N 3 28W A city in E Scotland, in Tayside Region on the Tay River. An early capital of Scotland, it was the scene of the assassination of James I (1437). There are dyeing, textiles, whisky distilling, and carpet industries and it is a popular tourist center. Population (1981): 42,000.

perturbations Small departures of a celestial body from the orbital path it would follow if subject only to the influence of a single central force. Short-term periodic disturbances arise from gravitational interactions with other bodies. Progressive disturbances or those of very long period can also occur.

Peru, Republic of A country in the NE of South America, on the Pacific Ocean. Narrow coastal plains rise to the high peaks of the Andes, reaching heights of over 21,000 ft (6500 m). The land descends again through an area of forested plateaus to the tropical forests of the Amazon basin. Most of the population is of Indian or mixed Indian and European descent. *Economy*: Peru is one of the world's leading fishing countries, the main product being fishmeal. Agriculture is important, now organized largely in cooperatives, and the main crops include corn, rice, sugarcane, cotton, and coffee. Large-scale irrigation projects are being undertaken. Livestock is particularly important to the economy, especially the production of wool. Rich mineral resources include copper, silver, lead, zinc, and iron; oil has been discovered in considerable quantities, both in the jungles and offshore. In recent years there have been considerable developments in industry and in industrial relations, including moves toward nationalization and worker participation, although such moves have been slowed down by changes of government. With its relics of ancient civilizations, Peru has a valuable tourist trade. The main exports include minerals and metals and fishmeal. *History*: Peru's precolonial history encompasses the civilization of the *Chimú and that of the *Incas, who were conquered by the Spanish under Pizarro in 1533. The viceroyalty of Peru, centered on Lima, enjoyed considerable prosperity in which the Indian population had little share. A revolt in 1780 led by Tupac Amarú was suppressed. Peru was the last of Spain's American colonies to declare its independence (1821) and the Spanish were finally defeated in 1824. Political stability was achieved by Gen. Ramón Castilla; (president 1845–51, 1855–62), who developed Peru's economy, based on guano deposits. However, the country's prosperity was undermined by the War of the *Pacific (1879–83) in which Peru lost the nitrate-rich province of Tarapacà to Chile. Since World War II, in which Peru declared war on Germany in 1945, the country has depended on US aid and has witnessed a series of coups and countercoups, such as in 1975, when Gen. Francisco Morales Bermúdez became president. In 1980, in Peru's first general elections to be held in 17 years, Fernando Beláunde Terry was elected president. The economy declined, violence escalated, and he was voted out of office in 1985. The new president, Alan García Pérez, was unable to halt economic decline or guerrilla violence. In 1990, Alberto Fujimori was elected president. His economic adjustment program was extreme, precipitating labor strikes. Violent fighting with the guerrilla movement Shining Path continued, as did problems with drug trafficking. In an April 1992 crackdown, Fujimori dissolved the congress and suspended parts of the constitution. Guerrilla fighting escalated and some cabinet members and government officials resigned, but Fujimori maintained his power and secured approval in 1993 of a new constitution that strengthened the presidency. Peru is a member of the OAS and LAFTA. Official languages: Spanish and Quechua; Aymará is also widely spoken. Official currency: sol of 100 centavos. Area: 496,093 sq mi (1,285,215 sq km). Population (1990 est): 21,904,000. Capital: Lima. Main port: Callao.

Peru Current. *See* Humboldt Current.

Perugia 43 07N 12 23E A city in Italy, the capital of Umbria. Originally an Etruscan city, it has 13th-century city walls, a 14th-century cathedral, an ancient fountain (the Maggiore Fountain), and a university (1200). Perugia is an agricultural trading center and its manufactures include furniture and textiles. Population (1991 est): 150,576.

Perugino (Pietro di Cristoforo Vannucci; c. 1450–1523) Italian Renaissance painter, born near Perugia. He worked on frescoes in the Sistine Chapel, including the *Giving of the Keys to St Peter* (1481–82). His spacious ordered compositions and graceful figure style influenced his pupil *Raphael.

Perutz, Max Ferdinand (1914–) British chemist, born in Austria, who developed the technique of *X-ray diffraction to determine the molecular structure of the blood pigment, hemoglobin. For his work he shared a Nobel Prize (1962) with J. C. *Kendrew.

Pesaro 43 54N 12 54E A city and resort in Italy, in Marche on the Adriatic coast. It is the birthplace of Rossini, who established a school of music there. Population (1990 est): 90,300.

Pescadores. *See* Penghu Islands.

Pescara 42 27N 14 13E A seaport in Italy, in Abruzzi on the Adriatic coast. Its chief industries are tourism, shipbuilding, and fishing. Population (1988 est): 130,500.

Peshawar 34 01N 71 40E A city in N Pakistan, situated at the E end of the Khyber Pass. One of the oldest cities in Pakistan, it has for centuries been a center of trade between the Indian subcontinent, Afghanistan, and central Asia. Industries include textiles, shoes, and pottery and it has a university (1950). Population (1981): 566,000.

Pestalozzi, Johann Heinrich (1746–1827) Swiss educator. A pioneer of mass education, Pestalozzi made several unsuccessful attempts to establish schools for poor children. His book *Wie Gertrud ihre Kinder lehrt* (1801) reflected his ideas on the intuitive method of education. Despite his apparent failures, his theories were of great importance to subsequent educational developments. Pestalozzi's work is commemorated in the **Pestalozzi International Children's Villages**, the first of which was established in 1946 for war orphans at Trogen (Switzerland). A second international village was established in 1958 at Sedlescombe (UK) for the care and education of selected children from developing countries.

pesticides. *See* herbicides; insecticides.

Pétain, (Henri) Philippe (1856–1951) French general and statesman. In World War I he distinguished himself at the defense of Verdun (1916), becoming marshal of France (1918). In World War II, when France was on the verge of defeat (1940), Pétain became prime minister. In June 1940, he signed an armistice with Hitler that allowed for a third of France to remain unoccupied by Germany. His government of unoccupied France at Vichy was authoritarian and from 1942 was dominated by *Laval and the Germans. Pétain was sentenced to death in August 1945, for collaboration but was then reprieved and imprisoned for life.

Peter (I) the Great (1672–1725) Tsar (1682–1721) and then Emperor (1721–25) of Russia, who established Russia as a major European power. Peter ruled with his half-brother Ivan V (1666–96) until Ivan's death and under the regency of his half-sister *Sophia until 1689, when he became effective ruler. Peter traveled in W Europe in the late 1690s, acquiring knowledge of Western technology and returning to Russia with Western technicians, who were to implement the modernization programs that marked his reign. He instituted many reforms in government and administration, trade and industry, and in the army. In the *Great Northern War (1700–21), he acquired Livonia, Estonia, and also Ingria, where in 1703 he founded St Petersburg (now *Leningrad). He campaigned less successfully against the Turks (1710–13) but gained territory in the Caspian region from war with Persia (1722–23). Peter's eldest son *Alexis died in prison, having been condemned to death for treason; Peter was succeeded by his wife, who became *Catherine I.

Peter I (1844–1921) King of Serbia (1903–18) and then of Yugoslavia (1918–21). Brought up in exile, Peter was elected king after the assassination of the last Obrenović monarch. His rule was marked by its constitutionalism.

Peter, St In the New Testament, one of the 12 Apostles. He was a fisherman on the Sea of Galilee until called by Jesus along with his brother *Andrew. He became the leader and spokesman for the disciples. Although his faith often wavered, notably at the crucifixion, when he denied Christ three times, Peter was named as the rock upon which the Church was to be built. He was also entrusted with the "keys of the Kingdom of Heaven" (Matthew 16.19)—hence his symbol of two crossed keys. After Christ's death, he dominated the Christian community for 15 years, undertaking missionary work despite imprisonment. Whereas Paul had responsibility for the Gentiles, Peter's was to the Jews. He is believed to have been martyred and buried in Rome. Feast day: June 29.

Peterborough 52 35N 0 15W A city in E central England, on the Nene River. The cathedral (begun in the 12th century) contains the tomb of Catherine of Aragon. Industries include sugar-beet refining, foodstuffs, engineering, and brick making and it is an important marketing center for the surrounding agricultural area. Population (1981): 114,108.

Peterborough 44 19N 78 20W A city in SE Canada, in Ontario. It is an important manufacturing center and the main commercial center for central Ontario. The largest deposit of nepheline in the world (used in the manufacture of glass) is nearby. Population (1991): 68,371.

Peter Damian, St (1007–72) Italian churchman; cardinal and Doctor of the Church. He is famous as a religious reformer who campaigned for clerical celibacy and attacked simony. Feast day: Feb 23.

Peter Lombard (c. 1100–60) Italian theologian. He studied in Rheims and in Paris, where, between 1136 and 1150, he taught theology at the school of Notre Dame. He became Bishop of Paris in 1159. His most famous work, the *Books of Sentences* (1148–51), was an objective summary of the beliefs of earlier theologians. It was a standard text in the universities until the 16th century and many medieval scholars wrote commentaries on it, including Thomas *Aquinas.

Peterloo Massacre (1819) The name given, by analogy with the battle of Waterloo, to the violent dispersal of a political meeting held in St Peter's Fields, Manchester, England. A peaceful crowd, numbering about 60,000, had gathered to hear a speech on parliamentary reform. The local officials, anxious about the size of the crowd, called in troops. The cavalry were ordered to charge and in the ensuing panic 11 people were killed.

Petersburg 37 13N 77 24W A city in SE Virginia, on the Appomattox River, SE of Richmond. A key Confederate supply base in the Civil War, Petersburg was besieged by Gen. Ulysses S. Grant from June 1864 until it fell in April 1865. Tobacco and peanut processing are important industries, and clothing, furniture, luggage, and paints are manufactured. Population (1990): 38,386.

Peter the Hermit (c. 1050–1115) French monk. A fervent supporter of the first *Crusade under Pope Urban II, he rallied over 20,000 peasants to follow him to the Holy Land, where many were massacred by the Turks. He later founded the monastery of Neufmoutier at Liège.

Petipa, Marius (1819–1910) French dancer and choreographer. He exercised an important influence on the Russian imperial ballet in St Petersburg, where he worked from 1847 until 1903. He became its chief choreographer in 1862. His many ballets include *Don Quixote* (1869) and *The Sleeping Beauty* (1890), on which he collaborated with its composer, Tchaikovsky.

Petit, Roland (1924–   ) French ballet dancer and choreographer. His innovative ballets, characterized by elements of fantasy and contemporary realism, include *Carmen* (1949) and *Kraanerg* (1969). He toured with his company in Europe and the US and also choreographed for Hollywood films.

petition of right The procedure by which a person formerly petitioned against the English crown for restoration of property rights. The petition might be for property that the crown had taken possession of or for money due by contract. Although still legal, this method of claiming against the crown, dating back to the reign of Edward I, has been replaced by ordinary court actions. A parliamentary declaration accepted by Charles I (1628) made illegal imprisonment without trial, taxation without parliamentary approval, and the billeting of soldiers on private individuals.

petit mal. *See* epilepsy.

Petőfi, Sándor (1823–49) Hungarian poet. He came from a peasant background and elements of traditional folk song occur in his early poetry, notably in the narrative poem *Janós the Hero* (1845). His later poetry was chiefly concerned with the cause of nationalism. He disappeared during the battle of Segesvar (1849), in which the Hungarian revolutionary army was defeated by the Austrians and Russians.

Petra An ancient town in S Jordan. It was the capital of the Nabataeans, nomadic Arabs who settled along the caravan routes from Arabia to the Mediterranean. Petra was a great trading center from the 3rd century BC. It was incorporated in the Roman Empire in 106 AD and was superseded by *Palmyra in the 2nd century. Accessible only through a narrow gorge, Petra is renowned for its rock-cut temples and dwellings.

Petrarch (Francesco Petrarca; 1304–74) Italian poet. He was born in Florence, but his family was banished and he lived mostly in Provence from 1312 to 1353, when he returned to Italy. He traveled widely in Europe and in 1341 was crowned as poet laureate in Rome. His humanist works of scholarship anticipated the Renaissance in their combination of classical learning and Christian faith. His other works include *Secretum meum*, his spiritual self-analysis, and *Africa*, a Latin verse epic on Scipio Africanus, but he is remembered chiefly for the *Canzoniere*, a series of love poems addressed to Laura. His work greatly influenced writers throughout Europe, including *Chaucer.

Petrea A genus of tropical climbing plants (about 30 species), native to tropical America and the West Indies. Up to 30 ft (9 m) high, they have oblong leaves and sprays of bluish-purple flowers, each with five widely spaced strap-shaped petals and colored sepals. Popular ornamental species include *P. volubilis* and *P. kohautiana*. Family: *Verbenaceae*.

petrel A marine bird belonging to a widely distributed family (*Procellariidae*; 55 species) characterized by a musky smell, thick plumage, webbed feet, and a hooked bill with long tubular nostrils; 11–35 in (27–90 cm) long, petrels are well adapted for oceanic life, feeding on fish and mollusks and only coming ashore to breed. Diving petrels belong to a family (*Pelecanoididae*; 5 species) occurring in the S hemisphere; they are 6–10 in (16–25 cm) long, have short wings, and feed mostly on crustaceans. Order: *Procellariiformes. See also* fulmar; prion; shearwater; storm petrel. □oceans.

Petrie, Sir (William Matthew) Flinders (1853–1942) British archeologist. After surveying British prehistoric sites, Petrie went to Egypt (1880), where his painstaking excavations and meticulous study of artifacts revolutionized and set new standards for archeology. He excavated numerous sites, including *Naukratis, *Tell el-Amarna, and *Abydos, finally leaving Egypt for Palestine in 1926.

Petrified Forest National Park A national park in E central Arizona, E of Flagstaff. The Puerto River runs through the park. Established as a national monument in 1906 and a national park in 1962, it contains petrified multicolored wood, ruins of ancient Indian life, including petroglyphs (prehistoric rock drawings or carvings), and part of the Painted Desert. Area: 147 sq mi (381 sq km).

petroleum. *See* oil.

petrology The study of rocks, including their formation, structure, texture, and mineral and chemical composition. **Petrogenesis** is the origin or mode of formation of rocks; **petrography** is the description and classification of rocks from hand specimens or thin sections.

Petronius Arbiter (1st century AD) Roman satirist. He was appointed "Arbiter of Taste" at the court of Nero. The *Satyricon*, his picaresque novel of which only fragments survive, relates the scandalous adventures of the youths Encolpius and Ascyltos and includes the famous satirical portrait of a coarse and vulgar millionaire, Trimalchio. Petronius committed suicide after being falsely accused of conspiring against Nero.

Petropavlovsk 54 53N 69 13E A city in N Kazakhstan, on the Ishim River. It is an important junction on the Trans-Siberian Railway and has varied industries. Population (1991 est): 248,300.

Petropavlovsk-Kamchatskii 53 03N 158 43E A port in E Russia, on the Kamchatka Peninsula. Long a major naval base, it was attacked by the French and British during the Crimean War. Fishing, fish processing, and ship repairing are the principal activities. Population (1991 est): 272,900.

Petrópolis 22 30S 43 06W A city and mountain resort in SE Brazil, in Rio de Janeiro state. Notable buildings include the Museum of the Empire (formerly the royal palace) and the gothic-style cathedral. Population (1980): 241,500.

Petrozavodsk 61 46N 34 19E A city in NW Russia, the capital of the Karelian associated republic, on Lake Onega. It was founded (1703) by Peter the Great: engineering and lumbering are important activities and there are many educational institutions. Population (1991 est): 278,200.

Petsamo. *See* Pechenga.

Petunia A genus of tropical American herbs (about 40 species), cultivated for their showy funnel-shaped flowers, which are sometimes frilled at the edges. Ornamental species include *P. integrifolia*, with pink, blue, or purple flowers, the white-flowered *P. axillaris*, which has a pleasant night fragrance, and hybrids between them. Family: *Solanaceae.

Pevsner, Antoine (1886–1962) Russian sculptor and painter, who worked in Paris from 1923. His early career was spent in W Europe but it was in Russia that he and his brother Naum *Gabo pioneered *constructivism in their *Realist Manifesto* (1920). His most characteristic abstract constructions consist of curving and thrusting shapes in striated metal.

pewter An *alloy of tin with lead or copper, antimony, and bismuth. It was formerly used to make plates, spoons, and other utensils.

peyote A blue-green *cactus, *Lophophora williamsii*, also called mescal, native to Mexico and the SW US. About 3 in (8 cm) across and 2 in (5 cm) high, it bears white to pink flowering heads, which, when dried, are known as "mescal buttons." They contain the alkaloid *mescaline, which produces hallucinations when chewed.

Pforzheim 48 53N 08 41E A city in SW Germany, in Baden-Württemberg. It was an important medieval trading center and is a center of the German watch and jewelry industry. Population (1991 est): 112,944.

pH A measure of the acidity or alkalinity of a solution, equal to the logarithm to the base 10 of the reciprocal of the number of moles per liter of hydrogen ions it contains. Thus a solution containing 10^{-6} mole of hydrogen ions per liter has a pH of $\log_{10}(^1/_{10}{}^{-6}) = 6$. In pure water there is a small reversible dissociation into equal amounts of hydrogen and hydroxide ions: $H_2O \rightarrow H^+ + OH^-$. The product of the concentrations of these ions (moles/liter) is about 10^{-14}: $[H^+][OH^-] = 10^{-14}$. In neutral solutions, therefore, the hydrogen ion concentration is 10^{-7} and the pH is consequently 7. In acid solutions the pH is less than 7; the lower the pH, the more acidic the solution. Conversely, alkaline solutions have pH values greater than 7. The pH scale is logarithmic; for example, a solution with a pH of 2 is 10 times more acidic than one with a pH of 1. *See also* acids and bases.

Phaedra In Greek mythology, the daughter of *Minos and Pasiphaë and the wife of Theseus. She fell in love with her stepson *Hippolytus. When he rejected her, she hanged herself, having first written a letter to Theseus accusing Hippolytus of having seduced her.

Phaedrus (1st century AD) Roman writer. Born a slave in Macedonia, he gained his freedom in the household of the emperor Augustus. He wrote poetic versions of the Greek prose fables ascribed to *Aesop. His work was popular in medieval Europe.

Phaethon In Greek mythology, the son of the sun god Helios, who granted him his wish to drive the chariot of the sun for one day. Unable to control the horses, he was about to burn the earth when Zeus struck him down with a thunderbolt.

phaeton A four-wheeled open carriage usually drawn by two horses. Various modifications of the phaeton (pony phaeton, Victoria phaeton, Stanhope phaeton, etc.) were fashionable in the 19th century for pleasure driving.

phagocyte A cell that engulfs and then digests particles from its surroundings: this process is called phagocytosis. Many protozoans are phagocytic, but the word specifically refers to certain white blood cells that protect the body by engulfing bacteria and other foreign particles.

phalanger A small herbivorous *marsupial of the family *Phalangeridae* (48 species), occurring in woodlands of Australia, (including Tasmania), and New Guinea. They range in length from 5–48 in (12–120 cm) and are adapted for climbing trees, having strong claws and prehensile tails. The family includes the *cuscuses, *flying phalangers, *honey mouse, *koalas, and *possums.

Phalaris (c. 570–c. 554 BC) Tyrant of Agrigento in Sicily, who established its prominence by subjugating the indigenous Sicels and defying the Phoenicians. Phalaris was noted for his cruelty and was overthrown.